Handbook of Consumer Behavior, Tourism, and the Internet

Handbook of Consumer Behavior, Tourism, and the Internet has been co-published simultaneously as *Journal of Travel & Tourism Marketing,* Volume 17, Numbers 2/3 2004.

The *Journal of Travel & Tourism Marketing*™ Monographic "Separates"

Editor-in-Chief: K. S. (Kaye) Chon

Below is a list of "separates," which in serials librarianship means a special issue simultaneously published as a special journal issue or double-issue *and* as a "separate" hardbound monograph. (This is a format which we also call a " DocuSerial.")

"Separates" are published because specialized libraries or professionals may wish to purchase a specific thematic issue by itself in a format which can be separately cataloged and shelved, as opposed to purchasing the journal on an on-going basis. Faculty members may also more easily consider a "separate" for classroom adoption.

"Separates" are carefully classified separately with the major book jobbers so that the journal tie-in can be noted on new book order slips to avoid duplicate purchasing.

You may wish to visit Haworth's website at . . .

http://www.HaworthPress.com

. . . to search our online catalog for complete tables of contents of these separates and related publications.

You may also call 1-800-HAWORTH (outside US/Canada: 607-722-5857), or Fax 1-800-895-0582 (outside US/Canada: 607-771-0012), or e-mail at:

docdelivery@haworthpress.com

Handbook of Consumer Behavior, Tourism, and the Internet, edited by Juline E. Mills, PhD, and Rob Law, PhD (Vol. 17, No. 2/3, 2004). *"WORTHWHILE. . . . RECOMMENDED. . . . The assembled research talent between the covers of this long-overdue (and much-needed) book represents writing from some of the most insightful thinkers in the field." (Andrew J. Frew, PhD, Professor and Chair, IT and Tourism; Director, SITI, Faculty of Business and Arts, Queen Margaret University College, United Kingdom)*

Management Science Applications in Tourism and Hospitality, edited by Zheng Gu, PhD (Vol. 16, No. 2/3, 2004). *"A THOROUGH BLUEPRINT for graduate students and industry executives." (Michael Kwag, PhD, CHA, CHAE, Associate Professor, Boston University)*

Safety and Security in Tourism: Relationships, Management, and Marketing, edited by C. Michael Hall, PhD, Dallen J. Timothy, PhD, and David Timothy Duval, PhD (Vol. 15, No. 2/3/4, 2003). *Examines tourism safety and security issues in light of the September, 2001 terrorist attacks on the United States.*

Wine, Food, and Tourism Marketing, edited by C. Michael Hall, PhD (Vol. 14, No. 3/4, 2003). *"One of the world's foremost researchers in culinary tourism takes the field to a new level. . . ." (Erik Wolf, MA, Director, International Culinary Tourism Association)*

Tourism Forecasting and Marketing, edited by Kevin K. F. Wong, PhD, and Haiyan Song, PhD (Vol. 13, No. 1/2, 2002). *"A valuable resource for policymakers in both the private and public sectors . . . Makes a significant contribution to the field of tourism forecasting by bringing together many different research methodologies with data on tourism flows from around the world." (Pauline J. Sheldon, PhD, Interim Dean and Professor, School of Travel Industry Management, University of Hawaii at Manoa)*

Japanese Tourists: Socio-Economic, Marketing and Psychological Analysis, edited by K. S. (Kaye) Chon, Tustomo Inagaki, and Taji Ohashi (Vol. 9, No. 1/2, 2000). *Presents recent studies on the socioeconomic, marketing, and psychological analysis of Japanese tourists.*

Geography and Tourism Marketing, edited by Martin Oppermann, PhD (Vol. 6, No. 3/4, 1997). *"Casts much light on how insights from geography can be applied to, and gained from, tourism promotion. . . . Well-written, informative, and interesting, and the issues are important." (David Harrison, PhD, Co-ordinator of Tourism Studies, School of Social and Economic Development, University of the South Pacific, Suva, Fiji)*

Marketing Issues in Pacific Area Tourism, edited by John C. Crotts, PhD, and Chris A. Ryan, PhD (Vol. 6, No. 1, 1997). *"A significant volume on the marketing issues that face the region. Nicely complements existing texts and will carve its own distinctive niche as a reference work. . . . Valuable to students of tourism marketing both inside and outside of the Pacific region." (C. Michael Hall, PhD, Professor and Chairperson, Tourism and Services Management, Victoria University of Wellington, New Zealand)*

Recent Advances in Tourism Marketing Research, edited by Daniel R. Fesenmaier, PhD, Joseph T. O'Leary, PhD, and Muzaffer Uysal, PhD (Vol. 5, No. 2/3, 1996). *"This book clearly marks the current advancement in tourism marketing research. . . . Tourism marketing researchers and academics can gain useful insights by reading this text." (Journal of the Academy of Marketing Science)*

Economic Psychology of Travel and Tourism, edited by John C. Crotts, PhD, and W. Fred van Raaij, PhD (Vol. 3, No. 3, 1995). *"A fresh and innovative volume that expands our understanding of consumers in the tourism market. . . . Will be a useful reference for scholars and graduate students working in tourism psychology and marketing."* (Dr. Stephen L. J. Smith, Professor, Department of Recreation and Leisure Studies, University of Waterloo, Ontario, Canada)

Communication and Channel Systems in Tourism Marketing, edited by Muzaffer Uysal, PhD, and Daniel R. Fesenmaier, PhD (Vol. 2, No. 2/3, 1994). *"Loaded with information on a variety of topics that provides readers with a solid background of the topic as well as introduces them to new ideas. . . . A valuable resource."* (Robert M. O'Halloran, PhD, Associate Professor, School of Hotel, Restaurant & Tourism, University of Denver)

Handbook of Consumer Behavior, Tourism, and the Internet

Juline E. Mills
Rob Law
Editors

Handbook of Consumer Behavior, Tourism, and the Internet has been co-published simultaneously as *Journal of Travel & Tourism Marketing,* Volume 17, Numbers 2/3 2004.

Routledge
Taylor & Francis Group

NEW YORK AND LONDON

Transferred to Digital Printing 2008 by Routledge
270 Madison Ave, New York NY 10016
2 Park Square, Milton Park, Abingdon, Oxon, OX14 4RN

First Published by

The Haworth Hospitality Press®, 10 Alice Street, Binghamton, NY 13904-1580 USA

The Haworth Hospitality Press® is an imprint of The Haworth Press, Inc., 10 Alice Street, Binghamton, NY 13904-1580 USA.

Handbook of Consumer Behavior, Tourism, and the Internet has been co-published simultaneously as *Journal of Travel & Tourism Marketing,* Volume 17, Numbers 2/3 2004.

The development, preparation, and publication of this work has been undertaken with great care. However, the publisher, employees, editors, and agents of The Haworth Press and all imprints of The Haworth Press, Inc., including The Haworth Medical Press® and Pharmaceutical Products Press®, are not responsible for any errors contained herein or for consequences that may ensue from use of materials or information contained in this work. Opinions expressed by the author(s) are not necessarily those of The Haworth Press, Inc.

Cover design by Jennifer M. Gaska

Library of Congress Cataloging-in-Publication Data

Handbook of consumer behavior, tourism, and the Internet / Juline E. Mills, Rob Law, editors.
   p. cm.
   "Co-published simultaneously as Journal of travel & tourism marketing, volume 17, numbers 2/3, 2004."
   Includes bibliographical references and index.
   ISBN 0-7890-2599-X (pbk. : alk. paper)
   1. Tourism–Computer network resources–Handbooks, manuals, etc. 2. Tourism–Handbooks, manuals, etc. 3. Internet marketing–Handbooks, manuals, etc. I. Mills, Juline E. II. Law, Rob. III. Journal of travel & tourism marketing.

G149.7.H36 2004
910'.68'8–dc22

2004014894

Publisher's Note
The publisher has gone to great lengths to ensure the quality of this reprint
but points out that some imperfections in the original may be apparent.

Indexing, Abstracting & Website/Internet Coverage

This section provides you with a list of major indexing & abstracting services and other tools for bibliographic access. That is to say, each service began covering this periodical during the year noted in the right column. Most Websites which are listed below have indicated that they will either post, disseminate, compile, archive, cite, or alert their own Website users with research-based content from this work. [This list is as current as the copyright date of this publication.]

[continued]

Special Bibliographic Notes related to special journal issues [separates] and indexing/abstracting:

- indexing/abstracting services in this list will also cover material in any "separate" that is co-published simultaneously with Haworth's special thematic journal issue or DocuSerial. Indexing/abstracting usually covers material at the article/chapter level.
- monographic co-editions are intended for either non-subscribers or libraries which intend to purchase a second copy for their circulating collections.
- monographic co-editions are reported to all jobbers/wholesalers/approval plans. The source journal is listed as the "series" to assist the prevention of duplicate purchasing in the same manner utilized for books-in-series.
- to facilitate user/access services all indexing/abstracting services are encouraged to utilize the co-indexing entry note indicated at the bottom of the first page of each article/chapter/contribution.
- this is intended to assist a library user of any reference tool [whether print, electronic, online, or CD-ROM] to locate the monographic version if the library has purchased this version but not a subscription to the source journal.
- individual articles/chapters in any Haworth publication are also available through The Haworth Document Delivery Service [HDDS].

Handbook of Consumer Behavior, Tourism, and the Internet

CONTENTS

ABOUT THE EDITORS

Juline E. Mills is Assistant Professor of Hospitality and Tourism Ecommerce at Purdue University. Dr. Mills has over ten years of education and managerial hotel industry experience in the United States and the Caribbean and has received specialized training in the area of E-Commerce and Computer Education and Cognitive Systems as it applies to hospitality and tourism. Dr. Mills conducts research in Hospitality and Tourism Marketing, E-consumer Behavior, Information Technology, Web Design and Development, Online Liability Issues, Electronic Surveying Methodologies, and Structural Equation Modeling. Dr. Mills has published numerous articles in scholarly journals and has received the Emerald Management Review Citation of Excellence Award. In addition to serving as an editorial board member and manuscript reviewer for various journals, Dr. Mills is currently the Guest Editor of the *Journal of Foodservice Business Research* special issue on Hospitality Information Technology.

Rob Law is Associate Professor of Information Technology in School of Hotel & Tourism Management, the Hong Kong Polytechnic University. Prior to joining the Hong Kong Polytechnic University in 1995, Dr. Law has worked in Canada and Hong Kong in academia and industry. Dr. Law's research areas include Information Technology, Internet/E-Commerce, Modeling/Forecasting, and Computer Assisted Education. Dr. Law actively serves research and professional bodies in hospitality and tourism, and publishes widely in leading research journals. He is the Internet Editor of *Journal of Travel & Tourism Marketing*, has served as Guest Editor of *Journal of Convention & Exhibition Management*, and an editorial board member of *Tourism Management*, *Journal of Hospitality & Leisure Marketing*, *FIU Hospitality Review*, *Information Technology in Hospitality*, and *Information Technology & Tourism*. He also serves many other research journals as a referee.

Preface

HANDBOOK OF CONSUMER BEHAVIOR, TOURISM, AND THE INTERNET

Whether it is used for academic research, industrial applications, or for consumer purchases, the Internet, has been, and will be, an increasingly valuable tool for travelers. Growth in online travel is noted world-wide with online travel sales doubling in the US, Europe, and Asia. As consumers continue to use the Web for travel and hospitality resources there is a need to examine the business-to-consumer online environment and the issues facing the continued acceptance and use of the Web by consumers. Research is therefore needed to aid businesses understand, for example, why consumers come to their Websites? Why consumers leave quickly or stay and browse? Are online travel, tourism, and hospitality businesses meeting the needs of consumers? Are the Web users the right e-consumers? These questions and many more surrounding the online travel and hospitality business certainly deserve in-depth investigations.

In noting the need to provide answers and suggest directions for academic and practitioner based research that may aid online travel and hospitality businesses, this special volume is a compilation of articles exploring the topic of e-consumer behavior. As a testament to the continuous growth and importance of e-consumer based research the articles in this special volume were written by international researchers from Asia, Europe, and the United States using a variety of research methodologies and data analyses techniques. Data analyses techniques used by authors ranged from qualitative data analysis using artificial neural network analysis, experimental design, through to non-parametric statistical tests, and structural equation modeling. The special volume is divided into six sections. Each section begins with a model/diagram that overviews the topic under discussion. Two to four full length manuscripts are next presented in each section followed by a section commentary recommending areas where future research is needed.

The special volume begins appropriately with an examination of travel and hospitality users, their characteristics, and their search behavior. Section one showcases articles in the area of online travel consumer search behavior where researchers explore barriers to online consumer search as well as examine the online search process of consumers when making travel arrangements. The second section examines travel Website user characteristics from general buyer characteristics, college student purchasing online to exploring the differences between broadband and narrowband users.

Section three gives the reader insights into the arena of quality and perception of lodging brands primarily from a business standpoint. The section points out the need for business to continue internal examinations in order to meet online consumer needs. Section four examines the emerging field of e-complaint behavior. Consumers are now taking to the Web to voice their complaints about travel services. The special volume concludes with a look at two areas that could be considered as the start of e-commerce research and enquiries that of Website design and the subsequent evaluation of these designs to ensure that they are meeting the needs of consumers. These two sec-

[Haworth co-indexing entry note]: "Preface." Mills, Juline E. and Rob Law. Co-published simultaneously in *Journal of Travel & Tourism Marketing* (The Haworth Hospitality Press, an imprint of The Haworth Press, Inc.) Vol. 17 No. 2/3, 2004, pp. xxxv-xxxvi; and: *Handbook of Consumer Behavior, Tourism, and the Internet* (eds: Juline E. Mills, and Rob Law) The Haworth Hospitality Press, an imprint of The Haworth Press, Inc., 2004, pp. xv-xvi. Single or multiple copies of this article are available for a fee from The Haworth Document Delivery Service [1-800-HAWORTH, 9:00 a.m. - 5:00 p.m. (EST). E-mail address: docdelivery@haworthpress.com].

http://www.haworthpress.com/web/JTTM

tions present advances in the area from analysis of online picture presentations to the importance and significance of maintaining travel agent Websites in section five to a review of the balanced scorecard and its use in evaluating Websites in section six.

The special volume has received an unprecedented number of submissions and the Editors wish to thank the twenty-one reviewers with reputable expertise in e-commerce and information technology who helped to make this special volume a success. These reviewers are as follows:

- Andrew Frew, *Queen Margaret University College* (UK)
- Billy Bai, *University of Nevada, Las Vegas* (USA)
- Bo Hu, *Oklahoma State University* (USA)
- Brian Miller, *University of Delaware* (USA)
- Brian Tyrrell, *University of Nevada, Las Vegas* (USA)
- Cathy Hsu, *Hong Kong Polytechnic University* (China)
- Cihan Cobanoglu, *University of Delaware* (USA)
- Clark Hu, *Temple University* (USA)
- Dan Connolly, *University of Denver* (USA)
- Dimitrios Buhalis, *University of Surrey* (UK)
- Joan Clay, *University of North Texas* (USA)
- Joseph Ismail, *Purdue University* (USA)
- Karl Woeber, *Vienna University of Economics and Business Administration* (Austria)
- Liping Cai, *Purdue University* (USA)
- Marianna Sigala, *University of Strathclyde* (Scotland)
- Pauline Sheldon, *University of Hawaii* (USA)
- Peter O'Connor, *Institute de Management Hotelier International (IMHI Cornell ESSEC)* (France)
- SooCheong (Shawn) Jang, *Kansas State University* (USA)
- Sunny Ham, *University of Kentucky* (USA)
- Vincent Heung, *Hong Kong Polytechnic University* (China)

- William Werner, *University of Nevada, Las Vegas* (USA)

The Editors also wish to thank Dr. Kaye Chon, Chief Editor of the *Journal of Travel & Tourism Marketing,* for his continued advice throughout the special volume as well as Dr. Fred DeMicco at the University of Delaware who helped us with refining the idea for the special volume.

As editors we hope that the information presented in this special volume is not only interesting and informative but will provide directions for future research in the area. We believe that the articles in this special volume are of high quality and signify the growing interest of tourism and hospitality researchers in this area we affectionately call Hospitality E-Business Analysis, Research, and Development (HEARD).

Juline E. Mills
Assistant Professor of Hospitality
and Tourism Ecommerce
Purdue University, USA

Rob Law
Associate Professor
of Information Technology
Hong Kong Polytechnic University, China

SECTION 1:
ONLINE TRAVEL CONSUMER
SEARCH BEHAVIOR

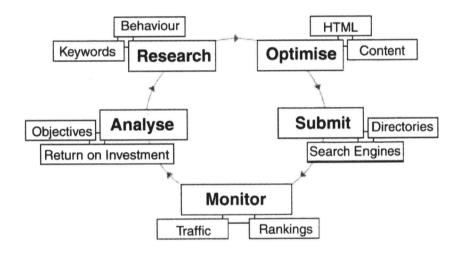

The Search Engine Marketing Model
Adapted from: http://www.searchenginestrategies.co.nz/sem-model.html

Consumer Objectives and the Amount of Search in Electronic Travel and Tourism Markets

Anssi Öörni

SUMMARY. This paper examines the effect of Internet-based travel and tourism markets on pre-purchase consumer search. It specifically aims to address the question of whether consumer search in electronic markets is substantially different from search in conventional markets judged by the objectives and amount of search. A self-administered mail survey of 871 subjects provides the empirical basis for the paper. The findings suggest that Internet-based leisure travel markets have, so far, affected pre-purchase consumer search less than has been expected. Online shoppers have not extended pre-purchase search. Further, they seem to advance convenience related objectives instead of attempting to optimize the purchase. *[Article copies available for a fee from The Haworth Document Delivery Service: 1-800-HAWORTH. E-mail address: <docdelivery@haworthpress.com> Website: <http://www.HaworthPress.com> © 2004 by The Haworth Press, Inc. All rights reserved.]*

KEYWORDS. Electronic commerce, electronic markets, travel, tourism, consumer search, empirical research

INTRODUCTION

Electronic markets benefit from increasing productivity of information technology, since product information can be disseminated at increased speed, quantity, and quality. This enhanced exchange of information is commonly believed to mollify information related market imperfections by allowing consumers to update their market knowledge more extensively than is feasible in most conventional consumer markets. As search costs decrease, consumers will be better able to find the best offerings, and sellers will be forced to seek either greater differentiation or lower prices (Bakos, 1997, 1998).

While increasing performance/price ratio of information and telecommunication technology is a fact, it is less clear if enhancements in data transmission alone will substantially change consumer behavior. Largely, the expected positive effects of electronic markets rest on indirect observations, e.g., on reports of the domestic air travel markets in the United States in the 1980s (Bakos, 1991b; Copeland & McKenney, 1988; Hopper, 1990). Higher levels of price competition were reported, and these observations were attributed to the de-

Anssi Öörni is Assistant Professor, Department of Information Systems Science, Helsinki School of Economics, Finland (E-mail: oorni@hse.fi).

[Haworth co-indexing entry note]: "Consumer Objectives and the Amount of Search in Electronic Travel and Tourism Markets." Öörni, Anssi. Co-published simultaneously in *Journal of Travel & Tourism Marketing* (The Haworth Hospitality Press, an imprint of The Haworth Press, Inc.) Vol. 17, No. 2/3, 2004. pp. 3-14; and: *Handbook of Consumer Behavior, Tourism, and the Internet* (ed: Juline E. Mills, and Rob Law) The Haworth Hospitality Press, an imprint of The Haworth Press, Inc., 2004, pp. 3-14. Single or multiple copies of this article are available for a fee from The Haworth Document Delivery Service [1-800-HAWORTH, 9:00 a.m. - 5:00 p.m. (EST). E-mail address: docdelivery@haworthpress.com].

velopment of computerized reservation systems (Bakos, 1991b). However, many other factors, such as deregulation, affected these markets simultaneously (Copeland & McKenney, 1988). Also, a number of studies have revealed rising airfares in the same time frame (Bailey & Williams, 1988; Dempsey, 1990; Joesch & Zick, 1990).

This work follows several other studies concerned with the effects of electronic commerce on consumer search. These reports have shown inconsistent support for the expected high efficiency of electronic consumer markets. Brynjolfsson and Smith (2000) demonstrated that substantial price dispersion existed in electronic markets for books and compact discs while the average prices were somewhat lower. Clemons et al. (2002) found substantial price dispersion for domestic airline tickets offered by online travel agents in the US. Experimental evidence suggests that the advantages of the Web seem to be smaller and the related uncertainties higher than often assumed (Anckar & Walden, 2002; Crichton & Frew, 2000; Öörni & Klein, 2003).

Previous research has employed experiments or measures such as average prices and price dispersion to study the efficiency of information search in electronic consumer markets. While these studies provide valuable information on the efficiency of the Internet as a source of product information, they also have limitations that should be addressed to increase our confidence in the results. Market prices, for example, may reflect events other than seller reactions to consumer search.

This paper examines the effect of Internet-based electronic markets on consumer search in the travel and tourism industry. It addresses the question whether consumer search in electronic markets is different from search in conventional markets. The topic question will be refined by the following sub-problems that examine both motivational and efficiency aspects of consumer search:

1. Have consumers extended their pre-purchase search in electronic markets when compared to the amount of search observed in conventional markets?

2. Do the objectives that consumers pursue in electronic markets deviate from those related to conventional markets?

Simon (1987) argues that when studying behavior, the context of the study must be comprehensive enough to encompass goals, the definition of situation, and computational resources. In the following section travel and tourism literature will be reviewed to construct the context of consumer search for travel and tourism products. Next, the research hypotheses are constructed through a review of electronic markets and consumer behavior literature discussing the amount of search and consumer objectives related to direct sales channels. The research questions will be addressed through comparative statistical analyses utilizing data from a self-administered mail survey. Finally, implications of the analyses on electronic travel and tourism markets will be discussed.

CONSUMER SEARCH IN TRAVEL AND TOURISM CONTEXT

A lot of variation in consumer search in travel and tourism markets emanates from varying consumer characteristics and decision contexts. Some of the related factors are likely to encourage consumers to resort to extended search and to rely heavily on external information sources; yet, this variation may also act as friction and reduce the positive effects of electronic markets. While purchases of travel services often involve extended problem-solving behavior, they may also become a routine (Moutinho, 1987) with limited or no search involved. According to Snepenger, Meged, Snelling and Worrall (1990), four major factors influence information search in the tourism context: (1) the composition of vacation groups, (2) the presence of family and friends at the destination, (3) prior visits to destination, (4) the degree of novelty associated with the destination. Greater planning efforts are related to groups with tight bonds. Especially, the inclusion of children increases the need for planning because of coordination of schedules and meeting of differential needs (Wilkes, 1995). Family-size and education are found to have a positive association with the use of destination-specific literature and other external information sources while age (Gitelson & Crompton, 1983) and occupation (Woodside & Ronkainen, 1980) seem to correlate with use of travel agencies. Interpersonal communication is frequently observed and multiple sources are typically used to retrieve information in vacation planning (Capella & Greco, 1987; Myers & Moncrief, 1978; Nichols & Snepenger, 1988). Importance of interpersonal sources seems to increase with age (Capella & Greco, 1987). First-time visitors to a destination are observed to rely more on professional sources than seasoned visitors (Snepenger, Meged, Snelling, & Worrall, 1990; Van Raaij, 1986). The novelty of a vacation is reported to increase both the length of the search and the number of information sources used (Engel, Kollat, & Blackwell, 1973; Snepenger, 1987).

Services of low complexity coupled with high customer knowledge are generally well suited for automated distribution since there is limited need to assist consumers in transactions (Apte & Vepsalainen, 1993). In the tourism context, such standard products comprise last minute offerings, single component products, and packaged tours (Werthner & Klein, 1999, p. 53). The more complex the product, the more uncertainty is involved in the transaction, and the less suitable the product class is for automation of purchase by providing consumers with direct access to the products (Werthner & Klein, 1999, p. 22). Travel and tourism products vary in complexity, and the complexity is related to both the product class and the context of use (*ibid.*). Consumer knowledge is negatively associated with product complexity and consumers vary in their knowledge of the product class. Hence, increase in product complexity will likely lead to more dispersed and, on average, lower consumer knowledge.

The Amount of Search

Information economics suggests that changing identity of sellers and fluctuations in supply and demand result in uncertainty, since information becomes obsolete (Stigler, 1961). Buyers must therefore update their information, and there is often no better means to do

that than search. Search is not, however, without costs. Stigler (*ibid.*) proposes, that high search costs will lead value maximizing consumers to limit their pre-purchase search, which results in less than perfectly informed purchase decisions. This is reflected in multiple prices in most consumer markets.

The amount of consumer search is inversely related to the level of search costs. The number of sellers visited, in particular, reflects the search costs that value maximizing consumers face. If low search costs prevailed in electronic markets, value-maximizing consumers would extend their pre-purchase search and visit a larger number of sellers than before–assuming that the benefits of search remain constant (Bakos, 1997).

Products are not alike judged by the costs related to evaluating them. As previously discussed, high product complexity is often associated with relatively low consumer knowledge. High product complexity raises need for information processing (Bettman, Johnson, & Payne, 1990), and thus increases the search costs. Variation in product complexity should be factored in when attempting to evaluate the amount of search across several product categories.

One further element that should be factored in is the total number of information sources used during the search process. Consumers rarely rely on a single information source only (Engel & Blackwell, 1982, p. 337). Rather, search is often a cumulative process; those who seek information from one source also turn to others. The mass media tend to be contributory and information sources tend to be complementary rather than competitive (Berelson & Steiner, 1964, p. 532; Katona & Mueller, 1955, p. 46). Hence, many consumers are likely to use the Web in combination with conventional sources and they may access various retailers through different channels. The effect that the Web may have on the amount of search should be distinguished from the indirect effect discussed above.

H1: Consumers using the Web to search for travel services visit a higher number of sellers than those abstaining from using the Web, when product class and the number of information sources used are controlled.

Objectives of Search

The expected positive effects of consumer search rest largely on the assumption that consumers try to optimize the total purchase costs. A number of authors (Akerlof & Yellen, 1985; Haltiwanger & Waldman, 1985; Russell & Thaler, 1985) have demonstrated that non-maximizing behavior can significantly affect equilibrium analyses. Small systematic deviations from value maximizing behavior can result in modest losses to individual actors. Yet, changes in the equilibrium of the systems are an order of magnitude larger.

A look into consumer objectives is necessary to assess whether consumers in any given markets behave according to the optimization paradigm previously discussed. The purchase decision is often treated in the electronic markets literature as a whole: price, product attributes, and search costs are combined to construct a single decision that can be optimized. In the direct sales literature, on the other hand, it is suggested that many consumers may separate product related decisions from decisions connected to the search process (see, e.g., Eastlick & Feinberg, 1994).

A number of objectives have been related to consumer search in electronic markets and direct sales literature. According to Bakos (1997), "the optimal strategy for a buyer in a market with search costs is to determine a 'price and fit' threshold, and keep searching until a satisfactory product is located." Degratu et al. (2000) compared online and offline supermarket customers and observed higher, if inconsistent, brand and price sensitivity among consumers in online supermarket environments.

Past research (Eastlick & Feinberg, 1994) has shown that convenience is a principal reason for patronage of direct channels. Eastlick and Feinberg (*ibid.*) argue that retail stores provide many benefits over direct channels: quicker gratification, opportunity for physical inspection, and easier product returns. According to them, in the absence of transportation costs, consumers would typically purchase from the retailer rather than the direct channel. Similarly, Donthu and Garcia (1999) found that Internet shoppers are less brand and price conscious than non-shoppers are. According to them, convenience seeking seems to drive use of the Internet markets.

The previous discussion offers multiple objectives that may drive use of the electronic markets. These objectives are often somewhat conflicting; yet, in order to evaluate their relative importance, they will be considered simultaneously. The hypothesis related to the objectives promoting use of electronic markets is formulated as:

H2:   Consumers using the Web are more price-sensitive, conscious of product quality, and seek to advance convenience more eagerly than do consumers abstaining from using the Web.

METHODOLOGY

The data were gathered by a self-administered post-purchase mail survey in December 2000 and January 2001. The recipients were randomly sampled from the customer base of Sonera Ltd., a major Internet service provider in Finland. The sample frame consisted of individual customers. The initial sample size was 3,000, which was reduced to 2,539 subjects during the preliminary screening. Industrial customers, erroneously labeled as individual customers, and duplicate entries of customers with multiple accounts were deleted from the sample.

The remaining 2,539 subjects were first contacted by an e-mail message, which included the URL of the HTML version of the questionnaire. Two weeks later those subjects, who had not taken part of the survey, were sent a letter and a printed version of the questionnaire. The total number of completed questionnaires was 871, which amounted to 34.4% response rate. Comparable response rates seem typical in social research and, hence, the response rate was deemed acceptable.

Data

To ensure that the sample did not deviate excessively from the sample frame or from the whole population, the sample demographics were compared to population statistics of census of 1999 by Statistics Finland (2000) and to the Internet tracking survey conducted by Taloustutkimus (2001). The following key demographics were identified in the consumer search literature as central person-related determinants of search behavior, which should be checked for possible biases: gender, age, education level, income, and location of residence. Table 1 exhibits both the sample and the population statistics.

Gender. While gender has little effect on one's cognitive abilities in relation to informa-

TABLE 1. Demographics

	Sample			Population
	Frequency	Percentage	Valid Percentage	Percentage
Gender				
Male	318	63.1	63.4	48.8
Female	550	36.5	36.6	51.2
Missing	3	0.3		
Total	871	100	100	100
Age				
0-10	0	0	0	12.2
10-14	3	0.3	0.3	6.1
15-19	32	3.7	3.7	6.4
20-24	44	5.1	5.1	6.3
25-29	62	7.1	7.1	5.9
30-34	107	12.3	12.3	6.9
35-39	118	13.5	13.5	7.4
40-44	136	15.6	15.6	7.5
45-49	127	14.6	14.6	7.8
50-54	111	12.7	12.7	8.2
55-59	58	6.7	6.7	5.5
60-64	39	4.5	4.5	5.0
65-69	21	2.4	2.4	4.4
70-74	9	1	1	4.0
75-79	2	0.2	0.2	3.1
80+	2	0.2	0.2	3.3
Total	871	100	100	100
Education				
Comprehensive school education	126	14.5	14.9	41.5
Upper secondary general school education	65	7.5	7.7	22.9
Vocational and professional education	242	27.8	28.5	12.7
Polytechnic education	234	26.9	27.6	12.6
University education	181	20.8	21.3	10.3
Missing	23	2.6		
Total	871	100		100

	Sample			Population
	Frequency	Percentage	Valid Percentage	Percentage
Income (FIM/year)				
0-19,999	51	5.9	6.4	9.9
20,000-29,999	10	1.1	1.3	5.3
30,000-39,999	10	1.1	1.3	8.9
40,000-49,999	5	0.6	0.6	7.6
50,000-59,999	11	1.3	1.4	7.4
60,000-79,999	37	4.2	4.7	11.0
80,000-99,999	42	4.8	5.3	9.7
100,000-140,999	245	28.1	30.9	22.3
150,000-199,999	184	21.1	23.2	9.8
200,000+	197	22.6	24.9	8.2
Missing	79	9.1		
Total	871	100	100.0	100
Community size				
The metropolitan area	155	17.8	17.9	18.3
Town, > 45,000 inhabitants	189	21.7	21.8	21.0
Town, < 45,000 inhabitants	255	29.3	29.4	21.1
Urban or semi-urban municipality	83	9.5	9.6	16.5
Rural municipality	186	21.4	21.4	23.1
Missing	3	0.3		
Total	871	100	100	100

tion processing, females have been found to associate positively with purchase involvement (Slama & Tashchian, 1985). Also, Eastlick and Feinberg (1994) have reported some gender differences in mail-order catalog patronage. According to them, females indicated that their salient motives were convenience-oriented while motives for males consisted mainly of merchandise and service-related factors. The major deviation between the sample and the population statistics is related to gender. Table 1 shows that of the subjects correctly identifying their gender, 63.4% were males and 36.6% females. The corresponding statistics in 1999 were 48.8% males and 51.2% females. Thus, the share of males in the sample is disproportionate to their percentage in the whole population. However, comparable statistics (Taloustutkimus, 2001) suggest that females accounted for approximately 40% of active (daily) Internet users. Thus, the data corresponded to the population of active Internet users fairly accurately.

Age. Age has been found to have a negative impact on the amount of pre-purchase search (Schmidt & Spreng, 1996) and the selection of information sources (Gitelson & Crompton, 1983). The age profile in the sample corresponds to that of the population excluding children and elderly people. Children under 10 were not included in the sample frame. Subjects over 60 years old, however, are underrepresented in the sample. The statistics of the Internet tracking survey (Taloustutkimus, 2001) reveal that elderly people have been relatively slow in adopting the Internet technology. The conclusion is that no serious biases exist in the data in this respect.

Education Level. Consumer behavior literature contains several studies in which education level is used as a determinant of information search. The reported results vary to some extent, yet, the basic finding is that higher levels of education lead to increased search activity (Claxton, Fry, & Portis, 1974; Katona & Mueller, 1955; Schaninger & Sciglimpaglia, 1981). This is interpreted to imply that the level of education is associated with one's ability to identify, locate, and assimilate relevant information (Schmidt & Spreng, 1996). The education level in the sample deviates substantially from that of the whole population, the share of highly educated people being larger than their share in the whole population. Thus, the subjects can be expected to display relatively high level of search, and caution should be exercised while generalizing the results to the whole population.

Income. One of the principal incentives of consumer search is to find the lowest price for a given level of quality. Past research has shown that the cost of product is positively associated with the search activity. Udell (1966) finds that the number of stores consumers visit increases for more expensive product categories. A positive relation for the price level and the search activity has been reported across a variety of product categories including cars (Kiel & Layton, 1981), appliances (Newman & Staelin, 1972; Udell, 1966), and apparel (Dommermuth, 1965). However, studies on major durables (Claxton et al., 1974; Katona & Mueller, 1955) and on food (Bucklin, 1969) have failed to find significant relationship between household financial pressure and the amount of search. Even though little empirical evidence exists in support of the relationship between the amount of search and the per-

ceived financial sacrifice, it has a sound theoretical background, and may affect search activity. The sample is biased towards the higher income echelons. Thus, the income level of the subjects may reduce, on average, the perceived benefits of search and have a negative effect on the amount of search.

Location of Residence. Economics of information theory directly relates search costs to market efficiency; consumers facing high search costs commit themselves to limited pre-purchase information search. Newman and Staelin (Newman & Staelin, 1972) found a positive relationship between information seeking and city size of residence for buyers of cars, but not for appliances. Their finding suggests that access to retailers is a necessary, yet insufficient condition for increased search (Newman, 1977). The share of townspeople in the sample is, again, out of their proportion in the population. Thus, the location of residence may reduce the average search activity of our subjects.

RESULTS

In this section the results of the statistical analyses are reported. The hypothesis regarding the positive effect the Web is expected to have on the amount of pre-purchase consumer search is tested first. This will be followed by an analysis and discussion of consumer objectives that may affect consumers' decision to use the Web as an information source during the pre-purchase search process.

The Amount of Search

Only consumers who had bought travel services during the year 2000 and paid the purchased services themselves were selected to the analyses. Of the 871 respondents, 406 met these controls. The subjects were first categorized by their use or non-use of the Web as an information source during the pre-purchase search process related to their most recent purchase of travel and tourism products. This information is displayed in Table 2. One can observe that two thirds of the subjects had used the Web as an information source. The figure is rather high, but not entirely surprising if one

TABLE 2. Subjects Categorized by the Use of the Web

	Web Used	Frequency	Percent	Valid Percent
Valid	Yes	257	63.3	64.9
.	No	139	34.2	35.1
Missing		10	2.5	
Total		396	100.0	

TABLE 3. Subjects Categorized by the Type of Travel Service Purchased

	Type of Travel	Frequency	Percent	Valid Percent
Valid	Cruise	114	28.1	28.6
	Packaged tour	131	32.3	32.8
	Flight + hotel	46	11.3	11.5
	Unidentified	108	26.6	27.1
	Total	399	98.3	100.0
Missing		7	1.7	
Total		406	100.0	

keeps in mind that the subjects came from a sampling frame consisting of customers of a major ISP. Hence, it is reasonable to expect that most of them should have had both means and motivation to use the Web for search.

Product class is likely to affect the search process, as discussed in the theory section. The respondents were categorized based on the product type (see Table 3) and it was found that more than half of the products purchased were relatively simple, single component products (Werthner & Klein, 1999, p. 53) and, thus, well suited for electronic markets.

For the test of the first hypothesis (H1) a linear regression model was constructed. The model attempts to capture the factors discussed in the theory section of this paper, namely the use of the Web, the number of media employed during the search process and the type of the travel services searched for. The linear regression model has the following form:

$$\mu = \beta_0 + \beta_W X_W + \beta_M X_M + \beta_C X_C + \beta_P X_P + \beta_F X_F,$$

where

μ: the expected value for the "number of sellers visited."

X_W: the indicator variable for the use of the Web.

X_M: the number of media used in search.

X_C: the indicator variable for the "cruise" product type.

X_P: the indicator variable for the "packaged tour" product type.

X_F: the indicator variable for the "flight and hotel" product type.

For the independent variable of interest, the following hypotheses are considered:

$$H_0: \beta_W \leq 0 \text{ and } H_a: \beta_W > 0$$

The α risk was controlled at 0.05 when $\beta_W = 0$. Parameter β_0 was of no interest in this case and parameters β_C, β_P, and β_F were included in the model as controls to ensure that product class related differences did not hide the effect of the Web. Parameter β_M, on the other hand, was included to control the fact that the use of the Web is likely to increase the total number of information sources used. The ordinary least squares estimates of the parameters of the linear model (1) are given in Table 4.

The null hypothesis is concluded regarding the effect of the Web on the amount of search: the use of the Web does not, as such, seem to associate with higher number of sellers visited. However, the use of the Web seems to correlate with the number of media used. This could be interpreted to imply that those consumers who actively search for and compare travel services prior to purchasing them, have adopted the Web as an additional medium to their repertoire. Yet, it appears that something holds consumers back from extending their pre-purchase search–at least when measured by the number of sellers visited–so substantially that it would show up in the analysis.

The number of media used during the search process associates, as expected, with the number of sellers visited. This finding suggests that consumers tend to contact different sellers through different media. The type of travel service searched for had a mixed effect on the amount of search. Consumers tended to compare a limited number of sellers when searching for cruises. This reflects most likely the limited number of companies organizing international cruises in the markets under study.

TABLE 4. The OLS Estimates of the Regression Coefficients (p-values are calculated one-sided)

	Estimates	Std. Dev.	t-value	p-value
Intercept (β_O)	2.143	0.250	8.578	0.000
Use of the Web (β_W)	−0.223	0.269	−0.831	0.204
Number of Media (β_M)	0.201	0.072	2.791	0.003
Cruise (β_C)	−1.074	0.231	−4.656	0.000
Packaged tour (β_P)	−0.241	0.219	−1.103	0.136
Flight and Hotel (β_F)	−0.396	0.289	−1.369	0.086

Dependent variable: number of sellers visited.
$R^2 = 0.081$, Adjusted $R^2 = 0.069$, n = 365.

Objectives of Search

The results of the previously reported analysis suggest that consumers do not consistently visit a higher number of sellers when using the Web. Yet the sample data show that a substantial portion of consumers with access to the Web use it during pre-purchase search for travel products. To gain a better understanding of the motives that presently drive use of electronic media, pair-wise comparisons of the relative importance of decision criteria related to use and non-use of the Web were conducted. The subjects had reported decision criteria they used for selecting their latest purchase. These criteria were measured using the Osgood scales (a seven-point development of the Likert scale). The originally measured criteria were found to contain several anomalies. Criteria like price and quality showed strong positive correlation in the data. Since these criteria should be somewhat conflicting in most real life situations, it was decided to remedy the anomalies by scaling the variables as suggested by Hair et al. (1998). Thus, the average criteria score was subtracted from individual scores to obtain the relative importance of criteria.

The group means were compared with independent samples t-tests. The hypothesis $H2$ was formulated as:

$$H_0: \mu_E = \mu_C \quad \text{and} \quad H_a: \mu_E \neq \mu_C$$

The α-risk was controlled at 0.05 when $\mu_E = \mu_C$.

According to the results of the independent samples t-tests, shown in Table 5, the hypothesis $H_a: \mu_E \neq \mu_C$ was concluded only for the criterion "speed of search." Hence, consumers using the Web during pre-purchase search were not, on average, more price-sensitive and did not seek for higher quality than those consumers abstaining from using the Web. However, the subjects using the Web regarded speed of search as a more important criterion than did those using conventional information sources only. The conclusion is that consumers presently seem to use electronic information sources, on average, much for the same reasons as they use other direct sales channels–to avoid need to visit stores, and thus to speed up the transaction.

The results of the statistical analyses suggest that the majority of consumers searching for travel services on the Web also utilize conventional information sources. Thus, the Web does not presently appear to be vastly more effective as a source of product information. At least, in the travel services context it appears not to be the information source over all other sources as is sometimes posited. The Web is, rather, a complementary information source providing consumers with relatively easy access to electronic versions of travel catalogs and inventory information once the prospective sellers are identified. It appears to be a valuable source, especially for those consumers who try to lower the time related search costs. Our results imply that most consumers extend their search to electronic markets to improve the search process, not necessarily the quality of their purchase decision.

DISCUSSION

The observed travel services markets display little support for the hypotheses concerning efficient electronic consumer markets, although the observations are consistent with most previous empirical evidence concerning the effects of electronic commerce on differentiated consumer markets. It appears that low cost of information dissemination alone does not alleviate search as much as some spectators have expected, and that such tasks as lo-

TABLE 5. Decision Criteria by Information Sources Used (p-values are calculated two-sided)

Criterion	Use of the Web	n	Mean	Std. Dev.	t-value	Df	p-value
Price	yes	325	0.091	1.670	0.477	460	0.634
	no	137	0.011	1.630			
Quality	yes	325	0.876	1.331	0.251	460	0.802
	no	137	0.843	1.196			
Speed of search	yes	325	−0.032	1.495	2.059	220.485[a]	0.042
	no	137	−0.413	1.901			

[a]Degrees of freedom vary, since homogeneity of population variances is not assumed based on the results of the Levene 's test of homogeneity-of-variance ($\alpha = 0.05$).

cating sellers and evaluating products remain relatively costly even in electronic markets. Stigler (1961) attributed the need to search largely to a desire to update information that has become obsolete. The present electronic markets provide few means to substantially better the conventional markets in this regard. The problem of information becoming obsolescent seems to prevail in electronic markets as well.

There are a number of reasons related to product characteristics and consumer behavior why electronic travel services markets do not conform to the general expectations regarding electronic markets. Travel decisions are very much affected by forces outside the individual, such as role and family influences, reference groups, social classes, and culture and subculture (Moutinho, 1987). Consumer decisions in general are contingent on the social environment (Bettman et al., 1990); the need to justify the decision to others has been found to lead to more coherent decision strategies. More specifically, the social setting that characterizes the consumption of a product also influences the information search (Stayman & Deshpande, 1989). The composition of the traveling party heavily influences the behavior of leisure travelers (McIntosh & Goeldner, 1986), not least since leisure travel products are often consumed jointly with others and the travel activities reflect both the direct and indirect influence of all those traveling together (Chadwick, 1987).

Integration issues in tourism and travel markets are more urgent than in most other consumer markets (Werthner & Klein, 1999, p. 49). This need is largely dictated by the complementary nature of travel products which are often used in combination with other prod-

ucts and services, thus increasing the complexity of the purchase decision. A consumer, composing his/her vacation from components such as flights, accommodation, dining, and attractions to visit, is often faced with a very high number of possible combinations. Moreover, all these components must fit into a schedule. Travel agencies have traditionally provided consumers with combined service offerings tailored to the customer's needs (*ibid.*). Since the complexity of combined products is relatively high, there will be a continued need for such intermediate services in the electronic markets.

To summarize the findings presented in this work, the study concludes that there is still little evidence of electronic markets leading invariably to extended consumer search, which in turn puts into question the expected low information search costs. Further, consumers seem to advance convenience related objectives instead of attempting to optimize the purchase. Such behavior, if it persists, decreases the probability of increasing price competition in electronic markets.

REFERENCES

Akerlof, G. A., & Yellen, J. L. (1985). Can Small Deviations from Rationality Make Significant Differences to Economic Equilibria? *The American Economic Review*, 75(4), 708-720.

Anckar, B., & Walden, P. (2002). Self-Booking of High- and Low-Complexity Travel Products: Exploratory Findings. *Information Technology & Tourism, 4*, 151-165.

Apte, U., & Vepsalainen, A. P. J. (1993). High Tech or High Touch? Efficient Channel Strategies for Delivering Financial Services. *Journal of Strategic Information Systems*, 2(1), 39-54.

Bailey, E., & Williams, J. R. (1988). Sources of economic rent in the deregulated airline industry. *Journal of Law and Economics, 31*(1), 173-202.

Bakos, J. Y. (1991b). A Strategic Analysis of Electronic Marketplaces. *MIS Quarterly, 15*(3), 295-311.

Bakos, J. Y. (1997). Reducing buyer search costs: Implications for electronic marketplaces. *Management Science, 43*(12), 1676-1692.

Bakos, J. Y. (1998). The emerging role of electronic marketplaces on the Internet. *Communications of the ACM, 41*(8), 35-42.

Berelson, B., & Steiner, G. (1964). *Human Behavior.* New York: Harcourt.

Bettman, J. R., Johnson, E. J., & Payne, J. W. (1990). Consumer Decision Making. In T. S. Robertson & H. H. Kassarjian (Eds.), *Handbook of Consumer Behavior* (pp. 50-84). Englewood Cliffs, N.J.: Prentice-Hall.

Brynjolfsson, E., & Smith, M. D. (2000). Frictionless Commerce? A comparison of Internet and conventional retailers. *Management Science, 46*(4), 563-586.

Bucklin, L. P. (1969). Consumer search, role enactment and market efficiency. *Journal of Business, 42*, 416-438.

Capella, L. M., & Greco, A. J. (1987). Information Sources of Elderly for Vacation Decisions. *Annals of Tourism Research, 14*(1), 148-151.

Chadwick, R. A. (1987). Concepts, Definitions, and Measures Used in Travel and Tourism Research. In J. R. B. Richie & C. R. Goeldner (Eds.), *Travel, Tourism, and Hospitality Research.* New York: John Wiley.

Claxton, J. D., Fry, J. N., & Portis, B. A. (1974). A taxonomy of prepurchase information gathering patterns. *Journal of Consumer Research, 1*, 35-42.

Clemons, E. K., Hann, I.-H., & Hitt, L. M. (2002). Price dispersion and differentiation in online travel: An empirical investigation. *Management Science, 48*(4), 534-549.

Copeland, D. G., & McKenney, J. L. (1988). Airline Reservations Systems: Lessons From History. *MIS Quarterly, 12*(3), 353-370.

Crichton, E., & Frew, A. J. (2000). Usability of Information and Reservation Systems: Theory or Practice? In D. R. Fesenmaier, S. Klein & D. Buhalis (Eds.), *Information and Communication Technologies in Tourism 2000* (pp. 408-417). Wien, New York: Springer.

Degratu, A., Rangaswamy, A., & Wu, J. (2000). Consumer Choice Behavior in Online and Traditional Supermarkets: The Effects of Brand Name, Price, and Other Search Attributes. *International Journal of Research in Marketing, 17*(1), 55-78.

Dempsey, P. S. (1990). *Flying blind: The failure of airline deregulation.* Washington, DC: Economics Policy Institute.

Dommermuth, W. P. (1965). The Shopping Matrix and Marketing Strategy. *Journal of Marketing Research, 2*(May), 128-132.

Donthu, N., & Garcia, A. (1999). The Internet Shopper. *Journal of Advertising Research, 39*(3), 52-58.

Eastlick, M. A., & Feinberg, R. A. (1994). Gender differences in mail-catalog patronage motives. *Journal of Direct Marketing, 8*(2), 37-44.

Engel, J. F., & Blackwell, R. D. (1982). *Consumer Behavior.* Chicago, IL: Dryden Press.

Engel, J. F., Kollat, D., & Blackwell, R. D. (1973). *Consumer Behavior.* Hinsdale, IL: Dryden Press.

Gitelson, R. J., & Crompton, J. L. (1983). The Planning Horizons and Sources of Information Used by Pleasure Vacationers. *Journal of Travel Research, 21*(Winter), 2-7.

Hair Jr., J. F., Anderson, R. E., Tatham, R. L., & Black, W. C. (1998). *Multivariate data analysis* (4th ed.). Upper Saddle River, N.J.: Prentice-Hall.

Haltiwanger, J., & Waldman, M. (1985). Rational Expectations and the Limits of Rationality: An Analysis of Heterogeneity. *American Economic Review, 75*(3), 326-340.

Hopper, M. G. (1990). Rattling SABRE–New Ways to Compete on Information. *Harvard Business Review* (May-June), 118-125.

Joesch, J. M., & Zick, C. D. (1990). Growing Market Concentration and Changes in Consumer Welfare. *Journal of Consumer Policy, 13*(4), 321-353.

Katona, G., & Mueller, E. A. (1955). A study of purchase decisions. In L. H. Clark (Ed.), *Consumer Behavior: The Dynamics of Consumer Reaction* (pp. 30-87). New York: New York University Press.

Kiel, G. C., & Layton, R. A. (1981). Dimensions of Consumer Information Seeking Behavior. *Journal of Marketing Research, 18*(2), 233-239.

McIntosh, R. W., & Goeldner, C. R. (1986). *Tourism: Principles, practices and philosophies.* New York: John Wiley and Sons.

Moutinho, L. (1987). Consumer Behavior in Tourism. *European Journal of Marketing, 21*(10), 5-44.

Myers, P. B., & Moncrief, L. W. (1978). Differential Leisure Travel Decision-Making Between Spouses. *Annals of Tourism Research, 5*(1), 157-165.

Newman, J. W. (1977). Consumer External Search: Amount and Determinants. In A. G. Woodside, J. N. Sheth & P. D. Bennett (Eds.), *Consumer and Industrial Buying Behavior* (pp. 79-94). New York: North-Holland.

Newman, J. W., & Staelin, R. (1972). Prepurchase Information Seeking for New Cars and Major Household Appliances. *Journal of Marketing Research, 9*, 249-257.

Nichols, C., & Snepenger, D. (1988). Family Decision Making and Tourism Behavior and Attitudes. *Journal of Travel Research, 26*(4), 2-6.

Öörni, A., & Klein, S. (2003). Electronic Travel Markets: Elusive Effects on Consumer Behavior. In A. Frew, M. Hitz & P. O'Connor (Eds.), *Information and Communication Technologies in Tourism 2003* (pp. 29-38). Wien, New York: Springer.

Russell, T., & Thaler, R. (1985). The Relevance of Quasi Rationality in Competitive Markets. *American Economic Review, 75*(5), 1071-1082.

Schaninger, C. M., & Sciglimpaglia, D. (1981). The Influence of Cognitive Personality Traits and Demographics on Consumer Information Acquisition. *Journal of Consumer Research, 8*(September), 208-216.

Schmidt, J. B., & Spreng, R. A. (1996). A proposed model of external consumer information search. *Academy of Marketing Science Journal, 24*(3), 246-256.

Simon, H. A. (1987). Rationality in Psychology and Economics. In R. M. Horgarth & M. W. Reder (Eds.), *Rational Choice, The Contrast Between Economics and Psychology* (pp. 25-40). Chicago and London: The University of Chicago Press.

Slama, M. E., & Tashchian, A. (1985). Selected Socioeconomic and Demographic Characteristics Associated with Purchasing Involvement. *Journal of Marketing, 49*(1), 72-82.

Snepenger, D. J. (1987). Segmenting the Vacation Market by Novelty-Seeking Role. *Journal of Travel Research, 26*(2), 8-14.

Snepenger, D. J., Meged, K., Snelling, M., & Worrall, K. (1990). Information Search Strategies by Destination-Naive Tourists. *Journal of Travel Research, 29*(1), 13-16.

Snepenger, D. J., & Milner, L. (1990). Demographic and Situational Correlates of Business Travel. *Journal of Travel Research, 28*(4), 27-32.

Statistics Finland. (2000). *Finland in figures*, 2001, from *http://www.stat.fi/tk/tp/tasku/suomilukuina_en.html*

Stayman, D. M., & Deshpande, R. (1989). Situational Ethnicity and Consumer Behavior. *Journal of Consumer Research, 16*(December), 361-371.

Stigler, G. J. (1961). The Economics of Information. *The Journal of Political Economy, 69*(3), 213-225.

Taloustutkimus. (2001). *The Finnish Internet Tracking*, from *http://www.taloustutkimus.fi/tuotteet/internet/inet1e.htm*

Udell, J. C. (1966). Prepurchase Behavior of Buyers of Small Electrical Appliances. *Journal of Marketing, 30*, 50-52.

Van Raaij, W. F. (1986). Consumer Research on Tourism: Mental and Behavioral Constructs. *Annals of Tourism Research, 13*, 1-9.

Werthner, H., & Klein, S. (1999). *Information technology and tourism: A challenging relationship* (1 ed.). Wien: Springer-Verlag.

Wilkes, R. E. (1995). Household Life-Cycle Stages, Transitions, and Product Expenditures. *Journal of Consumer Research, 22*(1), 27-42.

Woodside, A. G., & Ronkainen, I. A. (1980). Vacation Planning Segments: Self-Planning vs. Users of Motor Club and Travel Agents. *Annals of Tourism Research, 7*, 385-393.

APPENDIX 1

Questionnaire Questions Relevant to the Study

Question 1
How would you describe your latest journey?
[   ] A cruise on a sea bordering Finland
[   ] A packaged vacation/group travel
[   ] A flight and hotel combination
[   ] Other trip abroad

Question 2
Who paid for this trip?
[   ] Myself
[   ] My spouse
[   ] My parents
[   ] My employer
[   ] Somebody else

Question 3
Please indicate, in order of importance, those information sources out of the twelve listed below that you used when choosing this journey.
Do not tick an alternative that you did not use.
(1 = most important, 2 = second most important, etc. If in your opinion some two alternatives were equally important, you may mark them with the same number.)

Service provider's	Travel agency's
(___) Outlet/office	(___) Outlet/office
(___) Telephone service	(___) Telephone service
(___) E-mail	(___) E-mail
(___) Web pages	(___) Web pages
(___) Brochure	(___) Brochure
(___) Advertisement	(___) Advertisement

Service provider here means tour organizers, airline companies, ferryboat operators, and hotels. A travel agency in turn means a company that sells travel services rendered by multiple different service providers.

Question 4

In choosing the travel arrangements the following were very important conditions:

	Totally agree ⇓						Totally disagree ⇓
Low price	[ ]	[ ]	[ ]	[ ]	[ ]	[ ]	[ ]
High quality	[ ]	[ ]	[ ]	[ ]	[ ]	[ ]	[ ]
Need to find the products quickly	[ ]	[ ]	[ ]	[ ]	[ ]	[ ]	[ ]

Question 5
How many sellers' offerings did you compare?_____

Information Search Behavior and Tourist Characteristics: The Internet vis-à-vis Other Information Sources

Man Luo
Ruomei Feng
Liping A. Cai

SUMMARY. The Internet as a new form of media is impacting tourist information provision and acquisition. A better understanding of the use of the Internet and other information sources by tourists will benefit the marketing efforts of destination organizations. Based on a general consumer behavior theory by Berkman and Gilson (1986), this study examined the relationships between tourists' use of the Internet vs. other information sources and their characteristics. It was found that demographic characteristics of gender and household income and situational factors of trip purpose and travel party type were significantly related to tourists' choices of information sources; and such behavior was associated with their trip outcomes of accommodation types and expenditure. The study's implications were discussed in the context of destination marketing. *[Article copies available for a fee from The Haworth Document Delivery Service: 1-800-HAWORTH. E-mail address: <docdelivery@ haworthpress.com> Website: <http://www.HaworthPress.com> © 2004 by The Haworth Press, Inc. All rights reserved.]*

KEYWORDS. Internet, tourist, information search behavior

INTRODUCTION

Nua Internet Surveys (2002) reported that 605.60 million people worldwide have Internet access. In the travel and tourism setting, the Internet is becoming a crucial medium for information delivery and acquisition. Past research (Peterson, Balasubramania, & Bronnenberg, 1997) suggested that three main aspects of products and services may have influences on Internet usage: (a) the cost and frequency of purchase, (b) the value proposition, and (c) the degree of differentiation. Travel and tourism-related products and services are believed to be well suited for Internet marketing because of distinctive high-prices, high involvement, and well-differentiated characteristics (Bonn, Furr, & Susskind, 1998). From the tourist perspective, Buhalis (1998) revealed that potential tourists have become more independent and sophisticated in using a range of tools to arrange their travel. The

---

Man Luo is affiliated with the Department of Mathematical Science, Ball State University, Muncie, IN 47306. Ruomei Feng is a PhD Candidate, Department of Hospitality and Tourism Management, Purdue University, West Lafayette, IN 47907 (E-mail: ruomei@purdue.edu). Liping A. Cai is Associate Professor, Department of Hospitality and Tourism Management, Purdue University, West Lafayette, IN 47907.

[Haworth co-indexing entry note]: "Information Search Behavior and Tourist Characteristics: The Internet vis-à-vis Other Information Sources." Luo, Man, Ruomei Feng, and Liping A. Cai. Co-published simultaneously in *Journal of Travel & Tourism Marketing* (The Haworth Hospitality Press, an imprint of The Haworth Press, Inc.) Vol. 17, No. 2/3, 2004, pp. 15-25; and: *Handbook of Consumer Behavior, Tourism, and the Internet* (ed: Juline E. Mills, and Rob Law) The Haworth Hospitality Press, an imprint of The Haworth Press, Inc., 2004, pp. 15-25. Single or multiple copies of this article are available for a fee from The Haworth Document Delivery Service [1-800-HAWORTH, 9:00 a.m. - 5:00 p.m. (EST). E-mail address: docdelivery@haworthpress.com].

Internet provides opportunities to reduce dependency on traditional intermediaries for remote, peripheral, and insular destinations. In addition, Buhalis (1998) suggested that the Internet provides a mechanism to develop and promote specialized products for mini-market segments.

Some studies (Bonn, Furr, & Susskind, 1998; Weber & Roehl, 1999) have examined the profile of the Internet users among tourists in the pleasure segment. This current study extends the existing research efforts with these objectives: (1) to investigate the relationships between tourists' demographic characteristics and their usage patterns of the Internet and other information sources; (2) to understand the effects of situational factors, such as number of previous visits, trip purpose, and travel party composition, on tourists' choice of the Internet vs. other information sources; (3) to analyze trip outcomes by comparing those who search for information on the Internet to those who use other information sources; and (4) to examine the effect of using the Internet as an information source on destination perception.

LITERATURE REVIEW AND HYPOTHESES

This study applied the theory of consumer behavior by Berkman and Gilson (1986) as the conceptual framework to understand tourist information search behavior. In their model, Berkman and Gilson (1986) posit that environmental influence and individual difference are two antecedents of consequent consumers' behaviors during the entire consumption process. Environmental influence refers to the influence from the external environment of consumers such as culture, social status, and family, while individual difference is concerned with consumer's individual internal characteristics such as motive, personalities, and attitude. An important feature suggested in Berkman and Gilson's model is that there are mutual effects among series of consequent behaviors.

Within the domain of environmental influence, the popularity of the Internet has become a remarkable cultural phenomenon from the end of the 20th century. It is profoundly changing the lifestyle of many people by offering new methods in communication and information provision and acquisition. There were 92 million Internet users in the U.S. and Canada (Lieb, 2000). Half of the Internet users got information for travel products via the Internet in 1999 (Travel Industry Association, 2000). The Internet as a cultural phenomenon has and will continue to have a major effect on consumer information search behavior (Peterson & Merino, 2003). According to Berkman and Gilson (1986), reference groups, as part of environmental influence, affect a consumer's behavior as well. One important form of reference group is social class membership. Previous studies have revealed that social class exerts an important effect on consumer behavior since consumption patterns and interaction networks are intimately related (Kahl, 1967). The family, as a consumption unit, has the most pervasive influence on consumer behavior (Berkman & Gilson, 1986). As such, it is reasonable to suggest that the behavior of a person searching for information online could also be influenced by his or her family members and friends.

In addition to environmental influence, a consumer's information search behavior is shaped by individual traits such as learning, perception, motivation, personality, and attitude. Extant research has revealed that the role of learning is essential in individual consumer behavior (Berkman & Gilson, 1986). During the learning process, consumers develop information search strategies that reflect the trade-off between the perceived benefits and cost of the search (Moorthy, Ratchford, & Taluksar, 1997). Consumers based on personality characteristics have different perceptions of benefits and costs involved in information search. The benefit of a search is determined by the perception of uncertainty in the environment, the importance placed on product, and the perceived risk. Meanwhile, consumers evaluate the costs of search efforts in terms of the time and money required to conduct the search as well as the cognitive efforts required to process information (Srinivasan & Ratchford, 1991). It is commonly shared that the

Internet helps consumers to be more efficient and effective in information search (Kennedy, 1996; Janal, 1996).

Although in the general consumer behavior context, external environmental influence and individual difference are proved to affect information search behavior, it is difficult to directly measure these factors. Instead, demographic characteristics and situational factors can be used as proxies to represent some of the environmental and individual factors that affect consumer behavior in general and information search behavior in specific as illustrated in Figure 1. During the process of information search, people choose different search strategies, of which there are at least three dimensions: spatial, temporal, and operational (Fodness & Murray, 1999). The spatial dimension of an information search strategy refers to the locus of search activity: internal (accessing the information from memory) and external (searching for information from the environment). The temporal dimension refers to the timing of search activity: a search can either be ongoing, building a knowledge base for future decisions, or pre-purchase, related to a current purchase problem. The operational dimension refers to the way the search is conducted and focuses on the particular sources used. In this study, the operational dimension of tourists' search strategies is examined.

Online Information Search and Demographic Characteristics

Information search behavior and tourist demographic characteristics are closely related. One of the earlier studies on the relationship found that people of higher socioeconomic class preferred to use travel agents as an information source (Woodside & Ronkainen, 1980). Gitelson and Crompton (1983) also noted that older people were more likely to use travel agents for information and that college-educated individuals were more likely to use destination specific literature. The more recent literature showed that demographic characteristics kept its influence on information sources preferences and choices over years. Eby, Molnar, and Cai (1999) reported that content preference for in-vehicle tourist information systems differs by education level. Several other studies (Prideaux, Wei, & Ruys, 2001; Dodd, 1998; Andereck & Caldwell, 1993) presented similar evidence as well. Some research revealed that Internet users are more likely to be white males who have a high socioeconomic status (Pitkow & Kehoe, 1996; Times, 1995; Yankelovich Partner Inc., 1995). Bonn, Furr, and Susskind (1998) suggested that gender, education, income, race, and occupation all have an influence on Internet usage. To improve further understanding of these relationships, this study de-

FIGURE 1. A Conceptual Framework of Tourist Online Information Search Behavior

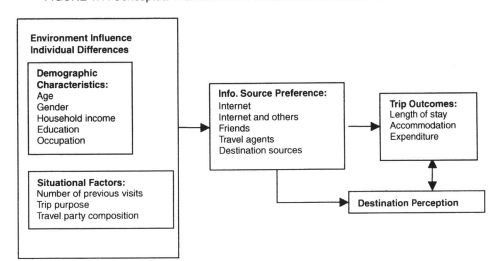

veloped the first five hypotheses for empirical testing:

H1: The use of the Internet and other information sources varies between senior and non-senior tourists.

H2: The use of the Internet and other information sources varies between female and male tourists.

H3: The use of the Internet and other information sources varies among tourists with low, medium, and high levels of household income.

H4: The use of the Internet and other information sources varies between tourists with college degree and those without college degree.

H5: The use of the Internet and other information sources varies among tourists with different occupations.

Information Search Behavior and Situational Factors

The influence of situational factors on tourist information search behavior is evident in previous literature. Regarding the determinants of information search in a travel purchase situation, Snepenger, Meged, Snelling, and Worrall (1990) identified four categories of variables: past experience, travel party composition, the presence of friends or relatives at the destination, and the degree of novelty associated with the destination. They found that prior experience with a destination could strongly affect information search behavior of destination-naive tourists. Chen and Gursoy (2000) and Dodd (1998) confirmed that there are differences existing between first-time and repeat visitors in using information sources. In addition, Moutinho (1987) suggested that purpose of trip remains the greatest influence on the tourist's behavior including information search. Cai, Lehto, and O'Leary (2001) investigated the U.S.-bound Chinese tourists and discovered that leisure tourists were more likely to use informal sources such as friends and relatives than tour-

ists with other purposes. Chen (2000) reported that in-flight information, national tourist office, and state/city tourist office are the only three information sources that are indistinguishable between the business travelers and leisure tourists of Korea, Japan, and Australia. These studies provided foundation for these three hypotheses:

H6: The use of the Internet and other information sources varies among tourists with different numbers of previous visits.

H7: The use of the Internet and other information sources varies among tourists on the three different trip purposes of pleasure, business, and personal.

H8: The use of the Internet and other information sources varies among tourists traveling with different party compositions.

Information Search Behavior and Trip Outcomes

The relationships between information search behavior and trip outcomes were supported in previous studies as well. Andereck and Caldwell (1993) concluded that trip characteristics are related to ratings of information source. Woodside, Cook, and Mindak (1987) found that frequent tourists could be distinguished from less frequent tourists in terms of media habits. Previous research has also revealed that tourists who reportedly use the Internet to gather travel and tourism-related information apparently spend more money on travel and tourism than nonusers (Bonn, Furr, & Susskind, 1998). Segmenting travel markets on the basis of information search behavior could be a useful way for destination marketers to reach their target markets' expectations by adopting effective media. If specific consumption travel patterns are found to be associated with sources used for information search, destination marketers could provide the right information to the tourists who adopt various search strategies. The following hypotheses were therefore proposed:

H9: There is a difference in length of stay among tourists who use the Internet vs. other information sources.

H10: There is a difference in accommodation usage among tourists who use the Internet vs. other information sources.

H11: There is a difference in travel expenditures among tourists who use the Internet vs. other information sources.

Information Search Behavior and Destination Perceptions

Some evidence of the relationship between information search behavior and destination perceptions can be found in the travel and tourism literature. Walmsley and Lewis (1984) suggested that tourists use information from various sources to compile pre-purchase destination images. These cognitive images serve as a basis for travel behavior (Aldskogius, 1977). The greater the match between the pre-purchase and after-purchase destination image the more likely that the tourist has favorable perceptions toward that destination. Lennon, Weber, and Henson (2001) investigated the influence of information resources on the perception of Northern Ireland. They reported that such sources of information as news media and word-of-mouth have a positive influence on perception while one (direct mail) has a negative influence. Baloglu (1999) also discussed that the variety (amount) and type of information sources (e.g., professional advices, word-of-mouth, advertisements, and non-tourism books/movies/news) determine tourists' perceptual/cognitive evaluation that form their affections about the tourist destination. It was thus hypothesized:

H12: There are differences in the destination perceptions among tourists who use the Internet vs. other information sources.

Figure 2 presents a graphic summary of the 12 proposed hypotheses.

METHODOLOGY AND EMPIRICAL FINDINGS

The study used the visitor profile data collected at four rural destinations (areas or counties) in the State of Indiana in the United States between 1998 and 2001. The data were collected on 16 fieldtrips through personal interviews. Each trip covered two weekdays and a weekend. The interview sites included major hotels and attractions. Tourists were approached by trained interviewers and asked if they were willing to participate in the study. Eighty to ninety percent of the individuals approached agreed to participate in the study. The respondents were presented with a list of information sources and asked to check those they used prior to their arrival at their destination. The information sources provided in the questionnaire included the Internet, friends and relatives, travel agents, and various destination-specific sources such as local convention and visitor bureaus. Other questions in the interview included trip characteristics, trip outcomes, demographics, and fourteen perceptual items. The destination perceptions were measured on a five-point Likert scale.

The sample included 716 respondents. Approximately 61.0% of the respondents were male. Of those respondents who were willing to provide information about their age, 26.0% were between the ages of 35 and 44, while 17.5% and 13.9% were in the age categories of 25-34 and 55-64 respectively. These three age categories comprised the majority of the respondents. Of those who answered the question regarding education, 18.8% of them had earned a high school diploma, 17.3% of them had been to college but had no degree, 30.7% reported that they had Bachelor's degrees, and 15.1% of them had Master's degrees. With regards to the income question, 528 respondents provided information on household income, where $50,000-$59,999 and $60,000-$69,999 were the most common answers, with 11.4% and 11.6% respectively.

This study explored five types of information usage choice: the Internet exclusively, destination sources, travel agents, friends and relatives, and a combination of the Internet and any of the aforementioned sources. With the differentiation of *the Internet* and *the*

FIGURE 2. Hypotheses Summary

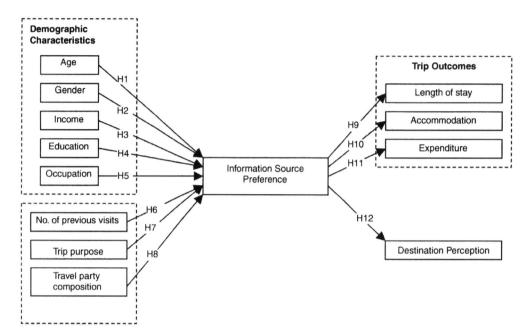

Internet and others, this study tried to investigate the two possible choices: using the Internet only and using the Internet complementarily. From H1 to H10, Chi-square analysis was used to test the associations between the row and column variables because such variables were measured on a discrete scale. This analysis examined whether differences exist in the usage of the Internet vs. other information sources among tourists of various demographics (H1-H5) and situational factors (H6-H8), and whether differences exist in trip outcomes of length of stay (H9) and accommodation usage (H10) among tourists who used different information sources. One-way ANOVA analysis was used to test the continuous variable of expenditure (H11) and destination perceptions (H12). The populations from which the samples were obtained were normally distributed. The samples were independent as well. This analysis examined the mean expenditures and the mean destination perceptions of tourists who used different information sources to test whether or not at least one mean is different.

It was revealed that, of the first five hypotheses, only H2 (gender, $\chi^2(4, n = 713) = 15.14$, $P = .004$) and H3 (household income, $\chi^2(8, n = 528) = 17.64$, $P = .024$) were accepted at the significance level of 0.05 (Table 1). The results show that tourists' use of the Internet and other information sources differs between the two genders, and among different levels of household income. These findings were consistent with the previous studies by Bonn, Furr, and Susskind (1988), which reported the effects of gender and household income of tourists on their usage of information sources including the Internet. No significant difference was found in information search behavior between senior and non-senior tourists (H1), between tourists with and without college education (H4), and among tourists in different occupations (H5).

Situational factors of various trip characteristics were tested in H6 through H8 (Table 2). Of the three hypotheses, H7 (trip purpose, $\chi^2(8, n = 713) = 25.63$, $P = .001$) was accepted, indicating that tourists adopted different sources for information, depending on their trip purposes. H8 (travel party composition, $\chi^2(12, n = 716) = 26.49$, $P = .009$) was also accepted. The types of traveling party composition were associated

TABLE 1. Chi-Square Results of Information Search Behavior and Demographic Characteristics

Demographic Characteristics	The Internet (%)	Internet and Others (%)	Dest. Sources (%)	Travel Agents (%)	Friends/ Relatives (%)	DF	χ^2	P-Value
H1: Age								
Under 50	11.1	11.1	21.5	30.9	25.4	4	4.74	0.315
50 and over	8.1	9.7	27.1	27.5	27.5			
H2: Gender								
Male	11.3	9.4	22.8	33.8	22.8	4	15.14	0.004*
Female	8.3	12.2	24.5	23.0	32.0			
H3: Household Income (Thousands)								
Under $40	3.9	10.8	17.6	32.4	35.3	8	17.64	0.024*
$40-$80	12.4	11.2	26.4	27.6	22.4			
$80 or over	11.9	12.5	22.2	34.7	18.8			
H4: Education								
Below college	10.4	7.8	25.0	27.2	29.5	4	7.58	0.108
College or above	10.5	12.9	21.5	31.3	23.9			
H5: Occupation								
Retired	7.1	10.2	27.6	25.5	29.6			
Manager	14.7	9.2	21.1	36.7	18.3			
Professional	10.8	12.6	23.4	29.4	23.8	16	17.58	0.349
Skilled worker	11.1	12.5	25.0	20.8	30.6			
Other	7.8	8.3	22.4	31.2	30.2			

TABLE 2. Chi-Square Results of Information Search Behavior and Situational Factors

Situational Factors	The Internet (%)	Internet and Others (%)	Dest. Sources (%)	Travel Agents (%)	Friends/ Relatives (%)	DF	χ^2	P-Value
H6: Number of Previous Visits								
First time	13.5	11.3	24.3	29.6	21.3	4	7.64	0.106
Repeat	8.5	10.1	22.9	29.7	28.9			
H7: Trip Purpose								
Pleasure	11.9	5.3	27.0	25.3	30.5			
Personal	10.1	13.0	18.9	30.8	27.2	8	25.63	0.001*
Business	8.1	14.7	22.4	33.6	21.2			
H8: Travel Party Composition								
Alone	9.5	10.4	20.7	33.3	26.1			
With family	12.3	9.2	27.6	24.6	26.3	12	26.49	0.009*
With friends	10.3	12.4	10.3	32.0	35.1			
With others	4.8	12.5	29.8	33.7	19.2			

with tourists' preferences for certain information sources such as the Internet. H6 (first-time vs. repeat visit) was rejected. No difference was noted in information search behavior between the first-time and repeat tourists.

H9 and H10 were examined with Chi-square analysis (Table 3), while H11 was tested with one-way ANOVA. It was found that tourists who searched for information on the Internet were more likely to be those staying at hotels (H10, $\chi^2(8, n = 700) = 26.63, P = .001$). Tourists who sought tourist informa-

tion on the Internet incurred significantly more trip expenditure than those who sought other sources (H11, $F = 3.56, P = .007$). H9 (length of stay) was rejected, as there was no significant difference in length of stay among tourists who use the Internet vs. other information sources.

H12 was tested using data collected from one destination, as the questions pertaining to the perceptions were destination specific. The hypothesis was rejected. The test results revealed no significant relationships between

TABLE 3. Chi-Square and ANOVA Results of Information Search Behavior and Trip Outcomes

Trip Outcomes	The Internet (%)	Internet and Others (%)	Dest. Sources (%)	Travel Agents (%)	Friends/ Relatives (%)	DF	χ^2	P-Value
H9: Length of Stay								
None	10.3	26.0	28.7	28.0	23.9			
1 night	30.9	23.3	22.6	29.4	30.6			
2 nights	35.3	21.9	18.9	15.2	20.6	16	22.92	0.116
3-4 nights	14.7	17.8	16.5	16.1	15.0			
5 nights or more	8.8	11.0	13.4	11.4	10.0			
H10: Accommodation								
Day trip	13.4	27.0	29.3	29.5	25.4			
Friends/relatives	4.5	2.7	5.4	5.8	14.6	8	26.63	0.001*
Hotels	82.1	70.3	65.3	64.7	60.0			
	Mean Value of Expenditure Range						F-value	
H11: Expenditure	4.61	4.72	3.42	4.13	3.29		3.56	0.007*

tourists' information sources and how positive or negative they perceived the destination on each of the 14 perceptual items (Table 4). This conclusion does not parallel previous research findings (Lennon, Weber, & Henson, 2001; Baloglu, 1999). A possible reason for this inconsistency is that the formation of tourists' destination perception is interactively influenced by information sources as well as some other variables, such as the long-term memory, since the information is acquired from varied sources over a lifetime (Mercer, 1971). Future research should further explore this issue by involving more variables. It was noted that tourists were quite positive about the destination overall. Table 5 summarized the conclusions for all hypotheses.

DISCUSSIONS

Punj and Staelin (1983) suggested that once a need for some consumption activity is recognized, the consumer is motivated to conduct a functional information search to enhance the quality of purchase outcomes. Today, the availability of tourist information sources has been extended by the Internet, which contains many of the features of television, radio, magazines, newspapers, telephone, and mail. It not only supports mass broadcasts but can also be applied in one-to-one communications with the features of text, images, audio, and video (McGaughey & Mason, 1998). The Internet user population is growing at a phenomenal

rate, and the Internet has become a global medium. Internet users can come from widely diversified cultural and social backgrounds. Geographical distances are no longer relevant when it comes to information provision and acquisition. Destination marketers can benefit from understanding the factors that influence the information search behavior, including the use of the Internet, in order to deliver appropriate messages.

The findings of the study confirm that tourist gender and household income are related to information source preference. Previous research found that male tourists with higher household incomes are more likely to be the Internet users (Pitkow & Kehoe, 1996; Times, 1995; Yankelovich Partner Inc., 1995). Similar conclusions can be deduced in this study. Destination marketers, therefore, should take into consideration the characteristics associated with these two demographics when developing contents and design of their websites. Future research is warranted to investigate the reasons underlying the influence of gender and household income on information search behavior. The current study found no difference in tourist information source preference among people with different demographics of age, education, and occupation. Such demographics are not barriers, one way or the other, in keeping people from searching information online. Destination marketers could use the Internet as an efficient marketing tool to attract the senior segment.

TABLE 4. ANOVA Results of Destination Perceptions and Information Search Behavior (H12)

Destination Perceptions	The Internet	Internet and Others	Mean Dest. Sources	Travel Agents	Friends/ Relatives	*F*-value	*P*-value
1. A good place for couples to visit	3.66	3.69	3.66	3.38	3.64	1.79	0.133
2. Does not have enough quality restaurants	2.45	2.48	2.74	2.68	2.38	1.44	0.223
3. A high degree of accessibility by road	3.29	3.86	3.57	3.50	3.62	1.60	0.175
4. Does not offer many activities for travelers	2.66	3.07	2.74	2.97	2.77	1.91	0.109
5. A safe travel destination	4.00	4.07	3.97	3.88	3.92	0.87	0.485
6. Difficult to find the way around the area	2.47	2.48	2.60	2.63	2.58	0.30	0.879
7. Affordable as a travel destination	3.66	4.07	3.86	3.67	3.83	1.91	0.110
8. The directional signs need to be improved	3.24	3.00	2.89	3.03	2.98	0.81	0.517
9. Has several unique attractions for vacationers	3.55	3.29	3.37	3.19	3.32	1.52	0.197
10. Does not have enough high-quality hotels	2.32	2.32	2.60	2.62	2.55	1.36	0.249
11. A good place to take children	3.61	3.57	3.37	3.40	3.42	0.88	0.477
12. A unique vacation travel destination	3.14	2.96	2.91	3.00	3.06	0.33	0.857
13. Offers several unique shopping opportunities	3.18	3.25	3.23	3.17	3.13	0.14	0.965
14. Not a good place for family weekends	2.58	2.43	2.69	2.82	2.87	2.09	0.083

TABLE 5. Summary for Hypothesis Testing

Hypothesis	Variable	Conclusion	Implication
H1	Age	Rejected	The use of the Internet and other information sources doesn't vary between senior and non-senior tourists.
H2	Gender	Accepted	The use of the Internet and other information sources varies between female and male tourists.
H3	Household income	Accepted	The use of the Internet and other information sources varies among tourists with low, medium, and high levels of household incomes.
H4	Education	Rejected	The use of the Internet and other information sources doesn't vary between tourists with college degree and those without college degree.
H5	Occupation	Rejected	The use of the Internet and other information sources doesn't vary among tourists with different occupations.
H6	No. of previous visits	Rejected	The use of the Internet and other information sources doesn't vary among tourists with different numbers of previous visits.
H7	Trip purpose	Accepted	The use of the Internet and other information sources varies among tourists on the trip purposes of pleasure, business, and personal.
H8	Travel party composition	Accepted	The use of the Internet and other information sources varies among tourists traveling with different party compositions.
H9	Length of stay	Rejected	There is no difference in length of stay among tourists who use the Internet vs. other information sources.
H10	Accommodation	Accepted	There is difference in accommodation usage among tourists who use the Internet vs. other information sources.
H11	Expenditure	Accepted	There is difference in travel expenditures among tourists who use the Internet vs. other information sources.
H12	Destination perceptions	Rejected	There is no difference in the destination perceptions among tourists who use the Internet vs. other information sources.

Trip purpose and travel party composition are associated with tourists' use of the Internet and other information sources. Destination marketers can benefit from understanding the relationship. For example, information for tourists traveling with families should contain distinctive features to cater to the needs of the segment. Destination marketers could also help tourists adapt to online information search by providing a platform that is similar to traditional sources. Tourists on pleasure trips are more likely to turn to friends or relatives for travel information (Cai, Lehto, & O'Leary, 2001). Thus, one-to-one relationship marketing should be emphasized in order to reach the segment more effectively. Destination marketers can communicate with tourists in the segment with more personalized approach. With the continuing advance of information technology, an online salesperson with a virtual image could be created to interact with pleasure tourists.

Whether or not a tourist searches for information online is also found to be an effective discriminator to distinguish trip outcomes. The findings of this research reveal that tourists who stay at hotels are more likely to search the Internet. Therefore it is possible for destination marketers to work with hotels in the local area to promote awareness of their Websites to targeted segments. The results from this study confirmed that tourists who search on the Internet tend to spend more at their destinations as compared to those who consult with other information sources (Bonn, Furr, & Susskind, 1998). Uysal, Fesenmaier, and O'Leary (1994) suggested that destinations should appeal to tourists who are likely to have the greatest economic impact. Understanding the relationship between destination product preference and the Internet users' social demographics and traveling characteristics would also assist destination marketers promote specific products that attract specific market segments such as male and higher socioeconomic tourists.

The data used in this study were collected in four rural counties of the State of Indiana. While implications of the findings can be discussed in the rural tourism settings, cautions should be taken in generalizing the results to other geographic areas. This research was conducted at different times during the period of 1998 to 2001. With the rapid advancement of information technology and the popularity of the Internet, the Internet information seekers also change very fast. For future research, it would be useful to duplicate similar studies in other destination areas. Detailed online behavior of tourists while searching on the Internet should be examined. For example, how early do they start to search the information before trips? What kinds of Websites do they visit for different types of travel information? Research questions along these lines would result in more valuable information for destination organizations in order to take full advantage of the Internet in meeting their marketing needs and better serve the traveling public.

REFERENCES

Aldskogius, H. (1977). A conceptual framework and a Swedish case study of recreational behavior and environmental cognition. *Economic Geography, 53,* 163-183.

Andereck, K. L., & Caldwell, L. L. (1993). The influence of tourists' characteristics on ratings of information sources for an attraction. *Journal of Travel & Tourism Marketing, 2*(2/3), 171-189.

Baloglu, S. (1999). A path analytic model of visitation intention involving information sources, socio-psychological motivations, and destination image. *Journal of Travel & Tourism Marketing, 8*(3), 81-90.

Berkman, H. W., & Gilson, C. (1986). *Consumer behavior: Concepts and strategies.* Boston, MA: Kent Publishing Company.

Bonn, M. A., Furr, H. L., & Susskind, A. M. (1998). Using the Internet as a pleasure travel planning tool: An examination of the sociodemographic and behavioral characteristics among Internet users and nonusers. *Journal of Hospitality & Tourism Research, 22*(3), 303-317.

Buhalis, D. (1998). Strategic use of information technologies in the tourism industry. *Tourism Management, 19*(5), 409-421.

Cai, L. A., Lehto, X. Y., & O'Leary, J. (2001). Profiling the U.S.-bound Chinese travelers by purpose of trip. *Journal of Hospitality & Leisure Marketing, 7*(4), 3-16.

Chen, J. S. (2000). A comparison of information usage between business and leisure travelers. *Journal of Hospitality & Leisure Marketing, 7*(2), 65-76.

Chen, J. S., & Gursoy, D. (2000). Cross-cultural comparison of the information sources used by first-time and repeat travelers and its marketing implications.

International Journal of Hospitality Management, 19(2), 191-203.

Dodd, T. H. (1998). Influences on search behavior of industrial tourists. *Journal of Hospitality & Leisure Marketing, 5*(2/3), 77-94.

Eby, D. W., Molnar, L. J., & Cai, L. A. (1999). Content preferences for in-vehicle tourist information systems: An emerging travel information source. *Journal of Hospitality & Leisure Marketing, 6*(3), 41-58.

Fodness, D., & Murray, B. (1999). A model of tourist information search behavior. *Journal of Travel Research, 37*(3), 220-230.

Gitelson, R. J., & Crompton, J. L. (1983). The planning horizons and sources of information used by pleasure vacationers. *Journal of Travel Research, 21*(3), 2-7.

Janal, D. S. (1996). Create a presence. *Credit Union Management, 19*(9), 42-45.

Kennedy, S. D. (1996). The Internet changes the way we live. *Information Today, 13*(8), 48-49.

Kahl, J. A. (1967). *The American class structure* (5th ed.). New York: Holt, Rinehart and Winston.

Lennon, R., Weber, J. M., & Henson, J. (2001). A test of a theoretical model of consumer travel behavior: German consumers' perception of Northern Ireland as a tourist destination. *Journal of Vacation Marketing, 7*(1), 51-62.

Lieb, J. (2000). 1999 U.S./Canada Internet Demographic Study. Retrieved November 1, 2002, from http://www.commerce.net/research/stats/analysis/99-USCanda-Study.pdf

McGaughey, R. E., & Mason, K. H. (1998). The Internet as a marketing tool. *Journal of Marketing Theory and Practice, 6*(3), 1-11.

Mercer, D. (1971). The role of perception in the recreation experience: A review and discussion. *Journal of Leisure Research, 3*, 261-276.

Moorthy, S., Ratchford, B. T., & Talukdar, D. (1997). Consumer information search revisited: Theory and empirical analysis. *Journal of Consumer Research, 23*(4), 263-277.

Moutinho, L. (1987). Role of budgeting in planning, implementing, and monitoring hotel marketing strategies. *International Journal of Hospitality Management, 6*(1), 15-22.

Nua Internet Surveys. (2002). How many Online? Retrieved December 9, 2002. from http://www.nua.ie/surveys/how_many_online/index.html

Peterson, R. A., Balasubramania, S., & Bronnenberg, B. J. (1997). Exploring the implications of the Internet for consumer marketing. *Journal of the Academy of Marketing Science, 25*(4), 329-346.

Peterson, R. A., & Merino, M. C. (2003). Consumer information search behavior and the Internet. *Psychology & Marketing, 20*(2), 99-121.

Pitkow, J. E., & Kehoe, C. M. (1996). Emerging trends in the WWW user population. *Communications of the ACM, 39*(6), 106-108.

Prideaux, B., Wei, S., & Ruys, H. (2001). The senior drive tour market in Australia. *Journal of Vacation Marketing, 7*(3), 209-219.

Punj, G. N., & Staelin, R. (1983). A model of consumer information search behavior for new automobiles. *Journal of Consumer Research 9*(3), 366-380.

Snepenger, D. J., Meged, K., Snelling, M., & Worrall, K. (1990). Information search strategies by destination-naïve tourists. *Journal of Travel Research, 29*(1), 13-16.

Srinivasan, N., & Ratchford, B. T. (1991). An empirical test of a model of external search for automobiles. *Journal of Consumer Research, 18*(9), 233-242.

Times Mirror Center for the People and the Press. (1995). *Technology in American household: Americans going on-line*. Washington, DC: Author.

Travel Industry Association. (2000). Technology and Travel. Retrieved April 14, 2000, from http://www.tia.org

Uysal, M., Fesenmaier, D. R., & O'Leary, J. T. (1994). Geographic and season variation in the concentration of travel in the United States. *Journal of Travel Research, 32*(3), 61-64.

Walmsley, D. J., & Lewis, G. J. (1984). *Human geography: Behavioural approaches*. New York: Longman.

Weber, K., & Roehl, W. S. (1999). Profiling people searching for and purchasing travel products on the World Wide Web. *Journal of Travel Research, 37*(3), 291-298.

Woodside, A. G., Cook, V. J., & Mindak, W. A. (1987). Profiling the heavy travelers segment. *Journal of Travel Research, 25*(4), 9-14.

Woodside, A. G., & Ronkainen, I. A. (1980). Vacation travel planning segments: Self-planning vs. user of the motor club and traveler agents. *Annals of Tourism Research, 7*(3), 385-394.

Yankelovich Partners, Inc. (1995). *The Yankelovich cybercitizen report*. Atlanta, GA: Author.

Barriers to Online Booking of Scheduled Airline Tickets

Stefan Klein
Frank Köhne
Anssi Öörni

SUMMARY. In the early years of e-Commerce, the tourism sector had high expectations for online booking. All the major airlines invested huge sums of money, not only to make booking features available, but also to integrate them into attractive, easy-to-use Web offerings. Nevertheless, even after years of investment and improvements, the booking ratio for all but the no-frills airlines is still disappointing. This paper discusses reasons for the slow adoption of online booking. Online booking systems are analyzed as consumer information environments for scheduled airline tickets. The analyses are based on two experiments conducted in 1999 and 2002 respectively. The negative effects of the underlying market structure and the product complexity in the adoption of online booking is also discussed. *[Article copies available for a fee from The Haworth Document Delivery Service: 1-800-HAWORTH. E-mail address: <docdelivery@haworthpress.com> Website: <http://www.HaworthPress. com> © 2004 by The Haworth Press, Inc. All rights reserved.]*

KEYWORDS. Tourism, electronic commerce, acceptance of online booking, consumer search, usability, uncertainty, price dispersion

PROTRACTED PROLIFERATION OF ONLINE FLIGHT BOOKING IN EUROPE

Tourism has been perceived both as a leading field of application and as a driver of Business-to-Consumer (B2C) e-Commerce (Werthner & Klein, 2000). Scheduled airline tickets seem especially appropriate for online distribution because they can be easily represented and distributed by electronic means.

However, with the exception of no-frills airlines such as easyJet or Ryanair, which enjoy online booking ratios well over 50%, the online booking ratio for incumbent airlines has remained below expectations and is only recently increasing (Marcussen, 1999, 2003). This sobering finding reflects neither the airlines' nor the travel agencies' reluctance to develop electronic retailing systems. On the contrary, millions of Euros have been invested in appropriate technologies and Web offerings

Stefan Klein is John E. Sharkey Professor of Electronic Commerce, MIS Department, University College Dublin, Belfield, Dublin 4, Ireland (E-mail: Stefan.Klein@ucd.ie). Frank Köhne is affiliated with the Department of Information Systems, University of Muenster, Germany. Anssi Öörni is Assistant Professor, Department of Information Systems Science, Helsinki School of Economics, Finland.

Address correspondence to Stefan Klein.

[Haworth co-indexing entry note]: "Barriers to Online Booking of Scheduled Airline Tickets." Klein. Stefan. Frank Köhne, and Anssi Öörni. Co-published simultaneously in *Journal of Travel & Tourism Marketing* (The Haworth Hospitality Press, an imprint of The Haworth Press, Inc.) Vol. 17, No. 2/3. 2004. pp. 27-39: and: *Handbook of Consumer Behavior, Tourism, and the Internet* (ed: Juline E. Mills, and Rob Law) The Haworth Hospitality Press. an imprint of The Haworth Press. Inc., 2004. pp. 27-39. Single or multiple copies of this article are available for a fee from The Haworth Document Delivery Service [1-800-HAWORTH. 9:00 a.m. - 5:00 p.m. (EST). E-mail address: docdelivery@ haworthpress.com].

have been continually expanded and improved in recent years. Airlines have made several attempts to bypass intermediaries and to distribute tickets directly to end customers. Lufthansa, for example, has initiated many innovations aimed at dealing directly with the end customer: the company runs a call center; has its own Website (at http://www.lufthansa. de); co-founded the online travel agency Opodo. com; and also operates a conventional travel agency called Lufthansa City Centre.

Initially, the promises of e-Commerce were high as it was expected to facilitate convenient shopping (Rayport & Sviokla, 1994), promote higher transparency of product and price information eventually leading to lower prices (Bakos, 1997). Experimental findings, however, have provided evidence that the advantages of e-Commerce are smaller and the uncertainties higher than was generally assumed (e.g., Anckar & Walden, 2002; Crichton & Frew, 2000; Consumer Reports, 2000): flight prices found in online travel outlets were not lower than those listed by conventional travel agencies; online searches were found to be time consuming and cumbersome; and, finally, searches yielded divergent results, especially when complex travel products were considered. In several cases, conventional travel agents yielded better results than their online counterparts (Öörni, 2002).

Using a consumer information environment point of view, this paper attempts to explain the negative empirical findings regarding the effectiveness of electronic air travel markets. The paper addresses the situation of the incumbent airlines. The so called no-frills airlines, which operate with a different business model, are used only for comparison. The focus is on the usability of the online booking environment, as well as on the product and market structure which are important drivers of the diffusion of e-Commerce. To achieve the goals of this paper, the information environment framework is first created by reviewing consumer behavior literature. Special attention is paid to how the characteristics of the environment can affect the consumer decision process. This is followed by a discussion of the distinctive characteristics of the scheduled airline ticket markets, as market structure is likely to affect the functionality of

the information environment. A number of propositions are put forth based on the existing literature. These propositions were evaluated in the light of two experiments conducted in 1999 and 2002. Finally, the implications of the findings on online markets for scheduled airline tickets are discussed.

CONSUMERS' INFORMATION ENVIRONMENT AND MARKET STRUCTURE

The perceived difficulty of consumer decisions is influenced by both the task structure and the provision of information in the consumer environment (Bettman, Johnson & Payne, 1991). The amount and quality of information available have a strong impact on the consumer's ability to choose. While fairly complete information on multiple alternatives promotes attribute based decision strategies, low quality or missing information may force consumers to make inferences and to resort to decision strategies that require less complete information, such as brand based choice. The amount and quality of information are positively related to decision quality. Attribute based choices, involving fairly complete and detailed information, lead to more precise decisions, yet they require more processing capacity and effort than, for example, brand based strategies.

Human cognitive abilities have often been found to be bounded or insufficient for real-life decision-making (Simon, 1982). This position promotes the importance of information environments; since mental processing capacity is a scarce resource (Simon, 1978), people tend to increase information search and processing if the mental effort of processing can be reduced (Bettman et al., 1991). The organization of information affects the difficulty of consumer choice. Product information, for example, is often available from a wide range of channels such as advertisements, brochures and consumer reports. These sources diverge on the amount and quality of information displayed. Advertisements typically highlight the strong points of the product while the weaknesses are not discussed. Furthermore, product information is typically displayed by alternative, i.e., one brand at a time, and only a subset of attribute information relevant to choice is revealed. Hence, consumers are effectively forced to retrieve information sequentially rather than simultaneously, which makes some decision strategies very difficult (Bettman, 1982). If information content is changed frequently, this effectively amounts to an increase in mental effort, less accurate decision strategies and lower quality decisions.

As previously suggested, consumer decisions are affected by both the task structure and the availability of relevant information in the consumers' information environment. Task structure is largely dictated by the product characteristics that are relevant to the decision. The complexity tends to increase with the number of product attributes factored into the decision. Access to information is paramount to consumer decisions. In online markets, technology largely dictates whether consumers will be able to retrieve the information they need to make informed decisions. The magnitude and frequency of changes in the consumer's information environment may further complicate the decisions by forcing consumers to update their information. For example, sellers enter and leave markets; new products are introduced and some products are discontinued. Furthermore, prices tend to vary both spatially and temporally. The following propositions apply the main features of the information environment to the characteristics of the online flight ticket market.

Proposition 1 "Product Properties"

The Complexity of Flights Offered Limits the Efficiency of Online Consumer Searches

Consumers vary in their knowledge of product categories and necessary consumer knowledge is related to product complexity. Hence, efficiency of a search and the acceptance of online ticket booking systems will be influenced by the characteristics of the offers made. Malone et al. (1987) introduced the notion of complexity of product descriptions to explain the effects of electronic markets on transaction costs. In their analysis, low levels of product description complexity render prod-

ucts better suited to electronic trade. In a similar vein, product complexity has been found to reduce the diffusion rate of innovations since consumers have more difficulties in learning about the product (Gatinon & Robertson, 1991). The higher the product complexity, the more uncertainty is involved in transactions, and the less suitable the product is for automation of purchases by letting consumers have direct access to the products (Werthner & Klein, 1999).

While air transportation is basically a homogeneous service, airlines have successfully managed to differentiate the product by dividing the available seats into diverse booking and service classes. Furthermore the cabins are divided by installing larger seats with more space for the first and business class passengers who pay premium fares (Lundberg, Krishnamoorthy & Stavenga, 1995). The complexity of purchase decisions is multiplied when tourism products, such as flight segments, accommodation or car rentals, are bundled. Hence, the current level of product complexity has lead to dispersed and, on average, relatively low consumer knowledge and—correspondingly—a high level of uncertainty. However, the no-frills airlines have demonstrated that product complexity and price dispersion are not inevitable They almost exclusively sell their point-to-point connections via their own direct distribution channels (Web and call centre). While these sites lack the convenience of online supermarkets with a huge collection of services from various sources, they are quite simple, straightforward and easy to understand.

Proposition 2 "Usability"

Increasing the Usability of Online Booking Systems Has Raised the Efficiency of Consumer Searches in Electronic Markets

Channel characteristics determine the consumer's efforts when searching. With the widening scope of functionality (and complexity) of online outlets, their usability has become increasingly important. There is a growing body of literature about Website quality assessment and recommendations for quality improvements (e.g., Totz & Riemer, 2001), which is indicative of a rising awareness of quality issues. Furthermore, search engine technology has advanced well and the utilization of search engines has become the major modus of interaction in the internet. However, few studies have been conducted to assess the quality of online reservation and booking systems for air travel (e.g., Law & Leung, 2000). It is proposed that airline and online travel agent Websites have shown notable quality improvements in the last years which have had a positive effect on their usability.

Proposition 3 "Online Booking Environment"

The Complexity of the Online Booking Environment Poses an Additional Hurdle for Consumers

The changing identity of sellers, as well as fluctuations in supply and demand, result in uncertainty, since information becomes obsolete (Stigler, 1961). Consumers must therefore update their information, and there is often no better means to do that than through search. Search is not, however, without costs and search costs prevent consumers from acquiring perfect information. While the quality of individual air travel Websites has significantly improved, the overall online air travel market is very dynamic and highly complex, with new entrants and, at the same time, concentration trends (Klein, 2002). There is widespread "co-opetition"; namely, there are numerous, competing business models and criss-crossing alliances among competing airlines and between airlines and distribution partners. Online-only brands are widespread, while only a few players pursue a channel integration strategy, which is regarded as advantageous for consumers (Görsch, 2003). In effect, it is not obvious for consumers which are the best online sources for airline tickets.

Proposition 4 "Price Dispersion"

Widespread and Persistent Price Dispersion Limits the Efficiency Gains in Online Retail Markets

Search theory is rather uniform in its definition of the implications of search costs for consumer behavior and price dispersion. Stigler (1961) proposed that high search costs will lead value-maximizing consumers to limit their pre-purchase search, which results in less than perfectly informed purchase decisions. The foremost premise attached to electronic markets holds that declining cost of transporting information over computer networks will decrease the cost of consumer search (Bakos 1997; Malone et al. 1987). Technology enables higher levels of market transparency over time: consumers should be more consistently able to locate the best offerings as search costs decline. As a result, prices should become less dispersed, since sellers would be forced to lower their prices towards the limit of marginal cost of production to attract customers (Bakos, 1997).

Despite these predictions, however, wide price dispersion has been consistently observed in electronic markets for scheduled airline tickets (Clemons, Il-Horn & Hitt, 2002; Öörni, 2002). The consequence of price dispersion, combined with dynamic differential pricing (based on yield management), is a high level of customer uncertainty. Wide price dispersion lessens the usability of price as a signal for product quality. It may also be more difficult to decide when to stop searching when wide price dispersion persists. Dynamic pricing results in temporal price variation, which may further lessen consumers' ability to search and compare scheduled airline tickets. Inexperienced consumers are likely to suffer the most as a result of wide price dispersion and seller-induced price fluctuation. Both price dispersion and dynamic pricing are considered obstacles for the proliferation of online booking.

METHODOLOGY AND EXPERIMENTAL SETTING

Our empirical data collection consists of two series of similar experiments with students which were conducted in 1999 and 2002 respectively. Between the first and second round of experiments, considerable changes have taken place in the online airline market. Even though new players have entered the market, in particular Opodo.com, a Pan-European travel service founded by nine airlines, the online flight ticket market has consolidated. Internet technology has matured and its adoption is proliferating. Given the progress that has been made over the course of these three years, it could be expected that the second series experiments would yield different results.

The research design is an experimental comparative static analysis. Two series of measurements are reported over a three year period. Unlike cohort analysis, it is not intended to describe effects within groups of individuals over time, but to describe market perception and changes in market perception from the perspective of similar samples. Based on the findings from the first experiment, the second experiment used an adapted experimental design by adding time pressure and varying the task complexity. The results are meant to be indicative of recent trends as they cover a fast moving environment and rely on quantitative as well as qualitative data. Due to the low number of data sets, advanced statistical methods like time series analysis could not be applied.

Figure 1 illustrates the framework for the experimental research. Test persons (students) were asked to search online for best offers for a given scheduled flight connection. It is assumed that the test person's disposition (expertise) and the structure and presentation of online offers (product properties) influence the performance of the search task, which is measured by the price as a result of the search (outcome). Moreover, the performance of the search task is influenced by the functional properties and usability of the online booking site and its environment (booking environment, usability), as well as the level of price

FIGURE 1. Research Framework

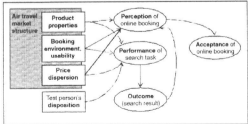

dispersion. The general acceptance of online booking is an indicator of whether the test persons will book online in the future. It is influenced by the perception of the booking process, which also reflects the satisfaction or uncertainty with the booking result. It must be noted that the experiments focused on the retrieval of product and price information. That is no reservations were made nor were any flights actually booked, in order to avoid distortion of the market as well as the risk of accidental bookings. The quality of the online booking environment as well as the structure of the travel market also affects the perception of online booking.

First Experiment

The first experiment was carried out in September 1999 at the Helsinki School of Economics, Finland. It consisted of two tasks: the subjects were asked to (1) arrange a conference journey to Hawaii in March 2000 and (2) to design a winter vacation for the season 1999-2000. The participants in the study had one week to complete these tasks, and they were free to schedule their work. They were also allowed to use all the information sources they wished. The destination of the conference journey was an information systems conference held in Hawaii in March 2000. The subjects were instructed to arrange flights to and from the conference destination, accommodation, and local transportation. The journey had to cover the conference dates. The subjects had at their disposal a grant of FIM 10,000 (approximately USD 1,800 at the time of the experiment). They were allowed to exceed the budget and pay the excess costs themselves. If the total budget of the conference journey was less than the grant, the subjects were allowed to "keep" the difference.

The second task of the experiment, the winter vacation, was designed for motivating the subjects. They were instructed to design a winter vacation with a total budget of FIM 4,000 (equivalent of USD 700). The vacation was to be arranged for the winter season 1999-2000. Every subject completing the tasks was awarded 10/100 points for the course grade. These points were not tied to the performance of the subjects and the assignment was not mandatory for passing the course. To further encourage the subjects, we announced that roughly half of them would be selected into a lottery based on their performance in the experiment. The prize of the lottery was one winter vacation with a budget of FIM 4,000–the winner was awarded the vacation designed in the second task of the experiment.

The experiment was an assignment in a university level course on electronic commerce. Thus, all subjects were undergraduate or graduate business students. The assignment was optional, yet the majority of the students initially participated in the study. The total number of students attending the experiment was 133. Eleven students did not complete their assignment and that left us with 122 observations (92%). We contacted all students with at least one missing item of data, and asked them to complete their assignment. After two rounds of requests to fill in the missing items, we had a fairly complete and rich data set.

Second Experiment

In the second experiment, carried out in July 2002, the test persons were instructed to search on the Internet for economy class airline ticket prices (including taxes and security fees) for specific destinations:

- Return flight (group A): Airport Münster/Osnabrück (FMO) which is the International Airport of Münster to Dublin Airport (DUB).
- Three leg flight (group B): FMO via DUB to Airport Cologne-Bonn (CGN).
- Bus or train transfers to or from other airports were not allowed.
- Flight dates: July 17, 2002 (first leg), July 18, 2002 (return).
- No preferences regarding departure/arrival time (but no intermediate stop should be longer than 5 hours) were specified.
- Student discounts were to be ignored.

In order to control for price effects, a less frequented destination in Europe was chosen, where flights might fill up quickly and where there are only a few connections. The experiment took place during the German holiday season with a high demand for airline tickets.

Further, by selecting destinations in the Euro zone, currency effects were avoided. The search time was restricted to 15 minutes for the return flight and 25 for the three leg flight. The time restrictions were meant to mimic a booking process via phone or via a visit to a travel agency respectively. The test groups were instructed to restrict their investigations to the Internet only (no phone calls, no visits to traditional travel agencies).

The subjects of the experiments were 44 Information Systems students in their 5th semester at the University of Muenster, Germany, who worked in 15 groups with one to four students. The return flight was searched for by 8 groups (23 individuals) and the three leg flight by 7 groups (21 individuals). All test groups completed the assigned task including the availability check. According to the participants' own judgment, the time restrictions (15 min and 25 min for return and three leg flight respectively) did not have a negative impact on the results. After completing their tasks, students were asked to comment on the quality of the Websites and in particular the quality of the support for these tasks.

Methodological Considerations and Limitations of the Research Design

According to Babbie (1998), experimentation is especially appropriate for hypothesis testing. He also states that experimentation is better suited for explanatory than for descriptive purposes. The major strength of experiments is that they enable researchers to isolate and control a small number of variables to be studied intensively (Babbie, 1998; Galliers, 1990). It was decided to investigate the efficiency of information search in experimental situations since they enable the researcher to treat the information channel, electronic or conventional, as the independent variable. Although the subjects were given pre-formulated problems, much effort was paid to avoid making the objectives too restrictive.

The artificiality of experiments is one of the strongest objections to the method. Galliers (1990) maintains that generalizability of the results is the major weakness of the experimental approach; due to the oversimplification of experimental situations and the exclusion of a number of relevant variables from the analyses, the observed relationships may only exist to a limited extent in the real world. Galliers (ibid.) further asserts that the use of students as surrogates for "real" decision makers may add to the sanitized nature of the laboratory situation. While Babbie (1998) agrees with Galliers (ibid.) on the artificiality of experiments, he maintains that this potential defect is less significant in explanatory research than it would be in descriptive research. Some authors argue that it is only necessary to reproduce the relevant characteristics and leave the superficial ones out of the experiment, in order to make generalizations (see, e.g., Locke, 1986). Berkowitz and Donnerstein (1982, p. 249) have reasoned that "the meaning the subjects assign to the situation they are in . . . plays a greater role in determining the generalizability of an experiment's outcome than does the sample's demographic representativeness or the setting's surface realism."

In both experiments, the student groups represented a convenience sample. Both groups were familiar with the Internet but had little knowledge or experience of the air travel market. The homogeneity of skills within and between the groups allows for a ceteris paribus examination of the research framework, as it is intended to explain market developments and not, for example, the developments of e-skills in a representative sample. The design of the two experiments was similar, however, the second experiment was not intended as a close replication of the first. Both experiments were self-administered. There was no evidence that the instructions were not followed.

EXPERIMENTAL FINDINGS

Barriers to Search

In the 1999 experiment, a list of barriers to online searches for flight information were identified. Availability of information was the most frequent source of complaints; 48 (39%) subjects reported that they experienced difficulties finding information relevant to choosing a flight. Of these subjects, 32 (26%) reported that they were unable to find all relevant information, i.e., flight schedules, prices, details

and availability of seats, in any one of the electronic sources they used. Ten subjects (8%) were more specific, reporting that comprehensive flight information was available through search engines (such as Travelocity.com), yet only for expensive business flights. A further 6 (5%) subjects complained that flight information was often disclosed only after registration or reservation.

Fourteen subjects (11%) experienced difficulty locating prospective sellers. Most of them reported that they could locate a number of sellers, but faced difficulties in evaluating them. Consumers with little prior knowledge of the market cannot differentiate a priori between sellers providing ample product information and those that are not able to meet their information needs. Similarly, it is difficult if not impossible to know in advance which sellers have attractive offers. Eight subjects reported frustration resulting from technical problems (7%) and flaws in search engine or interface design (6 subjects, 5%). Technical problems referred mostly to unreachable servers, while design issues comprised of low usability of electronic storefronts. Poor implementation of several search-engines caused difficulties in constructing multi-leg flights.

Table 1 provides an overview of the barriers of search identified in 1999. In summary, the majority of reported problems related to information content rather than technical issues. The lack of cohesive flight information can be traced to at least the high cost of systems integration. Law and Leung (2000), while investigating airlines' online reservation services on the Internet, reported that a higher number of airlines provided online flight schedule information than flight availability information. They also observed some regional differences in the provision of flight availability information, which they attributed to the high cost of integrating online Web services to airlines' central reservation systems.

Product Properties

The salience of information-related problems that has been reported by the students gives evidence of the perceived complexity of the product and the need for a rich product description. As a result of the selected task, stu-

TABLE 1. Barriers of Search in 1999

Barriers of search	Frequency		%	
Barriers of search related to information content	48		39	
• Flight information not available from a single source		32		26
• All relevant flight details available for expensive flights only		10		8
• Registration or reservation required to retrieve flight details		6		5
Finding and selecting the right Web services	14		11	
Technical problems	8		7	
Problems related to search engine or interface design	6		5	
Missing	46		38	
Total	122		100	

dents had to combine several flight segments and hence were confronted with a multitude of different options and possible routes. Complex pricing schemes employed to price-discriminate and sell unfilled seats contribute to consumer uncertainty (see the section *Price Dispersion and the Market Structure*). Not only do prices for the same destinations vary, but even for the same flight numbers, different prices are listed by different online sites. While the subsequent consumer uncertainty can be addressed in a personal interaction with the travel agent, the online consumer is confronted with a high level of complexity without a proper explanation. Hence, this poses an obstacle to the acceptance of online ticket booking.

Usability of Online Booking Sites

Usability subsumes the constructs' usefulness and ease of use, which are considered antecedents of information system acceptance in general (Davis, 1989). The usability of online booking sites can be operationalized as the perceived effectiveness and efficiency of the actual search and booking task. While task effectiveness describes if the tasks were successfully completed at all, the efficiency will be measured by the number of online booking sites considered per hour.

According to the diaries delivered in the 2002 experiment, not every selected Website provided enough information or was appropriate to fulfill the given task. The main problems were a lack of price information (e.g., Star Alliance, Lufthansa); lack of support for multi-leg flights (e.g., at http://www.flug.de); unclear terminology (e.g., Cabana used "Flugzentrale," [english translation "Flightcenter"] which is not generally associated with ticket booking); difficulties finding the departure airport due to a confusing use of airport names (e.g., http://www.airbroker24.de and http://www.Travel24.com used "Osnabrück" and not the official International Airport of Münster term "Münster-Osnabrück/FMO"); and booking restrictions because of the imminent departure date (e.g., http://www.Travel.de). According to the statements in the diaries, the student groups restricted their investigations from the 34 sites initially considered, to 27 different Websites in both groups. For the return flights, 19 out of the 25 sites initially considered were effective and for three leg flights, 14 out of 20 were effective (see Table 2).

On 24% of the Websites which were initially considered by the student group A and on 30% considered by group B, relevant information was not provided or could not be found. Furthermore, 23.5% (both groups) of the effective sites were described as problematic in terms of general usability or were perceived as confusing. This result, although still alarming, indicates a significant improvement

TABLE 2. Effectiveness and Efficiency of Search (sites considered per hour)

	Consideration set	Sites used	Sites used on avg.	Avg. efficiency
Group A (return)	25	19	3.4	13.5
Group B (multi-leg)	20	14	3.1	7.5

in terms of efficiency over the 1999 results. Table 3 analyzes the development of search efficiency for return flights over time.

Online search efficiency has greatly improved. In 1999, online search for return flight information was performed with, on average, 4.4 alternatives considered per hour. This in contrast to 13.5 alternatives in 2002. However, it is unclear if this observation is an effect of improved interface design, the differences in the experimental settings or changes in the market structure and online booking environment, e.g., via search engines. Further investigation shows that, in particular, information concerning the availability of seats, which is strictly necessary information for online booking, has become more accessible than in 1999. In the first experiment, only 15 of 68 subjects (22.1%) successfully retrieved this information on the Web. In the second experiment, all participants retrieved this information online.

Online Booking Environment

In contrast to the 1999 experiment, in 2002 all subjects were instructed to use only online information. Relevant Websites were found easily whereas in 1999 a certain difficulty in locating potential sellers was observed. Four patterns of provider selection were preferred in the 2002 experiment:

1. The Website is already known, e.g., from earlier experiences or advertising; examples are Expedia, Opodo, Flug.de, or Lufthansa (mentioned 27 times).
2. The Website is a query result using a popular search engine (or Web catalogue) like Google, Yahoo or Web.de or a sponsored link if too many results were found; examples are Ebookers, Airbroker24.de, or Travel Overland (mentioned 16 times).
3. The starting point for an investigation is one of the airports or an airline that operates on the itineraries; examples are airport Münster-Osnabrück, Ryanair, Eurowings, or Aer Lingus (mentioned 7 times).
4. The selection is based on "intuition," i.e., a generic travel term such as "fliegen" (English translation = fly); "reisen" (English translation = travel); or "Flüge"

(English translation = flights) is used as an URL. Examples were www.fliegen.de, www.fluege.de, or www.reisen.de (mentioned 6 times).

In one case, a typical "similar domain name" problem occurred. One student group had intended to visit the homepage of the Irish airline Aer Lingus (www.aerlingus.com). As a result of a typo (www.airlingus.com), they were directed to TravelNow's Website without realizing their error.

Even though online information had been at the student's fingertips in the 2002 experiment, the complexity of the online travel market had apparently increased. Although competitors are "just one click away," their sheer number has risen which makes the search a complex and opaque task. A search strategy that reduces the complexity and limits the price search to just one favorite site does not seem rational. In particular, inexperienced users will remain uncertain about the optimality of their search results regardless of their search efforts. According to Stigler (1961), uncertainty is induced by changes in the environment, e.g., the dynamics of the market structure with a multitude of new players and new business models.

Price Dispersion and the Market Structure

To allow for comparison between different product types, relative price deviations, which describe the price deviation relative to the minimal price in the sample, were computed in addition to the standard deviation (see Table 4). Not surprisingly the relative price deviation for return flights is lower in the 2002 experiment, which might be specific for the selected flights or a more general trend. However, the devia-

TABLE 3. Test of Identity of Mean Efficiency (not assuming equal variance)

	n	Mean	Std. Dev.	t-value	Sig. (two-sided)
Group A, 2002 (return)	8	13.5	3.7	−5.9	.000
1999 (return)	10	4.4	2.6		

TABLE 4. Price Dispersion

	n	Minimal Price	Std. Deviation	Relative Deviation
Group A (return)	8	1,044.58 EUR	90.45 EUR	9%
1999 (return)	13	4,625.00 FIM	1,222.39 FIM	26%
Group B (multi-leg)	7	457.85 EUR	242.73 EUR	53%

tions are highest in the case of the more complex multi-leg flights.

In order to gain a better basis for interpreting the experimental results, a few market parameters were monitored during the 2002 experiments: the price range among major online travel sites and functional properties of the Websites. A number of sites with heterogeneous backgrounds were chosen for monitoring: www.expedia.de (a spin-off of Microsoft Corp., owned by USA Networks, Inc.), www.flug.de (a spin-off of Cinetic Medientechnik GmbH, also founder of Web.de, a German Internet portal), www.lufthansa.de (a German airline), www.opodo.de (a platform formed by nine European airlines, among others Air France, British Airways and Lufthansa), www.travelocity.de (a tourism platform closely related to the Sabre reservation system), www.traveloverland.de (a platform initiated by Travel Overland, a traditional travel agency and a partner of Travelocity). Figure 2 depicts the observed prices which were mostly stable throughout the observed period but there were significant price differences among the competitors. The prices observed range from about EUR 1,200 (Traveloverland) to a maximum of about EUR 1,520 (Lufthansa/Travelocity).

The increase in Travelocity's price on July 5 can be interpreted as a result of yield management (e.g., if one booking class is fully booked, the next available class is offered instead). However, no plausible interpretation for the frequency and amplitude of changes observed at www.flug.de was found. Initially, it was planned to log the prices on these Websites automatically in order to repeat the price searches in constant intervals. However, the processing time of the queries varied significantly and thus complicated automatic logging. Minor changes in the interaction process

prevented automatic logging, even though the layout and content of the Websites were relatively static. Some Websites even changed their processes during the observation period, e.g., by adapting their sales procedures relative to the remaining time to take-off or by changing default values in forms. Moreover, pop-up windows appeared randomly, and on some Websites, flights were temporarily non-existent and reappeared shortly after. Although the automatic logging system was obviously easier to confuse than consumers, the difficulties encountered nevertheless give an indication of the intricacies and inconsistencies of online booking. Further, price changes during a search process could be reproduced, which indicates the use of caching mechanisms. Since only 0.5-5% of requests lead to a reservation while the travel agencies have to pay a fee to the reservation system provider on a per request basis (Clemons et al., 2002), caching is reasonable strategy to save transaction costs. The flip side of updating the price information on demand only is the risk to confuse customers and eventually to lose their trust in online price information.

In summary, despite increasing market transparency and intense competition, price dispersion prevails in the online market. The observations indicate that most of the price variations, which the test persons encountered in the experiment, were the result of price dispersion in the market, while yield management had only minor effects. While some price variations were the result of product variation, i.e., different carriers or different routes, a significant part of the price variations have to be attributed to the distribution system: different vendors use different global distribution systems, such as Sabre or Amadeus, and charge different prices for the identical product. Whether this is a result of differential wholesale prices, which the airlines charge to their distribution partners, or different pricing strategies lies beyond this analysis. Reports in the trade press suggest that wholesale prices reflect distribution partners' bargaining power and volume discounts. Price spread and volatility of prices are typically not transparent to the online customer, but may lead to confusion as different results will be reported at different times, whereas travel agents can selectively

FIGURE 2. Result of Selective Price Monitoring

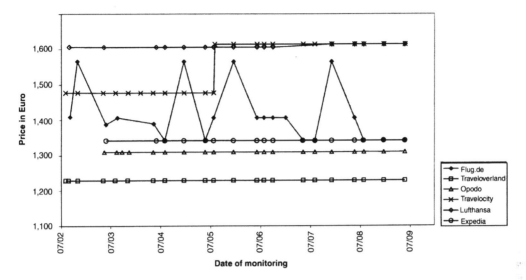

present the existing price spread and provide explanations and guidance.

CONCLUSIONS

Market research in the European travel market has provided evidence of a lackluster acceptance of online booking for scheduled air travel tickets (see Marcussen, 1999; 2003). In order to find possible explanations in a dynamic market environment, two sets of experiments had been carefully crafted to provide–albeit limited–empirical evidence:

- The sampling of Internet savvy test persons allowed a focus on travel related obstacles.
- The tasks and instructions were designed to provide insights into the comparative (dis-)advantages of the online channel.
- The repetition of the experiments, albeit in a modified form, provided some control over the advances in Website usability.

Our findings indicate that online vendors have learned over the past years and significantly improved their offerings with respect to the scope of functions, navigation, ease of do-

ing transactions and retrieving essential information. However, as the failed attempt to automatically log prices indicates, there are numerous little inconsistencies and variations among and within functionally equivalent Websites, which might be more irritating for less experienced users. As the search tasks were performed more efficiently in the 2002 experiment, the protracted adoption of online booking cannot only be attributed to a lack of search efficiency. Hence, further factors have to be identified.

Contrary to the theory (Bakos, 1997), a high level of price dispersion within the online market persists. In addition, product properties, especially the complexity of product description, as well as the booking environment were found to have an impact on the consumer's perception and acceptance of online booking. However, while Internet technology has become more mature, uncertainty is still an obstacle for the proliferation of online flight booking in Europe and different explanations for prevailing uncertainty in this setting are given. Research on online buying behavior has used measures like transaction costs (Malone et al., 1987) and search costs (Bakos, 1997) but little has been said about the impact of behavioral concepts like uncertainty on the adoption of online booking and possible mechanisms of uncertainty reduction in online markets.

The network structure of international air travel combined with a multitude of online distribution channels has lead to a confusingly large number of alternatives to consider and each offer is complex in itself. Huffman and Kahn (1998, p. 493) note: "The confusion a customer experiences with a wide assortment of options, however, is due to the perceived complexity, not necessarily the actual complexity or variety." In the experimental setting, homogeneity of the services was assumed and thereby subject's decision making was simplified. Subjects were limited to the consideration of price and availability information while airline flight tickets are actually more complex services with dimensions like quality of service, flight duration, number of stops, distance between airports and other locations to consider as well as frequent flyer programs and special offers combined with rental cars and hotel rooms. Research shows that consumers have trouble evaluating alternatives on more than two dimensions (Malhotra, 1982). Given that the air travel market cannot be reduced to simple "cut-throat" price competition, consumer search and decision making is probably less efficient than our findings indicate, which makes online booking even less attractive for consumers.

In the end it amounts to a strategic decision for the airlines: the diversity of channels and offerings in the current market environment structurally limits the extent of online booking. Traditional travel agents reduce this complexity by providing selected information and explanations where needed. No-frills airlines have reduced the complexity of the offer by focusing on direct flights to limited destinations and using their own Website and call centre as the only prime distribution channels. Aer Lingus, the national Irish carrier which has RyanAir as a direct competitor, is taking a middle road: they offer only a limited number of destinations (130) on their own Website. In return, the booking process is straightforward and quite simple. While their flights are available on numerous travel sites, they offer price incentives for booking on their Website. Furthermore, they consistently tell their customers that their best fares are available on aerlingus.

com. However, changing the product and distribution structure probably comes at a price which is too high for most of the incumbent airlines and might even lead to allegations of predatory disintermediation (Berghel, 2000).

REFERENCES

Anckar, B., & Walden, P. (2002). Self-Booking of High- and Low-Complexity Travel Products: Exploratory Findings. *Information Technology & Tourism, 4*, pp. 151-165.

Babbie, E. (1998). *The Practice of Social Research.* Belmont, CA, Wadsworth Publishing Company.

Bakos, J.Y. (1997). Reducing buyer search costs: Implications for electronic marketplaces. *Management Science, 43* (12), pp. 1676-1692.

Berghel, H. (2000). Predatory Disintermediation. *Communications of the ACM, 43* (5), pp. 23-29.

Berkowitz, L., & Donnerstein, E. (1982). External validity is more than skin deep. *American Psychologist, 37*, pp. 245-257.

Bettman, J.R. (1982). A functional analysis of the role of overall evaluation of alternatives in choice processes. In *Advances in Consumer Research, 9* (pp. 87-93). Ann Arbor, MI, Association for Consumer Research.

Bettman, J.R., Johnson, E.J., & Payne J.W. (1991). Consumer decision making. In T.S Robertson & H.H. Kassarjian (Eds.), *Handbook of Consumer Behavior* (pp. 50-84), Englewood Cliffs, NJ: Prentice-Hall.

Clemons, E.K., Il-Horn, H., & Hitt, L.M. (2002). Price dispersion and differentiation in online travel: An empirical investigation. *Management Science, 48* (4), pp. 534-550.

Consumer Reports. (2000). *"Lowest fares" online are all over the map.* Retrieved on April 14, 2003, from http://www.consumerreports.org.

Crichton, E., & Frew, A.J. (2000). Usability of information and reservation systems: Theory or practice? In D.R. Fesenmaier et al. (Eds.), *Information and Communication Technologies in Tourism* (pp. 408-417), Vienna, New York: Springer, pp. 219-228.

Davis, F.D. (1989). Perceived usefulness, perceived ease of use, and user acceptance of information technology. *MIS Quarterly, 13* (3), pp. 319-339.

Gatinon, H., & Robertson, T.S. (1991). Innovative decision processes. In T.S. Robertson & H.H. Kassarjian (Eds.), *Handbook of consumer behavior* (pp. 316-348). Englewood Cliffs, NJ, Prentice Hall.

Galliers, R.D. (1990). Choosing appropriate information systems research approaches: A revised taxonomy. In H.K. Klein, H.-E. Nissen, & Hirschheim, R. (Eds.), *Information systems research: Contemporary approaches & emergent traditions* (1, pp. 327-345), Amsterdam, North-Holland.

Görsch, D. (2003). *Multi-channel integration in the retail of physical products.* Copenhagen, Copenhagen Business School, PhD Series 12.2003.

Huffman, C., & Kahn B.E. (1998). Variety for sale: Mass customization or mass confusion. *Journal of Retailing, 74* (4), pp. 491-513.

Klein, S. (2002). Web impact on the distribution structure for flight tickets. In K. Wöber, A.J. Frew, & M. Hitz (Eds.), *Information and communication technologies in tourism 2002* (pp. 219-228). Vienna, New York: Springer.

Law, R., & Leung, R. (2000). A study of airline's online reservation services on the Internet. *Journal of Travel Research, 39* (2), pp. 202-211.

Locke, E.A. (1986). Generalizing from laboratory to field: Ecological validity or abstraction of essential elements? In Locke, E.A. (Ed.), *Generalizing from laboratory to field settings.* Lexington, Massachusetts, Lexington Books.

Lundberg, D.E., Krishnamoorthy, M., & Stavenga, M.H. (1995). *Tourism economics.* New York: John Wiley & Sons, Inc.

Malhotra, N.K. (1982). Information load and consumer decision making. *Journal of Consumer Research, 8* (March), pp. 419-430.

Malone, T.W., Yates, J., & Benjamin, R.I. (1987). Electronic markets and electronic hierarchies. *Communications of The ACM, 30* (6), pp. 484-497.

Marcussen, C.H. (1999). The effects of Internet distribution of travel and tourism services on the marketing mix: No-frills, fair fares and fare wars in the air. *Information Technology & Tourism, 2,* pp. 197-212.

Marcussen, C.H. (2003). *Trends in European Internet distribution of travel and tourism services,* Research Report. Retrieved on April 14, from http://www.crt.dk/uk/staff/chm/trends.htm (04/14/2003).

Öörni, A. (2002): *Consumer search in electronic markets.* Helsinki, Ph.D. thesis, Helsinki School of Economics.

Rayport, J.F., & Sviokla, J.J. (1994). Managing in the marketspace. *Harvard Business Review, 72* (6), pp. 141-150.

Simon, H.A. (1978). Rationality as a process and product of thought. *American Economic Review, 68,* 1-16.

Simon, H.A. (1982). *Models of bounded rationality.* Cambridge, MA: MIT Press.

Stigler, G.J. (1961). The economics of information. *Journal of Political Economy, 69* (3), pp. 213-225.

Werthner, H., & Klein, S. (1999). *Information technology and tourism: A challenging relationship.* Vienna: Springer.

Werthner, H., & Klein, S. (2000). ICT and the changing landscape of global tourism distribution. *EM-Electronic Markets, 9* (4), pp. 256-262.

The Past, Present, and Future Research of Online Information Search

SooCheong (Shawn) Jang

SUMMARY. Information technology has rapidly developed and accordingly online information search is increasingly important to both travelers and travel marketers. Despite the importance, there has not been given much attention to online information search behavior in the travel and tourism field. To stress the importance and urge researchers in advancing this area of research, this study briefly reviews (1) traditional views of information search, (2) the distinct features of online information search, (3) online benefits to travelers and marketers, and (4) online concerns and opportunities. In addition, potential issues on future research are suggested. *[Article copies available for a fee from The Haworth Document Delivery Service: 1-800-HAWORTH. E-mail address: <docdelivery@ haworthpress.com> Website: <http://www.HaworthPress.com> © 2004 by The Haworth Press, Inc. All rights reserved.]*

KEYWORDS. Online information search, online purchase, Internet, travelers' search behavior

INTRODUCTION

Information search has drawn attention from tourism researchers and practitioners since it is a significant part of the purchase decision process. To make selection decisions on destination, transportation, accommodation, meals, and entertainments, travelers seek corresponding information through different channels: travel agencies, friends and relatives, the Internet, newspapers and magazines, airline companies, and commercial advertisements.

From the tourism marketers' point of view, understanding travelers' information search behavior is important at the micro level for marketing management decisions, and at the macro level for public policy decisions (Schmidt & Spreng, 1996). It is also crucial for tourism marketers to understand consumer behavioral patterns in order to design effective marketing communication campaigns, because it represents the early stage at which marketing can provide information and can significantly influence travelers' decision-making. Research on information search further benefits tourism marketers by allowing them to recognize the underlying rationale of travelers' decisions, so that marketers can efficiently identify their prospective customers, communicate to them, and persuade them to purchase their products and services. From the travelers' perspective, information search is an effective tool as a

SooCheong (Shawn) Jang is Assistant Professor, Department of Hotel, Restaurant, Institution Management and Dietetics, Kansas State University (KSU), 104 Justin Hall, Manhattan, KS 66506-1404 (E-mail: jangs@ksu.edu).

[Haworth co-indexing entry note]: "The Past, Present, and Future Research of Online Information Search." Jang, SooCheong (Shawn). Co-published simultaneously in *Journal of Travel & Tourism Marketing* (The Haworth Hospitality Press, an imprint of The Haworth Press, Inc.) Vol. 17, No. 2/3, 2004, pp. 41-47; and: *Handbook of Consumer Behavior, Tourism, and the Internet* (ed: Juline E. Mills, and Rob Law) The Haworth Hospitality Press, an imprint of The Haworth Press, Inc., 2004, pp. 41-47. Single or multiple copies of this article are available for a fee from The Haworth Document Delivery Service [1-800-HAWORTH, 9:00 a.m. - 5:00 p.m. (EST). E-mail address: docdelivery@haworthpress. com].

means of reducing uncertainty and perceived risk (Urbany, Dickson, & Wilkie, 1989). It also enables travelers to enhance the quality of a trip with reduced uncertainty (Fodness & Murray, 1997).

The rapid development of information technology, particularly the Internet, has changed the socioeconomic context of tourism and is expected to stimulate further changes (Rayman-Bacchus & Molina, 2001). Since its introduction, the Internet has become a sales and marketing distribution channel for tourism businesses. Weber and Roehl (1999) asserted that the tourism industry has been one of the top product/service categories that may be significantly affected by the emergence of the Internet. Considering the importance of the Internet, research on online search behavior is increasingly necessary, particularly in a travel and tourism context. A number of research efforts have concentrated on general tourist information search behavior (Chen, 2000; Chen & Gursoy, 2000; Fodness & Murray, 1997, 1998, 1999; Gitelson & Crompton, 1983; Gursoy & Chen, 2000; Perdue, 1985; Schul & Crompton, 1983; Snepenger, Megen, Snelling, & Worrall, 1990; Vogt & Fesenmaier, 1998). However, insufficient research attention has been paid to online consumer search behavior in the travel and tourism field. To urge researchers in the advancement of this area of research, this study briefly reviews the following issues on online information search in terms of tourism marketing: (1) traditional views of information search, (2) the distinct features of online information search, (3) online benefits to travelers and marketers, (4) online concerns and opportunities, and (5) potential future research agenda.

TRADITIONAL INFORMATION SEARCH RESEARCH

Traditional Views

There are a few generally accepted views on information search behavior. According to Money and Crotts (2003), the theoretical background of information search behavior is rooted in Stinger's (1961) theory of economics of information: consumers continue ex-pending resources for search until the utility obtained from the search exceeds the cost. That is, the search behavior is a function of the utility and cost. Hofstede's (1980) research claimed five "uncertainty avoidance" dimensions, a measure of intolerance for risk: monetary (losing income), functional (does not meet the need), physical (personal illness or injury), social (unfashionable), and psychological (damages self-esteem). The dimensions were found to have a significant influence on differences in information search behavior among cultures (Dawar, Parker, & Price, 1996). Another widely cited view is "internal and external search" behavior. The internal search refers to the activity that retrieves information stored in long-term memory. It is the information that was created from previous experience, past information searches, and repeated exposure to marketing stimuli. People usually attempt to find information in their memory first, but if an internal information source does not provide sufficient information, they then go out and search for relevant information (Beatty & Smith, 1987). Thus, the external search means an activity to seek information that does not exist in memory. Beatty and Smith (1987) categorized the sources of external travel information into four groups: (1) personal (e.g., friends, relatives, and colleagues), (2) marketer-dominated (e.g., advertisements and promotions), (3) neutral (e.g., third-party such as travel agents and travel guides), and (4) experiential sources through direct contacts with retailer.

Empirical Tourism Research

Information search behavior has been empirically studied in a tourism context. Fodness and Murray (1999) proposed and tested a framework to identify whether tourist information search (information source) is related to situational variables (e.g., composition of traveling party), product characteristics (e.g., purpose of trip and mode of travel), tourist characteristics, and search outcomes (e.g., number of destinations visited), as an extension of their earlier study (1998) defining the dimensions of information search: spatial (internal or external), temporal (pre-purchase or ongoing during the trip), and operational (contributory or decisive in terms of the relative effectiveness for decision making). They found all the tested relationships to be significant, claiming that tourist information search is under a dynamic process in which travelers used various types and amounts of information sources in vacation planning.

Some studies explored linkages between information search behavior and travelers' socio-demographic characteristics, and argued that there is a significant relationship between the two (Gitelson & Crompton, 1983; Javalgi, Edward, and Rao, 1992; Mazursky and Hirschman, 1987). According to Javalgi et al. (1992), senior travelers engage less in external search, so they tend to buy more prepackaged tours than non-seniors. Gitelson and Crompton (1983) also reported that older vacationers were more inclined to use travel agents and that the higher education group was shown to use destination-specific literature. In the consumer product setting, individual consumers tend to be less dependent on external search than business consumers since individuals consider the search cost higher than organization customers (Mazursky and Hirschman, 1987).

More recent literature suggested that culture is a critical factor influencing travelers' information search behavior (Chen & Gursoy, 2000; Gursoy & Chen, 2000; Uysal, McDonald, & Reid, 1990). Indeed, culture is a key factor that gives a clue to common communication instruments and the patterns of purchase-decisions in international travel markets. For example, Uysal et al. (1990) proclaimed that travelers from different countries used different types of information with varying frequency. They reported that main sources of external information for British, German, and Japanese tourists were travel agents, family/friends, and books/library materials respectively. Even though cultural differences in information search have been extensively studied, online search has not drawn attention as a main source in the extant research. The studies have focused on more traditional sources of information such as travel agents, family/friends, brochures, pamphlets, magazine, newspaper articles, and TV and radio advertisements.

ONLINE INFORMATION SEARCH

Online information search usually refers to information search activity through the Internet. The Internet makes it possible for travelers to search and compare information at one sitting. Since the quality of travel product is not certain until it is experienced, travelers may want to make sure of the quality as much as possible before their departure. In this sense, it is not surprising that the travel industry has been identified as an industry greatly affected by the advent of the Internet (Weber & Roehl, 1999). In order to understand the uniqueness of online information search, it is important to note distinct features of information search through the Internet, what benefits it provides for travelers and travel marketers, and what concerns and opportunities it offers.

Distinct Features

As noted earlier, travelers can reduce the level of uncertainty and improve the quality of trip through information search since it is difficult to evaluate the quality before experiencing it (Fodness and Murray, 1997). Thus, the information search travelers undertake has significant implications for the purchases they eventually make (Money & Crotts, 2003). It is clear that online information search has greater influence on the reduction of uncertainty and the purchase decision (Fodness & Murray, 1997; Susskind, Bonn, & Dev, 2003). Consumers' online search usually involves multiple selections of suppliers, comparisons of facilities, prices, and availability, so travelers can reach optimal decisions through more sufficient information than traditional sources present. The Internet offers a rich environment for the information and resources to travelers (Susskind et al., 2003). On the other hand, suppliers, or marketers, can also get useful information from travelers' search and purchase records. For example, information intermediaries help suppliers profile travelers, and provide data on traveler's selection that is based on their needs (Palmer and McCole, 2000).

The relationship between online search/purchase and online advertising/selling is like two sides of a coin as presented in Figure 1. From a supply side, a buyer's search/purchase

FIGURE 1. Online Search/Purchase and Online Advertising/Selling

means advertising/selling. From the angle of demand side, online search/purchase is possible when online advertising and selling options are provided. One distinct feature is that consumer online information search is more directly connected with purchase, as opposed to other traditional sources, since tourism-related websites usually offer online reservation or purchase options. This feature clearly provides benefits to both travelers and marketers.

Benefits to Travelers and Marketers

Using the Internet and Web for information search is beneficial not only to travelers but also to tourism marketers because it aids with cost reduction and provides a real-time communication tool to both parties. Primary advantages of online search to travelers include its relative low cost, customized information, ease of product comparisons, interactivity, virtual community formation, and 24 hour accessibility (Hoffman & Novak, 1997; Wang, Head, & Arthur, 2002). Bellman, Lohse, and Johnson (1999) suggested that online purchasers believe that the online search using the Internet has improved the overall productivity of their purchase process.

Through the Internet, tourism marketers can enhance the efficiency of distributing information and selling products and services due to cost-effectiveness and immediate interactivity as well (Connolly, Olsen, & Moore, 1998). Another benefit to the marketers is that the Internet freely reaches anywhere in the world as far as the information line is connected, which means that the potential market has no national or international boundary. As Bonn, Furr, and Susskind (1998) suggested, online marketing may be a well-suited approach due to "the distinctive high-price, high-involvement, and well-differentiated characteristics of travel products and services." The advantages include global accessibility, convenience in updating, real-time information service, interactive communications features, and

unique customization capabilities (Bender, 1997). Buhalis (2000) expressed a similar opinion that using the Internet can enable travel destinations to enhance their competitiveness by increasing their visibility, reducing advertising costs, and facilitating local cooperation.

Concerns and Opportunities

According to Machlis (1997), people visit travel websites for information search, but less than five percent actually purchase travel products or services online. Among many possible reasons, researchers pointed out a few critical concerns: technical difficulties, credit card security, no assessment of product quality, and privacy issues (Szymanski & Hise, 2000; Weber & Roehl, 1999). Tourism marketers should seriously consider these concerns when they develop online marketing programs and design their websites.

Research studies claim that website features are a significant variable that relates online consumer information search to actual purchase (Chu, 2001; Metha & Shah, 2001; Murphy, Edward, Edward, & Brymer, 1996). To build competitive websites, marketers should pay attention to specifying information such as product perceptions, shopping experience, customer service, and consumer risks (Jarvenpaa & Todd, 1997). Tierney (2000) suggested that the types of information people need on the web include activities on the trip, travel regions/cities, sightseeing, maps, insider tips, lodging, shopping, special events/festivals, and reservations. Chu (2001) also noted that prospective travelers who were visiting airline and travel websites were expecting travel destination-related information, local tours, train passes, traveler's checks, travel insurance, and custom policies.

Research studies also indicate that online information users are young, predominantly male, well educated, and have well-paid occupations (Bonn, Furr, & Susskind, 1999; Fram & Grady, 1995; Pitkow & Kehoe, 1996). Morrison et al. (2001) found similar results that the 26-34 age group and people with higher education were more likely to buy travel online as opposed to offline. Weber and Roehl (1999) also support the findings by Morrison et al. (2001), arguing that those who search for or purchase travel product online are more likely to be young, to have higher incomes, to be employed in management jobs, and to have more online experience. These results present two facts: first, that the online consumer information search is still confined to a small segment of travelers. Second, as time goes by, the segment is more likely to grow because those young are expected to use Internet even when they are old, and people in the next decade are also expected to be more educated and more highly paid. Thus, more opportunities are coming online. In order to better understand future opportunities, it is currently of necessity to note the multidimensional relationships between the characteristics of travelers and their online search preference. The knowledge of the relationships can help expand the travel markets through the Internet.

POTENTIAL FUTURE RESEARCH

As mentioned earlier, little has been known on the online search behavior of travelers. There are many different subject areas that tourism researchers can address in the future research. First, researchers need to explore potential travelers' concerns and difficulties when planning and purchasing their trip online. Online security may be one of the most important topics that must be studied in depth to find suitable tasks (e.g., security policy and coordination of the implementation of security across the organization) to successfully minimize security problems such as personal information leakage, online fraud, and so forth. From a similar perspective, traveler's perceived risk can be a valuable subject. The risk studies (e.g., financial or temporal) will allow suppliers not only to understand what factors make online searchers perceive risk, but also help improve their websites through the findings, so that travelers can search and purchase more online in the future. In association with risk, researchers need to pay attention to trust. The literature supports the idea that trust plays a critical role in changing information-searchers into buyers under the uncertain online environments (Hoffman and Novak, 1998; Jarvenpaa, Tractinsky, and Vitale, 1999). The evidence in the tourism setting will offer meaningful results to tourism marketers.

Second, future research should be directed toward figuring out the underlying reasons why some travelers seek information but do not purchase products and services online. In this respect, a study regarding travelers' online attitude and search behavior is a necessary issue to examine. It will help explain how travelers' online search behavior changes according to attitudinal differences. To draw additional implications, the findings can be compared across different information sources. As an extension, an examination of the retention of online customers is also vital to marketers. The subject is connected with online customer relationship marketing (CRM). The results of online CRM research might contribute to comprehending how travel marketers create partner-like customers and spread positive word-of-mouth.

Third, to draw more in-depth relationships regarding information search, researchers need to challenge the association of online search behaviors with more psychographic variables such as satisfaction, value, image, and loyalty. As Deitel, Deitel, and Steinbuhler (2000) argued, the Internet has made it easy to select one product or service over another due to low switching costs. As such, loyalty has significant meaning for online marketers. A thorough understanding of the search factors that greatly influence online loyalty is critical in today's competitive business environment. In the same sense, past experience via the Internet can be an essential research factor in comprehending repeat users' behavior, predicting online loyalty, and suggesting future online search/purchase intention.

Last, but not least, as reviewed earlier, the cross-cultural impacts on tourists' online information search behavior under the above-mentioned research agenda are worthwhile issues for tourism marketers. Travelers' online search behaviors, like other research on consumer behavior, can be analyzed in multidimensional ways. An example is online search behavior across different nationalities. The results of studies focusing on the cross-cultural differences in online search behavior, concerns, and loyalty should be incorporated into website designing process to capture every cultural market segment since the Internet targets are worldwide.

REFERENCES

Beatty, S. E., & Smith, S. (1987). External information search: An investigation across several product categories. *Journal of Consumer Research, 14*, 83-95.

Bellman, S., Lohse, G., & Johnson, E. J. (1999). Predictors of online buying behavior. *Communications of the ACM, 42*(12), 32-38.

Bender, D. E. (1997). Using the web to market the hospitality, travel and tourism product or services. *HSMAI Marketing Review, 14*(3), 33-37.

Bonn, M. A., Furr, H. L., & Susskind, A. M. (1998). Using the Internet as a pleasure travel planning tool: An examination of the sociodemographic and behavioral characteristics among Internet users and nonusers. *Journal of Hospitality and Tourism Research, 22*(3), 303-317.

Bonn, M. A., Furr, H. L., & Susskind, A. M. (1999). Predicting a behavioral profile for pleasure travelers on the basis of Internet use segmentation. *Journal of Travel Research, 37*(4), 333-340.

Buhalis, D. (2000). Marketing the competitive destination of the future. *Tourism Management, 21*(1), 97-116.

Chen, J. S. (2000). Cross-cultural difference in travel information acquisition among tourists from three Pacific-rim countries. *Journal of Hospitality and Tourism Research, 24*(2), 239-251.

Chen, J. S., & Gursoy, D. (2000). Cross-cultural comparison of the information sources used by first-time and repeat travelers and its marketing implications. *International Journal of Hospitality Management, 19*(2), 191-203.

Chu, R. (2001). What online Hong Kong travelers look for on airline/travel websites? *International Journal of Hospitality Management, 20*(1), 95-100.

Connolly, D. J., Olsen, M. D., & Moore, R. G. (1998). The Internet as a distribution channel. *Cornell Hotel and Restaurant Administration Quarterly, 8*(4), 42-54.

Dawar, N., Parker, P. M., & Price, L. J. (1996). A cross-cultural study of interpersonal information exchange. *Journal of International Business Studies, 27*, 497-516.

Deitel, H. M., Deitel, P. J., & Steinbuhler, K. (2000). *e-Business & e-commerce for managers.* Upper Saddle River, NJ: Prentice Hall.

Fodness, D., & Murray, B. (1997). Tourist information search. *Annals of Tourism Research, 24*(3), 503-523.

Fodness, D., & Murray, B. (1998). A typology of tourist information search strategies. *Journal of Travel Research, 37*(2), 108-119.

Fodness, D., & Murray, B. (1999). A model of tourist information search behavior. *Journal of Travel Research, 37*(3), 220-230.

Fram, E. H., & Grady, D. B. (1995). Internet buyers: Will the surfers become buyers? *Direct Marketing, 58*(6), 63-65.

Gitelson, R. J., & Crompton, J. L. (1983). The planning horizons and sources of information used by pleasure vacationers. *Journal of Travel Research, 21*(3), 2-7.

Gursoy, D., & Chen, J. S. (2000). Competitive analysis of cross cultural information search behavior. *Tourism Management, 21*(6), 583-590.

Hoffman, D. L., & Novak, T. P. (1997). A new marketing paradigm for electronic commerce. *The Information Society, 13*, 43-54.

Hoffman, D. L., & Novak, T. P. (1998). Building consumer trust in online environments. *Communication of the ACM, 42*(4), 80-85.

Hofstede, G. (1980). *Culture's consequences.* Beverly Hills, CA: Sage Publications.

Jarvenpaa, S. L., & Todd, P. A. (1997). Consumer reactions to electronic shopping on the World Wide Web. *International Journal of Electronic Commerce, 1*(2), 59-88.

Jarvenpaa, S. L., Tractinsky, N., & Vitale, M. (1999). Consumer trust in an internet store: A cross-cultural validation. *Journal of Computer Mediated Communication, 5*(2), 32-69.

Javalgi, R., Edward, T., & Rao, S. R. (1992). Consumer behavior in the U.S. pleasure travel marketplace: An analysis of senior and non-senior travelers. *Journal of Travel Research, 31*, 14-20.

Machlis, S. (1997). Profits elude travel sites. *Computerworld, 32*, 53-54.

Mazursky, D., & Hirschman, E. (1987). A cross-organizational comparison of retail buyers' information search utilization. *International Journal of Retailing, 2*(1), 44-62.

Metha, K. T., & Shah, V. (2001). E-commerce: The next global frontier for small business. *The Journal of Applied Business Research, 17*(1), 87-94.

Money, R. B., & Crotts, J. C. (2003). The effect of uncertainty avoidance on information search, planning, and purchases of international travel vacations. *Tourism Management, 24*, 191-202.

Morrison, A. M., Su, J., O'Leary, J. T., & Cai, L. (2001). Predicting usage of the Internet for travel booking: An exploratory study. *Information Technology and Tourism, 4*(1), 15-30.

Murphy, J. F., Edward, J. W., Edward, C., & Brymer, R. A. (1996). Hotel management and marketing on the Internet. *Cornell Hotel and Restaurant Administration Quarterly, 37*(3), 70-82.

Palmer, A., & McCole, P. (2000). The role of electronic commerce in creating virtual tourism destination marketing organizations. *International Journal of Contemporary Hospitality Management, 12*(3), 198-204.

Perdue, R. R. (1985). Segmenting state information inquirers by timing of destination decision and previous experience. *Journal of Travel Research, 23*, 6-11.

Pitkow, J. E., & Kehoe, C. M. (1996). Emerging trends in the WWW user population. *Communications of the ACM, 39*(6), 106-108.

Rayman-Bacchus, L., & Molina, A. (2001). Internet-based tourism services: Business issues and trends. *Futures, 33*(7), 589-605.

Schmidt, J. B., & Spreng, R. A. (1996). A proposed model of external consumer information search. *Journal of the Academy of Marketing Science, 24*(3), 246-256.

Schul, P., & Crompton, J. L. (1983). Search behavior of international vacationers: Travel-specific lifestyle and sociodemographic variables. *Journal of Travel Research, 22*(3), 25-31.

Snepenger, D., Megen, K., Snelling, M., & Worrall, K. (1990). Information search strategies by destination-naïve tourists. *Journal of Travel Research, 29*(1), 13-16.

Stinger, G. J. (1961). The economics of information. *Journal of Political Economy, 69*, 213-225.

Susskind, A. M., Bonn, M. A., & Dev, C. (2003). To look or book: An examination of consumers' apprehensiveness toward internet use. *Journal of Travel Research, 41*(3), 256-264.

Szymanski, D. M., & Hise, R. T. (2000). E-satisfaction: An initial examination. *Journal of Retailing, 76*(3), 309-322.

Tierney, P. (2000). Internet-based evaluation of tourism website effectiveness: Methodological issues and survey results. *Journal of Travel Research, 39*(2), 212-219.

Urbany, J. E., Dickson, P. R., & Wilkie, W. L. (1989). Buyer uncertainty and information search. *Journal of Consumer Research, 16*, 208-215.

Uysal, M., McDonald, C. D., & Reid, L. J. (1990). Sources of information used by international visitors to U.S. parks and natural areas. *Journal of Park and Recreation Administration, 8*(1), 51-59.

Vogt, C. A., & Fesenmaier, D. R. (1998). Expanding the functional information search model. *Annals of Tourism Research, 25*(3), 551-578.

Wang, F., Head, M., & Arthur, N. (2002). E-tailing: An analysis of web impacts on the retail market. *Journal of Business Strategies, 19*(1), 73-93.

Weber, K., & Roehl, W. S. (1999). Profiling people searching for and purchasing travel products on the world wide web. *Journal of Travel Research, 37*, 291-298.

SECTION 2:
TRAVEL WEBSITE USER
CHARACTERISTICS

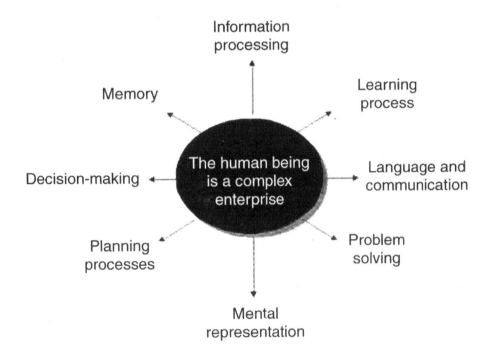

"It is by incorporating scientific knowledge into the design process that we can orient sites towards users."

Caffier, F. & Benchekroun, M. (2002). Web Site Ergonomics and User Tests. *Intranet Journal*. Available: *intranetjournal.com/articles/200201/er_01_16_02a.html*

Buyer Characteristics Among Users
of Various Travel Intermediaries

Kara Wolfe
Cathy H. C. Hsu
Soo K. Kang

SUMMARY. As online travel purchases increase, travel intermediaries must change to meet consumer demands. A survey was conducted to identify travelers' selection criteria and expectations of traditional travel agents. Responses from 382 individuals were compared by their methods of purchasing travel arrangements, including those who purchased online, offline, or both. Differences were found among the groups in terms of travel agent selection criteria and expectations; however, the groups were similar in their frequency of travel and number of information sources used. Results and conclusions identified strategies for travel intermediaries to attract and retain clientele. *[Article copies available for a fee from The Haworth Document Delivery Service: 1-800-HAWORTH. E-mail address: <docdelivery@haworthpress.com> Website: <http://www.HaworthPress.com> © 2004 by The Haworth Press, Inc. All rights reserved.]*

KEYWORDS. Travel agents, expectations, selection criteria, online purchasing, Internet

INTRODUCTION

The International Data Corporation predicted that worldwide e-commerce revenues will increase approximately eightfold in the next few years, growing from $634 billion in 2001 to more than $5 trillion in 2005 (Gantz, Glasheen, & Emberley, 2001). Travel and tourism accommodations have rapidly become the largest category of products sold over the Internet. In 2002, over 39 million people booked travel arrangements online (Travel Industry Association [TIA], 2002). As a result of these trends, Jupiter forecasted that the United States (US) online travel industry sales would increase from $18 billion in 2000 to $63 billion in 2006 (World Tourism Organization Business Council, 2001).

Kara Wolfe is Assistant Professor, Hospitality and Tourism Management, North Dakota State University. Cathy H. C. Hsu is Professor, Associate Head and Graduate Programs Director, School of Hotel & Tourism Management, The Hong Kong Polytechnic University. Soo K. Kang is Assistant Professor, Restaurant and Resort Management, Colorado State University.

Address correspondence to Kara Wolfe, Department of Apparel, Design, Facility and Hospitality Management, North Dakota State University, Fargo, ND 58105-5057 (E-mail: Kara.Wolfe@ndsu.nodak.edu).

The authors would like to thank the American Society of Travel Agents (ASTA) Foundation for its support and funding assistance.

[Haworth co-indexing entry note]: "Buyer Characteristics Among Users of Various Travel Intermediaries." Wolfe, Kara, Cathy H. C. Hsu, and Soo K. Kang. Co-published simultaneously in *Journal of Travel & Tourism Marketing* (The Haworth Hospitality Press, an imprint of The Haworth Press, Inc.) Vol. 17, No. 2/3, 2004, pp. 51-62; and: *Handbook of Consumer Behavior, Tourism, and the Internet* (ed: Juline E. Mills, and Rob Law) The Haworth Hospitality Press, an imprint of The Haworth Press, Inc., 2004, pp. 51-62. Single or multiple copies of this article are available for a fee from The Haworth Document Delivery Service [1-800-HAWORTH, 9:00 a.m. - 5:00 p.m. (EST). E-mail address: docdelivery@haworthpress.com].

This growth is not just a North American phenomenon. In New Zealand, 44% of Internet users went online to plan or book overseas holidays and 28% to plan or book domestic holidays (ACNielsen, 2001). Despite recent world conflicts, online purchases for the tourism, leisure, and entertainment sector in the United Kingdom (UK) and Europe for the first quarter of 2003 tripled that of the first quarter in 2002 (Visa Europe, 2003). Restaurant bookings and car rentals were also among the fastest growing segments in the industry (Visa Europe, 2003).

While consumers are changing, businesses are changing as well. The Internet has revolutionized the distribution channels and changed the way companies do business. Considering that commission payments represented the third or fourth largest operating expense for many international airlines (Standing & Vasudavan, 2000), cutting these costs means an increase in the bottom-line. In addition to commission cuts and caps, suppliers, such as airlines and hotels, made strategic decisions to target consumers directly and bypass the traditional distribution channels (Walle, 1996).

A recent report from the World Tourism Organization (WTO) Business Council (2001) indicated many small- to mid-size travel intermediaries have not incorporated the latest technology into their business strategy. Reasons for not doing so included: managers thought they were too far behind to catch up with industry leaders, they were afraid of the unknown, or they were not concerned with growth. While some analysts forecasted a pessimistic view and the demise of travel agencies, others believed that those agencies that develop new strategic plans will become leaders in the industry (Standing & Vasudavan, 2000). The call for new strategic plans means more research is needed on how managers can incorporate technology into their operation.

Comparing online and offline consumers' expectations of travel agents can help agents develop strategic plans and actions that could capture more travelers. Customer segmentation is important in determining e-commerce vendors' success (Berry, 1999). This study used behavioral segmentation to divide travelers into groups. As the Internet transforms the role of travel agents from order takers to that of consultants (Murphy & Tan, 2003; Raymond, 2001), it is important for travel intermediaries to know what consumers expect of them. Therefore, the purpose of this study was to explore differences among travelers who used various intermediary sources (i.e., traditional travel agent, Internet sites, and both) to purchase travel arrangements. Specific objectives were to (1) determine if there were differences in selection criteria and expectations among those who purchased travel products from a traditional travel agent, online, or both; and (2) profile the three segments by their demographic characteristics and unique travel behaviors, such as types of travel products purchased and information sources used.

TECHNOLOGY AND TRAVEL AGENTS

New technologies affect consumers' knowledge, attitudes, and behaviors (Wang, Head, & Archer, 2000). Not surprisingly, the Internet has contributed to increased expectations from consumers and competition within the tourism industry (Murphy & Tan, 2003; Raymond, 2001). Therefore, it is imperative for travel intermediaries to strive toward providing excellent service. Company profitability will depend on meeting travelers' expectations in an effort to satisfy consumers and gain their loyalty.

Parasuraman and Grewal (2000) contended that service quality enhances perceived value, which is linked to consumer loyalty. Consumers measure service quality by comparing a company's performance with their expectations. Technology has a major impact on this buyer-seller interaction because computer savvy travelers expect businesses to provide information via the Internet. Therefore, the websites providing high-quality information and user-friendly functions will be more likely to build consumer loyalty.

Businesses that provide outstanding services have a competitive advantage; this advantage can be enhanced with information technology (Picolli, Spalding, & Ives, 2001). For example, Travelocity® "Guides and Advice" provides air, hotel, and car reservations along with weather information and a currency converter. This site teams up with Frommer's travel guide to provide additional information, including attractions, suggested itineraries, and restaurant listings (Travelocity, n.d.). These services meet consumers' demands, and through technology, they are available anytime anywhere.

Past studies have provided profiles of Internet users, suggesting the types of people who would use travel websites. Researchers indicated that Internet users were likely to be under the age of 45 and college graduates (Bonn, Furr, & Susskind, 1999; Weber & Roehl, 1999). Weber and Roehl (1999) also found that those who had a four-year college degree or higher and those whose household income was above US$50,000 were more likely to purchase travel online. The Travel Industry Association of America (2002) found that approximately 96 million travelers had used the Internet, and online travel purchasers' characteristics reflected previous Internet users' profiles in that they tended to be younger and better educated. However, there has been a shift in the demographic profile of Internet users. As the Internet becomes more readily available, online travel purchase has become more common among the less affluent. This trend was evidenced by the decline in the average income of online travel purchasers three years in a row (TIA, 2002).

The Internet enables consumers to create their own itineraries, compelling travel intermediaries to concentrate on value-added products (Buhalis, 2000). As the number of Internet consumers continues to grow, it is important to learn more about them and the types of services they value the most. Lang (2000) surveyed travelers in the Seattle airport and found that 66% of respondents used the Internet to search for travel information and that most of them (59%) had been using the Internet for over two years. The respondents rated convenience, easy access to up-to-date information, easy to compare prices, and time as advantages of using the Internet for travel-related purposes. Chu (2001) conducted focus groups with Chinese and Caucasian travelers, which assisted in identifying travelers' needs and expectations of travel websites. Some travelers noted that one-stop shopping was expected, including hotel reservations, car rentals, customs, and weather reports. Respondents indicated they expected the site to be informative, interactive, and attractive.

If travel agents intend to embrace e-commerce, there are many facets to consider. Heung (2003) surveyed travel agents in Hong Kong on their barriers to e-commerce and found that cost, training, security, and complexity were listed as the top inhibitors. Analysts from Bear Stearns & Company predicted only 2 out of 10 individual commercial travel web sites will survive more than 3 years, yet online sales will quadruple over the next 4 years (Stoltz, 2000). This growth is forcing an increasing number of traditional travel agents to compete online. As a result, online and traditional travel agents are becoming more alike. For example, Expedia promotes its toll free number for people to call, and American Express advertises its services that allow travelers to price and purchase tickets online (Stoltz, 2000).

EXPECTATIONS OF TRAVEL AGENTS

Researchers have identified various aspects that are important to travelers in regards to selection criteria and expectations of traditional travel agents. These issues could be of importance to online consumers as well as offline purchasers. Heung and Chu (2000) found reputation, past experience with an agent, and travel knowledge were important selection criteria when choosing a travel agent. Another study found that knowledge, willingness to search for the lowest fares, and courteous/friendly agent were rated as very important service features among travel agent users (Persia & Gitelson, 1993). Integrity issues (e.g., providing services as promised), customer service (e.g., courteous), and knowledge were rated very high in terms of travelers' expectations of travel agents in a study by Ryan and Cliff (1997). Additionally, LeBlanc (1992) found that corporate image, competitiveness (e.g., personal service, competitive fares, and reliable service), and courtesy were predictors of satisfied customers.

Bitner (2001) claimed consumers' expectations have not changed due to the impact of technology–they still want good customer service. Meeting consumer expectations and providing good comprehensive service are critical to the survival of travel agents (Buhalis & Licata, 2002), because building Internet customer loyalty takes more than technology (Barnes & Cumby, 2002). Companies may try to use the lowest price tactic to attract customers; however, business' ability to meet consumers' expectations is the ultimate determinant of success (Wong & Kwan, 2001). To effectively target consumers, it is important to understand them and identify what they are seeking. These will help e-businesses allocate their limited resources (Bhatnagar & Ghose, in press).

METHODOLOGY

A questionnaire was developed that asked travelers about selection criteria and expectations of travel agents, travel booking behaviors, and demographic characteristics. Selection criteria and expectation items were adapted from past studies (Heung & Chu, 2000; Kendall & Booms, 1989; LeBlanc, 1992; Lowengart & Reichel, 1998; Persia & Gitelson, 1993; Ryan & Cliff, 1997). Travel agents in the local area (Manhattan, KS) were interviewed to identify challenges, services currently provided, and other operational and marketing issues. They were also asked to review the questionnaire and provide comments or suggestions for improvements. Results of the interviews were incorporated into the questionnaire. The questionnaire was pilot tested (n = 48) with respondents who had used a travel agent and who had booked travel arrangements online.

Travel agencies (n = 216) in the greater Kansas City area and the cities of Topeka, Kansas, and Columbia, Missouri, listed in the respective area telephone directories were contacted and asked if they would participate in the study. Letters were sent to the agencies to introduce the project, the researchers, and the purpose of the project along with a copy of the questionnaire. Approximately one week after the mailing, each travel agency was contacted by telephone to explain the request. The agency manager/owner was asked if he/she would be willing to participate in the study. The managers were provided with two options

for participating: (1) to provide a list of their current customers or (2) to receive pre-stuffed, postage paid envelopes containing the questionnaire, cover letter, and return envelope; then, the travel agent would place mailing labels of his/her clients on the envelopes and put them in the mail for delivery. Nine agents agreed to participate.

The participating agents provided a sample of 450 clients. The questionnaire and a cover letter explaining the purpose of the study were mailed to the clients. Three weeks after the initial mailing, a follow-up letter and questionnaire were sent to non-respondents from the list of clients provided by travel agents. Individuals who received questionnaires directly from the travel agents could not be identified. Therefore, non-respondents from this group did not receive a follow-up questionnaire. The mail survey resulted in 150 completed questionnaires, for a 33.3% response rate.

The questionnaire was also administered to travelers at the Kansas City International Airport to obtain information from individuals who purchased travel arrangements from various sources. Individuals were asked to complete the questionnaire in the airport and return it to one of the surveyors. The entire process resulted in 382 completed questionnaires, of which 232 (60.7%) were from the airport data collection.

DATA ANALYSIS

Responses from the two groups were checked for normality. Kurtosis tests of the demographic data were not significant at the .01 level (Mertler & Vannatta, 2002). Normality tests for selection criteria and expectation items were also conducted. Results showed that 11 of the 36 (30.6%) items did not have normal distribution based on the Kurtosis statistics (±2.58). However, "with moderate sample sizes, modest violations can be accommodated as long as the differences are due to skewness and not outliers" (Hair, Anderson, Tatham, & Black, 1998, p. 349). All the items that exceeded the ±2.58 Kurtosis statistics value had means above 6.00 and a median of 7, except convenient hours; and they all had small standard deviations (many 1.0 or less). Therefore, the evidence suggested the non-normality of data for those variables were caused by leptokurtosis, rather than outliers. In addition, multivariate techniques are robust and "work quite well when data vectors are not multivariate normally distributed, provided the data vectors still have independent probability distributions" (Johnson, 1998, p. 15). Therefore, further analysis of the data with multivariate statistics continued.

Results were compared by methods of purchasing travel arrangements (i.e., online, offline, or both). MANOVA should be used when comparing two or more groups on a large number of variables (Johnson, 1998), thus, MANOVAs of the selection criteria and expectations were conducted to determine if there were differences among the groups (Objective 1). The method of purchasing travel arrangements was used as the independent variable, and the dependent variables were the selection criteria in the first analysis and expectations in the second analysis. Chi-square tests and ANOVAs were used to compare the groups by demographics, and descriptive statistics were calculated on the types of items purchased and information sources used to identify characteristics of each group (Objective 2).

RESULTS

Respondent Profile

Of the 382 respondents, 43.8% of them were male, and 55.9% were female (Table 1). Nearly half of the respondents were 46 years and older (45.1%) and reported an annual household income of $75,000 or more (47.4%). Close to two-thirds of respondents (64.2%) had a college degree or higher and 22.8% had some college education. Over half (53.8%) of the respondents had purchased travel-related products (e.g., airline ticket, car rental reservation, hotel room reservation, cruise ship, attraction ticket, and visa/passport service) through the Internet. Almost three-fourths of respondents (72.5%) had used a travel agent for purchasing travel-related products in the past year.

TABLE 1. Demographics of Respondents

Gender	%
Male	43.8
Female	55.9
Age	
18-25	20.3
26-35	15.9
36-45	18.6
46-55	30.5
Older than 55	14.6
Annual Household Income	
Less than $30,000	15.8
$30,000-44,999	10.3
$45,000-59,999	9.5
$60,000-74,999	17.0
$75,000 or more	47.4
Education	
Grade school	0.3
High school diploma	12.8
Some college	22.8
College degree	36.7
Graduate degree	27.5
State of Residence	
Kansas	36.6
Missouri	28.3
Other	35.1

Selection Criteria and Expectations

Respondents were asked to rate the importance of items when choosing a travel agent and their agreement with expectation items. Of the selection criteria, trustworthiness (6.65) was rated the most important (Table 2). Criteria that were rated important regarding customer service issues included quality service (6.53), friendliness (6.21), and personalized service (6.14). Other items that were rated as important included ability to locate cheap fares (6.36), travel knowledge (6.33), and convenient business hours (6.02). When asked to rate their expectations of travel agents, respondents rated integrity issues among the top, with honesty (6.83) and reliability (6.77) rated as the highest expectations. They also rated solving problems (6.47) and clarifying the fine print (6.38), along with saving time

TABLE 2. Respondents' Ratings of Selection Criteria and Expectations of Travel Agents

Selection Criteria[a]	Overall Mean
Trustworthy	6.65
Quality service	6.53
Ability in locating the cheapest fares and rates	6.36
Travel knowledge or expert advice	6.33
Friendliness of travel agent	6.21
Personalized service	6.14
Convenient business hours	6.02
Past experience with travel agent	5.88
Reputation	5.88
Service charge	5.61
Free ticket delivery	5.42
Certified travel agent status	5.14
Friend's/Relative's recommendation	5.06
1-800 telephone number	5.07
Professional image of workplace	5.02
Location	4.82
Membership in a preferred travel club (e.g., AAA)	4.59
Size of travel agency	3.68
Expectations[b]	
Be honest	6.83
Be reliable	6.77
Save me time	6.49
Get problems solved when something inadvertently goes wrong (e.g., assist with refunds)	6.47
Save me money	6.45
Clarify the fine print (e.g., cancellation penalties and restrictions)	6.38
Provide precautionary advice (e.g., travel warnings or medical precautions)	5.98
Know details about the reservations (e.g., my room is pool side or I have an aisle seat)	5.95
Give advice on possible destination	5.90
Provide thorough information (e.g., sites or events to visit in addition to those requested)	5.73
Give advice on possible hotels	5.50
Offer trips with personalized itineraries (not packaged)	5.44
Offer packaged tours	5.31
I would rather my travel agent assess a flat rate fee rather than a percentage based commission	5.28
Give advice on local customs or cuisine	5.22
Inform me of new products or services on a regular basis	4.95
Enhance my cruise with value-added benefits and amenities (e.g., sending a bottle of wine, or providing additional land package)	4.95
Give advice on possible restaurants	4.69

[a]Importance scale: 7 = very important and 1 = not important.
[b]Agreement scale: 7 = strongly agree and 1 = strongly disagree.

(6.49) and saving money (6.45), among their top expectations of travel agents. The selection criteria and expectations ratings showed that, when respondents made travel arrangements, they wanted someone they can trust and who can provide good service, expertise, and convenience without costing too much. Other researchers also contend that establishing trust is very important when working with Internet consumers (Wang, Head, & Archer, 2000). Therefore, those embarking on e-commerce ventures should keep these issues in mind. The challenge is determining how a web site can exude trust and good service.

Respondents were asked the number of times they used a travel agent in the past 12 months and if they had purchased travel-related products through the Internet. Respondents who had not purchased travel services through a travel agent or the Internet were excluded (n = 48) from further analyses. Responses of those who had purchased travel arrangements through a travel agent, the Internet, or both were analyzed and compared.

MANOVAs were conducted to compare the selection criteria and expectations of the three groups. Results from the selection criteria by purchase arrangement indicated significant differences among the groups (Wilk's Lambda = .740, F = 2.444, p = .000) because the MANOVA test does not indicate where the differences occurred, post hoc tests were further conducted. These tests showed that respondents who only used a travel agent to purchase travel arrangements rated the following selection criteria higher than Internet purchasers: quality service, travel knowledge, friendliness, personal service, reputation, and past experience. Respondents who only purchased from the Internet rated service charge as more important (Table 3). Results of comparing expectations by purchase arrangement also showed differences among the three groups (Wilk's Lambda = .841, F = 1.489, p = .039). Post hoc tests revealed only 2 of the 18 expectation items were rated differently. Travel agent clients rated advice on hotels as a higher expectation than those who used both a travel agent and the Internet. Respondents who used the Internet to purchase travel items rated advice on restaurants as a higher expectation than those who used both intermediaries.

The findings could signify that travelers who used a traditional travel agent did so because they liked friendly, personal service and expert advice. It also showed that they chose their current travel agent based on past experi-

TABLE 3. Selection Criteria and Expectations by Purchase Arrangements

Selection Criteria[a]	Purchased travel from		
	Travel agent	Internet	Both
Quality service	6.65[c*]	6.26[c]	6.57
Travel knowledge or expert advice	6.49[c***]	5.89[cd]	6.37[d**]
Friendliness of travel agent	6.52[cd]	6.00[d**]	6.04[c***]
Personalized service	6.39[cd]	5.91[c*]	6.10[d*]
Reputation	6.08[c*]	5.72	5.76[c*]
Past experience with travel agent	6.02[c*]	5.41[cd]	5.97[d*]
Certified travel agent status	5.34[c*]	5.17	4.82[c]
Service charge	5.28[c***]	6.13[c]	5.57
Location	5.00[c*]	5.04	4.48[c]
Wilk's Lambda = .740, F = 2.444, p = .000			
Expectations[b]			
Give advice on possible hotels	5.66[c*]	5.45	5.33[c]
Give advice on possible restaurants	4.75[c*]	5.09[d***]	4.35[cd]
Wilk's Lambda = .841, F = 1.489, p = .039			

[a]Importance scale: 7 = very important and 1 = not important.
[b]Agreement scale: 7 = strongly agree and 1 = strongly disagree.
[cd]Items followed by the same letter were significantly different.
* $p \leq .05$, ** $p \leq .01$, and *** $p \leq .001$.

TABLE 4. Demographics by Purchase Arrangements

	Purchased travel from		
	Travel agent (n = 135)	Internet (n = 57)	Both (n = 142)
Gender			
Male	44.4%	37.5%	47.5%
Female	55.6	62.5	52.5
Age			
18-25	16.5	33.9	15.8
26-35	12.0	30.4	15.1
36-45	20.3	10.7	22.3
46-55	34.6	19.6	30.9
Over 55	16.5	5.4	15.8
$\chi^2 = 25.485$ (p = .001)			
Income			
< $30,000	13.1	32.1	9.8
$30,000-44,999	5.7	18.9	6.0
$45,000-59,999	11.5	11.3	6.8
$60,000-74,999	22.1	17.0	12.0
≥ $75,000	47.5	20.8	65.4
$\chi^2 = 43.089$ (p = .000)			
Education			
High school degree	15.1	10.7	7.3
Some college	24.6	19.6	21.2
Four year degree	31.7	39.3	41.6
Graduate degree	27.8	30.4	29.9

ence, reputation, and certified status. Travelers who purchased travel items online rated service charge as a more important selection criterion. This result may imply they used the Internet to avoid service charges that are often assessed by traditional travel agents.

When comparing demographics of the three groups, respondents were similar in terms of gender and education. However, there were some differences among the groups regarding age ($\chi^2 = 25.405$, p = .001) and income ($\chi^2 = 43.089$, p = .000). Respondents who purchased travel accommodations from a travel agent or both an agent and online tended to be older, whereas the Internet group had a higher representation from the younger age categories (Table 4). Travelers who used a travel agent were also more likely to be in the upper income categories, and approximately two-thirds of those who used both intermediaries were in the highest income group.

Travel Arrangements

When respondents were asked how they typically made leisure travel arrangements, using a travel agent and booking directly through the service providers (e.g., hotel, car

rental, and airline companies) ranked as the top modes. When comparing booking practices among the three groups, travel agent clients relied more on their agent, especially for airline tickets (Figure 1). However, they did not book hotel accommodations and car rental services through a travel agent as often as airline tickets. Online travel purchasers used a variety of sources, including direct booking, travel Internet sites, and specific company Internet sites. They also did not purchase lodging or car rental services from travel Internet sites as often as they purchased airline tickets. Close to two-thirds of the travelers who used a combination of travel agents and online providers relied on travel agents for airline tickets, and approximately one-third booked direct for lodging and car rental arrangements.

It appeared that the lodging and car rental customers are a market worthy of intermediaries' attention. As travel agents have transitioned

FIGURE 1. Leisure Travel Booking by Segment

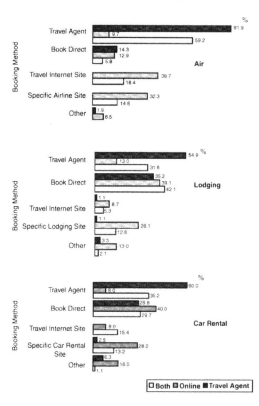

from relying on commissions from companies to earning fees from consumers for services rendered, capturing more opportunities to earn fees is important. Marketing activities should be developed to attract these customers to increase sales. For instance, traditional travel agents may try to entice travelers to increase purchases when they call to book an airline flight by offering additional services, such as making hotel and/or car rental reservations. To capture these "book direct" businesses, online travel agencies can use e-mails and pop-up advertisements to remind travelers that the Internet site can provide competitive rates and "one stop shopping" where visitors can enjoy the ease of making all types of reservations in one visit.

Besides marketing implications, the fact that more travelers booked direct for lodging and car rental services is an area that deserves further investigation. No other studies were found that addressed this issue. Possible rea-

sons for respondents' high likelihood to book direct for lodging accommodations included that they felt they may get a better room rate by negotiating with front desk or reservation employees, they did not want to book room reservations as far in advance as they were required for airline tickets, or they had specific questions to ask hotel employees (e.g., driving directions and area attractions).

Travel Behaviors

Respondents' frequency of travel and the number and types of information sources used were also compared by purchase arrangements. The three groups were compared with ANOVAs. Respondents who used both a travel agent and the Internet to purchase travel products appeared to travel more often (M = 13.09 trips per year) than those who purchased travel services from an agent (M = 7.81) or those who purchased travel services online (M = 9.42). However, the differences were not significant at the .05 level (F = 2.352, p = .097). Respondents used an average of 3.19 travel information sources, with no significant differences among the groups (F = .505, p = .604). When respondents were asked where they usually obtained travel information, the most commonly used sources were the Internet (68.6%), travel agents (62.3%), and friends/family (59.0%). When the information sources were compared by purchase arrangements, respondents who purchased travel arrangements on the Internet (92.8%) or used both the Internet and a travel agent (84.9%) were more likely to use the Internet as an information source than those who purchased only from a travel agent (40.8%). As expected, travelers who purchased from a travel agent (79.4%) and both a travel agent and the Internet (67.6%) were more likely to use a travel agent as an information source than those who purchased online (15.1%). Thus, travel agents who would like to capture some of the online travelers would want to have a web presence by either establishing their own web site or advertising on the Internet to provide travel product information.

The final analysis tabulated the reasons why respondents had not purchased travel products online. The most commonly reported reason was lack of personal service (41.4%), followed by security issues (40.4%), lack of experience (36.3%), and time consuming (30.8%). Therefore, travel companies and intermediaries that would like to increase the number of consumers who purchase travel arrangements online should continue to address these issues. Airlines and hotels have begun sending immediate e-mail responses to acknowledge and confirm travelers' reservations. This tactic along with e-mail messages that notify travelers of special promotions or miles accumulated may soon overcome consumers' perception of the lack of personalized service. As consumers become more familiar with the Internet, the lack of experience will diminish; as technology advances, increased security will become commonly available and consumers' concern for security problems will be eased. Security issues may also be addressed by building an environment of trust (Wang, Head, & Archer, 2000). Some ways to build consumer trust are to obtain and use branded websites and e-mail addresses, so that the brick and mortar company reputation is transferred to the e-commerce side of the business (Hanson, 2000; Ries & Ries, 2001). These tactics also will help overcome consumer privacy concerns (Wang, Head, & Archer, 2000). With these changes, the Internet is likely to continue its growth as an avenue for travel service purchases. Thus, travel intermediaries need to keep up with this trend.

CONCLUSIONS AND RECOMMENDATIONS

Travel Agencies

Of the buyer characteristics analyzed in this study, there was little difference in expectations of travel agents among travelers who purchased travel accommodations through different travel intermediaries. However, there were some differences in their ratings of selection criteria. Travelers who used only a travel agent were more focused on service, friendliness, and travel knowledge of the agent. Therefore, travel agents will need to use different strategies to retain existing clients and to attract travelers who have used alternative

means of making travel arrangements. For current clients, traditional travel agents should continue to focus on providing expert advice and friendly, personalized service, such as bon voyage cards or welcome home packages.

As the group that only purchased from a travel agent matures, it will be pertinent for traditional travel agents to capture the younger, upcoming market. Traditional travel agents may attempt to build customer relations with younger travelers by using both personalized and bulk e-mails to promote products. To capture online travel purchasers, traditional travel agents should also have an Internet site available for travelers' use. The Internet site is a good marketing tool, and the cost of maintaining the site could be offset by selling advertisements to travel service providers. The provision of Internet booking options with no service charge may result in attracting clients who will pay for other future services, such as personalized or international itineraries.

Online Travel Companies

On the other hand, online travel companies can try to capture part of the travel agent client market by emphasizing online agents' knowledge or amount of information available on the Internet. They can provide personalized service through e-mails and customized web sites that are built "on the fly" based on users' specific profiles and needs. Online travel agencies could also provide telephone numbers or e-mail contact information for consumers who are looking for one-on-one service or answers to specific questions. E-mail allows agencies to respond more promptly to consumers' inquiries and with as much personal, polite, professional, and promotional sense as postal mail and telephone calls (Murphy & Tan, 2003). E-mail also allows immediate responses to complaints, which can improve consumers' satisfaction and their intent to return (Matilla & Mount, 2003). These sites may have an advantage over a specific airline or lodging site. That is, they can provide "one-stop shopping," and they allow for comparison shopping by making several airline schedules and fees available from one site.

All Travel Service Providers

Travel service providers and online travel agencies trying to attract more online purchasers should emphasize their ability to provide travel accommodations at the lowest prices since travelers who only purchased from the Internet rated service charge as an important selection criterion. This tactic is also demographically logical because those who only used the Internet when making travel arrangements tended to have lower incomes. The Internet only group also had a higher percentage of respondents 35 years of age and younger. To retain these younger travelers, travel intermediaries need different strategies from those used to attract older travelers. Further studies are needed to identify what attracts younger travelers to specific Internet sites when purchasing accommodations online.

Both traditional travel agents and online travel companies should focus on those who used both travel agents and the Internet because this group is a large market and its members reported the highest income. Members of this group were also likely to do their homework online prior to calling the traditional travel agents. Because the Internet was the number one source of travel information, it is a smart business practice for all travel companies to have a web presence. To capture these travelers, it seems logical for travel companies to have live personnel available as well as online purchasing options.

This study contributed practical knowledge to the travel industry. Travel companies can use the buyer characteristics provided to tailor purchasing methods and services to meet consumer demand. Travel intermediaries (e.g., traditional travel agents and online travel agencies) as well as other travel companies (e.g., airlines, hotels, and car rental agencies) can continue to boost customer sales by increasing the perception of personal service and addressing Internet security issues. Addressing these issues will increase travelers' perceived value and satisfaction, leading to customer loyalty.

Travelers

As both online and offline travel agents realize the importance of providing online products and services, their use of new innovations will make e-consumers the ultimate winners. Advanced technology can improve customer service and products, thus increase consumers perceived value and satisfaction. Due to technology and competition, customers have and will continue to see improvements in services in the following manners. The Internet allows travelers to gather a plethora of information and become very knowledgeable about products and provides consumers the flexibility of purchasing anything, anywhere, anytime. The Internet allows companies to enhance service quality by improving customer relations and after-sales services (Wang, Head, & Archer, 2000). New technologies can shorten the time needed to perform back of the house tasks, allowing personnel to spend more time with consumers (Poon, 1993), which will attend to travelers' desires for friendly and personalized service. Other improvements consist of companies offering price discounts and bonus frequent flyer miles to consumers who purchase online (Law & Leung, 2000), which will appease those seeking the cheapest rates. Customers will continue to appreciate these improved services and products, as well as recognize the convenience and potential savings of using the Internet (Wang, Head, & Archer, 2000).

STUDY LIMITATIONS

Care must be taken in explaining the results of this study as there were several limitations. First, this study included mostly respondents in the midwestern cities of the United States. Those individuals were more likely to travel domestically. Therefore, the results here may not be representative of the selection criteria of travelers in other parts of the country or of international travelers. Second, due to the relatively small sample size, respondents' characteristics may not represent those of the population, hence limiting the general applicability of the study findings. Nevertheless, results of this study provided some insights on the characteristics of travelers who purchased travel arrangements through different means.

REFERENCES

ACNielsen. (2001). Travel search and booking behavior survey. Retrieved October 15, 2001, from http://www.acnielsen.co.nz/news.asp?newsID=124

Barnes, J. G., & Cumby, J. A. (2002). Establishing customer relationships on the Internet requires more than technology. *Australasian Marketing Journal, 10*(1), 36-46.

Berry, J. (1999, May 17). Why web sites fall short–according to CSC study, top management and IT are out of synch. *InternetWeek, 765*, 27-28.

Bhatnagar, A., & Ghose, S. (In press). A latent class segmentation analysis of e-shoppers. *Journal of Business Research.*

Bitner, M. J. (2001). Self-service technologies: What do customers expect? *Marketing Management, 10*(1), 10-11.

Bonn, M. A., Furr, H. L., & Susskind, A. M. (1999). Predicting a behavioral profile for pleasure travelers based on the basis of Internet use segmentation. *Journal of Travel Research, 37*(4), 333-340.

Buhalis, D. (2000). Trends in information technology and tourism. In W. C. Gartner & D. W. Lime (Eds.), *Trends in outdoor recreation, leisure, and tourism* (pp. 47-61). New York: CABI Publishing.

Buhalis, D., & Licata, M. C. (2002). The future of eTourism intermediaries. *Tourism Management, 23*(3), 207-220.

Chu, R. (2001). What online Hong Kong travelers look for on airline/travel websites? *International Journal of Hospitality Management, 20*(1), 95-100.

Gantz, J., Glasheen, C., & Emberley, D. (2001). The global market forecast for Internet usage and commerce: Based on Internet commerce market model [Version 7.1]. Framingham, MA: International Data Corporation.

Hair, J. F., Anderson, R. E., Tathan, R. L., & Black, W. C. (1998). Multivariate data analysis 5th ed. Upper Saddle River, NJ: Prentice Hall.

Hanson, W. (2000). *Principles of Internet marketing.* Cincinnati, OH: South Western College Publishing.

Heung, V. C. S. (2003). Barriers to implementing e-commerce in the travel industry: A practical perspective. *International Journal of Hospitality Management, 22*(1), 111-118.

Heung, V. C. S., & Chu, R. (2000). Important factors affecting Hong Kong consumers' choice of a travel agency for all-inclusive package tours. *Journal of Travel Research, 39*(1), 52-59.

Johnson, D. E. (1998). *Applied multivariate methods for data analysis.* Pacific Grove, CA: Brooks/Cole Publishing Company.

Kendall, K. W., & Booms, B. H. (1989). Consumer perceptions of travel agencies: Communications, images, needs and expectations. *Journal of Travel Research, 27*(4), 29-37.

Lang, T. C. (2000). The effect of the Internet on travel consumer purchasing behaviour and implications for travel agencies. *Journal of Vacation Marketing, 6*(4), 368-385.

Law, R., & Leung, R. (2000). A study of airlines' online reservation services on the Internet. *Journal of Travel Research, 39*(2), 202-211.

LeBlanc, G. (1992). Factors affecting customer evaluation of service quality in travel agencies: An investigation of customer perceptions. *Journal of Travel Research, 30*(3), 10-16.

Lowengart, O., & Reichel, A. (1998). Defining opportunities and threats in a changing information technology environment: The case of the travel agent. *Journal of Hospitality & Leisure Marketing, 5*(4), 57-71.

Matilla, A. S., & Mount, D. J. (2003). The impact of selected customer characteristics and response time on E-complaint satisfaction and return intent. *International Journal of Hospitality Management, 22*(2), 135-145.

Mertler, C. A., & Vannatta, R. A. (2002). *Advanced and multivariate statistical methods, 2nd ed.* Los Angeles, CA: Pyrczak Publishing.

Murphy, J., & Tan, I. (2003). Journey to nowhere? E-mail customer service by travel agents in Singapore. *Tourism Management, 24*(5), 543-550.

Parasuraman, A., & Grewal, D. (2000). The impact of technology on the quality-value-loyalty chain: A research agenda. *Journal of the Academy of Marketing Sciences, 28*(1), 168-174.

Persia, M. A., & Gitelson, R. J. (1993). The differences among travel agency users in the importance ratings of agency service features. *Journal of Travel & Tourism Marketing, 1*(4), 77-97.

Picolli, G., Spalding, B. R., & Ives, B. (2001). The customer-service life cycle: A framework for improving customer service through information technology. *Cornell Hotel and Restaurant Administration Quarterly, 42*(3), 38-45.

Poon, A. (1993). *Tourism, technology and competitive strategies.* Wallingford: CAB International.

Raymond, L. (2001). Determinants of Web site implementation in small businesses. *Internet Research, 11*(5), 411-422.

Ries, A., & Ries, L. (2001). *The 11 Immutable laws of Internet branding.* New York: HarperCollins.

Ryan, C., & Cliff, A. (1997). Do travel agencies measure up to customer expectation? An empirical investigation of travel agencies' service quality as measured by SERVQUAL. *Journal of Travel & Tourism Marketing, 6*(2), 1-31.

Standing, C., & Vasudavan, T. (2000). The impact of Internet on travel industry in Australia. *Tourism Recreation Research, 25*(3), 45-54.

Stoltz, C. (2000, May 14). Internet travel: Shakeout time; A vast majority of travel web sites are in the process of failing. *The Washington Post.* Retrieved June 10, 2003, from Proquest databases: http://proquest.umi.com/pqdweb?RQT=306&TS=1056054762

Travel Industry Association of America [TIA]. (2002). Online travel booking jumps in 2002, despite plateau in online travel planning. Retrieved December 17, 2002, from www.tia.org/Press/pressrec.asp

Travelocity®. (n.d.). Guides and Advice. Retrieved June 19, 2003 from http://leisure.travelocity.com/DestGuides/geo_frontdoor/0,,BF00013038787230661159,00.html

Visa Europe. (2003, May 20). Online spending in Europe doubles. *Press & Media*. Retrieved June 9, 2003, from: http://www.visaeu.com/press_release/press154.html

Walle, A. H. (1996). Tourism and the Internet: Opportunities for direct marketing. *Journal of Travel Research, 35*(1), 72-77.

Wang, F., Head, M., & Archer, N. (2000). A relationship-building model for the Web retail marketplace. *Internet Research, 10*(5), 374-384.

Weber, K., & Roehl, W. S. (1999). Profiling people searching for and purchasing travel products on the World Wide Web. *Journal of Travel Research, 37*(3), 291-298.

Wong, K. F., & Kwan, C. (2001). An analysis of the competitive strategies of hotels and travel agents in Hong Kong and Singapore. *International Journal of Contemporary Hospitality Management, 13*(6), 293-303.

World Tourism Organization Business Council. (2001). *E-business for tourism–Practical guidelines for destinations and businesses.* Madrid, Spain: Author.

Utilitarian Value in the Internet: Differences Between Broadband and Narrowband Users

Srikanth Beldona
Sheryl F. Kline
Alastair M. Morrison

SUMMARY. As homes across the world adopt broadband connectivity, there is a need to understand how it may impact consumer propensity to buy travel products on the Internet. The objective of this study is to evaluate differences in perceptions of utilitarian and social value on the Internet between broadband and narrowband users. The study also explores the relationship of utilitarian and social value on the Internet within the context of online travel purchase behavior. MANOVA results indicate differences between broadband and narrowband users when it comes to self-improvement and functional dimensions of utilitarian value. Practical and theoretical implications are also discussed. *[Article copies available for a fee from The Haworth Document Delivery Service: 1-800-HAWORTH. E-mail address: <docdelivery@haworthpress.com> Website: <http://www.HaworthPress. com> © 2004 by The Haworth Press, Inc. All rights reserved.]*

KEYWORDS. Perceived Internet value, online consumer behavior, technology adoption, broadband

INTRODUCTION

Broadband is considered to be a wide or high bandwidth medium that offers fast transmission speeds for high-volume data applications typically on the Internet. Home broadband penetration in the United States now stands at 26%, with another 29% planning to get broadband in the next two years (Kolko, Mcquivey, Gordon & Strohm, 2003). Broadband connectivity allows for the use of richer applications and an enhanced Internet experience compared to narrowband connectivity that works using a dial-up modem with limited bandwidth. A typical broadband customer has been categorized as progressive, success oriented, and ahead in the technology adoption curve (Jackson, Montigni, & Pearce, 2001). Significantly, research has indicated that broadband users show a greater likelihood of buying online (33%) com-

Srikanth Beldona is Assistant Professor, Department of Nutrition and Hospitality Management, College of Human Ecology, East Carolina University. Sheryl F. Kline is Assistant Professor, Department of Hospitality & Tourism Management, School of Consumer and Family Sciences, Purdue University. Alastair M. Morrison is Associate Dean, School of Consumer and Family Sciences, Purdue University.

Address correspondence to: Srikanth Beldona (E-mail: beldonas@mail.ecu.edu).

[Haworth co-indexing entry note]: "Utilitarian Value in the Internet: Differences Between Broadband and Narrowband Users." Beldona, Srikanth, Sheryl F. Kline, and Alastair M. Morrison. Co-published simultaneously in *Journal of Travel & Tourism Marketing* (The Haworth Hospitality Press, an imprint of The Haworth Press, Inc.) Vol. 17, No. 2/3, 2004. pp. 63-77; and: *Handbook of Consumer Behavior, Tourism, and the Internet* (ed: Juline E. Mills, and Rob Law) The Haworth Hospitality Press, an imprint of The Haworth Press, Inc., 2004. pp. 63-77. Single or multiple copies of this article are available for a fee from The Haworth Document Delivery Service [1-800-HAWORTH, 9:00 a.m. - 5:00 p.m. (EST). E-mail address: docdelivery@haworthpress.com].

pared to narrowband users (Yonish, Delhagen & Gordon, 2002). Broadband appeal has cata- pulted the Internet to a medium on par with television and radio, when it comes to time spent by consumers. In a typical broadband home, time spent on the Internet is equal to that of television and closely followed by ra- dio (Bouvard & Kurtzmann, 2002). This growth of broadband as a medium on par with television and radio is highlighting a paradigm shift in media consumption behavior. Other Internet consumption patterns also serve as key facts for input for future strategies. Com- pared to narrowband users (dial-up modem connection), broadband users are nearly four times as likely to download videos, 3.6 times likely to watch streaming videocasts and 3.07 times likely to listen to audiocasts (Kolko et al., 2003).

At a very broad level, participation in the Internet has been distilled into two distinct perspectives namely: utilitarian and social (Chung & Henderson, 2001). In the utilitarian perspective, the Internet is primarily viewed as an efficient marketplace as well as a conve- nient source of information. From the social perspective, the Internet is seen primarily as a conduit of communication that facilitates social interaction. These two perspectives have be- come increasingly important given the chang- ing landscape of Internet connectivity in American homes from narrowband to broad- band. However, except for findings mentioned in the trade press, there is no evidence of any literature that probes deeper or explains the nuances of these behavioral perspectives amongst broadband users. Value in the Internet can be derived from the varying reasons it is used for, an aspect reflective of its multifac- eted nature. Apart from being used as an infor- mation repository and a communication tool, it is used as a marketplace and is also consid- ered a social system (Maignan & Lukas, 1997). Each of these dimensions of Internet usage can induce value perceptions that can serve as antecedents of purchase behavior (Beldona, Morrison & Ismail, 2003). Argu- ably broadband users may perceive greater value in the Internet over narrowband users. Greater value in the medium indicates greater ease of use, which in turn explains the rela-

tively greater propensities to buy amongst broadband users.

The purpose of this paper therefore is to evaluate differences in perceived value in the Internet between broadband and narrowband users. Specifically, it derives utilitarian di- mensions of perceived Internet value to ex- plain differences between broadband and narrowband users. This is done based on a synthesis of literature spread across consumer behavior, social psychology and e-commerce. Identifying differences between these two groups (broadband and narrowband users) can help in developing a greater understanding of the drivers of online travel purchase behavior. This is all the more timely, because broadband is gradually altering media consumption be- havior amongst consumers. From a theoretical standpoint, the study bridges a gap by bringing perceived value into the Internet research do- main to explain behavioral differences be- tween two groups at varying points in the tech- nology adoption cycle.

Growth in broadband usage has significant implications for the travel industry particu- larly with the steady growth of complex travel products such as cruises, vacations, and desti- nations (NYU/PhocusWright Report, 2003). Complex travel products are highly intangible, and demand higher involvement in search be- cause of the depth and breadth of information they have to provide when compared with the relatively straight-forward booking of flights, hotels, and car rentals (Goossens, 1994; Vogt & Fesenmaier, 1998). Customers build expecta- tions of their prospective travel experience based on available information (Moutinho, 1987; Fodness & Murray, 1997; Vogt & Fesenmaier, 1998). In the traditional context, travel marketers used brochures and videos to enable customers to gain perceptions of what they may expect from their future travel expe- rience. However, the travel product is highly intangible, and customers make many deci- sions under conditions of uncertainty (Goos- sens, 1994; Vogt & Fesenmaier, 1998). It is here that travel marketers can enhance the quality of information provided through the use of broadband applications. Currently, the Internet is one of the most favorable informa- tion sources for travel, second only to "refer- ence information" (Kolko et al., 2003). Web based multimedia applications such as flash, streaming video, virtual tours may go a long way to improve the information context of the travel decision making process. Practically speaking, the findings of this study may help online travel marketers to proactively align strategies in concordance with the changing landscape of media consumption habits.

REVIEW OF LITERATURE

Broadband and Narrowband

A narrowband connection is accessed using a dial-up modem that is itself connected to the traditional copper wired telephone lines. Much of the growth of the Internet in the early to mid-'90s took place on this underlying infrastructure of telephone lines, a factor that helped in the rapid penetration of the Internet. Typically, narrowband connections transport data at speeds of 56 kilobytes per second or less (Paul, 2003). With Internet growth, the demand for richer forms of data such as video, audio, and rich images paved the way for technologies that enabled faster channels of access. Thereon, the Telecommunications Act of 1996 was introduced in the US, which provided a framework to encourage both competition and the development of advanced telecommunications services such as broadband. The Act enabled open access to telecommunications networks for consumers and service providers to leverage and enable the advent of futuristic services.

A direct and immediate result of this act was the introduction of digital subscriber line technology (DSL) by telecommunication carriers. DSL is a modem technology that uses existing twisted-pair telephone lines to transport high-bandwidth data, such as multimedia and video (Online Cisco Manual, 2003). The advantage of DSL is its ability to still leverage the existing telephone infrastructure, while simultaneously providing higher speed Internet access compared to narrowband connections (Paul, 2003). Since traditional copper wires are capable of handling much greater bandwidth (range of frequencies) DSL exploits this "extra capacity" to carry information on the wire by matching particular frequencies to

specific tasks (Franklin, 2003). There are several types and variations of DSL, although Asymmetric Digital Subscriber Line (ADSL) is the most prominent and widely used (Paul, 2003; Franklin, 2003). This is largely because typical home users tend to receive or download much more information than they actually send. ADSL suits this usage profile (Paul, 2003). ADSL divides up the available frequencies in a telephone line in a manner where the connection speed from the Internet to the user is three to four times faster than the connection from the user back to the Internet (Franklin, 2003).

Cable has also been the other alternative medium for accessing high speed Internet. This is done by leveraging existing TV cable lines provided by cable companies. Customers can use a cable modem to regulate the Internet connection at their end. Cable modem connections are comparable with DSL in terms of data transmission speeds. The actual cable wire is called a co-axial cable, where signals from the various channels are each given a 6-Megahertz slice of the cable's available bandwidth (Franklin, 2003). One co-axial cable can carry hundreds of megahertz of signals. Like any Cable TV channel, the Internet is also provided on this cable through a 6 Megahertz channel, although upstream Internet (for uploads) has a 2MHz slice. Cable companies were also pioneers in providing interactive services largely because of their first mover advantage (Paul, 2003). In the US, cable outperforms DSL with nearly twice as many subscribers.

There are other technologies that also fall under the heading of broadband namely T1 and T3. A T1 line is typically delivered by phone companies, has a fiber optic line (although copper wires are also used) and has data transmission speeds of 1.5 Megabits per second that is faster than DSL or cable (Brian, 2003; Campus-Wide Information Systems, 2001). As for T3, it is a high-speed connection capable of transmitting data at rates of up to 45 Mbps, and is comprised of 28 T1 lines (Brian, 2003). According to Paul (2003), electric companies are vying to provide broadband access using existing electrical wires, a fact that may further enhance broadband penetration in the US.

Broad and Narrowband Technologies and Online Travel Purchasing

There have been numerous studies that evaluate the predictors of online purchasing as a whole (Bellman, Lohse, & Johnson, 1999; Swaminathan, Lepkowska-White & Rao, 1999). Specific to online travel purchasing, a few studies have evaluated the predictors of purchase using behavioral and demographic variables (e.g., Beldona, Morrison, & Ismail, 2003; Morrison, Su, O'Leary & Cai, 2001; Weber & Roehl, 1999; Bonn, Furr & Susskind, 1998). However, there is no evidence of any study that explains the consumer's individual attachment to the underlying technology and evaluates this relationship within the context of online travel purchasing behavior.

Trade press research has highlighted broadband users to have a success-oriented outlook. They have demonstrated greater propensities to buy as well as adopt innovative technologies or business models that have emerged on the Web (Yonish et al., 2002). Broadband services enable richer functionality of applications for communication. For example, operating Webcams or using virtual tours are far more effective with broadband connectivity because of faster data speeds that result in richer quality of images. Interestingly, the use of these technologies in travel Websites has not increased the likelihood of purchase at travel or destination Websites (Forrester Report, 2002). Multimedia capabilities of the Internet can have a significant impact on the marketing of travel products (Cho, Wong & Fesenmaier, 2002). For example, operating Webcams or using virtual tours are far more effective with broadband connectivity because of faster data speeds that result in richer quality of images.

Economics of information theory (Nelson, 1970; Darby & Karni, 1973) categorized products into search, experience and credence types based on how consumers evaluate them. Products with search qualities can be fully evaluated prior to purchase, whereas experience based products must be first purchased and consumed before the consumer is able to evaluate. Darby and Karni (1973) extended this to include credence goods, which consumers can never fully evaluate even after pur-

chase and consumption. Zeithaml (1981) integrated this categorization to marketing, and posited that services exhibit more experience and credence qualities due to their unique characteristics of intangibility, non-standardization and inseparability. Bringing the realm of travel products within this search-experience-credence framework categorization provides cues on the nature of search and purchase on the online medium–especially, given that the Internet is an interactive tool that works in a computer mediated environment, and is able to provide greater detail on features of products sold using comparison charts in text form, virtual tours, video and still image formats. Klein (1998) contends that the Internet's rich interactivity and content can push experience based products into the searchable domain. For example, flights, accommodations and car rentals are standardized services that can be placed within the easier to evaluate context as there are more known parameters of tangibility (Zeithaml, 1981; Mittal, 1999). In contrast, complex travel products such as cruises, land based vacations, tours, activities and attractions can be arguably placed in the difficult to evaluate context.

It is with complex travel products that broadband technologies can play a significant role in improving searchable qualities. Environmental simulations such as sketches, photographs, and video are imperative towards communicating the image of a destination (Cho, Wang & Fesenmaier, 2002). For example, streaming video can give detail on tours and activities at destinations, as to where and when they start. Webcams can also provide real time glimpses of the destination, thereby increasing excitement value and providing a "feel" of the destination. Tools such as these can greatly enhance the reliability and effectiveness of marketing communication.

Incidentally, the use of rich video and related broadband application also tend to improve the experiential elements of travel information search, which in turn can impact the sensory and aesthetic needs (Vogt & Fesenmaier, 1998). Many resort hotels already provide virtual tours of facilities and accommodations. The real estate industry has used applications suited for broadband for a long time. Cho et al. (2002) expand on virtual tours in the travel context using the concept of virtual experiences. Virtual experiences provide both direct and indirect experiences to enable travelers to better anticipate the nuances of the prospective experience (Daugherty, Li & Biocca, 2001). Direct experience comprises aspects such as trial or inspection whereas the use of brochures or advertising implies indirect experiences (Hoch & Deighton, 1989).

Holbrook and Hirschmann (1982) proposed the experiential view of consumer choice that accommodates for the experience of the search itself. The experiential view includes consumer fantasies, imagination, affect and subjective reactions to consumption experiences that have an important influence on their behavior. Holbrook and Hirschman (1982), posited that leisure activities, aesthetic goods, and their like entail a different decision-making process from that suggested by the information-processing paradigm. Schmitt (1999) confirmed this perception of the experiential view of consumer decision making as key to representation of consumer choice than the more traditional models for all types of products.

Extending Hirschmann and Holbrook's (1982) experiential view into travel literature, Vogt and Fesenmaier (1998) stretched the functional travel information search framework to include four other dimensions, namely sign, hedonic, innovation and aesthetic needs. While the sign dimension symbolized the search for expression and social interaction, the hedonic aspect reflected the experiential contexts of emotion, sensory needs and phenomenology. They also found that consumers may seek innovation from travel information search as well as try and satisfy aesthetic needs as well. The five dimensions of search including the functional component were structured around travel information sources that were categorized as social, personal, marketing and editorial.

The Internet Medium and Technology Adoption

The Internet as a marketplace has been extensively researched illustrating the efficacy of the Internet as a medium for market exchange activities (Bakos, 1998). However, the Internet is also a vast information resource that serves as a key tool for improving the overall perceived productivity of individuals using it. From finding information pertaining to a particular health condition, to seeking key facts that help solve a problem with one's automobile, the Internet is increasingly becoming a valuable resource. In many ways, these issues highlight a greater perception of usefulness or value in the Internet as a tool in important activities. Greater reliability in the medium results in improved overall acceptability for commerce or exchange. In a very holistic sense, these developments have an impact on travel purchasing behavior because they indicate a shift in user beliefs towards an evolving medium. One may contend that such developments enhance the "Do it yourself" attitude amongst consumers when it comes to buying travel online. However, technology adoption in this context is better viewed through the framework provided by the Technology Adoption Model (TAM) (Davis, 1989), that is considered to be most widely used model of IT adoption.

According to TAM, IT adoption is influenced by two primary constructs, namely perceived usefulness and perceived ease-of-use, which determine an individual's behavioral intention to use the technology (Davis, Bagozzi & Warshaw, 1989). While perceived usefulness is more extrinsic in nature and is task-oriented, perceived ease of use is more intrinsic that relates to ease of learning, flexibility, and clarity of its interface (Gefen & Straub, 2000). However, applying TAM to e-commerce adoption requires the incorporation of barriers of perceived risk, due to the inherent characteristics of online transactional systems (Gefen & Straub, 2000; Pavlou, 2003; Pavlou, 2002). This is because e-commerce stretches beyond the domain of traditional information systems and any application of TAM must be integrated with the theory of marketing exchange (Sheth & Parvatiyar, 1995; Dwyer, Schurr & Oh, 1987). Lee, Park and Ahn (2000) expanded on the Technology Acceptance Model (TAM) and introduced an e-Com adoption model that included perceived risk with products/services, and perceived risk in the context of online transaction in addition to the existing perceived usefulness and perceived ease of use constructs. Salisbury, Pearson and Harrison (1998) found that the perceived usefulness of the Internet was a significant predictor of search, but not purchase. Perceived behavioral control and trust have also been acknowledged as key constructs in e-commerce adoption (Pavlou, 2002). Perceived behavioral control reflects beliefs pertinent to resources and opportunities required to facilitate behaviors that users may have (Ajzen, 1991). Trust on the other hand has been a key construct in the theory of marketing exchange (Hoffmann, Novak & Peralta, 1999).

From a strictly marketing perspective, the technology adoption cycle has been used to categorize users based on beliefs and attitudes (Parasuraman and Colby, 2003). The technology adoption cycle states that when a technology is introduced in the market, its adoption stages are characterized by five stages, namely Explorers, Pioneers, Skeptics, Paranoids, and Laggards (Parasuraman and Colby, 2001). Each segment varies based on a combination of optimism, innovativeness, discomfort, and insecurity in attitudes towards the technology. For example, low-end laggards are low in optimism and innovativeness, and high in discomfort and insecurity. Each segment develops over time to become a viable customer group. The process is not exactly sequential, although the categorization provides a strong set of guidelines for customer segmentation. Marketing strategies should be built upon an understanding of this adoption classification, by tailoring services to match the specific behavioral attributes and needs of each segment (Parasuraman and Colby, 2001).

The typical broadband customer has been categorized as an early adopter of technology. Studies have found significant association between demographics and attitudinal factors in the adoption of new technologies (Shimp and Beardon, 1982; Rogers, 1995; Dabholkar, 1996). Formative studies on Internet usage profiles suggest the importance of demographic factors such as education, race, and occupation are significant predictors of increased Web usage (Pitkow and Kehoe, 1996). These earlier studies found that Internet users were typically male and had higher incomes (Pitkow and Kehoe, 1996; Bonn, Furr and Susskind, 1998). This group can be typified as "explorers"

based upon Parasuraman and Colby's (2001) customer segmentation of technology adoption. Subsequently, Bonn et al. (1998) found significant differences in age, education, and the level of Internet use between pleasure travelers who would seek travel information online and those who do not.

Shopping experiences have been explained along two dimensions–utilitarian and hedonic (Babin, Darden & Griffin, 1994). This has been the case with the physical marketplace as well as the virtual marketspace that encapsulates the Internet as a shopping medium. When viewed from a consumption perspective, the Internet is akin to a shopping mall in a physical context, wherein there are features that eventually serve as catalysts to the purchase process. While a shopping mall may have parking, accessibility and good layout, that all build a shopping friendly environment, the Internet has a broader array of features that may largely depend on the users' perceptions of how it is used. Users' representations of the Internet as a source of information, communication tool, object/place of consumption, or social system (Maignan & Lukas, 1997) should be taken into account to understand their overall propensity to browse, buy or entertain themselves. This is based on the theory of reasoned action (Fishbein & Ajzen, 1975) which suggests that attitudes can be used to predict behavioral intentions and behaviors.

Research on the Internet as an object of consumption or a marketplace is prevalent in both information systems (IS) and marketing literature. O'Cass (2001) examined issues related to Internet involvement, subjective knowledge, thinking-feeling and personal and materialistic values related to the Internet as an object to be consumed. However, this scale of perceived usefulness of the Internet was uni-dimensional and did not effectively capture the multifaceted nature of the Internet as a medium. Chung and Henderson (2001) viewed the Internet medium from a participation perspective, and identified utilitarian and social dimensions. They found that utilitarian and the social participation perspectives played important roles in acceptance and use of the Internet. Bourdeau, Chebat and Couturier (2002) took it a step further and found five dimensions of the Internet usage, namely utilitarian, social, hedonic, learning and purchasing. However, they evaluated these dimensions across Web and email users only, and did not evaluate propensity to purchase.

The Internet as a medium for social interaction has also been studied extensively. Some have also termed the Internet as a "social technology" because of its ability to help connect with family and friends, as well as make new social connections (Kraut et al., 1998). Because of the continuous connectivity that is global in reach, there is potential to interact with multiple numbers of persons in differing geographical locations in real time. Technologies such as chat rooms and bulletin boards enable the development of new relationships and consequently expand one's social circle (Yamauchi and Coget, 2002).

RESEARCH METHODS

Data

Data used for the study were obtained from the March 2000 survey conducted by the Pew Internet Research Center. Of the 1,501 respondents only 862 reported themselves as Internet users. From this 862 set of Internet users, 715 cases qualified within the context of having either broadband or narrowband connections at home. The respondents for this study were 18 years of age or older, and the sample was randomly drawn from telephone exchanges across the continental United States. Random sampling was done by generating the last two digits of telephone numbers selected on the basis of their area code, telephone exchange, and bank number digit. This sample had representation of both listed and unlisted numbers (including not-yet-listed numbers). The survey was administered by telephone, and included both offline and online users. The dataset also included a weight variable which was derived from a demographic weighting procedure using parameters from the Current Population Survey, and balances for race and gender.

Methodology and Analysis

Of the total of 715 cases in the original dataset, 634 were categorized as narrowband

users and the remaining 81 as broadband users. This was based on a question posed to respondents that sought the type of Internet connection (dial up modem, T1, DSL, and Cable). With the exception of the dial-up modem connection type (narrowband), connections categorized as broadband were in compliance with the technological underpinning of a broadband connection (Paul, 2003). Before any analysis was performed, the 634 cases of narrowband users in the original dataset was reduced to 83 using a random selection of cases as provided by SPSS 11.0. SPSS 11.0 allows for random extraction of a percentage of cases from a dataset, and this procedure was used here. Final group sizes were 83 cases for narrowband and 81 cases representing broadband users.

The purpose of the above exercise was to achieve a fair level of parity in the number of cases between the two groups. This was required since the objective of the study is to evaluate differences between the two groups. Also, MANOVA (Multivariate Analysis of Variance) analysis, done further in the study, requires as key assumption equal cell sizes (Garson, 2001). MANOVA tends to be more robust when cell sizes are equal or close to equal. In addition cell size parity reduces the likelihood of violating the unequal variance assumption (Garson, 2001). Henceforth, mention of the phrase "two groups" means broadband and narrowband users, unless stated otherwise.

Statistical analysis for the study was undertaken in three stages. The first stage involved preliminary chi-square analysis to evaluate the differences of online travel purchase propensities between the two groups. This stage also involved descriptive statistics that explained for any differences between the two groups across a range of demographic variables. The second stage of the study involved the analysis of perceived Internet value dimensions using a principal components analysis (PCA). PCA was administered on the pooled number of cases (164) that included the 81 broadband and the 83 narrowband users. Items were drawn from questions that sought responses on how the Internet had improved respondents' lives in ten areas. For example, one question was, "How much, if at all, has the

Internet improved your ability to shop?" Principal components analysis is a data reduction technique that is based on the evaluation of the total variability that an item (variable) has to offer (Garson, 2003). PCA was chosen because the objective was to reduce the number of items into a smaller set of components. This is important as the study is exploratory in nature and uses items from a secondary dataset. Therefore, principal factor analysis (PFA) was not considered as it is more appropriate for latent variable identification and subsequent scale development (Bryant & Yarnold, 1998).

The third stage of the study involved the examination of differences in perceived Internet value between broadband and narrowband users. MANOVA was used to compare groups formed by categorical independent variables on group differences in a set of interval dependent variables (Garson, 2001). The dimensions identified from the PCA process served as the dependent variables, while the "type of Internet connection" (broadband and narrowband) was the independent variable. MANOVA was used as the items across each dimension captured different concepts, even though they were significantly correlated with each of the items across their respective dimensions. MANOVA also keeps Type I error rate down when dealing with multiple dependent variables that are somewhat correlated (Weinfurt, 1998). Lastly, separate MANOVA analyses were employed to evaluate differences across the three dimensions derived from principal components analysis between broadband and narrowband users.

RESULTS AND DISCUSSION

Results

Descriptive statistics for key demographic variables across both broadband and narrowband users are illustrated in Table 1. The sample profile indicates that narrowband users are only marginally older (mean = 43.62) compared to broadband users (mean = 41.17), although no significant differences were apparent. There were no differences in gender composition between the two groups. A larger number of broadband users had family incomes

TABLE 1. Descriptive Statistics

Variables	Broad-band	Narrow-band	F or χ^2
Age			
	41.17 (12.50)	43.62 (13.36)	F: 1.447
Gender			
Male	45.7%	53%	χ^2: 0.217
Female	54.3%	47%	
Income			
< $50,000	18.5%	45.8%	χ^2: 13.93***
> $50,000	81.5%	54.2%	
Education			
High School Incomplete	4.9%	0%	χ^2: 8.25
High School Grad	13.6%	22.9%	
Business, Tech, Vocational After School	4.9%	3.6%	
Some college/No 4 Yr Degree	19.8%	25.3%	
Bachelors' 4 Yr Degree	30.9%	30.1%	
Post Graduate	25.9%	18.1%	
First Went Online			
< 3 Yrs	43.2%	61.0%	χ^2: 5.15*
> 3 Yrs	56.8%	39.0%	
Online Travel Search			
Have Not Searched For Travel Information	19.8%	26.5%	χ^2: 1.05
Searched For Travel Information	80.2%	73.5%	
Online Travel Purchase			
Have Not Bought Travel	34.6%	56.6%	χ^2: 8.03**
Bought Travel	65.4%	43.4%	

*$p < 0.05$, **$p < 0.01$, ***$p < 0.001$.

over $50,000 as compared with narrowband users. This significant difference is glaring because a larger number of narrowband users belonged to the under $50,000 bracket when compared with the alternative in their own group. Education levels appear to be similarly spread out between both groups with greater numbers having attended some college or attained 4-year degrees and above. When it comes to when they first went online, broadband users show greater experience levels having been online for 3 years or more compared to narrowband users. In the narrowband group, the "less than 3 years" group is overwhelmingly greater than the "more than 3 years" group amongst narrowband users.

Chi-square tests of significance were administered to evaluate for differences between the broadband and narrowband users. Based on the cross tabulation matrix, conditional odds were computed to present the odds of buying travel of both broadband and narrowband users. Conditional odds are the odds of being in one category of a variable within another specific category of another variable (Rodgers, 1998). In our case here, the two variables are buying travel and the type of Internet connection, both of which have two categories each. Chi-square results indicate significant differences between broadband and narrowband users. Conditional odds that a broadband user picked at random will buy travel online is 1.89 compared to just 0.76 amongst narrowband users.

Principal components analysis indicated three dimensions that explained 59.15% of the total variance. A varimax rotation was administered and three value dimensions emerged namely: utilitarian (self-improvement), utilitarian (functional), and social. The components and respective factor loadings of each item are mentioned in Table 2. Items that had loadings below 0.50, or loaded on both components were discarded from the final solution (Hair et al., 1987). One item namely "ability to learn new things" loaded on two dimensions and was discarded. Before pursuing any other analyses, Cronbach's alpha was applied to test the reliability of the factor groupings. It is important to retain only those scales that report alphas above 0.60 for further analysis (Hair, Anderson, Tatham and Black, 1998). Utilitarian (self-improvement), and utilitarian (functional) reported alphas of 0.67 and 0.63 respectively and were retained. Since the alpha of the "social value" scale was 0.59, it was dropped from further analysis, and factor analysis was re-administered on the remaining selected items. The Kaiser-Meyer-Olkin measure of sampling adequacy and the Bartlett's test of sphericity were evaluated to ascertain the viability of principal components analysis for the study. The Kaiser-Meyer-Olkin statistic was 0.77, wherein values between 0.7 and 0.8 are considered good (Hair et al., 1998; Hutcheson and Sofroniou, 1999, pp. 224-225). The Bartlett's test was also significant ($p < 0.001$), therefore indicating that factor analysis was appropriate.

From Table 2, the first factor grouping reflects the self-improvement aspect of utilitarian value. Items on this factor showed an almost extracurricular aspect of day-to-day life that is tied to self-improvement. In comparison, the second dimension had a functional and periodic aspect attached to each of the three items. The fact that the "ability to meet new people" item loaded on the first dimension, and not on the social dimension, can be

TABLE 2. Factors of Perceived Value in the Internet (N = 160)

Factors (Reliability Alpha)	Loading	Eigen Value	Variance Explained
Factor 1: Utilitarian (Self-Improvement) Value (0.67)		2.94	21.84%
ability to meet new people	0.75		
ability to find ways to deal with problems	0.74		
the way you get information about health care	0.70		
the way you pursue your hobbies or interests	0.50		
Factor 2: Utilitarian (Functional) Value (0.62)		1.22	13.77%
ability to do your job	0.81		
the way you manage your personal finances	0.69		
ability to shop	0.66		
Factor 3: Social Value (0.59)		1.16	17.54%
improve connections to your friends	**0.79**		
improve connections to members of your family	**0.84**		

Note 1: KMO Measure of Sampling Adequacy was 0.77 and Bartlett's Test of Sphericity had an approx. chi-square value of 2447/64 and was significant at P < 0.001.

Note 2: One item, namely "ability to learn new things," was removed as it had cross-loadings across two factors at values above 0.40.

Note 3: Social value was tested in MANOVA because the Cronbach Alpha reliability was below 0.60.

explained by the wording in the question. It can be argued that the word "ability" induces a more utilitarian context to the question. Another distinction is between the ability to find or create new relationships rather than to improve existing ones. While this scale was dropped from the analysis, there is some pertinent information in this context that can be used for future studies. Social value can also be viewed from a perspective of re-connecting with friends and family that may have become dormant. The relative wording of the "social value" questions that use the words "connection," "friends," etc., may have also contributed to the difference in the perception of questions when compared with those in the self-improvement dimension. Put simply, social value comprised the value perception in improving connections with family and friends.

In the third and final stage of analysis, MANOVA was administered to evaluate differences in perceived Internet value between broadband and narrowband users (see Table 3). This was done on two derived dimensions of utilitarian value, namely self-improvement and functional. Social value was analyzed because of its low reliability alpha (0.59). In the test of assumptions, the Box's M test statistic was found to be non-significant ruling out any

TABLE 3. Value Perceptions Across Broadband and Narrowband Users

	Items	Broad-band Mean	Narrow-band Mean
Utilitarian Value (Self-Improvement)	the way you pursue your hobbies or interests	2.72	2.18
	the way you get information about health care	2.27	2.02
	ability to find ways to deal with problems	1.77	1.73
	ability to meet new people	1.53	1.46
Utilitarian Value (Functional)	ability to do your job	2.42	2.30
	ability to shop	2.56	2.04
	the way you manage your personal finances	2.05	1.72

Note: Respondents were asked to indicate their level of agreement on how the Internet had improved their lives along the above parameters (1: not at all; 2: only a little; 3: some; 4: a lot).

TABLE 4. Multivariate and Univariate Effects

Source	Multivariate		Univariate
	df	F	F
Utilitarian (Self-Improvement) Value	159	2.68*	
the way you pursue your hobbies or interests			9.66**
ability to find ways to deal with problems			0.06
ability to meet new people			0.21
the way you get information about health care			1.75
Utilitarian (Functional) Value	163	3.65*	
ability to do your job			0.34
ability to shop			9.29**
the way you manage your personal finances			3.50

*$p < 0.05$, **$p < 0.01$, ***$p < 0.001$.

significant differences in the covariance matrices of cells in the factor design matrix. Also, the Levene test for both MANOVA models showed non-significant differences between all other cells within each model thereby ruling out any violation of the unequal variances assumption. To evaluate the significance of the models, Pillai's trace was the chosen statistic. Pillai's trace is more robust than the other significance tests namely Wilks' Lambda and Hotelling's trace (Olson, 1976).

MANOVA results indicate significant differences between broadband and narrowband users in how they perceive utilitarian (self-improvement) value in the Internet. See Table 4 for MANOVA results that indicate both multivariate and univariate findings. Multivariate results indicate that broadband users perceive greater self-improvement utilitarian value compared to narrowband users. Except for the perceived value in the ability to pursue hobbies, univariate results show non-significance of all other items in this dimension. In the case of functional utilitarian value, the significant multivariate F in the model indicates overall differences between broadband and narrowband users. Mean differences between the two groups indicate that broadband users perceive greater value in the ability to shop over narrowband users. No significant differences were observed in the Internet's role in improving the ability to do one's job, and in the management of personal finances.

Discussion

At the outset, there are key differences in demographic characteristics between narrowband and broadband users. Income was a key differentiator between the two groups, with broadband users reporting higher incomes. As expected, broadband users came online much earlier compared to narrowband users, which validates their early majority status as technology users. While there were no differences between the two groups in online travel search, differences between propensities to buy travel amongst broadband users was significantly higher compared to narrowband users.

Differences between the two groups across both dimensions of utilitarian value (self-improvement and functional utilitarian value) indicate a fundamental distinction in how utilitarian value is perceived as a whole with regard to the Internet. In self-improvement utilitarian value, broadband users perceive the Internet's ability to pursue hobbies and interests to be significantly higher compared to narrowband users. This can be attributed to specific personality traits typical of broadband users. Viewed holistically, one may contend that the self-improvement dimension is more about the features of the Internet such as information richness, interactivity, and reach. Notably, the grouping of these variables together indicates a more extrinsic context. The fact that only "ability to pursue hobbies" was significant over health, people, and problems suggests that a more personality-type trait is evident rather than just the "relatively younger demographic in broadband users" argument. After all, early adopters are generally considered to be more innovate and are credited to have visions of their own (Parasuraman & Colby, 2001). Specific interests and hobbies can be better pursued on the Internet because of the vast information resource that it contains. Non-significant differences between other remaining parameters in this factor may be explained by the lack of their strong association with the early majority of users. It could also mean that both groups (broadband and narrowband) perceive similar levels of value in the Internet when it comes to solving problems, finding healthcare information and meeting new people.

With regard to the *functional* utilitarian value dimension, broadband users perceive greater value compared to narrowband users as a whole. They perceive greater value in the Internet's role with regard to their ability to shop compared to narrowband users. One plausible reason could be that their relatively greater participation in auctions and in the purchase of products, broadband users can be perceived to be more avid and accepting of emerging business models and buying propositions. In the case of handling personal finances, past research has found broadband users to have greater propensities to bank online as opposed to narrowband users (Forrester Research, 2002). However, our findings indicate that there are no significant differences in the perception of Internet's role in improving their ability to manage personal finances.

Differences across both dimensions of utilitarian value indicate that the early majority of broadband users see the Internet as a tool to improve their efficiency in general. However, there are only two univariate differences that suggest the need to delve further into the relative significance of the findings. For instance, only the "ability to shop" was found to differ significantly between the two groups in the functional dimension. That the remaining two were found non-significant highlights an underlying driver to this difference. Perceived control comes into mind because shopping is about exchange and also has physical activity associated with it in the traditional marketplace. Improving your ability in this direction

indicates that broadband users are more control oriented compared to narrowband users. One may argue that the "ability to manage personal finances" should be been significant too given the control argument. After all, physically going to a bank is a well recognized chore like shopping. Our contention here is that if this was revisited with a larger sample, likelihood of differences would improve on this variable, something that prior research has already indicated (Kolodinsky, Hogarth & Shue, 2000).

LIMITATIONS AND IMPLICATIONS

The study has its share of limitations that can be overcome in future studies. Firstly, this use of secondary data limited coverage of a few issues relevant to perceived value in the Internet. The limited number of broadband users and the resultant trimming down of the sample size to ensure parity in groups resulted in a loss of information. Future research can further validate these findings using a larger sample. The utilitarian value scale was well served, although dropping the social value scale was unavoidable. More relevant questions on the social value scale can greatly improve the reliability of the scale, and investigated in future studies. Questions pertaining to hedonic value were completely absent. Nevertheless, there is ground for strong generalizability of the findings based on the vast coverage (Continental United States) of the dataset. The study also could not control for online experience within the model, which would have provided added explanatory power to the results. It nonetheless attempted to incorporate this variable into the study, although largely different cell sizes induced a violation of the homogeneity of variance assumption in MANOVA.

There are several practical and theoretical implications that arise from the findings of the study. Firstly, the study makes a fine distinction between broadband and narrowband users based on their attitudes towards the Internet. It sieves through peripheral findings, and delves deeper into user perceptions that explains much of their consumption behaviors. For travel marketers, these findings provide strong underpinnings for the development of marketing strategies. For example, destination marketers can induce more broadband applications to promote key facets of their destinations. After all, destination Websites are content rich, and are aimed at improving destination image and improving the expectations of the travel experience. Findings of this study point to the fact that users who make use of functionality from broadband applications are more captive from a marketing standpoint and demonstrate greater propensities to buy travel services/products.

Travel marketers can also segment the market based on the findings of the study. A range of marketing initiatives can be developed to target broadband users. To gain more precision in marketing activities, special packages or promotion offers can be targeted first at this group. Developing marketing strategies for different stages of technology adoption improves precision of marketing efforts (Parasuraman and Colby, 2001). Travel marketers can also establish key alliances with broadband service providers, which in turn can give greater access to more captive markets. Another key implication for travel marketers from these findings is the potential for Web-based advertising. Not just with the "where to place messages," but also the types of message formats for maximum effectiveness. Web locations that vend services specific to broadband users can be suggestive venues for placing marketing messages. For example, online travel marketers can use chat rooms, online banking and stock trading sites to place marketing messages. Also, key alliances can be struck with partners engaged in online financial services to reach relatively more captive markets.

The significance of functional utilitarian value and social value as predictors of online travel behavior provide insights into the online travel consumer. Given the wider acceptability of broadband, different types of message formats can be explored now. While the viability of such a move requires more detailed study, developments in Internet usage habits using multimedia applications certainly indicate potential in this direction. The key here is to acknowledge changing media consumption habits through proactive measures. After all, travel is an information intensive product well suited for an information rich environment such as the Internet. How the industry reads signals from early adopters (broadband users) and understands their evolving needs will determine how well it exploits the capabilities of medium.

Theoretically, the study paves the way for a better understanding of the online travel consumer in an evolving domain of interest. Perceived value in the Internet as a predictor of online travel behavior has not been studied earlier, and this itself is a strong theoretical contribution. As an attitudinal construct, its role as an antecedent of travel buying behavior specific to complex travel products such as vacations and cruises will be interesting. If perceived risk is accounted for to some extent, to what extent will perceived value in the Internet impact buying propensities of complex travel products? Does this have anything to do with perceived control since the findings do indicate in the direction of broadband users perceiving more control from the Internet? Perhaps it can be argued that broadband users will be more likely buyers of complex travel products, and that cruise companies and other leisure operators should target this group online more effectively.

Future research should delve into potential differences in travel search behaviors between broadband and narrowband users using perceived value in the Internet as a moderator. One way of doing this is to focus on a more exhaustive scale that captures other dimensions of perceived value in the Internet, particularly the hedonic dimension. This way, marketers can extract much from the initial information search stage of the decision making process. Self-improvement utilitarian value can be specifically investigated around issues more relevant to travel. For example, particular hobbies that are more tied to or related to travel may have a significant impact on travel purchase behavior. In fact, a complete and tailored scale of perceived value constructed around strong relationships with the travel product and its features will pave the way for a finer understanding of purchasing behavior on a more widely acceptable medium.

REFERENCES

Ajzen, I. (1991). The theory of planned behavior. *Organizational Behavior and Human Decision Processes*, 50: 179-211.

Babin, B.J., Darden, W.R., and Griffin, M. (1994). Work and/or fun: Measuring hedonic and utilitarian shopping value. *Journal of Consumer Research*, 20, 644-656.

Bakos, Y. (1998). The emerging role of electronic Marketplaces on the Internet. *Communications of the ACM*, 41 (8), 35-42.

Beldona, S., Morrison, A.M., and Ismail, J., (2003). The impact of Internet usage characteristics on online travel behavior. *Advances in Hospitality and Tourism Research*, 8, 22-28. Paper presented at the Eighth Annual Graduate Conference in Hospitality and Tourism, Las Vegas, Nevada, January 5-7, 2003.

Bellman, S., Lohse, G., and Johnson, E. J. (1999). Predictors of online buying behavior. *Communications of the ACM*, 42 (12), 32-38.

Bonn, M.A., Furr, H.L., and Susskind, A.M. (1999). Predicting a behavioral profile for pleasure travelers on the basis of Internet use segmentation. *Journal of Travel Research*, 37, 333-340.

Bourdeau, L., Chebat, J.C., and Coutourier, C. (2002). Internet consumer value of university students: E-mail vs. Web users. *Journal of Retailing and Consumer Service*, 9, 61-69.

Bouvard, P., and Kurtzmann, W. (2002). The broadband revolution: How superfast Internet access changes media habits in American households [Online]. *Arbitron/Coleman Report*. Available www.arbitron.com/downloads/broadband.pdf [December 20, 2002].

Bryant, F.B., and Yarnold, P.R. (1998). Principal components analysis and exploratory and confirmatory factor analysis. In L.G. Grimm and P.R. Yarnold (eds.), *Reading and Understanding Multivariate Statistics*, 245-276. Washington, DC: American Psychological Association.

Cho, Yong-Hyun, Wang, Y., and Fesenmaier, D. (2002). Searching for experiences: The Web-based virtual tour in tourism marketing. *Journal of Travel & Tourism Marketing*, 12 (4), 1-18.

Chung, W., and Henderson, J.C. (2001). Americans on the Internet: Utilitarian and social participation perspectives [Online]. *Sprouts: Working Papers on Information Environments, Systems and Organizations*, 1. Available http://weatherhead.cwru.edu/sprouts/papers.html [Dec 01, 2002].

Dabholkar, P.A. (1996). Consumer evaluations of new technology-based self service options: An investigation of alternative models of service quality. *International Journal of Research in Marketing*, 13 (1), 29-51.

Darby, M.R., and Karni, E. (1973). Free competition and the optimal amount of fraud. *Journal of Law and Economics*, 16, 67-88.

Daugherty, T., Li, H., and Biocca, F. (2001). Consumer learning and 3-D ecommerce: Sequential exposure to a virtual experience relative to indirect and direct product experience, presented at 1st Experiential E-Commerce Conference, East Lansing, MI. Available at: http://mindlab.org/networkedminds/exp3d/sessions.htm

Davis, F.D. (1989). Perceived usefulness, perceived ease of use, and user acceptance of information technology, *MIS Quarterly*, 13 (3), 1989, 319-339.

Davis, F.D., Bagozzi, R.P., and Warshaw, P.R. (1989). User acceptance of computer technology: A comparison of two theoretical models. *Management Science*, 35 (8), 982-1003.

Dwyer, R.F., Schurr, P.H., and Oh, S. (1987). Developing buyer-seller relationships. *Journal of Marketing*, 51 (April), 11-27.

Fishbein, M., and Ajzen, I. (1975). *Belief, Attitude, Intention and Behavior: An Introduction to Theory and Research*. Reading, MA: Addison-Wesley.

Fodness, D. and Murray, B. (1997). Tourist information search. *Annals of Tourism Research*, 24 (3): 503-523.

Forrester Report (2001). What Europe's broadband users want [Online]. Forrester Research. Available http://www.forrester.com/ER/Press/Release/0,1769,665,00.html [Aug 28, 2002].

Franklin, Curt (2003). Howstuffworks–How DSL works [Online]. Available http://computer.howstuffworks.com/dsl1.htm [Jul 20, 2003].

Garson, D.G. (2001). PA 765 Statnotes [Online]. *An Online Textbook*. Available http://www2.chass.ncsu.edu/garson/pa765/statnote.htm [May 25, 2002].

Gefen, D., and Straub, D.W. (2000). The relative importance of perceived ease of use in IS adoption: A study of e-commerce adoption, *Journal of the Association for Information Systems*, 1 (Article 8), Available http://www.jais.org [Jul 29, 2003].

Goossens, C.F. (1994). External information search: Effects of tour brochures with experiential information. *Journal of Travel & Tourism Marketing*, 3 (3), 89-107.

Hair Jr., J.F., Anderson, R.E., Tatham, R.L. and Black, W.C. (1998). *Multivariate Data Analysis*, Prentice-Hall, NJ.

Hair, J.F., Anderson, R.E., Tatham, R.L., and Black, W.C. (1987). *Multivariate data analysis with readings* (3rd ed.), MacMillan, New York (NY).

Hoch, S.J., and Deighton, J. (1989). Managing what consumers learn from experience. *Journal of Marketing*, 53 (April), 1-20.

Hoffman, D.L., Novak, T.P., and Peralta, M. (1999). Building consumer trust online. *Communications of the ACM*. 42: 80-85.

Holbrook, M.B., and Hirschman, E.C. (1982). The experiential aspects of consumption: Consumer fantasies, feelings, and fun. *Journal of Consumer Research*, 9 (September), 132-140.

Jackson, P., Montigni, E., and Pearce, F. (2001). Turning on broadband users. Forrester Research [Online].

Forrester Research. Available http://www.forrester.com/ER/Research/Report/Summary/0,1338,12349,00.html [Nov 12, 2001].

Klein, L. (1998). Evaluating the potential of interactive media through a new lens: Search versus experience goods. *Journal of Business Research*, 41, 195-203.

Kolko, J., McQuivey, J.L., Gordon, J., and Strohm, C.Q. (2003). Benchmark June 2003 Data Overview [Online]. Forrester Research. Available http://www.forrester.com [June 17, 2003].

Kolodinsky, J., Hogarth, J.M., and Shue, J.F. (2000). Bricks or clicks? Consumers' adoption of electronic banking technologies [Online]. *Consumer Interests Annual*, 46. Available http://www.consumerinterests.org [July 15, 2002].

Kraut, R., Lundmark, V., Patterson, M., Kiesler, S., Mukopadhyay, T., and Scherlis, W. (1998). Internet paradox: A social technology that reduces social involvement and psychological well-being? *American Psychologist*, 53 (9), 1017-1031.

Lee, D., Park, J., and Ahn, J. (2001). On the explanation of factors affecting e-commerce adoption. *Proceedings of the 22nd International Conference on Information Systems* (ICIS 2001), 109-120. New Orleans, Louisiana, December 16-19, 2001.

Maignan, I., and Lukas, B. (1997). The nature and social uses of the Internet: A qualitative investigation. *The Journal of Consumer Affairs*, 31 (2), 346-371.

Mittal, B. (1999). The advertising of services: Meeting the challenge of intangibility. *Journal of Services Research*, 2 (Aug.) 98-116.

Morrison, A., Su, J., O'Leary, J., and Cai, L. (2001). Predicting usage of the Internet for travel bookings: An exploratory study. *Information Technology and Tourism*, 4 (1), 15-30.

Moutinho, L. (1987). Consumer behavior in tourism. *European Journal of Marketing*, 21 (10), 5-44.

Nelson, Philip (1970). Information and consumer behavior, *Journal of Political Economy*, 78 (March/April), 311-329.

NYU/PhocusWright Report (2003). Building the online vacation package marketplace: Survey results [Online]. Working Paper: Preston Robert Tisch Center for Sports and Recreation Management. School of Continuing and Professional Studies, New York University, NY. NYU. PhocusWright. Available 212.133.71.16/pdf/280103phocwright.pdf [April 15 2003].

O'Cass, A. (2001). Exploring the consumer-Internet relationship: A consumer behavior perspective. *Proceedings of the Australia New Zealand Marketing Academy Conference* (ANZMAC 2001). Auckland, New Zealand. December 3-5.

Olson, C. L. (1976). On choosing a test statistic in multivariate analyses of variance. *Psychological Bulletin*, 83, 579-586.

Online CISCO Documentation. (2003). CISCO Systems [Online]. Available at http://www.cisco.com/univercd/cc/td/doc/cisintwk/ito_doc/adsl.htm [Jul 29, 2003].

Parasuraman, A., and Colby, C. (2001). *Techno-ready marketing: How and why your customers adopt technology*. New York: The Free Press.

Paul, P. (2003). Hurry up and wait. *American Demographics*, 25 (5), 20-25.

Pavlou, P.A. (2002). What drives electronic commerce? A theory of planned behavior perspective, *Best Paper Proceedings of the Academy of Management Conference*, Denver, Colorado, August 9-14, 2002.

Pavlou, P.A. (2003). Consumer acceptance of electronic commerce–Integrating trust and risk with the Technology Acceptance Model. *International Journal of ElectronicCommerce*, 7 (3), 69-103.

Pitkow, J.E., and Kehoe, C.M. (1996). Emerging trends in the WWW user population. *Communications of the ACM*, 39, 106-108.

Rodgers, W. (1998). Analysis of cross-classified data. In L.G. Grimm and P.R. Yarnold (eds.), *Reading and Understanding Multivariate Statistics*, 245-276. Washington, DC: American Psychological Association.

Rogers, E.M. (1995). *Diffusion of Innovations*. New York: The Free Press.

Salisbury, W.D., Pearson, R.A., and Harrison, A.W. (2003). Who's afraid of the World Wide Web? An initial investigation into the relative impact of two salient beliefs on Web shopping intent [Online]. *Proceedings of the 1998 Association for Information Systems Americans Conference*. Available http://www.isworld.org/ais.ac.98/proceedings/track06/salisbury.pdf [Jan 21, 2003].

Schmitt, B. (1999). Experiential marketing. *Journal of Marketing Management*, 15, 53-67.

Sheth, J.N., and Parvatiyar, A. (1995). Relationship marketing in consumer markets: Antecedents and consequences. *Journal of the Academy of Marketing Science*, 23 (Fall), 255-271.

Shimp, T.A., and Beardon, W.O. (1982). Warranty and other extrinsic cue effects on consumers' risk perception. *Journal of Consumer Research*, 9, 38-46.

Swaminathan, V., Lepkowska-White, E., and Rao, B.P. (1999). Browsers or buyers in cyberspace? An investigation of factors influencing electronic exchange. *Journal of Computer Mediated Communication*, 5 (2), 1-23.

Tedeshci, B. (2002). Privacy is common issue online [Online]. E-commerce Report. *New York Times*. Available http://www.nytimes.com/2002/06/03/technology/03ECOM.html [Nov 05, 2002].

Vogt, C.A., and Fesenmaier, D.R. (1998). Expanding the functional information search model. *Annals of Tourism Research*, 25 (3), 551-578.

Weber, K. and Roehl, W.S. (1999). Profiling people searching for and purchasing travel products on the World Wide Web. *Journal of Travel Research*, 37, 291-298.

Weinfurt, K.P. (1998). Multivariate analysis of variance. In L.G. Grimm and P.R. Yarnold (eds.), *Reading and Understanding Multivariate Statistics*, 245-276. Washington, DC: American Psychological Association.

Yamauchi, Y., and Coget, J.F. (2002). Untangling the social impact of the Internet: A large scale survey. Information Systems Working Paper 1-02. The Anderson School at UCLA, California.

Yonish, S., Delhagen, K., and Gordon, J. (2002). Where the broadband shoppers are: Wholeview technographics research report [Online]. Forrester Research. Available http://www.forrester.com [Dec 18, 2002].

Zeithaml, V.A. (1981). How consumer evaluation processes differ between goods and services. In: Donelly, J.H. and George, E. (eds.), *Marketing of Services*, Illinois: American Marketing Association.

Online Travel Planning and College Students: The Spring Break Experience

Billy Bai
Clark Hu
Jeffrey Elsworth
Cary Countryman

SUMMARY. In the United States, spring break travel for college students has become a significant business for many tourism destinations. The purpose of the study was to investigate college students' online travel behavior in vacation planning through selected travel Websites. This exploratory study found that the respondents generally leaned toward satisfaction with their online travel planning experiences. Results of multinomial logistic regression indicated that the easiness of meeting the vacation budget and comfortability of providing credit card information increase the probability of college students' satisfaction with the online vacation planning process. The study also found that the more time that was used to search for an online vacation the less the likelihood of achieving higher levels of satisfaction. The study concludes with a discussion on marketing and business implications applicable to online consumer behavior. *[Article copies available for a fee from The Haworth Document Delivery Service: 1-800-HAWORTH. E-mail address: <docdelivery@haworthpress.com> Website: <http://www.HaworthPress.com> © 2004 by The Haworth Press, Inc. All rights reserved.]*

KEYWORDS. Online consumer behavior, online travel planning, spring break travel, Web travel service portals

INTRODUCTION

College students have become a major market for the travel industry with reported spending of approximately $14.8 billion annually on domestic and international travel (Borgerding, 2001). College students are highly motivated for spring break travel and considered technologically savvy enough to handle online activities. In order to capitalize on the size and economic value of this market, many online travel organizations have sprung up specializing in

Billy Bai is Assistant Professor, Department of Tourism and Convention Management, William F. Harrah College of Hotel Administration, University of Nevada, Las Vegas. Clark Hu is Assistant Professor, School of Tourism and Hospitality Management, Temple University. Jeffrey Elsworth is Assistant Professor, School of Hospitality Business, Eli Broad College of Business, Michigan State University. Cary Countryman is Assistant Professor and Director of Technology Research and Education Center, Conrad N. Hilton College of Hotel and Restaurant Management, University of Houston.

Address correspondence to Billy Bai (E-mail: billy.bai@ccmail.nevada.edu).

[Haworth co-indexing entry note]: "Online Travel Planning and College Students: The Spring Break Experience." Bai, Billy et al. Co-published simultaneously in *Journal of Travel & Tourism Marketing* (The Haworth Hospitality Press, an imprint of The Haworth Press, Inc.) Vol. 17, No. 2/3, 2004, pp. 79-91: and: *Handbook of Consumer Behavior, Tourism, and the Internet* (ed: Juline E. Mills, and Rob Law) The Haworth Hospitality Press, an imprint of The Haworth Press, Inc., 2004, pp. 79-91. Single or multiple copies of this article are available for a fee from The Haworth Document Delivery Service [1-800-HAWORTH, 9:00 a.m. - 5:00 p.m. (EST). E-mail address: docdelivery@haworthpress.com].

http://www.haworthpress.com/web/JTTM
© 2004 by The Haworth Press, Inc. All rights reserved.
Digital Object Identifier: 10.1300/J073v17n02_07

marketing travel products to college students. Chief among them are STA Travel, the world's largest student travel agency, specializing in cheap discount airfares and accommodation in more than 300 locations; and International Student Travel Confederation (ISTC) which promotes student travel and networks with 5,000 student travel organizations in over 100 countries (ISTC, 2003; STA Travel Inc., 2003). In the United States, the spring break travel for college student market has become a significant business for many tourism destinations (Butts et al., 1996; Clements & Josiam, 1995; Hobson & Josiam, 1992; Josiam, Clements, & Hobson, 1994; Josiam, Smeaton, & Clements, 1999).

While a number of studies have increasingly focused on online consumer behavior from the standpoint of both academicians and industry practitioners to enhance our understanding of consumer behavior on the Internet (e.g., Bonn, Furr, & Susskind, 1998; Connolly, Olsen, & Moore, 1998; Doolin, Burgess, & Cooper, 2002) there is a lack of revealing efforts examining how various consumer segments, specifically the college student market, actually behave during the online vacation planning process. Toward this end, the purpose of this exploratory study was to investigate college students' and their behavior in online vacation planning when using selected travel Websites. The study also attempted to examine influential factors that may contribute to satisfaction with the online travel planning process by college students.

THE COLLEGE STUDENT TRAVEL MARKET

The College Swim Forum, which began in 1935, is considered by many to be the beginning of spring break travel. College swim teams from the Northern portion of the United States began traveling to Fort Lauderdale, Florida, for competitions (Anonymous, 1998; Hobson & Josiam, 1992; Josiam, Hobson, Dietrich, & Smeaton, 1998). During World War II spring break travel grew further with Ivy Leaguers going to Fort Lauderdale, Florida instead of Bermuda due to the fear of German submarine attacks. Over the next three decades, Fort Lauderdale became known as the top destination for spring break. Daytona Beach, Florida, became prominent in 1981 by attracting 300,000 students compared to only 200,000 in Fort Lauderdale. In 1982, South Padre Island, Texas, became a destination for spring break travelers from Midwestern states. Fort Lauderdale reached a record in April of 1985 with 350,000 students and $140 million in spending. Corporate marketers such as Budweiser and AT&T also began to understand the marketing potential of spring break travel and in 1989 at Daytona Beach gave away T-shirts and promotional items to spring break travelers. Panama City Beach, Florida, was able to attract 500,000 students in 1992 and is now considered to be the nation's spring break capital. This is further substantiated by the fact that the Music Television Channel (MTV) moved its spring break headquarters to Panama City Beach in 1995. Since then, Panama City Beach has continued to attract 550,000 visitors annually (Anonymous, 1998).

Since 1998, the spring break travel market has become more fragmented with college students traveling to destinations other than Florida despite its continued popularity (Josiam et al., 1998; Klenosky, 2002). Other spring break travel destinations include Palm Springs, California; Lake Havasu, Arizona; Steamboat, Colorado; and several international destinations such as Cancun, Mexico and Nassau, Bahamas in the Caribbean. Many of these travel destinations relied heavily on the spring break travel market for a large percentage of their annual tourism receipts (Butts et al., 1996; Hobson & Josiam, 1992).

The spring break travel market has, however, witnessed some significant changes over time. These changes are manifested in the travel behavior, destination choice, and travel motivation of college students. More recently, Weinbach (2000) has observed that while a good portion of the $1 billion spring break market still makes its home in cheaper Florida and Texas beach towns, college students have begun spending more than ever on their spring break travel. In addition to visiting popular spots such as Cancun in Mexico, US college students are also lured to other surprising international destinations including Ireland, Costa Rica, and even Singapore (Higgins, 2002).

Moreover, the image of spring break travel is also changed from partying to giving back to the community. Bly (2002) reported that college students used their spring breaks to help build destination communities not only in the US but also overseas (e.g., church tours and visits to hospitals in Jamaica, cross-cultural service program in Peru, and teach conversational English in Mexico, Ecuador, Ireland, and Poland). Gender and religious beliefs were also found to affect destination choice for spring break travel (Mattila, Apostolopoulos, Sonmez, Yu, & Sasidharan, 2001).

E-SATISFACTION AND ONLINE SPRING BREAK PLANNING

In general, it is estimated that online air revenue will triple from $13 billion in 2000 to $39 billion in 2006 while online lodging revenue would grow from $4 billion in 2000 to $15 billion in 2006 (Swerdlow et al., 2001). Given the size of online travel and its economic value, it is critical and also imperative that travel and hospitality firms continue to focus their resources on this lucrative online market which includes the student travel segment. With regards to the Internet, college students are becoming leading edge Internet users so much so that their online habits could demonstrate the future direction of the Internet. In 2000, a joint study by Greenfield Online and YouthSteam Media Networks revealed that the Internet has become an integral element of college life, with nearly 31 percent of students describing themselves as "Internet dependent." In addition, 28 percent considered themselves "cybergeeks" (*Fairfield County Business Journal*, 2000).

College students are not only spending more on spring break travel but they are also researching the process more via the Internet. Borgerding (2001) reported findings about college student travel from a market survey conducted by Futurepages/Memolink.com. According to this survey, the Internet was found to be the most effective method to reach and communicate with the college student market. College students, being receptive to online promotions and discount deals, used the Internet for travel research more than recommendations from their friends. Borgerding further pointed out that more than 54% of 474 college students surveyed had purchased travel tickets online, over 14% had made travel arrangements exclusively online, and 27% had purchased travel through a discount travel Website such as Travelocity.com and Expedia.com. From a market segmentation perspective, Ismail, Xu, Mills, and Cai (2002) examined the college student market segment and their use of the Internet for travel information. They found that airlines, hotels, shopping, travel destinations, dance/music performance, sporting event tickets, and vacation and tour packages were among the most popular travel products being searched on the Internet.

Clearly, college students are a significant online travel market segment. Therefore it is imperative that online travel businesses focusing on spring break travel pay significant attention to college student attitude and satisfaction with their vacation planning process. Satisfied college students will not only become repeat business but will also promote online products through word-of-mouth. Understanding the factors related customer satisfaction with the vacation planning process is essential for the continued development of the online spring break market. Only when the needs and wants of college students planning the spring break vacation are known can the E-service provider design and deliver products and services that will meet and exceed their expectations.

In the area of customer satisfaction research, marketing professionals have embarked on a new direction of identifying the features or dimensions that are perceived necessary by online customers in general. While service quality impacts customer satisfaction in the virtual environment, various research approaches are needed to examine influential factors on e-customer satisfaction. E-satisfaction is defined as the contentment of the consumer with respect to his or prior purchasing experience with a given electronic commerce firm (Anderson & Srinivasan, 2003). Although the terms *satisfaction* and *quality* are sometimes used interchangeably, Zeithaml and Bitner (2000) argued that because service quality assessment focuses primarily on dimensions of service, perceived service quality is only a component of customer satisfaction that is also influenced by product quality, price, customer factors, and situational factors. In this study, customer satisfaction is operationalized as the overall satisfaction with the online travel planning process.

There are many benefits of e-customer satisfaction. Zeithaml (2000) provided a thorough overview of research findings on positive consequences of achieving customer satisfaction mostly in the offline environment. First, customer satisfaction contributes to customer loyalty. A positive relationship between customer satisfaction and customer retention was found in bank settings (Hallowell, 1996; Rust & Zahorik, 1993). Zeithaml, Berry, and Parasuraman (1996) found a positive and significant relationship between customers' perceptions of service quality, and their willingness to recommend the company and their purchase intentions. In addition, customer satisfaction can lead to profitability. In hospital settings, studies by Koska (1990) and Nelson et al. (1992) discovered positive relationship between patient satisfaction and hospital profitability. Heskett, Sasser, and Schlesinger (1997) also demonstrated the impact of customer satisfaction on a company's profits. After the extant literature reviews on service quality and benefits obtained as a result, Zeithaml (2000) suggested companies implement both defensive marketing strategies (focused on retaining customers) and offensive marketing strategies (focused on creating new customers) to increase profits, followed by a research agenda targeting at a deeper understanding of the relationship between service quality and profitability.

In a recent study by Anderson and Srinivasan (2003), e-satisfaction was found to have a positive impact on e-loyalty and this relationship was moderated by consumers' individual level factors and firms' business level factors. Using a qualitative approach, Szymanski and Hise (2000) developed a conceptual model of e-satisfaction to include convenience, merchandising (product offerings and product information), site design, and financial security. They empirically tested the model and concluded that convenience, site design,

and financial security are the dominant factors in consumer assessments of e-satisfaction.

Research has also shown the seriousness of the problem when companies have dissatisfied customers. Plymire (1991) found that 91 percent of a restaurant's dissatisfied customers will never come back; and what is even worse, they will typically tell eight to ten others about their negative experiences. According to a study by the International Customer Service Association and e-Satisfy.com, more than two-thirds of e-shoppers were dissatisfied with electronic customer service (Anonymous, 2000). These dissatisfied customers told twice as many people about their e-experience than those who are satisfied. Creating satisfied customers and retaining them are a constant challenge to companies both offline and online.

Linked to e-satisfaction is the concept of prior experience. Research has shown that past behavior is a good predictor of future behavior (Bentler & Speckart, 1981). Customer expectations on a certain product or service are related to their previous encounters with the product or service. Ravald and Grönroos (1996) found that for consumers, prior successful transactions help establish confidence in and commitment to the company. This is extremely important for the online environment where college students interact with the Web-based computer systems rather than service personnel. Especially for travel products, college students cannot feel, touch, or experience them because of their intangible characteristics. As a consequence, college students have to base their judgment mainly on the electronic information provided for decision-making. Prior behavior has also been proved to have an impact on online purchase intentions (Weber & Roehl, 1999) and an indirect effect on intention to use the Internet for purchase (Klein, 1998; Shim, Eastlick, Lotz, & Warrington, 2001). Customer attitudes toward Internet-based shopping are also found to affect the initial willingness of customers to e-shop on the Internet (Liao & Cheung, 2001). Pre-purchase expectations heavily rely on personal sources (Berry & Parasuraman, 1991). Prior purchase experience influences not only the customer's own behavior but also others through the word-of-mouth. Experience on the Internet is a good indicator of potential Internet usage for travel and tourism-related information and purchases. Weber and Roehl (1999) found that people purchasing travel online are more likely to have been online for 4 years or more. Having examined the data released by IntiMetrix on e-shoppers' spending patterns by experience, Simms (2002) observed that as they have more positive experiences, e-shoppers are more likely to return and purchase more. It seems that the longer people have access to the Internet, the more likely they will return for future purchase online. Trust can be built between the customer and the online company through positive experiences of past transactions. Based on the above discussions, it seems to suggest that prior experience may influence college student satisfaction with online spring break vacation planning.

In addition to prior experience, payment methods and the ability of the Website to meet the college student budget may have an effect on their e-satisfaction. For those that purchase travel online, one of the most important features of a Website is its secure payment methods (Law & Wong, 2003). However, those with more experience in purchasing travel online consider credit card security less of a concern than those that purchase travel through the more traditional means (Weber & Roehl, 1999). Perceptions of online transactional security and privacy play an important role not only in e-satisfaction (Szymanski & Hise, 2000) but also in e-loyalty (Hoffman, Novak, & Peralta, 1999). It can be concluded that online financial security is among the foremost concern to consumers when deciding whether or not to buy online. In this study, we wanted to find out whether the comfortability of releasing credit card information online contributes to college student satisfaction with their spring break vacation planning process. Meeting the travel plan budget is important for college students when they make travel plans, given their limited economic resources if they have to pay for the trip. Research has shown that not having enough money is the major barrier to travel during the spring break (Hobson & Josiam, 1995). It seems logical that if the online search results in a travel package that meets the

pre-determined budget, college students will be satisfied with their online planning process.

METHODOLOGY

Study Sample and Data Collection

College students of hospitality and tourism majors were solicited for voluntary participation in this study. A total of 60 students who majored in hospitality and tourism management participated in this study from three different universities located in separate cities (East Lansing, Michigan; Houston, Texas; and Las Vegas, Nevada) in the continental United States. The chosen subjects at each university performed planning tasks via all three major travel service Web sites: www.expedia.com, www.orbitz.com, and www.travelocity.com. These three travel service Websites are among the most popular Web travel service portals. In order to maintain operational consistency and simplicity, all participants were asked to plan a "standardized" vacation that would last five days and four nights for the 2002 spring break with a total budget of $2,000 for a party of two that cover the airfare, hotel accommodation and car rental. To avoid geographical unfamiliarity, the vacation trip was designed to originate from Las Vegas, Nevada, USA, to the destination point of Orlando, Florida, USA. Data were collected during March and April 2002 peak spring break travel periods. Each subject was scheduled to attend an individual session where the researcher administered data collection in a controlled environment. Three Web portals were pre-bookmarked in the Web browser (Internet Explorer v.6) of a designated and networked computer. Each of the three Websites was accessed by the subject without a particular order. With pre-assigned planning tasks as described above, all subjects were required to search each Website for needed travel information within the budget. Each subject then compared his/her search results and chose the Website that best satisfied planning requirements. The subject was finally asked to print out his/her itinerary without providing personal credit card information and give it to the researcher at each university. A post-planning survey was immediately distributed to the subject as soon as the planning tasks were completed.

Performance measures (total time spent and satisfaction level) regarding information search, vacation planning, and Web site choice were identified and examined. The participant's demographic information (age, gender, and year at school) and measurements of their Internet skills (online skillfulness and purchase experience) were also collected. Researchers also recorded the time spent at each Web travel portal by the respondent during his/her planning task and reported their comfortability of releasing credit card information while purchasing products online. Respondents were also asked to rate their satisfaction with the online vacation planning process on a 7-point Likert scale ranging from 1 (extremely dissatisfied) to 7 (extremely satisfied).

Data Analysis

Descriptive statistics including frequencies, percentages, and analysis of variance (ANOVA) were used to describe the sample characteristics. Given the nature of the categorical dependent variable–satisfaction with the online vacation planning process, ordinal (or ordered) regression modeling was first employed to examine influential factors on the satisfaction of online vacation planning. The ordered logistic model estimates the effects of independent variables on the log odds of having lower rather than higher scores on the dependent variable. The independent variables included the total time used, the prior experience of online vacation planning, the comfortability of releasing credit card information while purchasing products online, and the budget allocated to the online vacation planning process. Burke (2002) found that online shoppers are less satisfied with the slower speed of the shopping process. It is assumed that the total amount of time used to search for an online vacation package may influence customer satisfaction; that is, the longer the time used, the less satisfied the customer will be. Given the exploratory nature of the study, respondents were asked to hypothetically complete the time-consuming online travel planning process. A total useable 60 responses were collected. This sample size might affect

the generalizability of the results. However, it should also be reminded that the data collection process for this study was not a typical survey approach where people would have to recall what had happened a long time before. In this study, each participant was asked to complete a complex online travel planning process (air travel, hotel accommodation, and car rental) on all three Websites. The process was tedious and time consuming. Once the online travel planning process was over, the survey was administered to the participants. By doing so, the data collected were most recent and could reflect their immediate experiences of online travel planning. According to Hair, Anderson, Tatham, and Black (1998), the ratio of observations to independent variables should never fall below 5 to 1 to avoid the risk of "overfitting" the variate to the sample and the desired level is between 15 to 20 observations for each independent variable in the regression analysis. The sample size in this study was up to the desired level as indicated by Hair et al. (1998). Therefore, the sample size was considered appropriate.

Results of the ordered logistic regression showed that the test of parallel lines was statistically significant, indicating the violation of the assumption that the slop coefficients are the same across response categories. Long (1997) commented that the parallel regression assumption is frequently violated in ordered logistic regression. He suggested that the multinomial logistic model can be used to avoid the parallel regression assumption of the ordered regression models. Therefore, the present study adopted multinomial logistic regression to examine the factors that influence online vacation planning satisfaction.

RESULTS

In terms of demographics, relatively more female students (60%) than male ones (40.0%) participated in this study (Table 1). Students who fell in the age category of 19 to 22 years old (61.7%) dominated the sample. More than 78% of the respondents were junior or senior students and 20% were graduate students in their academic programs.

TABLE 1. Demographics of Respondents (*N* = 60)

Characteristic	Percentage	N
Gender		
Male	40.0	24
Female	60.0	36
Age		
19-22	61.7	37
23-30	29.9	18
Older than 30	8.4	5
School Year		
Sophomore	1.7	1
Junior	31.7	19
Senior	46.7	28
Graduate	20.0	12

TABLE 2. Profile of Respondents with Online Experiences and Online Purchases (*N* = 60)

Variable	Minutes	Percentage	n
Time Used For Web Sites			
Average Time Used For Total Three Web Sites	46		
www.expedia.com	13		
www.travelocity.com	17		
www.orbitz.com	17		
Computer Skills			
Novice/new user		1.7	1
Average user		61.7	37
Skilled user		36.7	22
Used a Travel Agent Before			
Yes		81.7	49
No		18.3	11
Preferred Choice of Online Travel Planning			
Yes		80.0	48
No		20.0	12
Use of Internet			
1-3 years		21.7	13
4-6 years		63.3	38
More than 6 years		15.0	9
Hours Spent on the Internet per Week			
Less than 5 hours		35.0	21
5-7 hours		23.3	14
More than 7 hours		41.7	25
Planned a Vacation Through a Travel Web Site			
Yes		45.0	27
No		55.0	33
Online Purchases at All			
Yes		86.7	52
No		13.3	8
Online Purchases During Last Six Months			
None		18.3	11
1-2 times		33.4	20
3-4 times		26.7	16
More than 4 times		21.6	13

The average time spend on online travel planning with all the three Web sites was 46 minutes with www.expedia.com being the shortest at 13 minutes (Table 2). Most of the respondents self-reported that they were competent with computer skills (98.4%). Eighty-two percent of the respondents reported that they had used a travel agent for their travel needs before. Table 1 also shows that 80% of the respondents indicated online travel planning as a preferred choice over the use of a travel agent. The majority of the sample (78.3%) reported that they had been using the Internet for four years and more. Sixty-five percent of the respondents spent five or more hours on the Internet each week. However, 55.0% of all participants reported no prior experience in planning a vacation through a travel Web site. A vast majority of the respondents had purchased online products (86.7%) and made online purchases (81.7%) over the past six months at the time this study was conducted.

As seen in Table 3, college students were generally satisfied with their Web site vacation planning experiences (Mean = 5.5 on a 7-point Likert-type scale) and their planning process (Mean = 5.4). Based on their planning experience, the findings indicated that they would recommend the use of www.expedia.com as the preferred choice for online vacation planning (Mean = 5.8) among the three selected Web travel service providers. However, the sample remained undecided regarding how comfortable they were in releasing their credit card information while purchasing products online (Mean = 4.3 where 7 = "ex-tremely comfortable" and 1 = "extremely uncomfortable").

The level of computer skills was found to have a significant impact on the comfortability of releasing credit card information between average and skilled users (Table 4). Skilled users were more comfortable to provide their credit card information than average users. Table 5 indicates that the longer the use of the Internet, the more comfortable the respondent was with providing credit card information for online purchases. Past online purchase experience made a difference on perceived comfortability of providing credit card information for online pur-

TABLE 3. Satisfaction, Easiness, and Comfortability with Online Travel Planning

Variable	Mean	Std. Dev.
Overall Satisfaction with Web Site Vacation Planning	5.5[a]	.93
Satisfaction with Planning Process	5.4[a]	1.14
Recommendation of Web Site		
www.expedia.com	5.8[b]	1.02
www.travelocity.com	4.4[b]	1.45
www.orbitz.com	3.8[b]	1.78
Easiness of Online Travel Planning Within the Budget	5.4[c]	1.24
Comfortability with Providing Credit Card Information	4.3[d]	1.80

Note:
a. 7 = extremely satisfied; 6 = satisfied; 5 = somewhat satisfied; 4 = neutral; 3 = somewhat dissatisfied; 2 = dissatisfied; 1 = extremely dissatisfied.
b. 7 = definitely recommended; 6 = probably recommended; 5 = somewhat recommended; 4 = neutral; 3 = somewhat not recommended; 2 = probably not recommended; 1 = definitely not recommended.
c. 7 = extremely easy; 6 = easy; 5 = somewhat easy; 4 = neutral; 3 = somewhat difficult; 2 = difficult; 1 = extremely difficult.
d. 7 = extremely comfortable; 6 = comfortable; 5 = somewhat comfortable; 4 = neutral; 3 = somewhat uncomfortable; 2 = uncomfortable; 1 = extremely uncomfortable.

TABLE 4. Level of Computer Skills and Release of Credit Card Information* (N = 59)

Level	Mean (Std. Dev.)	F	Sig.
		4.049	.049
Average User	4.0 (1.8)		
Skilled User	5.0 (1.7)		

* 7 = extremely comfortable; 6 = comfortable; 5 = somewhat comfortable; 4 = neutral; 3 = somewhat uncomfortable; 2 = uncomfortable; 1 = extremely uncomfortable.

TABLE 5. Use of the Internet and Release of Credit Card Information* (N = 60)

Number of Years	Mean (Std. Dev.)	F	Sig.
		4.082	.023
1-3 years	3.2 (1.5)		
More than 6 years	5.4 (1.5)		

* 7 = extremely comfortable; 6 = comfortable; 5 = somewhat comfortable; 4 = neutral; 3 = somewhat uncomfortable; 2 = uncomfortable; 1 = extremely uncomfortable.

TABLE 6. Online Purchase Experience and Release of Credit Card Information* (N = 60)

Online Purchase Experience	Mean (Std. Dev.)	F	Sig.
		7.980	.006
Yes	4.6 (1.8)		
No	2.8 (1.3)		

* 7 = extremely comfortable; 6 = comfortable; 5 = somewhat comfortable; 4 = neutral; 3 = somewhat uncomfortable; 2 = uncomfortable; 1 = extremely uncomfortable.

TABLE 7. Reasons for Purchasing Online Travel Services (N = 60)

Reason	Percentage [a]	n
Convenience	88.3	53
Discounted Prices	78.3	47
Past Experience	36.7	22
Recommendation from Someone	25.0	15
Company Reputation	11.7	7
Others[b]	5.0	3

Note:
a. Total percentage may not equal 100 due to multiple responses.
b. Respondents specified "other" reasons as: not paying travel agents, comparison, and better price.

quently mentioned reasons driving online travel purchases, following by past experience (36.7%) and recommendation by someone else (25%).

Multinomial logistic regression was found to replicate the observed distribution of outcomes on the dependent variable well. The Chi-square of −2 log likelihood for the fitted model was 62.343 at p < .0001. The Nagelkerke R-square value (.695) correlates the Cox and Snell value (.646). Such pseudo R-square measures indicate that the model performs fairly well. As seen in Table 8, the positive coefficients for meeting vacation budget across different levels of satisfaction indicates that the easiness to find a travel package that meets the vacation budget increases the probability of satisfaction with the online vacation planning process. Results also show that the higher comfortable levels of providing credit card information contributes to the likelihood of being extremely satisfied with the online vacation planning process at .10 level. The negative coefficient for total time used explains that the longer time used for the

chases (Table 6). Those who had previous online purchase experience felt more comfortable with releasing credit card information via the Web channel. Table 7 illustrates the top reasons why an online travel service would be used to purchase travel. Convenience (88.3%) and discounted prices (78.3%) were most fre-

TABLE 8. Results of Multinomial Logistic Regression: Online Vacation Planning Satisfaction (*N* = 60)

	Extremely Satisfied	Satisfied	Somewhat Satisfied
Providing credit card information	1.644* (.951)		
Total time used	−.430* (.255)		
Meeting vacation budget	10.181** (4.633)	2.071*** (.625)	.920** (.446)

Notes: Reference category for the equation is Somewhat Dissatisfied. Standard errors in parentheses.
* p ≤ .10; ** p ≤ .05; *** p ≤ .001.

vacation planning process the less likelihood of achieving satisfaction to the extreme possible at .10 level. The independent variables "Prior experience" was left out because it was not found to be significant in the model at .10 level.

DISCUSSION AND CONCLUSION

This exploratory study was designed to investigate college student online travel planning behavior in the context of spring break travel. The data collection was unique in that each participant completed the travel planning process using three popular travel Websites. The study found that the respondents generally leaned toward satisfaction with their online travel planning experiences. Results of multinomial logistic regression indicated that the easiness of meeting the vacation budget and comfortability of providing credit card information increase the probability of respondent satisfaction with the online spring break planning process, while the more time that was used to search for an online vacation the less the likelihood of achieving higher level of satisfaction.

Findings of this study suggest that Expedia.com is the preferred choice for spring break travel planning based on respondents' recommendation ratings. It should be noted, however, that this group of consumers are more educated and technologically savvy than general consumers. Total time used negatively influenced the higher level of satisfaction with the online vacation planning process experience. Websites must therefore be easy to navigate and their contents must be concise, up-to-date, and easy to understand. Otherwise, the possible outcome will be reduced traffic to the Website, and more importantly, prospective spring break travelers may switch to competitors for information searches and business transactions.

The present study found a significant difference among groups with different computer-skill levels in the comfortability of providing credit card information for online purchases. This finding suggests that the Web service companies must provide easy features to accommodate average users and continue to nurture/educate them. This may help to increase their online trust level. The risk associated with online purchases is always a stumbling block (Balfour, Farquhar, & Langmann, 1998; Belanger, Hiller, & Smith, 2002). It is up to the travel service companies to ensure security and build greater trust with college students. Online travel companies must provide privacy and security information. In addition, they should also inform customers of how transaction and personal data are secured (Shankar, Urban, & Sultan, 2002).

Prior experience of online purchases was found to enhance the comfortability of providing credit card information for online purchases. This is supported by Ravald and Grönroos (1996) who found that previous successful transactions help customers establish confidence in the service provider enabling customers to thus become more committed to the company. Additional marketing efforts should be directed to boosting first-time online purchases and helping college students reach the "comfort zone." While college students may seek convenient and discounted prices, travel service companies need to implement effective pricing strategies to lure more online business. The findings of this study also seem to suggest that word-of-mouth recommendations and company reputation may not be the best way to help drive college students into making online travel purchases at this time. One possible explanation would be that this consumer market is more price conscious and may ignore the other aspects that contribute to online purchases. This notion was confirmed by results of multinomial logistic regression where the easiness of meeting the vacation budget was the only positive influential factor that may increase the probability of respondent satisfaction with the online vacation planning process.

Spring break travel by college students has become a discrete self-contained phenomenon (Hobson & Josiam, 1995). The effect of online travel planning and booking on the travel industry is prominent. Thus, spring break travel presents both opportunities and challenges to travel service companies. Online travel planning is a preferred choice by college students in this study. It can be inferred that this travel market will use the Internet for travel planning more than traditional channels of distribution. This phenomenon is synonymous with the overall trend of online travel buyers. As described by Moran (2003), eight in 10 online travel buyers, in 2002, usually purchased their travel services online.

Understanding college students' behavior through online vacation planning is important to capitalize on this fast growing travel business on the Internet. Online purchases provide customers with a unique experience in that customers mainly depend on the Website that offers product related information, navigation, interactivity with the company, and transaction fulfillment (Hoque & Lohse, 1999; Kolesar & Galbraith, 2000; Lohse, Bellman, & Johnson, 2000; Lohse & Spiller, 1999). Consequently, the customer decision making process has become more complex in dealing with online products and services. Online service providers need to constantly monitor how e-travelers make their online travel plans so that they can design and deliver products and services that will meet and exceed the customer expectations. Online travel companies should prioritize business decisions to create and maintain satisfied college students. This exploratory study calls for more research devoted to the understanding of college students' travel behavior in the online environment. While the findings of the study provide meaningful implications for online travel companies, the

study remains exploratory in nature. One limitation with the study was the relatively small sample size. Future research should increase the number of subjects. Identification of additional variables that are theoretically related to customer satisfaction may reveal more insight into the understanding of college student behavior in the online environment.

REFERENCES

Anderson, R. E., & Srinivasan, S. S. (2003). E-satisfaction and e-loyalty: A contingency framework. *Psychology and Marketing, 20*(2), 123-138.

Anonymous. (1998, April 2). Spring break. *Rolling Stone*, 56, 58, 60, 62, 64, 66.

Anonymous. (2000). E-business misses the mark on customer service. *The Internal Auditor, 57*(3), 13-15.

Balfour, A., Farquhar, B., & Langmann, G. (1998). The consumer needs in global electronic commerce. *Electronic Markets, 8*(2), 9-12.

Belanger, F., Hiller, J. S., & Smith, W. J. (2002). Trustworthiness in electronic commerce: The role of privacy, security, and site attributes. *Journal of Strategic Information Systems, 11*(3-4), 245-270.

Bentler, P. M., & Speckart, G. (1981). Attitudes 'cause' behaviors: A structural equations analysis. *Journal of Personality and Social Psychology, 40*(3), 226-238.

Berry, L. L., & Parasuraman, A. (1991). *Marketing services: Competing through quality.* New York, NY: The Free Press.

Bly, L. (2002, February 8). Students build a better spring break: More forgo the beach to lend a helping hand. *USA Today*, p. E05.

Bonn, M. A., Furr, H. L., & Susskind, A. M. (1998). Using the Internet as a pleasure traveling planning tool: An examination of the sociodemographic and behavioral characteristics among Internet users and nonusers. *Journal of Hospitality and Tourism Research, 22*(3), 303-317.

Borgerding, T. (2001, April 2). *College students spend an estimated $14.8 billion on travel according to Futurepages/Memolink.com survey.* Retrieved May 13, 2002, from http://www.futurepages.com/pressrelease.cfm?articleID=43

Burke, R. R. (2002). Technology and the customer interface: What consumers want in the physical and virtual store. *Journal of the Academy of Marketing Science, 30*(4), 411-432.

Butts, F. B., Salazar, J., Sapio, K., & Thomas, D. (1996). The impact of contextual factors on the spring break travel decisions of college students. *Journal of Hospitality & Leisure Marketing, 4*(3), 63-70.

Clements, C. J., & Josiam, B. M. (1995). Role of involvement in the travel decision. *Journal of Vacation Marketing, 1*(4), 337-348.

Connolly, D. J., Olsen, M. D., & Moore, R. (1998). The Internet as a distribution channel. *Cornell Hotel and Restaurant Administration Quarterly, 39*(4), 42-55.

Doolin, B., Burgess, L., & Cooper, J. (2002). Evaluating the use of the Web for tourism marketing: A case study from New Zealand. *Tourism Management, 23*(5), 557-561.

Elliot, S., & Fowell, S. P. (2000). Expectations versus reality: A snapshot of consumer experiences with internet retailing. *International Journal of Information Management, 20*(5), 323-326.

Fairfield County Business Journal. (2000). Study shows college students Internet-savvy. Vol. 39, Issue 33, p. 11.

Furr, H. L., & Bonn, M. A. (1998). The Internet and the hospitality marketing professional. *Praxis: Journal of Applied Hospitality Management, 1*(1), 60-69.

Garbarino, E., & Johnson, M. S. (1999). The different roles of satisfaction, trust, and commitment in customer relationships. *Journal of Marketing, 63*(2), 70-87.

Hair, J. F., Jr., Anderson, R. E., Tatham, R. L., & Black, W. C. (1998). *Multivariate data analysis* (5th ed.). Upper Saddle River, NJ: Prentice Hall.

Hallowell, R. (1996). The relationship of customer satisfaction, customer loyalty, and profitability: An empirical study. *International Journal of Service Industry Management, 7*(4), 27-42.

Heskett, J. L., Sasser, W. E., & Schlesinger, L. A. (1997). *The service profit chain: How leading companies link profit and growth to loyalty, satisfaction, and value.* New York, NY: The Free Press.

Higgins, M. (2002, February 25). The breakaway spring break–Tour operators lure youths to surprising locations: Partying in Singapore? *Wall Street Journal,* p. W1.

Hobson, J. S. P., & Josiam, B. M. (1992). Spring break student travel: An exploratory analysis. *Journal of Travel & Tourism Marketing, 1*(3), 87-97.

Hobson, J. S. P., & Josiam, B. M. (1995). Spring break student travel: A longitudinal study. *Journal of Vacation Marketing, 2*(2), 137-150.

Hoffman, D. L., Novak, T. P., & Peralta, M. (1999). Building consumer trust online. *Communications of the ACM, 42*(4), 80-85.

Hoque, A. Y., & Lohse, G. L. (1999). An information search cost perspective for designing interfaces for electronic commerce. *Journal of Marketing Research, 36*(3), 387-394.

International Student Travel Confederation. (2003). *About ISTC.* Retrieved February 13, 2003, from http://www.aboutistc.org/about.html

Ismail, J., Xu, M., Mills, J., & Cai, L. A. (2002). *College student use of the World Wide Web: A travel markets pot of gold or potential nightmare?* Unpublished manuscript, West Lafayette, IN.

Josiam, B. M., Clements, C. J., & Hobson, J. S. P. (1994). Youth travel in the USA: Understanding the spring break market. In A. V. Seaton (Ed.), *Tourism:* *The state of the art* (pp. 322-331). Chichester, UK: Wiley, John & Sons.

Josiam, B. M., Hobson, J. S. P., Dietrich, U. C., & Smeaton, G. (1998). An analysis of the sexual, alcohol and drug related behavioural patterns of students on spring break. *Tourism Management, 19*(6), 501-513.

Josiam, B. M., Smeaton, G., & Clements, C. J. (1999). Involvement: Travel motivation and destination selection. *Journal of Vacation Marketing, 5*(2), 167-175.

Kasavana, M. L., Knutson, B. J., & Polonowski, S. J. (1997). Netlurking: The future of hospitality Internet marketing. *Journal of Hospitality & Leisure Marketing, 5*(1), 31-44.

Kaynama, S. A., & Black, C. I. (2000). A proposal to assess the service quality of online travel agencies: An exploratory study. *Journal of Professional Services Marketing, 21*(1), 63-88.

Klein, L. R. (1998). Evaluating the potential of interactive media through a new lens: Search versus experience goods. *Journal of Business Research, 41*(3), 195-203.

Klenosky, D. B. (2002). The "pull" of tourism destinations: A means-end investigation. *Journal of Travel Research, 40*(4), 385-395.

Knutson, B., Stevens, P., Wullaert, C., Patton, M., & Yokoyama, F. (1990). LODGSERV: A service quality index for the lodging industry. *Hospitality Research Journal, 14*(2), 277-284.

Kolesar, M. B., & Galbraith, R. W. (2000). A services-marketing perspective on e-retailing: Implications for e-retailers and directions for further research. *Internet Research: Electronic Networking Applications and Policy, 10*(5), 424-438.

Koska, M. T. (1990, March 5). High quality care and hospital profits: Is there a link? *Hospitals, 64,* 62-63.

Law, R., & Chen, F. (2000). Internet in travel and tourism–Part II: Expedia. *Journal of Travel & Tourism Marketing, 9*(4), 83-87.

Law, R., & Wong, J. (2003). Successful factors for a travel Web site: Perceptions of online purchasers in Hong Kong. *Journal of Hospitality and Tourism Research, 27*(1), 118-124.

Lennon, R., & Harris, J. (2002). Customer service on the Web: A cross-industry investigation. *Journal of Targeting, Measurement and Analysis for Marketing, 10*(4), 325-338.

Liao, Z., & Cheung, M. T. (2001). Internet-based e-shopping and consumer attitudes: An empirical study. *Information & Management, 38*(5), 299-306.

Liljander, V., van Riel, A. C. R., & Pura, M. (2001). *Customer satisfaction with e-services: The case of an online recruitment portal.* Retrieved June 28, 2003, from http://www.shh.fi/~liljande/vlarmprecr.pdf

Lohse, G. L., Bellman, S., & Johnson, E. J. (2000). Consumer buying behavior on the Internet: Findings from panel data. *Journal of Interactive Marketing, 14*(1), 15-29.

Lohse, G. L., & Spiller, P. (1999). Internet retail store design: How the user interface influences traffic and sales. *Journal of Computer-Mediated Communication, 5*(2), [Electronic version] Available http://www.ascusc.org/jcmc/vol5/issue2/lohse.htm.

Long, J. S. (1997). *Regression models for categorical and limited dependent variables.* Thousand Oaks, CA: Sage Publications.

Mattila, A. S., Apostolopoulos, Y., Sonmez, S., Yu, L., & Sasidharan, V. (2001). The impact of gender and religion on college students' spring break behavior. *Journal of Travel Research, 40*(2), 193-200.

Moran, S. J. (2003, April 3). *Consumer trends: Evolution of the online traveler-PhoCusWright's FYI.* Retrieved April 14, 2003, from http://www.wiredhotelier.com/news/WiredHotelier_-Editorial/4015397.html

Nelson, E. C., Rust, R. T., Zahorik, A. J., Rose, R. L., Batalden, P. B., & Siemanski, B. A. (1992). Do patient perceptions of quality relate to hospital financial performance? *Journal of Healthcare Marketing, 12*(4), 6-13.

Oliver, R. L. (1980). A cognitive model of the antecedents and consequences of satisfaction decisions. *Journal of Marketing Research, 17*(4), 460-469.

Oliver, R. L. (1997). *Satisfaction: A behavioral perspective on the consumer.* New York, NY: McGraw-Hill.

Parasuraman, A. (1996). *Understanding and leveraging the role of customer service in external, interactive and internal marketing.* Paper presented at the 1996 Frontiers in Services Conference, Nashville, TN.

Parasuraman, A. (2000). Technology readiness index (TRI): A multiple-item scale to measure readiness to embrace new technologies. *Journal of Service Research, 2*(4), 307-320.

Parasuraman, A., & Grewal, D. (2000). The impact of technology on the quality-value-loyalty chain: A research agenda. *Journal of the Academy of Marketing Science, 28*(1), 168-174.

Parasuraman, A., Zeithaml, V. A., & Berry, L. L. (1988). SERVQUAL: A multiple-item scale for measuring consumer perceptions of service quality. *Journal of Retailing, 64*(1), 12-40.

Phau, I., & Poon, S. M. (2000). Factors influencing the types of products and services purchased over the Internet. *Internet Research: Electronic Networking Applications and Policy, 10*(2), 102-113.

Plymire, J. (1991). Complaints as opportunities. *Journal of Consumer Marketing, 8*(2), 39-43.

Ratnasingham, P. (1998). The importance of trust in electronic commerce. *Internet Research: Electronic Networking Applications and Policy, 8*(4), 313-321.

Ravald, A., & Grönroos, C. (1996). The value concept and relationship marketing. *European Journal of Marketing, 30*(2), 19-30.

Rust, R. T., & Kannan, P. K. (Eds.). (2002). *e-Service: New directions in theory and practice.* Armonk, NY: M. E. Sharpe, Inc.

Rust, R. T., & Zahorik, A. J. (1993). Customer satisfaction, customer retention, and market share. *Journal of Retailing, 69*(2), 193-215.

Shankar, V., Urban, G. L., & Sultan, F. (2002). Online trust: A stakeholder perspective, concepts, implications, and future directions. *Journal of Strategic Information Systems, 11*(3-4), 325-344.

Shim, S., Eastlick, M. A., Lotz, S. L., & Warrington, P. (2001). An online prepurchase intentions model: The role of intention to search. *Journal of Retailing, 77*(3), 397-416.

Simms, D. (2002). Robots and gunslingers: Measuring customer satisfaction on the Internet. In R. T. Rust & P. K. Kannan (Eds.), *e-Service: New directions in theory and practice* (pp. 65-89). Armonk, NY: M. E. Sharpe, Inc.

STA Travel Inc. (2003). *STA Travel–Student travel worldwide offices.* Retrieved April 15, 2003, from http://www.statravel.com/contactus/worldwideoffices. asp

Steinbrink, S. (2003). *PhoCusWright consumer travel trends survey (5th ed.).* Sherman, CT: PhoCusWright Inc.

Stevens, P., Knutson, B., & Patton, M. (1995). DINESERV: A tool for measuring service quality in restaurants. *Cornell Hotel and Restaurant Administration Quarterly, 36*(2), 56-60.

Swerdlow, F. S., Kim, H., Kim, J., & Sehgal, V. (2001). *2001 U.S. travel forecast report* (Vision report). New York, NY: Jupiter Media Metrix, Inc.

Szymanski, D. M., & Hise, R. T. (2000). e-Satisfaction: An Initial examination. *Journal of Retailing, 76*(3), 309-322.

Travel Industry Association of America. (2001). *E-travel consumers–How they plan and buy leisure travel online* (Research report). Washington, DC: Travel Industry Association of America.

Travel Industry Association of America. (2001). *Travelers' use of the Internet (2001 Edition).* Washington, DC: Travel Industry Association of America.

Wang, H., Lee, M. K. O., & Wang, C. (1998). Consumer privacy concerns about Internet marketing. *Communications of the ACM, 41*(3), 63-70.

Weber, K., & Roehl, W. S. (1999). Profiling people searching for and purchasing travel products on the World Wide Web. *Journal of Travel Research, 37*(3), 291-298.

Weinbach, J. B. (2000). Beaches, babes . . . and a butler–Spring-break spending soars: Dude, does that hotel come with room service? *Wall Street Journal,* p. W1.

Wright, D. (2002). Comparative evaluation of electronic payment systems. *INFOR, 40*(1), 71-85.

Zeithaml, V. A. (2000). Service quality, profitability, and the economic worth of customers: What we know and what we need to learn. *Journal of the Academy of Marketing Science, 28*(1), 67-85.

Zeithaml, V. A., Berry, L. L., & Parasuraman, A. (1996). The behavioral consequences of service quality. *Journal of Marketing, 60*(2), 31-46.

Zeithaml, V. A., & Bitner, M. J. (2000). *Services marketing: Integrating customer focus across the firm* (3rd ed.). New York, NY: McGraw-Hill/Irwin.

Zeithaml, V. A., Parasuraman, A., & Malhotra, A. (2002). Service quality delivery through Web sites: A critical review of extant knowledge. *Journal of the Academy of Marketing Science, 30*(4), 362-375.

Reviewing the Profile and Behaviour of Internet Users: Research Directions and Opportunities in Tourism and Hospitality

Marianna Sigala

SUMMARY. Despite the wide-spread discussion of e-commerce advantages, research of e-commerce business models in the tourism literature has, to date, focused primarily on organisational, business and technical factors. In contrast, social considerations, i.e., factors related to the general societal context influencing the shape and adoption of e-commerce models in practice, have not been adequately addressed. As the wide success of e-commerce heavily depends on its adoption by society, it is imperative to develop a better understanding of the profile and behaviour of Internet surfers and shoppers. Thus, robust research on the adoption of e-commerce needs to consider the societal issues/factors affecting people and their environment. In this vein, by reviewing a great amount of literature from different disciplines, this paper aims to develop a holistic perspective for examining online tourists by integrating the study of individual, organisational, industrial, societal, and technological aspects of e-business. By consolidating and synthesizing a great number of studies, the paper also aims to identify and discuss future research opportunities and directions aiming to further examine Internet users and their behaviour. *[Article copies available for a fee from The Haworth Document Delivery Service: 1-800-HAWORTH. E-mail address: <docdelivery@haworthpress. com> Website: <http://www.HaworthPress.com> © 2004 by The Haworth Press, Inc. All rights reserved.]*

KEYWORDS. E-commerce, users' behaviour and profile, tourism, hospitality

INTRODUCTION

Although there has been wide-spread discussion of the advantages of ICT, Internet and e-commerce practices for both individuals and companies (Kosiur, 1997; Hoffman et al., 1996; Sigala, 2001 and 2002), the definition and research of e-commerce business models has, to date, focused primarily on organisational, business and technical factors. In contrast, social considerations, that are factors related to the general societal context, influencing the shape and adoption of e-commerce models in practice, have not been adequately addressed (Pouloudi, Vassilopoulou, & Ziouvelou, 2002). However, ultimately the wide success of e-commerce models heavily depends on their adoption by society. Moreover, with the increasing importance of online sales for tourism and hospitality products (Visa Eu-

Marianna Sigala is a Lecturer of Hospitality Management and Assistant Director of Research, Scottish Hotel School, University of Strathclyde (E-mail: M.Sigala@strath.ac.uk).

[Haworth co-indexing entry note]: "Reviewing the Profile and Behaviour of Internet Users: Research Directions and Opportunities in Tourism and Hospitality." Sigala. Marianna. Co-published simultaneously in *Journal of Travel & Tourism Marketing* (The Haworth Hospitality Press. an imprint of The Haworth Press. Inc.) Vol. 17. No. 2/3, 2004, pp. 93-102; and: *Handbook of Consumer Behavior, Tourism, and the Internet* (ed: Juline E. Mills, and Rob Law) The Haworth Hospitality Press, an imprint of The Haworth Press, Inc., 2004, pp. 93-102. Single or multiple copies of this article are available for a fee from The Haworth Document Delivery Service [1-800-HAWORTH, 9:00 a.m. - 5:00 p.m. (EST). E-mail address: docdelivery@haworthpress.com].

rope, 2003) and the growing number of online tourists patronising tourism Webstores, it is imperative to develop a better understanding of the profile and behaviour of Internet surfers and shoppers. Such investigation becomes even more important since research indicates that 81% of those that browse Websites for goods and services, do not make online purchases (Gupta, 1996; Graphic, Visualisation and Usability Center (GVU), 1999) and while many Web users are motivated to start a Web purchase transaction, 75% discontinue (cancel) the transaction (termed abandoning their shopping cart) (BizRate, 1999). Of greater concern to web retailers should be the fact that 80% of web users do not revisit web sites (NVision, 1999).

Therefore, robust research on the benefits and adoption of e-commerce needs to consider the dynamic capabilities that emerge from new business models as well as the societal issues/factors affecting people and their environment. Specifically, in investigating the take-up of e-business models, a holistic perspective should be adopted that integrates the study of individual, organisational, industrial, societal, and technological aspects of e-business. This research becomes even more important since the impact of social factors in e-commerce is underinvestigated not only in the generic literature but also in the context of e-travel and–tourism in particular. In this vein, it is the purpose of this paper to review and critically assess studies examining and evaluating the importance and implications of e-factors on e-commerce adoption and use. In other words, this paper aimed to collect and integrate research reporting on the impact of factors such as satisfaction and service quality affecting tourists' adoption and use of tourism and hospitality Webstores. By consolidating and synthesizing a great number of studies from different approaches found both in the tourism and mainstream literature, the paper also aims to identify and discuss future research opportunities and directions that would aim to further examine Internet users and their behaviour within the tourism and travel context.

E-FACTORS AFFECTING INTERNET USERS AND BEHAVIOUR: A REVIEW OF THE LITERATURE

There are a plethora of studies investigating the factors impacting on the adoption and use of Internet technologies. Overall, research at a local, regional, national, and global scale revealed that these factors can be categorised in socio-economic, geographical, educational, attitudinal and generational factors, or even to users' physical disabilities (Servon, 2002). Specifically, findings indicated that Internet users share the following characteristics. In terms of socio-demographic profile, studies revealed that gender, age, educational level, race/ethnicity, economic profile, technology and Internet skills and experience affect Internet use and adoption (Katz, & Aspden, 1997; Teo, 2001; Weber, & Roehl, 1999). Studies have generally shown that users are predominately males and that men took to the Internet faster than females (Zeffane, & Cheek, 1993; GVU, 1999; Harrison, & Rainer, 1992). This coupled with past research on computer predispositions which have generally shown that males are more interested in learning about computers than females (Qureshi & Hoppel, 1995) as well as that females demonstrate greater computer anxiety than males (Igbaria & Chakrabati, 1990) probably justify findings of current studies revealing that men are more likely to be Internet users and use the Internet for more activities (Teo, 2001; Sexton, Johnson, & Hignite, 2002; Katz, & Aspden, 1997). Previous studies have also shown that levels of computer usage, computer skills and so, not surprisingly, levels and types of Internet usage are negatively related with respondents' age (Elder et al., 1987; Harrison, & Rainer, 1992; Zeffane, & Cheek, 1993; GVU, 1999; Teo, 2001; Sexton, Johnson, & Hignite, 2002; Katz, & Aspden, 1997). Educational level is not usually found as a main construct predicting Internet use, but most often it is related to Internet usage indirectly via computer anxiety, and perceived respondents' easy of use and usefulness. Indeed, the positive impact of educational level on the latter variables (Igbaria, 1993; Brancheau & Wetherbe, 1990) has been found to indirectly affect Internet usage (Teo, 2001).

Other studies (Katz & Aspden, 1997; Wynter, 1996; Kraut, Scherlis, Manning, Mukhopadhyay, & Kiesler, 1996) also indicated that Internet use is also positively related to the respondents' economic level and dependent on ethnicity/race (e.g., Blacks, and Hispanic groups) and the push factors from social/work networks and children in family. Such findings are globally true since they had been validated by both international (Lynch, Kent, & Srinivasan, 2001) and national (Foley, Alfonso, & Ghani, 2002; Schmitt & Wadsworth, 2002; Gartner Group, 2001; Hoffman & Novak, 1999; Hoest, 2001) research, e.g., studies in the USA (Donthu & Garcia, 1999), in Asia (Wee & Ramachandra, 2000; Kau, Tang, & Ghose, 2003) and in Europe (Teo, 2001).

Within the context of tourism, studies have provided similar profiles of Internet users and their browsing and buying behaviour in tourism and travel Websites. Specifically, Internet users are likely to be under the age of 45 and have a college degree (Bonn, Furr, & Susskind, 1999; Weber & Roehl, 1999). Weber and Roehl (1999) also revealed that those with a four-year college degree or higher and with a household income above US$50,000 were more likely to purchase travel online. The Travel Industry Association of America (2002) also provided evidence that online travel purchasers' characteristics reflected previous Internet users' profiles in that they tended to be younger and better educated. Men were also found to have higher average online travel spending than women (TIA, 2001), but race was not found to have a noticeable effect regarding the travel-related information searches or purchases via the Internet (Weber & Roehl, 1999). Among the travel products purchased online, airline tickets, overnight lodging, and rental cars are the top three products travel consumers bought online (TIA, 2001). More recent research on the adoption of e-commerce for the purchase of travel products such as travel packages (Christou & Sigala, 2003) and airline tickets (Athiyaman, 2002; Christou & Kassianidis, 2002) has illustrated that the type and characteristics of the product, such as level of involvement, price, standardisation, importance to consumer, experiential product features, were found to have an effect on whether travellers prefer to buy them online or not. For example, although e-commerce in

the low cost airline sector (a very standardised product with a low value/risk and customer involvement) is highly adopted leading also to the "casualisation" of travelling, the same cannot be concluded for specialised and customised travel products, e.g., honeymooners, religious tourism, etc. Overall, it can be concluded that products/services that have lower risks (including product performance risk, financial risk, personal risk/preferences) tend to be purchased online by a greater number of online travellers.

Socio-economic differences have been overstressed as the major reason of the digital divide. However, further research into attitudes and barriers preventing use of the Internet is necessary before socio-economic reasons alone are assumed to be the major barrier to participation in the information age (Cullen, 2001; Quay, 2001). This is because closely aligned with the lack of skills and support are cultural and behavioural attitudes towards the technology–e.g., the computers are for "brainy" people, for males, for the young, are difficult to use or belong to a middle-class "white" culture. Concern over the lack of security of personal data or that computers are "unsafe" for families because of the amount of unsuitable material on the Internet are also sometimes expressed (Botha et al., 2001; Wilhelm, 1998). Attitudinal barriers can also be culturally based. In many cultures, which place high value on oral culture, personal communication, and strong family and kinship networks, the use of computers for communication purposes is not a high priority (Cullen, 2001). Lack of awareness about the opportunities offered by the e-commerce as well as lack of trust towards network security have also been argued to greatly determine attitudinal barriers and beliefs towards the adoption and use of e-commerce practices (Papazafeiropoulou, & Pouloudi, 2001). In this vein, several studies have emerged investigating trust antecedents and consequences on e-commerce adoption (Corbitt, Thanasankit, & Yi, 2003; Hoffman, Novak, & Peralta, 1999; Jarvenpaa, Tractinsky, & Vitale, 2000).

Davis (1989) developed and tested the TAM model (Technology Acceptance Model) illustrating that technology adoption and use is affected by the perceived easy of use and perceived effectiveness. Later, Straub et al. (1997) revealed that the TAM's constructs are significantly influenced by the four cultural differences (Hofstede, 1984). The validity of the TAM model in e-commerce adoption has been tested by several authors (Brown, 2002; Jennex & Amoroso, 2002) as well as applied and validated in studies investigating the adoption of e-commerce in tourism (Christou & Kassianidis, 2002; Christou & Sigala, 2003). In summary, Pouloudi, Vassilopoulou, and Ziouvelou (2002) developed a comprehensive list of societal factors determining broad and sustainable adoption of e-commerce models that categorized factors in seven general categories (Table 1): Region/Geography, Culture, Legal/Regulatory/Policy, Economic, Ethical and Professional, as well as Social Capital/Social Networks and Social Structure.

However, a new stream of research emerged aiming to extend and further validate the appropriateness and inclusiveness of the TAM model into the specific characteristics and features of Web retailing contexts. Such research builds on later work by Davis et al. (1992) that explicitly illustrated the impact of intrinsic motivation on computer usage by including in the TAM model the construct named perceived enjoyment. Perceived enjoyment was defined as "the extent to which the activity of using the computer is perceived to be enjoyable in its own right, apart from any performance consequences that may be anticipated" (Davis et al., 1992). The validity of this construct was later confirmed not only in the context of computer usage (Atkison & Kydd, 1997; Teo et al., 1999), but also in the e-commerce context whereby recent studies (Heijden, 2003; Cass & Fenech, 2003) have adopted and extended the TAM model by validating the inclusion and positive impact of new constructs on e-commerce adoption such as perceived visual attractiveness, opinion leadership, impulsiveness, web shopping compatibility, Internet self-efficacy, perceived web security, satisfaction with Websites, and shopping orientation.

TABLE 1. Summary of e-Social Factors

Category	Factors
Region/Geography	Language–Vocabulary Environmental issues Country-specific issues
Culture	Values/Beliefs Religion Acceptance/Maturity of People Ideas Awareness Attitudes Communities Change Social Support Word-of-Mouth/"Word of Mouse"
Legal/Regulation/Policy	Security Policy makers/"Policy Intermediaries" Privacy Regulatory framework–Jurisdictions Freedom of Information Taxation Reliability Infrastructure Confidentiality e-Democracy Regulation
Economic	Economic environment in a regional and national level Market structure (concentration, competition) Access
Ethical and Professional	Identity Crisis Issues Anonymity Responsibility and Roles Free Speech Computer Crime/Computer Abuse Trust
Social Capital/Social Networks	A social network is a set of nodes (e.g., persons, organizations) linked by a set of social relationships (e.g., friendship, transfer of funds, overlapping membership) of a specified type (Laumman, Galaskiewicz and Marsden, 1978: 458)
Social Structure	Social Factors Wealth Income Level Ethnic background Education Status Social cohesion Social class (social rank)

This new stream of research in the Information Systems (IS) and Technology disciplinary area is very compatible and inline with the evolution of research in the marketing discipline regarding the adoption and profile of e-commerce users. Specifically, the focus of research in recent marketing studies has immigrated in investigating e-commerce users' profile and identifying other criteria than socio-demographic and IT attitudes/perceptions for segmenting online shoppers that go further and one level higher in explaining consumers' motivations and reasons for adopting and using Internet shopping. For example, studies such as Bhatnagar and Ghose (2002) and (2003), Kau, Tang, and Ghose (2003) provided evidence that profiling e-shopper segments based on benefits sought provide more effective marketing information than mere demographic profiling. Specifically, the studies investigated the issues, namely the important benefits that shoppers seek from online stores, the risks online shoppers perceive, and the performance of Webstores on these attributes. As a result, the following major findings were reported: (a) compared with other online purchase related attributes, getting the lowest price was not appeared to be a very important attribute for web shoppers (this finding may also indicate that prices on Websites are somewhat similar or higher, and consumers are moving on to other criteria to continue their evaluation process); (b) demographics do not discriminate between web buyers even though that has been the traditional focus with the Internet; and (c) there is also a large segment of web surfers that dislike buying on the Internet.

Within the context of tourism and hospitality, further research is required for investigating the validity of this research on online travellers. Results may differ depending on the type of tourism product purchase as well as on the cultural features and characteristics of online travellers (Christou & Sigala, 2003). The moderating effect of these variables should also be examined. By investigating the values/benefits sought by online travellers, more crucial and practical information will be revealed regarding the reasons for which online travellers are (de-)motivated to adopt e-commerce activities and the practices travel Webstores should engage in to increase

their adoption/use. Research on the benefits/value sought by travellers when using different distribution channels, e.g., Internet, call centers, travel agents, etc., is also valuable for predicting and investigating disintermediation effects, identifying criteria for travel market segmentation and for benefits that need to be met by distribution channels for satisfying their customers.

In the same vein as research in the IS and marketing context aim to investigate the value that motivates shopping behaviour, another recent stream of marketing studies also aim to identify e-shoppers' profile based on the experiential value that they seek from online shopping environments as well as the website design and functionality features that can significantly affect online adoption and behaviour. For example, Mathwick, Malhotra, and Rigdon (2001) used Holbrook's (1994) typology of experiential value for profiling online shoppers based on the shopping values (extrinsic/intrinsic) and activity (active/participative) that online consumers sought. Four online shoppers were identified: those seeking efficiency and economic value (i.e., customer return on investment); those seeking service excellence; those seeking escapism and enjoyment (i.e., playfulness); and those seeking visual appeal and entertainment (aesthetics). On the other hand, Eroglu, Machleit and Davis (2001) examined the atmospheric qualities of Webstores that can affect consumers' e-commerce adoption and behaviour. As a result a new stream of research has risen examining the impact and development of experiential Websites and sensory online features that can impact on induced arousal and pleasure and so, in turn, influence Website adoption and use (Menon & Kahn, 2002; Liang & Lai, 2002; Gretzel & Fesenmaier, 2003). The value, applicability and importance of such research in the context of tourism and hospitality promises several research opportunities and practical implications mainly due to the nature and features of the tourism product, i.e., very experiential and intangible. However, as research by Zahir, Dobbing, and Hunter (2002) illustrated, the cultural impact and differences among online shoppers should be considered and evaluated when investigating experiential issues. The type of the tourism product to be purchased as well as the personality traits (e.g., risk takers/averse, self-confidence) of online travellers may also have a significant intermediate or direct effect on the relation between experiential values and environmental cues with e-commerce adoption and use. Thus, in addition to conventional variables, Internet research is producing new constructs which, while irrelevant in traditional retail contexts, are very applicable to the e-shopping experience. One such construct is telepresence, which describes the extent to which consumers feel their existence in the virtual space (Schloerb, 1995). Overall, research into this area can provide more interesting results on the profile and reasons/factors for which online travellers patronize, use and purchase from particular travel Webstores or prefer other tourism distribution channels.

CONCLUSIONS: THEORETICAL FRAMEWORKS FOR STUDYING E-COMMERCE ADOPTION AND DIRECTIONS FOR FUTURE RESEARCH

In conclusion, it becomes evident that societal factors play a crucial role in e-commerce, as they form the general "context" or "environment" within which e-commerce takes place. In this vein, several studies have aimed to address and investigate the societal issues, e.g., demographic features, issues of trust, awareness and culture, affecting the adoption and use of e-commerce in general and in tourism and hospitality specifically. However, a comprehensive theoretical framework of societal factors that can be used for profiling and identifying online shoppers' characteristics and behaviour does not yet exist. To address this gap, Table 2 was produced for summarizing the social theories that have previously been applied for exploring Internet adoption and use. These theoretical frameworks can be adapted and further enhanced for developing robust research methodologies and investigat-

ing e-commerce adoption trends. Table 2 also illustrates the evolution and immigration of research from descriptive/demographic approaches to more diagnostic frameworks that offer more practical implications for designing effective Webstore functionalities and services.

Thus, unlike traditional demographic-based profiling studies, this paper has illustrated how vital and substantially crucial it is to understand the needs that consumers have with respect to being involved in e-commerce within the tourism and hospitality context. Diagnostic rather than merely descriptive information about online travellers should help tourism and hospitality firms make better decisions about their marketing strategies, segmentation and personalisation practices. Thus, in addition to demographics, tourism and hospitality marketers need to know the intrinsic as well as extrinsic benefits/value that e-shoppers seek when engaging in e-shopping as well as the atmospheric and environmental cues that can influence Webstore adoption and use. To achieve that, it is argued that future research should be benefited by adopting and using research from the environmental psychology and/or marketing servicescape theories that has already been applied in e-commerce. However, in addition to this stream of environmental psychology research, other under-utilised sub-fields of psychology can also be considered as potential explanatory paradigms of e-commerce adoption and use (Aldersey & Williams, 1996).

Specifically, psychophysics, for example, extends the field of ergonomics into the area of human visual and aural response and focuses on issues such as the legibility of typographic fonts on computer screens and desirable levels of brightness, colours, and contrasts. Cognitive psychology concerns itself with how we think, understand and remember and examines how best to present information and how much of it people can absorb. Finally, ecological psychology focuses on human perception and studies how individuals are affected by using the environment around them. All of these disciplines are full of constructs, which can enhance our understanding of how online atmospheric can affect e-commerce adoption, e-shoppers' online use and behaviour in Webstores.

TABLE 2. Theories for Investigating Societal Factors

Theories	Societal factors identified
Cultural Theory [e.g., Hofstede, 1994; Douglas,1978]	• Values and Beliefs • Communities • Awareness • Ideas and Attitudes • Community • Social Support • Social Networks
Socio-Cultural Theories [e.g., Piaget, 1928; Vygotsky, 1978]	• Social structure • Role • Social factors • Competition • Communities • Attitudes
Ethical Theories [e.g., Mason, 1995; Moor, 1985]	• Computer Crime • Responsibility • Professionalism • Anonymity • Trust • Free Speech
Cyberculture and Cyberpsychology [e.g., Turkle, 1995]	• Language • Linguistic • Anonymity • Identity Crisis • Free speech • Confidentiality • Trust • Computer Crime • Reliability
Diffusion of Innovation [e.g., Davies, 1979; Rogers, 1962]	• Competition • Economic • Government • Environmental • Roles • Social structure • Regulation/legislation • Cultural
Social Attitude Theories [e.g., Abelson, 1968; Heider, 1959; Triandis, 1971]	• Acceptance • Change • Attitudes • Ideas • TAM model • Competition • Roles • Social structure
Social Embeddedness [e.g., Granovetter, 1973; 1985]	• Social networks • Social capital • Social cohesion • Social support
Population Ecology [e.g., Hannah & Freeman, 1977]	• Acceptance level
Institutional Theory [e.g., DiMaggio & Powell, 1983; Zucker, 1987]	• Acceptance of business models • Diffusion of innovative business practices • The role of incubators in the adoption of particular business models

TABLE 2 (continued)

Theories	Societal factors identified
Stakeholder Theory [e.g., Freeman, 1984; Donaldson & Preston, 1995]	• Culture • Ethics • Decision-making • In-depth perspectives of decision makers
Environmental Psychology [e.g., Holbrook, 1994; Mehrabian & Rusell, 1974]	• Experiential value • Intrinsic/extrinsic shopping value • Passive/participative shopping behavior • Pleasure, Arousal, Dominance (PAD) emotional experience
Marketing theories for servicescape, atmospheric/ environmental cues/qualities [e.g., Baker, 1986; Bitner, 1992]	• Social, design and ambient factors • Ambient cues, layout and functionality, signs, symbols and artifacts • Structural, social, aesthetic visual elements

REFERENCES

Abelson, R. (1968). *Theories of Cognitive Consistency Theory*. Chicago: Rand McNally.

Aldersey-Williams, H.A. (1996). Interactivity with a human face. *MIT Technology Review*, February, 99 (3): 34-39.

Athiyaman, A. (2002). Internet users' intentions to purchase air travel online: An empirical investigation. *Marketing Intelligence & Planning*, 20 (4): 234-242.

Atkinson, M.A., & Kydd, C. (1997). Individual characteristics associated with WWW use: An empirical study of playfulness and motivation. *Data Base for Advances in Information Systems*, 28 (2): 53-62.

Baker, J. (1986). The role of environment in marketing services: The consumer perspective. In Czpeil, J.A., Congram, C., Shanaham, J. (eds.). *The Services Marketing Challenge: Integrated for Competitive Advantage*. Chicago: American Marketing Association, 1986, pp. 79-84.

Bhatnagar, A., & Ghose, S. (2004). A latent segmentation analysis of e-shoppers. *Journal of Business Research*, 57 (7): 758-767.

Bhatnagar, A., & Ghose, S. (2004). Segmenting consumers based on the benefits and risks of Internet shopping. *Journal of Business Research*, In press.

Bitner, M.J. (1992). Servicescapes: The impact of physical surroundings on customers and employees. *Journal of Marketing*, 56 (1): 57-71.

BizRate (1999). 75% of shoppers abandon carts. Cyberatlas. Available: *http://cyberatlas.internet.com/big-picture/demographics/article/0,1323,6061_230231,00.html* [08/11/1999].

Bonn, M.A., Furr, H.L., & Susskind, A.M. (1999). Predicting a behavioral profile for pleasure travelers based on the basis of Internet use segmentation. *Journal of Travel Research*, 37 (4): 333-340.

Botha, N., Small, B., Crutchley, P., & Wilson, J. (2001). Addressing the rural digital divide in the new Zealand. Wellington: MAFPolicy.

Brancheau, J.C., & Wetherbe, J.C. (1990). The adoption of Spreadsheet software: Testing innovation diffusion theory in the context of end-user computing. *Information Systems Research*, 1 (2): 115-143.

Brown, I. (2002). Individual and technological factors affecting perceived easy of use of web-based learning technologies in a developing country. *The Electronic Journal on Information Systems in Developing Countries*, 9 (5): 1-15.

Cass, A., & Fenech, T. (2003). Web retailing adoption: Exploring the nature of internet users Web retailing behaviour. *Journal of Retailing and Consumer Services*, 10: 81-94.

Christou, E., & Kassianidis, P. (2002). Examining the adoption of e-shopping for travel services: Determinants of perceptions. In K. Wober, A. Frew & M. Hitz (eds.). *Information and Communication Technologies in Tourism 2002* (pp. 55-64). Wien: Springer-Verlag.

Christou, E., & Sigala, M. (2003). Adoption of on-line shopping for holiday packages: A qualitative investigation. *1st Asia-Pacific CHRIE Conference: Hospitality & Tourism Research and Education*. Seoul, Korea: Hallym University, 21-23 May, 2003.

Corbitt, B., Thanasankit, T., & Yi, H. (2003). Trust and e-commerce: A study of computer perceptions. *Electronic Commerce Research and Applications*, 2 (3): 203-215.

Cullen, R. (2001). Addressing the digital divide. *Online Information Review*, 25 (5): 311-320.

Davies, S. (1979). *The Diffusion of Process Innovations*. Cambridge University Press.

Davis, F. (1989). Perceived usefulness, perceived easy of use and user acceptance of information technology, *MIS Quarterly*, 13 (3): 319-340.

Davis, F.D., Bagozzi, R.P., & Warshaw, P.R. (1992). Extrinsic and intrinsic motivation to use computers in the workplace. *Journal of Applied Social Psychology*, 22: 1111-1132.

DiMaggio, P.J., & Powell, W. (1983). The iron cage revisited: Institutional isomorphism and collective rationality in organizational fields. *American Sociological Review*, 48 (2): 147-160.

Donaldson, T., & Preston, L.E. (1995). The Stakeholder Theory of the Corporation: Concepts, evidence and implications. *Academy of Management Review*, 20 (1): 65-91.

Donthu, N., & Garcia, A. (1999). The Internet shopper. *Journal of Advertising Research*, May-June: 52-58.

Douglas, M. (1978). *Cultural Bias*. Occupational Paper 35. London: Royal Anthropological Institute.

Elder, V.B., Gardner, E.P., & Ruth, S.R. (1987). Gender and age in technostress: Effects on white-collar productivity. *Government Finance Review*, 3 (6): 17-21.

Eroglu, S., Machleit, K., & Davis, L. (2001). Atmospheric qualities of online retailing: a conceptual model and implications. *Journal of Business Research*, 54: 177-184.

Foley, P., Alfonso, X., & Ghani, S. (2002). The digital divide in a world city: A literature review and recommendations for research and strategy development to address the digital divide in London. London: Greater London Authority.

Freeman, R.E. (1984). *Strategic Management: A Stakeholder Approach*. Cambridge, MA: Ballinger.

Gartner Group (2000). The digital divide and American Society, *www3.gartner.com* [accessed 31/10/2000].

Granovetter, M.S. (1985). Economic Action and Social Structure: The Problem of Embeddedness. *American Journal of Sociology*, 91 (3): 481-510.

Granovetter, M.S. (1973). The strength of weak ties. *American Journal of Sociology*, 78 (6): 136-143.

Gretzel, U., & Fesenmaier, D. (2003). Experience-based Internet marketing: An exploratory study of sensory experiences associated with pleasure travel to the Midwest United States. In Frew, A., Hitz, M., & O'Connor, P. (eds). *Information and Communication Technologies in Tourism 2003*, pp. 49-57.

Gupta, S. (1996). The fourth WWW Consumer Survey. A Hermes Project, in collaboration with GVU Centre's 4th WWW User Survey. Available: *http://www.umich.edu/-sgupta/hermes* [06/06/1996].

GVU (1999). 10th WWW User Survey. Graphic, Visualisation and Usability Center. Available: *http://www.cc.gatech.edu/user_surveys/survey-1998-10/* [10/11/1999].

Hannan, M.T., & Freeman, J.H. (1977). The population ecology of organizations. *American Journal of Sociology*, 82: 929-964.

Harrison, A.W., & Rainer, R.K. (1992). The influence of individual differences on skill in end-user computing. *Journal of Management Information Systems*, 9 (1): 93-111.

Heider, F. (1959). *The Psychology of Interpersonal Relations*. New York: Wiley.

Heijden, van H. (2003). Factors influencing the usage of Websites: The case of a generic portal in the Netherlands. *Information & Management*, 40: 541-549.

Hoest, R. (2001). The European dimension of the digital economy. *INTERECONOMICS*, January/February: 44-50.

Hoffman, D., Novak, T., & Chatterjee, A. (1996). Commercial scenarios for the Web: Opportunities and challenges. In Kalakota, R. (ed.). *Readings in Electronic Commerce*, Addison-Wesley, pp. 29-53.

Hoffman, D., & Novak, T. (1999). The evolution of the digital divide: Examining the relationship of race to Internet access and usage over time. *Understanding the digital economy: Data, tools, and research*, Washington, USA.

Hoffman, D.L., Novak, T.P., & Peralta, M. (1999). Building consumer trust in online environments: The case for information privacy. *Communications of the ACM*, 42 (4): 80-85.

Hofstede, G. (1994). *Cultural Diversity in the Workplace*. Westport, CT: Quorum Books.

Holbrook, M. (1994). The nature of customer value: An axiology of services in the consumption experience. In Rust, R. and Oliver, R. (eds.). *Service Quality: New Dimensions in Theory and Practice*, Newbury Park, CA, Sage, pp. 21-71.

Igbaria, M. (1993). User acceptance of microcomputers technology: An empirical test. *OMEGA International Journal of Management Science*, 21 (1): 73-90.

Igbaria, M., & Chakrabati, A. (1990). Computer anxiety and attitudes towards microcomputer use. *Behaviour and Information Technology*, 9 (3): 229-241.

Jarvenpaa, S.L., Tractinsky, N., & Vitale, M. (2000). Consumer trust in an Internet store. *Information Technology and Management*, 1: 45-71.

Jennex, M., & Amoroso, D. (2002). e-Business and technology issues for developing countries: A Ukraine case study. *The Electronic Journal on Information Systems in Developing Countries*, 10 (5): 1-14.

Katz, J., & Aspden, P. (1997). Motivations for and barriers to Internet usage: Results of a national public opinion survey. *Internet Research: Electronic Networking Applications and Policy*, 7 (3): 170-188.

Kau, A., Tang, Y., & Ghose, S. (2003). Typology of online shoppers. *Journal of Consumer Marketing*, 20 (2): 139-156.

Kosiur, D. (1997). *Understanding Electronic Commerce*. Microsoft Press.

Kraut, R., Scherlis, W., Manning, J., Mukhopadhyay, T., & Kiesler, S. (1996). Home Net: A field trial of residential Internet services. *Communications of the ACM*, 30 (12): 232-249.

Laumman, E.O., Galaskiewicz, J. and Marsden, P.V. (1978). Community structure and inter-organizational linkages. *Annual Review of Sociology*, 4: 455-484.

Liang, T., & Lai, H. (2002). Effect of store design on consumer purchases: An empirical study of online bookstores. *Information & Management*, 39: 431-444.

Lynch, P.D., Kent, R.J., & Srinivasan, S.S. (2001). The global Internet shopper: Evidence from shopping tasks in 12 countries. *Journal of Advertising Research*, May/June: 15-23.

Mason, R. (1995). Applying Ethics to Information Technology Issues. *Communications of the ACM*, 38 (12): 55-57.

Mathwick, C., Malhotra, N., & Rigdon, E. (2001). Experiential value: Conceptualisation, measurement and application in the catalog and Internet shopping environment. *Journal of Retailing*, 77: 39-56.

Mehrabian, A., & Russell, J.A. (1974). *An approach to environmental psychology.* Cambridge, MA: MIT Press.

Menon, S., & Kahn, B. (2002). Cross-category effects of induced arousal and pleasure on the Internet shopping experience. *Journal of Retailing*, 78: 31-40.

Moor, J.H. (1985). What is Computer Ethics. *Metaphilosophy*, 16 (3): 266-275.

NVision (1999). Four out of 5 users never re-visit the average website. CyberAtlas. Available: *http://cyberatlas. internet.com/big_picture/demographics/article/0,1323, 5931_212071,00.html* [21/10/1999].

Papazafeiropoulou, A., & Pouloudi, A. (2001). Social issues in electronic commerce: Implications for policy makers. *Information Resources Management Journal*, Oct-Dec: 24-31.

Piaget, J. (1928). *Judgement and Reasoning in the Child.* New York: Harcourt Brace.

Pouloudi, A., Vassilopoulou, K., & Ziouvelou, X. (2002). Considering the societal implications in the adoption of e-business models. In Proceedings of ETHICOMP 2002–Lisbon, Portugal, 13-15 November.

Quay, R. (2001). Bridging the digital divide. *IN Planning* (American Planning Association), 67 (7): 12-17.

Qureshi, S., & Hoppel, C. (1995). Profiling computer predispositions. *Journal of Professional Services Marketing*, 12 (1): 73-83.

Rogers, P. (1962). *The diffusion of innovations.* New York: Free Press.

Schloerb, D.W. (1995). A quantitative measure of telepresence. *Presence, Teleoperators and Virtual Environment*, Winter, 24: 127-146.

Schmitt, J., & Wadsworth, J. (2002). *Give PCs a chance: Personal computer ownership and the digital divide in the United States and Great Britain.* Centre for Economic Performance, London School of Economics and Political Science, London.

Servon, L. (2002). Four myths about the digital divide. *IN Planning Theory and Practice*, 3 (2): 221-244.

Sexton, R., Johnson, R., & Hignite, M. (2002). Predicting Internet/e-commerce use. *Internet Research: Electronic Networking Applications and Policy*, 12 (5): 402-410.

Sigala, M. (2001). Modeling e-marketing strategies: Internet presence and exploitation of Greek hotels. *Journal of Travel & Tourism Marketing*, 11 (2/3): 83-103.

Sigala, M. (2002). The impact of multimedia on employment patterns in Small and Medium Hospitality and Tourism Enterprises (SMTHEs) in UK. *Information Technology and Tourism*, 4 (3/4): 175-189.

Straub, D., Keil, M., & Brenner, W. (1997). Testing the TAM across cultures: A three country study. *Information & Management*, 33 (1): 1-11.

Teo, T. (2001). Demographic and motivation variables associated with Internet usage activities. *Internet Research: Electronic Networking Applications and Policy*, 11 (2): 125-137.

Teo, T.S., Lim, V.K., & Lai, R.Y. (1999). Intrinsic and extrinsic motivation in Internet usage. *Omega, International Journal of Management Science*, 27: 25-37.

Travel Industry Association of America. (2002). Online travel booking jumps in 2002, despite plateau in online travel planning. Retrieved December 17, 2002, from *www.tia.org/Press/pressrec.asp*.

Travel Industry Association of America. (2001). *E-travel consumers–How they plan and buy leisure travel online* (Research report). Washington, DC: Travel Industry Association of America.

Triandis, H. (1971). *Attitude and Attitude Change.* New York: Wiley.

Turkle, S. (1995). *Life on the Screen: Identity in the Age of the Internet.* New York: Simon & Schuster.

Visa Europe (2003, May 20). Online spending in Europe doubles. *Press & Media.* Available: *http://www. visaeu.com/press_release/press154.html* [10/06/03].

Vygotsky, L.S. (1978). *Mind in Society: The Development of Higher Psychological Processes.* Harvard University Press.

Weber, K., & Roehl, W.S. (1999). Profiling people searching for and purchasing travel products on the World Wide Web. *Journal of Travel Research*, 37 (3): 291-298.

Wee, K.N.L., & Ramachandra, R. (2000). Cyberbuying in China, Hong Kong and Singapore: Tracking the who, where, why and what of online buying. *International Journal of Retail & Distribution Management*, 28 (7): 307-316.

Wynter, L. (1996). Business and race: Survey of black hackers shows an elite audience. *Wall Street Journal*, March 6, p. B1.

Zahir, S., Dobbing, B., & Hunter, M. (2002). Cross-cultural dimensions of Internet portals. *Internet Research: Electronic Networking Applications and Policy*, 12 (3): 210-220.

Zeffane, R., & Cheek, B. (1993). Profiles and correlates of computer usage: A study of the Australian telecommunications industry. *Computers in Industry*, 22: 53-69.

Zucker, L.G. (1987). Institutional theories of organization. *Annual Review of Sociology*, 13: 443-464.

SECTION 3:
PERCEPTION AND QUALITY OF ONLINE LODGING AND TRAVEL BRANDS

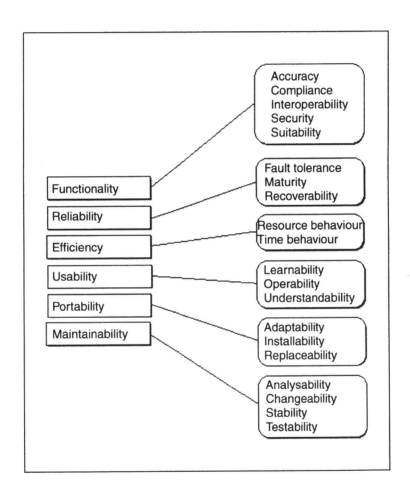

Quality Measures in IT and Software Development
Adapted from: Evaluation according to predefined quality models.
Available: *www.cse.dcu.ie/essiscope/sm4/services.html*

Comparison of Web Service Quality Between Online Travel Agencies and Online Travel Suppliers

Woo Gon Kim
Hae Young Lee

SUMMARY. The purpose of this study is to: (1) identify the underlying dimensions of Web service quality between online travel agencies and online travel suppliers; and (2) compare the magnitude of Web service quality dimensions between online travel agencies and online travel suppliers in explaining the overall level of customer satisfaction. The study found that online travel agencies and online travel suppliers share similar commonalities with regard to *information content, reputation and security, structure and ease of use*, and *usefulness* commonly derived dimensions of Web service quality. *Information content* was found to be the most important dimension of online travel agencies in explaining the overall level of customer satisfaction while *structure and ease of use* was thought of as the most important dimension of online travel suppliers. *[Article copies available for a fee from The Haworth Document Delivery Service: 1-800-HAWORTH. E-mail address: <docdelivery@haworthpress.com> Website: <http://www.HaworthPress.com> © 2004 by The Haworth Press, Inc. All rights reserved.]*

KEYWORDS. Web service quality, online travel agencies, online travel suppliers

INTRODUCTION

The development of Web technologies has provoked cut-throat competition between online travel agencies and online travel suppliers (Zellner, 2002). Within this study, online travel agencies are defined as travel agencies providing value-added travel services to potential customers only through the Web interface such as Expedia.com and Travelocity.com. While, online travel suppliers are defined as major airline companies and hotel companies providing their own travel re-sources to potential customers through the Web along with their traditional distribution channels. Major travel suppliers such as American Airlines are changing their Web-based business model and targeting their customers directly in order to minimize operating costs and realize profit while bypassing traditional travel agencies. This is because the Web removes the traditional physical limitations and allows online travel suppliers to communicate with customers directly (Lewis, Semeijn, & Talalaevsky, 1998; Maselli, 2002). This means that online travel agencies are not only enter-

Woo Gon Kim is Assistant Professor, School of Hotel and Restaurant Administration, Oklahoma State University. Hae Young Lee is a PhD candidate, School of Hotel and Restaurant Administration, Oklahoma State University.
Address correspondence to Woo Gon Kim (E-mail: kwoo@okstate.edu).

[Haworth co-indexing entry note]: "Comparison of Web Service Quality Between Online Travel Agencies and Online Travel Suppliers." Kim, Woo Gon, and Hae Young Lee. Co-published simultaneously in *Journal of Travel & Tourism Marketing* (The Haworth Hospitality Press, an imprint of The Haworth Press, Inc.) Vol. 17, No. 2/3, 2004, pp. 105-116; and: *Handbook of Consumer Behavior, Tourism, and the Internet* (ed: Juline E. Mills, and Rob Law) The Haworth Hospitality Press, an imprint of The Haworth Press, Inc., 2004, pp. 105-116. Single or multiple copies of this article are available for a fee from The Haworth Document Delivery Service [1-800-HAWORTH, 9:00 a.m. - 5:00 p.m. (EST). E-mail address: docdelivery@haworthpress.com].

ing into competition with offline travel agencies, but must also cope with the increasing competition from online travel suppliers (Zellner, 2002).

Given that the needs of online customers are diverse, if online travel agencies and online travel suppliers can find a way to meet the needs of customers exactly, the Web can be a great opportunity for both of them. Therefore, it is very important to understand each other's similarities and differences in Web service quality as perceived by customers. A better understanding would enable online travel agencies and travel suppliers to apply specialized service strategies to retain existing customers and attract potential customers at the same time (De Ruyter, Wetzels, & Kleijnen, 2001; Yang & Jun, 2002).

Much research has been done concerning Web service quality of travel-related businesses, nevertheless, there is a lack of research comparing Web service quality between online travel agencies and online travel suppliers. Therefore, the aim of this study is to: (1) identify the underlying dimensions of Web service quality between online travel agencies and online travel suppliers; and (2) compare the magnitude of Web service quality dimensions between online travel agencies and online travel suppliers in explaining the overall level of customer satisfaction. The results of this study will provide meaningful implications to operators and marketers of both online travel agencies and online travel suppliers.

LITERATURE REVIEW

Web Service Quality

Much research has been conducted to identify the crucial dimensions of Web service quality affecting customer satisfaction. A measure of Web service quality is important to successful Web marketing because it helps to estimate efficiencies of the Web. Donthu (2001) developed SITEQUAL to measure the perceived quality of an Internet shopping site. It can be divided into two major groups: site-related factors (ease of use, aesthetic design, processing speed, and security) and vendor-related factors (competitive value, clarity

of ordering, corporate and brand e-quality, product uniqueness, and product quality assurance). Rather than one outstanding attribute, Donthu (2001) pointed out that all nine dimensions are of equal importance, and no one dimension can be ignored if the overall goal is to maximize Web service quality.

Based on the two major dimensions of service quality by Garvin (1991) and Berry and Parasuraman (1991), Madu and Madu (2002) identified 15 dimensions for e-quality: performance, features, structure, aesthetics, reliability, storage capability, serviceability, security and system integrity, trust, responsiveness, product/ service differentiation and customization, Web store policies, reputation, assurance, and empathy. Madu and Madu (2002) also suggested that identified dimensions can be united according to the discretion of the individual researchers, because some of the dimensions may be closely associated with each other.

Hanna and Millar (1997) suggested that page design, managerial issues and information content should be discussed as three main categories to develop a Website. Hanna and Millar (1997) pointed out that every online business should keep Web information current and respond to customer information requests in a timely manner. Spiliopoulou (2000) stated that content, Web page design, and overall site design are three factors influencing the way customers perceive and evaluate a Website. Spiliopoulou (2000) mentioned that knowledge about the needs of potential customers and the ability to build personalized Web service satisfying these needs are essential to winning a competitive race. The Web should be personalized according to the requirements of each customer and customer navigation patterns.

Additional support can be found by Yang and Jun (2002), who suggested that personalization and access are common important dimensions of e-service quality between Internet purchasers and Internet non-purchasers. They also pointed out that while Internet purchasers think of the reliability dimension as the most important, Internet non-purchasers consider the security dimension to be the most important in explaining overall service quality assessment.

Web Service Quality Related to Travel and Tourism

Kaynama and Black (2000) introduced E-QUAL to measure Web service quality dimensions of online travel agencies. Based on SERVQUAL, E-QUAL has seven dimensions: content and purpose, accessibility, navigation, design and presentation, responsiveness, background, personalization and customization. They pointed out more detailed attributes such as easy-to-use interface, currency and accuracy of contents, and personalized e-mail response are needed for customer satisfaction. They also mentioned that in order to not be left behind by the competitors, online travel agencies should think of navigation and design as well as responsiveness as desperately needed dimensions.

Chu (2001) conducted focus group interviews to identify Internet user needs and expectations toward airline/travel Websites. He mentioned that customers expect informative, interactive, and attractive features from airline/travel Websites. Walle (1996) stated that ease of use is important to travel and tourism marketing and that advances in security would change the trends of facilitating the Web.

Law and Leung (2000) investigated airline's online reservation services on the Internet to determine whether there are any differences between the Web services provided by three regions. They indicated that product information, product pricing, online ordering information, extra benefits, fast loading speed, and the additional services or facilities are primary attributes contributing to a successful airline Website. They also pointed out that the efficiency in terms of processing time could make customers revisit a Website and purchase air tickets directly via the Web.

Jeong and Lambert (2001) suggested that a conceptual framework is needed for measuring information quality on lodging Websites. They mentioned that perceived usefulness and attitudes are two major determinants of information quality on lodging Websites. They also pointed out that perceived usefulness is the most influential variable affecting customers' perceived Web behavior: intention to use information, information use, and recommendation.

Consequently, based on the above literature review, several important dimensions of Web service quality were explored in this study. Table 1 presents brief definitions for six dimensions of Web service quality adapted from previous research. First, *ease of use* related to the Website structure and navigation was explored as a dimension of Web service quality, because it revealed that *ease of use* influences the initial decision to use a certain Website (Adams, Nelson, & Todd, 1992; Madu & Madu, 2002). Second, much research revealed that if online customers perceive a particular Website to be useful, they would be more satisfied and have a positive attitude (Adams et al., 1992; Bhattacherjee, 2001; Jeong & Lambert, 2001). Following this line of reasoning, *usefulness* was included and explored. Third, based on the notion that *Information content* influences the online customers' potential

TABLE 1. Dimensions of Web Service Quality

Dimensions	Definition	Source/reference
Ease of use	the degree to which a user believes that using the Internet would be free of effort	Donthu (2001), Jeong and Lambert (2001), Madu and Madu (2002)
Usefulness	the degree to which a user believes that using the Internet would be better than using the other competing ways	Jeong and Lambert (2001)
Information content	the degree to which a user believes that contents of the Websites are reliable	Jeong and Lambert (2001), Kaynama and Black (2000)
Security	the degree to which a user believes that using the Internet would be safe when processing sensitive personal information	Kaynama and Black (2000), Madu and Madu (2002)
Responsiveness	the degree to which a user believes that the promised service would be performed accurately and in a timely manner	Kaynama and Black (2000), Madu and Madu (2002)
Personalization	the degree to which a user believes that the individualized attention to user concerns and requests would be provided	Kaynama and Black (2000), Madu and Madu (2002)

buying behavior (Chu, 2001; Jeong & Lambert, 2001; Standing, 2000), *Information content* was included. In reality, *information content* is the essence of the Web service (Lederer, Maupin, Sena, & Zhuang, 2000). Fourth, *security* was also explored as a dimension of Web service quality, because security is one of the major obstacles of the Web-based transactions. If online customers could not have a sense of security when they process sensitive personal information, they are not willing to provide their personal information and to purchase any more (Madu & Madu, 2002; Suh & Han, 2002). Lastly, under the notion of differentiation, *responsiveness* and *personalization* were explored. Since both online travel agencies and travel suppliers provide basically the same reservation services, it is difficult to differentiate their online services each other (Kaynama & Black, 2000). Therefore, by providing quick and personalized attention to customer request, online businesses could make their customers more satisfied and have an intention to purchase (Madu & Madu, 2002).

Based on the above summary of Web service quality dimensions, this study attempts to answer the following research questions: (1) Are there any differences in the dimensions of Web service quality between online travel agencies and online travel suppliers? (2) Which dimensions of Web service quality between online travel agencies and online travel suppliers are more important in explaining the overall level of customer satisfaction?

METHODOLOGY

Research Instrument

A questionnaire was developed based on a comprehensive review of the tourism and Web service quality literature. The dimensions devised by Madu and Madu (2002), Donthu (2001), Kaynama and Black (2000), and attributes suggested by Jeong and Lambert (2001), and Law and Leung (2000) were used as a foundation to derive the measurements used in this study. The questionnaire was originally written in English, and the English version was translated into Korean. The Korean version was translated by the researchers to-

gether with two other native Korean speaking marketing managers working in Korea's tourism industry. In order to facilitate the respondents' clear understanding of both online travel agencies and online travel suppliers, the detailed definitions of online travel agencies and online travel suppliers were illustrated in the questionnaire with their specific examples.

The questionnaire was divided into two sections. The first section of the questionnaire contained 30 attributes concerning the Web service quality of online travel agencies and online travel suppliers. The respondents were requested to evaluate the performance of each Web service quality attribute based on their overall past experience using a five-point Likert-type scale ranging from strongly disagree (1) to strongly agree (5). A final question was asked about the overall level of customer satisfaction with Web service quality (1 = extremely dissatisfied, 5 = extremely satisfied). The second section of the questionnaires asked about the respondents' demographic background, such as gender, age, marital status, education level, and occupation. Thirty questionnaires were distributed for the purpose of pre-testing the questionnaire contents to 30 members of the travel-related online community in August 2002. Of the 30 questionnaires, 22 were returned. Based on the comments collected during the pilot test period, some modifications of the questionnaire were made and a complete questionnaire was developed.

Data Collection

This survey was conducted at the Kimpo Airport, Seoul, South Korea, from September 10, 2002 to October 11, 2002. A non-probability sampling method was used to select the samples. Data for the study were collected from departing Korean travelers. Every 20th traveler immediately after entering the departure lounge gate of the Kimpo Airport was interviewed at various times of the day on four weekdays and the weekends over a four-week period. Every effort was made to achieve a representative sample. Respondents were approached and informed about the purpose of the study in advance of being given the questionnaire. At the beginning of the questionnaire, one screening question was asked to identify whether or not the respondents had purchased any travel-related products or services from both online travel agencies and online travel suppliers through the Web within the last 12 months. The respondents were asked to complete both sections of the self-administered questionnaire. A total of 600 Korean travelers were approached, of which 376 (62.7%) responded and completed the questionnaires. Of the 376 returned questionnaires, 34 were discarded because they were not fully completed and 342 questionnaires were retained for further data analysis.

Analysis

The data analysis was completed in three steps. First, the paired samples *t*-test was used to examine any significant difference in the overall level of customer satisfaction between online travel agencies and online travel suppliers. Second, two factor analyses with varimax rotation were conducted to derive the underlying factors of the 30 Web service quality attributes. Principal component factors with eigenvalues of 1.0 or greater were rotated by the varimax analysis. Only factor loadings of 0.4 or higher were retained, indicating good correlations between the items and the factors to which they belonged (Hair, Anderson, Tatham, & Black, 1995). To test the reliability and internal consistency of each factor, Cronbach's Alpha of each factor was determined and the factors with Alpha of 0.6 were retained for further analysis (Kline, 1994). Third, two multiple regression analyses were used to compare the magnitude of Web service quality dimensions between online travel agencies and online travel suppliers in contributing to the overall level of customer satisfaction. Factors extracted in the factor analysis were used as the independent variables, and the overall level of customer satisfaction was the dependent variable. Factor scores were used to avoid the multicollinearity effect of the model due to the possibility of high correlations among independent variables (Kline, 1994). The stepwise method was used to rank the factors with various degrees of significance in order of importance by the Beta coefficients.

RESULTS

Respondents' Demographic Profile

As shown in Table 2, of the 342 respondents, 54.7% were male and 45.3% were female. Almost 66% of the respondents were aged between 28 and 37, and 22.5% were aged between 38 and 47. The majority of the respondents (64.9%) were single, while 35.1% were married. In terms of education level, 62.6% of the respondents received a four-year degree, while 15.5% of the respondents had completed two years of college. The survey also indicated that owner/partner represented the largest group of the respondents (32.8%), followed by professional (24.3%), and white-collar (21.1%). With the exception of occupation, other demographic categories of this study were very similar to that reported in 2002 Korea Internet White Paper. Therefore, the sample of this study was reasonably representative of general Internet users in South Korea.

TABLE 2. Descriptive Characteristics of Respondents (n = 342)

Variable	Frequency	Percentage
Gender		
Male	187	54.7
Female	155	45.3
Age		
18-27	36	10.5
28-37	225	65.8
38-47	77	22.5
48-57	4	1.2
58 or older	0	0
Marital status		
Married	120	35.1
Single	222	64.9
Education level		
High school	47	13.7
2-year college	53	15.5
4-year college/university	214	62.6
Graduate school	28	8.2
Occupation		
Owner/partner	112	32.8
White-collar	72	21.1
Professional	83	24.3
Housewife	19	5.6
Student	39	11.4
Other	17	5.0

Comparing the Overall Level of Satisfaction

The paired samples *t*-test was used to examine any significant difference in the overall level of customer satisfaction between online travel agencies and online travel suppliers, because the research design for this study involved measuring each subject twice: for online travel agencies and again for online travel suppliers. From Table 3, the *t*-value was 5.483 ($p < .001$), indicating that there was a statistically significant overall satisfaction difference between online travel agencies and online travel suppliers. The mean difference and standard deviation were −.19 (3.01-3.20) and .63, respectively. The mean of online travel suppliers reported having significantly higher than did online travel agencies.

Underlying Dimensions of Web Service Quality

A factor analysis was performed on the Web service quality attributes of online travel agencies to find the underlying dimensions. The Alpha coefficients ranged from .67 to .81, indicating that variables were considered to be internally consistent (Hair et al., 1995). A total of 20 attributes from the factor analysis resulted in five factors and explained 62.8% of the variance.

As shown in Table 4, the five factors identified with online travel agencies were *structure and ease of use, information content, responsiveness and personalization, reputation and security,* and *usefulness.* Factor 1, *structure and ease of use,* contained six items and explained 36.1% of the variance in the data, with an eigenvalue of 7.11. The six items were ease

of getting an overview of the structure, consistency of the structure, ease of navigation, ease of online reservation, ease of online cancellation, and overall Web speed. Factor 2, *information content,* was composed of three items and explained 7.7% of the variance in the data, with an eigenvalue of 1.53. The three items were accuracy of travel information, conciseness of travel information, and currency of travel information. Factor 3, *responsiveness and personalization,* was loaded with four items and explained 6.9% of the variance in the data, with an eigenvalue of 1.37. The four items were individualized attention to customer concerns, e-mail service, personalized information for repeat customers, and reply to customer reservations. Factor 4, *reputation and security,* referred to three items and explained 6.1% of the variance in the data, with an eigenvalue of 1.23. The three items were level of recognition of brand image, security for online purchase, and reliability of travel information. Factor 5, *usefulness,* contained four items and explained 6.1% of the variance in the data, with an eigenvalue of 1.22. The four items were variety of discount offering, variety of online purchase, variety of price comparison, and hyperlinks to relevant Websites.

Using the same process for the Web service quality attributes of online travel suppliers, four factors were identified and explained 59.6% of the variance. The Alpha coefficients ranged from .60 to .82. The four factors with online travel suppliers, as shown in Table 5, embraced *information content, structure and ease of use, reputation and security,* and *usefulness.* Factor 1, *information content,* included five items and explained

TABLE 3. The Paired Samples t-Test Result of the Overall Level of Satisfaction Between Online Travel Agencies and Online Travel Suppliers

	Mean Scores		Mean difference (Standard Deviation)	t-value	Sig. (2-tailed)
	Online travel agencies	Online travel suppliers			
Overall satisfaction	3.01	3.20	−.19 (.63)	5.483	.000

Based on mean value on a five-point Likert-type scale. where 1 = extremely dissatisfied, 3 = neutral, 5 = extremely satisfied.
Mean difference (Online travel agencies − Online travel suppliers).

TABLE 4. The Dimensions of Web Service Quality of Online Travel Agencies

Cronbach's Alpha	Variables	Factor Loading	Eigen Value	Variance Explained (%)
	FACTOR 1: *Structure and ease of use*			
	Ease of getting an overview of the structure	.703		
	Consistency of the structure	.666		
.80	Ease of navigation	.654	7.11	36.1
	Ease of online reservation	.527		
	Ease of online cancellation	.515		
	Overall Web speed	.502		
	FACTOR 2: *Information content*			
	Accuracy of travel information	.789		
.81	Conciseness of travel information	.759	1.53	7.7
	Currency of travel information	.712		
	FACTOR 3: *Responsiveness and personalization*			
	Individualized attention to customer concerns	.831		
.77	E-mail service	.661	1.37	6.9
	Personalized information for repeat customers	.563		
	Reply to customer reservation	.554		
	FACTOR 4: *Reputation and security*			
	Level of recognition of brand image	.787		
.79	Security for online purchase	.752	1.23	6.1
	Reliability of travel information	.558		
	FACTOR 5: *Usefulness*			
	Variety of discount offering	.733		
.67	Variety of online purchase	.693	1.22	6.1
	Variety of price comparison	.515		
	Hyperlinks to relevant Websites	.421		
	Total variance explained			62.8

TABLE 5. The Dimensions of Web Service Quality of Online Travel Suppliers

Cronbach's Alpha	Variables	Factor Loading	Eigen Value	Variance Explained (%)
	FACTOR 1: *Information content*			
	Accuracy of travel information	.797		
	Currency of travel information	.583		
.78	Conciseness of travel information	.578	6.48	38.1
	Uniqueness of travel information	.572		
	Variety of travel information	.486		
	FACTOR 2: *Structure and ease of use*			
	Consistency of the structure	.746		
	Ease of getting an overview of the structure	.679		
.82	Ease of navigation	.670	1.36	8.0
	Ease of online reservation	.494		
	Ease of online cancellation	.428		
	FACTOR 3: *Reputation and security*			
	Level of recognition of brand image	.727		
.70	Security for online purchase	.686	1.19	7.0
	Security for providing personal information	.633		
	Reliability of travel information	.502		
	FACTOR 4: *Usefulness*			
	Variety of discount offering	.729		
.60	Variety of price comparison	.696	1.22	6.1
	Hyperlinks to relevant Websites	.570		
	Total variance explained			59.6

38.1% of the variance in the data, with an eigenvalue of 6.48. The five items were accuracy of travel information, currency of travel information, conciseness of travel information, uniqueness of travel information, and variety of travel information. Factor 2, *structure and ease of use*, contained five items and explained 8.0% of the variance in the data, with an eigenvalue of 1.36. The five items were consistency of the structure, ease of getting an overview of the structure, ease of navigation, ease of online reservation, and ease of online cancellation. Factor 3, *reputation and security*, was composed of four items and explained 7.0% of the variance in the data, with an eigenvalue of 1.19. The four items were level of recognition of brand image, security for online purchase, security for providing personal information, and reliability of travel information. Factor 4, *usefulness*, was loaded with three items and explained 6.1% of the variance in the data, with an eigenvalue of 1.22. The three items were variety of discount offering, variety of price comparison, and hyperlinks to relevant Websites.

Comparing the Magnitude of Web Service Quality Dimensions

Two multiple regression analyses were used to compare the magnitude of Web service quality dimensions between online travel agencies and online travel suppliers in contributing the overall level of customer satisfaction. The adjusted R^2 values of online travel agencies and online travel suppliers were .538 and .413, respectively, which indicates that approximately 53.8% and 41.3% of the variation in the dependent variables could be explained by the regression equations. F-values of both equations were 37.52 ($p < .001$) and 29.85 ($p < .001$), which explains that the results of the regression equations could hardly have occurred by chance. Therefore, the regression equations achieved a satisfactory level of goodness of fit in predicting the variance of the overall level of customer satisfaction in relation to the dimensions examined in the factor analysis. In other words, at least one of the factors identified in the factor analysis

was important in contributing to the overall level of satisfaction.

From Table 6, it was observed that all five independent variables were statistically significant ($p < .001$). The Beta coefficients of each variable reflect the relative importance of variables in the regression equation. It indicated that the information content factor (Beta = .419) had the strongest impact on the overall level of customer satisfaction with the Web service quality of online travel agencies, followed by the reputation and security factor (Beta = .337), the usefulness factor (Beta = .320), the responsiveness and personalization factor (Beta = .284), and the structure and ease of use factor (Beta = .284).

From Table 7, it can be also noted that the structure and ease of use factor (Beta = .473) was the most important factor in explaining the overall level of customer satisfaction with the Web service quality of online travel suppliers, followed by the information content factor (Beta = .332), the usefulness factor (Beta = .281), and the reputation and security factor (Beta = .123).

DISCUSSION AND IMPLICATIONS

The online customers' satisfaction level between online travel agencies and online travel suppliers was compared. The overall level of customer satisfaction in Web service indicated a significant difference between online travel

TABLE 6. Regression Results: Factors Affecting Customer Satisfaction of Online Travel Agencies

Variable	Stepwise regression Standardized Beta Coefficient	*t*	Sig.
Information content	.419	7.717	.000
Reputation and security	.337	6.214	.000
Usefulness	.320	5.901	.000
Responsiveness and personalization	.284	5.228	.000
Structure and ease of use	.284	5.225	.000

Dependent Variable: the overall level of customer satisfaction with the Web service quality of online travel agencies.
Only variables significant at the .05 level or better are listed.
Note: F = 37.524; Sig. = .000; R^2 = .552; Adjusted R^2 = .538.

TABLE 7. Regression Results: Factors Affecting Customer Satisfaction of Online Travel Suppliers

Variable	Stepwise regression Standardized Beta Coefficient	t	Sig.
Structure and ease of use	.473	7.901	.000
Information content	.332	5.543	.000
Usefulness	.281	4.693	.000
Reputation and security	.123	2.055	.042

Dependent Variable: the overall level of customer satisfaction with the Web service quality of online travel suppliers.
Only variables significant at the .05 level or better are listed.
Note: $F = 29.847$; Sig. $= .000$; $R^2 = .427$; Adjusted $R^2 = .413$.

agencies and online travel suppliers. More specifically, online customers showed that the satisfaction level of the online travel suppliers was perceived to be much higher than that of the online travel agencies. In turn, satisfied customers are more likely to stay on the Web with a positive attitude, while dissatisfied customers may switch to an alternative service provider (Bhattacherjee, 2001).

Although the combination of attributes was slightly different between online travel agencies and online travel suppliers, the four Web service quality dimensions (*information content, structure and ease of use, reputation and security,* and *usefulness*) were found to have a significantly positive relationship with customer satisfaction. The results of the study showed also that there are some differences in the dimensions of Web service quality between online travel agencies and online travel suppliers in explaining the overall level of customer satisfaction.

A somewhat surprising result was that *responsiveness and personalization* was not derived as an important dimension of online travel suppliers, although much research revealed it is one of the most important Web service quality dimensions (Griffith & Krampf, 1998; Hanna & Millar, 1997; Kaynama & Black, 2000; Spiliopoulou, 2000; Yang & Jun, 2002). One plausible conclusion is that customers consider online travel suppliers to be a Website for comparing prices rather than to be a Website for personalized Web service. In other words, the customers search the Websites of online travel suppliers when they cannot

find what they want to acquire from online travel agencies. However, this tentative conclusion leaves more to be investigated and answered in the light of further research.

It is noteworthy that *information content* had a significantly positive effect on customer satisfaction between online travel agencies and online travel suppliers. *Information content* is absolutely essential for attracting and retaining customers, because it influences the customers' potential buying behavior (Chu, 2001; Jeong & Lambert, 2001; Standing, 2000). The customers' intention of using the Web is either to get information or to purchase travel-related products or services. If they are not satisfied with the Web service at the stage of searching for information due to the low quality of information content (e.g., inaccuracy, inconsistency, incompleteness, etc.), the customers will not make a purchase (Jeong & Lambert, 2001; Yang & Jun, 2002).

While *reputation and security* was the second most important dimension affecting the overall level of customer satisfaction with Web service quality of online travel agencies, it was the least important dimension of online travel suppliers. The observed differences in the relative importance could be explained by the relative level of recognition of brand image between online travel agencies and online travel suppliers. The customers generally have a high degree of confidence in the information they receive through the Web; however, they are often concerned about the risk related to online purchase (Walle, 1996). Although some of the online travel agencies have a high level of brand image recognition, since online travel agencies do not exist in the traditional travel market and do not provide offline services to customers, their customers want to know whether or not a certain online travel agency is trustworthy (Madu & Madu, 2002; Standing, 2000). Contrarily, most online travel suppliers exist in traditional travel markets and give offline service to customers, so customers are less concerned about the risk regarding online purchase in online travel suppliers. It could be because the promoted level of brand image would minimize their customers' concerns in regard to purchasing travel-related products or services (Madu & Madu, 2002; Yang & Jun, 2002). Therefore, online travel agencies should persevere more in their efforts to keep and improve the level of brand image recognition than do online travel suppliers. In addition, online travel agencies may need to ensure that all customer information would be saved safely and would not be used for any other purposes.

Although the result of this study showed that its relative importance was not equal, *usefulness* exerted a significant impact on the overall level of customer satisfaction with Web service quality of both online travel agencies and online travel suppliers. *Usefulness* refers to the degree to which using a Website would enhance benefits for customers' decision-making. When customers perceive a Website as useful, they will recommend the Website to others and keep using that Website (Jeong & Lambert, 2001). Much research also revealed that *usefulness* affects the customers' real usage (Adams, Nelson, & Todd, 1992; Davis, 1989; De Ruyter et al., 2001; Jeong & Lambert, 2001).

Of special interest is that the importance of *structure and ease of use* had quite the opposite trend. That is, while *structure and ease of use* was the least important dimension affecting the overall level of customer satisfaction with Web service quality of online travel agencies, it was also thought of as the most important dimension of online travel suppliers. Here, structure means making information ready in such a way that it can be accessed quickly and efficiently (Gloor, 2000). The observed differences in the relative importance of *structure and ease of use* could be rooted from the contrasting evolution history of the Web-based business model. In the early stage of Web utilization, the Websites of online travel suppliers were primarily used as another means of delivering information about the companies, products, and services, because they already established a physical (off-line) channel of distribution. Of course, nowadays, it is quite natural for online travel suppliers to use the Web as a means of facilitating transactions through value-added features (Angehrn & Meyer, 1997; Doolin, Burgess, & Cooper, 2002; Walle, 1996). In the process of evolution, however, online suppliers were relatively less concerned about the consistency and ease of use than about information quality (Law & Leung, 2000). On the other hand, since the

Websites of online travel agencies were originated to make a profit through Web-based transactions with customers, the information structure and the Web-based transaction structure were equipped with the features of consistency and ease of use to complete Web-based transactions (Kaynama & Black, 2000).

In addition, the lack of *consistency and ease of use* between information structure and Web-based transaction structure could be partly attributed to the inefficient outsourcing practices of Korean online travel suppliers. Most Korean online travel suppliers outsourced some of their Web management for the purpose of overcoming the limited range of products and services in the process of adopting Web-based transactions features. In this case, it is normally anticipated that outsourcing would help to efficiently manage the business. However, since certain outsourcing practices of Korean online travel suppliers were not properly managed by the systematic business strategy, the sizable number of Websites of Korean online travel suppliers failed to provide the customers with easy to use features. Therefore, it is essential that they find the best fit between their goals and their outsourcing (Law & Leung, 2000).

CONCLUSIONS

This study has attempted to identify the underlying dimensions of Web service quality between online travel agencies and online travel suppliers and to compare the magnitude of Web service quality dimensions between online travel agencies and online travel suppliers in explaining the overall level of customer satisfaction. The findings of this study indicate that *information content* is a commonly important Web service quality dimension of both online travel agencies and online travel suppliers. Travel-related businesses are highly dependent on accurate and current information, which draws potential customers to the site (Standing, 2000). Therefore, it is essential that both online travel agencies and online travel suppliers improve *information content* presented on the Web before providing a Web-based transaction and reservation service to their customers.

Two of the most important conclusions that may be drawn from this study are differences of the relative importance of *reputation and security* and *structure and ease of use* between online travel agencies and online travel suppliers in explaining the overall level of customer satisfaction. While online travel agencies need to improve *reputation and security* rather than other Web service quality dimensions (*structure and ease of use, responsiveness and personalization, and usefulness*), online travel suppliers need to improve *structure and ease of use* by integrating their Web resources. Since online travel agencies and online travel suppliers may have a different target segment, marketers should develop differentiated marketing strategies and Website designers should consider those discriminating factors while establishing and updating their Websites.

Limitations

As with all studies, this study has its limitations. First, this study encompassed only Korean online travelers. Since the respondents may possess certain cultural attributes that differ from those people in other countries, generalizations of the present findings should be cautioned. Therefore, more diversified random samples to verify the relative importance should be used in future research. Second, this study was based on respondents' subjective perceptions to identify the level of overall satisfaction. Since a subjective perception does not always accurately reflect actual purchase behavior, a longitudinal design should be used that includes measures of actual purchase. Lastly, this study did not include various demographic, behavioral, and travel-related variables, such as type of travel, size of party, number of online purchases, income, etc., to examine the difference of customers between online travel agencies and online travel suppliers. However, this information could provide more meaningful insight to the results. Therefore, various demographic, behavioral, and travel-related variables should be considered in future research.

REFERENCES

Adams, D. A., Nelson, R. R., & Todd, P. A. (1992). Perceived usefulness, ease of use, and usage of information. *MIS Quarterly, 16*(2), 227-247.

Angehrn, A., Meyer, J. (1997). Developing mature Internet strategies. *Information System Management, 14*(2), 37-43.

Berry, L. L., & Parasuraman, A. (1991). *Marketing service–competing through quality.* New York: The Free Press.

Bhattacherjee, A. (2001). An empirical analysis of the antecedents of electronic commerce service continuance. *Decision Support Systems, 32*(2), 201-214.

Chu, R. (2001). What online Hong Kong travelers look for on airline/travel Websites? *International Journal of Hospitality Management, 20*, 95-100.

Davis, F. (1989). Perceived usefulness, perceived ease of use, and user acceptance of information technology. *MIS Quarterly, 13*(3), 319-340.

De Ruyter, Wetzels, M., & Kleijnen, M. (2001). Customer adoption of e-service: An experimental study. *International Journal of Service Industry Management, 12*(2), 184-207.

Donthu, N. (2001). Does your Website measure up? *Marketing Management, 10*(4), 29-32.

Doolin, B., Burgess, L., & Cooper, J. (2002). Evaluating the use of the Web for tourism marketing: A case study from New Zealand. *Tourism Management, 23*(5), 557-561.

Garvin, D. A. (1991). *Competing on the eight dimensions of quality: Unconditional Quality.* Cambridge, MA: Harvard Business Review.

Gloor, P. (2000). *Making the e-business transformation.* London: Springer-Verlag.

Griffith, D., & Krampf, R. (1998). An examination of the Web-based strategies of the top 100 U.S. retailers. *Journal of Marketing Theory and Practice, 6*(3), 12-23.

Hair, J. F., Anderson, R. E., Tatham, R. L., & Black, W. C. (1995). *Multivariate data analysis* (4th ed.). London: Prentice-Hall International.

Hanna J. R. P., & Millar, R. J. (1997). Promoting tourism on the Internet. *Tourism Management, 18*(7), 469-470.

Jeong, M., & Lambert, C. U. (2001). Adaptation of an information quality framework to measure customers' behavioral intentions to use lodging Websites. *International Journal of Hospitality Management, 20*(2), 129-146.

Kaynama, S., & Black, C. (2000). A proposal to assess the service quality of online travel agencies: An exploratory study. *Journal of Professional Services Marketing, 21*(1), 63-88.

Kline, P. (1994). *An easy guide to factor analysis.* New York: Routledge.

Law, R., & Leung, R. (2000). A study of airline's online reservation services on the Internet. *Journal of Travel Research, 39*(2), 202-211.

Lederer, A. L., Maupin, D. J., Sena, M. P., & Zhuang, Y. (2000). The technology acceptance model and the World Wide Web. *Decision Support Systems, 29*(3), 269-282.

Lewis, I., Semeijn, J., & Talalayevsky, A. (1998). The impact of information technology on travel agents. *Transportation Journal, 37*(4), 20-25.

Madu, C. N., & Madu, A. A. (2002). Dimensions of e-quality. *International Journal of Quality & Reliability Management, 19*(3), 246-258.

Maselli, J. (2002, March 25). E-ticketing threatens travel agents. *Information Week, 881,* 28.

Spiliopoulou, M. (2000). Web usage mining for Web evaluation. *Association for Computing Machinery, 43*(8), 127-134.

Standing, C. (2000). *Internet commerce development.* Norwood, MA: Artech House Inc.

Suh, B., & Han, I. (2002). Effect of trust on customer acceptance of Internet banking. *Electronic Commerce Research and Applications, 1*(3-4), 247-263.

Walle, A. H. (1996). Tourism and the Internet: Opportunities for direct marketing. *Journal of Travel Research, 35*(1), 72-77.

Yang, Z., & Jun, M. J. (2002). Consumer perception of e-service quality: From Internet purchaser and non-purchaser perspectives. *Journal of Business Strategies, 19*(1), 19-41.

Zellner, W. (2002, April 1). Online travel takes wing. *Businessweek, 3776,* 77.

A Study of the Perceptions of Hong Kong Hotel Managers on the Potential Disintermediation of Travel Agencies

Rob Law
William Lau

SUMMARY. The wide-scale integration of the Internet in the hospitality and tourism industry has drawn the attention of researchers worldwide to the issue of the disintermediation of travel agencies. Despite the existence of numerous prior studies on disintermediation, only a very limited number of published articles have focused on the perceptions of industry practitioners of the impact of the Internet on the role of travel agencies. This empirical study makes an attempt to investigate the perceptions of Hong Kong hotel managers of the impact of Internet technology on the role of travel agencies as an intermediary. Using a survey of 88 hotel managers, the study shows that the perception of disintermediation can be initially grouped into five dimensions: (i) Price, (ii) Product, (iii) Participants, (iv) Place and (v) Process. Experimental results show that hotel practitioners do not perceive that disintermediation of travel agencies will occur. However, the respondents also predicted that the share of e-business in total hotel room sales will increase. *[Article copies available for a fee from The Haworth Document Delivery Service: 1-800-HAWORTH. E-mail address: <docdelivery@haworthpress.com> Website: <http://www.HaworthPress.com> © 2004 by The Haworth Press, Inc. All rights reserved.]*

KEYWORDS. Internet, disintermediation, hotel, Hong Kong, travel agency

INTRODUCTION AND BACKGROUND

The rapid growth of the travel industry has meant that sophisticated information technologies (ITs) are required to manage the increasing volume and quality of tourism services/products. Prior studies have indicated that modern travelers are demanding more high quality products, travel services, information and value for their money (Christian, 2001; Lubetkin, 1999; Samenfink, 1999). The emergence of new tourism services and products, together with the rapid development in tourism demand, has driven the wide-scale adop-

Rob Law is Associate Professor, Information Technology, School of Hotel & Tourism Management, The Hong Kong Polytechnic University, Hung Hom, Kowloon, Hong Kong (E-mail: hmroblaw@polyu.edu.hk). William Lau is an Independent Researcher.

Address correspondence to Rob Law.

The authors acknowledge the constructive comments offered by the anonymous reviewers about an earlier version of this paper.

This research was supported in part by a research grant from The Hong Kong Polytechnic University under contract number: G-T569.

[Haworth co-indexing entry note]: "A Study of the Perceptions of Hong Kong Hotel Managers on the Potential Disintermediation of Travel Agencies." Law, Rob, and William Lau. Co-published simultaneously in *Journal of Travel & Tourism Marketing* (The Haworth Hospitality Press, an imprint of The Haworth Press, Inc.) Vol. 17, No. 2/3, 2004, pp. 117-131; and: *Handbook of Consumer Behavior, Tourism, and the Internet* (ed: Juline E. Mills, and Rob Law) The Haworth Hospitality Press, an imprint of The Haworth Press, Inc., 2004, pp. 117-131. Single or multiple copies of this article are available for a fee from The Haworth Document Delivery Service [1-800-HAWORTH, 9:00 a.m. - 5:00 p.m. (EST). E-mail address: docdelivery@haworthpress.com].

tion of ITs in general, and the Internet in particular, as an electronic intermediary. In other words, the Internet is serving as a new communication and distribution channel for customers and suppliers of travel services and products. According to Jeong and Lambert (1999), the World Wide Web is playing an important role in mediating between customers and hotel companies by serving as a place where information can be acquired and business transacted. Liu (2000) argues that the Internet can serve as an ideal channel for tourism marketing. This new channel is thus enabling tourism businesses to improve their competitiveness and performance.

Tourism researchers have long been emphasizing the importance of the Internet for travel and tourism (Barnett & Standing, 2001; Buhalis, 1998; Kasavana, Knutson, & Polonowski, 1997). From the perspective of travel suppliers, the Internet is providing a way for them to sell their products globally to potential travelers at any time (Giaglis, Klein, & O'Keefe, 2002; Morris & Morris, 2002). These suppliers can remotely control their servers to display information on services and products at an electronic speed (Phau & Poon, 2000; Sweeney, 2000). Therefore, more and more companies are developing and exploring business opportunities on the Internet. This, in turn, is causing a demand for business-to-customer (B2C) e-commerce over the Internet (Liao & Cheung, 2001).

It is generally agreed that Websites should have a commercial value in terms of profitability (Lang, 2000; Sweeney, 2000). Hence, in the hospitality industry, many hotels have established Websites in order to make it easier for their customers to make online reservations (Murphy et al., 1996; van Hoof & Combrink, 1998; Wan, 2002). From the perspective of hoteliers, the factors that make a hotel Website successful are lower distribution costs, higher revenues and a larger market share. For hotel guests, the Internet allows them to communicate directly with hotels to request information and to purchase services and products at any time and in any place (Olmeda & Sheldon, 2001).

To the extent that the Internet enables e-travelers to easily arrange and purchase their own services and products, the future of travel agencies–the traditional intermediary–becomes uncertain. Academic researchers argue that the direct and immediate contact between suppliers and customers, coupled with the decrease in transaction costs, have made a strong case for Internet-driven disintermediation (Berthon, Ewing, Pitt, & Naude, 2002; Jallat & Capek, 2001; Vandermerwe, 1999). Different tourism researchers have debated the topic of disintermediation, particularly the elimination of the middleman in the customer-agent-destination/supplier network in the travel industry of the future (Buhalis, 1998; Walle, 1996). To some researchers, the accessibility of online travel Websites is reducing the importance of travel agencies, and might ultimately result in their being bypassed altogether (Barnett & Standing, 2001; Buhalis, 1998). However, Palmer, and McCole (1999) as well as Walle (1996) have argued that a key strength of travel agencies is their ability to provide personal information and advice to travelers continuously. The role of the travel agency will consequently remain secure if its advice-offering capability is strengthened by the presence of the Internet, rather than if an agency acts according to the more negative image of being simply a "booking agency." While hospitality and tourism researchers have investigated the views of travel agencies (Fong & Law, 2002; Law, Law, & Wai, 2003), academics and consultants (Buhalis & Licata, 2002), and travelers (Law, Leung, & Wong, 2004), the views of suppliers have largely been overlooked in the hospitality and tourism literature. In other words, it is generally unclear whether suppliers judge travel agencies as being less valuable with the presence of online distribution channels. The absence of prior studies on the views of suppliers in the debate over the disintermediation of travel agencies is particularly true in the context of hotels in Hong Kong, a major sector of the tourism industry in a leading Asian travel destination.

Thus, this study makes an attempt to examine the views of Hong Kong hotel managers on the potential disintermediation of travel agencies. In other words, the primary objective of this research is to seek the opinions of hotel managers about the elimination of the middleman in reserving hotel accommodation. More specifically, using the marketing mix concept, this research aims to examine how hotel managers in Hong Kong view the trend towards disintermediation, and whether these managers perceive disintermediation positively or negatively. The outcomes of this study will benefit the Hong Kong hotel industry, and possibly the hotel industry at large, by allowing them to better plan for future e-business development. Another contribution of this study is to offer further insights on the issue of disintermediation in the customer-agent-destination/supplier network. This will help hoteliers better serve e-consumers by improving the quality of their online offers, expanding the quality of services, and developing more competitive prices e-distribution channels.

The study begins with the development of the supporting framework for examining the perceptions of hotel managers on the potential disintermediation of travel agencies. A discussion of the methodology used in the study and empirical analysis follows. The study concludes with a discussion on the implications of the results as well as offers suggestions for future research.

MODEL DEVELOPMENT

Generally speaking, travel agencies serve as the major broker of travel and tourism services. These agencies function as an intermediary between industry suppliers and consumers. As previously stated, with the advent of the Internet, consumers are able to develop and purchase their own travel itineraries, and for this reason, the future role of travel agencies has become uncertain. Buhalis (1998) has stated that the Internet can potentially change the role of tourism intermediaries, particularly the travel agencies, on the arrangement and purchase of travel related services and products. Once customers realize that they can arrange a larger proportion of their own travel itineraries, and at a lower cost, directly with the suppliers, they will very likely bypass the travel agencies (Poon, 2001). This research, hence, makes an attempt to apply the concept of marketing mix to the context of disinterme-

diation of travel agencies from a hotel managers' perspective.

The ways in which services and products can be distributed to customers in an effective and efficient manner have been a major area of investigation for marketing researchers. Borden (1965) originally introduced the concept of marketing mix. Kotler and Armstrong (1994) further stated that a marketing mix consists of everything that a firm can do to influence the demand for products. Known as the 4Ps, that is, Product, Price, Place, and Promotion (Kotler, 1976), the marketing mix is based on the idea that there is a set of controllable variables that can have an effect on the customer's decision to purchase (Shapiro, 1985). Booms and Bitner (1981), in applying the concept of marketing mix to the service industry, extended the 4Ps to 7Ps. The additional Ps are Participants, Physical Evidence and Process. Based on Booms and Bitner's 7Ps framework, Rafiq and Ahmed (1995) conducted an exploratory study to assert the appropriateness of the 7Ps framework as a more generic model for marketing mixes.

With the growing popularity of the Internet and e-commerce, the process of developing and modeling of online marketing has been discussed by various researchers. For instance, Angehrn (1997) presented a model of Internet marketing which consists of 4 virtual business spaces for information, communication, distribution, and transaction (ICDT). This ICDT model described the major business opportunities such as increasing visibility and reducing cost, and threats like competitive pressures on the Internet. Angehrn further argued that the ICDT model offers an environment for e-business strategies, and a new approach for a company's strategy-building process. On the basis of the ICDT model, Sigala (2001) proposed an e-marketing mix and applied it to 93 Greek hotels. Empirical results showed that hotels in different categories did not perform equally in terms of the composition of their e-marketing mix, indicating that there is need for hotels to examine their positions in the industry.

In addition, Zott, Amit, and Donlevy (2000) advocated that the strategies for value creation in e-commerce can enhance transaction efficiency and convenience, as well as strengthening the supply chain. Azzone, Blanchi, and Noci (2000) also made a similar claim that the Internet can improve the marketing effort in several dimensions. Studies performed by O'Connor and Horan (1999) and Procaccino and Miller (1999) demonstrated that different sectors of the hotel and tourism industries have utilized the Internet as a marketing channel, but their resulting efforts differed largely on technical capability and business functionality.

This research aims to revise and apply the 7Ps marketing mix concept presented by Booms and Bitner (1981) and Rafiq and Ahmed (1995) to facilitate a better understanding of the relationship among different marketing dimensions in the context of hospitality and tourism. In this way, a more thorough comprehension of the disintermediation and redistribution of travel distributing channels can be achieved. The following paragraphs depict the sketch of the research framework use in this study.

Having examined the components of the 7Ps in detail, the Promotion and Physical Evidence dimensions of the 7Ps are excluded in this study. Promotion is excluded because most of its functions have already been integrated into Product. The removal of Physical Evidence is simply due to its inapplicability in the virtual marketing environment. Such removals are to validated by a focus group comprises hotel managers. Figure 1 presents the modified 5Ps framework used in this research that groups the appropriate dimensions for evaluation. The modified framework consists of five dimensions, namely, Price, Product, Participants, Place, and Process. In this study, Price relates to discounts, allowances, payment terms, and customers' own perceived value. The Product dimension is associated with brand name, service line, and warranty. Similarly, Participants refer to personnel, interpersonal communications, and other customers' behavior/degree of involvement. While Place refers to distribution channels, distribution coverage, location, accessibility, tangible knowledge, and delivery. Lastly, Process is for mechanization, policies, and flow of activities.

FIGURE 1. A Framework of the Views of Hotel Managers on the Potential Disintermediation of Travel Agencies

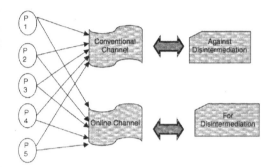

P1 = Price, P2 = Product, P3 = Participants, P4 = Place, P5 = Process.

METHODOLOGY

A structured questionnaire was used to collect data from hotel managers. Due to the relative lack of instruments to specifically measure the perceptions of Internet-induced disintermediation, the study adapted the questionnaires that were used to examine the views of travel agencies (Fong & Law, 2002) and travelers (Law, Leung, & Wong, 2004) on the issue of disintermediation in the context of Hong Kong. The attributes in both studies were originated from Buhalis (1998), who demonstrated the arguments for and against disintermediation of the tourism distribution channel. The attributes used in previous studies (Fong & Law, 2002; Law, Leung, & Wong, 2004) were modified and rephrased to ensure that they are applicable to the Hong Kong hotel industry. Having carefully evaluated the applicability of these arguments, the final questionnaire contained 18 attributes, with half of the questions supporting disintermediation and the other half opposing it. These attributes were grouped into the five dimensions as depicted in Figure 1. Prior to the survey, the questionnaire was pilot-tested by four hotel practitioners and researchers. The pilot test did not show any problems with wording or understanding.

In addition, a focus group discussion session was organized with the participation of seven managers from the above departments of the hotels. These focus group participants included 3 Marketing and Sales managers, 3

Front Office managers, and 1 Electronic Data Processing (EDP) manager. Additionally, these managers were from 1 High Tariff A hotel, 4 High Tariff B hotels, and 2 Medium Tariff hotels. The focus group discussion served two purposes. First, the group verified the five marketing dimensions as presented in Figure 1. More importantly, the participants, with their professional experiences, verified the attributes that were included in each of the five dimensions. They all agreed with the proposed dimensions. In addition, following their recommendations, two attributes were repositioned to more appropriate dimensions.

The target population for the survey consisted of all member hotels of the Hong Kong Hotels Association (HKHA). In Hong Kong, hotels are classified into three categories: High Tariff A (luxury), High Tariff B (mid-priced), and Medium Tariff (economy) hotels (HKTA, 1998). A total of 77 qualified hotels were identified. These hotels were members of HKHA and had established their own Websites. Two hundred and thirty-one questionnaires were sent to managers in the Marketing and Sales, Front Office, and Management Information Systems (MIS)/EDP departments of these qualified hotels, as they are involved in e-business of their hotels. One hundred and sixty follow-ups were performed to increase the response rate. At the end of February 2003, 88 usable questionnaires were received from all categories of hotels in Hong Kong, representing a response rate of 38.1%.

FINDINGS

Profiles of the Respondents and Hotels

In this study, data were collected on the respondents' working experience, work department, age group, gender, and educational background. Table 1 summarizes the descriptive results of the respondents' demographic data. Seventy-seven percent of the respondents had more than 10 years of experience working for hotels. This implies that the opinions expressed in the questionnaires were mostly from hotel managers with a good knowledge of and experience in the industry. It is, however, also interesting to note that 55

TABLE 1. Profile of Respondents

Demographic Variables		Percentage (n = 88)
Working experience in the hotel industry (in years)	0-5	4.6
	6-10	18.4
	11-15	35.6
	16-20	32.2
	21-25	5.7
	26-30	1.1
	Over 30	2.3
Number of years working in the present hotel	0-5	55.2
	6-10	28.7
	11-15	11.5
	16-20	3.4
	21-25	0
	26-30	0
	Over 30	1.1
Department in the present hotel	FO	47.1
	M & S	36.8
	MIS/EDP	16.1
Age group	20-29	4.6
	30-39	56.3
	40-49	33.3
	50 or above	5.7
Gender	Male	80.5
	Female	19.5
Educational background	Secondary	21.4
	Vocational	14.3
	Undergraduate degree	42.9
	Postgraduate degree	21.4

percent of the respondents had been working for their present hotel for less than six years. This can probably be explained by the high demand for experienced managers and the high rates of turnover in Hong Kong hotels (HKTB, 2003). A majority of the respondents were Front Office managers (47%), in the age group of 30-39 (56%), male (81%), and holders of an undergraduate degree (43%).

Besides the hotel managers' demographics, the questionnaire identified the profile of the hotels at which the respondents worked. This part included the history and classification of the hotel, its background of Internet usage, share of business from travel agencies, and prediction of changes in business share. Table 2 outlines the results of the profile of the hotels. The hotels participating in this study had operating histories of varying length, with the majority having been in business for 11 to 15 years (36%). Seventeen percent of the hotels involved in this study had been operating for 6 to 10 years. Similarly, 17 percent of hotels in the study had also been in business for 31 to 35 years. In addition, the hotels fell evenly into the categories of High Tariff A, High Tariff B, and Medium Tariff. Furthermore, although most hotels were using the Internet (n = 79), less than half of them had been using the technology for business-to-business (n = 35) and business-to-customer (n = 43) purposes in the past three years. Such a relatively low percentage of e-business application could account for the finding that for most of the hotels (86%) less than 20% of total room sales were from e-business. Still, most hotels (79%) expected that the share of business from the Internet would increase in the coming years. The hotels, however, also relied heavily on travel agencies for their room sales. The majority of them (37%) had received more than half of their business from travel agencies, and most hotels (54%) predicted that their share of business from travel agencies would remain unchanged in the next 12 months.

Perceptions of Disintermediation

As previously stated, the 18 attributes used in the questionnaire were equally divided into arguments for and arguments against disintermediation. The arguments for disintermediation addressed issues such as the development of the Internet, customers' propensity to use the technology, and the traditional role of travel agencies. In contrast, the arguments against disintermediation covered the value-adding services provided by travel agencies, the professionalism of travel agencies, and the limitations of the Internet. The hotel managers were requested to indicate their level of agreement towards these attributes on a five-point Likert scale, with 1 representing "Strongly Disagree" and 5 representing "Strongly Agree." Tables 3 and 4 summarize the findings.

TABLE 2. Profile of the Hotels

Variables		Percentage (n = 88)
Operating history of the hotel (years)	0-5	6.0
	6-10	16.7
	11-15	35.7
	16-20	9.5
	21-25	9.5
	26-30	6.0
	31-35	16.7
Hotel classification	High Tariff A	33.7
	High Tariff B	30.2
	Medium Tariff	36.0
Number of years of using the Internet (including e-mail)		
Using the Internet (n = 79)	0-3	20.2
	4-6	28.2
	7-9	31.4
	10 years or above	20.2
Operating B2B (n = 35)	0-3	62.9
	4-6	28.6
	7-9	5.8
	10 years or above	2.9
Operating B2C (n = 43)	0-3	58.2
	4-6	32.6
	7-9	7.0
	10 years or above	2.3
Share of hotel's business from travel agencies to total room sales in the past 12 months	Below 9%	0
	10-19%	8.3
	20-29%	15.5
	30-39%	16.7
	40-49%	22.6
	50% or above	36.9
Prediction regarding this share (i.e., business from travel agencies) in the coming 12 months	Increase	25.0
	Decrease	21.4
	Remain Unchanged	53.6
Share of the hotel's e-business (B2B plus B2C) to total room sales in the past 12 months	Below 10%	52.5
	10-19%	33.8
	20-29%	12.5
	30-39%	1.3
Prediction of this share (i.e., e-business) in the coming 12 months	Increase	78.8
	Decrease	2.5
	Remain Unchanged	18.8
On whether the company provides training on using the Internet	Yes	51.2
	No	48.8

In Table 3, all but one attribute received mean values of above 3, indicating general agreement among the hotel managers on the arguments for disintermediation. In other words, managers agreed that the Internet can offer convenient hotel room reservation ser-

TABLE 3. Arguments for Disintermediation (n = 88)

Question	Mean	Standard Deviation
1. Travel agencies are more eager to sell hotel accommodations that offer higher commissions or markups than to cater to the needs and interests of customers.	3.57	0.956
2. Commissions or markups to travel agencies eventually increase the price of hotel accommodations.	3.40	0.989
3. Travel agencies add little value to hotel accommodations as they merely manage information and undertake reservations.	3.15	0.870
4. Personnel in travel agencies are often inadequately trained and inexperienced.	3.10	0.831
5. Experienced hotel guests are more knowledgeable than travel agencies, especially for specialized markets.	3.66	0.725
6. Room rates that hotel Websites offer to consumers are lower than the room rates that travel agencies offer to consumers.	2.44	0.756
7. Technology enables hotel guests to undertake most functions from the convenience of their armchairs.	3.86	0.571
8. Online hotel reservations are boundary-free and have an around-the-clock presence.	4.20	0.697
9. The re-engineering of the hotel industry (e.g., Internet and hotel loyalty programs) facilitates disintermediation.	3.27	0.707

Scale: 1 = Strongly Disagree, 2 = Disagree, 3 = Neutral, 4 = Agree, 5 = Strongly Agree.

TABLE 4. Arguments Against Disintermediation (n = 88)

Question	Mean	Standard Deviation
1. Travel agencies offer a human touch and a human interface with their customers.	3.97	0.686
2. Travel agencies add value by offering free counseling services and advice on hotel accommodations.	3.91	0.768
3. Travel agencies use expertise to save time for hotel guests.	3.72	0.762
4. Visiting a travel agency for hotel reservations is convenient.	3.22	0.850
5. Travel agencies offer greater flexibility and more choices on hotel accommodations than do hotel Websites.	3.33	1.069
6. Travel agencies can offer better room rates by buying in bulk or through consolidators.	3.84	0.741
7. The more complex computers and the Internet become, the more expertise people need to make online hotel reservations.	3.42	0.893
8. Online hotel reservations are not secure and reliable.	2.51	0.802
9. A large number of travelers are computer illiterate and therefore not ready for online hotel reservations.	2.83	0.847

Scale: 1 = Strongly Disagree, 2 = Disagree, 3 = Neutral, 4 = Agree, 5 = Strongly Agree.

vices that are free from geographical and time limits. The respondents also agreed that travel agencies are business oriented and that these agencies may place their business interests ahead of the customers' interests.

Different from the findings listed in Table 3, the respondents thought that there is still a need for travel agencies to offer the personal services that cannot be matched by technology (Table 4). In particular, hotel managers perceived that several factors would prevent travel agencies from being bypassed. These factors mainly re-late to the ability of travel agencies to offer value-added services, a human touch and interface, as well as competitive room rates.

Relationship Between Perception of Disintermediation and Hotel Categories

One-way Analysis of Variance (ANOVA) was used to determine whether any of the observed differences were significant. Since different hotel categories have different financial background, business origins, and market origins, it is worthwhile to investigate whether the perception of disintermediation differ among different hotel categories. Tables 5 to 9 show the results of the relationships between hotel categories and disintermediation attributes in the five dimensions, namely: Price, Product, Participants, Place, and Process. Luxury hotels usually receive more resources to develop e-business, and their managers might be expected to have a more positive view towards the potential disintermediation of travel agencies. However, as revealed in Tables 5 to 9, none of these attributes shows a significant difference among the various hotel categories. This, in turn, indicates that hotel managers in Hong Kong do not hold different perceptions towards disintermediation. This finding contradicts a previous study in which Siguaw, Enz, and Namasivayam (2000) claimed that levels of technological sophistication and integration are directly related to hotel category, and therefore hoteliers have different views on the application of technology.

Relationship Between Perceptions of Disintermediation and Hotel Departments

This study also attempted to compare the relationship between the disintermediation attributes and the departments in which the hotel managers worked. Kotler, Bowen, and Makens (1999) stated that hotel practitioners have dissimilar roles in different functional areas. Therefore, the different job natures of Front Office, Marketing and Sales, and MIS/EDP departments necessitate the adoption of dissimilar approaches by managers to deal with e-business and room reservations. Hence, managers' perceptions towards the disintermediation of travel agencies could be different. Tables 10 to 14 summarize the ANOVA results of hotel departments and disintermediation attributes in the five dimensions.

Similar to the findings of the relationships between disintermediation attributes and hotel categories, all but one of the ANOVA results in Tables 10 to 14 showed no significant difference between the attributes and hotel departments. This implies that Front Office, Marketing and Sales, and MIS/EDP managers held the same views towards the disintermediation of travel agencies. The only attribute that showed a significant difference among the opinions of managers in different departments is in the Process dimension (Table 14), which relates to the association of computer technology and human expertise. A post-hoc Duncan analysis used to find the relationship among different groups of respondents shows that, significantly, Front Office managers and MIS/EDP managers viewed the attribute differently from the Marketing and Sales managers. Such a difference could be explained by the more operational and technology-based job nature of Front Office and MIS/EDP departments.

DISCUSSION

The research findings of this study have suggested that hotel managers generally perceived

TABLE 5. Comparisons of Perceptions of Disintermediation by Hotel Classifications on Price

Question	Mean (std)			F-value	Sig.
	High tariff A Hotel (n = 29)	High tariff B Hotel (n = 26)	Medium tariff Hotel (n = 31)		
Commissions or markups to travel agencies eventually increase the price of hotel accommodations.	3.55 (0.910)	3.50 (1.140)	3.10 (0.870)	1.965	0.147
Travel agencies can offer better room rates by buying in bulk or through consolidators.	3.79 (0.675)	3.77 (0.908)	3.94 (0.680)	0.418	0.660
The room rates that hotel Websites offer to consumers are lower than the room rates that travel agencies offer to consumers.	2.52 (0.785)	2.38 (0.752)	2.45 (0.723)	0.213	0.809

Note: Due to 2 missing cases, total n = 86.

TABLE 6. Comparisons of Perceptions of Disintermediation by Hotel Classifications on Product

Question	Mean (std)			F-value	Sig.
	High tariff A Hotel (n = 29)	High tariff B Hotel (n = 26)	Medium tariff Hotel (n = 31)		
Travel agencies are more eager to sell hotel accommodations that offer higher commissions or markups than to cater to the needs and interests of customers.	3.55 (1.055)	3.50 (1.068)	3.61 (0.761)	0.098	0.907
Travel agencies add little value to hotel accommodations as they merely manage information and take reservations.	3.07 (0.842)	3.16 (1.068)	3.19 (0.749)	0.157	0.855
Travel agencies add value by offering free counseling services and advice on hotel accommodations.	3.69 (0.712)	4.00 (0.824)	4.03 (0.836)	2.037	0.137
Online hotel reservations are not secure and reliable.	2.45 (0.783)	2.50 (0.990)	2.58 (0.672)	0.201	0.818

TABLE 7. Comparisons of Perceptions of Disintermediation by Hotel Classifications on Participants

Question	Mean (std)			F-value	Sig.
	High tariff A Hotel (n = 29)	High tariff B Hotel (n = 26)	Medium tariff Hotel (n = 31)		
Travel agencies offer a human touch and a human interface with their customers.	3.76 (0.577)	4.04 (0.824)	4.10 (0.651)	2.037	0.137
Travel agencies use expertise to save time for hotel guests.	3.63 (0.565)	3.73 (0.778)	3.87 (0.846)	0.771	0.466
Personnel in travel agencies are often inadequately trained and inexperienced.	3.17 (0.928)	3.08 (0.796)	3.10 (0.790)	0.101	0.904
Experienced hotel guests are more knowledgeable than travel agencies, especially on specialized markets.	3.76 (0.636)	3.69 (0.736)	3.55 (0.810)	0.647	0.526
A large number of travelers are computer illiterate and therefore not ready for online hotel reservations.	2.72 (0.882)	2.92 (0.845)	2.87 (0.846)	0.406	0.668

TABLE 8. Comparisons of Perceptions of Disintermediation by Hotel Classifications on Place

Question	Mean (std)			F-value	Sig.
	High tariff A Hotel (n = 29)	High tariff B Hotel (n = 26)	Medium tariff Hotel (n = 31)		
Visiting a travel agency to make hotel reservations is convenient.	3.14 (0.789)	3.12 (0.864)	3.39 (0.882)	0.939	0.395
Travel agencies offer greater flexibility and more choices on hotel accommodations than do hotel Websites.	3.45 (0.985)	3.04 (1.280)	3.52 (0.851)	1.690	0.191
The re-engineering of the hotel industry (e.g., Internet and hotel loyalty programs) facilitates disintermediation.	3.34 (0.670)	3.35 (0.689)	3.06 (0.680)	1.695	0.190
Online hotel reservations are boundary-free and have an around-the-clock presence.	4.14 (0.639)	4.38 (0.752)	4.13 (0.718)	1.158	0.319

TABLE 9. Comparisons of Perceptions of Disintermediation by Hotel Classifications on Process

Question	Mean (std)			F-value	Sig.
	High tariff A Hotel (n = 29)	High tariff B Hotel (n = 26)	Medium tariff Hotel (n = 31)		
Technology enables hotel guests to undertake most functions from the convenience of their armchairs.	3.79 (0.559)	3.88 (0.711)	3.90 (0.473)	0.300	0.741
The more complex computers and the Internet become, the more expertise people need to make online hotel reservations.	3.38 (0.775)	3.54 (0.905)	3.48 (0.890)	0.248	0.781

TABLE 10. Comparisons of Perceptions of Disintermediation by Hotel Department on Price

Question	Mean (std)			F-value	Sig.
	Front Office (n = 42)	Marketing and Sales (n = 32)	MIS/EDP (n = 14)		
Commissions or markups to travel agencies eventually increase the price of hotel accommodations.	3.57 (0.887)	3.13 (1.129)	3.43 (0.852)	1.910	0.154
Travel agencies can offer better room rates by buying in bulk or through consolidators.	3.93 (0.677)	3.75 (0.880)	3.79 (0.579)	0.568	0.569
Room rates that hotel Websites offer to consumers are lower than the room rates that travel agencies offer to consumers.	2.55 (0.739)	2.41 (0.756)	2.29 (0.825)	0.727	0.486

TABLE 11. Comparisons of Perceptions of Disintermediation by Hotel Department on Product

Question	Mean (std)			F-value	Sig.
	Front Office (n = 42)	Marketing and Sales (n = 32)	MIS/EDP (n = 14)		
Travel agencies are more eager to sell hotel accommodations that offer higher commissions or markups than to cater to the needs and interests of customers.	3.59 (0.836)	3.59 (1.103)	3.43 (1.016)	0.161	0.851
Travel agencies add little value to hotel accommodations as they merely manage information and make reservations.	3.22 (0.759)	2.90 (1.012)	3.50 (0.760)	2.576	0.082
Travel agencies add value by offering free counseling services and advice on hotel accommodations.	4.02 (0.749)	3.91 (0.777)	3.64 (0.842)	1.281	0.283
Online hotel reservations are not secure and reliable.	2.55 (0.832)	2.31 (0.780)	2.71 (0.825)	1.402	0.252

that the service of hotel reservations, which are traditionally provided by travel agencies, can largely be performed by the Internet. The managers, however, also believed that travel agencies would still be needed to plan and reserve hotel rooms for guests in the future, due to the need for personal services and the existence of technology-related barriers. In other words, this study has found that, on the whole, the respondents are optimistic about the outlook for travel agencies. Among the attributes in the five dimensions, the respondents agreed that traditional travel agencies have an advantage in making room reservations, and that Internet-based marketing and distribution channels are capable of accomplishing the same

TABLE 12. Comparisons of Perceptions of Disintermediation by Hotel Department on Participants

Question	Mean (std)			F-value	Sig.
	Front Office (n = 42)	**Marketing and Sales** (n = 32)	**MIS/EDP** (n = 14)		
Travel agencies offer a human touch and a human interface with their customers.	3.95 (0.731)	4.00 (0.622)	4.00 (0.784)	0.050	0.951
Travel agencies use expertise to save time for hotel guests.	3.76 (0.624)	3.73 (0.785)	3.57 (1.089)	0.308	0.736
Personnel in travel agencies are often inadequately trained and inexperienced.	3.10 (0.759)	3.13 (0.976)	3.00 (0.679)	0.110	0.896
Experienced hotel guests are more knowledgeable than travel agencies, especially for specialized markets.	3.71 (0.844)	3.63 (0.660)	3.57 (0.514)	0.221	0.802
A large number of travelers are computer illiterate and therefore not ready for online hotel reservations.	2.78 (0.759)	2.88 (1.040)	2.93 (0.616)	0.201	0.818

TABLE 13. Comparisons of Perceptions of Disintermediation by Hotel Department on Place

Question	Mean (std)			F-value	Sig.
	Front Office (n = 42)	**Marketing and Sales** (n = 32)	**MIS/EDP** (n = 14)		
Visiting a travel agency to make hotel reservations is convenient.	3.17 (0.853)	3.16 (0.884)	3.43 (0.756)	0.579	0.563
Travel agencies offer greater flexibility and more choices on hotel accommodations than do hotel Websites.	3.27 (1.001)	3.22 (1.184)	3.71 (0.994)	1.139	0.325
The re-engineering of the hotel industry (e.g., Internet and hotel loyalty programs) facilitates disintermediation.	3.40 (0.627)	3.09 (0.689)	3.29 (0.914)	1.794	0.173
Online hotel reservations are boundary-free and have an around-the-clock presence.	4.10 (0.735)	4.25 (0.718)	4.43 (0.514)	1.267	0.287

TABLE 14. Comparisons of Perceptions of Disintermediation by Hotel Department on Process

Question	Mean (std)			F-value	Sig.
	Front Office (n = 42)	**Marketing and Sales** (n = 32)	**MIS/EDP** (n = 14)		
Technology enables hotel guests to undertake most functions from the convenience of their armchairs.	3.88 (0.600)	3.94 (0.435)	3.64 (0.745)	1.323	0.272
The more complex computers and the Internet become, the more expertise people need to make online hotel reservations.	3.60 (0.798)	3.06 (0.948)	3.71 (0.825)	4.458	0.014*

*Significant at the 0.05 level.
*Front Office, MIS/EDP > Marketing and Sales.

task. These findings are similar to prior studies on the issue of the potential disintermediation of travel agencies with travelers (Law, Leung, & Wong, 2004) and travel consultants (Fong & Law, 2002) in Hong Kong. In other words, travelers and hotel practitioners all perceived that travel agencies will remain important in the travel and tourism industry. The parties involved, however, also realize the high potential of online reservations.

In spite of the Internet's potential to pose a threat to travel agencies in the area of hotel accommodation counseling and room reservations, hotel managers felt that technology-based hotel room reservations still have many problems. Examples of these problems include the difficulty of locating the relevant Website, and therefore the required information, as well as issues of security and privacy, information overload, and the lack of a human interface (Kasavana, Knutson, & Polonowski, 1997; Lang, 2000; van Hoof & Combrink, 1998). That is, the Internet cannot replace the knowledge that travel agencies possess of the products, destinations, and the needs of their customers. This knowledge enables travel agencies to recommend the best combination of hotel accommodations to suit the needs of guests. This finding is in accord with the claim made by tourism researchers that there is a continuing need for travel agencies to supply specialized information relating to travelers' desires and to do so professionally (Buhalis, 2000; Kotler, Bowen, & Makens, 1999; Poon, 2001). Lastly, it is interesting to note that, based on hotel managers' experience, room rates offered by hotel Websites are not lower than the room rates offered by travel agencies. This finding should be of particular interest to most e-consumers. In particular, e-consumers may benefit from knowing that travel agencies can give customers the full range of products and services that they need, and that the agencies can always produce personalized offerings to suit the unique needs of individuals.

To remain competitive, the present hotel industry has largely made its presence felt on the Internet (van Hoof & Combrink, 1998). In addition to hotel Websites, numerous international online travel Websites such as expedia.com and travelocity.com have been established to offer a wide range of travel-related services, including hotel room reservations (Samenfink, 1999). While the number of consumers who are turning to the Internet keeps increasing, prior studies have shown that people tend to utilize the Internet to search for information instead of to make online purchases (Citrin et al., 2000; Lang, 2000). This technology-assisted searching instead of technology-assisted purchasing behavior directly applies to the local hotel industry in Hong Kong.

As shown in Table 2, more than half of the hotels saw less than 10 percent of their total room sales coming from e-business. Leong (2001) in his study of Singapore hotels also obtained a similar result, in which Internet reservations accounted for less than 10 percent of room sales in most hotels.

In the context of Hong Kong, official statistical data show that the local hotel industry is unique in several ways (HKTB, 2002; HKTB, 2003). First, visitors consistently contribute more than 90 percent to the overall business of hotels. Next, hotels in Hong Kong have always been able to achieve an occupancy rate of 80% or above. Third, most visitors to Hong Kong are from Mainland China (37%) and Taiwan (17%). More importantly, most visitors from Mainland China and Taiwan travel to Hong Kong in tour groups operated by travel agencies (Kwong, 1997). Zhang (2000) further states that travelers from Mainland China seldom use the Internet to purchase travel products. Inevitably, these factors mean that hotels in Hong Kong rely upon the distribution networks of travel agencies to attract hotel customers, especially those from Mainland China and Taiwan. Apparently, hotels in Hong Kong offer their best available rates to travel agencies because the agencies can guarantee a certain volume of business. As a consequence, even though hotels intend to engage in more direct e-business, sales volumes and room rates from the online channel are not as competitive as those from travel agencies.

The findings of this research have a major effect on e-consumer behavior. At present, purchasing online is still unpopular in the context of hospitality and tourism. Law and Wong (2003) performed a recent study to investigate Hong Kong residents' online purchasing behavior. In this study, only 22.5% of the 952 respondents had visited at least one travel Website. Among these e-lookers, only 6.5% of them had actually purchased some services/products from travel Websites. In view of the low propensity of online purchases, together with the strong support from hotel managers about the need to have travel agencies, hospitality and tourism Websites must be extremely intuitive to users in order to achieve e-satisfaction and eventually the loyalty and retention. Some examples of the required features on the hospitality and tourism Websites are the provision of updated information, competitive price, user-friendly interface, and rapid response that mimic the service provided by travel agencies.

CONCLUSIONS AND FUTURE RESEARCH

This study has investigated the perceptions held by Hong Kong hotel managers on the potential for the disintermediation of travel agencies. In general, hotel managers in Hong Kong do not believe that the Internet will threaten the role of travel agencies as an intermediary between hotels and customers. The research, however, was limited in terms of sample size and geographical area. For this reason, it is unable to draw any general conclusions about the issue for the hotel industry at large. Despite such limitations, there are several implications in this research for travel agencies in Hong Kong and possibly in other regions. First, since hoteliers generally recognize the importance of travel agencies in the customer-agent-destination/supplier network, practitioners in travel agencies should not worry about their future employment. The local travel and tourism industry in Hong Kong basically offers a unique environment that shields travel agencies from being disintermediated. Second, although the Internet provides a new distribution channel for hotel room reservations, a pleasant purchase experience to many hotel customers always requires the professional assistance of a friendly and helpful travel agent. It is even possible that the need for personal communications and interactions will increase as a consequence of the technological revolution. In other words, travel agencies will therefore safely maintain their position as an intermediary.

Last and most importantly, travel agencies should appreciate the potential of the Internet in the service of providing hotel accommodation. They should learn how to take advantage of the technology, and to view the technology as an opportunity rather than a threat. To fully utilize the benefits of both cyberspace and physical businesses, travel agencies can transform their "bricks and mortar" business model to a "clicks and mortar" approach. Maintain-

ing physical outlets gives travel agencies the advantage in providing personal interaction and serving traditional customers who are reluctant to turn to the Internet. At the same time, their presence on the Internet enables travel agencies to enjoy the benefits that technology provides, such as enhanced reach and streamlined operations.

From the perspective of hotels, cooperation should be maintained with travel agencies in order to have a stable business environment. Travel agencies can serve as base business partners for hotels in the present market. However, the importance of electronic business-to-customer development should not be ignored because the Internet has a large potential to be a major distribution channel that can provide the benefits of direct communications with hotel customers, and hence cost effectiveness.

Both hotel managers and travel agencies should be aware that the rapid pace of technological advancements may make business strategies that are highly successful today obsolete in the near future. While the search for a successful strategy will lead to a better chance of survival in the future, practitioners in the hospitality and tourism industry should monitor their operating environment closely. Perhaps the only way for a business to remain an ongoing success is to be flexible and adaptable at all times.

Moreover, the study offers e-consumers the opportunity to know the need for the existence of travel agencies. As previously discussed, e-consumers will be satisfied and purchase if the hospitality and tourism Websites are more accessible, more price competitive, and more user-friendly. Consequently, hotels and travel agencies need to bear these requirements in mind when they are developing their Websites.

The research results presented in this paper are positive about the view of hotel managers on the future role of travel agencies in hotel room reservations. Other research questions have yet to be investigated in future studies. These research questions may include, for example: How is the degree of disintermediation to be measured? What are the characteristics of the hotel customers who prefer to reserve hotel rooms through the Internet and those who prefer to purchase through travel agencies? To what extent should room rates be reduced to encourage customers to purchase online rather than to purchase from traditional channels? These research questions undoubtedly deserve in-depth examination in the future.

REFERENCES

Angehrn, A. (1997). Designing Mature Internet Business Strategies: The ICDT Model. *European Management Journal*, 15(4), 361-369.

Azzone, G., Bianchi, R., & Noci, G. (2000). The company's Website: Different configurations, evolutionary path. *Management Decision*, 38(7), 470-479.

Barnett, M., & Standing, C. (2001). Repositioning Travel Agencies on the Internet. *Journal of Vacation Marketing*, 7(2), 143-152.

Berthon, P., Ewing, M., Pitt, L., & Naude, P. (2002). Understanding B2B and the Web: The acceleration of coordination and motivation. *Industrial Marketing Management*, 5549, 1-9.

Booms, B.H., & Bitner, M.J. (1981). Marketing strategies and organization structures for service firms. In Donnelly, J.H. and George, W.R. (Eds), *Marketing of Service* (pp. 47-51). Chicago: American Marketing Association.

Borden, N.H. (1965). The concept of the marketing mix. In Schwartz, G. (Eds), *Science in Marketing* (pp. 386-397). New York: John Wiley & Sons.

Buhalis, D. (1998). Strategic use of information technologies in the tourism industry. *Tourism Management*, 19(5), 409-421.

Buhalis, D. (2000). Marketing the competitive destination of the future. *Tourism Management*, 21(1), 97-116.

Buhalis, D., & Licata, M.C. (2002). The future of eTourism intermediaries. *Tourism Management*, 23(3), 207-220.

Christian, R. (2001). Developing an online access strategy: Issues facing small to medium-sized tourism and hospitality enterprises. *Journal of Vacation Marketing*, 7(2), 170-178.

Citrin, A.V., Sprott, D.E., Silverman, S.N., & Stem, D.E., Jr. (2000). Adoption of Internet shopping: The role of consumer innovativeness. *Industrial Management & Data Systems*, 100(7), 294-300.

Fong, C., & Law, R. (2002). A Study of Hong Kong Travel Agencies' Perception of Disintermediation. *Proceedings of the 8th Joint International Computer Conference*, November, Ningbo, China, pp. 691-701.

Giaglis, G.M., Klein, S., & O'Keefe, R.M. (2002). The role of intermediaries in electronic marketplaces: Developing a contingency model. *Information Systems Journal*, 12, 231-246.

HKTA (1998). *HKTA Hotel Classification System 1998*, Hong Kong: Hong Kong Tourist Association.

HKTB (2002). *A Statistical Review of Hong Kong Tourism 2001*. Hong Kong: Hong Kong Tourism Board.

HKTB (2003). *Hotel Room Occupancy Rate Report*. Available online at: www.partnernethktb.com [Accessed: March 21, 2003].

Jallat, F., & Capek, M.J. (2001). Disintermediation in Question: New Economy, New Networks, New Middlemen. *Business Horizons*, March-April, 55-60.

Jeong, M., & Lambert, C. (1999). Measuring The Information Quality on Lodging Websites. *International Journal of Hospitality Information Technology*, 1(1), 63-75.

Kotler, P. (1976). *Marketing Management*. Englewood Cliffs, New Jersey: Prentice-Hall.

Kotler, P., & Armstrong, G. (1994). *Principles of Marketing*, 6th ed. Englewood Cliffs, New Jersey: Prentice-Hall.

Kotler, P., Bowen, J., & Makens, J. (1999). *Marketing for Hospitality and Tourism*. New Jersey: Prentice Hall.

Kwong, K.S. (1997). *Tourism and the Hong Kong Economy*. Hong Kong: City University of Hong Kong.

Kasavana, M.L., Knutson, B.J., & Polonowski, S.J. (1997). Netlurking: The Future of Hospitality Internet Marketing. *Journal of Hospitality & Leisure Marketing*, 5(1), 31-44.

Lang, T.C. (2000). The effect of the Internet on travel consumer purchasing behaviour and implications for travel agencies. *Journal of Vacation Marketing*, 6(4), 368-385.

Law, R., Law, A., & Wai, E. (2001). The Impact of the Internet on Travel Agencies in Hong Kong. *Journal of Travel & Tourism Marketing*, 11(2/3), 105-126.

Law, R., Leung, K., & Wong, J. (2004). The impact of the Internet on travel agencies. *International Journal of Contemporary Hospitality Management*, 16(2), 100-107.

Law, R., & Wong, J. (2003). Successful Factors for a Travel Website: Perceptions of Online Purchasers in Hong Kong. *Journal of Hospitality & Tourism Research*, 27(1), 118-124.

Leong, C.C. (2001). Marketing practices and Internet marketing: A study of hotels in Singapore. *Journal of Vacation Marketing*, 7(2), 179-187.

Liao, Z., & Cheung, M.T. (2001). Internet-based e-shopping and consumer attitudes: An empirical study. *Information & Management*, 38(5), 299-306.

Liu, Z. (2000). *Internet Tourism Marketing: Potential and Constraints*. Available online at: http://www.hotel-online.com/Neo/Trends/ChiangMaiJun00/InternetConstraints.html [Accessed: November 15, 2002].

Lubetkin, M. (1999). Bed-and-breakfasts: Advertising and promotion. *Cornell Hotel & Restaurant Administration Quarterly*, 40(4), 84-90.

Morris, L.J., & Morris, J.S. (2002). The changing role of middlemen in the distribution of personal computers.

Journal of Retailing and Consumer Services, 9, 97-105.

Murphy, J., Forrest, E.J., Wotring, C.E., & Brymer, R.A. (1996). Hotel Management and Marketing on the Internet. *Cornell Hotel and Restaurant Administration Quarterly*, 37(3), 70-82.

O'Connor, P., & Horan, P. (1999). An Analysis of Web Reservation Facilities in the Top 50 International Hotel Chains. *International Journal of Hospitality Information Technology*, 1(1), 77-85.

Olmeda, I., & Sheldon, P. (2001). Data Mining Techniques and Applications for Tourism Internet Marketing. *Journal of Travel & Tourism Marketing*, 11(2/3), 1-20.

Palmer, A., & McCole, P. (1999). The Virtual Re-intermediation of Travel Services: A Conceptual Framework and Empirical Investigation. *Journal of Vacation Marketing*, 6(1), 33-47.

Phau, I., & Poon, S.M. (2000). Factors influencing the types of products and services purchased over the Internet. *Internet Research: Electronic Networking Applications and Policy*, 10(2), 102-113.

Poon, A. (2001). The Future of Travel Agents. *Travel & Tourism Analyst*, 3, 57-80.

Procaccino, J.D., & Miller, F.R. (1999). Tourism on the World Wide Web: A Comparison of Websites of United States- and French-based Businesses. *Information Technology & Tourism*, 2(3/4), 173-183.

Rafiq, M., & Ahmed, P.K. (1995). Using the 7Ps as a generic marketing mix: An exploratory survey of UK and European marketing academics. *Marketing Intelligence & Planning*, 13(9), 4-15.

Samenfink, W.H. (1999). Are you ready for the new service user? *Journal of Hospitality & Leisure Marketing*, 6(2), 67-73.

Shapiro, B.P. (1985). Rejuvenating the marketing mix. *Harvard Business Review*, September/October, 28-34.

Sigala, M. (2001). Modelling E-Marketing Strategies: Internet Presence and Exploitation of Greek Hotels. *Journal of Travel & Tourism Marketing*, 11(2/3), 83-103.

Siguaw, J.A., Enz, C.A., & Namasivayam, K. (2000). Adoption of Information Technology in U.S. Hotels: Strategically Driven Objectives. *Journal of Travel Research*, 39(2), 192-201.

Sweeney, S. (2000). *Internet Marketing for Your Tourism Business*. Gulf Breeze, Florida: Maximum Press.

Vandermerwe, S. (1999). The Electronic 'Go-Between Service Provider': A New 'Middle' Role Taking Centre Stage. *European Management Journal*, 17(6), 598-608.

van Hoof, H.B., & Combrink, T.E. (1998). U.S. Lodging Managers and the Internet. *Cornell Hotel & Restaurant Administration Quarterly*, 39(2), 46-54.

Walle, A. (1996). Tourism and Internet: Opportunities for Direct Marketing. *Journal of Travel Research*, 35(1), 72-77.

Wan, S.S. (2002). The Websites of international tourist hotels and tour wholesalers in Taiwan. *Tourism Management*, 23, 155-160.

Zhang, S. (2000). The impact of computer networks on China's travel services. *International Journal of Contemporary Hospitality Management*, 12(5), 331-335.

Zott, C., Amit, R., & Donlevy, J. (2000). Strategies for Value Creation in E-Commerce: Best Practice in Europe. *European Management*, 18(5), 463-475.

Building E-Loyalty of Lodging Brands:
Avoiding Brand Erosion

Brian Miller

SUMMARY. In the early days of the Internet, lodging Websites used the principle of "if we build it they will come." However, with the proliferation and growth of travel Websites and consumers' willingness to book hotel arrangements online, hotel-owned Websites are not capturing the same share of room bookings as achieved through offline distribution channels. Using proprietary Websites to attract, satisfy, and ultimately retain loyal e-consumers will become more critical in maintaining a competitive advantage in a marketplace being dominated by online travel agencies. This paper describes the importance of building e-consumer's loyalty through the proprietary Websites of lodging brands. This paper explores hotel-owned Websites' search engine exposure and salient factors that should be considered by the developers of hotel-owned Websites to positively impact e-loyalty of e-consumers. A framework for future empirical exploration is proffered. *[Article copies available for a fee from The Haworth Document Delivery Service: 1-800-HAWORTH. E-mail address: <docdelivery@ haworthpress.com> Website: <http://www.HaworthPress.com> © 2004 by The Haworth Press, Inc. All rights reserved.]*

KEYWORDS. E-consumer loyalty, hotel proprietary Websites, travel industry intermediaries, e-consumer satisfaction, hotel-owned Websites

INTRODUCTION

In 1999, Bear Sterns reported that the Internet would be the best thing since the toll free telephone call for the lodging industry (Greenspan, 2003a). However, this premise has been hotly debated as being wrong (Starkov, 2002; Stock, 2003; Bergen, 2003; & Welch, 2003). What has proven to be accurate is that the convenience of the Internet has lured travelers to search online when making travel plans and this shift has resulted in significant gains for online travel agencies such as Expedia, Travelocity, and Orbitz. In April 2003, these online travel agencies brought 8.7, 7.2, and 6.6 million visitors to their sites respectively (Greenspan, 2003a). While these e-travel agent sites have grown, in e-consumer visitation (looker behavior), bookings, and ultimate satisfaction, this has not been the case for Websites owned and operated by lodging brands. Top ten ratings of e-consumer satisfaction with travel Websites, compiled by Nielsen Net ratings, do not include any proprietary Websites of lodging brands. The top ten included eight airlines as well as the travel

Brian Miller is Assistant Professor, Hospitality IT, Hotel, Restaurant and Institutional Management, University of Delaware, Newark, DE 19716 (E-mail: blm@udel.edu).

[Haworth co-indexing entry note]: "Building E-Loyalty of Lodging Brands: Avoiding Brand Erosion." Miller, Brian. Co-published simultaneously in *Journal of Travel & Tourism Marketing* (The Haworth Hospitality Press, an imprint of The Haworth Press, Inc.) Vol. 17, No. 2/3, 2004, pp. 133-142; and: *Handbook of Consumer Behavior, Tourism, and the Internet* (ed: Juline E. Mills, and Rob Law) The Haworth Hospitality Press, an imprint of The Haworth Press, Inc., 2004, pp. 133-142. Single or multiple copies of this article are available for a fee from The Haworth Document Delivery Service [1-800-HAWORTH, 9:00 a.m. - 5:00 p.m. (EST). E-mail address: docdelivery@haworthpress.com].

intermediaries Expedia and Travelocity (Pastore, 2001). Nielsen Net Ratings also projects that 57 percent of e-consumers researched for lodging online compared to 52 percent who research for air travel online (Greenspan, 2003a) suggesting that e-consumers, if given the appropriate enticement, would visit and book more rooms with hotel-owned branded Websites.

In 2002, hotel bookings on the Internet, at $6.4 billion, accounted for roughly nine percent of total hotel room bookings (PhoCus Wright, 2003). This growth in online hotel reservation is forecasted to continue unabated and is expected to rise to $14.8 billion (Greenspan, 2003a). However, hotel-owned Websites are steadily losing ground to online travel agencies or intermediary travel Websites. Between 1999 and 2002, hotel-owned Websites have gone from capturing 57% to 51% of total online hotel room bookings (Starkov & Price, 2003; Greenspan, 2003b). Additional stress to hoteliers' profits is created in the average room rate that the hotels receive through the various online distribution channels. The average room rate booked directly at the hotel's Website is approximately $110.00 compared to $76.80 offered at travel intermediary Websites (Starkov, 2002).

Discussions occurring in the lodging industry about what has gone wrong with the industry's failure to capitalize on the direct sales opportunity provided via the Internet conclude that a lack of understanding of the phenomenon of online distribution and limited efforts to identify the impact of the Internet on e-consumer purchasing behavior, resulting in the slow adoption by hoteliers to leverage the Internet as a distribution medium have contributed to the predicament that lodging brands are currently facing (Starkov, 2002). Hoteliers realizing the need to capitalize on the power of the Internet are now under pressure to define viable frameworks for improving their proprietary Websites. This research note examines the challenges facing proprietary lodging Websites in an environment of declining market share of online room reservations through their Websites. The paper concludes with the discussion on developing a framework and identifying salient factors that can be deployed

by hotel-owned Websites to impact e-consumer loyalty positively.

THE E-COMMERCE OF HOTEL ROOMS

In 1996, KPMG Peat Marwick maintained that the Internet would provide significant opportunities for hotel companies to extend a "brand lock" on the consumer (KPMG, 1996). By 2000 most hotel organizations had agreed with this position and were placing hotel room inventory online for consumers to access through their Websites. However, as Burns (2000) noted, too many organizations only paid attention to updating and managing the sites during slow occupancy periods. Unfortunately, this failed strategy of managing the potential for electronic distribution through proprietary lodging brand Websites has led to a continued slippage in the conversion of room sales when compared to online travel agents and third-party Websites (PhoCus Wright, 2003).

Since the explosion of the Internet as a marketing tool, the lodging industry has struggled with the implications of travelers booking rooms online (Greenspan, 2003b; Marta, 2002b; McAuliffe, 2003; O'Connor, 2003; PhoCus Wright, 2003). The Internet as a medium for the distribution of rooms has changed the environment for consumers as well as the hotel industry. In the pre-Internet environment there was information scarcity with respect to who had access to hotel inventory (Frank, 1997). Today, the marketplace has evolved into an information democracy where anyone with access to the Web can receive, use, and diffuse information. Lodging organizations are therefore finding it more difficult to control their inventory and to sustain a competitive advantage with their branded Website. One result of this greater access to information awarded to customers is that they have become more empowered than they were prior to the advent of the Internet (Ostrom & Iacobucci, 1995). Customers can more easily initiate and control information, thus altering the traditional supply and demand balance. Moreover, with the astonishing amount of information provided by different travel sites, consumers are spending more time browsing the Internet in search of relevant information and competitive prices (Stock, 2003). Consequently, in a world where information overload is substituting for information shortage, customers are weakening the traditional buyer-seller relationship (Frank, 1997).

Between the years 1991 and 2000 the demand for hotel rooms increased by 22.9 percent, while supply of rooms during the same period increased by 22.8 percent (Smith Travel, 2001) indicating that the demand for hotel rooms has only matched the pressure from the increase supply of rooms in the marketplace. The phenomenon of the increased access of information to consumers through the development of the Internet as a distribution strategy however, has not resulted in a significant increase in the demand for hotel room nights. In contrary, it has resulted in a shift of power from the supplier (hotels) to the consumer (Stock, 2003).

On the flip side, the advances of the Internet and Web technologies have expedited the development of e-commerce in the sale of hotel rooms. Travel start-up Websites have developed new business portals and provided the marketplace with larger inventories of rooms thereby expanding their markets and creating greater business opportunities (Pastore, 2001). However, the exponentially increasing information, consumer control, along with the rapid expansion of e-businesses have created a situation in which hotel operators are losing control of their room inventory. E-consumers' access to this information coupled with hoteliers' inability to provide competitive information on their own Websites is resulting in a larger supply of rooms being sold through travel intermediaries with higher distribution costs and at lower average room rates for lodging organizations (Marta, 2002a; PhoCus Wright, 2003). As the number of channels for the distribution of hotel rooms online escalated hoteliers embraced this new distribution channel as a way to sell off dead inventory. However, the results of this strategy are leading hoteliers to feel that these new distribution modes have resulted in losing control of their hotel room inventory (McAuliffe, 2003).

Of the four primary distribution channels utilized in the lodging industry with respect to transaction cost, traditional travel agent ($13.50),

online travel agent ($10.50), central reservation system (CRS) ($8.50), and hotel proprietary Website ($1.50), the least expensive channel available to the industry is through the lodging brand's proprietary Website. The variance between selling hotel rooms through a traditional travel agent (most expensive) and selling it through the lodging brand's Website is approximately $12 per transaction (Starkov, 2002). Similarly, after collecting room rates from Internet Websites of the 25 largest international hotel chains and four intermediary Websites, Expedia, Travelocity, TravelWeb, and WorldRes for selected dates, O'Connor (2003) reported that the mean room rate quoted from hotels' proprietary Websites was $159 compared to $152 from Expedia. Moreover, when the hotels' central reservation system (CRS) was called by phone the mean rate received was $163. It appears that hoteliers are discounting room rates offered on their brand's Website as compared to those rates quoted off the CRS reflecting a savings from the lower transaction cost. However, when compared to third-party travel intermediaries the lodging brand's Website was higher.

Additional pressure on room rates has been the adoption by online intermediaries of the merchant model. In utilizing the merchant model, intermediaries purchase large blocks of distressed rooms from hoteliers at deep discounts and are reported to sell them at 15 to 30 percent higher to the e-consumer (Marta, 2002b; PhoCusWright, 2003). This practice is providing record profits from Expedia and others, while hoteliers are struggling to survive (Starkov, 2002). Using the Internet to distribute hotel rooms has several other negative consequences for hoteliers, which include but are not limited to increasing the cost of distribution, reducing average room rates resulting in a degradation of the lodging brand's pricing integrity, and no significant expansion in the demand for hotel rooms.

HOTEL-OWNED WEBSITES RECEIVE LIMITED EXPOSURE ON MAJOR SEARCH ENGINES

Before hotel proprietary Websites can begin to significantly make an impact on reducing the slide in market share of online room sales from third party travel sites they must identify and understand e-consumer search behavior. Windham and Orton (2000) found that 80 percent of respondents or Internet users in their study expected to turn to the Internet more often than current practice for making online purchases. More importantly, sixty-five percent regularly visited a search engine to begin their Internet search activities with travel purchases among the tenth most popular product purchased online. However, there has been mixed messages as to how e-consumers and e-businesses can maximize their efforts and expand their capture rate in the online market respectively. Greenspan (2003a) found that 56% of Internet users give up their search before going past the second page of search engine results. Moreover, over a quarter will move onto another search engine site before refining their keywords. Even with the potential of creating a competitive advantage through the development of proprietary brand Website, hotel companies have missed opportunities to generate traffic on their branded Websites by not considering a strategy to improve their Website visibility in search engines (CyberAtlas, 2001b).

To further examine this concept this author conducted an exploration of finding proprietary lodging brand Websites through search engines using intuitive keywords. After identifying the top seven search engines being used by e-consumers in 2003, this researcher ran a search using keywords to identify how e-consumers can easily locate hotels for booking rooms online. The seven most popular search engines used today in order of their popularity are Google, AlltheWeb, Teoma, Yahoo, Altavista, MSN, and Lycos (CyberAtlas, 2001a). For each search engine, a common keyword was used to identify the results of hotel proprietary Websites returned from the search. Four keywords were used and included "hotel," "hotels," "lodging" and "travel." Tables 1 and 2 present the results from each of the seven most popular search engines when using "hotel" (Table 1) and "hotels" (Table 2). When using "hotel" as the keyword Yahoo returned the most proprietary lodging Websites in the first two pages with 15 out of 40 links. AlltheWeb and MSN returned only four and

six proprietary lodging Website links respectively within the first two pages. Similar results occurred when using the keyword "hotels." Surprisingly, when the keyword used was "lodging" only Teoma (12) and MSN (6) returned any links to proprietary Websites. The results were even more discouraging for proprietary lodging Websites when using the keyword "travel" which resulted in no hotel-owned Websites found in the search results within the first two pages. It seems clear that one part of the Internet strategy that lodging brands need to address to overcome the lack of market share in online room bookings is to get more exposure with the popular search engines when using intuitive keywords.

When searching under the keyword "travel," Expedia and Travelocity came up within the first two non-sponsored listings in each of the seven most popular search engines. Given the current state of affairs, e-consumers in search of hotel rooms on the Internet may very well find that using third party travel agents represents the most efficient search strategy in terms of time and cost. Hotel-owned Websites must begin developing a better strategy to position their Websites on Internet search engines to drive customers to their Websites. Conventional wisdom seems to contend that a large section of the e-commercial marketplace gravitates toward the sites that listed in their searches and ultimately purchase rooms online based on price alone (Starkov, 2002).

EMERGING HOTEL STRATEGIES

The marketplace is beginning to see evidence that hoteliers are attempting to take back control of their room inventories. Marta (2002a) suggests that hotel companies are being careful when directing activities toward their online sales efforts. However, a select few hotel brands are taking an aggressive approach. Recently, several hotel companies have announced e-commerce initiatives that guarantee e-consumers that the lowest Internet price at their hotels will be found on their proprietary Website. These promotions are a direct effort to increase the percentage of direct sales of hotel rooms purchased online toward those being achieved off-line.

TABLE 1. Web Search Results When Using Keyword Hotel

Keyword: Hotel

Search Engine						
Google	**AlltheWeb**	**Teoma**	**Yahoo**	**Altavista**	**MSN**	**Lycos**
Hilton	Radisson	Marriott	Hilton	Days Inn	Country Inns & Suites	Radisson
Marriott	Sheraton (Starwood)	Hilton	Marriott	Hilton	Marriott	Sheraton
Radisson	Marriott	Ramada	Radisson	Marriott	Days Inn	Marriott
Sheraton (Starwood)	InterContinental	Sheraton (Starwood)	Sheraton	Radisson	Ramada	Doubletree
InterContinental		Days Inn	Hyatt	Sheraton	Motel 6	InterContinental
Westin (Starwood)		Holiday Inn	Westin	Ramada	Hyatt	
Fairmont		Westin (Starwood)	Fairmont	Holiday Inn		
Westin (Starwood)		Hyatt	InterContinental			
Wyndham		Radisson	Wyndham			
Omni		Bellagio	Marriott			
		Crowne Plaza Hotels (Inter-Continental)	Days Inn			
		Wyndham	Embassy Suites			
			Clarion Inn			
			Doubletree			
			Hyatt			

Notes: There are 84,100,000 links found when searching "hotel" under Google search engine.
There are 45,017,594 links found when searching "hotel" under AlltheWeb search engine.
There are 15,480,000 links found when searching "hotel" under Teoma search engine.
There are 75,600,000 links found when searching "hotel" under Yahoo search engine.
There are 21,546,177 links found when searching "hotel" under Altavista search engine.
There are 122,152 links found when searching "hotel" under MSN search engine.
There are 65,519,943 links found when searching "hotel" under Lycos search engine.

Wyndham spent $4 to 5 million on upgrading their Website to include faster connections and technology to build repeat customer relationships. Additionally, they have rolled out a program, Wyndham.com WEBRATES, which guarantees e-consumers the lowest available Wyndham rate found on the Internet. With the new Webmatch Guarantee, if e-consumers find a lower Wyndham rate for the same property on another Website, Wyndham will match it (Wyndham Hotels and Resorts, 2003).

InterContinental Hotels Group is seeing an 80 percent increase in Internet revenue after their launching of "The Lowest Internet Rate Guarantee." InterContinental Hotels Group proclaims to be the first hotel company to offer Web bookings more than eight years ago. The hotel company is reporting that their lowest Internet rate guarantee is proving to be a win-win-win situation for their customers, the individual hotels and for InterContinental Hotels Group. The company contends that since the launch of the "Lowest Internet Rate Guarantee" program, more people are booking direct on their Website than ever before. InterContinental Hotel Group, whose brands include the InterContinental, Holiday Inn, Holiday Inn Express, Crowne Plaza and Staybridge, ensures that guests can book with confidence the confidence that they will always get the best available rate, that their reservation will be there when they arrive, and that their security and privacy are always protected (InterContinen-

TABLE 2. Web Search Results When Using Keyword Hotels

Keyword: Hotels

Search Engine						
Google	**AlltheWeb**	**Teoma**	**Yahoo**	**Altavista**	**MSN**	**Lycos**
Hilton	Hyatt	Marriott	Hyatt	Days Inn	Country Inn & Suites	Hyatt
Marriott	Radisson	Hilton	Radisson	Hilton	Marriott	Radisson
Hyatt	Sheraton (Starwood)	Radisson	Sheraton	Marriott	Days Inn	Sheraton
Radisson	InterContinental	Ramada	Hilton	Radisson	Ramada	InterContinental
Sheraton (Starwood)	Westin (Starwood)	Wyndham	Westin (Starwood)	Sheraton	Motel 6	Doubletree
Westin (Starwood)	Starwood	Hyatt	Marriott	Ramada	Hyatt	Westin (Starwood)
InterContinental	Wyndham	Holiday Inn	Fairmont	Holiday Inn		Starwood
Fairmont	InterContinental	Westin (Starwood)	Starwood	Concorde		Wyndham
	Omni	Sheraton	Six Continents	Fairmont		InterContinental
	Holiday Inn	Days Inn	Wyndham	Starwood		Omni
	Loews	Renaissance	Omni			Holiday Inn
		Comfort Hotels & Suites	Holiday Inn			
		Four Seasons	Renaissance			
		Crowne Plaza Hotels	Omni			
		Fairmont	Wyndham			
			Starwood			

Notes: There are 69,000,000 links found when searching "hotels" under Google search engine.
There are 33,520,645 links found when searching "hotels" under AlltheWeb search engine.
There are 11,890,000 links found when searching "hotels" under Teoma search engine.
There are 61,800,000 links found when searching "hotels" under Yahoo search engine.
There are 14,406,569 links found when searching "hotels" under Altavista search engine.
There are 122,152 links found when searching "hotels" under MSN search engine.
There are 40,871,865 links found when searching "hotels" under Lycos search engine.

tal Hotel Group, 2003). Since launching the Internet guarantee in May 2002, the InterContinental Hotel Group's Websites booked more than $3 million in a single day (InterContinental.com, 2003).

Cendant Corporation's hotel group has also announced a best available rate guarantee that promises to provide online customers with the lowest rates available anywhere on the Internet for its Days Inn, Super 8, Ramada, Travelodge, Howard Johnson, Knights Inn, Villager, Wingate Inn and AmeriHost Inn hotel brands. Under the guarantee, if customers find lower published rates for any of their hotel properties in the United States and Canada through any other online travel site, they will receive the lower rate plus an additional 10 percent discount. Rudnitsky, CEO of Cendent's hotel group, states "As the world's largest hotel franchisor, we are committed to ensuring our customers' trust and confidence in our brands. With the best available rate guarantee, our customers will get the best deals as well as quick, convenient service through our branded Websites" (Cendent Corporation, 2002). How effective these pricing strategies prove to be will be determined in the future, however, hotelier strategies should go beyond competition with the intermediary Websites, they must incorporate strategies that are gleaned from research findings to create an experience for the consumer which will build e-commerce loyalty to their brand, thus averting their product from becoming a commodity.

CONSUMER E-LOYALTY

Building e-consumer loyalty will be vital to the success of hotels in reversing the trend of losing market share in the online room booking market and reducing distribution costs. Without motivating e-consumers to their proprietary Websites hoteliers have limited opportunities to present their value proposition to the consumer and will be left to compete online solely on price. Therefore, consideration should be given to identifying strategies for increasing consumer e-loyalty with hotel proprietary brand Website.

Customer loyalty may be defined as the propensity of the consumer to hold an approving disposition toward a brand or company, which is exhibited through a sustained commercial relationship over time with a brand or company. Srinivasan, Anderson, and Ponnavolu (2002) defined e-loyalty as a "customer's favorable attitude toward the e-retailer that results in repeat buying behavior" (p. 42). One factor that hotel companies need to hone in is whether consumer loyalty has any relationship to consumer's price sensitivity (Krishnamurthi & Raj, 1991; Mela, Gupta & Lehmann, 1997; Wernerfelt, 1991). Researchers that have addressed this topic have generally found that increases in consumer loyalty does reduce consumer's sensitivity to price as well as permitting businesses to charge a premium over existing competitors and serving as a defense against lower-priced emergent competitors (Krishnamurthi & Papatla, 2003). Both of these assertions lead credence to the argument that hoteliers can positively impact the capture rate of online room bookings as compared to third party travel sites.

Srinivasan et al. (2002) identified seven factors that were found to be important to e-consumers while conducting commerce with retailers electronically. These factors have an impact on e-loyalty of e-consumers when visiting e-retailers' Websites. The eight factors that were deemed to be important on e-retail-

ers' Websites were customization, contact interactivity, care, community, convenience, cultivation, choice, character, and trust. An eighth factor has already been described and that is trust. A brief discussion of each follows.

Customization

Customization relates to the ability to provide individualized products or services through flexible processes. Customization of the online hotel room purchase experience must allow for the consumer to change and direct the interface of the Website to better meet their needs. This would include identification of the e-consumer on return visits, multiple search strategies, variable options for delivery of search results, production and retrieval of travel itineraries, and multiple methods of payment for services. Other benefits derived by providing for more customization for the e-consumer are increased perception of choice (Shostak, 1987), reduced confusion (Lidsky, 1999), and improved conversion from search to purchase (Ostrom and Iacobucci, 1995).

Contact Interactivity

To stimulate interest in the lodging brand's Website it is important that the e-consumer can structure their search in a manner that is intuitive and relevant. Too often hotel Websites are created with the organization's or programmer's perspective. Website interactivity has the ability to bring together sales, service, and support effort of the hotel organization online because it is driven by the e-consumer. It requires integration between legacy brick and mortar systems and e-commerce communication systems. LaMonica (1999) writes that the value of interactive Web-based sites increases almost exponentially as they are integrated into other service channels.

Care

Efforts should be made by proprietary lodging Websites to communicate with the e-consumer during the pre- and post-purchase phase (Srinivasan et al., 2002). Collaborative e-commerce software tools should be considered as will allow the organization to interact online with potential customers as well as current and past customers in a real time manner.

Community

Hagel and Armstrong (1997) and Frank (1997) suggest that building virtual communities promote the advantages of word-of-mouth advertising strategies and provide for an opportunity to compare information regarding e-consumers' experiences respectively. Since 1997 the development of virtual communities has been seen by marketing and advertising worlds and the future to mass customization. In travel and tourism, the industry has attempted to create a "virtual plaza" where e-consumers could congregate and share information while carrying out their travel related e-purchases. Wang, Yu, and Fesenmaier (2002) suggests that there are operational issues that must be considered when setting up virtual communities. These surround the people, purpose, policy, and computer systems that are to be used.

Cultivation

The characteristic of the business transaction of reserving a room in the hotel provides lodging organizations with robust collection of consumer information. By utilizing this information lodging organizations can build e-consumer relationships that enhance the experience for the guest and provide opportunities to guide them through the purchasing experience. The traditional means for cultivating customers is to offer points for each room booked. These points are kept by the traveler and can be redeemed for prices and/or savings on future planned stays. Once an e-consumer has visited the Website, successful hotel Websites can begin to a carefully developed strategy to turn lookers into booker. Creating this experience for the e-consumer should not be seen as unnecessary, time-consuming, and burdensome.

Choice

Bergen, Dutta, and Shugan (1996) suggest that there are costs to the e-consumer when searching across multiple vendors. Their research found that shopping with vendors that offer multiple product lines reduce the cost of inconvenience to the e-consumer and that those vendors who appear to offer greater choice will garner improved e-loyalty.

Character

The Website of the lodging brand should be more than a brochure of the collection of hotel properties. It should be designed to reflect the image that the organization wishes to portray in the marketplace. By keeping the site fresh and updated with relevant e-consumer information, hotels can use the Website to not only promote the sale of rooms but also to create an important resource for travel information that goes beyond their facility.

Trust

Developing e-loyalty in a virtual environment and moving the e-consumer from a browser to electronic commerce require an essential prerequisite: trust (Papadopoulou, Andreau, Kanellis, & Martakos, 2001). Much more research into this dynamic component is needed to be learned before Website developers will truly know how to approach this factor. Additionally, as encoding software becomes more powerful and trusted in the marketplace, the mechanics of securing data electronically should become more routine. However, regardless of the technical merits required to secure customer data, hoteliers must apply ethical practices in the sale and delivery of their product. Practices of overstating property characteristics, hidden charges, and confusingly worded promotions will further exacerbate the challenge of promoting trust to e-consumers.

CONCLUSION

The e-commerce of hotel rooms will see double-digit growth into the foreseeable future. Hotel-owned Websites have seen a decline in market share of converting lookers to bookers against their online travel agents and third-party travel Websites. In addition to online booking of hotel rooms at proprietary hotel brand Websites at a slower rate than offline proprietary channels, hoteliers are faced with an increase in distribution costs and a decrease in realized average daily rates (Starkov, 2002). The hotel industry will need to gain confidence in the prudence of this strategy through the efforts of research conducted by academics in the field of travel and tourism marketing. Research should help to construct a clearer picture of e-consumer behavior and identify actionable strategies for proprietary lodging brand Websites developers to capture and retain more online hotel room sales.

Potential research topics include: (1) An empirical review of reported factors that prior research have identified as salient in the development of e-loyalty. Survey instruments should collect information from e-consumers of lodging proprietary Websites. This type of research will provide greater precision as to the extent that e-consumers of hotels products expect when conducting e-commerce of hotel products. (2) Compare retail trends of other retail goods (such as books and music), which have been dramatically altered by consumers' attraction to using the Internet purchasing these productions online. These efforts may lead to identifying similar themes and strategies that are applicable to those found in the change and growth of how consumers are purchasing hotel rooms. For example, airlines have been quick to accept the potential of direct sales of seats in an online environment (Bergen, 2003). This type of research could identify what element(s) were in place to produce this phenomenon. (3) Conduct qualitative research of decision makers in lodging organizations to identify long-term strategies for the distribution of their room inventory. How are the leaders in the lodging industry framing the problem of declining market share in online bookings, increasing distribution costs and the reduction of average room rates? To what effect are these strategies impacting the challenges being faced by the hotel industry of flat hotel demand, lower average room rates, and lower occupancy? Further exploration along these lines will identify if specific Internet distribution strategies transcends service level products. (4) Through the use of the case study research method, researchers should identify hoteliers that are achieving higher direct online room bookings than the average proprietary lodging Websites. Through this research

salient factors can be identified and verified with traditional consumer loyalty research to determine any variation with those that are found to be significant in moving the consumer toward e-loyalty of similar products purchased online. Completing an analysis of these successful proprietary lodging Website designs will provide information toward improving e-consumer visitation and satisfaction. Conducting auxiliary analysis of findings, which compare results to a similar evaluation of e-travel agents and online third-party travel sites, could expand this line of research.

Developing hotel proprietary Websites that build e-consumer loyalty for their brands should foster reestablishing the hotel organization's control of room inventory, which will ultimately have a positive effect on room rates and reduce distribution costs while cultivating e-consumer loyalty toward their hotel brands.

REFERENCES

Bergen, K. (2003). Hotel company Websites pulling 51% of online bookings in 2002: Internet strategies in play to reduce third-party bookings. Retrieved December 21, 2003 from *www.Hotel-online.com/News/PR2003_1st/Jan03_BookingSites.html*

Bergen, M., Dutta, S. & Shugan, S. (February, 1996). Branded variants: A retail perspective. *Journal of Marketing Research*, 33, 9-19.

Brown, G. (June 9, 1952). Brand loyalty: Fact or fiction? *Advertising Age*, 23, 53-55.

Burns, J. (Fall, 2000). Understanding and maximizing a hotel's electronic distribution options. Retrieved June 6, 2003 from *www.hotel-online.com/News/PressReleases2000_4th/Oct00_ElectronicDistrib.html*

Cendant Corporation. (2003). Corporate Website. Retrieved June 28, 2003 from *www.cendant.com*

CyberAtlas. (2001a). Google grabs globe, U.S. to Yahoo. *CyberAtlas*. May 1, 2001. Retrieved June 22, 2003 from *cyberatlas.internet.com*

CyberAtlas. (2001b). Companies lack sound search engine strategies. *CyberAtlas*. September 13, 2001. Retrieved June 2, 2003 from *cyberatlas.internet.com*

Frank, M. (1997). The realities of Web-based electronic commerce. *Strategy and Leadership*, 5(5), 30-32.

Greenspan, R. (2003a). Hotel industry makes room for online bookings. *CyberAtlas*, January 9, 2003.

Greenspan, R. (2003b). Traveler's first trip is often the Internet. Retrieved May 27, 2003 from *cyberatlas.internet.com*

Hagel, J. & Armstrong, A. G. (Winter, 1997). Net gain: Expanding markets through virtual communities. *McKinsey Quarterly*, 140-147.

InterContinental Hotel Group. (2003). Corporate Website. Retrieved June 23, 2003 from *www.intercontinental. com*

KPMG Peat Marwick (1996). Five major trends today create opportunities for hospitality industry tomorrow. Retrieved from *http://www.hotel-online.com/ Trends/KPMG/Articles/14jun1996.html* on June 30, 2003.

Krishnamurthi, L. and Raj, S. (Spring, 1991). An empirical analysis of the relationship between brand loyalty and consumer price elasticity. *Marketing Science,* 10, 172-183.

Krishnamurthi, L. & Papatla, P. (2003). Accounting for heterogeneity and dynamics in the loyalty-price sensitivity relationship. *Journal of Retailing,* 79(2), 121-135.

LaMonica, M. (November, 1999). Putting together the interactivity puzzle. *Infoworld,* 21(44), 35.

Lidsky, D. (October 5,1999). Getting better all the time: Electronic commerce sites. *PC Magazine,* 98.

Marta, S. (November, 2002a). Competition to sell discounted hotel rooms over the Internet heats up. *Hotel-Online.com.* Retrieved January 16, 2003 from *www.hotel-online.com/News/PR2002_4th/Nov02_ Commidity.html*

Marta, S. (January, 2002b). Hotels look for ways to lure more customers back to their Websites; want to take back the reins on distribution. *Hotel-Online.com.* Retrieved January 22, 2003 from *www.hotel-online. com/News/PR2003_1st/Jan03_WebBookings.html*

McAuliffe, S. (January, 2003). Wresting back control from the online wholesalers. *Hotel-Online.com.* Retrieved January 21, 2003 from *www.hotel-online. com/News/PR2003_1st/Jan03_RateParity.html*

Mela, C., Gupta, S. and Lehmann, D. (May, 1997). The long-term impact of promotion and advertising on consumer brand choice. *Journal of Marketing Research* 34, 248-261.

O'Connor, P. (2003). Online pricing: An analysis of hotel-company practices. *Cornell Hotel and Restaurant Quarterly,* 44(1), 88-96.

Ostrom, A. & Iacobucci, D. (1995). Consumer tradeoffs and evaluation of services. *Journal of Marketing,* 59(1), 17-28.

Papadopoulou, P., Andreau, A., Kanellis, P., & Martakos, D. (2001). Trust and relationship building in electronic commerce. *Internet Research: Electronic Networking Applications and Policy,* 11(4), 322-332.

Pastore, M. (2001). Online Travel Market Largely Avoids Economic Slowdown. *CyberAtlas.com.* Retrieved April 17, 2003 from *http://cyberatlas. internet.com/markets/travel/article/0,,6071_749671, 00.html#table*

PhoCus Wright (2003). PhoCus Wright's FYI: Hotels' efforts to control distribution could backfire. Retrieved December 16, 2002 from *www.Webtravelnews.com/ archive/article.html?id=929*

Shostak, G. (1987). Breaking free from product marketing. *Journal of Marketing,* 41(4), 73-80.

Smith Travel Research (2001). Hotel operating statistics: 2001 report for the year 2000. Hendersonville, TN.

Srinivasan, S., Anderson, R., & Ponnavolu, K. (2002). Customer loyalty in e-commerce: An exploration of its antecedents and consequences. *Journal of Retailing,* 78(1), 41-50.

Starkov, M. (October, 2002). The Internet: Hotelier's best ally or worst enemy? *Hotel Online Special Report.* Retrieved October 9, 2002 from *hotel-online. com/News/PR2002_4th/Oct02_InternetAlly.html*

Starkov, M. & Price, J. (2003). Are hoteliers ready to meet the new challenges in online business travel? *Hospitalitynet.* Retrieved March 5, 2003 from *www.hospitalitynet.org/news/4014923.html*

Stock, T. (2003). Getting hotel consumers to click. Retrieved February 3, 2003 from *www.lodgingnews. com/subs/learnincenter/whitepapers/sdnal.asp*

Wang, Y., Yu, Q., & Fesebnauer, D. (2002). Defining the virtual tourist community: Implications for tourism marketing. *Tourism Management,* 23(4), 407-417.

Ward, J. & Ostrom, A. (2003). The Internet as information minefield: An analysis of the source and content of brand information yielded by net searches. Retrieved June 18, 2003 from *www.sciencedirect.com*

Welch, R. (2003). E-commerce marketing: The race for success. Retrieved January 22, 2003 from *www.hotel-online.com/News/PR2003)1st/Jan03_eCommerceRace. html*

Wernerfelt, B. (Summer, 1991). Brand loyalty and market equilibrium. *Marketing Science,* 10, 229-245.

Windham, L. & Orton, K. (2000). *The soul of the new consumer: Attitudes, behavior, and preferences of e-consumers.* Allworth Press: New York, NY.

Wyndham Hotels and Resorts. (2003). Corporate Website. Retrieved June 28, 2003 from *www.wyndham.com*

SECTION 4:
E-COMPLAINT BEHAVIOR

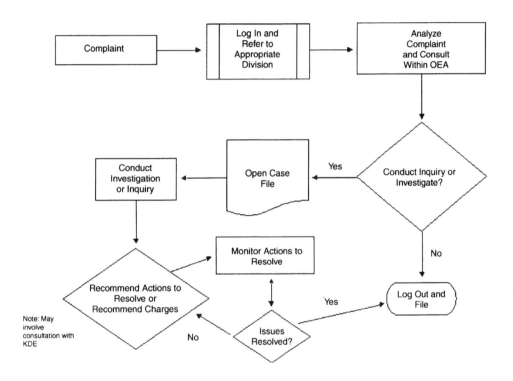

The Complaint Resolution Process
Adapted from: www.lrc.state.ky.us/oea/process.htm

Internet Diffusion of an E-Complaint:
A Content Analysis of Unsolicited Responses

Linda Shea
Linda Enghagen
Ashish Khullar

SUMMARY. "Yours Is A Very Bad Hotel," a customer complaint in the form of a PowerPoint presentation, earned a degree of notoriety when it spread worldwide via the Internet even though it was not intended for public distribution. While none were solicited, its authors received over 4,000 e-mail responses to their e-complaint. This paper presents a content analysis of 1,000 of those responses. The results of the content analysis yielded interesting patterns of diffusion that have implications for hospitality practitioners and academics. The findings include geographic diffusion within and outside the U.S. as well as diffusion through professional groups and organizations over time. Patterns with respect to gender, employment sector, affective response, intention to communicate with other individuals and groups, and intentions for further usage of the complaints are also presented. Comparisons to theories of diffusion of innovations were also undertaken. *[Article copies available for a fee from The Haworth Document Delivery Service: 1-800-HAWORTH. E-mail address: <docdelivery@haworthpress.com> Website: <http://www.HaworthPress.com> © 2004 by The Haworth Press, Inc. All rights reserved.]*

KEYWORDS. E-mail, e-complaint, complaint behavior, diffusion, word-of-mouth communication, service recovery

INTRODUCTION

While the customer isn't always right, it's also true that the customer isn't always wrong. In fact, from management's perspective, the more compelling truth is that who is right and who is wrong is largely irrelevant. Managing complaints with the goals of service recovery and customer retention are more important than assessing and laying blame. For example, the cost of finding a new customer is five to ten times that of retaining an existing customer. In addition, nineteen dissatisfied customers do not complain for every one that

Linda Shea and Linda Enghagen are Associate Professors, Department of Hospitality and Tourism Management, Isenberg School of Management, the University of Massachusetts at Amherst. Ashish Khullar is affiliated with Expedia.

Address correspondence to Linda Shea (E-mail: LJShea@ht.umass.edu).

The authors wish to acknowledge Tom Farmer of Solid State Information Design and Shane Atchison of ZAAZ for providing the case study, data and ongoing guidance for this project.

[Haworth co-indexing entry note]: "Internet Diffusion of an E-Complaint: A Content Analysis of Unsolicited Responses." Shea, Linda, Linda Enghagen, and Ashish Khullar. Co-published simultaneously in *Journal of Travel & Tourism Marketing* (The Haworth Hospitality Press, an imprint of The Haworth Press, Inc.) Vol. 17, No. 2/3, 2004, pp. 145-165; and: *Handbook of Consumer Behavior, Tourism, and the Internet* (ed: Juline E. Mills and Rob Law) The Haworth Hospitality Press, an imprint of The Haworth Press, Inc., 2004, pp. 145-165. Single or multiple copies of this article are available for a fee from The Haworth Document Delivery Service [1-800-HAWORTH, 9:00 a.m. - 5:00 p.m. (EST). E-mail address: docdelivery@haworthpress.com].

does (Coca-Cola USA, 1981a; TARP, 1986). This is consistent with the work of Bitner, Booms and Tetreault (1990) who found that while customers expect to experience some service failures, the extent of their satisfaction or dissatisfaction rests on the manner in which the failure is resolved. Worse yet, research indicates that in more than half of those instances in which a company attempts to resolve a customer's complaint, the customer becomes more dissatisfied based on how the complaint is handled (Hart, Heskett & Sasser, 1990). The potential for lost business from customer complaints is significantly increased with the widespread use of the Internet and e-mail communications. *"Yours Is A Very Bad Hotel"* is one example of a relatively straightforward e-complaint earning unexpected notoriety as the result of unintended Internet diffusion.

"YOURS IS A VERY BAD HOTEL"
INCIDENT

On November 15, 2001, two consultants traveling on business were refused a room at an overbooked Houston hotel despite holding guaranteed reservations and membership in an elite level frequent guest program. They responded with what became a widely distributed and now well-known complaint in the form of a PowerPoint presentation entitled "Yours Is a Very Bad Hotel." At the time, they sent it to the General Manager of the hotel and forwarded copies to a relative and two friends with no intention or expectation that it be further disseminated (Farmer, 2002). Nevertheless, in a matter of weeks it became "Urban Legend" as, via the Internet, the presentation made its way throughout the United States and around the world. It filtrated many sectors of the economy including business (hospitality and tourism in particular), education, government, and the media. The authors themselves received over 4,000 e-mail responses from individuals who received the PowerPoint presentation (Farmer, 2002). Furthermore, it was widely reported by the media with articles appearing in such publications as *ADWEEK* (Terror of Night Clerk Mike, 2002), *Fast Company* (Cheat Sheet, 2002), *Financial Post*

(Vardy, 2001), *PR Week* (Holmes, 2002), *The Seattle Times* (Soto, 2002), *USA Today* (Bly, 2002), and the *Wall Street Journal* (Guzman, 2001). This unique form of complaint has also raised various questions in the minds of academics and practitioners from varied backgrounds (Farmer, 2002). For instance, e-mail respondents representing business school educators, media consultants and managers within product and service industries questioned the meaning of the word "guarantee" as applied to hotel rooms. Furthermore, they have inquired as to the effectiveness of this form of communication in achieving a response from the hotel company involved (Farmer, 2002). Some of the issues most relevant to hospitality educators and managers include overbooking, complaint behavior, service quality, employee training, and communications, to name a few.

Using this case for analysis, this project provides insight into the diffusion process relevant in today's world of electronic communication. This study involves a content analysis of the e-mail responses and determines the extent and directional flow of electronic word-of-mouth communication as the message diffused.

DIFFUSION MODELS

The diffusion of innovation is the aggregate of the individual adoption process whereby an individual passes from knowledge, to formation of an attitude, to a decision to adopt or reject, to implementation of the new idea, and to confirmation of the decision (Rogers, 1983). It refers to the process and rate at which various groups of individuals adopt an idea or innovation in a given society. Adopter groups are identified as innovators, early adopters, early majority, and laggards or non-adopters (Rogers, 1983). Adopter groups can be described by personal characteristics, socio-economic status, or by their exposure to communications and subsequent influence on others.

Communication channels through which information travels are categorized as interpersonal or mass media in nature. Interpersonal channels usually involve a face-to-face exchange between two or more individuals. These can be marketer-dominated sources (sales personnel, travel agents) or non-marketer dominated (friends, family) forms of word-of-mouth communication. Mass media channels include radio, television, newspapers, and direct mail (Rogers, 1983). Channel usage by different adopter categories also determines the flow of communication and differentiates between the categories on the basis of the awareness and the dissemination of information (Rogers, 1983).

The use of Internet communications is of particular interest because it can be considered both a source of interpersonal and mass communication among e-consumers. Furthermore, it is a rather informal non-marketer dominated form of communication (even within formal organizations) that itself had not yet diffused throughout the population when diffusion/adoption theories were initially developed and studied (Leslie, 1994). Leslie (1994) estimated that by the end of 2003, business email usage would quintuple the 1993 rate of 16 million messages per year. It is widely accepted that the use of the Internet in the form of emails and to some extent web sites, adds a new dimension to available methods of communication among networks of individuals and groups, both formal and informal (Leslie, 1994).

Not all individuals in a social system adopt an innovation or an idea at the same time. Rather, they adopt in a time sequence, and they are classified into adopter categories on the basis of when they employ the idea (Rogers, 1983). The diffusion effect is the cumulatively increasing degree of influence upon an individual to adopt or reject an innovation, resulting from the activation of peer networks about an innovation in the social system (Rogers, 1983). The diffusion effect depends on the degree of interconnectedness. While diffusion of an e-complaint is different from diffusion of an innovation, the conceptual linkages are apparent. It is the communication flow, dissemination of information and interconnectedness that are relevant in this case. Communication and diffusion of information referred to in the original diffusion model that pre-dates Internet usage, was largely based on physical, geographic proximity of individuals (Rogers, 1983). As an example, the diffusion of solar panels tended to occur in geographically concentrated areas where individuals were connected

and communicated within neighborhoods (Rogers, 1983). In contrast, communication via email allows information to spread more quickly in a rather geometric fashion due to the extensive interconnectedness of individuals and groups (Wilson, 2003; Leslie, 1994). Using the Internet, individuals are able to connect easily with social and professional groups. The communication flow is likely multi-directional and these patterns are of particular interest in this study.

In this paper, the trickle-down, trickle up, and trickle-across theories of diffusion relative to Internet communication are examined. The classical model posits a trickle-down process whereby information and influence flow sequentially from the top down through socio-economic classes within a social system. Later, a two-step flow of communications model was proposed as a second theory (Rogers, 1983). Known as the trickle-across theory, it implies a layer of opinion leaders who seek out information and influence others within formal and informal, social, and work groups. Finally, a third theory referred to as the trickle-up process suggests that some innovations begin at the lower end of the socio-economic population and move upward through the classes. The three diffusion processes are depicted in Figure 1 (Rogers, 1983).

The conceptual equivalent of the trickle down process for business could be viewed as the movement of information or ideas from top management filtering through layers of

FIGURE 1. Three Diffusion Models

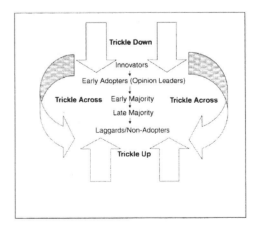

managers and employees. The trickle across process implies the receipt of information by opinion leaders in an organization with subsequent passage to others. Finally, the trickle up process suggests that lower level employees pass information to those in higher ranked positions. Diffusion models traditionally have implicated strategies for marketer-dominated communications and in fact were developed long before Internet usage began its own diffusion process. Word-of-mouth communication has been a part of the model since its inception; however, considering the speed and extent of diffusion through the Internet, this non-marketer-dominated communication channel introduces a unique element to this process. It is well accepted by marketing scholars and managers that non-marketing dominated sources of information, including negative word-of-mouth messages, are given substantial consideration in forming opinions and making purchase decisions–particularly in the context of services (Richins, 1983). On the Internet, word-of-mouth marketing is referred to as "viral marketing" (Wilson, 2000).

VIRAL MARKETING AND THE IMPACT OF E-MAIL MESSAGES

Viral marketing describes any strategy that encourages individuals to pass on a marketing message to others, creating the potential for exponential growth in the message's exposure and influence (Wilson, 2000). The notion of a virus pertains to the reliance on rapid multiplication that spreads to thousands and even millions of people. The extent that the message spreads depends on the "pass-along rate"–the percentage of people who pass on a file or message to their friends, relatives, co-workers, and other formal and informal groups (marketingterms.com, 2003). Pass-along rates are essentially a measure of word-of-mouth marketing. Messages passed through email and other files often contain humor and entertainment, news, or shopping promotions (marketingterms.com, 2003). They tend to be relatively short and informal, as casual conversations, a phone call, or a postcard (Leslie, 1994). Internally, companies have identified

electronic mail as a coalition-building tool largely due to the members of an organization being less inhibited in their input (Romm & Pliskin, 1998).

Literature related to viral marketing often suggests a deliberate strategy developed and executed by a company to encourage pass along rates (Wilson, 2000; Parker, 2003). For instance, Wilson (2000) outlines six principles or elements of a viral marketing strategy. Of particular note is his reference to communication networks. Similarly, Parker (2003) offers four characteristics that little has been related to potential negative word-of-mouth consequences to firms. One of these important characteristics is that the sender of an e-mail message to people on their own mailing lists is typically considered a trusted source of information.

In contrast, there is a paucity of research on the unintentional, negative consequences of e-mail messages. The term vile viral refers to negative word-of-mouth generated when people use e-mail messages, Websites and other types of files to warn others of negative experiences with a product, service or company (Rohrbacher, 2000). The fact that many of these negative viral marketing instances are unintentional points to the lack of control and potential damage toward firms. Ritson (2003), noted that with help from the Internet, "viral marketing" allows individual customers to damage and potentially destroy multinational organizations.

Since hospitality consumers subjected to a complaint as recipients of e-mail messages may subsequently form opinions about the company that is the object of the complaint, it is an issue that warrants a broader understanding. This study, therefore, explores the patterns of diffusion of this case of e-communications and the influence on e-consumer behavior.

METHODOLOGY

A sample of 1,000 responses was randomly generated from the total of more than 4,000 responses that the two consultants received. One-fifth of the e-mail responses had previously undergone a rather rudimentary organization into several batches that were treated as strata, based on industry segments such as hospitality, media, and consulting. A perusal of the categories deemed them incomplete and inaccurate; hence, they were essentially treated as part of the total sampling frame. Every fourth subject was selected from each segment. The content analysis framework shown in Table 1 was developed to extract and organize information included in the responses.

A total of 36 variables were used in the framework including physical or movement characteristics of the message, demographic sender characteristics and message content details such as affective response and nature of anecdotal information. The message characteristics were intended to extract an estimate of the nature and extent of movement. Determining how subjects received the original message, to whom it was then forwarded, for what the PowerPoint complaint would be used, and what they intended to do with the message are important in examining diffusion.

Since many of the e-mail responses included personal anecdotes of service failures, measures of the subject and content of those were also of interest. The potential of those variables to help explain what triggered the reaction seemed relevant. The variables in the personal anecdote category relate to the gap model of service quality (Zeithaml, Parasuraman & Berry, 1990) and the five dimensions of service quality as identified by Parasuraman, Zeithaml, and Berry (1988).

The gap model identifies four potential points where discrepancies in perception and reality lead to a reduction in overall service quality (see Zeithaml, Parasuraman & Berry, 1990 for a complete explanation). The first gap is represented by the difference between consumer expectations and management's perception of consumer expectations. Gap 2 represents the difference between management's perception of consumer expectations and the subsequent translation into a service design to meet those expectations. Gap 3 is the difference between the service design capabilities and service delivery. Gap 4 is created by the difference between service delivery and what the company's implied or explicit communication with customers about service de-

TABLE 1. Analytical Framework

Message Characteristics	
Message Length	**Sender Characteristics**
Date of Origin	Gender
Number of Times Forwarded	Geographic Location
Forwarding Further	Employment Sector
Number of Recipients Forwarded To	
Purpose of Further Usage	
Request for Permission to Use	
Request for Copy	**Message Content**
	Mention of Mike
Personal Anecdotes (99 responses)	Mention of XXXXXXXXXXXXXXXXXX
Customer Expectations	Mention of XXXXXXXXXXXXXXXXX Response
Management Awareness	Overall Purpose
Service Design	Affective Response
Service Delivery	Focus of Response—Humor
External Communication	Focus of Response—Distributive Justice
Reliability	Focus of Response—Procedural Justice
Assurance	Focus of Response—Interactional Justice
Tangibles	Mention of Guarantee
Empathy	Mention of Hotel Company Policy
Responsiveness	Reference to Formal Litigation Complaint

livery. Gap 5 is a function of the sum of Gaps 1 through 4 and is articulated as the difference between customer expectations of service quality and the consumer's perceived service quality. Therefore, in the content analysis, clues were searched to see whether a specific service quality gap emerged as a dominant theme. This would include such content as the mention of expectations not being understood (Gap 1) or over-promises made by the company in its advertisements (Gap 4).

Similarly, a reference in the e-mail to any of the service quality dimensions identified by Parasuraman, Zeithaml, and Berry (1988) (reliability, responsiveness, assurance, empathy, and tangible attributes) was also sought. For example, if there was a mention of slow reactions from staff (responsiveness) or a perceived lack of understanding by an employee (empathy), it was noted in the analysis.

Identifying the gender, geographic location and employment sector of the responders offered potential insight into the geographic directions and industry concentration of diffusion. Finally, additional message content factors listed in Table 1 seemed relevant in terms of the impact the original complaint had on individuals receiving it. Noting the brand name of the hotel, the employee name, or the guarantee policy mentioned in the complaint would imply specificity in the recollection of the message. Although 36 variables were included in the analytical framework, the results reported in this paper focus on the most significant and relevant findings in each of the four variable categories.

Three independent raters participated in the analysis using the reliability procedures outlined by Kassarjian (1977) and used previously in the hospitality context (Manickas & Shea, 1997; Shea & Roberts, 1998). The content analysis yielded some useful information about the diffusion of the PowerPoint complaint.

It should be noted that the analysis of sender characteristics was limited to the data extractable from the e-mail responses to the e-complaint. Hence, gender, geographic location of the sender, employment status and other information was extracted from signature blocks and other textual notations in the messages. It represents a limitation of the content analysis method since unlike a prepared survey, it relinquishes control of information from the re-

searchers. In this context, then, the "respondents" are not individuals who responded to a survey, but rather those who voluntarily created and sent a message to the creators of the complaint making them "responders" to the PowerPoint message.

RESULTS

The results of the content analysis of 1,000 e-mail responses to the PowerPoint complaint yielded a number of interesting findings. Some of the frequencies of responses are presented in Table 2. Given that e-mail communications tend to be informal and brief, it is not surprising that 94.8 percent of the messages analyzed were less than one print page (8-1/2" × 11") in length. Patterns of diffusion were examined from multiple perspectives. The total message responses generated by males (57 percent) exceeded that generated by females (38 percent) over the 15-week period. However, in the early weeks, it was more evenly split. For example, in week two, exactly 50 percent of the e-mails analyzed were from each gender.

For nearly half of the messages, the sender's place of origin was noted. Geographically, diffusion was broad and variable, with few concentrations in regions, states or cities. The senders represented 46 states and 21 countries from Australia to Argentina to Ireland, Japan and Maldives.

Looking at the diffusion through employment sectors revealed that the largest identifiable segment was hospitality-related businesses (17.5 percent did not specify and 36 percent fell into the "other" category). Individuals employed in the hospitality sector, including such companies as Disney World, Australian Tourist Commission, Continental Airlines, Enterprise Rent-a-Car, Hyatt Hotels, Taco Bell, and Royal Caribbean Cruise Lines, sent almost 21 percent of the e-mails. The consulting (9.3 percent) and media (8.9 percent) sectors followed the hospitality sector in number. Responses from individuals in the media included major print publications such as *The Wall Street Journal*, the *New York Times*, and *USA Today*. A complete list of media outlets including web sites from our sample of re-

TABLE 2. Message Analysis

	Number of Reponses	%		Number of Responses	%
Message Length			**Intention to Forward**	374	42.7
Less than One Page	830	94.9			
More than One Page	45	5.1	**Request for Copy**	156	17.8
Total	875	100			
			Employment Sector		
Purpose of Further Usage			Consulting	81	9.3
Classroom	40	4.6	Education	59	6.7
Hospitality Training	73	8.3	Hospitality	183	20.9
Business Training	51	5.8	Media	78	8.9
Other Uses	119	13.6	Others	319	36.5
			Not Specified	155	17.7
Gender					
Male	498	56.9	**Geographic Location**		
Female	332	37.9	Within U.S. (46 States)	335	38.3
Not Specified	6	0.7	Other Countries (21)	71	8.1
Ambiguous	39	4.5	Not Specified	469	53.6

sponses is presented in Table 3. Additionally, many of these organizations posted or published articles about the PowerPoint complaint.

Furthermore, a number of major corporations and organizations were represented in the 36 percent "other" category: Bank of Tokyo, American Marketing Association, American Medical Association, Citicorp, Dell Computer, Enron, Ford Motor Company, KPMG, Paramount Studios and Sony Corporation. The range of businesses and organizations through which the e-complaint diffused is depicted in Table 4.

Individuals from both private and public institutions of higher education generated another 6.7 percent of the messages analyzed. Again, major educational institutions were represented. They include: Yale, Northwestern, Georgetown and Cornell Universities as well as the Universities of Calgary, Minnesota, and Massachusetts. The 35 academic institutions are listed in Table 5.

Despite the geographic coverage and the sheer number of recipients, the diffusion of the electronic complaint occurred very rapidly. Figure 2 shows the rate of responses over time. Nearly half of the messages were received within approximately three weeks of the initial distribution of the complaint. The fifth week represents the time between Christmas and New Year's Day. A small surge after the New Year may have been influenced by a newspaper report published in *USA Today*. Interestingly, the pattern of early response held true between genders and industry sectors. Percentages of male and female respondents were nearly identical. The earliest responders (within a week) represent the hospitality industry, but the pattern for all sectors for the remaining weeks do not differ significantly.

While it was evident from the number of e-mail responses that more than 4,000 individuals had seen the electronic complaint, many responders in the sample of 1,000 forwarded the presentation on to other individuals and groups and many had intentions of further usage for the PowerPoint. A total of 76 individuals indicated they had already shared the complaint with others. The numbers they had shared with ranged between 1 and 10,000 people, with a median of 36 individuals. Ten sub-

TABLE 3. Web Sites and Publications

www.c-interface.com	Customer Interface
www.consultingcentral.com	Denver Post
www.craphound.com	Houston Chronicle
www.despair.com	Los Angeles Times
www.drive-you-nuts.com	New York Times
www.hyperorg.com	The Wall Street Journal
www.icon-nicholson.com	Travel Weekly
www.madskipper.com	USA Today
www.mainmail.com	US Golf Association Newsletter
www.mindleaders.com	Lodging Hospitality
www.secure.presenter.com	
www.sissyfight2000.com	
www.snopes.com	
www.weeklybitch.com	
www.worsthotels.com	

jects specifically mentioned forwarding the message to other groups.

More than 43 percent of individuals indicated an intention to forward the message in the future. Of the 173 individuals that noted an intended future usage for the complaint presentation, about eight percent was for hospitality training, nearly six percent for business training, and about five percent indicated classroom use. Furthermore, 155 of the 1,000 e-mail senders requested additional copies of the presentation. Surprisingly, 101 individuals asked for permission from the authors to use the presentation in the future.

The responses to the complaint were overwhelmingly positive in tone. Nearly 95 percent of the messages were rated as positive in nature, compared to 4 percent neutral and 1 percent negative. Nine individuals placed blame on the authors of the complaint and only one message represented a personal attack against the complainers. An astounding 75 percent of the messages contained the actual name of the hotel and/or parent company. More than half of the messages contained a reference to the humor in the complaint and 50 individuals asked if it was a hoax. Nearly a third inquired about the hotel management's response. Almost a fourth of the respondents asked about the employee's response. Ninety-nine individuals offered personal anecdotes about negative service encounters. About one-fourth of those involved the same hotel brand

as the PowerPoint complaint, another fourth involved other services and well over a third (38) involved other hotels. The hotels, airlines, and other services that were the subject of the complaints included anecdotes concerning destinations. These are listed in Table 6. Further analysis of these anecdotes and other service quality issues are superfluous to the diffusion and hence will be reported elsewhere.

CONCLUSION AND DISCUSSION

The content analysis of the PowerPoint complaint indicates a widespread and rapid diffusion of colossal proportions. The original e-mail message generated a strong pass-along rate. Within a few weeks, it reached individuals virtually all over the world, threaded its way into dozens of Fortune 500 companies, and made its way into numerous publications and web sites, and is being used as a learning/training tool in universities, consulting firms, and other public and private organizations.

Interestingly, there do not seem to be clear patterns or boundaries of diffusion in the message's progression geographically, through industry sectors or across genders. The analysis provides evidence that the message diffused through 46 states, 31 countries, 35 public and private universities, and more than 70 organizations, associations, and corporations. While altogether more males than females responded to the PowerPoint complaint, the early responders (over 50 percent of messages were received within 3 weeks of initial distribution), were equally split between the genders. Similarly, while 20 percent of the respondents represented the hospitality industry in one way or another, many other sectors were penetrated and there was no clear progression from one sector to another. Diffusion of products tends to concentrate geographically, primarily due to the influence of marketer-dominated sources of information, namely, advertising that is shown in specific geographic markets and because of informal social circles that tend to be constrained by geographic boundaries. The Internet as a communication distribution channel blurs those patterns. As Wilson (2000) explained, if messages make their way into existing communication networks between people, the dispersion rate

TABLE 4. List of Organizations the PowerPoint Diffused

A.T. Kearney	Discovery Networks	National Broadcasting Company
America West Airlines	Disney World	Nokia
American Dental Association	Donna Karan New York	Oracle
American Marketing Association	Enron	Pacific Bell
American Medical Association	Enterprise Rent-A-Car	Palm Inc.
Anderson LLC	ESPN	Paramount Studios
Anheuser Busch	Ford	PWC Global
Aramco	Fox Cable Network	Royal Caribbean Cruise Lines
AT&T	GE Capital	Sara Lee Corp.
Australian Tourist Commission	Glaxo SmithKline	Sears and Roebuck
Bank of Tokyo–Mitsubishi	Hewlett-Packard	Six Continent Hotels
Bank One	Honeywell	Sony Corporation
Bell Atlantic	Hyatt Hotels	Sprint PCS
Best Western International	International Business Machines	Starwood Hotels
Bloomberg	Intel	Taco Bell
Boeing	J.D. Power & Associates	The Wall Street Journal
British Petroleum	Kodak	United Airlines
Cisco Systems	KPMG Consulting, Inc.	Timberland
Citicorp	Lockheed Martin	USA Today
Continental Airlines	Marriott International	Volkswagen of America
Dell Computer Corp.	Microsoft	Walt Disney
Deloitte Touche	Motorola	Warner Corp.
Delta Airlines	National Aeronautics and Space Administration	And more . . .

TABLE 5. Academic Institutions

Boston University	Niagara College	University of Nevada-Las Vegas
Centennial College, Toronto	Oklahoma State University	University of New Hampshire
College of Charleston, OH	Roosevelt University, Chicago	University of New Orleans
Colorado Mountain College	Rutger's School of Law, Newark	University of North Carolina
Cornell University	Southern Methodist University	University of Northern Colorado
Dakota State University	The State University of West Georgia	University of Houston
De Paul University, Chicago	Trinity University, TX	University of North Florida
George Brown College	University of Calgary	University of Pennsylvania
Georgetown University	University of Houston	University of Phoenix
Georgia Southern University	University of Iowa	University of Western Ontario
Harvard Business School	University of Maryland	University of Wisconsin
Indiana University-Purdue University Indiana	University of Massachusetts-Amherst	Vanderbilt University
Kellogg Business School	University of Michigan	Virginia Tech.
Northwestern University	University of Minnesota	Whitworth College, WA
Monash University, Australia	University of Montana	Yale University

FIGURE 2. Diffusion of PowerPoint Complaint

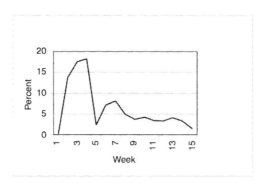

will rapidly multiply. More than half of the respondents made a reference to the humorous nature of the e-mail complaint, a factor that tends to increase the pass-along rate (Wilson, 2000; Rohrbacher, 2000).

It should be noted that the extent of diffusion of the PowerPoint complaint indicated in this research is clearly a gross underestimation and represents merely the tip of the iceberg. First, this study analyzed only one-fourth of the unsolicited e-mail responses sent to the complainers. A tracking of the additional 3,000 e-mail messages would undoubtedly broaden the geographic distribution and lengthen the lists of states, countries, companies, institutions and other recipients of the message. Secondly and more importantly, many more individuals heard the negative word-of-mouth message that did not write to the consultants who sent the complaint. For instance, of the three authors of this study, only one sent a message to the consultant. One author showed the PowerPoint complaint in several university classes, and one of the authors forwarded it to an e-mail list exceeding 350 individuals (students, friends, employees of multinational corporations, etc.) spread throughout the world. The authors also showed and discussed it at a University Chancellor's Conference and an academic conference, both comprised of several hundred people. Thirdly, virtually all of the 4,000 individuals responding to the original complaint did not receive it directly; instead, they received it from someone else. The consultants sent copies of the original complaint to only four individuals and none of them are part of the 4,000 who responded. Finally,

within this sample group, 155 individuals requested additional copies of the PowerPoint complaint, 102 asked for permission to use it for another purpose, and more than 40 percent of them indicated intentions to forward the complaint. These factors imply that the unmeasured diffusion likely exceeds the measured rate.

Some theoretical connections to diffusion are apparent. While we were unable to extract specific numbers of each type of diffusion due to the methodology employed here and because a survey was not part of it, the analysis suggests the occurrence of a simultaneous combination of three types of diffusion: trickle-down, trickle-up and trickle across patterns. The evidence for this was gleaned from individual response messages, each of which comprises inconsistent information. The complaint flowed from the top down and bottom up (depending who received the presentation first, an employee or student versus a manager or professor) through dozens of universities, hospitality organizations and multinational corporations as indicated in Tables 3, 4 and 5. Many mentioned passing the presentation to students and trainees (top down); others suggested passing it to their supervisors and top management (trickle up). The intentions to forward also indicate a trickle across pattern with the message senders acting as opinion leaders within certain formal and informal groups. For example, middle managers within the hospitality industry served as opinion leaders for those to whom they sent the message both inside and outside of the industry. In other words, they influenced both formal and informal groups simultaneously. In Table 2, the purpose of further usage indicates an intention by more than 17 percent of respondents to use the PowerPoint presentation in educational, hospitality and business training. This suggests both trickle up and trickle down patterns of diffusion. Furthermore, the number of individuals that respondents reported forwarding the message to ranged from 1 to 1,000, with a median of 36. These messages being forwarded would have to be sent exclusively to managers, consultants, professors, and other "top officials" or "opinion leaders" to exclude the occurrence of a trickle-up process.

Therefore, the evidence does suggest each of these patterns.

There are some differences, however, in the diffusion of negative word-of-mouth and diffusion/adoption of a product or service. In this case study, 95 percent of the responses were positive in nature, 4 percent neutral, and only 1 percent negative. This does not mean that the information was accepted as the truth or would affect subsequent buying behavior.

The number of mentions of the specific hotel brand and employee involved indicates the apparent occurrence of cognitive processing of this negative word-of-mouth communication, however. The list of hospitality and other services in Table 6 (other firms referred to by respondents sharing their own complaints) indicates some degree of "adoption" and believ-

ability of the complaint. This is not surprising given that the messages were passed along from sources likely perceived as trusted (Parker, 2003). Another difference in the diffusion process is that traditionally, the first source of information is communicated through formal, yet neutral, often scientific sources. The PowerPoint complaint began with an informal, non-neutral, non-scientific source and the Internet created a much more rapid rate of diffusion.

IMPLICATIONS

Hospitality managers cannot lightly dismiss the potential financial impact resulting from dissatisfied customers. While at one time they were concerned about the negative impact of a complainer telling a dozen or so others about an incident, this case illustrates that thousands and perhaps hundreds of thousands of other potential guests may hear about a negative experience. Furthermore, the fact that this information is not company controlled makes it potentially more damaging. E-consumer behavior in the form of written communication may carry a façade of credibility compared to verbalized hearsay, as details are less likely to be altered, and the message retains its specificity. The authors of the e-complaint did not intend to generate this expansive, worldwide reach and impact, yet the speed, the simultaneous convergence of trickle theories, the replicability, and the uncontrollable nature of diffusion created a reaction previously undocumented in e-consumer behavior.

More specifically, there are some implications for hospitality managers. The potential damage (image and financial) that can be done through viral marketing points to the importance of service recovery. As indicated in the PowerPoint complaint outlined in the Appendix, there were several opportunities for complaint handling before the written complaint was made. There was inadequate financial and emotional compensation (no apology), no empathy from the employees, and very little interest in the recovery process. Had the complaint been handled fairly, promptly, and efficiently, the written complaint may not have been sent. Hart, Heskett and Sasser (1990) found that

TABLE 6. Services Identified in Anecdotes

Airlines	Hotels
Air Canada	Boston Sheraton
American Airlines	Days Inn
British Airways	XXXXXX XXXX XXXXXXXX
Delta Airlines	XXXXXX XXXX XXXXXX XXX
Northwest Airlines	XXXXX XXXX XXXXXX
United Airlines	XXXXXX XXXX XXXXXXX
	XXXXXX XXXX XXXXXXXX, XXXXXXX
Cities and Countries	XXXXXX XXXX XXX XXXXX
Amsterdam	XXXXXX XXXX XXXXXX
Edmonton	XXXXXX XXXX XXXXXX
England	XXXXXX XXXX XXXXXX, XX
Florida	Embassy Suites, Secaucus
Indianapolis	Holiday Inn, Montreal
Las Vegas	Holiday Inn, Bloomington
Thailand	Hyatt Regency
	Le Meridien, Dallas
Other Services	Marriott Albany
AT&T	Marriott Atlanta
Circuit City	Marriott Courtyard, Columbus
Hertz	Marriott Courtyard Sugarland
Sea Wind Cruise Line	Marriott Courtyard Plano
UHAUL	Marriott Westside, Houston
UPS	Radisson Astrodome TX
	Regency NY
	Waldorf Astoria
	Westin Santa Clara

about half of customers become dissatisfied by the manner in which a complaint is addressed and resolved. Furthermore, Bitner, Booms and Tetreault (1990) found that individuals understand many of the problems that arise, but their satisfaction rests on the handling of the initial complaint. The apparent rate of diffusion in a matter of weeks is a strong indicator for managers to employ recovery efforts immediately. The timing of recovery efforts should be a focus in training, because with diffusion via the Internet, communication is neither controllable nor retractable. Furthermore, managers must ensure that all employees (even night auditors, as in this case) are trained in service recovery procedures. Finally, hospitality managers should avoid using the term "guaranteed room" unless it is an unconditional guarantee. At the very least, customers need to be informed of any conditions that apply (such as time of arrival or membership in loyalty programs) prior to the service experience.

This exploratory study suggests that more attention to Internet diffusion and its effect on e-consumer behavior is warranted. Research on the trickle theories, tracking word-of-mouth communication, and the influence of humor and visuals on responses to interpersonal, non-marketing dominated sources of information are some areas worthy of further exploration.

REFERENCES

Bitner, M. J., Booms, B. H. & Tetreault, M. S. (1990, January). The service encounter: Diagnosing favorable and unfavorable incidents. *Journal of Marketing, 54*, 71-84.

Bly, L. (2002, January 4). Online complaint about bad hotel service scores bull's-eye. *USA Today*, 6D.

Cheat sheet. (2002, September). *Fast Company*, 38.

Coca-Cola USA. (1981a). Customer complaint handling in America: An update study, part 2 (Technical Assistance Research Project). Atlanta, GA.

Coca-Cola USA. (1981b). Measuring the grapevine, consumer response and word of mouth (Technical Assistance Research Project). Atlanta, GA.

Farmer, Tom, telephone interview, 14 March 2002.

Guzman, R. (2001, December 14). Takeoffs & landings. *The Wall Street Journal*, W7.

Hart, C. W. L., Heskett, J. L. & Sasser, Jr., W. E. (1990, July-August). The profitable act of service recovery. *Harvard Business Review*, 148-156.

Holmes, P. (2002, January 14). To protect your reputation, every employee must be a member of the PR staff. *PR Week*, 9.

Johnson, L. K. (2003, Fall). Does e-mail escalate conflict? *MIT Sloan Management Review, 44*, 14-15.

Kassarjian, H. H. (1977). Content analysis in consumer research. *Journal of Consumer Research, 4*, 8-18.

Leslie, J. (1994, March). Mail Bonding. *www.wired.com.* 1-6.

Manickas, P. A. & Shea, L. J. (1997). Hotel complaint behavior and resolution: A content analysis. *Journal of Travel Research, 36*(2), 68-73.

Parasuraman, A., Zeithaml, V. A. & Berry, L. L. (1988). "SERVQUAL: A multiple-item scale for measuring consumer perceptions of service quality," *Journal of Retailing, 64*(2), 12-40.

Parker, P. (2003, July 4). Learning from the (urban) legend. *www.clickz.com.*

Richins, M. L. (1983). Negative word-of-mouth by dissatisfied consumers: A pilot study. *Journal of Marketing, 47*(1), 68-78.

Ritson, M. (2003). Prepare for a virtual battering if you fail to deal with complaints. *Marketing*, (March), 16.

Rogers, E. (1983). *Diffusion of Innovations, 3rd edition.* New York: Free Press.

Rohrbacher, B. (2000, November 8). The power of viral marketing. *www.clickz.com.*

Romm, C. T. & Pliskin, N. (1998, January). Electronic mail as a coalition-building information technology. *ACM Transactions on Information Systems, 16*, 82-100.

Saunders, C. (2002, May 9). User satisfaction key to viral marketing. *Internet Advertising Report.*

Shea, L. & Roberts, C. (1998). A content analysis for postpurchase evaluation using customer comment logbooks. *Journal of Travel Research, 36*(4), 68-73.

Soto, M. (2002, April 18). No room in the inn leads to worldwide lesson. *Seattle Times*, C1.

Technical Assistance Research Program (TARP) (1986). *Consumer Complaint Handling in America: An Update Study.* Office of Consumer Affairs, Washington, D. C.

Terror of night clerk Mike: A viral e-mail skewers XXXXXXXX hotels (shop talk). (21 January 2002). *ADWEEK, 43*(4), 34.

Vardy, J. (2001, December 15). You know you're in a bad hotel when . . .: Houston resort's service failure posted on net for all to see. *Financial Post*, FP1.

Wilson, R. (2000, February 1). The six principles of viral marketing. *Web Marketing Today*, 70.

Zeithaml, V. A., Parasuraman, A. & Berry, L. L. (1990). *Delivering Quality Service: Balancing Customer Perceptions and Expectations.* New York: The Free Press.

APPENDIX

The complete PowerPoint presentation created by Tom Farmer and Shane Atchison is reproduced in this Appendix with their permission.

Yours is a Very Bad Hotel

A graphic complaint prepared for:

XXXXXXX

General Manager

XXXXXXX

Front Desk Manager

XXXXXXXXXXXXX

XXXXXXX XXXX

Houston, Texas

APPENDIX (continued)

*In the Early Morning Hours of
November 15, 2001, at the* **XXXXXXXXX**
Houston, We Were Treated Very Badly Indeed.

- We are Tom Farmer and Shane Atchison of Seattle, Washington.
- We held guaranteed, confirmed reservations at the **XXXXXXXXX** for the night of November 14-15.
- These rooms were held for late arrival with a major credit card.
- Tom is a card-carrying **XXXXXXXXXXX** VIP...
- Yet when we arrived at 2:00am... *we were refused rooms!*

*Refused Rooms... Even When We're
"Confirmed" and "Guaranteed"?*

- Mike, your Night Clerk, said the only rooms left were off-limits because their plumbing and air-conditioning had broken!
- He'd given away the last good rooms three hours ago!
- He'd done nothing about finding us accommodation elsewhere!
- And he was deeply unapologetic!

Quotations from Night Clerk Mike

"Most of our guests don't arrive
at two o'clock in the morning."

-- 2:08 am, November 15, 2001

Explaining why it was
OUR fault that the **XXXXXXXXXX**
could not honor our guaranteed reservation

We Discussed With Mike the Meaning
of the Term "Guarantee."

guar·an·tee (g r n-t), *n.*

1. Something that assures a particular outcome or
   condition: *Lack of interest is a guarantee of failure.*

   a. A promise or an assurance, especially one given in writing, that
      attests to the quality or durability of a product or service.

   b. A pledge that something will be performed in a specified
      manner.

   (Save this for your future reference.)

APPENDIX (continued)

Mike Didn't Much Care.

- He seemed to have been betting that we wouldn't show up.
- When we suggested that the least he should have done was line up other rooms for us in advance... Mike bristled!

Quotations from Night Clerk Mike

"I have nothing to apologize to you for."

-- 2:10 am, November 15, 2001

Explaining why we were wrong to be upset that our "guaranteed" rooms weren't saved for us

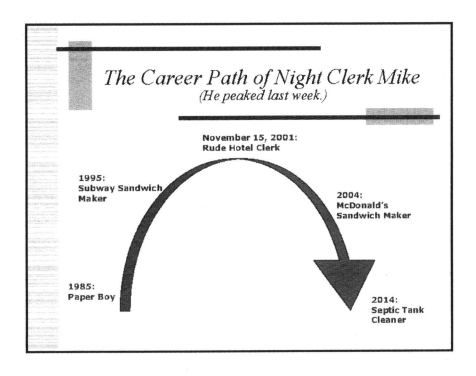

The Career Path of Night Clerk Mike
(He peaked last week.)

November 15, 2001:
Rude Hotel Clerk

1995:
Subway Sandwich
Maker

2004:
McDonald's
Sandwich Maker

1985:
Paper Boy

2014:
Septic Tank
Cleaner

Mike Wasn't Too Optimistic About Finding Us a Place to Sleep.

- 2:15 in the morning is a heck of a time to start looking for two spare hotel rooms!

- Mike slowly started dialing around town.

APPENDIX (continued)

Quotations from Night Clerk Mike

"I don't know if there ARE any
hotel rooms around here... all these
hotels are full."

-- 2:12 am, November 15, 2001

*Just starting to look for alternate
accommodation for us, even though he'd filled
his own house up by 11:00pm*

Mike Finally Found Us Rooms Here.

XXXXX
XXXXX

+ XXXXXXXXXXXXXXXX is a **dump**.
+ It is six miles further away from downtown Houston, which makes a difference in morning rush-hour traffic.
+ Had we wanted to stay at **XXXXXX**, we would have called them in the first place.
+ We could only get smoking rooms.

The Experience Mike Provided Deviated from Usual Treatment of an **XXXXXXXXX** Member.

Expected **XXXXXXXXX** Member Benefits	Actual Benefits Provided by **XXXXXXXXXX** 11/15
Confirmed reservation	Ignored reservation
Upgraded room when available	No room available
Free continental breakfast	Free confusing directions to shabby alternate hotel
XXXXX points *plus* frequent-flyer miles	Insolence *plus* insults

Even After We Left the **XXXXXXXX**, Our Troubles Weren't Over, as This Timeline Shows.

Jon, a colleague, was arriving in Houston on an overnight flight and coming to join us at the **XXXXXXXXXX** *first thing in the morning. As we had to go stay elsewhere, we wrote Jon a note and left it in care of Mike the Night Clerk.*

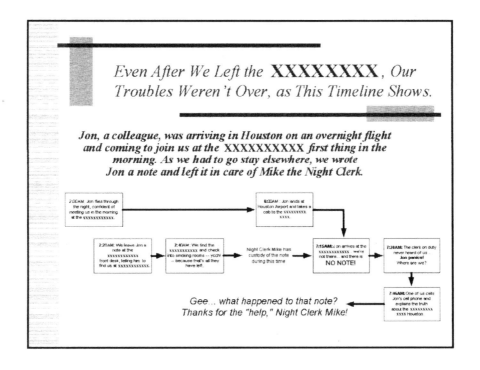

APPENDIX (continued)

We Are Very Unlikely to Return to the **XXXXXXXXXXXX** *Houston.*

Lifetime chances of dying in a bathtub: **1 in 10,455**

(National Safety Council)

Chance of Earth being ejected from the solar system by the gravitational pull of a passing star: **1 in 2,200,000**

(University of Michigan)

Chance of winning the UK Lottery: **1 in 13,983,816**

(UK Lottery)

Chance of us returning to the **XXXXXXXXX** Houston: **worse than any of those**

(And what are the chances you'd save rooms for us anyway?)

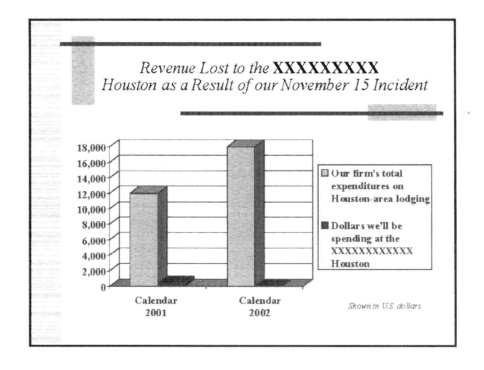

We'll Be Sending This Presentation to XXXXXXXXXXX.

- And to some friends.
- We hope they'll share it with *their* friends!
- If you'd like a hard copy, email us at: **XXXXXXXX**.
- Good luck!
- And give our best to Mike!

Analyzing Hotel Customers' E-Complaints
from an Internet Complaint Forum

Charles Changuk Lee
Clark Hu

SUMMARY. Recent web technology advancement has enabled online customers to express their concerns and negative experiences about the hotel services over the Internet. This exploratory study attempts to provide some insights into this recent phenomenon by analyzing self-selected hotel customers' online complaints recorded on a specialized complaint forum, eComplaints.com. A content analysis of those e-Complaints in 18 problem categories revealed that online customers were mostly unhappy with fundamental service failures (i.e., declined service quality and rude employees) in the hotel service encounter. Surprisingly, only one in every five e-Complaints received a response from the hotel company in the identified top-five complaint categories. The authors further used text-mining software to identify most frequently complained keywords and examine their relational associations. Business implications of the research findings were also discussed. *[Article copies available for a fee from The Haworth Document Delivery Service: 1-800-HAWORTH. E-mail address: <docdelivery@haworthpress.com> Website: <http://www.HaworthPress.com> © 2004 by The Haworth Press, Inc. All rights reserved.]*

KEYWORDS. E-Complaints (online complaints), company response, complaint handling, hotel service quality, service recovery

INTRODUCTION

Managers in the hospitality industry have the best intentions to provide quality services to customers. However, service failures frequently occur when the lodging company and its customers interact with each other. As a result, hotel management should consider service failures as a serious problem as well as take the lead to act on why customers are dissatisfied with the hotel's services. The fundamental reason for attending to consumer complaints, instead of trying to block them, is rather simple because it is more cost effective to maintain existing customers than to invest extra marketing budgets to find new ones (Harrison-Walker, 2001). Thus, service providers should not only monitor consumer issues but also encourage dissatisfied consumers to help remedy service problems.

Responsive handling of complaints not only facilitates effective resolution of con-

Charles Changuk Lee and Clark Hu are Assistant Professors, School of Tourism and Hospitality Management, Temple University.

Address correspondence to Charles Changuk Lee (E-mail: charlesl@temple.edu).

[Haworth co-indexing entry note]: "Analyzing Hotel Customers' E-Complaints from an Internet Complaint Forum." Lee, Charles Changuk, and Clark Hu. Co-published simultaneously in *Journal of Travel & Tourism Marketing* (The Haworth Hospitality Press, an imprint of The Haworth Press, Inc.) Vol. 17, No. 2/3, 2004, pp. 167-181; and: *Handbook of Consumer Behavior, Tourism, and the Internet* (ed: Juline E. Mills, and Rob Law) The Haworth Hospitality Press, an imprint of The Haworth Press, Inc., 2004, pp. 167-181. Single or multiple copies of this article are available for a fee from The Haworth Document Delivery Service [1-800-HAWORTH, 9:00 a.m. - 5:00 p.m. (EST). E-mail address: docdelivery@haworthpress.com].

http://www.haworthpress.com/web/JTTM
© 2004 by The Haworth Press, Inc. All rights reserved.
Digital Object Identifier: 10.1300/J073v17n02_13

sumer problems but also provides opportunities to improve long term relationships with customers (Estelami, 2000; Kirkby, Thompson, & Wecksell, 2001; Mitchell, 1993). Research has shown that customers rate service performance higher if a failure occurs and the contact personnel successfully addresses the problem than if the service had been delivered correctly the first time (Hoffman & Bateson, 2001). Specifically, customers who are satisfied with the complaint handling process are found to be up to 8% more loyal than if they have had no problem at all (Goodman, 1999). It is also not surprising that sometimes dissatisfied customers are actually more beneficial to a company than satisfied ones since unhappy customers provide insights into service failures (Harrison-Walker, 2001).

Thanks to fast changing technology developments, recent marketing shifts toward customer retention has revolutionized the way the hotel industry reaches out to customers. Hotel companies are becoming increasingly dependent on technology-based approaches, such as Internet marketing. Technology-based marketing creates substantial managerial implications for both corporations and clients. Internet technology has been widely used in the hotel industry as a powerful marketing tool because of its capability for instant two-way communications and real time information sharing (Page, Brunt, Busby, & Connell, 2001). Most hotel companies use the Internet as a distribution channel to transmit information to technology-savvy customers (Connolly, Olsen, & Moore, 1998). Van Hoof and Combrink (1998) indicated that American lodging managers have climbed on the Internet bandwagon by using their own Web pages to promote the services they provide to customers. Furthermore, each intermediary in the electronic distribution chain is trying to bypass other intermediaries further down in the distribution chain and transact business directly with the hotel customers (O'Connor & Frew, 2002). Therefore, the Internet provides both an opportunity and a challenge for hotel marketers. While the opportunity lies in reaching customers directly through Websites, the challenge is to maintain guests' attention long enough to tell their stories.

While hotel companies work on the kinks of managing the online operation, consumers are sharing their concerns about their hotel experiences on popular Web-based complaint forums such as www.eComplaints.com and www.planetfeedback.com. Gelb and Sundaram (2002) reported that this relatively new form of electronic consumer forums (i.e., electronic complaints or e-Complaints) offer customers confidentiality while they share negative experiences with the public. On the flip side, these forums also present real time opportunities for the company to monitor Websites where products and services are likely to be discussed, as well as to inform the customers that the firm supports the subject in question.

RESEARCH OBJECTIVES

Although there has been plenty of research related to consumer complaints, little is known to hospitality researchers about how customers complain and the recovery process in online environments. In the area of traditional offline hospitality service failures, Manickas and Shea (1997) investigated complaint logbooks of a hotel while Davidow (2000) studied organizational responses to the complaints of restaurant patrons. Both studies provided information on specific areas of hotel guest complaints and the hotel companies' responsiveness to these complaints. The findings of these studies are helpful in general but have not successfully translated into research investigating customer complaint behavior on the Web. More recently, Harrison-Walker (2001) examined the nature of airline passengers' complaints on the Internet. Mattila and Mount (2003) examined the impact of customers' technology readiness and response time on satisfaction in the complaint handling process and return intent via e-mail. It seems logical to continue expanding the body of knowledge in the area of online consumer complaint behavior.

Given the dearth of hospitality research about understanding complaint behavior on the Internet, the following research objectives are developed for this study:

1. to report descriptive nature of the online customer complaints on a specialized Internet complaint forum,
2. to understand the pattern of hotel company responses to the customers' e-Complaints about dissatisfied hotel services, and
3. to identify most frequently complained keywords and examine their relational associations from collected e-Complaints.

LITERATURE REVIEW

Technology-Based Marketing

The hotel industry has witnessed the recent marketing shift from a traditional focus on market share of a company to technology-based customer retention. Hotel companies' use of technology in the customer interaction process is growing at a fast pace (Mattila & Mount, 2003). Similarly, customers are dealing with services that are becoming increasingly sophisticated from a technological standpoint. As such, the nature of company-customer interactions is undergoing fundamental revolution with far-reaching managerial implications for both companies and customers (Parasuraman, 2000). Parasuraman (1996) proposed a "pyramid model" of services marketing and argued that his model is an extension of a traditional "triangle model" where company and employees interact with customers without substantial support of technology. The "pyramid model" considers the impact of technology in conceptualizing the marketing activities. Due to the fast utilization of technology into the service delivery process, technology has been incorporated as a new dimension into the two-dimensional triangle model. The new model highlights three links–company-technology, technology-employee, and technology-customer–that need to be managed well to maximize marketing effectiveness (Parasuraman, 1996). In the hospitality literature, Lee's service quality process model broadened the understanding of the causality of service quality by considering the impacts of information and technology on interdepartmental connectedness and perceived service quality (Lee, 2001). Contrary to the traditional approach to service quality in hospitality research that has investigated the SERVQUAL concept and its employee empowerment and interaction with customers, Lee's new approach expands the understanding of the causality of service quality by considering the relationships of information and technology, management leadership, empowerment, interdepartmental connectedness, and perceived service quality.

The essence of current information technology lies in the advent of Web technology since the Web generates boundless business environment by allowing individual customers to view companies' virtual color catalogues, to make room reservations, and to provide feedback on hotel services. As the Web becomes a virtual information source for cyber hotel business, many researchers have raised their interests in the quality of Web information. For instance, Jeong and Lambert (1999) examined the quality of information on lodging Websites by proposing a conceptual framework for measuring information quality associated with customers' perceived beliefs to use information on the Web (i.e., perceived usefulness, perceived ease of use, and perceived accessibility). More theoretical standpoint, Zeithaml, Parasuraman, and Malhotra (2002) critically reviewed and synthesized the literature about service quality delivery through Web sites and develop an agenda for needed research. They defined electronic service quality (e-SQ) as service quality through Web sites including information availability and content, ease of use or usability, privacy and security, graphic style, and fulfillment. Also, they demonstrated how e-SQ can be measured. Specifically, they illustrated the different ways of measuring e-SQ even though the measurement of service quality delivery through Web sites is in its infant stage. One example can be using categories like ease of use, customer confidence, reliability, relationship services (i.e., reuse of customer information to facilitate future interactions), and timeliness of response. On the other hand, some researchers have started to establish comprehensive e-SQ scales based on more rigorous empirical testing. Loiacono, Watson, and Goodhue (2000) established a WEBQUAL scale with 12 dimensions: informational fit to task, interaction, trust, response time, design, intuitiveness, visual appeal, innovativeness, flow (emotional appeal), integrated communication, business process, and substitutability. Overall, the WEBQUAL scale is geared toward helping Website designers to better design Websites to affect the interaction perceptions of the users. The scale is more pertinent to interface design than to service quality measurement (Zeithaml, Parasuraman, & Malhotra, 2002).

The Internet is both an opportunity and a challenge for hotel marketers. The opportunity lies in reaching customers directly through Internet sites and the challenge is to get the guests' attention long enough to tell their stories. Mostly hotel companies use the Internet as a powerful distribution channel to transmit hotel information to technology-savvy customers (Connolly, Olsen, & Moore, 1998). Van Hoof and Combrink (1998) concluded that America's lodging managers have climbed on the Internet bandwagon by having their own Web pages to promote the services they provide to customers. The managers are convinced of its benefits and believe that it is going to be of vital importance in the future. At the same time, though, the respondents made it clear that short-term operational concerns must be resolved before they will be assured of the Internet's long-term benefits.

Service Failures

One of the concerns that hotel managers have to face on a daily basis is the problem of service quality. Service failures are inevitable breakdowns in delivering hotel service because they usually come from hotel service variations and line employees' occasional lack of patience dealing with demanding customers (Hoffman & Bateson, 2001). As a result, service failures directly impact customers' perception of core service offerings. Bitner, Booms, and Tetreault's (1990) seminal work categorized service failure into *the* three main themes: (1) responses to service delivery system failures; (2) responses to customer needs and requests; and (3) unprompted and unsolicited employee actions. First, service delivery system failures consist of the following failures: unavailable service, slow service, and other core service failures (i.e., rude customer service at front desk). The second type of ser-

vice failures focus on employee responses to individual customer needs and special requests. The third type of service failures concern unprompted and unsolicited employee behaviors that are totally unexpected by the customer. Subcategories in this group include level of attention (e.g., negative employee attitudes) and cultural norms (e.g., unfair employee activities).

Despite these significant implications, there has been limited hospitality research in investigating complaint behavior from a consumer perspective. By adopting Bitner, Booms, and Tetreault's (1990) research, Chung and Hoffman (1998) studied service failure at a restaurant utilizing three failure categories: service delivery failure, implicit or explicit customer requests, and unprompted and unsolicited employee reactions. The study found product defects (i.e., poorly prepared food) was the most common error. Manickas and Shea (1997) presented content analysis of complaints recorded in a logbook of a luxury hotel. The data was classified by time of complaint, type of complaints, solutions to the complaints, and guests' responses to the solutions. The majority of complaints were focused on service failures, equipment failure, and guest failure during their stay at the hotel. The hotels replied to the customers by correcting problems, sending out follow-up letters, and upgrading rooms. As a result, the majority of the guests were satisfied with the solutions provided by the hotel.

As we have seen from the above discussions, customers traditionally express dissatisfaction with the service provider by calling or writing letters to the companies. Goodman (1999) pointed out only 1% to 5% of unhappy customers complain to management or corporate headquarters, while 50% of individuals who encounter problems do not complain at all. Current Internet technology facilitates individuals to express their complaints on the Internet and provides effective tools for the company to handle complaint management (Mattila & Mount, 2003). In fact, unhappy consumers want to inform others of their bad experiences, influence others' evaluations of similar complaints, solicit sympathy, and generate consensus of the complaints by utilizing convenience of the Internet (Harrison-Walker,

2001; Hoffman & Bateson, 2001). Opinions disseminated via electronic consumer forums come from individuals who have strong views about brands and the willingness to express total negative opinions about service (Gelb & Sundaram, 2002). For a practical purpose, electronic consumer forums provide a virtual channel to consumers who hope that the company will pay attention to complained matters and act appropriately to respond. In some extreme cases, angry consumers even develop websites to voice their frustration and address their concerns to service providers. By using qualitative methods, Harrison-Walker (2001) analyzed the www.untied.com which functions as a complaint forum against United Airlines and identified the nature of the complaints as well as the company responses to the problems. The majority of the complaints expressed on the Web were about wrong information from employees, employee incompetence, employee rudeness, delayed flights, and baggage mishandling. It is also interesting to note that only several individuals who filed their complaints on the Web received responses from the company (Harrison-Walker, 2001).

Online Complaints

Hospitality researchers have accumulated very little knowledge about how technology (for instance, Internet and e-mail) affects customer evaluations of service complaints and recovery process. The lack of understanding of how hotel guests perceive complaint handling processes and the hotel company gives any attention to the complaints on the virtual world is rather surprising since poor complaint management results in lost customers and negative word-of-mouth (Mattila & Mount, 2003). "Cyberostracism," coined by Williams, Cheung, and Choi (2000), describes consumer reactions to the delay in company responses including failures to prompt responses to the complaints expressed through e-mails and negative impacts on customer perceptions of hotel's online service quality.

In services marketing literature, Zeithaml, Parasuraman, and Malhotra (2002) reported that the three dimensions–responsiveness, compensation, and contact–become salient only when online customers have questions or run into problems. These three dimensions have been conceptualized as the e-SERVQUAL scale. Responsiveness measures the e-retailers' ability to provide appropriate information to customers when a problem occurs, to have mechanisms for handling complaining process, and to provide online guarantees. Comprehension is the dimension that involves receiving money back and returning shipping and handling costs. The contact dimension of the e-SERVQUAL scale requires seamless multiple channel capabilities which include communicating with online customer service agents or speaking to the customer service department by phone.

On the other hand, there has been some research about organizational responses to the complainants. Davidow (2000) tested a model of complainants' perceptions of the restaurant's responses and the impact of the organizational response on post-complaint customer behavior. He found that attentiveness–referring to the interaction between the company representative and the complainant–was the most influential variable affecting satisfaction, word-of-mouth likelihood, and intention of repurchase. Davidow (2003) advanced the idea of organizational response to customer complaints and their impacts on post-complaint customer responses. He used a conceptual framework that divides these organizational responses into six separate dimensions (i.e., timeliness, facilitation, redress, apology, credibility, and attentiveness) and categorized post-complaint customer responses into three dimensions (i.e., word-of-mouth likelihood, intent to repurchase, and 3rd party complaint). Mount and Mattila (2000) examined the effectiveness of a customer relations call center in handling hotel guests' complaints. The phone survey suggested that the positive customer responses to the call center depend on the company's response to their complaints. The authors also suggest that a chain hotel needs to provide effective communication with specific actions about the guest problems with a hotel property. Recently, Mattila and Mount (2003) investigated the impact of Cyber customers' technology readiness and return intent via e-mail and found that satisfaction with the e-problem handling and repurchase intentions are directly related to the response time from the hotel company.

E-WOM (Electronic Word-Of-Mouth)

The above form of sharing consumers' attitudes and behavior on the Internet is often called electronic word-of-mouth (e-WOM) communication. Electronic WOM, coming from individuals with strong views about brands, is a great tool to disseminate such strong opinions via chat rooms and electronic consumer forums (Gelb & Sundaram, 2002). Those opinion leaders, as influencers to other customers' behavior and perception toward a certain service, have willingness to express total negativity of their experiences with hotels and theme parks (Buttle, 1998). Much of the existing WOM research focuses on the favorableness of the communication (i.e., whether the communication is favorable or unfavorable to the brand or service) and intention to pass along WOM information to other customers (Walker, 2001). This emerging e-WOM is evolved from traditional approaches of WOM. According to Buttle (1998), WOM is defined as oral, person-to-person communication between a receiver and a communicator.

Consumers rely on WOM to reduce the perceived risks and uncertainty associated with purchase decision (Walker, 2001). Walker (2001) found that consumers tend to engage in WOM when it is positively related to the level of dissatisfaction or negatively related to the consumers' perception of the company's responses to complaints. According to Anderson (1998), WOM is often related to consumers' satisfaction or dissatisfaction with previous purchasing experiences. He also found that extremely dissatisfied customers engage in greater word-of-mouth than highly satisfied ones. Dissatisfied consumers usually blame the company's operation and marketing rather than themselves or their own behavior and are more likely to engage in negative WOM (Richins, 1983). These findings are clear indication that consumers' tendency to engage in negative WOM was largely dependent on their perception of justice as it relates to the complaints. In particular, research in hospitality and service marketing also suggests that WOM lends itself to the communi-

cation of subjective perceived quality rather than objective prices (Chung & Hoffman, 1998; Harrison-Walker, 2001; Manickas & Shea, 1997).

Need for Qualitative Research on the Topic/Limitations

Much of the existing service complaint research uses subjective methods and focuses on the customers' perceived experiences whether or not consumers favor to the brand or service (Walker, 2001). Specifically, most studies on customer complaints have utilized qualitative methods to gain insights regarding critical incidents of service mishaps using customers' descriptive comments on hospitality and airline services (Chung & Hoffman, 1998; Harrison-Walker, 2001; Johnson, 2002; Manickas & Shea, 1997).

Fundamentally, Hobson (2003) argues the need for more exploratory and qualitative tourism research. It makes sense given the fact that hospitality research in the area of e-Complaint is still in its infant stage. In other words, hospitality researchers need to explore qualitative online contexts since e-Complaints are such context-specific experiences (Hobson, 2003). Golden-Biddle and Locke (1997) promoted qualitative research as a systematic and empirical strategy for answering questions about people in a bounded social context. The Internet, online purchases, and e-Complaints can all be considered as examples in the bounded social context. This type of exploratory research is so essential since it will provide building blocks for future research. Similarly, the grounded theory approach uses a systematic set of procedures to develop a theory about a social phenomenon such as public forum on the Internet. The purpose is to develop a theory that uncovers what lies behind any unknown phenomenon by identifying major categories and context of the situation (Strauss & Corbin, 1997).

Like other methods used in marketing studies, qualitative research has limited generalizability. This may be considered as a reasonable price to pay for improving the depth and quality of research in the area of e-customer behavior. The expected outcome is to develop a comprehensive idea of how the respondents perceive the issue and, in turn, will allow the researchers to understand shared characteristics that may be applicable to other respondents.

RESEARCH METHODS

The Sample and the Data

Limited studies on hospitality complaint behavior drove the authors to explore hotel customers' complaints on the Web environment. The study sample consisted of self-selected online participants who were drawn to the specialized complaint forum (www. e-complaints.com) to report their negative hotel experiences. The Web site has distinguished and experienced corporate council members to promote outstanding customer service and customer-centric business practices. This Web complaint site was chosen because (1) the complaint forum was a very popular site for active online users, (2) it had a relatively long history of collecting customer e-Complaints, and (3) it had well organized data to answer the study's research objectives. On the main Web page of this forum, there was a full list of many industry categories (including travel, communications, entertainment, utilities, health care services, and consumer products) from which an individual complainant could conveniently select a specific industry and register his/her complaints. The main page allows a complainant to perform search queries, reads complaints, issue a complaint, and look for consumer and business information.

The hotel industry section allows hotel customers to freely communicate service failures by filling out complaint information: company name, type of problem, date of incident, complaint log, company response, satisfaction ratings to the company's response, and last word from the customer. Since the last two items appeared quite spare, they were not included in this study. A well-trained graduate assistant was instructed to collect hotel data from the complaint forum. The types of hotel service problems were pre-identified by the Web forum. A total of 222 individual valid complaints over the five-year period, starting from

Jan. 1, 1996 to Jan. 15, 2001, were collected and analyzed. The contents (complaint logs) of all 222 individual complaints were compiled into a single text (ASCII) dataset for further analysis in the stage two. Data cleaning was performed to identify and unify "text representation" for similar keywords such as "booking," "booked," and "bookings" (to be corrected as a single representation of "booking") and to eliminate highly frequent but non-essential words that bear insignificant meanings such as "will," "that," "only," "been," "go," etc. In addition, highly frequent and too-specific words were also excluded in the text data. These words are highly related to "complaint" such as "complaints," "complain," "argue," and so on. The following are two cases of e-Complaint data examples collected during the study period. Although the hotel property's name is available in the dataset, it should be noted that the identity of the specific hotel company and its property are kept anonymous to protect the complainant's confidentiality.

Case 1
Problem category: 01
Hotel property: Anonymous
Date: 26/09/2000
Response: 0 (No response from the company)
Complaint log:
"When we booked the reservations months ago, we requested a king-sized bed and we pre-paid for the room. When we checked in we were told they had no more king-sized beds, even though we had pre-paid in advance. We get to our room and there are 2 almost twin sized beds. My husband is 6'3" and I am 5'8" and when I lay on the bed, my feet hung over and I took up the whole thing. There was no way 2 of us were going to fit. And, this being our honeymoon, we really didn't want to sleep in separate beds. So, we had to push the 2 beds together and slept long ways across the 2 so that we wouldn't fall into the crack. The bed was very uncomfortable and the feather pillows were even worse. My back still aches from nights spent there. Also, the bathroom in our room was dirty. There was hair and debris leftover from the previous guests and

the sink and bath tub were clogged. We tried to call for assistance, but we were put on hold and never gotten back too. The sink and drain finally drained sometime later. The beach on the property had bottle caps and glass on it."

Case 2
Problem category: 10
Hotel property: Anonymous
Date: 11/06/2000
Response: 1 (Company responded to the complaint)
Complaint log:
"Disappointing and exceptionally poor service at La Coquina restaurant. Wonderful hotel staff at check in, valet, etc. Hyatt would benefit by ensuring the same quality service at their in-house restaurant. Much needed 1 night romantic getaway for my husband and I turned sour by the lack of restaurant service. Waiter did not extend any info on specials; I ordered wine with dinner that didn't show up until I asked specifically for it again. No apologies were extended. We would, however, like to extend our great satisfaction with the kitchen staff, i.e., cook."

Data Analysis

Stage One: Descriptive Content Analysis

The content analysis method used for this study is similar to series of recent studies where qualitative self report was reported to gain insights about customer behavior. A recent study in service marketing field by Harrison-Walker (2001) utilized similar qualitative analysis of an Internet complaint forum against United Airlines. Further, this research method is often used to understand critical incidents by grouping customers' descriptive comments about hotel service mishaps (Chung & Hoffman, 1998; Johnson, 2002; Manickas & Shea, 1997). This methodology approach fits the suggestion by Hobson (2003) who advocates the need for more exploratory and qualitative tourism research. Given the fact that hospitality research in the area of e-Complaints is still in the formative stage, it makes sense to explore qualitative online context since

e-Complaints are derived from context-specific experiences.

Stage Two: Qualitative Text-Mining

Qualitative research concentrates on studying the perceptions, opinions, beliefs, and practices of individuals so that an underpinning meaning can be assigned to these views (Patton, 1990). This type of research method is often viewed as an interpretive approach where much attention is focused on research assumptions and subjective views of respondents. The goal is to discover and interpret respondents' individual and collective thinking and action that bear an intelligible meaning (Minichiello, 1995). Qualitative data of e-Complaints are particularly suitable for this methodological approach because it allows researchers to explain consumers' complaint behavior in terms of the underlying meaning reflected by e-Complainants who have access to Internet and are willing to put forward their strong opinions about dissatisfactory hotel services. The expected outcome is to develop a comprehensive idea of how the respondents perceive the problematic service issues and, in turn, will facilitate researchers' understanding on various service-related characteristics (as portrayed by associated keywords) of online complaints. This is essentially an application of building ontologies. The word "ontology" was borrowed from the discipline of philosophy where it means a systematic explanation of being (Corcho, Fernández-López, & Gómez-Pérez, 2003). In the knowledge engineering community, an ontology defines the basic terms and relations comprising the vocabulary of a topic area and the rules for combining terms/relations to define extensions to the vocabulary (Neches et al., 1991).

In order to achieve the last research objective, the text-mining software called CATPAC (Woelfel & Woelfel, 1997) was employed to analyze most frequently mentioned "unique" words that appeared in the complaint text. Based on neural network algorithms, CATPAC has been used in tourism research to identify keywords from open-ended text sources. For example, Mohsin and Ryan (1999) studied 38 travel agents in Kuala Lumpur, Malaysia, to explore the potential demand of residents in

Kuala Lumpur for their holiday travel in Darwin and the Northern Territory, Australia. They used CATPAC to perform clustering tasks on narrative responses. Their results suggested the respondents' lack of knowledge about the Northern Territory and an existence of a niche market for Darwin as a stop-over destination or one of two destinations in multi-destination holidays. Later, Ryan (2000) suggested that phenomenographic analysis by CATPAC may be one approach that permits both a revelation of individual experience while allowing model building of the shared consensus of what is actually happening. Mills (2002) and Mills and Morrisson (2003) determined factors that contributed to customer satisfaction with travel agent Websites. Their study also utilized CATPAC to examine 119 open-ended survey questions from respondents who were members of various travel-related LISTSERV and newsgroups. They found that the majority of respondents were "fairly well" satisfied with travel agent Websites and that satisfied respondents desired information that is accessible, accurate, available, clear, comparable, complete, flexible, trustworthy, varied, and up-to-date.

In this study, CATPAC was used to examine e-Complaints in two ways: (1) keyword frequency analysis–discovering important keywords' frequencies appeared in the e-Complaints, and (2) cluster analysis–examining keyword association by grouping identified important keywords based on the Ward's clustering method. The Ward's method is sometimes called the minimum variance method in which similarity is measured by joining the cluster pair and minimizing the increase in the total within- group SSE (error sum of squares) to generate homogeneous clusters (Mojena, 1988).

One of the most difficult tasks in CATPAC maneuver is setting up the neural network parameters. This requires researchers' experiences learned from trials and errors. The neural network settings used in this study are presented in Figure 1. Some practical advice regarding those more difficult settings are provided as follows:

1. Number of unique words: CATPAC selects these keywords based on frequency counts. In most cases, specifying the top 15 to 30 unique words is sufficient.

2. Window size: This number controls how CATPAC will move and read through text data. It indicates the number of words read by the software at a time. Each time a certain word is read in the window, the corresponding neuron becomes active and connections among active neurons are strengthened. Therefore, words that are close to each other in the text tend to associate with each other. A good window size to start with is usually 7.

3. Number of cycle: CATPAC tries to simulate real-time parallel connections in biological neurons by switching neurons on and off. The entire network is updated periodically all at once. Each update is called a cycle or epoch. Specifying cycle more than one allows CATPAC to detect higher-order relationships among the words to be considered. Normally 1 or 2 will be enough.

4. Decay rate: The decay rate specifies how soon the neurons return to their "off" condition after being activated (in a cycle). The default rate of 0.9 is a good starting point, which means that each neuron will lose 90% of its activation each cycle if it is not reactivated.

5. Learning rate: When neurons have similar patterns in activation, the connection strength between them is reinforced. The learning rate is usually a small number between 0 and 1. Larger numbers mean faster learning in each cycle but may be learning the same things all the time and the learning becomes memorization. Starting with 0.01 and changing the value by a factor of 10 is a good experimental practice.

6. Clamping: An action forces all neurons to remain in an activated state and this makes CATPAC less likely to "forget" the word in the learning process. It is suggested to start learning with this option checked.

7. Sliding mechanism: The "full window" method only looks for words that are part of your analysis. Therefore, this method has the speed advantage. Novice users should start with this option.

8. Transfer function: The most commonly used transfer function is sigmoid function, a logistic function varying between −1 and +1. New users should try this function first.

RESULTS AND DISCUSSIONS

Descriptive Content Analysis

E-complaints in the top five categories made up almost three-fourth of all filed complaints (n = 165, 74.32%). These e-Complaints were related to service delivery failures include "service provided not as agreed upon" (n = 40, 18.02%), "service declined in quality" (n = 37, 16.67%), "rude customer service representatives" (n = 32, 14.41%), "service never provided" (n = 29, 13.06%), and "overcharging" (n = 27, 12.16%). The results support past studies' findings that customers were not happy with fundamental services such as service delivery failures and inappropriate employee behaviors in hospitality industry (Bitner, Booms, & Tetreault, 1990; Chung & Hoffman, 1998; Manickas & Shea, 1997). Furthermore, these top complained areas are similar to those found in a study about the Internet complaints to the airline industry that include inattentive employees and rude employee attitudes toward customers (Harrison-Walker,

FIGURE 1. Neural Network Settings Used in CATPAC

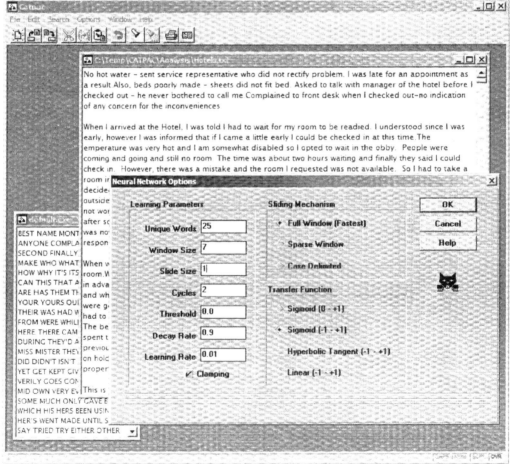

2001). No complaint was filed in *the* three problem categories: "payment credited incorrectly," "undercharged," and "unsolicited marketing calls." Table 1 provides a more detailed descriptive summary of e-complaints in 18 problem categories pre-defined by the www.e-complaints.com.

Hotel companies may be held responsible for what customers complain about. When a complaint is filed, the company is expected to respond to the customer complaint at least. In the online environment, we found that this expectation was rather difficult to realize. Of all 222 e-Complaint cases, only 31 were

TABLE 1. Lodging Cases of e-Complaints in 18 Problem Categories

No.	Complaint Category	Cases[a]	(%)	Rank[b]
01	Customer service contact confusing/inefficiency	7	(3.15)	8
02	Failed to credit promotional discount	2	(0.90)	14
03	Misleading advertising	13	(5.86)	6
04	Overcharged	27	(12.16)	5
05	Payment credited incorrectly	0	(0.00)	n/a
06	Payment was not credited	1	(0.45)	15
07	Refused to adjust fees as guaranteed	5	(2.25)	10
08	Refused to honor cancellation as guaranteed	4	(1.80)	12
09	Rude customer service representatives	32	(14.41)	3
10	Service declined in quality	37	(16.67)	2
11	Service never provided	29	(13.06)	4
12	Service provided not agreed upon	40	(18.02)	1
13	Service stopped	3	(1.35)	13
14	Undercharged	0	(0.00)	n/a
15	Unexpected/hidden fees added to the bill	7	(3.15)	8
16	Uniformed service representatives	5	(2.25)	10
17	Unresponsive to requests for assistance	10	(4.50)	7
18	Unsolicited marketing calls	0	(0.00)	n/a
	Total e-Complaint cases (N):	222	(100.0)	
	Total e-Complaints responded by companies:	31	(13.96)	

a. Collected data included hotel e-Complaints that were posted up to January 15th, 2001.
b. n/a: Not applicable.

responded to by lodging companies in the forum. In other words, only about 14 cases out of 100 were addressed by the responsible hotel companies. It is interesting to note that almost all responses to e-Complaints were found in the top five problem categories but that only one responded case was found in the category "unresponsive to requests for assistance." Table 2 reveals "company response rate" in each of the top five complained categories. Only 18.18% of the companies (n = 30) responded to the 165 top five e-Complaints. The remaining 81.82% (n = 135) did not receive any response from the companies involved. Thus, about one e-Complaint in every five received a certain attention from a hotel company. Compared with the previous e-Complaints study by Harrison-Walker (2001) that revealed only 7 consumers had received feedback from the airline company, this finding seemed to suggest that hotel companies are more responsible than airline companies in the online platform. In this study, the company response rates were on "rude customer service representatives" (n = 9, 28.13%), "service never provided" (n = 6, 20.69%), "service declined in quality" (n = 7, 18.92%), "service provided not as agreed upon" (n = 5, 12.5%), and "overcharged" (n = 3, 11.11%), respectively. Interestingly, these findings indicated that lodging companies tended to respond to more frequently complained categories. Thus, the troubled hotel companies need to allocate resources (e.g., line employees and customer service repre-

TABLE 2. Lodging Companies' Responses to Top Five e-Complaint Categories

Rank	Complaint Category[a]	Cases	Responded[b]	(%)
1	Service provided not agreed upon	40	5	(12.50)
2	Service declined in quality	37	7	(18.92)
3	Rude customer service representatives	32	9	(28.13)
4	Service never provided	29	6	(20.69)
5	Overcharged	27	3	(11.11)
	Total:	165	30	(18.18)

a. The category "unresponsive to requests for assistance" has 1 responded case but not listed here.
b. Responded cases by lodging companies through online postings in the complaint forums.

sentatives at call centers) redress the complained problems.

Qualitative Text-Mining

The 25 unique keywords (with highest frequencies) were identified from a total of 1,791
words by the CATPAC. The most frequently
mentioned keywords are ROOM, STAFF,
SERVICE, and CUSTOMER. Note that these
keywords represent certain meanings. The
chances are higher to be used in a complaint if
the keyword has a higher frequency. Figure 2
shows most settings of neural network parameters and the results of the keyword frequency
analysis in a descending order. This frequency
list helps a researcher examine how frequently

a particular keyword appears in the complaint
data.

Using the Ward's clustering method, the
CATPAC found associations among the identified 25 keywords and presents the results in a
dendogram (see Figure 3) as commonly seen
in the traditional cluster analysis. This "dendogram" looks similar to the skyline of a city
and the "buildings" underneath the words show
keywords clustered together. This data analysis seemed to suggest a four-cluster solution.
Within each cluster, grouped keywords were
associated with one another. These identified
clusters were {REFUND, WANTED, STAFF,
SERVICE, ROOM, CUSTOMER}, {RUDE,
SUITE, RESPONSE, FULL, HOUR}, {SIT-
UATION, BUSINESS, CREDIT, POOL, IN-

FIGURE 2. Results of Unique Keyword Frequency Analysis

```
TOTAL WORDS           1791    THRESHOLD          0.000
TOTAL UNIQUE WORDS      25    RESTORING FORCE    0.100
TOTAL EPISODES        1785    CYCLES                 2
TOTAL LINES           2445    FUNCTION           Sigmoid (-1 - +1)
                              CLAMPING               Yes


      DESCENDING FREQUENCY LIST                 ALPHABETICALLY SORTED LIST
                         CASE CASE                                 CASE CASE
WORD           FREQ PCNT FREQ PCNT    WORD           FREQ PCNT FREQ PCNT
-------------- ---- ---- ---- ----    -------------- ---- ---- ---- ----
ROOM           466 26.0 1395 78.2     AVAILABLE       28  1.6  180 10.1
STAFF          179 10.0  849 47.6     BATHROOM        47  2.6  253 14.2
SERVICE        151  8.4  730 40.9     BEACH           29  1.6  118  6.6
CUSTOMER       148  8.3  715 40.1     BED             44  2.5  232 13.0
PHONE           90  5.0  411 23.0     BOOKED          55  3.1  281 15.7
CHARGE          70  3.9  321 18.0     BUSINESS        29  1.6  164  9.2
CREDIT          63  3.5  294 16.5     CHARGE          70  3.9  321 18.0
BOOKED          55  3.1  281 15.7     CREDIT          63  3.5  294 16.5
BATHROOM        47  2.6  253 14.2     CUSTOMER       148  8.3  715 40.1
BED             44  2.5  232 13.0     FULL            27  1.5  187 10.5
REFUND          39  2.2  217 12.2     HOUR            27  1.5  173  9.7
WANTED          39  2.2  234 13.1     INFORMED        30  1.7  169  9.5
RATE            38  2.1  167  9.4     PHONE           90  5.0  411 23.0
RUDE            38  2.1  230 12.9     POOL            31  1.7  143  8.0
WATER           34  1.9  163  9.1     RATE            38  2.1  167  9.4
POOL            31  1.7  143  8.0     REFUND          39  2.2  217 12.2
RESPONSE        31  1.7  186 10.4     RESPONSE        31  1.7  186 10.4
INFORMED        30  1.7  169  9.5     ROOM           466 26.0 1395 78.2
BEACH           29  1.6  118  6.6     RUDE            38  2.1  230 12.9
BUSINESS        29  1.6  164  9.2     SERVICE        151  8.4  730 40.9
SITUATION       29  1.6  182 10.2     SITUATION       29  1.6  182 10.2
SUITE           29  1.6  132  7.4     STAFF          179 10.0  849 47.6
AVAILABLE       28  1.6  180 10.1     SUITE           29  1.6  132  7.4
FULL            27  1.5  187 10.5     WANTED          39  2.2  234 13.1
HOUR            27  1.5  173  9.7     WATER           34  1.9  163  9.1
```

FIGURE 3. Cluster Analysis Results Shown as a Dendogram

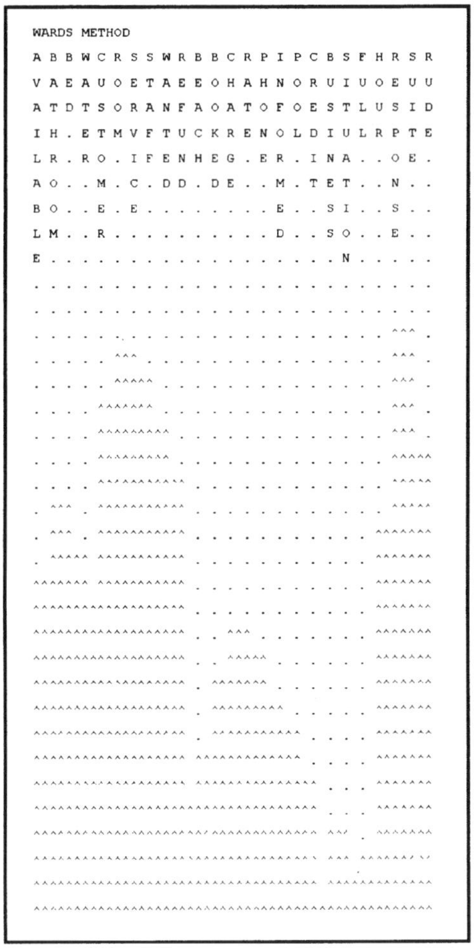

```
WARDS METHOD
A B B W C R S S W R B B C R P I P C B S F H R S R
V A E A U O E T A E E O H A H N O R U I U O E U U
A T D T S O R A N F A O A T O F O E S T L U S I D
I H . E T M V F T U C K R E N O L D I U L R P T E
L R . R O . I F E N H E G . E R . I N A . . O E .
A O . . M . C . D D . D E . . M . T E T . . N . .
B O . . E . E . . . . . . . . E . . S I . . S . .
L M . . R . . . . . . . . . . D . . S O . . E . .
E . . . . . . . . . . . . . . . N . . . . .
```

FORMED, PHONE, RATE, CHARGE, BOOKED, BEACH} and {WATER, BED, BATHROOM, AVAILABLE}. Clustering these associated keywords allows the researchers to discern linkages between certain keywords within each cluster. For example, as seen in Figure 3, the words "ROOM" and "SERVICE" cluster very closely together. The words "STAFF" and "CUSTOMER" join this cluster at a slightly lower level, followed with the word "WANTED" at even lower level, and then "REFUND" at lowest level within this cluster. Since all texts were extracted from customers' complaints, the negative implication of "complaining about the problem" should be embedded in the interpretation of the "key" clusters. Therefore, the aforementioned example may suggest that "CUSTOMERs complained about ROOM SERVICE STAFF and WANTED the REFUND."

LIMITATIONS AND FUTURE IMPLICATIONS

Conducting research on the Internet contents has its own limitations. For instance, there may be some self-bias problems since the respondents might give inaccurate complaint information. The use of the Internet may be linked to complainers' higher income level. Thus the study may reflect high incomers' sentiment towards negative hotel experiences. Further, the researchers recently found that the Web site is temporarily out of operation due to slow economy. However, information we have investigated until January 2001 is still very valuable.

This research yielded managerial guidelines and future research implications. The company needs to be attentive to the e-Complainants and take immediate actions to the guest problems (Davidow, 2000; Mount & Mattila, 2000). Thus, hotel management should place structured electronic complaint management procedures to efficiently deal with the unsatisfied customers. The call center or customer relations department at the corporate level should regularly log on to the e-Complaint site to monitor the aggregated complaint data and report it to the general managers or supervisors in relevant hotel properties to fix the alluded problems. Hotels can further publicize the company response by posting them at www.eComplaints.com. The hotel company can also benefit from well-designed Web management system which enables the complaint information of the Web site sent directly to the corporate headquarters and the hotel property. For instance, the system can utilize auto reply (or a personalized follow-up) to the customer and mention that the company is working on specific actions to correct the problem or eliminating the problem.

Further research may focus on investigating customer usage pattern (i.e., length of relationship with the hotel) and types and number of previous complaints stored on the Web pages. Further, hospitality researchers should develop potential model of e-Complaint behavior by investigating the relationships among severity of service failure, types of complaints on the Internet, satisfaction with the company responses, and e-WOM. For instance, investigating customers' satisfaction with the company's response to their complaints will expand our understanding of e-Complaint behavior.

In all, consumers' online comments on the Web page are a treasure for underutilized customer information. The hotel industry needs to address the service failure issues by working closely with the troubled hotel property with sophisticated complaint management system. Consumers look at the company's response to their requests as a tally of how hotel organizations care about service issues. It is hoped that this study will encourage additional research on e-Complaints and would facilitate faster business responses to customer concerns.

REFERENCES

Anderson, E. (1998). Customer satisfaction and word of mouth. *Journal of Service Research, 1*(1), 5-17.

Bitner, M. J., Booms, B. H., & Tetreault, M. S. (1990). The service encounter: Diagnosing favorable and unfavorable incidents. *Journal of Marketing, 54*(1), 71-84.

Buttle, F. A. (1998). Word of mouth: Understanding and managing referral marketing. *Journal of Strategic Marketing, 6*(3), 241-254.

Chung, B., & Hoffman, K. D. (1998). Critical incidents: Service failures that matter most. *Cornell Hotel and Restaurant Administration Quarterly, 39*(3), 66-77.

Connolly, D. J., Olsen, M. D., & Moore, R. (1998). The Internet as a distribution channel. *Cornell Hotel and Restaurant Administration Quarterly, 39*(4), 42-55.

Corcho, O., Fernández-López, M., & Gómez-Pérez, A. (2003). Methodologies, tools and languages for building ontologies: Where is their meeting point? *Data & Knowledge Engineering, 46*(1), 41-64.

Davidow, M. (2000). The bottom line impact of organizational responses to customer complaints. *Journal of Hospitality and Tourism Research, 24*(4), 473-490.

Davidow, M. (2003). Organizational responses to customer complaints: What works and what doesn't. *Journal of Service Research, 5*(3), 225-250.

Estelami, H. (2000). Competitive and procedural determinants of delight and disappointment in consumer complaint outcomes. *Journal of Service Research, 2*(3), 285-300.

Gelb, B. D., & Sundaram, S. (2002). Adapting to "word of mouse." *Business Horizons, 45*(4), 15-20.

Golden-Biddle, K., & Locke, K. (1997). *Composing qualitative research.* Thousand Oaks, CA: Sage Publications, Inc.

Goodman, J. (1999, June). Basic facts on customer complaint behavior and the impact of service on the bottom line. *Competitive Advantage,* 1-5.

Harrison-Walker, L. J. (2001). E-complaining: A content analysis of an Internet complaint forum. *Journal of Services Marketing, 15*(5), 397-412.

Hobson, J. S. P. (2003). The case for more exploratory and grounded tourism research. *Pacific Tourism Review, 6*(2), 73-81.

Hoffman, D. L., & Bateson, J. (2001). *Essentials of services marketing: Concepts, strategies, and cases.* Mason, OH: South-Western.

Jeong, M., & Lambert, C. (1999). Measuring the information quality on lodging web sites. *International Journal of Hospitality Information Technology, 1*(1), 63-75.

Johnson, L. (2002). An application of the critical incident technique in gaming research. *Journal of Travel & Tourism Marketing, 12*(2-3), 45-63.

Kirkby, J., Thompson, E., & Wecksell, J. (2001). *Customer experience: The voice of the customer* (Research note No. TG-14-9567). Stamford, CT: Gartner, Inc.

Lee, C. C. (2001). The impact of information technology on hotel service quality. *International Journal of Hospitality Information Technology, 2*(1), 57-68.

Loiacono, E. T., Watson, R. T., & Goodhue, D. L. (2000). *WebQual™: A web site quality instrument.* Retrieved June 30, 2003, from *http://piano.dsi. uminho.pt/grupok3/bibdig/WebQual_Draft.pdf*

Manickas, P., & Shea, L. (1997). Hotel complaint behavior and resolution: A content analysis. *Journal of Travel Research, 36*(2), 68-73.

Mattila, A. S., & Mount, D. J. (2003). The impact of selected customer characteristics and response time on e-complaint satisfaction and return intent. *International Journal of Hospitality Management, 22*(2), 135-145.

Mills, J. E. (2002). *An analysis, instrument development, and structural equation modeling of customer satisfaction with online travel services.* Unpublished doctoral dissertation, Purdue University, West Lafayette, IN.

Mills, J., & Morrison, A. M. (2003, August 6-10). *Examining customer satisfaction with travel agent websites: A qualitative neural network analysis approach.* Paper presented at the 2003 Annual International CHRIE Conference and Exposition, Palm Springs, CA.

Minichiello, V. (1995, May 19). CRC seminar series: Designing qualitative research. *Qualitative Research Forum by Victoria University of Technology.*

Mitchell, V. W. (1993). Handling consumer complaint information: Why and how? *Management Decision, 31*(3), 21-28.

Mohsin, A., & Ryan, C. (1999). Perceptions of the Northern Territory by travel agents in Kuala Lumpur. *Asia Pacific Journal of Tourism Research, 3*(2), 41-46.

Mojena, R. (1988). Ward's clustering algorithm. In S. Kotz & N. L. Johnson (Eds.), *Encyclopedia of Statistical Sciences* (Vol. 9, pp. 529-532). New York, NY: John Wiley & Sons.

Mount, D. J., & Mattila, A. S. (2000). The final opportunity: The effectiveness of a customer relations call center in recovering hotel guests. *Journal of Hospitality and Tourism Research, 24*(4), 514-525.

Neches, R., Fikes, R., Finin, T., Gruber, T., Patil, R., Senator, T. et al. (1991). Enabling technology for knowledge sharing. *AI Magazine, 12*(3), 36-56.

O'Connor, P., & Frew, A. (2002). The future of hotel electronic distribution. *Cornell Hotel and Restaurant Administration Quarterly, 43*(3), 33-45.

Page, S. J., Brunt, P., Busby, G., & Connell, J. (2001). *Tourism: A modern synthesis.* London, UK: International Thomson Business Press.

Parasuraman, A. (1996). *Understanding and leveraging the role of customer service in external, interactive, and internal marketing.* Paper presented at the 1996 Frontiers in Services Conferences, Nashville, TN.

Parasuraman, A. (2000). Technology readiness index (TRI): A multiple-item scale to measure readiness to embrace new technologies. *Journal of Service Research, 2*(4), 307-320.

Patton, M. P. (1990). *Qualitative evaluation and research methods* (2nd ed.). London, UK: Sage Publications, Ltd.

Richins, M. L. (1983). Negative word-of-mouth by dissatisfied consumers: A pilot study. *Journal of Marketing, 47*(1), 68-78.

Ryan, C. (2000). Tourist experiences, phenomenographic analysis, post-positivism and neural network software. *International Journal of Tourism Research, 2*(2), 119-131.

Strauss, A., & Corbin, J. (1997). *Grounded theory in practice.* Thousand Oaks, CA: Sage Publications, Inc.

van Hoof, H. B., & Combrink, T. E. (1998). U.S. lodging management and the Internet: Perceptions from the industry. *Cornell Hotel and Restaurant Administration Quarterly, 39*(2), 46-54.

Walker, L. J. (2001). The measurement of word-of-mouth communication and an investigation of service quality and customer commitment as potential antecedents. *Journal of Service Research, 4*(1), 60-75.

Williams, K., Cheung, C., & Choi, W. (2000). Cyberostracism: Effects of being ignored over the Internet. *Journal of Personality and Social Psychology, 79*(5), 748-762.

Woelfel, J. K., & Woelfel, J. D. (1997). CATPAC for Windows (Version 2.0) [Computer program]. Amherst, NY: The Galileo Company.

World Tourism Organization. (1999). *Marketing tourism destinations online: Strategies for the information age.* Madrid, Spain: World Tourism Organization Business Council (WTOBC).

Zeithaml, V. A., Parasuraman, A., & Malhotra, A. (2002). Service quality delivery through web sites: A critical review of extant knowledge. *Journal of the Academy of Marketing Science, 30*(4), 362-375.

E-Complaints:
Lessons to Be Learned
from the Service Recovery Literature

Brian Tyrrell
Robert Woods

SUMMARY. This study looks at the recent phenomenon of online or e-consumer complaints often referred to as e-complaints and stresses that travel and tourism professionals should address such complaints. E-complaints are then examined using the service recovery process. A detailed examination of the service recovery literature is undertaken. Suggestions for the future direction of e-complaint research are also made. *[Article copies available for a fee from The Haworth Document Delivery Service: 1-800-HAWORTH. E-mail address: <docdelivery@haworthpress.com> Website: <http://www.HaworthPress.com> © 2004 by The Haworth Press, Inc. All rights reserved.]*

KEYWORDS. Complaints, e-complaints, service failure, service recovery

INTRODUCTION

The complaining traveler is something with which all travel and tourism professionals are familiar. Albrecht and Zemke (1996) highlight some often cited statistics with respect to consumer complaints: less than 5 percent of dissatisfied customers actually voice their complaints; satisfactorily resolved complaints will lead to a 54 to 70% retention rate of customers and up to 95% if resolved quickly; and complainers typically tell more than 20 acquaintances about their problem. Such figures suggest the importance of both listening to customer complaints and encouraging those that do not voice their complaints to do so.

Recognizing and reacting to guest complaints is nothing new in the travel and tourism industry. Even the most customer service-oriented business will find that unexpected circumstances arise where the customer experiences a service failure. How the company deals with the circumstance once they have received the complaint can help to define a customer service-oriented business. Indeed, research suggests that both customer retention and loyalty are enhanced when complaints are handled well (Sing and Wilkes, 1996). Service providers that can analyze consumer complaints will benefit from the perspective of their customers. Those that do not might find their deficiencies broadcast to a rather wide

Brian Tyrrell is Assistant Professor and Robert Woods is Professor, both of the Department of Hotel Management, William F. Harrah College of Hotel Administration, University of Nevada, Las Vegas.
Address correspondence to Brian Tyrrell (E-mail: Brian.Tyrrell@ccmail.Nevada.edu).

[Haworth co-indexing entry note]: "E-Complaints: Lessons to Be Learned from the Service Recovery Literature." Tyrrell, Brian, and Robert Woods. Co-published simultaneously in *Journal of Travel & Tourism Marketing* (The Haworth Hospitality Press, an imprint of The Haworth Press, Inc.) Vol. 17, No. 2/3, 2004, pp. 183-190; and: *Handbook of Consumer Behavior, Tourism, and the Internet* (ed: Juline E. Mills, and Rob Law) The Haworth Hospitality Press, an imprint of The Haworth Press, Inc., 2004, pp. 183-190. Single or multiple copies of this article are available for a fee from The Haworth Document Delivery Service [1-800-HAWORTH, 9:00 a.m. - 5:00 p.m. (EST). E-mail address: docdelivery@haworthpress.com].

audience. Such was the case in 1996 when Jeremy Cooperstock and a colleague wrote United Airlines® about several unpleasant experiences they had encountered during both legs of a round-trip flight from Toronto to Tokyo. After hearing no response after six weeks a follow-up letter was sent expressing concern that their attempt at pointing out service failures to the company was not responded to. This second letter was responded to only by a form letter which did not address the specific concerns of Cooperstock. This incident prompted Cooperstock to start a "Poor Show" Website which later became Untied (untied.com), a complaint Website for disgruntled customers of United Airlines to visit and post their own concerns. Consumers wishing to complain online have found that the process is not necessarily a difficult one. On the Website Untied. com a complaint form is readily available for visitors to the site to gripe about United Airlines.®

The above incident highlights why e-complaints should be brought to the forefront of complaint research. However, little empirical research has been directed to e-complaints. Harrison-Walker (2001) conducted a content analysis of an Internet complaint forum and suggested that in analyzing the content of complaints, companies can create products and or services to remedy the problem areas. While Harrison-Walker added to the body of literature on service recovery, little was offered which would indicate how a business should respond to a complaint. It is with this in mind that the current paper attempts to describe e-complaint behavior and then discuss such behavior in light of the service recovery literature. The paper begins with a general discussion about what constitutes e-complaining. It then turns its attention to the service recovery literature, drawing parallels between phenomenons addressed in the literature with behavior exhibited online. Suggestions for future research conclude the article.

THE TYPOLOGY
OF CONSUMER E-COMPLAINTS

Where once negative publicity about a company required a media outlet interested in publishing a consumer's concerns, today, with the proliferation of the Internet, everyone can be an author and the world is their audience. Recently e-complaining has entered mainstream society with an increase in the number of individuals becoming familiar with Web publishing. Wolrich (2002) describes four complaint sites directed at specific companies (Allstate®, PayPal®, Microsoft®, and American Express®). The complaint site on PayPal® (www.paypalsucks. com) was started not necessarily because of the complaint the creator had with the company but rather the company's lack of interest in their complaint. The creator of PayPalsucks.com writes:

> I called PayPal to inquire about a very simple question. I don't even recall what the problem was now . . . just a simple question. But the person I spoke with could not answer it. After repeated requests to get a supervisor online, they hung up on me. I called back and believe it or not, got a different person and they hung up on me too. I felt like I was in the twilight zone.

The growth of e-complaints has also been aided by the introduction of companies attempting to profit from consumers wishing to express their opinions online. Consumers are turning to these sites and others to register e-complaints in record numbers. In 2000 one commercial site, Planetfeedback.com, boasted 500,000 unique visitors per month and 500 consumer letters per day (Neff, 2000). Such numbers suggest a growing need for tourism and hospitality firms to take notice and address e-complaints as a marketing priority. Unfortunately, it seems that some tourism and hospitality firms have not taken notice of e-complaints. According to Adams (2000), at least three major airlines currently do not respond to a large portion of e-complaints. Indeed, the former Website eComplaints.com reported that less than one percent of complaints registered are responded to by the companies who are the worst offenders (Appelman, 2001; Lee, 1999). Some companies will also not accept e-complaints from their customers. Adams (2000) notes that three airlines in particular (American®, US Airways®, and

Southwest®) have determined that they cannot justify the expense associated with answering all e-complaints, particularly ones that are general complaints about the company. Southwest quotes "we cannot justify adding the numerous employees who would be needed to filter through the . . . emails."

Singh (1988) developed a typology of consumer complaint responses, classifying complaining behavior as either third party (complaints lodged with some independent organization), voice (complaints lodged with the faltering company), or private (complaints lodged with family or friends), all three of which are present in e-complaints. Consumers are using the third party option to gripe about companies and will likely continue this practice. PlanetFeedback.com is a good example of a third party receiving and disseminating e-complaints. The site has a form which allows participants to identify a company by name and industry, and even provides a classification for your feedback (complaint, compliment, question or suggestion). Companies in their database will then have an option for the complainer to select from a list of common complaint topics. For instance, if one were to enter Hilton in the complaint form, a drop down menu of complaint topics would include check-in, checkout, food service, front desk and housekeeping, among others.

Complaining to the company via an e-mail address (voice) is also common. Unfortunately, companies sometimes are reluctant to do anything but respond to the consumer directly, thereby missing out on third party options. Wal-Mart® representatives contend that "If we went to complaint sites or negative sites and attempted to deal then we'd be energizing something that doesn't need to be energized" (Appelman, 2001). So while it is encouraging to find that companies are at least attempting to provide a means of communicating e-complaints directly, they should not be seen as the sole method of voicing complaints online.

In addition to the likely thousands of private e-mails discussing poor service encounters that companies might never hear about, there is at least one example of an e-complaint meant to be private that turned out to be anything but. Khullar and Enghagen (2003) describe a PowerPoint® presentation that was created for the General Manager of a hotel in Houston, TX as well as a relative and two friends. The subsequent press that the complaint received went far beyond anything the disgruntled travelers had imagined. The General Manager of the hotel claims they did not send the complaint on to anyone else suggesting that it was the private parties that began the widespread dissemination of the humorous yet serious complaint lodged against the hotel.

SERVICE RECOVERY'S ROLE IN THE STUDY OF E-COMPLAINTS

It is well established in the service industry that it is much less expensive to retain existing customers than to spend marketing dollars in attracting new ones. In the past this has meant a careful examination of the complaints lodged by consumers and appropriate action to remedy the situation both for the existing customers as well as potential future ones. For researchers, this meant conducting research on service failures and complaint resolution, or service recovery. Currently, there exists very little research into e-complaints; however, the research on service recovery is well established. This segment summarizes the literature on service recovery, and discusses this literature in light of the recent phenomenon of e-complaining.

Service recovery can be defined as "putting right what has gone wrong" (Bailey, 1994). Effective service recovery processes can, and usually do, have a dramatic positive impact on both customer satisfaction and the bottom line (Mattila, 2001, p. 593). In their seminal work on service recovery, Hart (1990) discusses the importance of making it easy for customers to complain. We can assume that these authors would be pleased to see the trend in growth of e-complaints because such vehicles make it easier for the customer to complain. Others share in this sentiment as well. Ahmad (2002), referring to the customers' ability to communicate their concerns, suggests, "the need for multiple channels of communication is of utmost importance" (p. 19). An understanding of the service recovery concept is necessary to fully comprehend current issues with e-complaints.

Scholars have looked at service recovery from different vantage points. In this paper we concentrate on an aspect not fully discussed in the literature to date. Our approach involves understanding some concepts often discussed in organizational behavior, industrial psychology and sociology. Applying these concepts to service recovery helps one understand the important role that recovery plays in customer satisfaction as well as the intention to complain. For instance, several scholars have suggested that such factors as affect-balance, equity, attribution, and the degree of customer voice/no voice likely influence how customers perceive service recovery efforts. In effect, these concepts likely determine whether or not a customer will return to the same provider again. Each of these topics are discussed below.

Affect-Balance Theory

Affect-balance theory contends that events in life alternate between the positive and the negative and instances of one do not preclude the other (Andreassen, 2000). This means that individuals typically experience variations in service delivery and recovery, that they are influenced by such events and that a positive (or negative) event does not preclude the opposite from occurring. Therefore, one might say that while providing service recovery processes will likely lead to greater customer satisfaction, just "having" such a program does not necessarily mean that customers will be more satisfied. Services are particularly subject to affect-balance emotions because there is such a large number of potential attributes in each service encounter which customers may perceive as negative or unpleasant (Oliver in Andreassen, 2000, p. 3).

Consider a simple visit to a chain restaurant. During this visit the customer encounters first the appearance of the outside of the building and signage, the appearance of the lot, landscaping, then the personality and proficiency of the greeter, the server, the bartender, sometimes the manager and finally the greeter again in one simple service encounter. Within each of these events are actually a series of potential service encounters. Any one of these encounters can cause a customer to feel dissatisfied with the overall experience.

Equity

Parties in an exchange must feel like they got fair treatment. In a service recovery environment this means that customers who perceive that they have received poor service experience a sense on inequity and are, therefore, more likely not to use the service provider again. Equity theory is based on a comparison of output to outcome. In effect, the greater the output from a customer, the greater the expectations of a desirable outcome with the service experience. By definition, then, the more involved the customer is with the creation and delivery of service, the higher his/her expectations will be. People want to feel a sense of balance in the amount of output they invest and the amount of outcome they experience. If the output is considered by the customer to be fair and equitable in return for their investment in time, money and other resources then s/he will have a greater sense of equity-balance in the transaction.

The opposite is also true. Customers who believe that they invested more than they got are unlikely to experience satisfaction because they perceive an equity-imbalance. For example, one of the authors recently had a negative customer service experience with Amazon.com. In this event, the author purchased a book for his daughter. The book was to be delivered to the daughter's address and the author/buyer paid for overnight delivery. Unknown to the customer was that Amazon.com allows its delivery associates (UPS, FEDEX, etc.) to decide whether or not a package is deliverable with or without a signature for receipt of delivery. Amazon.com does not explain this fact to customers. Instead, Amazon.com's position is that it sells the customer a book and "engages on their behalf" a delivery service. Whatever actions the delivery service takes are not the responsibility of Amazon.com. In the service event with Amazon.com delivery was not made "the next day" as the customer had paid for in his order. Instead, the delivery company decided that they needed a signature for delivery and, instead of delivering the book, left a note to contact the delivery company and arrange for signature. In discussing this problem with Amazon.com our author learned that Amazon.com takes no responsibility for delivery, only for sales. How and when the delivery agent decides to deliver the product is not part of their contract with the customer, according to the Amazon.com agent who fielded a service recovery call from the author-buyer. In other words, while Amazon.com agreed to accept payment for the book and delivery, it does not guarantee when delivery will be made, regardless of what type of delivery the customer pays for with his/her order.

Attribution

The Amazon.com situation may lead to what is known in organizational behavior, industrial psychology and sociology as an "attribution theory" scenario. Attribution theory is simple. Humans like to blame someone for their problems. Who the customer blames (in this case Amazon.com or UPS) is an example of attribution theory at work. Typically a customer will blame the service provider from whom s/he purchased the products or services, not the agent who delivers the products or services. Therefore, in the case of Amazon.com, the customer is more likely to blame Amazon.com than UPS because their "deal" was made with Amazon.com. Failure is thus attributed to Amazon.com and the customer believes that his/her investment far outweighed the return from Amazon.com. The result is a dissatisfied customer.

It is natural for people to want to attribute events to certain actions and decisions. Interestingly, the importance of attribution in service recovery is tied somewhat to the socio-economic status of the buyer. This is because of the effect that locus of control has on people's actions. Locus of control is a measure of the extent to which individuals feel like they are in control of events in their lives. People with a high internal locus of control (people who believe that they control events in their lives) believe that they are in control of events. When a service error occurs it throws them off, because it is not something that they can control. As a result, they are more likely to place blame on the company for their service problems. This is especially true when they have invested time and energy into attempting to fix the problem by calling it to the attention of the company. Returning to the discussion of why Untied.com was started, Jeremy Cooper-

stock and his colleague in their second attempt to contact the company via traditional means are quoted as stating "after all the time and effort we spent politely explaining the incidents that occurred, in addition to providing suggestions as to how United could improve its service, we certainly did not expect to be further insulted by having our letter ignored." Clearly their notion of what United Airlines® should have done contributed to their outrage.

Voice/No Voice

Behavior in service environments is dependent on the extent to which customers perceive that they have a voice (or no voice) in actions resulting from prior service failures. Those with a voice or opinion that is heard are more likely to believe that the service recovery effort succeeded. However, those who are accustomed to being able to voice their position are easily angered when this is taken away from them. For these people, the extent to which a customer is satisfied with service recovery depends on the extent to which they have the opportunity to voice their opinions (Beadren and Teal, in Andreassen, 2000, p. 3). People with low internal locus of control have likely learned that their opinion is neither wanted nor needed, in contrast. It is when these individuals become frustrated that their concerns are not heard that they might be more likely to turn to a third party to complain. Lee (1999, p. 4) quotes the President of Caveat Emptor (cemptor.com) Bill Tran as saying "A lot of people have tried to handle problems themselves, but they're frustrated and angry. They want to forget about it, that's when I jump in." Perhaps the anonymity of the Internet provides the encouragement for those with "no voice" to speak up regardless of whether the company wants to listen or not.

TYPES OF SERVICE RECOVERY IMPORTANT TO HANDLING E-COMPLAINTS

While so far we have spoken of service recovery as if there is a single type in which companies should engage, this is definitely not the case. Different levels of service recovery are needed depending on the following factors:

1. Problem severity (denial or delay).
2. Criticality levels (low–high).
3. Which deviation is it (first, second, third) and how prior attempt to fix are evaluated.
4. Compensation by company for problems encountered.

The lesson this offers is that service recovery efforts are different based on the product/service. Service recovery efforts must be tailored to the given situation. Most service recovery programs also focus on how to fix problems. However, this is only part of the battle for service providers. Effective service recovery programs not only fix the problem but also include processes that help customers feel comfortable with the solution (i.e., equity theory) (McDougal, 1999).

In a study of restaurant patrons and their observations about service recovery efforts, Palmer (2000, 13) found that whether or not the customer has a sense of equity is significantly correlated to their intent to purchase again. Palmer also noted that demographics play a role in customer acceptance of service recovery efforts. In fact, Palmer noted that service providers should be aware of the "demographic profile" of the customer and the person attempting to fix their problem. When both customer and employee are from same demographic profile, customers are more likely to accept recovery then when not. Palmer also found that customers are more satisfied when the service recovery is initiated and completed by a line-level employee than they are when a manager becomes involved. This is because customers perceive a company as willing to empower employees to fix problems and must therefore be more interested in satisfaction (Jones and Sasser, 1995).

Service recovery efforts often forget to include an apology. Interestingly, Mack found in a study of restaurants that while many companies engaged in some type of service recovery, only 15.3% of them apologized for the problem. No apology leaves customers thinking that the company did not really believe that they had done something wrong in the first place. Indeed, the founder of Untied suggests that some of the Website (untied.com) would never have begun if an apology was forthcoming in the first place.

In e-complaints customers often want to talk to someone about problems but are prevented from doing so because they can only respond by e-mail, with no options provided for contacting the business by telephone. The service provider understands that using e-purchasing practices can and does lower its human capital costs because it eliminates personnel. However, companies that do not provide a phone contact method for customers do not understand that the customer does not consider such responses to be adequate in terms of their affect-balance or equity perceptions. When replies from service providers involve only generic responses (e-mail or live) customer sense on inequity goes up, not down. And, why shouldn't it? From the customer perspective they have invested more time and money into purchasing a product or service and into the service recovery process when the purchase goes bad so does the service provider.

Ahmad also found that 67.5% of customers who purchase products online prefer e-mail (to 31.5% who prefer telephone contact) for generic questions. However, this relationship is reversed when contact involves a service recovery issue over an already-purchased product or service. In fact, customers who have already experienced a service problem and are attempting to find correction prefer telephone to e-mail 51.4% to 48.6% and this is only on the first attempt at service recovery. If the problem is not fixed with the initial customer effort, expectations by the customer that they need to communicate by telephone with a live person increases dramatically (Ahmad, 2002, p. 23).

In examining service failures during online shopping experiences, Ahmad (2002) correlates consideration of shopping at the same site again with whether or not customers had a bad experience. Ahmad found a strong negative correlation (-0.53) between whether customers would shop at a provider who provided poor service and/or recovery efforts. Further evidence from the same study suggests that bad experiences typically lead to the shopper discouraging as many as eight to ten others from using the service provider. Ahmad also found that it is not enough for the online shop to provide a means of contacting them, or of simply making an effort at resolving the customer's complaint, but rather the problem must be satisfactorily resolved. If the problem is satisfactorily resolved, customers are more likely to shop at the same provider again (0.88) and to recommend it positively to others (0.81).

SERVICE RECOVERY AND DIRECTION FOR E-COMPLAINT RESEARCH

The current study has attempted to describe a recent phenomenon, e-complaining. It has also described research on service recovery's role in resolving guest complaints. It is suggested by the authors that the lessons learned from the service recovery literature should be applied to both the resolution of e-complaints by service providers as well as help to guide the future research of e-complaints by academics. It is important to keep in mind that e-complaining is simply another outlet by which customers who are dissatisfied can voice their opinion about perceived inequity. Furthermore, while e-complaining is often viewed by the customer as an easier means of complaining, research highlighted above indicates that it should not replace traditional means of contacting a service provider. Nor should e-complaints be ignored while traditional means of communication are being addressed in service recovery efforts. In short, all complaints should be handled by the same service recovery processes in an organization.

Rather than discouraging e-complaints, it is important that service providers encourage such communication. E-complaints registered to a company are much more manageable from a public relations standpoint than e-complaints registered to some third party and posted for the world to read. This, coupled with the ideas expressed within the framework of service recovery, suggests that e-complaints should take the same priority as would a complaint over the telephone, through traditional mail or in person. A greater understanding of e-complaint behavior through replications of the work done in service recovery will assist these providers in understanding the importance or complaint resolution in the virtual world. Models of exploration to consider are needed.

A great deal more research is needed on e-complaints. In this article we have described the phenomenon which has become a staple method of remedy for many Americans. We need to know much more. Who uses e-complaints and in which type of occasions would greatly enhance an organization's ability to turn e-complainers into loyal customers. More needs to be learned about how e-complaints affect the service recovery process, as well. We have identified the relationship between service recovery and e-complaints in this paper. Hopefully other researchers, both within academia and the hospitality industry, will further clarify the relationship and the impact of various types of e-complaint resolution behavior. We do not yet know what will make a hospitality e-complainer happy. Opening the door of knowledge to illuminate the link between service recovery and e-complaints could save the industry millions of dollars. E-complaints may also provide an excellent means of identifying how successful new product or services are with customers. At this point, so little has been done in understanding e-complaints in tourism and hospitality that understanding virtually any aspect of the process would improve customer relations somehow.

REFERENCES

Adams, M. (2000, April 18). More fliers land on the Internet to air complaints: Government, some airlines post links to e-mail forms. *USA Today*, p. B12.

Ahmad, S. (2002). Service failures and customer defection: A closer look at online shopping experiences. *Managing Service Quality, 12*, (1), 19-29.

Alexander, E.C. (2002). Consumer reactions to unethical service recovery. *Journal of Business Ethics, 36*, (3), 223-237.

Albrecht, K. and Zemke, R. (1985). *Service America! Doing business in the new economy.* Homewood, IL: Dow Jones-Irwin.

Andreassen, T.W. (2000). Antecedents to satisfaction with service recovery. *European Journal of Marketing, 34*, (1/2), 156.

Appelman, H. (2001, March 4). I Scream, You Scream: Consumers Vent Over the Net. *New York Times*, p. 3.13.

Bailey, D. (1994). Service recovery: A ten-stage approach in the training of front-line staff. *Training & Management Development Methods, 8*, (4), 4-8.

Beyette, B. (1999, November 2). Feeling a Tad Stressed Over Your Job? *The Los Angeles Times*, pp. E1:3.

Bowen, D.E., & Johnston, R. (1999). Internal service recovery: Developing a new contract. *International Journal of Service Industry Management, 10*, (2), 118-131.

Brown, S.W. (2000). Practicing best-in-class service recovery. *Marketing Management, Chicago, 9*, (2), 8-9.

Brown, S.W. (1996). Service recovery: Its value and limitations as a retail strategy. *International Journal of Service Industry Management, 7*, (5), 32.

Durvasula, S., Lysonski, S., & Mehta, S.C. (2000). Business-to-business marketing service recovery and customer satisfaction issues with ocean shipping lines. *European Journal of Marketing, 34*, (3/4), 433-452.

Eccles, G. (1998). Complaining customers, service recovery and continuous improvement. *Managing Service Quality, 8*, (1), 68.

Harrison-Walker, L.J. (2001). E-complaining: A content analysis of an Internet complaint forum. *Journal of Services Marketing, 15*, (5), 397-412.

Hart, C.W.L. (1990). The Profitable Art of Service Recovery. *Harvard Business Review, 68*, (4), 148-156.

Khullar, A., Shea, L., & Enghagen, L. (2003). Negative word-of-mouth via the Internet: Diffusion of a PowerPoint complaint. *Proceedings of the Eight Annual Graduate Education and Graduate Students Research Conference in Hospitality and Tourism, Las Vegas, NV, January 5-7*, 246-250.

Lee, J. (1999, July 8). Addition to Consumers' Arsenal: Net Complaint Services for Hire. *New York Times*, p. 4.

Lewis, B.R. (2001). Service failure and recovery in UK theme parks: The employees' perspective. *International Journal of Contemporary Hospitality Management, Bradford, 13*, (4/5), 166-175.

Lewis, D. (2001, September 10). Nationwide customer view: Insurer deploys low-cost Web app to get complete view of complaints. *InternetWeek*, p. 50.

Mattila, A.S. (2001). The effectiveness of service recovery in a multi-industry setting. *The Journal of Services Marketing, 15*, (6/7), 583-596.

McDougall, G.H.G. (1999). Waiting for service: The effectiveness of recovery strategies. *International Journal of Contemporary Hospitality Management, 11*, (1), 6.

Neff, J. (2000, October 2). PlanetFeedback happy to hear consumer gripes. *Advertising Age, 71*, (41), pp. 48-52.

Palmer, A., Beggs, R., & Keown-McMullan, C. (2000). Equity and repurchase intention following service failure. *The Journal of Services Marketing, 14*, (6), 513-528.

PlanetFeedback.com. (2003, July 9). Search ratings. Available online at: http://www.planetfeedback.com/ratings/0,2502,,00.html

Singh, J. (1988). Consumer complaint intentions and behavior: Definitional and taxonomical issues. *Journal of Marketing, 59*, (1), 93-107.

Singh, J., & Wilkes, R.E. (1996). When consumers complain: A path analysis of the key antecedents of consumer complaint response estimates. *Journal of the Academy of Marketing Science, 24*, (1), 350-365.

Wolrich, C. (2002). The best corporate complaint sites. Available online at: http://www.forbes.com/home/2002/08/21/0821hatesites.html

SECTION 5:
WEBSITE DESIGN AND DEVELOPMENT IN TRAVEL AND TOURISM

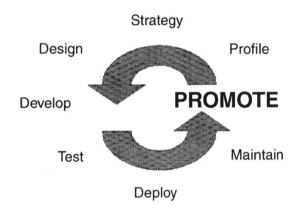

Adapted from: Project Process Approach. Available: *www.imogenmedia.com/appr.htm*

Effects of Picture Presentations on Customers' Behavioral Intentions on the Web

Miyoung Jeong
Jiyoung Choi

SUMMARY. As the Web is becoming a major communication channel to bridge hotels and customers, great marketing efforts have been made to attract new customers and repeat business. A wide variety of studies have been conducted to identify factors that could affect customers' purchase behavior on the Web. Little research, however, has been documented that assessed the effects different pictures presented on the Web had on customers' online purchase behavior. Based on the content analyses with 203 existing hotel Websites, this study examined the potential effects of Website format, Website contents, and Website realism on customers' behavioral intentions. Results indicate that the content and realism of picture presentations are important predictors of customers' attitudes toward the Website. The attitudes appear to be a strong predictor of behavioral intentions on the Web. Suggestions and implications are included for the lodging industry and future research. *[Article copies available for a fee from The Haworth Document Delivery Service: 1-800-HAWORTH. E-mail address: <docdelivery@haworthpress.com> Website: <http://www.HaworthPress. com> © 2004 by The Haworth Press, Inc. All rights reserved.]*

KEYWORDS. Hotel Websites, picture presentations, online, Website design, e-commerce, behavioral intentions

INTRODUCTION

With an exponential growth and great success, the Internet is becoming a powerful marketing medium directly connecting companies and customers by sharing information about and enabling instant transactions of products and services. In particular, online retail sales in the United States are estimated to reach nearly $230 billion in 2008, which will account for 10% of total US retail sales (John-son, Delhagen, & Yuen, 2003). As the second largest e-commerce business, the travel industry predicts that US online travel sales will reach up to $43 billion in 2003 (Blank, Card, & Sehgal, 2003). Customers also are becoming more dependent upon the Internet for searching information, planning their travel, and making online transactions.

Keeping up with the current trend of the Internet business, lodging companies have accelerated their marketing efforts to establish

Miyoung Jeong is Assistant Professor, Program of Hotel, Restaurant, and Institution Management, and Jiyoung Choi is a Doctoral Student, Department of Apparel, Educational Studies, and Hospitality Management, both at Iowa State University.

Address correspondence to Miyoung Jeong (E-mail: mjeong@iastate.edu).

[Haworth co-indexing entry note]: "Effects of Picture Presentations on Customers' Behavioral Intentions on the Web." Jeong, Miyoung, and Jiyoung Choi. Co-published simultaneously in *Journal of Travel & Tourism Marketing* (The Haworth Hospitality Press, an imprint of The Haworth Press, Inc.) Vol. 17, No. 2/3, 2004, pp. 193-204; and: *Handbook of Consumer Behavior, Tourism, and the Internet* (ed: Juline E. Mills, and Rob Law) The Haworth Hospitality Press, an imprint of The Haworth Press, Inc., 2004, pp. 193-204. Single or multiple copies of this article are available for a fee from The Haworth Document Delivery Service [1-800-HAWORTH, 9:00 a.m. - 5:00 p.m. (EST). E-mail address: docdelivery@haworthpress.com].

their brand names and expand their markets through the Internet. Well-designed Websites are becoming a crucial way for hotels to communicate with customers, attract more businesses, and generate repeat businesses by delivering appropriate information to meet customer needs before making·purchase decisions. Jupiter Media Metrix predicted that 22% of all travel-related bookings can be made via the Internet by 2007 (Haussman, 2002).

Despite the continuous growth of electronic commerce, especially through companies' Websites, little research has been reported to show how such Website design factors as pictorial presentation influence Web customers' purchase behavior. To date, researchers (Strader & Shaw, 1997; Sawyer, Greely, & Cataudella, 2000) have stressed mainly information quality and its effects on customers' attitudes toward a Website and future purchase decisions. These studies have found that relevancy, accuracy, timeliness, and completeness of information on the Web are frequently used attributes to measure information quality. These attributes, however, pertain to text-based information only rather than graphics or pictures embedded on the Web.

This study aimed to examine the effects different picture presentations have on customers' online purchase intentions. Elaborating on pictorial presentations on Websites, this study attempted to determine the potential impact that different formats, contents, and realism of picture presentations on Websites have on customers' online purchase-related behavior. This study also attempted to contribute to website theory development in the travel and tourism discipline by understanding how customers perceive pictures on the Web, and to aid hotels with developing and improving their Websites.

STUDY BACKGROUND

The advent of the Web in the current business environment has changed the way companies do business with their customers. As a major communication and distribution channel, the Web is replacing the major roles conventional advertising media (e.g., TV, radio, and magazine) have fulfilled by providing up-to-date information and building close and interactive relationships with customers. In the hospitality industry, in particular, the Web is playing a critical role in delivering information and offering online transactions so that customers can make their travel plan prior to visiting a travel destination or staying at a hotel.

The Web's versatile capabilities to deliver both text-based and picture-based information including videos and 3 dimensional (3D) features are key to its success as an advertising medium. The·importance of advertising to the customer's decision making process had become a common notion in the business community, even before the Web market became available (see Edell, Julie, and Staelin, 1983). Edell et al. (1983) reported that when people decided to take a trip, more than 55% of them were likely to be influenced by advertising on their choice of a destination. Among a variety of forms of advertising, pictures were considered one of the most effective communication tools that is capable of projecting desirable visual images and conditions of products and services into the customer's mind.

With regard to advertising formats, researchers reported that pictures outperformed text in the function of customers' recall of the products and services companies offer (Alesandrini & Sheikh, 1983; Edell & Staelin, 1983; Unnava & Burnkrant, 1991; Leong, Ang, & Tham, 1996). These researchers also reported that pictures can be used to measure the effectiveness of advertising messages in drawing customers' attention, providing information about how and who to use the product, and creating a brand image. Leong et al. (1996) stated that pictures are more memorable and easier than text for creating an image about products and services in the customer's mind.

The comparative effects between picture and text advertising can be explained by the *picture superiority effect*, which means that picture advertising results in better memorability of products and services as compared to text (Leong et al., 1996). Picture advertising is believed to create dual code capabilities in customers' memory (i.e., imaginary and verbal codes), while text advertising generates only verbal codes. With these two different types of codes, picture advertising can help customers easily visualize the target product and service. Embedded with non-verbal cues and visual reinforcement, pictures are more likely to produce a superior learning and be more persuasive than text (Stewart, Hecker, & Graham, 1987). For example, more than 50% of advertisement response variability has been related to nonverbal factors such as pictures, sounds, and smells (Hecker & Stewart, 1998).

In the hospitality industry, however, little research has been reported on the effects of picture advertising on customer purchase behavior, especially addressing the implications of pictorial presentations on Websites. Olsen, McAlexander, and Roberts (1986) indicated that pictures improved effectiveness of informational advertising (i.e., improved the customers' attitudes toward the ad and the agency), while text-only advertising was believed to distract customers' attention to products and services. Such distractions could eventually result in loss of customers' interest in further search for the target product on the Internet.

Similar to the conventional wisdom of consumer marketing, the ultimate goal of the Internet business is to find what customers need in the online business environment. If a hotel understands what information customers are looking for on the Internet and provides need-satisfying information, customers would develop favorable attitudes toward the hotel and its Website. Many hotels attempt to identify factors associated with customers' purchase behavior on the Web. Information quality or Web design can be critical factors to be considered in Web-based marketing. In particular, different picture presentations on the Web can affect customers' behavioral intentions because pictures easily represent the target hotel's overall image and product conditions.

Use of pictures on the Internet is one of the strategies that can be employed to overcome disadvantages associated with the intangibility of the hotel product and service in the pre-purchase stage of the consumer decision making process (Koernig, 2003). Both traditional and Internet advertisings indicated that making services more tangible helped increase advertising effectiveness (Berry & Clark, 1986; Krentler & Guiltinan, 1984; Li, Daugherty, & Biocca, 2001). Berry and Clark (1986) developed a typology of four communication strate-gies that could help the service industry provide customers with more tangible cues: physical representation, association strategy, visualization, and documentation strategy. These four strategies focus on the tangible elements that are important parts of the service, including service personnel, place, events, and figures that could be presented effectively in picture formats. They also identified that visualization helped engage customers in mentally picturing the benefits of the service and imagining actually experiencing the service.

Krentler and Guiltinan (1984) examined three types of advertising messages to improve the effectiveness of tangibility, including ads that emphasized the service personnel, ads that associated the service with a tangible object, and ads that provided a tangible representation of the service. In particular, the ads that emphasized the service personnel elicited more favorable perceptions of benefits related to trust. Thus, pictures of products and services are believed to stimulate customers' potential online purchase behavior by making them enrich virtual product experience and feel present at a hotel (Klein, 2003).

Li et al. (2001) examined the effects of two dimensional (2D) versus three dimensional (3D) picture presentations on the creation of virtual product experiences. In their experimental study, they concluded that customers exposed to 3D pictures could enhance their knowledge about products and services, feeling of "being there" with products, and perceptions of the relevance of products to themselves more than when treated with 2D pictures. Such picture-related effects could well be associated with customers' brand attitude, product knowledge, and purchase intention. Thus, these previous studies (Berry & Clark, 1986; Koernig, 2003; Krentler & Guiltinan, 1984; Li et al., 2001) support that, in the computer-mediated environment such as the Internet, pictures can add tangible cues, enable customers to obtain a virtual experience of the product beforehand, and make them feel more present with the company's products and services. All these advantages can be achieved through providing carefully designed Websites in which the way of presenting pictures become critical.

METHODOLOGY

In this section, we briefly present the results of a pilot study in which we content-analyzed existing hotel Websites to understand how hotel companies were using pictorial presentations on their Websites. Then, such pilot study results lead to developing a conceptual framework for the current study and research propositions related to pictorial presentations that are tested subsequently. An experimental study designed to empirically test the propositions is introduced with detailed explanations of construct measurement.

Content Analysis of Hotel Websites

Objectives

Due to the limited number of studies on the effects of picture presentations on customers' behavioral intentions on the Web, this study conducted a content analysis with 203 existing hotel Websites based in New York City in order to capture the current trends of picture presentations on hotel Websites. The hotels in New York City were selected for several reasons. First, New York City ranked second, after Orlando, for the volume of Internet hotel bookings in 1999 (Lodging, 2000). Second, most hotel reservations in Orlando are believed to be more for leisure, while hotel reservations in New York City are for both business and leisure purposes. In addition, New York City is the host of many lodging companies representing chains and independents with different levels of services. Thus, it was believed that the hotels in New York City could reflect the current trends of the lodging industry as well as lodging Websites.

Procedures

The content analysis was conducted covering a period from October 8 to October 13, 2001. A list of the 203 hotel Websites in New York City was retrieved from wholesaler Websites such as Travelocity.com or Expedia.com. Throughout the data collection process this study used the same IBM computer, the same Internet Service Provider (ISP; MSN), and the same Internet browser (i.e., IE) in order to maintain consistency and validity of the content analysis. Based on both ownership and level of service, hotels were categorized each into two (chain vs. independent) and four (luxury, upscale, mid-scale, and budget) groups so as to assess whether ownership and level of service could affect types of picture presentations on hotel Websites.

Results of Content Analysis

Of the 203 hotels, approximately 60% (122 out of 203) were independently-owned. More than one-fourth of the hotels in New York City consisted of independently-owned budget hotels, followed by independently-owned mid-scale hotels (22%), chain-operated upscale hotels (14%), and independently-owned upscale hotels (12%) (see Figure 1).

The results of the content analysis indicated that hotel Websites had different schemes in their picture presentations such as the number of pictures, areas of facilities, and format of picture display. The majority of the hotels (65%) provided more than six pictures on their Websites, while five percent of hotels had no pictures at all. Regardless of the ownership of the hotels, main areas of the pictures presented on their Websites were bedroom, lobby, building, restaurant, meeting rooms, and lounge (see Figure 2). Especially, more than a third of the hotels had guests or staff members in their pictures in order to help potential guests feel comfortable and have a pseudo-experience with various amenities prior to an actual stay.

Figure 3 presents different formats of pictures on hotel Websites by the ownership. Typically, two different formats were used by hotels to present pictures on the Web includ-

FIGURE 1. Distribution of Hotels by Ownership and Level of Service in New York City

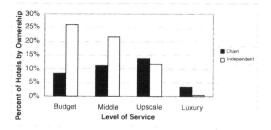

FIGURE 2. Areas of Picture Presentations on the Web by Hotel Ownership

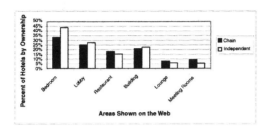

FIGURE 3. Formats of Picture Presentations on the Web by Hotel Ownership

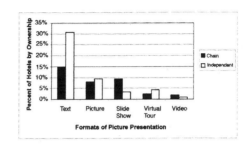

ing pictures with text and a separate section for pictures. In the separate section for picture presentations, there were four different ways to display pictures such as picture gallery, slide show, 3D virtual tour, and video. More than half of the hotel Websites (55%) had a separate section for picture presentations. Among them the largest group was picture gallery (17.2%), followed by slide show (12.3%), 3D virtual tour (6.9%), and video (2.5%). Chain hotels used more slide or video shows than independent hotels, while independent hotels used more picture gallery and text with pictures than chain hotels.

Conceptual Framework and Research Propositions

Pictures can be a more important attribute than just descriptions in a text format because of their capability to make products and services more tangible, to draw customers' attention to their potential place to stay in and to present a wide variety of hotel amenities. Based on the content analyses of the existing hotel Websites and previous studies in the areas of traditional and Internet advertising (e.g., Berry & Clark, 1986; Krentler & Guiltinan, 1984; Li et al., 2001), this study developed three experimental treatments, format, content, and realism of picture presentations, as major factors potentially influencing customers' online purchase-related behavioral intentions. Location of pictures on the Web was not considered as an influential factor for customers' behavioral intentions based on Murphy's findings (1999). Murphy (1999) reported that customers' perceptions of picture location on the Web such as right vs. left or top vs. bottom did not exert a significant influence on behavioral intentions.

These three treatments as exogenous variables were assumed to have direct impacts on customers' attitudes toward Websites and online behavioral intentions.

Customers' attitudes toward Websites were believed to form as a result of combined effects of attitudes toward outcomes and perceived behavioral control (Klobas, 1995). In this study, attitudes toward outcomes refer to how customers use pictures on the Web to form their behavioral intentions. Perceived behavioral control implies the extent to which customers believe their control over pictures for their behavioral intentions. Thus, customers' behavioral intentions on the Web were believed to form after evaluating a Website and developing positive or negative attitudes toward it. After customers have experienced a Website, they are also believed to establish a willingness to recommend a hotel Website to others. Figure 4 presents potential relationships between exogenous (three treatments) and endogenous variables (attitudes and behavioral intentions) along with four hypothesized propositions.

P_1: Separate picture presentations, such as in the format of 3D, will result in more positive attitudes toward the Website and higher behavioral intentions than still picture presentations with text.

P_2: Pictures of various areas (i.e., bedroom, lobby, restaurant, etc.) presented on the Web will result in more positive attitudes toward the Website and higher behavioral intentions than pictures showing only one area (i.e., bedroom).

P_3: Pictures with people (i.e., lobby area with staff members or guests) presented on the Web will result in more positive attitudes toward the Website and higher behavioral intentions than pictures without people.

P_4: A positive relationship exists between customers' attitudes toward the Website and their behavioral intentions.

Experiment Design

Design of the Study

A $2 \times 2 \times 2$ between-subjects design was employed with the format, content, and realism of pictures presented on Websites as the three factors. Based on the first three propositions and two treatment levels for each factor, eight hypothetical Websites were designed for the subjects' evaluations. All of the Websites featured identical logos, backgrounds, color schemes, and information about the hotel but they were differentiated only by different ways of picture presentations. Each factor was presented at one of two conditions, high or low, resulting in the eight possible combinations (see Table 1).

As an exploratory research project, this study used a self-administered survey with a convenience sample of undergraduate students majoring in hospitality management and business administration at a large mid-Western university in the United States. Although it would be ideal to conduct the survey with active lodging customers, use of a student sample was also recommended based on several reasons (Oh, 2000). First, in order to test hypotheses in a between-subjects design, a relatively homogeneous sample was desired. Second, the results of the study could be more valid by minimizing potential experience effects. Third, the student sample could provide useful insights just focusing on information processing in an experimental study. And finally, students are likely to be active Internet users in the near future for hotel reservations (see Oh, 2000).

A survey questionnaire was distributed to 560 students, indicating the URL (Uniform Resource Locator) of the Website they would visit to evaluate effects of picture presentations on customers' attitudes as well as their behavioral intentions in the Internet environment. An equal number of students (70) were assigned randomly to one of the eight Websites. Prior to visiting the Website for evaluations, respondents were provided a hypothetical travel situation in which they assumed to travel to Miami, Florida for their spring break and tried to make an online reservation at a hotel. Respondents seemed to be satisfied with information about location, room rate, and local attractions

FIGURE 4. A Conceptual Framework to Measure the Impact of Picture Presentations on Respondents' Attitudes Toward the Website and Behavior Intentions

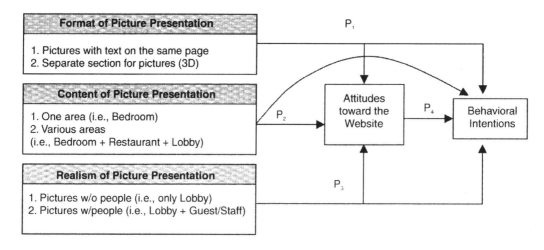

TABLE 1. The Eight Experimentally-Designed Hotel Websites

Website	Label	Format of Picture Presentations[a]	Content of Pictures[b]	Realism of Pictures[c]
Site 1	HHH	H	H	H
Site 2	HHL	H	H	L
Site 3	HLH	H	L	H
Site 4	HLL	H	L	L
Site 5	LHH	L	H	H
Site 6	LHL	L	H	L
Site 7	LLH	L	L	H
Site 8	LLL	L	L	L

[a] H: separate section for picture presentations (i.e., 3D, slides, video), L: pictures with texts.

[b] H: pictures of various areas (i.e., bedroom, restaurant), L: pictures of one area.

[c] H: pictures with people (i.e., lobby with guests), L: pictures without people.

of the hotel. For the purpose of the study, respondents were asked to concentrate on pictures presented on the Website and evaluate them to make a final decision. The questionnaire was composed of three parts: demographic information, Website evaluations, and attitudes toward Websites and behavioral intentions. Seven demographic questions were employed to identify the characteristics of the study subjects.

Endogenous Variables and Item Reliability Estimates

Two endogenous variables (attitudes and behavioral intentions) were measured with multiple questions to enhance construct validity. Seven questions were modified from the study of Jeong and Lambert (2001) to measure customers' attitudes toward the Website, using 7-point semantic differential scales. The questions included "visiting this Website is unenjoyable/enjoyable," "using this Website is difficult/easy," "obtaining information via this Website is useless/useful," "obtaining information via this Website is helpless/helpful," "obtaining information of the hotel by this Website is inefficient/efficient," "searching information on this Website is uninteresting/interesting," and "likeliness of using the Web to make a hotel room reservation." In order to measure behavioral intentions, four

questions were developed by anchoring from 1: strongly disagree to 7: strongly agree. The questions were: "I will visit this hotel Website for obtaining information," "I will use this hotel Website for making a room reservation," "I will recommend this hotel Website for obtaining information to others," and "I will recommend this hotel Website for making a room reservation to others."

Two endogenous variables were constructed by averaging the item responses for each variable, based on Cronbach's reliability alphas of .88 and .94 for attitudes and behavioral intentions, respectively. These scores were deemed sufficiently high, given the recommended standard of .7 by Nunnally (1978).

RESULTS AND DISCUSSIONS

Subject Characteristics

Five hundred sixty questionnaires were distributed to evaluate the eight Websites. Of the 560 subjects, 364 questionnaires were returned, resulting in a response rate of 65%. The number of responses to each Website was quite evenly distributed, from smallest 41 to largest 51, across the eight Websites. The characteristics of the subjects are summarized in Table 2. More than half of the subjects (58%) were female and nearly 65% were aged 19 to 22. The majority of the subjects (81%) owned a personal computer and reported having a wide variety of online shopping experiences. More than 70% of the subjects indicated that they used the Internet at least 10 hours per week.

Manipulation Check

The effects of manipulation were checked using a series of *t*-test based on the three measurement items of format, content, and realism of picture presentations. Three measurement items were employed to assess the effects of manipulation: "this Website had a link for hotel pictures" for format, "the pictures of the hotel were various areas of the hotel" for content, and "the pictures on this Website included people" for realism. Table 3 presents the results, along with cell mean scores and

TABLE 2. Socio-Demographic Characteristics of Subjects (n = 364)

Socio-Demographic Characteristics	n (%)
Gender	
Female	212 (58.2)
Male	149 (40.9)
Age	
19-22	235 (64.5)
23-25	53 (14.6)
over 25	73 (20.1)
PC Ownership	
Yes	294 (80.8)
No	67 (18.4)
Time on Internet per Week (Hours)	
1-9	105 (28.8)
10-19	142 (39.0)
20-29	58 (15.9)
30-39	36 (9.9)
over 40	20 (5.5)
Online Shopping Experience	
Yes	294 (80.8)
No	64 (17.6)
Times for Online Shopping in Year 2001	
0	14 (3.8)
1-4	158 (43.4)
5-9	60 (16.5)
Over 10	69 (19.0)

sample sizes. The manipulation of the three exogenous variables produced desired treatment effects that were statistically significant ($p < 0.01$).

Proposition Testing

Multivariate analysis of variance (MANOVA) was employed to test the effects postulated in the study's propositions (see Tables 4 and 5). As a result, Proposition 1 should be rejected that there was no positive effect of different formats of picture presentations (separate picture presentation vs. still picture presentations with text) on customers' attitudes toward the Website and behavioral intentions ($p < .05$). The MANOVA test indicated that customers did not benefit differently from the two different features in their virtual experience with products and services. Especially, the 3D effects placed on a separate Webpage could be viewed as hassle to customers because they were required to go to a linked page in order to see the virtual tour of the hotel.

Proposition 2 predicted that the more pictures the Website offered, the more favorable attitudes customers had and the higher behavioral intentions they develop. As shown in the findings of Koernig's study (2003), a variety of physical representations such as bedrooms, lobby, restaurant, and other hotel service areas elicited more favorable attitudes and higher intentions than single area pictures in a hotel. The MANOVA test revealed that a significant main effect of pictures of various areas of the hotel on customers' attitudes and behavioral intentions ($p < .01$). The result supported Proposition 2 and suggested that a variety of pictures of the hotel could increase tangible cues for customers and provide a vivid image and conditions of the hotel, which subsequently evoked more positive attitudes and behavioral intentions.

Proposition 3 could be partially supported that the pictures with people definitely made customers feel more present at the hotel and more associated with the service provided than pictures without people, which evoked more favorable attitudes toward the Website ($p < .05$). Interestingly, the MANOVA test indicated that there was no main effect of pictures with people on behavioral intentions ($p < .05$). However, there were significantly positive interaction effects between format and realism on customers' attitudes and behavioral intentions. That is, picture presentation format could be an important factor when it is, and should be, considered in combination of the picture's realism. If the Website provided customers with 3D pictures of people, it would be effective in increasing service tangibility and improving customers' virtual experience. Similar to the findings in previous studies, this study could not reject Proposition 4 ($p < .05$). When respondents had favorable attitudes toward the Website, they began to form strong behavioral intentions to use the Website or recommend it to others.

A path analysis via a series of multiple regression analyses was employed to test the proposed conceptual model. As shown in Table 5, the explanatory ability of the model for attitude was quite low (.08), given the three treatment variables. That is, the three independent variables included in the model were not sufficient enough to predict respondents'

TABLE 3. Results of Manipulation Check

Manipulated Variable		n	Mean (No. in each cell)		t-value
			High	Low	
Format	This Website had a link for hotel pictures	364	5.81 (186)	2.42 (178)	18.84*
Content	The pictures of the hotel were various areas of the hotel	363	5.37 (188)	2.70 (175)	15.37*
Realism	The pictures on the Website included people	364	5.96 (182)	1.49 (182)	31.89*

*Significant at *p* < .01.
Note: The High and Low columns indicate the cell mean value, and the cell size is in parentheses.

TABLE 4. MANOVA Results–Dependent Variables

Variables	Main Effect						Interactive Effects							
	Format (F)		Content (C)		Realism (R)		F × C		F × R		C × R		F × C × R	
	F	p	F	p	F	p	F	p	F	p	F	p	F	p
Attitude towards the Website	1.59	.208	23.32	.000	4.98	.026	.59	.444	4.88	.028	.10	.758	.77	.380
Behavioral Intentions	1.19	.277	27.91	.000	.83	.362	.01	.943	4.07	.044	.45	.502	3.24	.073

TABLE 5. Regression Estimates of the Attitude and Intentions

	Model 1[a]			Model 2[b]		
	Partial Regression Coefficients		t-value	Partial Regression Coefficients		t-value
	Unstandardized	Standardized		Unstandardized	Standardized	
Format	.15	.06	1.21	.03	.00	.10
Content	.58	.24	4.68**	.25	.08	2.33*
Realism	.30	.12	2.42*	−.12	−.04	−1.14
Attitude				.96	.76	21.48**
Intercept	3.74		30.57**	−.94		−4.79**
R^2	.08[c]			.60[c]		

[a] Dependent variable is attitude.
[b] Dependent variable is intention.
[c] F < .01
*p < .05   **p < .01

attitudes toward the Website. Several reasons are plausible for the low explanatory power. First, the model included only Website-related variables; other variables capturing the information about the sample hotel's product and service, such as price, brand name, and quality, were not considered in the model as they were beyond the scope of the current study. Thus, missing variables could have caused a relatively small amount of variance explained.

Second, the three treatment variables were represented in the model in a dichotomous variable (0 and 1), which again could lower the explanatory ability of the model (Hair et al., 1995). Measuring the treatment effects with quantitative scales may improve the model's predictive ability. Although the model's predictive power was rather lower than expected, the focus of this study was not on prediction; the study attempted to explore potentially important variables determining consumer attitudes toward hotel Websites. Therefore, despite the small amount of variance explained, this study needs to be viewed as providing a useful starting point for building and refining a Website attitude model.

In model 2 of Table 5, the squared multiple correlation appeared to be strong (.60). As expected, attitudes appeared to be a strong predictor of customers' behavioral intentions on hotel Websites. As mentioned earlier, among the three treatments, the content of picture presentations could be another predictor of customers' behavioral intentions, which implies that customers could have a strong behavioral intention if a hotel Website featured a variety of pictures of the hotel facilities including bedrooms, lobby, restaurant, and other public areas of the hotel. Overall, model 2 is useful to predict customers' behavioral intentions to use the Website or recommend it to others.

CONCLUSIONS

As an exploratory study, this study attempted to measure the effects of picture presentations on a hotel Website on customers' attitudes and behavioral intentions. Since no *a priori* studies have been reported in this area, this study designed eight hypothetical hotel Websites by using the three treatments (format, content, and realism of picture presentations), based on the content analyses of the 203 existing hotel Websites in New York City and previous studies in the areas of traditional advertising and Internet advertising.

Findings of this study indicated that if a hotel Website provided a variety of pictures of the hotel and featured service personnel or guests in the pictures, customers tended to have more favorable attitudes toward the hotel Website because they could mentally picture the overall image of the hotel and benefits of the service, and imagine actually experiencing the service. Even though there was no main effect of the format of picture presentations on customers' attitudes and behavioral intentions, a significant interactive effect existed between the format and realism of picture presentations. When the service personnel or guests were included in the 3D virtual tour or

slide shows, customers were more likely to have favorable attitudes toward the hotel Website and higher behavioral intentions.

Even though the model's explanatory power to predict respondents' attitudes toward the hotel Website was quite low (.08), the two treatments, *content* and *realism of picture presentations*, appeared to be powerful indicators of attitudes ($p < .05$). By looking at pictures presented on the Web, respondents preferred to have a wide variety of pictures of the hotel and people in the pictures so that they were able to evaluate how others enjoyed their stay at the hotel prior to staying at the hotel and increase service tangibility by reviewing available hotel facilities and services. In this study, however, effects of room rates, location, and brand of the hotel were excluded. Another way to look at the low r-squared value is that attitudes may not be a powerful mediator of the three treatment variables toward online behavioral intentions.

The effects of picture presentations on hotel Websites on respondents' behavioral intentions are very minimal in the sense that only one treatment, *content of picture presentations*, appeared to have a statistically positive relationship with behavioral intentions. Approximately 60% of variation in behavioral intentions could be explained by the content treatment and attitudes toward the Website. Attitudes were the most powerful predictor of respondents' behavioral intentions. Thus, hotel Websites should provide a wide variety of pictures about the hotel and then the pictures on the Website should deliver useful, clear, and complete information for customers to establish strong behavioral intentions by only reviewing them.

SUGGESTIONS AND IMPLICATIONS FOR FUTURE RESEARCH

Even though this study was carefully designed to strengthen internal validity, the experimental nature of this study could undermine external validity. In order to improve the external validity of the study, future research should use real hotel customers and evaluate effects of pictures of real hotel Websites at the same time, considering effects of brand, location, and room rates in an actual purchase setting. Thus, the study results may not be generalized to all hotel Websites and customers.

The proposed model could be extended to include socio-economic characteristics of online customers such as purposes of visiting a hotel Website (i.e., information search or online reservations) and previous experience with the Website. Customers' hedonic or utilitarian attitudes should also be included to measure the effects of pictures presented on a hotel Website on their global attitudes toward the Website, because different motivational attitudes tend to result in different needs or perceptions of picture presentations.

As an initial attempt to measure the effects of picture presentations on hotel Websites on customers' attitudes and behavioral intentions, the study could provide groundwork for future research in this area and a practical guideline for hotel management and Website developers. Since customers' attitudes are a strong predictor of behavioral intentions, future research should pay more attention to ways to establish favorable attitudes toward a hotel Website incorporating other interactive or customized features on the Web, which were omitted in this study. Also, as the study results indicated that the *content* and *realism* of picture presentations had significant partial relationships with customers' attitudes toward hotel Websites, hotel management or Website developers should carefully incorporate these features when developing and improving Websites such as in pictures of various areas of the hotel that include its staff members or guests.

Another lesson that this study could provide to hotel management would be that hotels should not overlook the importance of tangible cues that pictures could provide on the Web. Conventional wisdom supports the notion that increasing the tangibility of intangible services should result in a more positive response and more positive evaluations of the Website (Koernig, 2003). The results of this experimental study imply that the joint effects of format and realism of picture presentations could elicit more favorable attitudes and higher behavioral intentions. In order to increase customers' tangible cues of service and improve their virtual experience, a hotel Website should provide more dynamic and interactive virtual tour of the property, showing service personnel catering guests or guests enjoying its facilities and services.

REFERENCES

Alesandirini, K. & Sheikh, A. (1983). *Research on imagery: Implications for advertising*. New York, NY: John Wiley.

Berry, L.L. & Clark, T. (1986). Four ways to make services more tangible. *Business*, 53-55.

Blank, J., Card, D., & Sehgal, V. (2003). Jupiter research forecast report. Available at *http://www.jup. com/bin/item.pl/research:vision*

Edell, Julie A. & Staelin, R. (1983). The information processing of pictures in print advertisement. *Journal of Customer Research, 10*(1), 45-61.

Haussman, G. (2002). Jupiter predicts online travel booking increase. Available at *http://www.hotelinteractive. com/news/articleView.asp?articleID=1447&Sess_ ID...:06%20A.*

Hecker, S. & Stewart, D. (1998). Nonverbal in Communication. Lexington: Lexington Books.

Jeong, M. & Lambert, C. (2001). Adaptation of an information quality framework to measure customers' behavioral intentions to use lodging Web. *International Journal of Hospitality Management, 20*(2), 129-146.

Johnson, C.A., Delhagen, K., & Yuen, E.H. (2003). Highlight: US ecommerce hits $230 billion in 2008. Available at *http://www.forrester.com/ER/Research/ Brief/Excerpt/0,1317,17217,00.html*

Klein, L.R. (2003). Creating virtual product experiences: The role of telepresence. *Journal of Interactive Marketing, 17*(1), 41-55.

Klobas, J.E. (1995). Beyond information quality: Fitness for purpose and electronic information resource use. *Journal of Information Science, 21*(2), 95-114.

Koernig, S.K. (2003). E-Scapes: The electronic physical environment and service tangibility. *Psychology & Marketing, 20*(2), 151-167.

Krentler, K.A. & Guiltinan, J.P. (1984). Strategies for tangibilizing services: An assessment. *Journal of the Academy of Marketing Science, 12*, 77-93.

Leong, S., Meng, A., Swee, H., & Tham, L. (1996). Increasing brand name recall in print advertising among Asian customers. *Journal of Advertising, 25*(2), 65-81.

Li, H., Daugherty, T., & Biocca, F. (2001). Characteristics of virtual experience in electronic commerce: A protocol analysis. *Journal of Interactive Marketing, 15*(3), 13-30.

Lodging (2000). Pegasus business intelligence outlook. *25*(6), 48.

Murphy, J. (1999). Surfers and searchers: An examination of Website visitors' clicking behavior. *Cornell*

Hotel and Restaurant Administration Quarterly, 40(2), 84-95.

Nunnally, J.C. (1978). *Psychometric Theory.* McGraw-Hill, New York.

Oh, H. (2000). Customer value and behavioral intentions. *Journal of Hospitality & Tourism Research,* 24(2), 136-162.

Olsen, J., McAlexander, J., & Roberts, S. (1986). *Tourism Marketing.* Cleveland, OH: Cleveland State University.

Sawyer, R., Greely, D., & Cataudella, J. (2000). *Information Content: Creating Stores on the Web.* Berkeley, CA: Peachpit Press.

Stewart, D., Hecker, S., & Graham, J. (1987). It is more than what you say: Assessing the influence of nonverbal communication in marketing. *Psychology and Marketing, 4,* 303-322.

Strader, T.J., & Shaw, M.J. (1997). Characteristics of electronic markets. *Decision Support Systems, 21,* 185-198.

Unnava, H.R., & Burnkrant, R.E. (1991). An imagery-processing view of the role of pictures in print advertisement. *Journal of Marketing Research, 28* (2), 226-231.

Developing, Operating, and Maintaining a Travel Agency Website: Attending to E-Consumers and Internet Marketing Issues

Jenny Ji-Yeon Lee
Heidi H. Sung
Agnes L. DeFranco
Richard A. Arnold

SUMMARY. Travel agencies have increasingly utilized agency Websites on the Internet to enhance their marketing efforts. This exploratory study aims to provide an analysis of the Internet use by travel agencies in the United States. A survey conducted with 102 travel agency professionals collected primary data to examine the perceived value and contribution of a Website to the agency business, purposes for developing and operating a Website, and benefits and challenges faced in operating a travel agency Website. The results of this study not only identified various issues in developing, operating, and maintaining a travel agency Website but also made various suggestions to address those issues. Implications are discussed as to how travel agencies could better understand e-consumer behavior and effectively market their product offerings online. *[Article copies available for a fee from The Haworth Document Delivery Service: 1-800-HAWORTH. E-mail address: <docdelivery@haworthpress.com> Website: <http://www.HaworthPress.com> © 2004 by The Haworth Press, Inc. All rights reserved.]*

KEYWORDS. Travel agency, Websites, Internet use, e-consumer, online marketing

INTRODUCTION

In recent years, the Internet has substantially affected virtually all sectors of the tourism industry. From its initial purpose created for national defense three decades ago, the Internet has reshaped the way that business is conducted and provided new perspectives and opportunities for the tourism industry (Dev & Olsen, 2000) which has become an information intensive, highly segmented business sector (Poon, 1993; Gunn, 1994). The surge of Internet use and availability has been phenomenal in recent years (Christou & Kassianidis 2002; Perry, 1997). Today, the travel and tourism industry has become the Internet's second

Jenny Ji-Yeon Lee is a Graduate Research Assistant, Heidi H. Sung is Assistant Professor, Agnes L. DeFranco is Associate Professor, and Richard A. Arnold is Information Technology Manager, all at the Conrad N. Hilton College of Hotel & Restaurant Management, University of Houston.
Address correspondence to Heidi Sung (E-mail: hsung@uh.edu).

[Haworth co-indexing entry note]: "Developing, Operating, and Maintaining a Travel Agency Website: Attending to E-Consumers and Internet Marketing Issues." Lee, Jenny Ji-Yeon et al. Co-published simultaneously in *Journal of Travel & Tourism Marketing* (The Haworth Hospitality Press, an imprint of The Haworth Press, Inc.) Vol. 17, No. 2/3, 2004, pp. 205-223; and: *Handbook of Consumer Behavior, Tourism, and the Internet* (ed: Juline E. Mills, and Rob Law) The Haworth Hospitality Press, an imprint of The Haworth Press, Inc., 2004, pp. 205-223. Single or multiple copies of this article are available for a fee from The Haworth Document Delivery Service [1-800-HAWORTH, 9:00 a.m. - 5:00 p.m. (EST). E-mail address: docdelivery@haworthpress.com].

largest application area after the computer hardware sector (Robinson, 2002). It the largest revenue generator among consumers on the Internet, which is responsible for 21% of total e-commerce revenue (Susskind, Bonn, & Dev, 2003). Online leisure travel sales in the United States alone totaled $22.7 billion in 2002 and are expected to increase up to $50 billion by 2007 according to Forrester Research (Nua Internet Survey, 2002).

The Internet has competitive advantages for both users and marketers over traditional marketing tools such as direct mailing. This is particularly true in travel information search because: (1) it enables travel and tourism suppliers to communicate with their customers directly; (2) it eliminates the unequal barriers for customers and suppliers; (3) it creates the environments of equal competence among companies with different backgrounds; and (4) it forces companies to reorganize their marketing efforts and pricing strategies in order to differentiate prices on various groups of customers (Law, 2000). The use of the Internet in the tourism marketing field, however, appears to be still in its developing stage (Kasavana, Knutson, & Polonowski, 1998; Liu, 2000). Several limitations of Internet use such as information overload, irrelevant advertisements and links, and misleading or inaccurate information (Susskind et al., 2003) are crucial for many sites to draw customers' attention or to enhance revenue-generating transactions. The hospitality and tourism industry has paid more attention to satisfying the immediate demands of Website users rather than capturing business by utilizing the full marketing capabilities of the Internet (Cano & Prentice, 1998; Christou & Kassianidas, 2002).

Travel agencies have been the primary intermediary dominating the traditional travel distribution channel with most of its business generated from commission-based revenue by suppliers (Cook, Yale, & Marqua, 2001). Nevertheless, the number of travel agency locations in the United States has decreased by 16 percent over the four-year period, with 27,235 in 2001 compared to 33,500 in 1997 (Travel Weekly, 2002). It seems that such decline might have been affected not only by external constituents such as recent economic downturn or 9/11 but also by industry-specific

environment such as bypassing agencies through direct distribution from providers to consumers (Dorsey, 1998; Siebenaler & Groves, 2002). Direct on-line purchase of a hotel room, for instance, would cost only $1.50 per each sale by using a company operated Website, whereas traditional travel agent-GDS-CRS distribution route might cost $13.50 for each transaction (O'Connor, 2003).

According to 2002 Travel Industry Survey (Travel Weekly, 2002), both the number of U.S. travel agency locations and total agency sales revenue had been decreased between 1999 and 2001 by 16% (from 32,238 to 27,235 locations) and 5% (from $142.8 billion to $136.4 billion), respectively. Despite this decline, it is noticeable that revenue per agency location climbed by 13% during the same period. This might be due to the enhanced agency productivity by automation (i.e., using Global Distribution System [GDS] or Computerized Reservation System [CRS] for direct or interactive inventory control with providers) or shifting revenue mix (i.e., from airline commission that is $35-50 fee-based or 3-5% of the ticket price to cruise package sales with 12-15% rebates expected). Results of the same survey (Travel Weekly) also indicated that less than 20 percent of larger agencies accounted for more than half of the entire industry revenue and that the number of travel agency employees averaged 6.2 per agency location in 2001. Overall, most of travel agencies in the U.S. have made a profit over the last decade, and travel agencies still appear to be the sales specialists dominating the distribution channel of tourism products or services.

It is remarkable that 77% of the respondents to a recent survey of 2002 American Travelers (NFO Plog Research, 2002 as cited in Travel Weekly, 2002) still rely on travel agents as top information source in their travel decision-making process followed by printed materials and Internet (59 and 56%, respectively). The same survey also reported that these travel agent users exhibited stronger travel patterns than non-users both in terms of number of trips taken (7.5 versus 5.0) and amount spent on leisure travel in past year ($4,334 versus $2,493 on average). From this, travel agency users overall can be seen as heavy users of tourism products and services, signaling agencies the need to develop effective strategies to target, satisfy, and retain a more clearly defined group of consumers.

To effectively cater to these travelers, travel agencies should reinforce customer relationship based upon traditional service framework and also develop and operate agency Websites focusing on consumers' Internet usage patterns so as to attract, inform, educate, and retain consumers. In addition to focusing on these consumer behavioral components, travel agencies should clearly identify the utility of agency Websites in formulating effective marketing strategies as to how to link their product and service offerings to target segments. Tourism researchers have come to recognize an immediate need to provide a useful guideline for business practitioners so that they may utilize their Websites as powerful marketing tools to gain competitive advantage in today's marketplace.

In an effort to enhance online marketing activities of travel agencies in the U.S., the purposes of this study were: (a) to provide an analysis of Internet use by travel agencies in the United States; (b) to identify issues regarding developing, operating, and maintaining a travel agency Website; and (c) to suggest effective online marketing strategies for travel agencies in the United States. The results of this study will provide the U.S. travel agency industry with a comprehensive analysis of Internet use and practice and help agency managers and marketers address specific issues in utilizing the Website as a marketing tool. The findings will also offer useful information to formulate effective online marketing strategies.

LITERATURE REVIEW

Internet Use and Travel Agencies

Travel agencies have increasingly utilized the Internet to enhance their business activities and marketing efforts. The number of travel agencies in the United States with access to the Internet has increased from 24 percent of 33,593 agencies in 1995 to 94 percent of 27,235 agencies in 2001 (Travel Weekly,

2002). A majority of travel agencies have used the Internet in the U.S. in gathering travel products, vendor, and destination information. According to a recent survey conducted by Travel Weekly (2002), approximately 60 percent of all agencies had a Website in 2001 and roughly three quarters of travel agencies used the Internet to receive travel requests as well as to confirm bookings.

Maintaining a Website has become more and more crucial for a travel agency in order to sustain the competitive strength in today's marketplace. On the supply side, commissions and caps have been continuously reduced since United Airlines cut off commissions from airline ticket sales in 1995 (Siebenaler & Groves, 2002). The commission cuts have compelled travel agencies to adjust their business strategies in the shifted revenue mix. Direct marketing and selling of the tourism products to customers by suppliers and wholesalers through their Websites was another reason that agencies needed to develop new long-term strategies and initiate structural changes (Buhalis, 1998; Siebenaler & Groves, 2002). On the demand side, travel agencies should identify the needs of their customers who are more sophisticated, knowledgeable, demanding, and familiar with computers. The number of Internet users has dramatically grown over seven years, reaching 59.1 percent of the total U.S. population in 2001 from 6.7 percent in 1995 (NUA, 2001). As the number of travelers using the Internet increased, airline and travel agency Websites have continued to grow in popularity and total revenue from bookings has also increased (Disabatino, 2001).

In order to satisfy consumers' demands and survive in the long-term competition, travel agencies ought to adapt technology and adjust their businesses to enhance the interactivity with their target market (Buhalis, Jafari & Werthner, 1997; Rach, 1997). Travel agencies are also required to reengineer their business processes and structures so that they could cater to potential customers by providing timely and accurate information due to the intangibility and perishability of tourism products and services (Buhalis, 1998). Therefore, the Internet could play a vital role as an information source and facilitator for travel agency services (Sheldon, 1997).

Internet Marketing Strategy and Travel Agencies

The use of the Internet now tends to be not just as a selling vehicle but as a marketing and management tool centered on Web-based operating system (Ho, 2002; Murphy et al., 2003). This allows agencies to build and update their database systems constantly, by which they can identify and understand the group of customers they are dealing with. Once identified, existing customers can be placed in an agency's relationship marketing management system, so that customer information can be streamlined and ready to serve specific marketing efforts by various categories. Travel agencies must adopt a long-term strategy of Internet use as a marketing tool that is geared for the potential changes in today's business structure.

The Internet would create strategic feasibility and competitive advantage for travel agencies if they could satisfy certain conditions such as "long term planning and strategy," "innovative business processes re-engineering," "top management commitment," and "training throughout the hierarchy" (Buhalis, 1998). Furthermore, agencies should not only weigh costs and profitability involved with utilizing a Website but also consider the strengths and weaknesses of a Website in the planning stage (Law, Law, & Wai, 2001). Still, some researchers argued that no significant relationship between costs and profitability of information technology was found since it was hard to justify the gap between what companies spent on implementation of the Website and what benefits they got from it (Gamble, 1990/1992; Strassman, 1990; Yuan, Gretzel, & Fesenmaier, 2003). Given this, travel agencies should proactively choose a business model that could support an effective online strategy (Barnett & Standing, 2000). Burn and Barnett (1999) suggested a model to delineate the range of business strategies and structures for virtual tourism organizations including virtual faces, co-alliances, star alliances, value alliances, market alliances, virtual brokers, and virtual spaces (see Table 1).

A few studies have suggested various stages of Internet technology adaptation and use in tourism-related businesses. A study of the analy-

sis of the functionality of 50 Australian travel agencies' Websites determined the types of business strategies adopted in relation to Internet technology and e-commerce (Standing & Vasudavan, 1999). Another study (Yuan, Gretzel, & Fesenmaiser, 2003) also showed that American convention and visitor bureaus were classified into five adopter groups along with different Internet technology implementation and use. These adopters were laggards, sophisticated followers, knowledge adopters, early light adopters, and late light adopters. According to the study results, American CVBs with different stages of technology implementation and use differed significantly in their use of Internet applications, their perceived value of Internet technology, and its impacts on their business activities.

One framework for analyzing Websites was developed from the business process reengineering (BPR), which was an advanced approach within the scope of the business process change model (Talwar, 1996). The model is divided into three stages: (1) process improvement; (2) process re-engineering; and (3) transformation. According to the study's application to BPR, process improvement represents the simple supplementation or enhancement of existing business process while business process re-engineering would be that travel agencies strategically repositioned their businesses via the Web. Moreover, process re-engineering involves the redesign of an entire process in order to accomplish noticeable improvements in the organization. In the study, the researchers concluded that most of Internet commerce strategies used by travel agencies in Australia could be categorized into process improvement stage with a few exceptions.

In accordance with the concept of BPR, Shankar (1999) highlighted four phases of e-commerce evolution in typical organizational settings. In Phase I, "WebPresence" phase, the Website with basic design, navigation and data collection functions is in the process of creating business strategies. In Phase II, "WebService" phase, the Website is capable of processing to product and service inquiries online, which can play a role as the marketing department. In Phase III, "WebTransaction" phase, the Website has transaction features such as online order and

TABLE 1. Different Types of Virtual Tourism Organizations

Type	Characteristics	Strategy
Virtual faces	• Existing companies with the Website to provide value-added services to customer • Low budget approach–Obstacles to afford transaction features, to keep updating, to promote effectively	• Using the Web to promote the company and market products and services
Co-alliances	• Shared partnerships to form a consortium providing supports on specific functions	• Developing more sophisticated and effective Website
Star alliances	• Interconnected networks reflecting a core surrounded by satellite organizations • Franchising	• The core companies provide expertise to members
Value alliances	• Based on the value or supply-chain model • Bringing products, services, and facilities together in one package	• Taking advantage of communications efficiencies not previously available • Changing components quickly in response to market
Market alliances	• Existing primarily in cyberspace • Bringing non-competing products and services together in one package	• Virtual community • Serving as a portal for some products of the group
Virtual brokers	• Third-party value-added suppliers, information brokers • Highest level of flexibility	• Providing a virtual structure around specific business information services
Virtual spaces	• Wholly depending on virtual contact with the customers	• Constructing online marketing channel for distribution of products and services

payment. In Phase IV, "Integrated Web" phase, Extranet and Intranet have included beyond a function of transaction not only to create e-value but also to facilitate proactive e-communications. A survey of the top 50 U.S. Websites (*Netmarketing*, 1998) revealed that most of organizations were in Phase I, II, and III, while less than 50 percent of the organizations are in the Integrated Webphase. The conceptual framework linking BPR and phases of E-Commerce evolution to e-consumer behavior can be illustrated in Figure 1.

Advantages and Challenges of Internet Use

An increasing number of recent studies recognized the value of the Internet as a marketing tool and suggested how it could be adapted to the hospitality and tourism industry. The presence of a Website has provided strategic advantages with travel agencies such as cost reduction, revenue growth, niche marketing, improved customer satisfaction, quality improvement, and addressing other critical business or customer needs (Buchanan & Lukaszewski, 1997). Travel agencies which adopted e-commerce facilitate many aspects including customer relationships

management, marketing and product development, partnerships with other related industry, and direct selling (Standing & Vasudavan, 1999). In addition, the Internet appeared to be competent in differentiating the quality of intangible goods that might require high financial expenditures but were seldom procured (Peterson, Balasubramanian, & Bronnenberg, 1997). More importantly, the Internet could possibly help travel agencies improve their negotiating power with vendors through effective, interactive communication and easy access to a wide variety of product offerings.

However, it was presumable that most travel agencies were not early adopters of the Internet technology mainly due to the fear that the Internet might be going to put them out of business. Bypassing travel agencies and selling directly to consumers appeared to be compelling to tourism providers such as airlines and hotel companies in order to reduce costs. It appears that some travel agencies might have constraints to creating and maintaining the Websites primarily due to the availability of financial resources or their managerial capability at various levels. King, Bransgrove, and Whitelaw (1998) discussed that small tourism

FIGURE 1. Conceptual Framework Linking Business Process Reengineering [BPR] (Standing & Vasudavan, 1999) and Phases of E-Commerce Evolution (Shankar, 1999) to E-Consumer Behavior

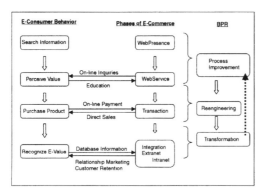

businesses had a relatively low level of explicit and formal strategic management due to a lack of managerial expertise and the absence of staff. Moreover, the computer-mediated, impersonal environments might introduce some negative perceptions to travel agencies.

Considering the fact that hospitality and tourism business has centered in highly interpersonal relationships, major challenges for retail travel agencies to marketing online might also include disintermediation and reintermediation (Coupey, 2001). The direct marketing has enabled the suppliers to eliminate intermediaries, a process defined as disintermediation (Palmer & McCole, 1999), which resulted as the threat of the survival of travel agencies. It has been predicted that there would be no need for travel agencies in the near future due to that fact that prevalence of the Internet might lead to simplification of structures in distribution channel through direct marketing between travel suppliers and consumers.

Given the fact that the primary focus of using the Internet has been on generating direct sales in the retail travel market, both communication and transaction play a crucial role for both providers and consumers. While the Internet offers a dynamic environment with an easy access to a wide variety of information covering products, price ranges, and providers to choose from, Internet users often face several limitations. Susskind et al. (2003) suggested that such limitations might include: (1) the absence of rules to govern the *credibility* of Internet posting, leading to

false, outdated, or misleading information; (2) *incompatible technology* features that might limit the accessibility to certain data types over the Internet; (3) *security* of consumers' personal and payment information that might keep potential buyers from on-line purchasing; and (4) lack of personal *attention* to customer service. The same study examined consumers' apprehensiveness toward Internet use and reported that an individual's resistance to, or fear of, both the Internet as a form of communication and engaging in commerce-based transactions over the Internet were negatively related to online spending and, therefore, could be adequate indicators of Internet use intentions as well as behavior. As Morrison et al. (1999) discussed challenges and disadvantages of online marketing of the small hotel operations, there were some issues that fit into the context of travel agencies (see Figure 2).

Researchers, nevertheless, have underlined the importance of travel agencies because most suppliers have limited capabilities in identifying their target segments and directly approaching to suppliers and consumers. In addition, the delivery of effective and efficient one-stop shopping experiences linking providers to consumers is unique and only available with travel agencies. In this context, reintermediation has emerged noticeably as a result of numerous Websites offering travel products to

FIGURE 2. Issues of Internet Marketing for Retail Travel Agencies from the Perspectives of Consumers and Marketers (Source: Buhalis, 1998; Morrison et al., 1999; Susskind et al., 2003)

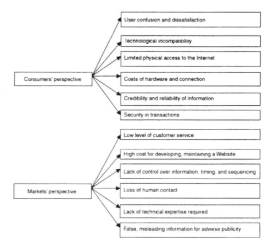

consumers through sophisticated profiling and intelligent agents as well as the expansion of business-to-business information exchange online. According to Palmer and McCole (1999), reintermediation created new value between consumers and suppliers on the Internet by harnessing the elements of marketing the four Ps and by customizing consumption experience in conjunction with logistics, information, and service. Therefore, it has become necessary for travel agencies to reengineer their channel of product distribution toward extensive marketing opportunities.

Internet Marketing Research in Hospitality and Tourism Industry

Recent studies in hospitality and tourism marketing have made several attempts to evaluate the effectiveness of Websites (Murphy, Forrest, & Wotring, 1996; Morrison et al., 1999; Countryman, 2000; Choi & Hsu, 2001; Perdue, 2001). It is arguable, however, that selecting the evaluation criteria remains a critical issue to satisfy both internal and external validity. That is, it was difficult for researchers to establish valid or parsimonious criteria because of continuous design improvement, evolution of technological applications, and establishment of enhanced customer relations (Kasavana, 2002).

A few studies have focused on travel agencies and their perceptions towards the adaptation of the Internet. Yung (1997/1998) evaluated the perceptions of travel agencies in Taiwan on marketing travel products online. The study concluded that travel agencies in Taiwan used the Internet as a source of data gathering and means of transactions with the conditions of improving the security, developing more sophisticated computer technology, and rationalizing cost related issues. Similarly, Law et al. (2001) conducted a study of the impact of the Internet on travel agencies in Hong Kong. The study found that Hong Kong travel agents generally had positive attributes towards Internet applications in order to provide their customers with value-added services. Nevertheless, not many agencies in Hong Kong have fully developed and utilized the Internet. The study also noticed significant

relationships between company size, age, and some Internet attributes.

Another effort was made to position different types of travel agencies in order to reflect business strategies and structures at different technological adaptation stages. According to Siebenaler and Groves (2002), there were four types of travel agencies in association with their adaptation styles of information technology such as entrepreneurship, traditional travel agents, technological innovators, and Webmanager. Small travel agencies operating independently with limited resources were grouped as entrepreneurship, which were dependent upon relationships with consolidators and adapted their business model through trial and error strategy and benchmarking from the airlines. Traditional travel agencies had depended upon airline reservations and increased operational efficiency by controlling costs, enhancing automation, and establishing a Website. Technological innovators, which had their business bases wholly on the Web by offering limited services, quickly responded to technology and made efforts to provide more information about prices and shopping. Their business success is directly dependent on an effective Website design. Webmanagers were travel agencies that were exclusively web-based and had no business foundation until e-commerce developed. They were indirectly involved with a travel agency by way of using Websites to shop for travel products but made their reservations in another location.

Travel agencies in this study can be loosely grouped into two major types: (1) independent agencies and (2) non-independent agencies. Independent agencies refer to the agencies that are operated independently without any franchise or corporate affiliations, while non-independent agencies are agencies involved with affiliations or alliances to have networks. Among the eight agency types adapted and modified from Cook et al. (2001), independent agencies, specialty agencies, home-based agencies, and Internet agencies appear to belong in the "independent agency" category, while the remaining four agency types–agency chains (wholly owned or franchised), consortium-affiliated agencies, corporate travel agencies, and corporate travel department–are considered to belong in the "non-independent" category. One underlying assumption was that travel agencies might exercise different strategies in developing and maintaining agency Websites by different agency types, suggesting further exploration might provide some meaningful results in conjunction with the hypothesized factors in this study. For this, testing hypotheses included cross-examination of the factors by travel agency types–independent and non-independent agencies.

The overall purpose of this study was to provide an analysis of the Internet use by travel agencies in the U.S. with specific emphases on identifying various issues in developing, operating, and maintaining a travel agency Website to enhance effective online marketing strategies. For empirical examination of the study purposes, this study aimed to examine the following specific research hypotheses:

H1.   There is no significant difference between independent and non-independent travel agencies in their developing, operating, and maintaining the agency Websites.

H2.   A travel agency Website might contribute to the agency business with no significant difference between independent and non-independent agencies.

H3.   Purposes for developing and operating a travel agency Website might not differ between independent and non-independent agencies.

H4.   Benefits and challenges faced in operating a travel agency Website might not be different between independent and non-independent agencies.

METHODOLOGY

Study Site and Subjects

The subjects of this study were travel agency professionals representing their agencies located in the United States. The focus of this study was on the Internet usage and its practice among travel agencies in the U.S. This appeared to be appropriate since the Internet is the most popular in the U.S. travel and tourism industry in terms of registered Websites and users.

The World Travel Congress, which was held by ASTA (the American Society of Travel Agents) in Hawaii was chosen as the venue to collect primary data for this study. Being the largest travel trade association with 24,000 travel industry professionals and business entities in North America and worldwide, ASTA aims to pursue professionalism and profitability of members by effectively representing various issues and identifying the needs of industry, education and training. The study site was chosen because it offered an opportunity to access a large number of travel agency professionals in the United States due to its confinement within a specific location and period of time. ASTA has a majority of travel agencies in the United States as its members, and The World Travel Congress is the major annual gathering of travel agencies registered in ASTA. This allowed the sample surveyed in the conference could be assumed to represent the travel agency population in the U.S.

The survey was conducted on-site over a three-day period from November 4 to November 7, 2002. Questionnaires were distributed to the attendees of ASTA's 2002 Annual World Travel Congress at various locations including registration booth, hallway, and dining venues. Using name tags indicating travel agency information, non-travel agency attendees were screened out. Of those, approximately 3,000 travel agents or travel industry professionals attended the 2002 Annual World Travel Congress, the exact number of travel agency professionals was unknown. A total of 800 survey questionnaires were distributed to the prospective respondents for this study who were travel agency professionals. With a brief description of the purpose of this study by the researcher, those screened attendees were asked to complete a survey questionnaire and return it to designated drop-off locations during the conference. Those who were unable to complete the questionnaire on-site were provided with a self-addressed stamped envelope to mail it back to the researcher. A total of 102 completed questionnaires were collected at the conference. No questionnaires have been mailed back.

In the current survey, the response rate cannot be calculated since the number of eligible units in the sample was not exactly known. This was because: (1) some questionnaires were placed in unattended public locations such as registration booth to be picked up at no control or screening of the subjects by the researcher; (2) the classification of business category between travel and non-travel agents were not always accurately or clearly indicated in the name tags provided; and (3) some subjects might have received more than one survey questionnaire at different locations. Beyond the unknown response rate, the number of completed surveys cannot be seen too great, raising an issue of potential non-response bias. It is generally agreeable that low response rates are one of the more frequent sources of bias in marketing research (Burns & Bush, 2003). According to Vogt (1999, p. 193), this is the kind of bias that occurs when some subjects choose not to respond to particular questions and when the nonrespondents are different in some way (i.e., they are not a random group) from those who do respond. For example, it was presumable that those who did not have an agency Website might not actively participate in the current survey.

This became evident among 86.3% (N = 88) of the respondents with the agency Website while the industry reported only 62.3% of travel agencies with Webpresence (Travel Weekly, 2002). It is arguable that those who did not turn in completed questionnaires in the current survey might be different from those who did and that their missing information would bias the survey results. Nevertheless, the study focus was on Internet use, and the fact that the survey respondents might overrepresent the agencies with Websites should not be treated as a critical program in applying the study results to achieving the specific research objectives.

Measures

A three-page, self-administrative questionnaire was used to gather the primary data for this study. The survey questionnaire consisted of five sections, using various levels of measurement scales. The first section of the questionnaire was designed to examine how a

Website contributes to the agency business. Travel agency professionals were asked to evaluate how valuable the Website was to their agency business, using a 7-point Likert scale to rate the level of importance, with score 1 being the least valuable and 7 being the most valuable.

The second section examined primary purposes to create and operate a travel agency Website. Eight attributes were identified assessing agency's needs and purposes to have a Website. These attributes included: (1) to effectively disseminate information; (2) to enhance marketing efforts; (3) to expand distribution channel; (4) to have direct communication with customers and vendors; (5) to build partnership with other related hospitality industry; (6) to use as an advertising medium; (7) to provide value-added services; and (8) to use as a reservation tool. These attributes were scored on a five-point scale measuring the needs in terms of the level of importance: (1) most important; (2) somewhat important; (3) not applicable; (4) not very important; and (5) least important.

The third section of the questionnaire evaluated benefits that the Website could possibly offer to travel agency business. Ten attributes for determining the benefits and challenges from Web development were examined. These attributes for the benefits were identified: (1) cost reduction; (2) direct selling; (3) ease of marketing; (4) ease of product development; (5) partnership; (6) revenue growth; (7) improved customer satisfaction; (8) quality improvement; (9) addressing other business issues; and (10) unlimited operating hours. The question asked the respondents to select five most beneficial aspects to have a Website, ranging from the most beneficial to the fifth most beneficial aspect. In addition, major challenges in developing and maintaining a Website were asked in a separate question with 5 listed items for the respondents to choose from: (1) no time to update; (2) limited Website outsourcing available; (3) low level of marketing strategy; (4) limited technical expertise; and (5) lack of financial resources.

The fourth section assessed the extent to which travel agencies in the United States have adapted the Internet. This section included developmental and maintenance-related issues such as how many years travel agencies have had a Website, how much money they invested initially to develop the Website and how much they were spending monthly on maintenance of the Website, and by whom agency Websites were being operated and maintained. The last section asked participants to provide general information of travel agencies including number of years in business, business volumes, agency sizes, and types of agency they focused on.

In an effort to ensure validity and reliability of the study and minimize confusion in completing the questionnaire, a pilot test was employed with selective travel agencies in Greater Houston area during October 2002. Modifications to the phrasings in the questionnaire were made from the result of the pilot study.

RESULTS AND DISCUSSION

The Profile of Respondents

The overall purpose of this study was to provide an analysis of the Internet use by travel agencies in the United States. Nearly three-quarters (71.9%) of the respondents identified themselves as independent agencies, including independent agency (59.4%), specialty agency such as cruise-oriented (6.3%) or home-based agency (4.2%), and Internet agency (2.1%). Agencies in these types tend to target mostly unknown, general public who are likely to be leisure or pleasure travelers seeking out one-on-one assistances in finding travel information, bargain fares, and perhaps sending an inquiry before making a reservation. The remaining respondents (28.1%) were from a group of non-independent agencies, which were consortium-affiliated agency (17.7%), agency chain (6.3%), and corporate travel agency or department (4.2%). These "non-independent" agencies are more inclined to the business clientele through specialty channel of distribution such as incentive travel agencies or meeting planners, where a great deal of business is based upon an existing relationship between the corporation (or specialty channel) and the affiliated providers of travel related services.

In terms of years in business, the respondents were almost evenly distributed to three categories: (1) 1 to 10 years; (2) 11 to 20 years; and (3) more than 20 years (representing 36.3%, 28.4%, and 32.4%, respectively). A majority of respondents were operating their business in small or medium profit margin and size. On average, gross revenue per year was $3.9 million and number of employees in each agency location equaled 14.6 persons. Only 23.5 percent of travel agencies generated more than $5 million of annual revenue, leaving a majority (76.5%) in the $5 million or less. Since the aftermath of September 11, the gross revenue of agencies has been down from a far decreased traffic in U.S. domestic tourism. This might have affected an industry trend toward downsizing in order for agencies to become more cost effective. The same trend can also be seen in a recent survey of the U.S. travel agencies, the results of which reported an overall decrease in terms of both number of agency locations and gross industry revenue (Travel Weekly, 2002) as discussed earlier. The summary of descriptive statistics (Table 2) provides a general profile of the study respondents including type of agency business, years in business, gross annual revenue, and number of employees.

Developing, Operating and Maintaining a Travel Agency Website

The first research hypothesis was to examine how a travel agency Website is developed, operated, and maintained by independent and non-independent travel agencies. This might assess up to which extent and how the Internet has been adopted in the current travel agency business. The criteria included in the analysis were: (1) the length of agency Website; (2) initial investment spent on the Website development; (3) monthly expenses to maintain the Website; (4) frequency of the weekly maintenance of the Website; and (5) by whom the agency Website is operated and maintained.

As discussed earlier, the respondents appeared to be heavy users of the business Websites compared to the industry average (86.3% had a Website versus 62.3%). Of those (N = 88), ninety percent have developed a Website within the past five years, while the

TABLE 2. Profile of Respondents

Variables with Descriptions	Frequency	%	M	SD
Type of the Business (*N* = 96)				
Independent Agency (N = 69, 71.9%)				
Independent agency	57	59.4		
Specialty agency	6	6.3		
Home-based agency	4	4.2		
Internet agency	2	2.1		
Non-Independent Agency (N = 27, 28.1%)				
Agency chain	6	6.3		
Consortium-affiliated agency	17	17.7		
Corporate travel agency/department	4	4.2		
Years in Business (*N* = 99)			19.2	22.4
1-10 years	37	36.3		
11-20 years	29	28.4		
More than 20 years	33	32.4		
Annual Gross Revenue (*N* = 81)			$3,960,852	$4,782,189
Less than 1 million	22	27.2		
1-5 million	40	49.4		
More than 5 million	19	23.5		
Number of Employees (*N* = 99)			14.6	41.7
Less than 15 employees	77	77.8		
15-30 employees	14	14.1		
More than 30 employees	8	8.1		

rest (10%) had a Website for more than five years. It was found that, on average, independent agencies had a Website for a shorter period of time than non-independent agencies (2.7 years and 4.9 years, respectively). Most agency types had a Website for less than 5 years (3.3 years on the average overall) with ranging from 1.8 years (home-based agency) to 3.8 years (specialty agency) with a distinct outlier of corporate travel agency with the longest history in the 12.4 years. It is probable that the corporate travel agencies in the U.S. are operating their business primarily based upon business relationship with selective corporate clients and that they need to cater to their niche who had recognized the utility of a Website relatively earlier than other business types (see Table 3).

In terms of initial development costs of the Website, a little more than half of respondents (53%) spent less than $1,000 while 17% of them spent more than $5,000. The remaining 30% were in the $1,000 to $5,000 expenditure group. On average, the respondents spent $5,101.06 in developing a Website, with four times of difference between $3,120 by independent agencies and $11,777.27 by non-independent agencies including agency chains (wholly owned or franchised), consortium-affiliated agencies, corporate travel agencies, and corporate travel department. For operating and maintaining a Website, some (58.7%) of the respondents spent less than $500 on their Websites per month, while 30.4% spent between $100 and $500, and 10.9% spent more than $500. Stated differently, the respondents also spent, on average, $273.83 on operating

TABLE 3. Factors in Developing/Operating/Maintaining a Travel Agency Website

Factors		Descriptive Statistics			Independent Sample T-Test		
		Mean	SD	N	t	df	Sig. (2-tailed)
Number of	Independent	2.70	1.50	64			
years of Web	Non-	4.90	1.90	24			
presence	Total	3.29	3.80	88	−2.456	86	0.016***
Initial cost on	Independent	$3,120.00	$6,846.87	35			
development	Non-	$11,777.27	$26,647.53	11			
	Total	$5,101.06	$14,248.79	46	−1.782	44	0.082*
Monthly cost on	Independent	$242.94	$437.14	36			
maintenance	Non-	$422.22	$624.56	9			
	Total	$273.83	$473.55	45	−1.007	43	0.319
Number of	Independent	2.38	2.60	63			
weekly update	Non-	2.00	2.34	23			
	Total	2.28	2.51	86	0.617	84	0.539

and maintaining the Website every month between US$242.94 and $422.22 by independent and non-independent agencies, respectively.

Among the non-independent category, the consortium-affiliated agency spent the greatest amount of money among other types of businesses, on the average of $13,131.25 for initial cost on Website development and $491.67 for monthly operating and maintaining expenses. It is probable that these agencies might have paid a consortium some significant amount of money for developing and maintaining the Website compared to their counterpart in different business categories since they are linked together and receive the financial benefits through the chain system. On the contrary, independent agencies spent the least amount of money to develop ($3,120.00) and maintain ($242.94) their Websites. Considering their financial resources dedicated to Website development might be scarce.

In addition to the above factors, the availability and capability of human resources can also play a significant role in developing, operating, and maintaining a travel agency Website. In-house staff appears to be the major force (52.3%) for both independent (49.2%) and non-independent agencies (60.9%). Using external services and expertise also tends to be popular (37.5% overall) but more with independent agencies (40.0%) than with non-inde-

pendent agencies (30.4%). Shown in Table 4 are the results of cross-tabulation for the major entities who operate and maintain the agency Website, reporting no significant difference between independent and non-independent agencies (χ^2 = 0.812 with the significance level at 0.666).

As discussed, the results of both independent sample T-tests (Table 3) and Chi-Square statistics (Table 4) suggest an outline of the hypothesized factors in developing, operating, and maintaining a travel agency Website in the United States. Two out of the five hypothesized, number of years of Web presence (t = −2.456 at the 0.01 significance level) as well as initial cost on the site development (t = −1.782 at the 0.10 significance level), appear to significantly vary across the two agency types. The null hypothesis of no significant difference in those factors between independent and non-independent agencies (H1) was partly supported.

Contribution of a Website to Travel Agency Business

The second research hypothesis was to examine how a Website contributes to the travel agency business between independent and non-independent agencies. As shown in Figure 3, the overall average mean value of a

TABLE 4. Crosstabulation for "By Whom the Website Is Operated/Maintained?"

Agency Website Operated/Maintained by:	N	Independent Agencies (%)	Non-Independent Agencies (%)	χ^2	p
				0.812	0.666
In-house staffs	46	49.2	60.9		
Outsourcing	33	40.0	30.4		
Others	9	10.8	8.7		

Website to the travel agency business was 4.63 without indicating any significant difference between independent and non-independent agencies (Mean = 4.71 and 4.45, respectively, where score 1 being not at all important and 7 being extremely important). The fact that some (15.8%) of the respondents evaluated their Websites as being "not at all valuable" might have affected the overall mean value to be lower than expected. However, one should also note that a considerable proportion of the respondents evaluated their Websites being "somewhat valuable" (14.7%) or "extremely valuable" (18.9%).

Non-independent agencies appear to agree that agency Websites were significantly contributing to communicating general information (Mean = 5.06) and enhancing marketing and promotion efforts (Mean = 4.97). However, the contribution of an agency Website to transaction features, improving consumer relationship, and tangibility of products and services were more strongly perceived by independent agencies (Mean = 4.58, 4.67, and 4.61, respectively) than by the non-independent group. The results indicated that the respondents overall did not highly perceive or recognize the value of their Website as an important attribute to the agency business. As shown in Table 5, the results of MANOVA statistics for the 6 hypothesized variables revealed no significance difference among the variables across two business types. The second hypothesis of no significant difference in the Website contribution to the travel agency business between independent and non-independent agencies (H2) was also supported by multivariate test statistics (Wilks' lambda F = 0.764 with the significance level at 0.601).

Purposes for Developing and Operating a Travel Agency Website

Figure 4 illustrates various purposes or needs for an agency Website in terms of mean level of importance by two agency types. This was to address the third research hypothesis of testing primary purposes for developing and operating a Website. Overall, travel agencies might use their Websites primarily to enhance marketing efforts (Mean = 5.72 with score 1 being not at all important and 7 being extremely important), to effectively disseminate information, or to use as an advertising medium (Mean = 5.63 with both purposes). On the other hand, the need of a Website to be used as a direct reservation channel or for building a partnership was not perceived to be highly important. On the seven-point scale used, these two were considered somewhat important (Mean = 3.90 and 4.24, respectively).

While the mean scores indicating the importance of primary purposes in developing and operating a Website were not significantly different between independent agencies and non-independent agencies (see Figure 4), the purpose for expanding distribution channels varied significantly across the two agency types. It appeared that independent agencies might be more strongly focused on the needs of a Website to expand the channel of tourism product distribution than those who were already with agency chains or affiliated with other methods (Mean = 5.34 versus 4.71). The same can be seen also in the results of MANOVA (Table 6), where all hypothesized purpose variables did not indicate any significant differences by two agency types with the only exception of the purpose for expanding

FIGURE 3. Mean Level of Importance for Contribution of a Travel Agency Website to the Agency Business

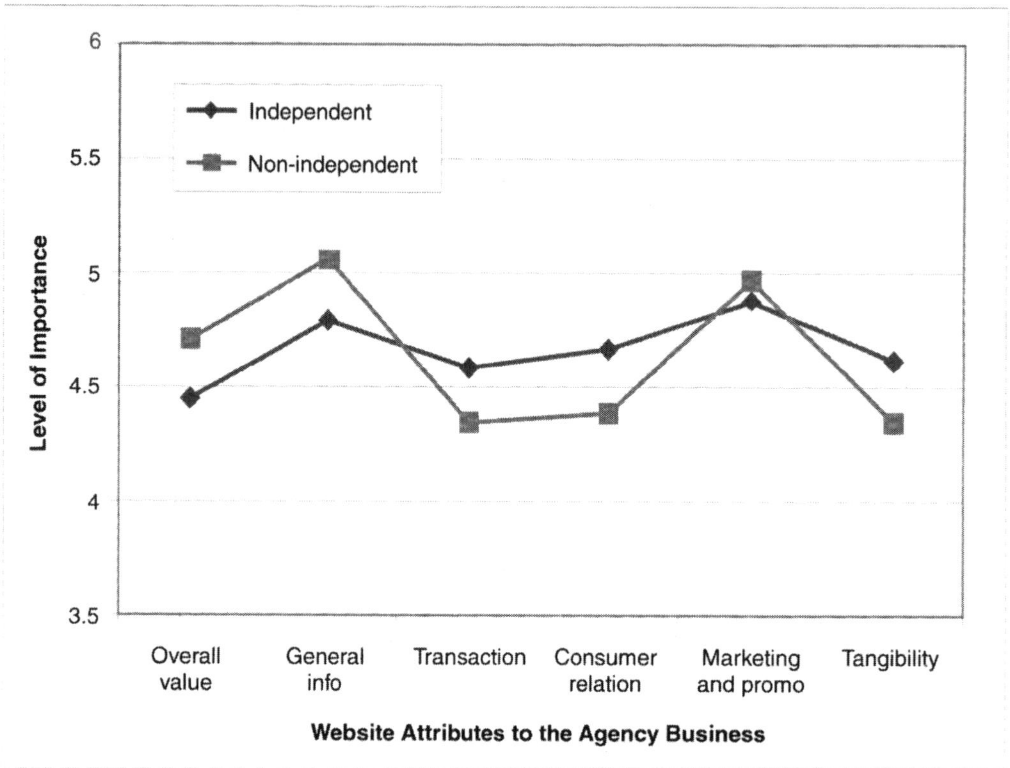

Note: Level of importance was measured in a 7-point scale with 1 being "Not at all important" and 7 being "Extremely important."

TABLE 5. MANOVA for Contribution of a Travel Agency Website to the Agency Business by Agency Types (Independent versus Non-Independent Agencies)

Contribution Variables	df	MSE	F	Sig.*
Overall value of the Website to business	1	0.942	0.295	0.589
General information	1	0.954	0.841	0.362
Transaction features	1	0.769	0.158	0.693
Consumer relation	1	1.147	0.506	0.479
Marketing and promotion	1	0.113	0.054	0.816
Tangibility of products and services	1	0.988	0.348	0.557

*No variable is significant at the 0.10 level.

distribution channels. The null hypothesis of no difference in purposes for developing and operating a travel agency Website between independent and non-independent agencies (H3) was also supported by multivariate test statis-

tics (Wilks' lambda F = 1.291 with the significance level at 0.260).

Benefits and Challenges in Operating an Agency Website

The fourth research hypothesis was to evaluate benefits and challenges in operating an agency Website. The respondents were asked to provide five most beneficial aspects of their Websites, generating a total of 446 multiple responses among 10 benefits suggested. As shown in Table 7, travel agency professionals participated in the study considered that operating a Website was the most beneficial in making marketing efforts easy (80.3%). In addition, they sought opportunities to sell directly to consumers (57.8%), to take the advantage of the 24-hour availability of operating their business (56.9%), to increase revenue (48.0%),

FIGURE 4. Mean Level of Importance for Purposes for Developing and Operating an Agency Website

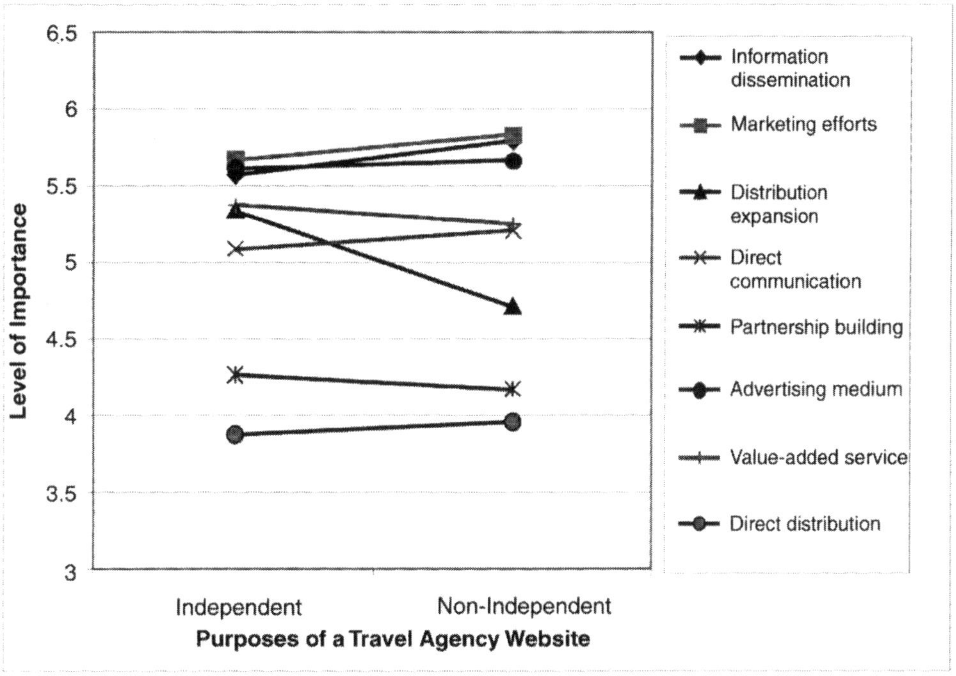

Note: Level of importance was measured in a 7-point scale with 1 being "Not at all important" and 7 being "Extremely important."

TABLE 6. MANOVA for Purposes for Developing and Operating an Agency Website by Agency Types

Purpose Variables	df	MSE	F	Sig.
To effectively disseminate information	1	0.867	0.349	0.556
To enhance marketing efforts	1	0.429	0.228	0.634
To expand distribution channel	1	6.960	2.918	0.091*
Direct communication with clientele	1	0.236	0.084	0.772
Partnership building	1	0.158	0.044	0.834
To use it as an advertising medium	1	0.046	0.019	0.892
To provide value-added services	1	0.249	0.091	0.763
To use it as a direct distribution channel	1	0.116	0.025	0.876

*Significant at the .10 level.

and to improve customer satisfaction (48.0%). Added to this, some respondents thought an agency Website would be useful for making the ease of product development or for addressing other business issues (23.5% and 26.5% of the responses, respectively). Interestingly, non-independent agencies appeared to consider a Website as being a less important tool to accomplish their business goals than independent agencies. Nevertheless, the results of Chi-Square statistics ($\chi^2 = 9.260$ with the significance level at 0.321) did not support any significant differences, supporting the null hypothesis of no difference in benefits between those two groups (H4).

A total of 174 responses were generated in reply to major challenges in operating and maintaining a travel agency Website (Table 8). Of those, almost all respondents (93.1%) pointed out that they did not have enough technical expertise to maintain a Website. Other challenges came from the lack of financial resources (34.3%), a low level of established ex-

TABLE 7. Benefits of Operating/Maintaining a Travel Agency Website

Benefits	Frequency	%
Ease of marketing	82	80.3
Direct selling	59	57.8
No limitation of operating hours	58	56.9
Revenue growth	49	48.0
Improved customer satisfaction	49	48.0
Cost reduction	35	34.3
Quality improvement of services and products	32	31.4
Partnership with other related organizations	31	30.4
Addressing other business issues	27	26.5
Ease of product development	24	23.5
Total	446*	

*N = 446 from multiple responses.

TABLE 8. Challenges in Operating/Maintaining a Travel Agency Website

Challenges	Frequency	%
Limited technical expertise	95	93.1
Lack of financial resources	35	34.3
Low level of explicit and formal marketing strategy	24	23.5
Limited human resources	12	11.8
Limited Website outsourcing availability	8	7.8
Total	174*	

*N = 174 from multiple responses.

plicit and formal marketing strategy (23.5%), limited human resources causing time constraint to update the Website (11.8%), and limited Website outsourcing available (7.8%). An open-ended response option was included in the survey to capture additional challenging aspects, if any. These six suggested categories appeared to be valid and comprehensive in covering various issues that the U.S. travel agency professionals were challenged by the use of their Websites. Testing differences in major challenges in operating and maintaining a Website between independent and non-independent agencies (H4) was also performed by Chi-Square statistics, reporting no significant differences between the two groups (χ^2 = 7.792 with the significance level at 0.351). The null hypothesis of no difference in benefits and challenges (H4) was supported overall.

Limitations of Study

A few limitations should be reported with the results of this study. First, the sample drawn for the study may not represent the entire population of travel agency professionals in the United States. Although the biggest gathering of travel agency gatherings worldwide, the study site chosen (ASTA's Annual World Travel Congress) was specific to one organization, which might raise an issue of a systematic exclusion of travel agencies without being affiliated with the ASTA membership. It should be noted that the survey distribution was concentrated only on travel agency professionals in the United States. Therefore, the findings of this study primarily apply to the travel agency industry in the U.S.

Second, the size of sample could be relatively small to yield quantitative results with statistical significance. This small sample size resulted from the limited time frame for data collection since the data were gathered only for three days during the conference sessions. Even though the self-addressed, stamped envelopes were also provided for participants who did not have the time during the conference to complete the survey but agreed to complete the survey afterwards, their responses by mailing were not too great. However, no strong indication of biased response was found in validity and reliability of the survey questionnaire. For the study results to be more representative, additional efforts to include more travel agency professionals in the sample might help ensure the validity or reliability of the results of this study.

CONCLUSIONS AND IMPLICATIONS

This study was designed primarily to analyze Internet use and practice by U.S. travel agencies and identify issues on their Website development, operation, and maintenance. A survey of 102 travel agency professionals in the United States has found that the majority of travel agencies are being operated independently with small agency size and thin profit margins. It is probable that these agencies might not have enough resources and technical expertise for their online marketing efforts.

An increasing number of recent studies indicated the effectiveness of online marketing in the travel and tourism industry worldwide. Consumers today can have an unlimited, immediate access to a wide variety of online services offered by mega-size agencies such as Expedia, Travelocity, Orbitz, and Priceline, just to name a few. These agencies offer not only online booking but also provide a toll free number for consumers to ask questions and communicate directly. If consumers are at a loss in the reservation process or do not want to bother to go through all the screens of procedures and prefer some human interaction, they can also book tickets, hotel rooms, and other services through the toll free numbers just like calling their own travel agency in the neighborhood. Most importantly, the price points offered by online agencies are often lower than those by traditional travel agencies. Travelers for instance, book a last minute 3-day Caribbean Cruise on a new Carnival ship at $299 when they book on-line through Expedia.com, while they would have paid $399 for the same through travel agencies. Hotel and airline companies also have their own Websites to directly book consumers into their systems. However, the result of this study reports that travel agencies today have not maximized the utility of the agency Website for an effective, valuable marketing tool. So, what does this mean from the standpoint of these travel agencies, and more importantly, for the consumers?

This contradiction is not new. In fact, this was consistent with Yung's findings (1997/ 1998) which emphasized issues and concerns regarding operation, security, and cost-effectiveness to be resolved first in order for travel agencies to take a full advantage of their Websites. Most respondents of this survey had a Website within the last 5 years although the differences in its duration between agency types were found. These travel agencies have recently recognized the value of the Website

and establish it in order to use it more efficiently and effectively. It appears that this contradiction or gap may only be a function of time. However, in business, time is money. This gap of more consumers using the Internet for their travel needs and travel agencies not fully utilizing their Websites need to be minimized as soon as possible. As more and more consumers become savvy with using the Internet, travel agencies need to build Websites that are easily navigable and offer products at competitive price points.

Besides operation and security issues, it always comes down to the monetary resources available. It is noted that a significant amount of investment on the Website is required unless travel agencies have technical expertise of managing every aspect of the Website development and maintenance. Travel agencies, on the average, spent $5,101.06 in setting up the Website and $278.83 in operating and maintaining it every month. Website development and maintenance costs also varied depending on agency types. Non-independent agencies spent more money in developing, operating, and maintaining their Websites than independent agencies. A majority of travel agency professionals also indicated lack of technical expertise as the major challenge to develop, operate, and maintain their agency Websites. Independent agencies had difficulty in keeping up the Website because of limited financial resources and non-independent agencies had no time to keep it up frequently.

It is, therefore, recommended for travel agencies to measure the effectiveness of Internet marketing related to business performance and justify the costs associated with implementation of the Website and the benefits that it could offer. Without addressing such issues, a Website might be able to offer only a relative advantage, not a competitive one. This also opens the door for online entrepreneurs who may wish to provide services to travel agencies at a more reasonable price range. If online booking services can survive and multiply, so can Websites of travel agencies. If it's setup costs and maintenance costs that are prohibitive, smart entrepreneurs can find a way to utilize the economies of scale also and offer small travel agencies some competitive and reasonable pricing.

One item that travel agencies need to capitalize on is their relationship with their clients, the consumers. Besides using a Website for booking business, the agencies can further utilize a Website to diverse channels of product distribution and to establish a direct communication link to their customers as well as vendors. They would like to take advantage of the Internet operating business with continuity and accessibility. The comparative analysis of the needs, benefits, and challenges showed that independent travel agencies had different approaches to the underlying needs and beneficial attributes of the Website from non-independent travel agencies. The usage of customer relationship management and also of a more personal way is of utmost importance. Travel agencies can capitalize on this point to retain and expand their market share.

The Internet is not a fad. It has enjoyed a phenomenal growth in almost every aspect of economies during the past decade and continues to grow in years to come. Travel agencies that have been operating in the traditional way need to examine the viability of a good and robust Website and have a strong presence on the Internet as a viable sales and marketing tool. The 21st Century will only take the Internet to another level, and the utility of Internet in the travel and tourism industry needs to adopt changes to cater to consumers' needs and demands in today's ever changing marketplace.

REFERENCES

Barnett, M. & Standing, C. (2000). Repositioning travel agencies on the Internet. *Journal of Vacation Marketing, 7*(20): 143-152.
Buchanan, R.W., & Lukaszewski, C. (1997). *Measuring the Impact of Your Website: Proven Yardsticks for Evaluating.* New York: John Wiley & Sons.
Buhalis, D., Jafari, J., & Werthner, H. (1997). Information technology and the re-engineering of tourism. *Annals of Tourism Research, 24*(1): 245-248.
Buhalis, D. (1998). Strategic use of information technologies in the tourism industry. *Tourism Management, 19*(5): 409-421.
Burn, J. & Barnett, M. (1999). Communicating for advantage in the virtual organization. *IEEE Transactions on Professional Communication, 42*(4): 215-222.
Cano, V., & Prentice, R. (1998). Opportunities for endearment to place through electronic 'visiting': WWW homepages and the tourism promotion of Scotland. *Tourism Management, 19*(1): 67-73.
Choi, J.J., & Hsu, C.H.C. (2001). Native American casino marketing on the Web. *Journal of Travel & Tourism Marketing, 10*(2/3): 101-117.
Christou, E., & Kassianidis, P. (2002). Consumer perceptions and adoption of online buying for travel products. *Journal of Travel & Tourism Marketing, 12*(4): 93-107.
Cook, R.A., Yale, L.J., & Marqua, J.J. (2001). *Tourism: The Business of Travel.* Upper Saddle River, NJ: Prentice Hall.
Countryman, C.C. (2000). Designing effective bed & breakfast Websites. In C.B. Mok & A.L. DeFranco (Eds.). *Advances in Hospitality & Tourism Research* (pp. 430-432). The Fifth Annual Graduate Education and Graduate Students Research Conference in Hospitality and Tourism, held at Houston, Texas (January 6-8).
Coupey, E. (2001). *Marketing and the Internet: Conceptual Foundations.* Upper Saddle River, NJ: Prentice Hall.
Dev, C. & Olsen, M. (2000). Marketing challenges for the next decade. *Cornell Hotel & Restaurant Administration Quarterly, 41*(1): 41-47.
Disabatino, J. (2001). Travel industry showing growth in online sales. Retrieved February 23, 2003 from *Computerworld* on the World Wide Web: *http://www.computerworld.com/managementtopics/ebusiness/story/0,10801,59766,00.html*
Dorsey, J. (1998, October 8). Survey forecast: Smaller retailers will be casualties of Internet boom. *Travel Weekly, 57*(180): 1-6.
Gamble, P. (1990). Culture shock, computers and the art of making decisions. *International Journal of Contemporary Hospitality Management, 2*(1): 4-9.
Gamble, P. (1992). The Strategic role of information technology systems. In R. Teare & M. Olsen (Eds.), *International Hospitality Management: Corporation Strategy in Practice.* London: Pitman.
Gunn, C.A. (1994). *Tourism Planning: Basics, Concepts, Cases.* Washington, DC: Taylor & Francis.
Ho, J.K. (2002). Easy-to-use multilingual communication over the Internet: Facilitating "e-business" for the hotel industry. *Cornell Hotel and Restaurant Administration Quarterly, 43*(2): 18-25.
Kasavana, M.L., Knutson, B.J., & Polonowski, S.J. (1998). Netlurking: The future of hospitality Internet marketing. *Journal of Hospitality & Leisure Marketing, 5*(1): 31-34.
Kasavana, M.L. (2002). eMarketing: Restaurant Websites that click. *Journal of Hospitality & Leisure Marketing, 9*(3/4): 161-178.
King, B., Bransgrove, C., & Whitelaw, P. (1998). Profiling the strategic marketing activities of small tourism businesses. *Journal of Travel & Tourism Marketing, 7*(4): 45-49.

Law, R. (2000). Internet in travel and tourism. *Journal of Travel & Tourism Marketing, 9*(3): 65-71.

Law, R., Law, A., & Wai, E. (2001). The impact of the Internet on travel agencies in Hong Kong. *Journal of Travel & Tourism Marketing, 11*(2/3): 105-126.

Liu, Z. (2000). Internet tourism marketing: Potential and constraints. Retrieved April 4, 2002 from *Hotel Online* on the World Wide Web: *http://www.hotel-online. com/Neo/Trends/ChinaMaiJun00/InternetConstraints. html*

Morrison, A.M., Taylor, J.S., Morrison, A.J., & Morrison, A.D. (1999). Marketing small hotel on the World Wide Web. *Information Technology & Tourism, 2*(2): 97-113.

Murphy, J., Forrest, E., & Wotring, C.E. (1996). Restaurant marketing on the World Wide Web. *Cornell Hotel & Restaurant Administration Quarterly, 37*(1): 61-71.

Murphy, J., Olaru, D., Schegg, R., & Frey, S. (2003). The Bandwagon effect: Swiss hotels' Web-site and E-mail management. *Cornell Hotel and Restaurant Administration Quarterly, 44*(1): 71-87.

NUA Analysis (2001). How many online? Retrieved February 21, 2003 from *NUA Internet survey* on the World Wide Web: *http://www.nua.ie/surveys/how_ many_online/n_america.html*

NUA Analysis (2002). Online leisure travel spending to double. Retrieved March 12, 2003 from *NUA Internet survey* on the World Wide Web: *http://www. nua.ie/surveys/index.cgi?f=VS&art_id=905358614& rel=true.*

O'Connor, P. (2003). On-line pricing: An analysis of hotel-company practices. *Cornell Hotel and Restaurant Administration Quarterly, 44*(1): 88-96.

Palmer, A., & McCole, P. (1999). The virtual reintermediation of travel services: A conceptual framework and empirical investigation. *Journal of Vacation Marketing, 6*(1): 33-47.

Perdue, R.R. (2001). Internet site evaluations: The influence of behavioral experience, existing images, and selected Website characteristics. *Journal of Travel & Tourism Marketing, 11*(2/3): 21-38.

Perry, P.M. (1997). Honing your home page. *National Restaurant Association, 17*(8): 21-25.

Peterson, R.A., Balasubramanian, S., & Bronnenberg, B.J. (1997). Exploring the implications of the Internet for consumer marketing. *Journal of Academy of Marketing Science, 25*(4): 329-346.

Poon, A. (1993). *Tourism, Technology and Competitive Strategies.* Wallingford, CT: CAB International.

Rach, L. (1997). The connected consumer: Implications for hospitality sales and marketing. *Hospitality Sales and Marketing Association International, 13*(3): 23-26.

Robinson, T. (2002, August 19). Online sales spike, led by computers, travel. Retrieved February 23, 2003 from *E-Commerce Times* on the World Wide Web: *http://www.ecommercetimes.com/perl/story/19079.html*

Shankar, V. (1999). E-Commerce: Now and in the future. *HSMAI Marketing Review, 16*(1): 28-29.

Sheldon, P.J. (1997). *Tourism Information Technology.* New York: CAB International.

Siebenaler, T.C. & Groves, D.L. (2002). Travel agents and their survival. *Journal of Human Resources in Hospitality & Tourism, 1*(1): 1-16.

Standing, C., & Vasudavan, T. (1999). Internet marketing strategies used by travel agencies in Australia. *Journal of Vacation Marketing, 6*(1): 21-32.

Strassmann, P. (1990). *The Business Value of Computers: An Executive Guide.* Connecticut: The Information Economics Press.

Susskind, A.M., Bonn, M.A., & Dev, C.S. (2003). To look or book: An examination of consumers' apprehensiveness toward Internet use. *Journal of Travel Research, 41*(3): 256-264.

Talwar, R. (1996). Re-engineering: A wonder drug for the 90's. In C. Coulson-Thomas (Ed.), *Business Process Re-Engineering.* London: Kogan Page.

Travel Weekly. (2002). 2002 U. S. Travel Industry Survey: New market, new rules, new people. *Travel Weekly, 61*(42): 11-47.

Vogt, W.P. (1999). *Dictionary of Statistics & Methodology: A Nontechnical Guide for the Social Sciences* (2nd ed.). Thousand Oaks, CA: Sage Publications.

Yuan, Y., Gretzel, U., & Fesenmaier, D.R. (2003). Internet technology use by American convention and visitors bureaus. *Journal of Travel Research, 41*(3): 240-255.

Yung, C. (1997/1998). Internet marketing: The perception of travel agencies in Taipei, Taiwan. *Asia Pacific Journal of Tourism Research, 2*(1): 67-74.

Conflicting Viewpoints on Web Design

Peter O'Connor

SUMMARY. While design undoubtedly affects a Website's success, two ideologically opposite schools of thought have developed as to what is meant by good design. The approaches differ fundamentally in terms of how to balance two interrelated but conflicting elements–presentation and usability. Supporters of the aesthetic school argue that the graphical/multimedia features of the Web should be used to enhance the visitor experience. Functionalists, on the other hand, argue for less emphasis on visual design and more focus on content. This article reviews both approaches and examines their applicability to the travel product. *[Article copies available for a fee from The Haworth Document Delivery Service: 1-800-HAWORTH. E-mail address: <docdelivery@haworthpress.com> Website: <http://www.HaworthPress.com> © 2004 by The Haworth Press, Inc. All rights reserved.]*

KEYWORDS. E-Commerce, website design, travel

INTRODUCTION

The development of the Web has undoubtedly had a major effect on the way in which travel goods and services are being marketed, distributed and sold. Due to its dependence on visual representation (Morgan, Pritchard et al., 2001) and its intangible, heterogeneous nature, travel is thought to be very suitable for sale on the Web (O'Connor, 1999). In practice, it has become one of the most frequent items sold online, with recent figures placing the value of leisure and unmanaged business travel online sales in the United States alone at approximately US$23 billion in 2002 (Forrester Research, 2003). Furthermore, sales volumes are forecast to at least double over the next five years. Estimates from Marcussen (2003) place the equivalent European figure at approximately US$7 billion, with Asian fig-

ures much lower at about US$3.5 (Ong, 2002). However, sales volumes in both Europe and Asia are forecast to grow even more aggressively. None of the above figures include sales influenced by, but not transacted through online channels, which are thought to be quite substantial. For example, PhoCusWright (2003) estimates that as much as 55% of travellers are looking online but booking offline, placing the true value of travel influenced by the Web at nearly US$60 billion or over 35% of global travel and tourism market (Caroll & Siguaw, 2003).

For companies wishing to exploit this potential, a key issue is the design of their Websites. How should sites be structured and laid out in order to gain maximum benefit for the organisation? For the purposes of this paper, it is presumed that such owners are travel and tourism principals, and that for the most

Peter O'Connor is Associate Professor, IMHI, Essec Business School, Ave Bernard Hirsch, Cergy Pontoise Cedex, France (E-mail: oconnor@essec.fr).

[Haworth co-indexing entry note]: "Conflicting Viewpoints on Web Design." O'Connor, Peter. Co-published simultaneously in *Journal of Travel & Tourism Marketing* (The Haworth Hospitality Press, an imprint of The Haworth Press, Inc.) Vol. 17. No. 2/3, 2004, pp. 225-230; and: *Handbook of Consumer Behavior, Tourism, and the Internet* (ed: Juline E. Mills, and Rob Law) The Haworth Hospitality Press, an imprint of The Haworth Press. Inc., 2004. pp. 225-230. Single or multiple copies of this article are available for a fee from The Haworth Document Delivery Service [1-800-HAWORTH, 9:00 a.m. - 5:00 p.m. (EST). E-mail address: docdelivery@haworthpress.com].

http://www.haworthpress.com/web/JTTM
© 2004 by The Haworth Press, Inc. All rights reserved.
Digital Object Identifier: 10.1300/J073v17n02_17

part their objectives are to inform customers about their products (with the ultimate objective of making a sale) and also where possible to facilitate that sale online. While in certain circumstances, such as with national or regional tourist boards, these objectives may not be entirely accurate, for the most part this generalisation is appropriate. Thus this article reviews current research on Web design to illustrate how it contributes to both the communication and sale of the travel and tourism product.

WEB DESIGN IN THEORY

The topic of Web design is highly complex and at its broadest level can be thought of as including elements of content, information architecture, graphic design, search strategy, navigability, and usability. However the core of Web design can be thought of as *presentation* and *usability*–in essence how the content is represented on the Web page and how the user interacts with this content (Robbins & Stylianou, 2003). However, this simple definition reveals a conflict in terms of the theory of Web design. Good design implies balancing these two interrelated but often conflicting elements. Certain authors and practitioners focus on the multimedia capabilities and marketing/advertising potential of the Web and stress the need to use these facilities to their full potential. Gathered around designer David Siegel, supporters of this approach argue for emphasis on the graphical design, aesthetic and entertainment aspects of Web design (Siegel, 1997). Their opponents–known as functionalists and centered on usability-guru Jakob Nielsen–argue for a decreased priority to be given to graphical features in order to focus more on content and function (Nielsen, 2000). In essence supporters of the latter approach argue for substance rather than style, and campaign against excessive (or even moderate) graphic design, preferring instead to focus on content. Thus (conceptually at least) it is clear that Web design has split into two camps that seem to represent extreme ideological opposites. While it is clear that both approaches have merit, for the purposes of explanation it is useful to examine each philosophy separately.

THE AESTHETIC SCHOOL OF WEB DESIGN

Although from a graphical perspective, Web pages have undergone radical changes since the introduction of the Web browser in 1994, having developed from primitive wall-to-wall text displays to interactive multimedia presentations featuring animation, sound and video, little research has been carried out on the implications of such changes for the customer. Engholm (2002) does however provide a useful overview of the different stages that commercial Websites have gone through in terms of their aesthetic styles. As both HTML (Hypertext Markup Lanuguage) and Web browser technology have been refined, designers have gained increasing amounts of leeway over how their pages are displayed on users' screens. While presented as a historical overview, Engholm's classifications for the most part still holds true today and represents a useful way to highlight the various approaches used within this school of thought.

At the most basic level of aesthetics is the simple text and hyperlink based page, sometimes supplemented by a logo or banner to add some graphical interest. Known as HTML-design, such sites have traditionally been built by programmers or other technology professionals with little if any graphical flair. Their primary focus is on presenting information rather than trying to influence or sell to the customer (see, for example, http://www.microtelinn.com). Supporters of the aesthetic school claim that the rival functional approach is only a small progression from this category, as it places emphasis on user friendliness and fitness for the task rather than graphical design (Engholm, 2002). While Nielsen and his supporters maintain that users visit a Website for its content and thus it makes little sense wasting time on its packaging (Nielsen, 1993), others argue that good graphical design enhances content and adds value. For example, the so-called Swiss-style can be seen as a more design conscious version of the functional school. In this school of thought, form and function are seen not as separate issues but as two sides of the same coin (Zeldman, 2001). The style is characterised by an airy typography, primary but muted colors on a white, black or grey background and large amounts of empty space which give a modern feel, and is often used by companies that want to project a serious and contemporary image online without compromising functionality (see, for example, http://www.fourseasons.com).

Next on the hierarchy is what is known as branded-style, which uses more advanced Web technology and multimedia seamlessly in an effort to create an aura for the company and its products (see, for example, http://www.ianschrager.com). Branded-style sites reflect a fundamental change in philosophy, moving responsibility for the Website out of the hands of technology professionals and giving more influence to marketers. Web presence is usually integrated with the other aspects of a company's communications, and the primary focus starts to become less on content and navigation, and more on image and how the company is being projected online.

Lastly, at the opposite extreme of the graphical design spectrum is what Engholm (2002) terms the avant-garde or trash style of Web design. Such sites range from lo-fi-grunge, which ignores the traditional grid like structure that invisibly controls "normal" Web pages, to Pixel-style, which is characterised by isometric graphics presented at a 45 degree angle and which tries to emulate a computer game rather than the real world. Avant-garde style digresses radically from established and accepted norms in terms of user interface and human-computer-interaction, and in most cases the emphasis seems to be on how the page looks rather than the information it contains or how the user will interact with it (see, for example, http://www.lebristolparis.com). Such a departure may be caused by the trend where younger Web users value sensory impact more than their older peers (Lightner, 2001), and such sites are designed primarily to appeal to this youth culture.

It is interesting to note the similarities between the classifications provided above by Engholm (2002) and those outlined by Siegel (1997) when discussing different generations of Website design. Functional style corresponds broadly with Siegel's first generation in that it is characterised by a simplistic linear structure dictated largely by the technical constraints of basic HTML. Similarly Swiss-style broadly corresponds with Siegel's second generation in that it follows a similar linear structure, but with a stronger focus on aesthetics aspects as a result of increased use of images and icons and a stronger orientation towards graphical features. As with third generation sites, Engholm's branded style is characterised by a consistent design concept for the entire site in order to create a complete and coherent user experience. Siegel's classification does not mention avant-garde sites, but this to a large extent is due to their comparatively recent development.

THE FUNCTIONAL SCHOOL OF WEB DESIGN

As was discussed briefly above, the functional school of Web design places emphasis on usability and navigability rather than on aesthetics. Proponents of this approach argue that a well designed Website should provide easy and well ordered access to information to all possible users rather than present fancy graphics or multimedia. Simplicity in text, layout, language and style is emphasized (Yale Centre for Advanced Instructional Media, 1997). Good design should direct users towards information rather than distract from it (Smith, 2001). Functionality and usability are the key design issues, and this approach largely ignores beauty and finesse. For example, most functionalists counsel against the use of "splash pages" (multimedia rich pages presented to the user on their initial access to a Website)–a key technique used as sites move along the aesthetic continuum described above, or against techniques such as animation except where it directly adds to the content of the Website (Nielsen, 2002).

Clearly, usability is an important issue. When faced with a site that has poor usability, users are likely to abandon their visit in favor of more usable sites (Nielsen, 2000). Souza et al. (2000) report that 65 percent of visitors to retail Websites leave due to usability barriers. Similarly, Nielsen and Tahir (2001) found that users looking for a desired item on ecommerce sites cannot find it nearly one third of the time, leading to lost opportunities for sales. As a result, usability is a key issue affecting commercial Websites. A study by Tedeschi (1999) revealed that when the usability of their sites was improved, IBM achieved an increase in sales of nearly 400%, while another study (Creative Good, 1999-2001) estimated that improving the customer experience increases the number of buyers by 40% and increases order sizes by 10% on selected sites.

One challenge with the functional approach is that a large number of very specific guidelines are available, most of whose origins and validity are questionable (see Park & Noh, 2002; Tullis, 1997; Robbins & Stylianou, 2003). For example, two commonly accepted functional Web design rules are the "three-click" rule (which states that users should be able to access any Website feature or piece of information within three clicks of the mouse, otherwise they will be dissatisfied) and the "AOL" rule (which advises designers to keep the file size of Web pages below 40K–a guideline based on the supposed length of time a user connecting to the Web over a conventional modem would be prepared to wait for a page to download) (Nielsen, 2002). While both rules make sense, there is little if any empirical evidence to support either claim. Similarly there are a large number of reports dealing with Web design produced by Internet research companies. However, their quality is often difficult to judge as such studies rarely tell the reader how their recommendations were formulated. To generalise a little too much (as these studies often do), where details of the underlying "study" are presented, the methodology used often does not stand up to the rigours of academic scrutiny, and thus such findings should be approached with caution. For that reason, rather than repeating hearsay and half-truths, the discussion below will focus on outlining the principal functional guidelines for which sufficient empirical evidence could be found.

A challenge with presenting an overview of Web design from a functional perspective is how to structure the vast number of very specific guidelines that are available. Moving from the general towards the more specific, Rosenfeld and Morville (1998) suggest that there are five broad dimensions to Website design: Language (the choice of words used to present content on the Webpage); Layout (how elements are visually rendered on the page); Information architecture (how a site's content and features are arranged); User Interface (how navigation through the content is facilitated); and General issues on design and maintenance. Similarly, Smith (2001) identifies four sets of factors: Ease of navigation; whether pages are clear and uncluttered; whether standard HTML is used; and whether the design allows the site to be accessed at low bandwidth and by users with less advanced technology or with disabilities. Other similar sets of broad advice can easily be found in the literature–see for example Sears (2000) or Diaper and Waelend (2000).

In terms of more specific guidelines, the functional style stresses that each Web page should be an appropriate length, uncluttered and clearly laid out. A simple look and feel should be consistent throughout the entire Website (Koyani & Nall, 1999). Most research draws a distinction between navigation pages and content pages with most researchers recommending that the former be less than one screen in length (Lynch & Horton, 1999). There is also support for the common practice of placing the main navigation menu from the top left-hand side of a Web page, as deviations from this location significantly decrease search time and overall usability (Park & Noh, 2002), (van Schaik & Ling, 2001). Of course with the functional school content is king, and information should be presented in sharp, easy to understand textual copy (Gerhardt-Powals, 1996). Colour schemes should be muted. For example, Park and Noh (2002) stress that retail sites should use a light background colour, as dark backgrounds make users feel uneasy. Graphics should only be used that enhance content or that lead to a better understanding of the information being presented (Spool, Scanlon et al., 1997). Large or complex graphics are discouraged as they both detract from the information content and also decrease load time (Bouch, Kuchinsky et al., 2000). At all times, the emphasis is on simplicity to help increase usability. However, despite guidelines such as these (and a vast number of others that have not been empirically proved), usability is clearly still an issue with many Websites. Proctor et al. (2002) point out how there are few graduate programs in applied user interface design, leading to an inadequate number of designers with expertise in usability, and that few people perform usability evaluations early and throughout the Web design process. Thus there seems to be a mismatch between theory and reality.

CONCLUSION AND POTENTIAL FUTURE RESEARCH

The number one challenge for marketers today is clearly converting browsers into buyers. As was mentioned in the introduction, most travel sites suffer from a relatively low look to book ratio, with the majority of site visitors preferring to complete the purchase through some other distribution channels. Despite this, the majority of travellers have indicated that they would like to purchase travel online (Yesavitch, Pepperdine & Brown, 2002), but for some reason practice differs from their desires. Some analysts suggest that this may be because current non-buyers are stubborn and need to be lured to their first online purchase. Effective Web design is thus a key element in encouraging this conversion. As can be seen from the above discussion, Web design philosophies fall into two opposing camps-one focused on aesthesis and the other on usability. It is clear that both have merit, and in fact more recent authors–see for example Zeldman (2001)–advocate a less extreme stance, recommending an integration of form and function.

Little research has been carried out in relation to Web design issues in the travel and tourism sector. Williams and Palmer (1999) suggest that "inadequate design resulting in inferior Websites and poor quality information" is one of the key issues limiting tourism marketing on the Web, but offer few concrete suggestions as to how to improve matters. Schegg et al. (2002) suggest a large number of design elements (over 200) and use them successfully to benchmark the content of Swiss hotels, but make no attempt to assess their relative importance. There is some evidence to suggest that adopting a purely functional approach may not be appropriate for travel and tourism Websites. For example, a study by Morgan, Pritchard and Abbott (2001) highlights the importance of photos on travel Websites. Potential purchasers, having become accustomed to glossy paper brochures both place emphasis on the graphic design of a site when assessing its quality and want to see as wide a range of high quality photographs to help aid in their purchase decision. Similarly, a study by Lightner and Jackson (2001) found that a combination of text and pictures is more effective at selling the tourism product than simply using textual descriptions alone. Clearly there is an expectation that information presented online is not only useful but also attractive and well presented (Hinton, 1998).

In terms of future research, it is clear that there are many potential topics in this area. Irrespective of whether you support the aesthetic or the usability school of thought, or lie somewhere in between, many issues remain unproven, both in general terms and as they related to the tourism product. At a fundamental level, is marketing, distributing or selling tourism online any different from selling any other product, and what effect does this have on the way in which Websites and Web pages are designed? We (and I include myself in such a statement) in the tourism sector frequently claim that there is something unique about the tourism product, but is selling travel online any different from selling any other product from a design perspective? Similarly, as was mentioned above, converting lookers into bookers is of critical importance in the tourism sector. How can the design of a Web page aid in or hinder this process? Do any of the issues highlighted above–aesthetics, navigation, usability or any other factors–have an influence on a consumer's propensity to buy online? Common sense would indicate yes, but to date the area is relatively unexplored, giving vast potential to academics brave enough to tackle the area.

REFERENCES

Bouch, A., Kuchinsky et al. (2000). *Quality is in the eye of the beholder: Meeting users' requirements for Internet quality of service.* CHI 2000.

Carroll, B. and J. Siguaw (2003). Evolution in Electronic Distribution: Effect on Hotels and Intermediaries. Ithaca, NY, Centre for Hospitality Research, Cornell University.

Creative Good (1999-2001). The dotcom survival guide. *http://www.creativegood.com/survival.*

Diaper, D. and P. Waelend (2000). World Wide Web working whilst ignoring graphics: Good news for Web page designers. *Interacting with computers* (13): 163-181.

Engholm, I. (2002). Digital style history: The development of graphical design on the Internet. *Digital Creativity* 13(4): 193-211.

Forrester Research (2003).*US Managed and Unmanaged Business Travel, 2002-2007*. Cambridge, MA, Forrester Research Inc.

Gerhardt-Powals, J. (1996). Cognitive engineering principles for enhancing human-computer performance. *International Journal of Human-Computer Interaction* 8(2): 189-211.

Hinton, S. (1998). From home page to home site: Effective Web resource discovery at the ANU. *Computer Network and ISDN Systems* (30): 309-316.

Koyani, S. and J. Nall (1999). *Website Design and Usability Guidelines*. Bethesda, MD, National Cancer Institute.

Lightner, N. (2001). Strategies for designing usable interfaces for Internet applications. *Usability evaluation and interface design: Cognitive engineering, intelligent agents and virtual reality*. M. Smith, G. Salvendy, D. Harris and R. Koubek. Mahwah, NJ, Lawrence Erlbaum Associates. 1: 1387-1389.

Lynch, P. and S. Horton (1999). *Web Style Guide: Basic Design Principles for Creating Websites*. New York, Yale University Press.

Marcussen, C. (2003). *Trends in European Internet Distribution of Travel and Tourism Services*. Bornholm, Danish Centre for Regional and Tourism Research.

Morgan, N., A. Pritchard et al. (2001). Consumers, travel and technology: A bright future for the Web or television shopping. *Journal of Vacation Marketing* 7(2): 110-124.

Nielsen, J. (1993). *Usability engineering*. San Diego, Academic Press.

Nielsen, J. (2000). *Designing Web usability*. Indianapolis, New Riders Publishing.

Nielsen, J. (2002). *Homepage Usability: 50 Websites Deconstructed*. Indianapolis, New Riders.

Nielsen, J. and Tahir (2001). Building Websites with depth. *Webtechniques* (2): (online).

O'Connor, P. (1999). *Electronic Information Distribution in Hospitality and Tourism*. Oxford, CAB International.

Ong, C. (2002). Zuji launch to rival Priceline in Hong Kong. *South China Morning Post*, November 26, p. 4.

Park, H.-S. and S. J. Noh (2002). Enhancement of Web design quality through the QFD approach. *Total Quality Management* 13(3): 393-401.

Proctor, R., K.-P. Vu et al. (2002). Content Preparation and Management for Web Design: Eliciting, Structuring, Searching and Displaying Information. *International Journal of Human Computer Interaction* 14(1): 25-92.

Robbins, S. and A. Stylianou (2003). Global corporate Websites: An empirical investigation of content and design. *Information & Management* (40): 205-212.

Schegg, R., T. Steiner et al. (2002). Benchmarks of Website Design and Marketing by Swiss Hotels. *Information Technology in Tourism* 5(1): 73-89.

Sears, A. (2000). Introduction: Empirical studies of WWW usability. *International Journal of Human Computer Interaction* (12): 167-171.

Siegel, D. (1997). *Creating killer Websites: The art of third generation site design*. Indianapolis, Hayden Books.

Smith, A. (2001). Applying evaluation criteria to New Zealand government Websites. *International Journal of Information Management* (21): 137-149.

Souza, R., H. Manning et al. (2000). The best of Retail Site Design. *Techstrategy. http://www.forrester.com/ER/Research/Report?summary/0,1338,10003,FF.html*, Forrester Research. 2002.

Spool, J., T. Scanlon et al. (1997). *Website Usability: A Designer's Guide*. North Andove, MA, User Interface Engineering.

Tedeschi, B. (1999). Good Website design can lead to healthy sales. *New York Times e-commerce report*. New York: 30.

Tullis, T. (1997). Screen Design. *Handbook of human-computer-interaction*. M. Helander, T. Landauer and P. Prabhu. Oxford, Elsevier: 503-531.

van Schaik, P. and J. Ling (2001). Design Parameters in Web Pages: Frame Location and Differential Background Contrast in Visual Search Performance. *International Journal of Cognitive Ergonomics* 5(4): 459-471.

Williams, P. and A. Palmer (1999). Tourism destination brands and electronic commerce: Towards synergy? *Journal of Vacation Marketing* 5(3): 263-275.

Zeldman, J. (2001). *Taking your talent to the Web. A guide for the transitional designer*. Indianapolis, New Riders.

SECTION 6:
WEBSITE EVALUATION
IN HOSPITALITY AND TOURISM

A General Model for Website Evaluation
Adapted from: Website Evaluation Methods.
Available: *http://www.hopkinsmedicine.org/ccp/ppt/casey/eval.htm*

Website Evaluation in Tourism and Hospitality: The Art Is Not Yet Stated

Alastair M. Morrison
J. Stephen Taylor
Alecia Douglas

SUMMARY. Millions of dollars have been invested in Website development, often without much thought of how to evaluate the effectiveness of sites. This paper reports on the past, present, and likely future of one of the recommended approaches for evaluating tourism and hospitality Websites, the modified Balanced Scorecard approach. It traces the use of the approach from its beginning in 1999 to the present time. A thorough review of other approaches to Website evaluation is also provided. The article suggests that Website evaluation approaches can be classified into four groups based upon why and when the evaluation is done (formative vs. summative evaluation) and whether efficiency or effectiveness is being measured. It concludes with a call to action for industry leaders, academics, and consultants to develop a unified procedure for Website evaluation in tourism and hospitality. *[Article copies available for a fee from The Haworth Document Delivery Service: 1-800-HAWORTH. E-mail address: <docdelivery@haworthpress.com> Website: <http://www.HaworthPress. com> © 2004 by The Haworth Press, Inc. All rights reserved.]*

KEYWORDS. Balanced Scorecard (BSC), critical success factors (CSFs), efficiency, effectiveness, formative evaluation, summative evaluation, Web metrics, Website evaluation

INTRODUCTION

In the mid-to-late 1990s, practitioners and academics struggled to understand the Web and the people who were using it to for travel information and bookings (Bonn, Furr, & Susskind, 1998, 1999; Jung, 1999; Kasavana, Knutson & Polonowski, 1997; Smith & Jenner, 1998; Walle, 1996; Weber & Roehl, 1999). In a virtual sea of new terminology and techniques, Website performance and evaluation were neglected topics of concern. Millions of dollars were poured into Website development without much thought given to their effectiveness in meeting specific organizational objectives. As the broader field of Internet marketing has matured, there is now a greater focus on measuring the performance of individual Websites

Alastair M. Morrison is Distinguished Professor of Hospitality and Tourism Management and Associate Dean for Learning, School of Consumer and Family Sciences, Purdue University. J. Stephen Taylor is Lecturer, The Scottish Hotel School, University of Strathclyde. Alecia Douglas is a Master's Candidate, Department of Hotel, Restaurant, and Institutional Management, University of Delaware.

Address correspondence to Alastair M. Morrison (E-mail: alastair@cfs.purdue.edu).

[Haworth co-indexing entry note]: "Website Evaluation in Tourism and Hospitality: The Art Is Not Yet Stated." Morrison, Alastair M., J. Stephen Taylor, and Alecia Douglas. Co-published simultaneously in *Journal of Travel & Tourism Marketing* (The Haworth Hospitality Press, an imprint of The Haworth Press, Inc.) Vol. 17. No. 2/3, 2004, pp. 233-251; and: *Handbook of Consumer Behavior, Tourism, and the Internet* (ed: Juline E. Mills, and Rob Law) The Haworth Hospitality Press, an imprint of The Haworth Press, Inc., 2004, pp. 233-251. Single or multiple copies of this article are available for a fee from The Haworth Document Delivery Service [1-800-HAWORTH, 9:00 a.m. - 5:00 p.m. (EST). E-mail address: docdelivery@haworthpress.com].

and benchmarking them against competitive sites and industry standards.

As suggested by Tierney (2000), the evaluation of Website effectiveness is needed because of the significant setup and maintenance costs. He also pointed out that, although online sales are a good way to measure Website effectiveness, many tourism sites, such as destination marketing organizations, do not have this feature since they generate little or no revenues of their own. Website evaluations are needed to facilitate continuous improvements as well as to judge site performance against competitors and industry peers. Organizations may also wish to track the performance of their Websites over successive time periods.

A variety of approaches have been suggested or used for measuring the effectiveness of tourism and hospitality Websites. Murphy, Forrest, Wotring and Brymer (1996a) analyzed the Websites of 36 hotels in late 1995, and identified 32 categories of hotel Website features, which they subsequently grouped into promotion and marketing, service and information, interactivity and technology, and management. They did not perform an overall evaluation of each of the hotel sites, but rather calculated the percentages that had each of the 32 features, and developed a classification system for the categories of content in these sites. In another study, Murphy, Forrest and Wotring (1996b) analyzed 37 restaurant Websites and checked to see if they had specific features (e-mail contact, online sales promotions, frequent specials, directions, reservations, e-mail newsletter, franchising, coupons, recruiting, and contests). They concluded that restaurants should expand the ways they use the Web to communicate with a variety of audiences.

Similarly, Kasavana et al. (1997) provided a useful set of benchmarks for evaluating marketing on hospitality Websites (audience measurement, audience recall, bandwidth, user friendliness, use of e-commerce, and use of new technologies to enhance online marketing), although they did not assess specific sites. Kasavana (1997) also suggested various features that a private club Website should include to be effective. Ho (1997) evaluated 1,000 North American Websites from 20 different industrial sectors, including 25 sites

each from airlines, hotels/resorts, and travel. He evaluated four types of value creation by Websites; timeliness, customization, logistic value (built-in propositions), and sensational value (excitement created by graphics).

In an assessment of 130 Websites promoting tourism in Scotland, Cano and Prentice (1998) found that Website performance varied greatly, and concluded that overall the sites were underselling Scotland as a destination. Connolly, Olsen and Moore (1998) examined hotels' use of the Internet as a distribution channel, and questioned the return on investment on the significant costs of Website development. They briefly described the Websites of five luxury hotel chains. The authors concluded that these chains were not fully embracing the online booking potential of the Internet, but rather using the Web as a way to disseminate hotel information in an electronic directory format.

Historically, as Kasavana (2002) suggested, it has been difficult to create a set of criteria against which to evaluate Website effectiveness. NetGenesis/SPSS (2003a: 5) suggest, "Defining specific metrics for measuring the success of a Web site is a daunting task." However, several approaches have been used to comprehensively measure Website effectiveness. This paper reports on the past, present, and likely future of one of the recommended approaches, the modified Balanced Scorecard (BSC), for evaluating tourism and hospitality Websites. It traces the use of the approach from its beginning in 1999 to the present time. Before describing the history of the modified BSC approach, the original BSC must be explained.

THE ORIGINAL BALANCED SCORECARD EXPLAINED

One of the most influential management tools to have appeared on the corporate scene in the past two decades is the Balanced Scorecard (BSC). Developed just over a decade ago by Robert Kaplan and David Norton (1992; 1993), the proliferation of its use in managing and assessing organizational performance today has been exceptional. The success of this relatively new measure can be attributed to the fact that it came at a time when there was a need to break away from measuring company performance on solely financial measures. The BSC was used by at least 60 percent of Fortune 1000 companies in the U.S. at the end of 2001, while 39 percent of Fortune 100 companies in the U.K. had adopted it (Bourne, 2002). However, it is imperative to look beyond the statistics and focus on the foundation of the BSC to fully understand its relevance in Website evaluation.

The BSC in the most basic terms is a set of carefully selected measures originating from the organization's vision and strategy (Niven, 2002). In expanding this definition Niven (2002) further describes the BSC as a tool used by company executives to communicate to employees and shareholders the outcomes of the company's value drivers and their success in achieving the vision and objectives. The Balanced Scorecard Collaborative (2002) defines the BSC as "a tool that translates an organization's mission and strategy into a comprehensive set of performance measures that provide the framework for a strategic measurement and management system."

The BSC specifies that performance should be measured from four perspectives: customer, financial, learning and growth, and internal business processes. It captures both the financial and non-financial elements of a company's strategy, and examines the cause-and-effect relationships that drive business results. This allows organizations to be more strategic in their approach by using lead indicators as against following the traditional system by using lag indicators that were more suited for the "Old Economy." Lead indicators are defined by Niven (2002) as the drivers of future economic performance, while the lag indicators, such as financial measures, represent the outcomes of actions previously taken, which provide an excellent account of historical performance and events.

Operating under the basic premise that measurement motivates, or in other words, "what gets measured, gets done," the BSC is so influential that it commands attention even when there are no incentives linked to the achievement of specific goals (Balanced Scorecard Collaborative, 2002). In one single management report, many of the seemingly disparate elements of a company's competitive agenda are brought together in such a way that management is led to consider the effects of one activity on another (Kaplan & Norton, 1992). Consequently, a company's vision and strategy are seamlessly translated into logical performance measures that are easily associated at the various levels of the organization.

The performance measures as subdivided by Kaplan and Norton (1992; 1993) are described as follows. The financial perspective addresses the question of "How do we look to shareholders?" Essentially, traditional monetary measures such as profitability, revenue growth, and shareholder value are monitored. The second perspective is that of the customer and answers the question of "How do customers see us?" It measures indicators such as service levels, satisfaction ratings, customer retention, as well as market share. The third perspective examines internal business processes and procedures and their efficiency at driving the business. It is critical here that management identifies the core competencies and subsequently decides at which processes and competencies they must excel, as well as specifying measures for each. The final perspective deals with innovation, learning, and growth. With a focus on the organization's people and infrastructure, these indicators include intellectual assets, market innovation, and skill development.

Due to intense competition both locally and globally, and in a bid to remain competitive, companies have to continually improve their products/services and processes, a measure that is tied directly to value. Figure 1 shows the integrated relationship among the key parts of the BSC approach; vision, strategy, and the four perspectives. Balance is achieved through the use of the four perspectives, the decomposition of the organization's vision into business strategy and then into operations, and the translation of strategy into the contribution each member of the organization must make to successfully meet goals (Rohm, 2002).

An evaluation of the BSC's usefulness and relevance to corporate financial performance also deserves some discussion. As noted previously, the BSC arose out of the need to measure company performance on more than just

FIGURE 1. Basic Design of a Balanced Score Card Approach

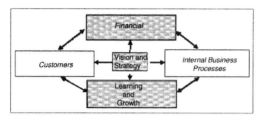

Source: Rohm, H. (2002). Performance measurement in action. *Perform*, (2) 2, 2-5.

financial measures. These measures were acceptable in business up until the late 1980s, when there was a widespread fixation with measuring and managing financial performance. Performance measurement was reliant on reporting systems focused on the past rather than looking toward the future, and this paralleled management's inward looking view (Bourne, 2002). As Kaplan and Norton (1992) stated, today these measures are out of step with the skills and competencies companies are trying to master. The BSC was developed to keep companies looking and moving forward instead of backward, and thus helps organizations compete in the new millennium.

Within tourism and hospitality, Hilton Hotels, the City of Charlotte, North Carolina, and White Lodging Services have used the BSC. With the BSC, Hilton created a systematic business approach to drive consistently high levels of service across its hotels. Using the BSC approach, guest satisfaction rose to 6.25 on a 7-point scale, customer retention rose from 6 per cent to 56 per cent, and revenue per available room increased 2.7 per cent from 1998 to 1999. The City of Charlotte is the second largest financial center in the U.S. and enjoys an annual growth rate of 20 per cent. The BSC is reported to have enabled Charlotte's council-manager government to achieve its vision of creating a "community of choice for living, working, and leisure activities" by focusing Charlotte's varied departments on the City's five stated strategic themes (Balanced Scorecard Online, 2003). By applying the BSC approach, White Lodging Services Corporation, which manages a hotel portfolio chiefly comprising Marriott limited-service franchises, primarily Courtyard, Fairfield Inn,

and Residence Inns, developed a unified measure of how well its hotels were performing from both the managers' and owners' viewpoints (Denton and White, 2000).

THE EVOLUTION OF THE MODIFIED BALANCED SCORECARD (BSC) APPROACH

The Beginning

Morrison, Taylor, Morrison and Morrison (1999) noted that not much had been written about the evaluation of Website effectiveness in the tourism and hospitality literature. These authors recognized that measuring a Website's performance was multi-dimensional, meaning that there was more than one dimension on which a site should be measured. One of the team members, J. Stephen Taylor of the University of Strathclyde's Scottish Hotel School, suggested using an approach that was roughly modeled around Kaplan and Norton's (1992, 1993) BSC approach. It is of interest to note here that Sterne (2002: 50) acknowledges the growing popularity of using the BSC approach for Website evaluation in the broader field of business.

To that end, Morrison et al. (1999) identified four perspectives for hotel Website evaluation; customer, technical, marketing, and internal (Figure 2). They applied a modified BSC approach in evaluating a group of small Scottish hotels, operationalizing each perspec-

FIGURE 2. The Modified BSC Approach

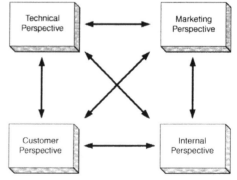

Source: Morrison, A. M., Taylor, J. S.. Morrison, A. J. & Morrison, A. D. (1999). Marketing small hotels on the World Wide Web. *Information Technology & Tourism*, 2 (2). 104.

tive through a set of critical success factors (CSFs). Huotari and Wilson (2001) attributed the CSF concept to Daniel (1961) and Rockart (1979), stating that in any organization certain factors are critical to its success, and the organization will fail if it does not achieve the objectives associated with these factors. In tourism and hospitality Website evaluation, the CSFs represent criteria that a Website must meet in order to be effective. Table 1 shows a list of 25 CSFs for hotel Website evaluation as suggested by Morrison et al.

Although the authors acknowledged the importance of the internal perspective, they were unable to measure all of its CSFs since they did not have access to this information. Additionally, although not acknowledged at that time, the authors recognized that the reliability of the scoring system used in the preliminary study could be questioned. As noted by Ismail, Labropoulos, Mills and Morrison (2002), the use of many Likert scales in the Morrison et al. study introduced a high level of subjectivity into the scoring. Another limitation to the Mor-

rison et al. study was that, although the rater was highly qualified in Website design and marketing, only one of the research team members evaluated all of the Websites of the small Scottish hotels.

Other criticisms that can be made of the Morrison et al. study include how the four perspectives were selected, and whether there might be other viable perspectives for evaluating Website performance or effectiveness. For example, the study certainly did not measure the return on investment of the small hotel Websites. An expert Web designer evaluated the customer's perspective, not the customers themselves. In addition, no one from the subject hotels was involved in the evaluation, so truly the internal perspective was not present. Chung and Law (2003) also criticized the Morrison et al. (1999) study for failing to incorporate the views of hoteliers into the development of the research instrument.

Other authors have also acknowledged that different perspectives can be adopted. For example, according to a literature review by Blum and Fallon (2002), there are three broad directions of Website evaluation: (1) business perspective; (2) customer perspective; and (3) combination of business and customer perspectives. The business evaluation perspective has a focus on the use of a Website for business transformation; that is, moving its Web presence from being information based to transaction based. The customer evaluation perspective has two views; the first has an emphasis on site design issues, and the second is based on consumer behavior theory. Blum and Fallon (2002) placed the modified BSC approach into the combination of business and customer perspectives group.

Another flaw in the original work was that the final scores for the four perspectives were unbalanced; the maximum scores were customer (25), customer (25), technical (22), and internal (5). Finally, it may be said that just evaluating Websites at one point in time is insufficient to reflect the variability in sites over time.

The Evolution

Research Studies

Subsequent studies have applied the modified BSC approach beyond the field of hotels.

TABLE 1. Critical Success Factors for Effective WWW Sites

PERSPECTIVES	CRITICAL SUCCESS FACTORS
Technical	• Currency of links • Effective use of HTML • Reciprocal hyperlinking • Registration with search engines • Short download time • Traffic monitoring and analysis
Marketing	• Positioning approach • Market segmentation and target marketing • Marketing research and database marketing • Relationship marketing • Partnerships • Tangibilizing of hotel services • Marketing evaluation
Internal	• Ease of site maintenance • Schedule for site maintenance and updating • Skills to maintain site
Customer	• Attractiveness • Availability and reservations • Content and organization • Currency of information • Interactivity • Needs of special customer groups • Response verification and speed • Security of purchases • User friendliness

Source: Morrison, A. M., Taylor, J. S., Morrison, A. J. & Morrison, A. D. (1999). Marketing small hotels on the World Wide Web. *Information Technology & Tourism.* 2 (2). 105.

Kim, Morrison and Mills (2002) conducted an evaluation of the performance of the Websites of 10 first-tier U.S. convention centers using the same perspectives as in the original Morrison et al. (1999) study. However, the customer CSFs were modified to reflect the unique needs of convention and meeting planners. Again, only one of the research team members evaluated the 10 convention center sites, so this analysis had the same limitations as the Morrison et al. study. In a follow-up study, Kim et al. (2003) enhanced the Morrison et al. methodology by evaluating the same 10 sites one year later. As such, they were able to track the trends in evaluation scores over a one-year period, and comment upon the individual and overall improvement in Website effectiveness for these major U.S. convention centers. The authors noted in their discussion of limitations that there was a need to also measure more tangible outcomes of tourism and hospitality Websites, including reservations generated and cost reductions through online marketing when compared with traditional promotional methods.

Three subsequent studies modified and improved upon the original Morrison et al. (1999) methodology. Ismail et al. (2002) adopted the modified BSC approach in evaluating the marketing of culture on the Websites of European national tourism organizations (NTOs). The authors substituted a cultural aspects perspective for the internal perspective in the original Morrison et al. study. This was appropriate since they were evaluating the cultural information contents of the NTO Websites, and also because they recognized the difficulties in measuring the internal CSFs. Ismail et al. (2002) renamed the customer perspective as the site visitor relationship aspects, and reorganized the evaluation criteria into four groups, ease of navigation, ease of contact, attractiveness of the site, and general availability of travel and tourism links.

More importantly, the measurement scales were changed from Likert formats to dichotomous "yes/no" questions indicating the presence or absence of specific site features. This removed the aforementioned level of subjectivity noted in the Morrison et al. study. The Ismail et al. (2002) study introduced a more sophisticated approach to ranking Websites,

employing Kendall's Coefficient of Concordance. Non-parametric rather than parametric statistical techniques were applied recognizing both the type of data and the small number of cases involved. Denmark was ranked first in the study, followed by Spain, Finland, and Holland. The authors also found that some countries with impressive cultural resources (e.g., Greece and Portugal) were not using the Web effectively to promote these assets.

Similarly, Feng, Morrison and Ismail (2003) evaluated and compared destination marketing organization (DMO) Websites in China and the U.S. using the modified BSC approach. The four perspectives measured were marketing strategies, Web page design, marketing information, and technical quality. The marketing information perspective replaced the cultural aspects in the Ismail et al. (2002) study, and measured the broader destination information content of sites. Three qualified researchers evaluated a total of 64 Websites (30 in the U.S. and 34 in China). Both English and Chinese language Websites were rated. The results showed that the performance of U.S. DMO Websites was superior to their Chinese counterparts, and especially with respect to marketing strategies and information. U.S. convention and visitor bureau Websites received the highest evaluations among all DMO tiers (local, state, and national).

So and Morrison (2002) applied the modified BSC approach in evaluating the Websites of 14 NTOs in East and South East Asia. The overall approach was somewhat similar to the Feng et al. (2003) study, using the four perspectives of technical, marketing, customer, and destination information. A weighting procedure was used to ensure that each of the four perspectives made an equal contribution to the total score for each NTO Website. The So and Morrison (2002) study used only one qualified evaluator, and all of the DMO sites that were rated were in English. Using a similar approach to Kim et al. (2003), So and Morrison (2003) completed a second analysis of the 14 Websites using the same criteria. In both 2002 and 2003, Singapore, Hong Kong, and South Korea received the best evaluations. However, it was concluded that most of the other countries were not making the most effective use of their Websites.

Practical and Industry Applications of the Modified BSC

Since 1999, the modified BSC approach has been used to evaluate convention and visitor bureau (CVB) Websites as part of the Certified Destination Management Executive (CDME) program. With over five years of use in two of the International Association of CVB's CDME courses, the perspectives and items in the modified BSC approach have been found to be both valid and practical by several hundred CVB senior executives and marketing managers. However, while doing the CDME Website evaluations, the drawbacks in the initial modified BSC instrument were recognized. During the summer of 2000, Mills and Morrison designed a standardized evaluation form based on the modified BSC. The aim was to have an instrument that could be used by customers, expert panels, and businesses with enough flexibility to make changes based on the industry sector under investigation (e.g., hotels, destination marketing organizations, tour operators, etc.). This instrument formed the basis of the Feng, Morrison and Ismail (2003) study as well as the So and Morrison (2002) and Kim et al. (2003) studies.

A copy of the standardized form is shown in Appendix 1. New perspectives added in the standardized form were legal compliance, trip planner assistance, and link popularity. The standardized form designed for CVB Website evaluation is comprised of seven main categories; technical aspects, user friendliness, site attractiveness, marketing effectiveness, link popularity, trip planner assistance, and legal compliance. Each category receives its own score and then the seven category scores are combined to provide an overall score for the Website. In the first category, ratings on technical aspects are achieved by allotting scores for link check, html check, browser compatibility, load time, and spell check on Net Mechanic (accessible at www.netmechanic.com). The scores for technical aspects, which are determined on a scale of 1 to 5, are obtained directly from Net Mechanic. All other categories with the exception of the fifth category, link popularity, use a scale of 0 to 4 where 0 is the lowest score representing a feature not present on the site, while 4 is the highest score representing an excellent representation of a feature. Zero was noted as

important to the rating system as some features that are important to the site may not be present at the time of evaluation; therefore, strong arguments for its inclusion could be made. In evaluating site attractiveness, the Website is scrutinized on text, contrast, aesthetics, and use of space. Marketing effectiveness is determined by the information, research, products, segmentation, and positioning evident from perusing the site. Additionally, the site is judged on how effectively the product is tangibilized, existence of partnerships, globalization, and customer service.

The fifth category determines the link popularity of the site by searching for the number of hits on search engines such as Altavista, Google and Hotbot (accessible at www.linkpopularity.com). In trip planner assistance, the site is evaluated on the information provided to visitors with respect to getting around the destination, essential visitor information, travel documents, weather, bank information, and things to do. Finally, the legal compliance category seeks to clarify the position of the site owners as it relates to copyright disclaimers, trademark displays, usage terms, and privacy issues.

The modified BSC approach was also used as the basis for a comprehensive student project in a graduate level marketing class at Purdue University. Over a three-year period, the approach was applied to airlines, CVBs, cruise lines, luxury hotels, resorts, restaurants, state tourism offices, tour operators, theme parks, travel agencies, and volunteer vacation organizations. This indicated the need to slightly modify the BSC approach to better fit the unique characteristics of each type of tourism and hospitality organization. Other university programs have used the modified BSC approach, including students at the University of Delaware in an E-service Management class who have also evaluated a variety of tourism and hospitality Websites.

Other Website Evaluation Approaches

Other researchers have attempted evaluation studies of tourism and hospitality Websites by using the content analysis methodology. For example, Benckendorff and Black (2000) evaluated the Websites of 16 regional tourism authorities (RTAs) in Australia. They proposed the concept of an Internet Marketing Star, with four points comprising site planning, design, content, and management characteristics. Weeks and Crouch (1999) did a content analysis of 20 sites from six tourism and hospitality sectors in Australia. Park (2003) evaluated the Websites of 23 large Korean travel agencies through a content analysis that measured factors such as the availability of online reservations, a home page in English, tourism information and company background, electronic boards, interactive communication tools, product search engines, links, cyber events, special prices, and customized products.

Blum and Fallon (2002) did an evaluation of 53 Websites of Welsh visitor attractions using six groups of features (product, price, promotion, place, customer relations, and technical aspects). They categorized the attractions in Wales into seven distinct categories and then evaluated the Websites using content analysis to determine which features were present. Blum and Fallon (2002) found that the attractions' Websites failed to make adequate use of the place (online purchases and distribution), promotion, and customer relations features. Perdue (2001) evaluated major North American ski resorts using four general Website characteristics; speed and quality of site accessibility, ease of navigation, visual attractiveness of the site, and quality of information content. Fifty students studying business at a U.S. university did the ratings in a controlled, computer laboratory setting. Using regression analysis, a conceptual model was tested, and it was found that the perceived quality of a resort as presented through its Website, was primarily a function of the site's navigation, visual attractiveness, and information content.

Certain specialized evaluations of Websites have also been completed with a focus on specific aspects of the sites. Law and Leung (2000) did an analysis of the Websites of 30 airlines around the world to evaluate their online reservation services. The results were presented for three components of reservation services (flight schedules and availability; airfares; and online ordering information). Differences were found in what was provided on the Websites according to the three regions of the airlines (North America; Europe and Middle East; and Asia and Australia). Using the experi-

mental design method, Jeong and Lambert (2001) had 250 conference attendees evaluate the information quality of eight hypothetical hotel Websites. A content analysis of hotel Websites to determine the extent to which they were applying relationship marketing techniques was conducted by Gilbert and Powell-Perry (2002). The results indicated the current usage rates of various Web-based relationship marketing mechanisms, including information, reservations, loyalty programs, newsletters, special gestures, feedback, customer service, public relations, value-added services, employee Websites, channel member Websites, and customized research.

Countryman (1999) conducted a content analysis on all 50 official state tourism Websites in the U.S. The study evaluated the application of marketing concepts in the design and creation of state tourism Websites. The evaluation criteria included accessibility, segmentation, positioning, consumer research based on the use of cookies, design, content, and hyperlinks. Based on his findings, Countryman (1999) concluded that many of the state tourism Websites had not taken the full advantage of the interactive nature of the Internet. His research also suggested that state tourism Websites should better integrate market segmentation to offer more specific information to interest groups such as meeting planners, travel agents, state residents, and others.

In a similar effort, Wan, Su and Shih (2000) conducted an evaluation using content analysis of the Websites of 60 international tourist hotels and 78 wholesalers in Taiwan. The evaluation criteria used in this study were user friendliness, variety of information, community, and online reservations systems. Their results showed that while user interface rated the highest, most sites were rated low on the variety of information offered, with only a few of them having a virtual community on their Websites. Additionally, the findings revealed that online reservations were more prevalent on hotel rather than on tour operator sites.

Chung and Law (2003) defined five major hotel Website dimensions (facilities information, customer contact information, reservations information, surrounding area information, and management of Websites) to measure the performance of Hong Kong hotels. Choi (2003) used a content analysis to evaluate the effectiveness of the Web marketing of 100 U.S. fine dining restaurants. Seven types of content were evaluated; information clearing house, public relations, interactive brochure, virtual storefront and direct sales, marketing research, encouragement, and other Internet activities. The author concluded that Web marketing by restaurants was still in its infancy, as they were not yet taking full advantage of e-commerce potential. Table 2 provides a summary of the previously discussed Website evaluation studies.

Additionally, there are Website evaluation systems and services available through the private sector. For example, Randall Travel Marketing produces the *Annual Tourism Destination Website Comparative Study*, which ranks CVB and state tourism office Websites in the U.S. on four major criteria (search engine optimization, site navigation and content, quality assurance, and technical interface) (Randall

Travel Marketing, 2003). On a broader industry scale, AC Nielsen offers a Website evaluation and e-strategy service (AC Nielsen, 2003).

Qualitative approaches are also in use for Website analysis. For example, Nielsen and Tahir (2002) produced a Website usability text, which evaluates all aspects of the site using a discussion type approach with the authors acting as qualified expert panelists in the area of Web usability. The authors used a qualitative approach to examine and discuss various features present on the Website and to obtain what they term "a screen real estate" output.

A final topic that should be addressed is the array of units of measurement available for measuring the success of Websites, the so-called Web metrics (Sterne, 2002). According to NetGenesis/SPSS Inc. (2003b), the data-gathering power of the Web requires non-traditional metrics, or *e-metrics* that measure

TABLE 2. Summary of Website Evaluation Studies in Tourism and Hospitality

Approach and Authors	Industry Sector Focus and Geographic Area	Method	Evaluators/Evaluations
Modified BSC			
Morrison et al. (1999)	Small hotels; Scotland	Content analysis (16)	One expert; one evaluation
Kim et al. (2002)	Large convention centers; USA	Content analysis (10)	One expert; one evaluation
So et al. (2002)	National tourism organizations; East and South East Asia	Content analysis (14)	One expert; one evaluation
Feng et al. (2002)	Destination marketing organizations; USA and China	Content analysis (64)	Three experts; one evaluation
Ismail et al. (2002)	National tourism organizations; Europe	Content analysis (15)	One expert; one evaluation
Kim et al. (2003)	Large convention centers; USA	Content analysis (10)	One expert; two evaluations
So et al. (2003)	National tourism organizations; East and South East Asia	Content analysis (14)	One expert; two evaluations
Other			
Murphy et al. (1996)	Hotel chains and independent hotels; USA	Content analysis (36)	One expert (*); one evaluation
Cano and Prentice (1998)	Tourism marketing agencies; Scotland	Content analysis (130)	One expert (*); one evaluation
Weeks and Crouch (1999)	Six industry sectors; Australia	Content analysis (20)	One expert (*); one evaluation
Benckendorff and Black (2000)	Regional tourism authorities; Australia	Content analysis (16)	One expert (*); one evaluation
Law and Leung (2000)	Airlines; worldwide	Content analysis (30)	One expert (*); one evaluation
Jeong and Lambert (2001)	Hotels; hypothetical	Experimental design (8)	Conference attendees; one evaluation
Perdue (2001)	Top 50 downhill ski resorts; USA and Canada	Content analysis (50)	Students (50); one evaluation
Blum and Fallon (2002)	Attractions; Wales	Content analysis (53)	One expert (*); one evaluation
Gilbert and Perry (2002)	Hotels; worldwide	Content analysis (140)	One expert (*): two evaluations
Choi (2003)	Fine dining restaurants; USA	Content analysis (100)	One expert (*); one evaluation
Chung and Law (2003)	Hotels; Hong Kong	Content analysis (80)	One expert (*); one evaluation
Park (2003)	Travel agencies; South Korea	Content analysis (23)	One expert (*); one evaluation

(*) Assumed because not specifically stated in the articles or proceedings.

Website success. Patton (2002) identified Web metrics for business-to-consumer (B2C) Websites (net dollar per visitor, clickstream, customer drop-off rates), content sites (loyalty index, customer satisfaction), and business-to-business (B2B) sites (site performance, user efficiency, average time spent on system). NetGenesis/SPSS Inc. (2003a) offer an even greater range of Web metrics or what they call e-metrics. These include stickiness, slipperiness, focus, and velocity, which are four measures of customer behavior on a Website. From the perspective of promotional investment in Websites, they suggest the metrics of acquisition cost, cost per conversion, net yield, and connect rate. Also mentioned are the use of recency, frequency, and monetary value to determine a Website's best customers. Inan (2002) offers another useful set of Web metrics divided into reach, acquire, convert, and retain stage measures. He also recommends best customer analysis. Sterne (2002), NetGenesis/SPSS Inc. (2003a; 2003b), and Inan (2002) provide many valuable yardsticks to measure the success of Websites. However, all three acknowledge that there is a plethora of perspectives and measures available, but a general lack of standards and measurement criteria.

The Future

The preceding analysis provides adequate proof there is a need to develop more standardized approaches and measurement criteria for tourism and hospitality Websites. In the private sector, this need will intensify in the future, as companies will demand to know the ROIs of their Websites, and the sites' performance relative to more traditional information and promotional media such as advertising. As more e-commerce is transacted through tourism and hospitality Websites, there will be a greater ability in the private sector to measure more tangible outcomes such as bookings and sales. In the non-profit and government sector, the growing demand for accountability will bring increased scrutiny to all forms of marketing, including that done on the Internet. The modified BSC approach has some poten-

tial in providing a standardized approach for the evaluation of tourism and hospitality Websites. As acknowledged by its originators, this approach currently has its limitations. The following are some suggestions as to how the modified BSC approach could be used more effectively in the future.

Industry sectors: With certain modifications, the modified BSC approach can be applied to all sectors of tourism and hospitality. To date, however, the approach has not been used with rental car companies or the full range of attractions (e.g., museums, national and state parks), and service organizations. There is also considerable scope for using it with restaurants and other food service operations. The use of a standardized instrument, criteria, and measures will allow sector-to-sector comparisons in the future. This will be vital to determining within-sector performance, and for judging an organization's Website performance versus its peers. There are no such standards of performance existing at present.

Evaluators: Qualified subject matter experts in tourism and hospitality, marketing, and Website design have been used as the evaluators in almost all previous applications of the modified BSC approach. In future, other groups of people can and should be incorporated into the process, including customers and managerial staff from the organizations involved. Groups of customers could be asked to complete the evaluations of the customer perspective or to validate the customer perspective scores of expert evaluators through focus groups or other methods. Managers from the organizations could be involved in measuring the internal perspective. In addition, a panel of marketing managers might be used to validate the scores on the marketing perspective. Finally, it is recognized that using more expert evaluators and other steps are needed to improve and measure inter-rater reliability in the application of the modified BSC approach.

Timeframes: Most of the previous applications of the modified BSC approach included only one evaluation at a specific time; giving just a "snapshot in time" as Ismail et al. (2002) suggested. Added value will be gained from performing several evaluations with a standard methodology and instrument over a certain time period. This was clearly demonstrated in the Kim et al. (2003) and So and Morrison (2003) studies, as they were able to track changes in individual Websites and overall within the sectors between two points in time. It was also very beneficial in Gilbert and Powell-Perry's (2002) study as it enabled them to trace the progression in the use of online relationship marketing techniques by hotels between May 1997 and November 1999.

The Web environment and technology is constantly changing, and Websites are also in a continuous state of evolution. In such a dynamic situation, a one-time evaluation of a site is certainly interesting, but inadequate. There is a need in tourism and hospitality to develop a set of standardized evaluation perspectives and measures, and to have these applied at least once a year to determine the evolution of Website performance in specific sectors of the business.

Perspectives and measures: Certainly there is scope to add other perspectives to the modified BSC approach and to have other yard-sticks to measure Website performance. Log file analyzer programs, such as WebTrends (NetIQ), provide very useful statistics on the traffic to individual Websites, which Inan (2002) refers to as *Website-traffic analysis*. However, these data are proprietary to individual sponsoring organizations and group comparisons could not be made without a voluntary pooling of the data from the log file analyzer programs. The conversion rate is another measure that can be employed, and this has been used by several DMOs to determine the proportions of the people who visit their Websites that eventually also visit the destination. McLemore and Mitchell (2001) found a very high conversion rate for those who visited Arkansas' state tourism Website. Some 64.6 per cent of the Website visitors who requested a vacation planning kit visited Arkansas. A similar result was found in the *2001 Nova Scotia Tourism Evaluation Study* (Tourism Nova Scotia, 2002), in which the provincial tourism Website had a conversion rate of 43 per cent.

Seeking to add a benchmarking and more rigorous approach for Website analysis, while also including analysis from the customer perspective, Mills and Morrison (2003) employed a structural equation modeling approach to evaluate consumer evaluation of various Website factors. Based on a review of literature, the authors developed and tested the model shown in Figure 3. Contending that customer satisfaction should be the outcome of Website evaluation, the model proposed that customer satisfaction is a direct result of the customer's experience at a Website. The customer's Website experience, in turn, was seen as a multi-dimensional construct impacted by the travel Website interface, perceived quality of the services and products offered by the travel Website, and the perceived value of the travel Website to the customer. A positive experience at the travel Website was expected to lead to higher levels of e-satisfaction (E-SAT) with the travel Website. The model also proposed that the three constructs of interface, quality, and value were second-order factors and collectively, were a function of 14 first-order factors including access, loading, appearance, and other factors as shown in Figure 3. The model was tested using a total sample of 611 college students in an online forum. The testing phase using confirmatory factor analysis and structural equation modeling supported the proposed model.

Website evaluation cannot be accomplished unless a clear set of objectives has been established for a site. These objectives themselves must be appropriate based upon the organization's resources and the Website's capabilities. Kaplan and Norton (1992) in their original *Harvard Business Review* article recommended that goals be established for the four BSC perspectives. Likewise, greater value can be created from using the modified BSC approach if an organization establishes clear and appropriate objectives for each of the perspectives included in the Website evaluation.

FORMATIVE AND SUMMATIVE EVALUATION OF EFFICIENCY AND EFFECTIVENESS

It is clear that there are many potential ways to evaluate tourism and hospitality Websites, and the modified BSC approach is just one of them. As mentioned earlier, some have argued that there are three broad categories of evalua-

FIGURE 3. Model of Customer Satisfaction with Travel Websites

Source: Mills, J. E. and Morrison, A. M. (2003). Measuring Customer Satisfaction with Online Travel. *International Federation of Information and Communications Technologies in Tourism 2003 Conference Proceedings*. Helsinki, Finland, January 27-February 1, 2003.

tion approaches, business, customer, and combined business and customer (Blum & Fallon, 2002). Another view of Website evaluation techniques is to classify them into either formative or summative evaluations. Formative evaluation occurs during the time a program or activity is being implemented, mainly to measure performance on a regular basis so that strengths and weaknesses can be detected and corrective actions taken. Summative evaluation takes place after a program or activity has been completed, and essentially documents the program or activity results.

Two other concepts of evaluation are whether efficiency or effectiveness is being measured. Although there are many arguments over the exact meanings of these two terms, effectiveness here is defined as the ability to meet pre-specified objectives measured by tangible outcomes. Efficiency typically means getting the most out of organizational resources at the lowest comparative cost. However, with promotions it is usually interpreted as measuring indicators of levels of customer activity in response to specific promotions, e.g., enquiries received, coupons redeemed, and hits on a Web page. Table 3 combines the concepts of formative and summative evaluation with efficiency and effectiveness, and indicates general measures for Website evaluation.

Table 4 lists more specific measures for Website evaluation. It suggests that the modified BSC approach can be classified as a summative evaluation technique to measure Website effectiveness. It also indicates that there are other summative measures of effectiveness that must be determined, such as amount of e-commerce transactions and return on investment.

Undoubtedly, the ultimate measure of the success of a tourism and hospitality Website is its return on investment (ROI). With the increasing incorporation of online sales and booking features into private sector Websites, it will be possible to compare Website sales versus costs. However, as mentioned earlier,

non-profit and governmental organizations will continue to face difficulties in accurately measuring the ROIs of their Websites.

Table 5 provides a suggested set of reasons for doing Website evaluations many of which could be translated into objectives for Websites. The first column shows the perspectives within which Website objectives can be framed. The second column indicates the reasons for formative Website evaluations. These involve monitoring and tracking Website performance, continually assessing strengths and weaknesses, and taking corrective action if needed. The third column lists the potential reasons for summative Website evaluation. These include getting results through using an approach like the modified BSC, and gathering data on annual Website traffic volumes, reservations and bookings, costs, and sales. They also incorporate comparisons

TABLE 3. General Measures for Website Evaluation

	Efficiency	Effectiveness
Formative Evaluation	• Measuring levels of activity on a Website during the year or other planning period	• Measuring progress towards objectives during the year or other planning period
Summative Evaluation	• Measuring levels of activity on a Website for the whole year or other planning period	• Measuring the degree of achievement of objectives at the end of the year or other planning period

TABLE 4. Specific Measures for Website Evaluation

	Efficiency	Effectiveness
Formative Evaluation	• Website traffic analysis (e.g., hits, page views, unique visits by week or month) • Number of bookings or reservations by week or month	• E-commerce transactions (e.g., sales resulting from bookings or reservations for week or month)
Summative Evaluation	• Website traffic analysis (e.g., hits, page views, unique visits for year) • Number of bookings or reservations for year	• E-commerce transactions (e.g., total sales resulting from bookings or reservations for year) • Modified BSC approach scores • Return on investment on Website costs (development and maintenance)

TABLE 5. Reasons for Conducting Website Evaluations

Perspectives	Formative	Summative
Financial	• Track costs associated with Website maintenance and redesign	• Determine all costs associated with Website • Determine online sales • Calculate return on investment
Marketing	• Monitor volumes of Website traffic and traffic patterns (hits, page views, unique visits) • Monitor numbers of reservations and bookings • Determine marketing strengths and weaknesses • Improve marketing approaches on Website	• Calculate total traffic to Website through log file analyzer software • Determine the impact of specific promotions on Website traffic volume • Track numbers of reservations and bookings • Compare Website marketing effectiveness to performance last year (e.g., through BSC)
Customer Service	• Determine strengths and weaknesses in customer service aspects • Improve customer service features of Website	• Compare Website customer service effectiveness to performance last year (e.g., through BSC)
Competitors	• Identify competitors with the most effective Websites • Determine strengths and weaknesses relative to competitors • Improve Website relative to competitors	• Compare performance relative to competitors • Compare performance relative to industry norms or standards
Website Design	• Determine strengths and weaknesses in Website design • Improve Website design	• Compare Website technical effectiveness to performance last year (e.g., through BSC)

with the previous years, with competitors, and with industry standards.

CONCLUSIONS

In summary, it is fair to say that Website evaluation in tourism and hospitality is still in its early stages of development. As yet there are no standardized criteria, tools or techniques for evaluating sites. For the past eight years, academics, consultants, and practitioners have been experimenting with different approaches, and the modified BSC has been one of these. As acknowledged by its originators, the modified BSC approach has its limitations, which to some extent have been corrected in follow-up studies. In addition, it does not measure all aspects of a tourism and hospitality Website, nor does it evaluate a Website from every possible perspective. However, the major contribution of the modified BSC approach is in suggesting an organizing framework for Website evaluation. This framework forces site evaluators to consider multiple perspectives of a Website, and to give equal weighting to each perspective in arriving at the overall measurement of performance. Kaplan and Norton (1992, p. 71), the originators of the BSC, argued, "no single measure can provide a clear performance target or focus attention on the critical areas of the business." Likewise no single perspective or set of measures of a Website can produce a full assessment of its effectiveness.

It seems imperative that any holistic Website evaluation approach must have at its foundation an assessment of the technical details of the site design. Insufficient attention to site design and search engine positioning greatly reduce the value of good content and sound marketing. Viewing a site from the customer's or other user's perspective should be another element of a comprehensive evaluation process. Almost every previous research study has examined elements of user friendliness, interactivity, and relationship building. Although not exclusively a marketing channel, tourism and hospitality organizations primarily use their sites to promote and sell their services and products. Therefore, evaluating the marketing effectiveness of sites is warranted. Another perspective in site evaluation can either be a customized content analysis,

or an overall assessment of the site from the organization's internal perspective, which may incorporate an ROI calculation. Checking the legal compliance of the site is another aspect of evaluation that should be considered. Most of these perspectives, with the exception of ROI, have been addressed in the applications of the modified BSC.

In conclusion, this article has cited many different attempts, including modified BSC approach studies, to determine the effectiveness of groups of Websites in different tourism and hospitality sectors. While these studies have differences in approaches, there are also similarities among them in evaluation criteria and methods (primarily content analysis). There is a definite need in the future to draw together these approaches into a unified evaluation procedure.

Allowances will have to be made for the unique characteristics of certain groups of organizations (e.g., cruise lines vs. tour operators), but most of the perspectives or evaluation criteria and measures can be standardized across tourism and hospitality. Industry leaders within trade associations should work together with academics and private consultants to develop greater standardization in Website evaluation methods. There remain methodological issues that academics still have to resolve, some of which have been identified earlier. Industry leaders and consultants can provide valuable advice on the perspectives and specific evaluation criteria that are most useful to them. Sterne (2002: 65) clearly supports this conclusion in saying, "We have to agree on definitions of terms and agree on methodologies of measurement. We have to find a way to discuss best practices to determine how to collect the numbers, what formulas to use, and which results are common enough to be called benchmarks."

It is impossible at this point to pinpoint the state of the art in Website evaluation for tourism and hospitality. Academics have proposed a variety of approaches and research methodologies in the past eight years, and have not reached a consensus on what are the best criteria and practices. Additionally, practitioners and consultants are struggling to fill the void with a hodgepodge of solutions, none of which provide comprehensive Website evaluations. Given this situation, the paper's sub-title, "The

Art Is Not Yet Stated," seems a most appropriate description of Website evaluation to date in tourism and hospitality. The gauntlet has certainly been thrown down for the industry to set its own standards, but one must wonder if in the absence of such standards, consumer groups and their advocates will seek to fill the void. Given the often significant costs of travel, is the *Consumer Reports* of tourism and hospitality Websites a concept that is just around the corner in the future?

REFERENCES

AC Nielsen. (2003). Website evaluation & e-strategy. Retrieved June 9, 2003, from http://www.acnielsen.com.au/product.asp?ProductID=58

Balanced Scorecard Collaborative (2002). *Executing strategy with the balanced scorecard: An introduction to the strategy-focused organization.* Retrieved September 24, 2002, from http://www.bscol.com

Balanced Scorecard Online, (2003). *Balanced Scorecard Hall of Fame.* Retrieved May 30, 2003, from http://www.bscol.com/bsc_online/learning/hof/index.cfm?id=F33F0A47-B9D1-4AC0-AA564C6D1B9F764A

Benckendorff, P. J., & Black, N. L. (2000). Destination marketing on the Internet: A case study of Australian Regional Tourism Authorities. *Journal of Tourism Studies*, 11 (1), 11-21.

Blum, V., & Fallon, J. (2002). Welsh visitor attraction Websites: Multipurpose tools or technological tokenism. *Information Technology & Tourism*, 4, 191-201.

Bonn, M. A., Furr, H. L., & Susskind, A. M. (1998). Using the Internet as a pleasure travel planning tool: An examination of the sociodemographic and behavioral characteristics among Internet users and nonusers. *Journal of Hospitality & Tourism Research*, 22 (3), 303-317.

Bonn, M. A., Furr, H. L., & Susskind, A. M. (1999). Predicting a behavioral profile for pleasure travelers on the basis of Internet use segmentation. *Journal of Travel Research*, 37 (4), 333-340.

Bourne, M. (2002). The emperor's new scorecard. *Financial World.* Retrieved April 2, 2003, from www.financialworld.co.uk/magazine/mag.pdf/augustpdf/P48-50BALANCEDSCORECARD_C3.pdf

Cano, V., & Prentice, R. (1998). Opportunities for endearment to place through electronic 'visiting': WWW homepages and the promotion of Scotland. *Tourism Management*, 19 (1), 67-73.

Connolly, D. J., Olsen, M. D., & Moore, R. G. (1998). The Internet as a distribution channel. *Cornell Hotel and Restaurant Administration Quarterly*, 39 (4), 42-54.

Choi, Y. S. (2003). The Web marketing strategy for fine dining restaurants. *Advances in Hospitality and Tourism Research, Volume 8: Proceedings of the Annual Graduate Education and Graduate Student Research Conference in Hospitality and Tourism*, 98-99.

Chung, T., & Law, R. (2003). Developing a performance indicator for hotel Websites. *International Journal of Hospitality Management*, 22, 119-125.

Countryman, C. C. (1999). Content analysis of state tourism Websites and the application of marketing concepts. *Advances in Hospitality and Tourism Research, Volume 4: Proceedings of the Annual Graduate Conference in Hospitality and Tourism*, 210-218.

Daniel, R. H. (1961). Management data crisis. *Harvard Business Review.* Sept-Oct, 111-112.

Denton, G., & White, B. (2000). Implementing a balanced-scorecard approach to managing hotel operations. *Cornell Hotel and Restaurant Administration Quarterly*, 41 (1), 94-107.

Feng, R., Morrison, A. M., & Ismail, J. A. (2003). East versus west: A comparison of online destination marketing in China and the U.S. *Journal of Vacation Marketing*, 10 (1), 43-56.

Gilbert, D., & Powell-Perry, J. (2002). Exploring developments in Web based relationship marketing within the hotel industry. *Journal of Hospitality & Leisure Marketing*, 9 (3/4), 141-159.

Ho, J. (1997). Evaluating the World Wide Web: A global study of commercial sites. *Journal of Computer-Mediated Communication*, 3 (1). Retrieved September 25, 2002, from http://www.ascusc.org/jcmc/vol3/issue1/ho.html

Huotari, M.-L., & Wilson, T. D. (2001). Determining organizational information needs: The Critical Success Factors approach. *Information Research*, 6 (3). Retrieved October 10, 2002, from http://www.shef.ac.uk/~is/publications/infres/paper108.html

Inan, H. (2002). *Measuring the success of your Website.* Frenchs Forest, NSW: Pearson Education Australia.

Ismail, J. A., Labropoulos, T., Mills, J. E., & Morrison, A. M. (2002). A snapshot in time: The marketing of culture in European Union NTO Websites. *Tourism, Culture & Communication*, 3 (3), 165-179.

Jeong, M., & Lambert, C. (2001). Adaptation of an information quality framework to measure customers' behavioral intentions to use lodging Web sites. *International Journal of Hospitality Management*, 20 (2), 129-146.

Jung, H. S. (1999). The analysis of demographic profiles and prospects of Internet users in national tourism organizations. Case study: Korea National Tourism Organization (KNTO). *Information Technology & Tourism*, 2, 131-138.

Kaplan, R. S., & Norton, D. P. (1992). The balanced scorecard–measures that drive performance. *Harvard Business Review*, January/February, 71-79.

Kaplan, R. S., & Norton, D. P. (1993). Putting the balanced scorecard to work. *Harvard Business Review*, September/October, 134-142.

Kasavana, M. L. (1997). Critiquing club Websites on the Internet. *Club Management*, November-December, 63-70.

Kasavana, M. L. (2002). eMarketing: Restaurant Websites that click. *Journal of Hospitality & Leisure Marketing*, 9 (3/4), 161-178.

Kasavana, M. L., Knutson, B. J., & Polonowski, S. J. (1997). Netlurking: The future of hospitality Internet marketing. *Journal of Hospitality & Leisure Marketing*, 5 (1), 31-44.

Kim, D.-Y., Morrison, A. M., & Mills, J. E. (2002). Examining the Web-based marketing efforts of first-tier city convention centers in the U.S., in Wober, K., Frew, A. J., & Hitz, M. (eds.), *Information and Communication Technologies in Tourism*: 2002, 195-206.

Kim, D. Y., Morrison, A. M., & Mills, J. E. (2003). Tiers or tears? An evaluation of the Web-based marketing efforts of major city convention centers in the *U.S. Journal of Convention & Exhibition Management*, in press.

Law, R., & Leung, R. (2000). A study of airlines' online reservation services on the Internet. *Journal of Travel Research*, 39 (2), 202-211.

McLemore, C., & Mitchell, N. (2001). An Internet conversion study of *www.arkansas.com*: A state tourism Website. *Journal of Vacation Marketing*, 7 (3), 268-274.

Mills, J. E., & Morrison, A. M. (2000). Updated Balanced Score Card Instrument. Available: http://www.htmresearch.atfreeweb.com/BSC.

Mills, J. E., & Morrison, A. M. (2003). Measuring Customer Satisfaction with Online Travel. *International Federation of Information and Communications Technologies in Tourism 2003 Conference Proceedings*. Helsinki, Finland, January 27-February 1, 2003.

Morrison, A. M., Taylor, J. S., Morrison, A. J., & Morrison, A. D. (1999). Marketing small hotels on the World Wide Web. *Information Technology & Tourism*, 2 (2), 97-113.

Murphy, J., Forrest, E. J., Wotring, C. E., & Brymer, R. A. (1996a). Hotel management and marketing on the Internet. *Cornell Hotel & Restaurant Administration Quarterly*, 37 (3), 70-82.

Murphy, J., Forrest, E. J., & Wotring, C. E. (1996b). Restaurant marketing on the Worldwide Web. *Cornell Hotel & Restaurant Administration Quarterly*, 37 (1), 61-71.

NetGenesis/SPSS Inc. (2003a). *E-metrics. Business metrics for the new economy*. Retrieved June 28, 2003, from http://www.spss.com/netgenesis

NetGenesis/SPSS Inc. (2003b). *Measuring success in the new economy*. Retrieved June 28, 2003, from http://www.spss.com/netgenesis

Nielsen, J., & Tahir, M. (2002). *Homepage usability: 50 Websites deconstructed*. Indianapolis: New Riders Publishing.

Niven, P. R. (2002). *Balanced scorecard step-by-step: Maximizing performance and maintaining results*. New York: John Wiley & Sons Inc.

Park, C. (2003). A content analysis of travel agency Websites in Korea. *Asia Pacific Journal of Tourism Research*, 7 (1), 11-18.

Patton, S. (2002). *Web metrics that matter*. Retrieved June 27, 2003, from http://www.cio.com/archive/111502/matter.html

Perdue, R. R. (2001). Internet site evaluations: The influence of behavioral experience, existing images, and selected Website characteristics. *Journal of Travel & Tourism Marketing*, 11 (2/3), 21-38.

Randall Travel Marketing (2003). The 2001/02 annual tourism destination Website comparative study. Retrieved June 9, 2003, from http://www.rtmnet.com/comparative_study.html#Methodology

Rockart, J. F. (1979). Chief executives define their own data needs. *Harvard Business Review*, 57 (2), 238-241.

Rohm, H. (2002). Performance measurement in action. *Perform*, (2) 2, 2-5.

Smith, C., & Jenner, P. (1998). Tourism and the Internet. *Travel & Tourism Analyst*, 1, 62-81.

So, S.-I., & Morrison, A. M. (2002). Virtually there? An evaluation of the Websites of Asian national tourism organizations. *Tourism in Asia: Development, Marketing & Sustainability: The Fifth Biennial Conference*, 539-549.

So, S.-I., & Morrison, A. M. (2003). Internet marketing in tourism in Asia: An evaluation of the performance of East Asian National Tourism Organization Websites. *Journal of Hospitality & Leisure Marketing*, in press.

Sterne, E. (2002). *Web metrics. Proven methods for measuring Web site success*. New York: Wiley Publishing, Inc.

Tierney, P. (2000). Internet-based evaluation of tourism Website effectiveness: Methodological issues and survey results. *Journal of Travel Research*, 39 (2), 212-219.

Tourism Nova Scotia (2002). *Nova Scotia Tourism & Culture 2001 Nova Scotia Tourism Advertising Evaluation Study*. Halifax, Nova Scotia.

Walle, A. H. (1996). Tourism and the Internet: Opportunities for direct marketing. *Journal of Travel Research*, 35 (1), 72-77.

Wan, C. S., Su, A., Y, & Shih, C. C. (2000). A study of Website content analysis of international tourist hotels and tour wholesalers in Taiwan. *Advances in Hospitality and Tourism Research, Volume 5: Proceedings of the Annual Graduate Conference in Hospitality and Tourism Research*, 132-137.

Weber, K., & Roehl, W. S. (1999). Profiling people searching for and purchasing travel products on the World Wide Web. *Journal of Travel Research*, 37 (3), 291-298.

Weeks, P., & Crouch, I. (1999). Sites for sore eyes: An analysis of Australian tourism and hospitality Websites. *Information Technology & Tourism*, 2, 153-172.

APPENDIX 1

Mills and Morrison (2002) Standardized Website Evaluation Form

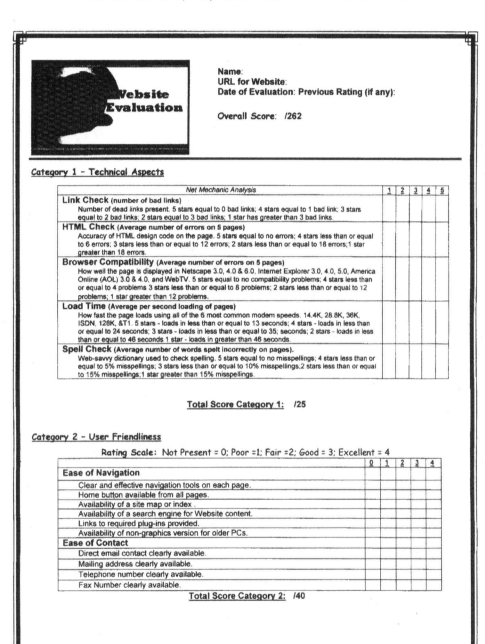

Website Evaluation

Name:
URL for Website:
Date of Evaluation: Previous Rating (if any):

Overall Score: /262

Category 1 – Technical Aspects

Net Mechanic Analysis	1	2	3	4	5
Link Check (number of bad links) Number of dead links present. 5 stars equal to 0 bad links; 4 stars equal to 1 bad link; 3 stars equal to 2 bad links; 2 stars equal to 3 bad links; 1 star has greater than 3 bad links.					
HTML Check (Average number of errors on 5 pages) Accuracy of HTML design code on the page. 5 stars equal to no errors; 4 stars less than or equal to 6 errors; 3 stars less than or equal to 12 errors; 2 stars less than or equal to 18 errors; 1 star greater than 18 errors.					
Browser Compatibility (Average number of errors on 5 pages) How well the page is displayed in Netscape 3.0, 4.0 & 6.0, Internet Explorer 3.0, 4.0, 5.0, America Online (AOL) 3.0 & 4.0, and WebTV. 5 stars equal to no compatibility problems; 4 stars less than or equal to 4 problems 3 stars less than or equal to 8 problems; 2 stars less than or equal to 12 problems; 1 star greater than 12 problems.					
Load Time (Average per second loading of pages) How fast the page loads using all of the 6 most common modem speeds. 14.4K, 28.8K, 36K, ISDN, 128K, &T1. 5 stars - loads in less than or equal to 13 seconds; 4 stars - loads in less than or equal to 24 seconds; 3 stars - loads in less than or equal to 35; seconds; 2 stars - loads in less than or equal to 46 seconds 1 star - loads in greater than 46 seconds.					
Spell Check (Average number of words spelt incorrectly on pages). Web-savvy dictionary used to check spelling. 5 stars equal to no misspellings; 4 stars less than or equal to 5% misspellings; 3 stars less than or equal to 10% misspellings; 2 stars less than or equal to 15% misspellings; 1 star greater than 15% misspellings.					

Total Score Category 1: /25

Category 2 – User Friendliness

Rating Scale: Not Present = 0; Poor =1; Fair =2; Good = 3; Excellent = 4

	0	1	2	3	4
Ease of Navigation					
Clear and effective navigation tools on each page.					
Home button available from all pages.					
Availability of a site map or index .					
Availability of a search engine for Website content.					
Links to required plug-ins provided.					
Availability of non-graphics version for older PCs.					
Ease of Contact					
Direct email contact clearly available.					
Mailing address clearly available.					
Telephone number clearly available.					
Fax Number clearly available.					

Total Score Category 2: /40

APPENDIX 1 (continued)

Category 3 – Site Attractiveness

Rating Scale: Not Present = 0; Poor =1; Fair =2; Good = 3; Excellent = 4

Site Attractiveness	0	1	2	3	4
Clear and readable text.					
Clean and uncluttered pages.					
Sufficient contrast between background and text.					
Effective and aesthetically appealing backgrounds.					
Availability of pictures to reinforce text content.					
Other images used to improve aesthetics of the site.					
Use of color to improve the visual appeal of the site.					
Too long scrolling pages.					
Overall appeal of site.					
Effective use of Web page space.					

Total Score Category 3: /40

Category 4 – Marketing Effectiveness

Rating Scale: Not Present = 0; Poor =1; Fair =2; Good = 3; Excellent = 4

	0	1	2	3	4
Marketing Information					
Current and timely Information.					
Separate links page provide detailing all links available on the site.					
Maps and driving directions.					
Marketing Research					
Contact information gathered from visitors.					
Marketing Products					
Links to hotels and accommodations.					
Links to restaurants.					
Links to local attractions and events.					
Market Segmentation (Provision of specific Information for the following groups:)					
Business travelers					
Children					
Convention/Meeting Groups					
Couples					
Families					
Honeymooners					
Tour Groups					
Culture and arts activities provided.					
Outdoor recreation activities.					
Sporting activities provided.					
Market Positioning					
Mission and purpose of the organization clearly stated.					
Stated theme carried throughout the site.					
Tangibilizing of Products					
Virtual tour and/or map of city.					
Testimonials and/ or awards posted.					
Photo Gallery.					
News Releases.					
Partnership					
Hyperlinks provided to partner organizations.					
Globalization					
Foreign language, special interest sites for foreigners.					
Customer Service					
Inquiries encouraged.					
FAQ					
Guest-book					

Total Score Category 4: /112

<u>**Category 5 – Link Popularity**</u> (Total number of web sites that link to your site)

Rating Scale: average of 0-199 links =1; 200-399=2; 400-699= 3; 600 -1000= 4; Over 1000=5; Not Applicable= N/A

Link Popularity Report **www.linkpopularity.com**	
Altavista number of links **Google** number of links **Hotbot** number of links	

Total Score Category 5: /5

<u>**Category 6 – Trip Planner Assistance**</u>

Rating Scale: Not Present = 0; Poor =1; Fair =2; Good = 3; Excellent = 4

	0	1	2	3	4
Getting around.					
Essential information.					
Documents needed by International travelers.					
Local Weather Information.					
Local Bank Information.					
Things to Do.					

Total Score Category 6: /24

<u>**Category 7 – Legal Compliance**</u>

Rating Scale: Not Present = 0; Poor =1; Fair =2; Good = 3; Excellent = 4

	0	1	2	3	4
Copyright disclaimers.					
Trademark prominently displayed.					
Site usage terms.					
Privacy policy.					

Total Score Category 7: /16

General Comments: (example comments below)

- Very attractive site!

- Navigation can be expanded so that user does not have to continually return to the homepage to access most of the other areas of the site.

- Contact information not readily available. Not having your email, fax, tel. no., and address on the first page can cost you good business, as visitors not wanting to surf a Website for contact information will click away and take their business somewhere else. Also at the top of the contact page, place the contact information clearly so users do not have to read through or scan the entire page to find the CVB address.

Exploring Bed & Breakfast Websites:
A Balanced Scorecard Approach

Sheryl F. Kline
Alastair M. Morrison
Andrew St. John

SUMMARY. This exploratory study was designed to evaluate the Websites of Bed & Breakfast(s) (B&B) belonging to the Indiana B&B Association (IBBA). Using the Balanced Scorecard (BSC) approach, four evaluation perspectives were considered: (1) user friendliness, (2) site attractiveness, (3) marketing effectiveness, and (4) technical aspects. A team of trained evaluators rated a random sample of 20 IBBA property Websites. The study found that the major strength of the B&B Websites evaluated was their attractiveness, but improvements were needed in all four categories. The B&B modified BSC instrument used in this research also showed good inter-rater reliability. *[Article copies available for a fee from The Haworth Document Delivery Service: 1-800-HAWORTH. E-mail address: <docdelivery@haworthpress.com> Website: <http://www.HaworthPress.com> © 2004 by The Haworth Press, Inc. All rights reserved.]*

KEYWORDS. Balanced Scorecard (BSC), Bed and Breakfasts (B&Bs), Internet marketing, Website evaluation, Web marketing

INTRODUCTION

A B&B stay is an interactive experience both for the guest and the owner. It therefore follows that B&Bs should be marketed in an engaging and an interactive manner to their target markets. The Internet and more specifically the Web is one tool that can be used to achieve the goal of interactive or I-marketing. In support of I-marketing for B&Bs Countryman (2000) points out that the Internet provides B&B owners and operators with greater exposure allowing potential guests to see what is offered prior to arriving at the property. However, Lituchy and Rail (2000) argue that innkeepers could use the Internet more, but they are not as many B&B owners are not aware of what to do to enhance their Website marketing effectiveness. Selz and Schubert (1998) note that it is unclear as to what makes a viable, effective B&B Website. Despite this lack of consensus innkeepers now consider the

Sheryl F. Kline is Assistant Professor and Director, Center for the Study of Lodging Operations, Department of Hospitality and Tourism Management, Alastair M. Morrison is Distinguished Professor of Hospitality and Tourism Management and Associate Dean for Learning, School of Consumer and Family Sciences, and Andrew St. John is a Master's Degree candidate, all at Purdue University.

Address correspondence to Sheryl F. Kline (E-mail: klines@purdue.edu).

[Haworth co-indexing entry note]: "Exploring Bed & Breakfast Websites: A Balanced Scorecard Approach." Kline, Sheryl F., Alastair M. Morrison, and Andrew St. John. Co-published simultaneously in *Journal of Travel & Tourism Marketing* (The Haworth Hospitality Press, an imprint of The Haworth Press, Inc.) Vol. 17, No. 2/3, 2004, pp. 253-267: and: *Handbook of Consumer Behavior, Tourism, and the Internet* (ed: Juline E. Mills, and Rob Law) The Haworth Hospitality Press, an imprint of The Haworth Press, Inc., 2004, pp. 253-267. Single or multiple copies of this article are available for a fee from The Haworth Document Delivery Service [1-800-HAWORTH, 9:00 a.m. - 5:00 p.m. (EST). E-mail address: docdelivery@haworthpress.com].

Web to be their primary marketing tool (Eimer, 2000). Further research on Website marketing is needed to assist B&B owners in building more effective Websites (Countryman, 2000).

In an effort to fill this research gap, the specific objectives of this exploratory research study are as follows:

1. To develop and test an instrument and procedure to objectively evaluate B&B Websites using the modified Balanced Scorecard (BSC) approach.
2. Based on the BSC assess the relative strengths and weaknesses of existing B&B Websites from the marketing, customer, and technical aspects perspectives.
3. To provide a set of recommendations to assist B&B operators to improve the design and marketing of their Websites.

BED AND BREAKFASTS IN THE UNITED STATES

Brief History of the B&B Industry in the U.S.

Traditionally B&Bs were owner-occupied homes converted into lodging establishments (PAII, 2003). Most B&Bs may have one to 20 rooms and these small properties typically serve breakfast which is included in the price of the room rate. B&Bs also offer historical, architectural, or other uniquely charming or memorable features that make each property distinct. Different authors have traced the origins of the development of B&Bs in the U.S. to the 1960s and 1970s (Buchanan & Espeseth, 1991; Lanier & Berman, 1993). In 1968, there were only 15 locations offering B&B accommodations and they were primarily in California (Notarius & Brewer, 2001). Today one can find B&Bs in every state in a range of locations from metropolitan to rural areas. According to a 2000 study, B&Bs, country inns, and small hotels represent 31% of the U.S. lodging industry and are comprised of small businesses renting rooms to travelers (Lodging Resources Workshops & Lanier Publishing, 2003). The Professional Association of Innkeepers International (PAII) has identified approximately

18,000 B&Bs in the U.S. (Valhouli, 2002). As of 2003, 45 states had their own B&B association (BedandBreakfast.com, 2003).

Definition and Distinctions Among B&Bs

Many states and associations attempt to define B&Bs and or differentiate them from hotels. State government licensing divisions each have specific definitions indicating the differences between B&Bs and hotels. For example, Indiana defines a B&B as "an owner-occupied residence that provides sleeping accommodations to the public for a fee, has no more than 14 guest rooms, provides breakfast to its guests as part of the fee, and provides sleeping accommodations for no more than 30 consecutive days to a particular guest (Rule 410 IAC, Section 1)" (Indiana Bed & Breakfast Association, 2003). In contrast, the state of Kansas requires all licensed B&Bs to have four or more rooms that can accommodate eight or more guests. Each guest room must have a private bath (Kansas Bed and Breakfast Association, 2003). PAII is the largest association of B&Bs and divides B&Bs into six categories that range from a homestay of one to three rooms to a B&B hotel with 30-plus rooms located in an historic structure (PAII, 2003). In another attempt to categorize this segment of the lodging industry, Clark (1992) divided the category of B&Bs into a number of subsets: B&Bs, country inns, homestays, and B&B hotels.

While taking into consideration the customers' perspective, another definition of the B&B segment of the lodging industry can be loosely formed. A B&B is a lodging property that offers its guests personal attention and an architecturally interesting or historic structure. It is a property where the owner is highly involved with the daily operation and has a great deal of guest contact (PAII, 2003). The property size and owner interaction is a function of the definition. Therefore, the larger the property, the more likely it is viewed as a hotel. Also, the less the owners are involved with the business, the greater the perception is that this lodging facility is a hotel and not a B&B.

The involvement of the owners is an integral part of any B&B property. Most B&Bs are operated by owners who live on the property and consider themselves to be professional innkeepers (Hotch & Glassman, 1992; Notarius & Brewer, 2001). The personality and hospitality of the innkeeper add to the guest's experience, making the innkeeper's presence and personal touch an important part of the property's uniqueness.

WEB MARKETING AND B&Bs

Traditionally, B&B innkeepers used a range of marketing vehicles to promote and advertise. They have relied on word-of-mouth, association memberships, and promotion through local chambers of commerce or convention and visitor bureaus (CVBs) (Clark, 1992). Print advertising has also been a popular marketing tool, with B&Bs primarily using brochures, newsletters, magazine and phonebook advertisements, and placement in guidebooks (Hotch & Glassman, 1992; Notarius & Brewer, 2001). By the close of the 20th century, the Internet had become the new major source of business for B&Bs in the U.S. In 2000, over 40 percent of new guests located a B&B online. The other 60% relied upon the more traditional marketing vehicles (Notarius & Brewer, 2001). The *Fifth Annual Innkeeper Tracking Study: 2001* noted that 50% of all guests found B&Bs on the Internet, which was a 12 percentage point increase over 1999 (Schleim & Saint-Amour, 2001). Fewer guests found B&Bs from travel guides, print media, and CVBs. The total change in those guest sources declined a total of seven percent from 1999 to 2001. This trend indicates the rising importance of the Internet as a source for new and returning guests.

The fact that B&B guests are using the Internet to view and book their lodging arrangements is only part of a compelling argument for innkeepers to establish and promote their property online. Web users are likely to spend more money at their destinations than non-users (Bonn, Furr, & Susskind, 1998). Older, mature travelers are also using the Internet more often. The Travel Industry Association of America (2001) notes that mature travelers tend to take longer trips (3.9 nights) compared to 3.4 nights on average for travelers overall. Just over half (52%) stay in a hotel, motel or B&B, while 43% stay with friends or relatives. Morrison, Pearce, Moscardo, Nadkarni, and O'Leary (1996) found that the guests of B&Bs tended to be more highly educated and had higher incomes, matching the characteristics of online users. Both the younger, well-educated and mature markets are important to B&Bs.

The benefits of Web marketing can be viewed through the unique characteristics of the innkeeper/owners' circumstances. B&B owner operators are well suited for marketing in the online environment. Web marketing is especially appropriate for B&Bs for at least five reasons: (1) the limited financial resources of B&Bs coupled with the potentially low cost of Web marketing; (2) the aforementioned market profile of online users; (3) the content-rich environment offered by the Web; (4) the uniqueness of each B&B property; and (5) when compared to branded hotels, these innkeepers have a limited ability to compete, gain exposure, and lack the marketing expertise and resources (Countryman, 2000).

Marketing on the Web can be easy and relatively inexpensive. Due to their small size and limited budgets, there is no justification for a full-scale marketing and sales management team at a B&B. The Web therefore represents an affordable and efficient channel for B&Bs to appeal to target markets on a national and even international level. An effective Website may be designed for just under $500 (Morrow, 2001). Kasavana (2002) indicates that with the Web it is possible to have a 24 hour a day, 7 day a week presence and exposure with minimal risk.

However, although the Web is both very important and appropriate for marketing B&Bs very little is known as to how effectively B&Bs are using the Web. A study of small hotels on the Web, to which B&Bs can be compared, found that they were not marketing their Websites as effectively as they could (Morrison, Taylor, Morrison & Morrison, 1999). The authors suggested that small hotel owners needed to improve their Web marketing efforts. When selecting a B&B on the Web, potential guests do not know what to expect in terms of quality giving chain hotels a clear advantage of brand identity as, although not unique, their high levels of market awareness and consistency attract guests. Many small lodging property Websites continue to frustrate Web users who are expecting to book on-line but are unable to make reservations because of a lack of availability of contact information via e-mail, fax or telephone. Countryman (2000) also states that potential guests are often unable to gather sufficient information, via the Website, about a destination prior to traveling. The need therefore exists to develop a standardized instrument to objectively measure various marketing aspects of B&B Websites. This exploratory study attempts to fill this gap through the use of a modified BSC approach using a sample of B&B Websites from Indiana, U.S.

METHODOLOGY

Population and Sample

The Indiana Bed and Breakfast Association (IBBA) is an association of B&B owners that adheres to a high level of operating standards, including an inspection process, and these innkeepers generally employ more sophisticated marketing practices than other B&Bs. IBBA members are regularly reviewed and monitored to ensure that properties meet the association's published standards and practices. At the time of this study, 70 member properties were listed on the IBBA Website, 54 of which had links to their own Websites. Using a random number generator within Microsoft Excel (command *Rand()*), a random number was generated for each B&B. The properties were then sorted from the lowest to highest number, and the first 20 properties were selected for evaluation.

Indiana state law regulations limit B&B properties to renting from one to 14 rooms, and most of the B&Bs are on the lower end of this stated limit. In this study's sample, the number of rooms ranged from two to eleven, with a mean of 5.1. All the B&Bs in this sample offered breakfast as part of the room rate which ranged from $43-$175 per night. The overall average room rate was $92 per night. The lowest average rate was $71.05 with a high of $114.60 per night (Table 1).

Modified BSC Instrument and Measurement Criteria for the Study

Schwartz (1999) identified subjectivity as a problem in Website evaluation, and suggested that a larger variety of measures should be used to reduce it. Due to the subjective nature of evaluating Websites, the modified BSC approach was used because it balances different measures of Website effectiveness. Morrison et al. (1999) adapted the BSC approach from Kaplan and Norton (1992; 1993) to evaluate the Websites of small hotels in Scotland. They analyzed critical success factors (CSFs) from four perspectives: technical, marketing, internal, and customer. They supported Schwartz's contention that Website evaluation is subjective in nature and must be performed with a balanced set of measures.

The researchers in this study used an evaluation approach based on the previous work of Morrison et al. (1999), Garcia (2002), Ismail et al. (2002), and Feng et al. (2003), all stemming from the original Kaplan and Norton (1992; 1993) BSC model. In addition, Countryman (2000), Clark (1992), Hotch and Glassman (1992), and Notarius and Brewer (2001) recommended evaluation criteria specific to B&Bs. Using this as the foundation, the modified BSC instrument developed within this study included four perspectives: quadrant 1 (user friendliness), quadrant 2 (site attractiveness), quadrant 3 (marketing effectiveness), and quadrant 4 (technical aspects), as detailed in Table 2.

User Friendliness (Quadrant 1)

User friendliness was evaluated with nine different yes/no items (Table 2), and one overall question with a four-point Likert scale response. Based on the literature review, these items were all important aspects of B&B Website design. A Website that is easy to navigate enables a potential guest to freely click in and out of pages without causing confusion or distress. The more user-friendly a Website, the more a potential guest is likely to continue to view the B&B information and want to find out more about the property. When a home button is clearly available on every page, this makes it easy to find information without getting con-

TABLE 1. Demographics of Sample of Indiana B&Bs

B&B Name	Region	# Rooms	Lowest Rate	Highest Rate
1877 House Country Inn B&B	South	3	$75.00	$125.00
Angola's Tulip Tree Inn	North	4	$90.00	$125.00
Apple Inn Museum B&B	Central	10	$60.00	$135.00
Big Locust Farm B&B	South	3	$60.00	$90.00
Castlebury Inn	South	6	$60.00	$85.00
Commandant's Home B&B	Central	6	$85.00	$125.00
Gothic Arches B&B	South	5	$69.00	$119.00
Hilltop Farm B&B	Central	2	$79.00	$79.00
Historic Loeb House Inn	Central	5	$85.00	$175.00
Honeymoon Mansion B&B and Wedding Chapel	South	7	$79.00	$169.00
James Wilkins House	South	3	$55.00	$65.00
Katie Scarlett B&B*	Central	3	$43.00	$53.00
Queen Anne B&B	North	6	$70.00	$110.00
Ruddick-Nugent House	Central	4	$69.00	$99.00
The Cottage at West Point	South	3	$75.00	$150.00
The Homespun Country Inn	North	5	$59.00	$79.00
The Inn at Aberdeen, Ltd.	North	11	$97.00	$154.00
The Old Bridge Inn	South	4	$65.00	$115.00
The Oliver Inn B&B	North	7	$94.00	$145.00
The White House on Park Avenue	North	5	$52.00	$95.00
Total	Mean	5.1	$71.05	$114.60
	Mode	3		

*This B&B's data was removed from the analysis due to problems with the Website on the day of evaluation.

fused and lost. This also prevents the user from accidentally closing the browser. Of course, clearly displaying contact information of all kinds (phone, fax, address, and e-mail) is vitally important to communicate with potential guests. The use of buttons enables the user to click from page to page without having to scroll through multiple pages to find information.

Site Attractiveness (Quadrant 2)

Nine specific aspects of site attractiveness were evaluated with yes/no responses (Table 2). An overall question with a four-point Likert scale response was included. If a B&B Website does not have clear and readable text, color, hyperlinks, and good quality photographs and images, then Web page space is being misused. A B&B Website should not be a photocopy of a print brochure, but an interactive display of what is available at the property. Cluttered and unclear pages decrease a

Website's effectiveness. The B&B Website should entice the user's interest, and not turn them away. If the Website is not attractive, then a guest will feel that the B&B itself is not appealing.

Marketing Effectiveness (Quadrant 3)

The researchers identified 18 specific marketing effectiveness criteria (Table 2) to evaluate with yes/no responses. An overall evaluative question with a four-point Likert scale response was again incorporated. The aspects evaluated were all determined to be important for an interactive B&B Website that follows sound marketing principles. These include that the B&B Website should define the uniqueness of the B&B and its surrounding environs by providing information on the history of the property, as well as information about the innkeepers, local events, rates, photographs, awards, testimonials, packages, and

TABLE 2. Modified BSC Quadrant Descriptions

Quadrants	Factors Examined
1. User friendliness (9 items)	**Ease of navigation:** *examples of items:* Site search, Site map, Home button, Navigation tools, Limited scrolling
	Contact information: *examples of items:* Direct e-mail contact, Mailing address, Telephone number, Fax number
2. Site attractiveness (9)	**Visual appeal:** *examples of items:* Pictures, Clear and uncluttered pages, Text readability, Background color
3. Marketing effectiveness (18)	**Product:** *examples of items:* House and room pictures, Virtual tour
	Information availability: *examples of items:* Rate availability, Target markets addressed, Unique aspects of B&B and innkeepers, Local activities and links to activities
4. Technical qualities (5)	**NetMechanic test:** Link check, HTML check, Browser compatibility, Load time, Spell check

promotions. These factors make the virtual experience of the B&B more tangible for the user.

Technical Aspects (Quadrant 4)

The use of NetMechanic.com allowed the researchers to develop an accurate evaluation of the technical design aspects of each Website. The NetMechanic service allows up to five pages to be freely tested per Website. The NetMechanic system conducts link check, hypertext markup language (HTML) check, browser compatibility, load time, and spell check components for each Website. NetMechanic uses a five-star rating per aspect per page (NetMechanic, 2003). Not all the Websites had five or more pages to be evaluated, so comparisons were based on the average scores for the pages assessed.

Pilot Testing of the Instrument

In tandem with the first objective of this study which was to develop and test a Website evaluation instrument specifically designed for B&Bs the instrument was pilot tested. An instrument needs to have validity and reliability in order to be of value to its users. Together with the literature review of B&B marketing data and studies, and the Website evaluation analyses using the modified BSC approach the authors also visited over 100 B&B Websites and piloted a previous version of the instrument (St. John et al., 2003). The instrument was revised based on the feedback from the first instrument. In particular, quadrant 3 was totally redesigned and incorporated more specific marketing effectiveness questions. Therefore, the current instrument has strong content validity with respect to B&B operations and Website marketing.

Data Collection

The researchers invited hospitality and tourism Master's degree students from a U.S. Mid-West university to participate in this study as raters. Nine students were selected to evaluate the 20 B&B Websites. All of the evaluators had prior experience in Website evaluations and each had taken a graduate-level marketing class with a specific focus on Website marketing and evaluation. Evaluations were conducted by the students within the same computer laboratory during the same time frame.

The evaluators were asked to assess the first three quadrants in the study (user friendliness, site attractiveness, and marketing effectiveness) by recording 36 aspects of each of the 20 B&B Websites with a yes (1) if present and a no (0) if not present. A four-point Likert scale measure was also employed to rate the three overall aspects of the quadrants, which was later used to examine the reliability of the measures. The evaluators did not rate the fourth quadrant, as its five attributes were evaluated using the services of NetMechanic. com.

Prior to doing the site evaluations, they participated in a 30-minute training session that provided specific instructions on how to use the modified BSC. The researchers identified and defined each question on the instrument and showed examples from B&B Websites. The B&B Websites used during the training were not part of the sample. For practice, the evaluators rated two B&Bs, not included in the sample, using the BSC instrument. During this training phase, the evaluators were given an opportunity to ask questions and improve their ability to use the instrument. Through this question and answer session definition and qualities outlined in each evaluation item of the instrument were also refined. Prior to collecting the data, the evaluators were advised that they could not talk or look at anyone's score cards while collecting the data.

After the training, the evaluators were given scorecards and a list of the 20 B&B Websites. They were told that they had an unlimited amount of time to complete the evaluations. They were not limited on time to simulate actual Web surfing for travel information. All the evaluators used the same browser (Internet Explorer 6.0) to ensure that they were viewing the Websites in exactly the same way. Due to a potential learning curve effect and social response bias, each evaluator was given the B&B Websites list with a randomly assigned starting point. Therefore, no two evaluators were evaluating a particular B&B at the same time. This was done to prevent a bias toward any of the B&B Websites based upon the order of evaluation.

Throughout the Website evaluation process, three proctors were in the computer laboratory. The proctors ensured that the evaluators did not communicate with each other, thereby controlling for social response bias. The proctors also provided assistance to the evaluators when questions arose with respect to the B&B Websites or measurement criteria.

Statistical Analysis

After all of the evaluation data were collected, the BSC scores were checked for inter-rater reliability. The nine evaluators had used two types of measures on three of the quadrants. The fourth quadrant which was rated by NetMechanic.com and therefore was not checked for inter-rater reliability. Since the evaluation instrument had two scales, two methods were used to check for inter-rater reliability. For the dichotomous questions on the 1 = yes and 0 = no scale, the Kendall's Coefficient of Concordance was calculated. Kendall's Coefficient of Concordance is used when determining inter-rater reliability with three or more evaluators and when the data is dichotomous and then ranked. Because there were nine evaluators and dichotomous ranked data, this statistic was used to determine inter-rater reliability (Wuensch, 2000). Using the SAS software program version 8.02, the coefficient of concordance is calculated as $W = \dfrac{\chi^2}{J(n-1)}$. The chi-square was calculated by using Friedman's chi-square, where n was the number of B&Bs and J equaled the number of evaluators. The Cronbach Coefficient of Alpha was used to compare the Likert-scale responses for the overall ratings of the three quadrants. This analysis determines how well a set of items (or variables) measures a single uni-dimensional latent construct (UCLA Academic Technology Services, 2003). This was also calculated using the SAS software program.

This BSC evaluation measure used two scales, dichotomous and Likert. The relationships between these rankings of the B&Bs on each scale were correlated. The Wilcoxon Signed ranks test for non-parametric statistics was used to determine if there was a statistically significant difference for each quadrant ranking and on the total BSC ranking. This statistic is used with non-parametric statistics and is appropriate for determining whether or not there is a significant association between a dichotomous variable and a continuous variable with independent samples (Wuensch, 2002).

RESULTS

Inter-Rater Reliability

The inter-rater reliability tests for the dichotomous and Likert scale data were performed on the evaluations of the nine raters for quadrants 1, 2, and 3. The Kendall's Coefficient of Concordance was W = 0.6569 with a chi-square of 106.411. The W is always between zero and one, with zero representing complete disagreement and one representing complete agreement. A result in the 0.4 to 0.6 range is considered to indicate a moderate level of agreement, while a 0.6 to 0.8 statistic reflects a substantial level of agreement (Landis & Koch, 1977). The result for the inter-rater reliability of the nine evaluators in this study showed a substantial level of agreement. The Cronbach's Coefficient of Alpha for the four-point Likert scale data was 0.747, an acceptable level of inter-rater reliability (Nunnaly, 1978).

The two scales were compared to see if the dichotomous ranked data was significantly different from the Likert scale ranked data. Using the Wilcoxon Signed ranks test for non-parametric statistics, each scale was compared for the three quadrants and the total BSC ranking. There were no significant differences between the Likert BSC ranks and the dichotomous BSC ranks for all quadrants and the total ranks. The p-value ranged from 0.317 to 0.930. The outcomes of this test were not significant at p < 0.05. Therefore there was no difference between the dichotomous and ranked data. Based on these results, it can be inferred that the two methods of evaluating the B&Bs resulted in the same rankings.

Overall B&B Website Rankings

This research determined which B&B had the best Website based upon a final ranking that gave equal weight to the four quadrants of the BSC. The three quadrants rated by all the evaluators were summed using the following method. The rank for quadrant 1 (user friendliness) was comprised of nine aspects and the nine evaluators rated each B&B on these nine aspects. A score was also given between one and four for the Likert-scale question for user

friendliness. The total for quadrant 1 was computed by adding all the evaluators' scores. The B&Bs were then ranked in order from the highest to lowest total scores for user friendliness (Table 3). The same procedure was repeated for quadrant 2 (site attractiveness) and quadrant 3 (marketing effectiveness).

NetMechanic gives one to five stars for five technical aspects. It was necessary to convert the NetMechanic data into either a four-point Likert-scale or a dichotomous scale in order to rank the B&Bs on quadrant 4. For the Likert scale rankings, the star ratings were converted to a one-to-four Likert scale. For the dichotomous scale, the stars were converted to either a one or zero. Stars three and four equaled one and stars one and two equaled zero on the dichotomous scale. After converting the NetMechanic star results, the data were then ranked using the same method as in the first three quadrants.

The rankings in Table 4 reflect the total points achieved in each quadrant by 19 of the B&Bs. The quadrant 1, 2, and 3 rankings reflected the total scores for the dichotomous responses. This study did not find a significant difference between the rankings on the Likert and dichotomous scales. Since there were no significant differences between these ranked scales, it would be redundant to report the details of the Likert-scale findings. The quadrant 4 rankings were based on the four-point Likert scale scores from NetMechanic for the technical analysis, which is explained in further detail in Table 4.

Strengths and Weaknesses of the B&B Websites

The second study objective was to assess the relative strengths and weaknesses of existing B&B Websites. To achieve this objective, descriptive statistics were used with the dichotomous scale data to assess the relative strengths and weaknesses of existing B&B Websites from the customer (user friendliness and site attractiveness), marketing, and technical perspectives. The dichotomous data had more aspects for comparing the B&Bs and therefore it was used in this analysis. The Likert-scale data had only one measurement per quadrant for the first three quadrants.

TABLE 3. B&B Balanced Scorecard Rankings

Inn Name	Quad 1 (UF) Rank	Quad 2 (SA) Rank	Quad 3 (ME) Rank	Quad 4 (TA) Rank	Total BSC Rank
Historic Loeb House Inn	6	1	3	1	1
James Wilkins House	1	3	6	7	2
The Oliver Inn B&B	10	5	1	1	2
The Inn at Aberdeen, Ltd.	3	10	2	4	4
Ruddick-Nugent House	1	2	5	17	5
Commandant's Home B&B	5	6	6	11	6
Honeymoon Mansion B&B and Wedding Chapel	11	11	6	1	7
The White House on Park Avenue	4	4	6	17	8
Gothic Arches B&B	13	7	11	4	9
Queen Anne B&B	16	11	4	7	10
The Homespun Country Inn	9	9	13	7	10
The Old Bridge Inn	6	8	10	17	12
Angola's Tulip Tree Inn	11	14	16	4	13
Castlebury Inn	6	14	18	11	14
1878 House Country Inn B&B	13	16	12	11	15
The Cottage at West Point	15	13	17	10	16
Apple Inn Museum B&B	19	19	13	11	17
Big Locust Farm B&B	16	18	15	16	18
Hilltop Farm B&B	18	17	19	11	18

TABLE 4. Technical Analysis Rating Scale

Technical Aspect	4 Star Rating	3 Star Rating	2 Star Rating	1 Star Rating
Link Check	0 bad links	1 bad link	2 bad links	More than 2 bad links
Load Time	< or = 13 seconds	< or = 24 seconds	< or = 35 seconds	> 35 seconds
HTML	0 errors	1-6 errors	7-12 errors	Greater than 12 errors
Browser	0 problems	1-4 problems	5-8 problems	More than 8 problems
Spell Check	0 misspellings	Up to 5% misspellings	Up to 10% misspellings	Greater than 10% misspellings

Table 5 shows the means and standard deviations for all of the items measured. Also indicated are the percentages of the total points earned by the 19 properties for each of the four quadrants. The results show that the greatest strength of these B&B Websites was in their attractiveness, earning around 88.5 percent of the total points available. The B&B Websites received a passing score on the technical aspects, capturing 74.8 percent of the total points available. The technical features of these Websites can be improved through better use of HTML and by lowering load times. In the area of user friendliness, this sample ranked significantly lower at 63.7 percent of the total points available, indicating there was considerable scope for site improvements in this aspect.

The major weakness of the B&B Websites overall was in marketing effectiveness, securing just 40.2 percent of the total points available. This finding corresponds to that of the Morrison et al. (1999) analysis of small hotels,

TABLE 5. Evaluation Scores by Quadrant

Quadrant 1: User-Friendliness (UF)	Mean	SD	Percent
Telephone number clearly available	8.60	0.75	
Mailing address clearly available	8.10	1.76	
E-mail contact clearly available	7.90	1.59	
Limited vertical and horizontal scrolling	6.75	2.54	
Home button available on all pages	6.40	2.94	
Clear and effective navigation tool on each page	5.75	2.54	
Fax number clearly available	3.80	3.75	
Site map or index available	2.35	2.03	
Site content search function available	1.95	0.39	
Total	51.60	7.48	
Percentage of Total (51.6/81)			63.7%
Quadrant 2: Site Attractiveness (SA)			
Text clear and readable	9.00	2.31	
Hyperlinks easy to read	9.00	2.45	
Pages clean and uncluttered	8.67	1.99	
Photos and images are good quality	8.00	2.39	
Effective use of Web page space	8.00	2.41	
Pictures and images reinforce text	7.89	1.24	
Sufficient contrast between background and text	7.00	2.39	
Background effective and appealing	7.00	2.42	
Use of color improves visual appearance	7.00	2.60	
Total	71.67	15.07	
Percentage of Total (71.67/81)			88.5%
Quadrant 3: Marketing Effectiveness (ME)			
House pictures available	8.42	1.12	
Guest room pictures available	7.79	2.68	
Are the rates available?	7.63	2.31	
Text describe uniqueness of the B&B (architect, historical, etc.)	6.16	1.83	
Local activities and events listed on site	5.26	2.16	
Links to activities and area attractions	4.21	2.86	
Are special packages offered?	4.05	4.02	
Hyperlinks to sponsor/advertisements available	3.32	2.19	
Text describe innkeepers or owners	2.79	2.35	
Logo reflected on the Website	2.68	2.06	
Can you make a reservation online?	2.68	3.20	
Special promotions addressed	2.26	2.26	
Special target markets addressed (children, pets, ADA, etc.)	2.16	1.50	
Calendar of events available	2.05	2.25	
Testimonial information available	1.16	2.63	
Virtual tour available	1.05	2.82	
Mission statement available	1.00	1.20	
Awards information available	0.37	0.83	
Total	65.05	19.55	
Percentage of Total (65.05/162)			40.15%
Quadrant 4: Technical Aspects (TA)			
Link check	3.58	0.51	
HTML check	2.42	1.12	
Browser compatibility	3.00	0.75	
Load time speed	2.47	0.96	
Spell check	3.47	0.51	
Total	14.95	2.34	
Percentage of Total (14.95/20)			74.75%

which also concluded that the small hotels were not effectively applying marketing principles within their Websites. Although one could argue that small hotels in Scotland and B&Bs in the U.S. are very different populations, they are in fact very similar in size and in the nature of the innkeepers' involvement with the operations.

Rankings of Individual B&B Properties

A ranking of the 19 properties was performed. Quadrant 1 resulted in a tie between the James Wilkins House and Ruddick-Nugent House for the most user-friendly Website. The Hilltop Farm B&B and Apple Inn Museum B&B placed 18th and 19th with the lowest scores for user-friendliness. The Historic Loeb House Inn had the top ranking for quadrant 2, indicating it was the most attractive site. The least attractive site was Hilltop Farm B&B, ranking 19th on the cumulative scores from all the evaluators. The top-ranked Website for quadrant 3 was The Oliver Inn B&B, making it the most effective in the application of marketing principles. The lowest scoring property for marketing effectiveness was again the Hilltop Farm B&B.

The NetMechanic analysis for quadrant 4 resulted in three-way ties for both the most technically-sound Website and the least technically-sound Website. The Historic Loeb House Inn, The Oliver Inn B&B, and the Honeymoon Mansion B&B, and Wedding Chapel received the highest scores, while the Ruddick-Nugent House, The White House on Park Avenue, and The Old Bridge Inn had the most technical problems and lowest scores. The total BSC rank was computed by summing the quadrant ranks for each B&B to arrive at a total BSC rank score (Table 3). The B&B with the lowest total received the highest ranking and this was the Historic Loeb House Inn with a score of 11. It ranked first in site attractiveness and technical aspects, third in marketing effectiveness, and sixth in user friendliness. A screen capture of the Historic Loeb House's Website is shown in Figure 1. The James Wilkins House (17) and The Oliver Inn B&B (17) tied for second place, while the Big Locust Farm B&B (65) and Hilltop Farm B&B (65) tied as the lowest ranked Websites.

Another important observation about these Website evaluations is the large level of variation in the relative rankings for the four quadrants among most of these B&Bs. For example, while the Ruddick-Nugent House tied for the top rank on user-friendliness, it also tied as the poorest performing Website on technical aspects. The White House on Park Avenue earned the fourth best rankings for user-friendliness and site attractiveness, but was tied for last place for the technical aspects. The Oliver Inn B&B earned the top place for marketing effectiveness but was tenth-ranked for user-friendliness. This indicated a high level of inconsistency in performance across the four evaluation quadrants. Once again, it also confirmed the advisability of using a multi-perspective approach such as the one in the BSC.

Table 6 shows more detailed technical characteristics of each B&B Website as well as the Web addresses. The number of links per site tested ranged from 9 to 79 with a mean of 32.84. The number of pages per site was not particularly extensive, ranging from 2 to 34 with a mean of 10.84.

CONCLUSIONS AND RECOMMENDATIONS

Any B&B innkeeper can evaluate the strengths and weaknesses of their Website using the instrument developed in this study. Each of the four quadrants in the instrument supplies a set of aspects that provide for a user friendly, attractive, effectively marketed Website that is technically sound. The overall goal of a B&B Website should be to clearly describe the experience of staying there and convey the special qualities, and characteristics of the property and personality of the innkeepers. In essence, the Website should reflect the guest's experience at the property, and it gives the innkeeper the opportunity to communicate and interact directly with potential guests. As recent statistics suggest, a Website is a powerful tool to generate business for a B&B (Schleim & Saint-Amour, 2001).

This study concluded that there is room for improvement in all the four aspects of existing B&B Websites. Site attractiveness reflects to the visual aesthetics of a Website. This sample

FIGURE 1. Screen Capture of the Homepage of The Historic Loeb House: The Best Overall Website

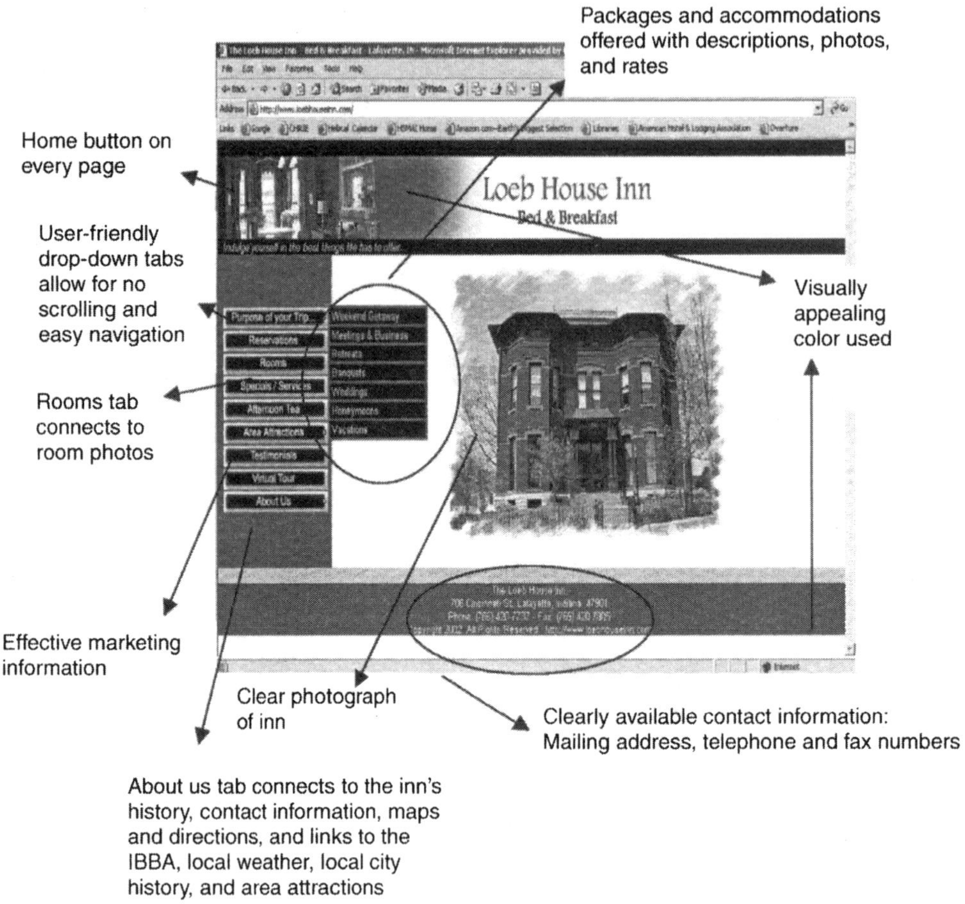

of B&Bs scored extremely well on site attractiveness, with an overall score of 88.5 percent. The contrast of text with the use of appealing color to improve the visual appearance is important to the appeal of a site. Innkeepers can improve their sites with the use of appealing backgrounds paired with contrasting text. Another area that can be improved is in ensuring that the photographs and images are reinforced by adjacent text.

For user friendliness, although several Websites offered a homepage button on every page, there is considerable scope left to enhance the user's ability to search sites. In particular, there is a need to incorporate more navigation tools such as site maps and searches, and to add fax contact details. Although this may seem to be an obvious and essential part of a Website, not all of the B&Bs prominently displayed a telephone number, address, and e-mail contact. Contact information needs to be displayed clearly with a working link for the e-mail address. B&Bs scored lower for providing a fax number, but this may be due to the increased use of communications through e-mail and lesser reliance on fax machines. However, if a B&B has a fax machine on property, the number should be displayed on the Website.

This sample of B&Bs performed very poorly in the marketing effectiveness of their Websites. Earlier, the point was made that B&Bs are well suited for the online environment due to their uniqueness, coupled with the content-rich nature of the Web. In marketing

TABLE 6. B&B Technical Information

B&B Name	Web Address	# Links per Site	# Pages per Site
Historic Loeb House Inn	http://loebhouseinn.com/	23	34
James Wilkins House	http://www.jameswilkinshousebnb.com/	37	6
The Oliver Inn B&B	http://www.oliverinn.com/	39	15
The Inn at Aberdeen, Ltd.	http://www.innataberdeen.com/	64	29
Ruddick-Nugent House	http://www.ruddick-nugent-house.com/index.shtml	33	8
Commandant's Home B&B	http://www.commhomeb-b.com/	34	11
Honeymoon Mansion B&B and Wedding Chapel	http://www.bbonline.com/in/honeymoon/	38	7
The White House on Park Avenue	http://www.bnb-on-parkave.com/	47	14
Gothic Arches B&B	http://www.gothicarches.com/	36	7
Queen Anne B&B	http://www.queenanneinn.net/	25	7
The Homespun Country Inn	http://www.homespuninn.com/	23	5
The Old Bridge Inn	http://www.oldbridgeinn.com/	32	8
Angola's Tulip Tree Inn	http://www.tuliptree.com/	20	2
Castlebury Inn	http://www.castleburyinn.com/	14	4
1877 House Country Inn B&B	http://www.1877house.com/	23	9
The Cottage at West Point	http://www.cottageatwestpoint.com/	16	5
Apple Inn Museum B&B	http://www.appleinninc.com/	79	22
Big Locust Farm B&B	http://ourworld-top.cs.com/joellindley22/index.htm	32	7
Hilltop Farm B&B	http://www.hilltopfarm.com/	9	6
Mean		32.84	10.84

principles terminology, a Website provides a great opportunity to tangibilize the uniqueness of a B&B for the Web user. However, although most of these Websites included photographs of the property and the guest rooms, almost all lacked virtual tours. Here the major purpose of the Website is to reflect the guest experience and communicate the unique personality of the B&B. To achieve this, the site must include more than still photographs of the interior, exterior, and various rooms at the property. A virtual tour more effectively tangibilizes the B&B experience, taking the Website to a higher level of comprehension for the user.

The Website text must also convey the personality of the B&B. Although most sites had photographs, fewer provided narrative descriptions highlighting the uniqueness of the properties. A description of the architecture, history, special location, or other unique feature of the B&B should complement the photographs and convey the core personality of the property. This is also true for the innkeepers. Very few Websites had photographs or descriptions of the innkeepers. The absence of

this information may convey that the owners are not managing the property or are not on-site. More importantly, however, the Website must convey the personality of the innkeepers, their backgrounds, and interests. According to BedandBreakast.com (2001), B&B innkeepers need to use or express three Ps on their Websites: professionalism, personality, and pictures. Under personality, the Web provides a prime opportunity for innkeepers to introduce themselves to virtual guests and welcome them to their B&Bs. This greeting should be in text, but it can also be done virtually in the same manner as the virtual tour. For example, the innkeeper could welcome the guest and describe the B&B in the virtual tour. Several techniques can be used to bring the innkeepers and B&B to life. Virtual tours, sound or movie clips that feature the innkeepers welcoming their virtual visitors can better engage visitors online and bring the Website experience closer to the experience of a real visit. The addition of sound and video takes the online experience beyond the static brochure-on-the-Web experience that one finds on most existing B&B Websites.

The main product and service of B&Bs is the rental of rooms. Although many properties had the rates on their sites, very few provided the ability to make online reservations. As indicated in the literature, an increasing proportion of guests are finding B&Bs online. B&Bs need not create complicated room reservation HTML code to accomplish this. Some of the B&Bs in this sample used existing Web-based reservation services to allow online booking. The most popular system was through an online reservation product offered by *http://www.netbookings.com*. The other method used by some B&Bs was through their property management systems and this online system was provided as part of *SuperInn*, a product offered by *http://www.sarktech.com/*. Of course, there are other products that make online booking an option for B&Bs. As more guests shop on the Web for B&Bs, the trend to offer online booking will become more important, and eventually will be a necessity.

Overall, there is much room for improvement in other facets of marketing effectiveness. Innkeepers need to expand the description of packages and special promotions, as well providing more links to area attractions. Awards, guest testimonials, and vision and mission statements are all opportunities for innkeepers to make their properties more concrete for Web users by providing positive evidence and opinions on the qualities of their B&Bs.

For the fourth quadrant, good spelling, links that work, and quick load time speeds offer the Web visitor a well functioning Website that looks and works professionally. A technically-sound Website adds to the visit experience. It is also a reflection of the innkeeper's ability to maintain the B&B. If the site is well maintained, one can make the assumption that the B&B is also well maintained, and the opposite can also be inferred.

Limitations and Needs for Future Research

There are a number of limitations to this research study that must be acknowledged. One of these is the lack of direct involvement of B&B innkeepers in the design of the Website evaluation instrument. In the future, it is suggested that these operators should be consulted about the specific criteria incorporated in the B&B Website evaluation instrument. It may also be desirable to have the sites evaluated by former guests of B&Bs, who may have greater insight than trained evaluators on the inherent qualities of these properties.

Another recognized limitation of the study was the omission of criteria related to the provision of breakfasts in a B&B. In future, the instrument needs to be augmented by items relating to breakfast, such as a description of the meals, menus, and recipes. Additionally, the availability of specific driving directions to the B&B needs to be verified in the instrument.

The B&B Websites evaluated in this study may reflect a sample of typical B&Bs in the U.S. The results of this study show that there is much opportunity to improve B&B Websites particularly in their marketing effectiveness. However, it may also be argued that the sample of properties was too small and only from one state, and that the results are not representative of all B&Bs in the U.S. While acknowledging this work as an exploratory study, there is a great opportunity in the future to increase the geographical scope of this research, as well as evaluating a larger pool of B&Bs.

While the inter-rater reliability found in this study was at an acceptable level, it may have been possible to increase it. For example, this might have been accomplished by having two evaluation sessions, one acting as a pilot and the second being the evaluation proper. The researchers could have used the pilot session to pinpoint where the major variations in scoring were occurring among the evaluators. This could have then been used as the basis for a second training session to encourage greater consistency in evaluator ratings.

REFERENCES

BedandBreakfast.com. (2001). *Can you pick an inn from its web site?* Retrieved July 13, 2003, from *http://www.bedandbreakfast.com/report/Mar01/v2i2j_00_tips.htm*.

BedandBreakfast.com. (2003). B&B associations. Retrieved June 30, 2003, from *http://www.bedandbreakfast.com/associations/index.aspx*.

Buchanan, R. D., & Espeseth, R. D. (1991). *Developing a Bed & Breakfast Business Plan*. North Central Region Extension Publication 273. Urbana, Illinois: University of Illinois Ag Publication Office.

Bonn, M. A., Furr, L. H., & Susskind, A. M. (1998). Using the Internet as a pleasure travel planning tool: An examination of the sociodemographic and behavioral characteristics among Internet users and nonusers. *Journal of Hospitality and Tourism Research*, 22 (3), 303-317.

Clark, W. S. (1992). Colorado's bed and breakfast industry. Colorado Springs, CO: Holden House-1902 Bed & Breakfast Inn.

Countryman, C. C. (2000). Designing effective bed and breakfast web sites. *Proceedings of the Fifth Annual Graduate Education and Graduate Students Research Conference in Hospitality and Tourism*, 5, 430-432.

Eimer, M. (2000, November). B&B Internet marketing: The innside story. *Library Journal*, 125 (18), 150.

Feng, R., Morrison, A. M., & Ismail, J. A. (2003). East versus west: A comparison of online destination marketing in China and the U.S. *Journal of Vacation Marketing*, 10 (1), 43-56.

Garcia, A. (2002). *Website evaluation for bed and breakfasts*. Retrieved May 15, 2002, from *http://www.cfs.purdue.edu/htm/pages/pdf/bbevaluation.pdf*.

Hotch, R., & Glassman, C. A. (1992). *Start and run your own bed and breakfast inn*. Harrisburg, PA: Stackpole Books.

Indiana Bed & Breakfast Association. (2003). *Application for Active Membership*. Retrieved February 25, 2003, from *http://www.indianabedandbreakfast.org/Docs/Active%20Membership.pdf*.

Ismail, J. A., Labropoulos, T., Mills, J. E., & Morrison, A. M. (2002). A snapshot in time: The marketing of culture in European Union NTO Web sites. *Tourism, Culture & Communication*, 3 (3), 165-179.

Kansas Bed and Breakfast Association. (2003). Retrieved August 26, 2003 from: BedandBreakfast. com. (2001). *Can you pick an inn from its web site?* Retrieved July 13, 2003 from *http://www.kbba.com/join.shtml*.

Kaplan, R. S., & Norton, D. P. (1992). The balanced scorecard—measures that drive performance. *Harvard Business Review*, January/February, 71-79.

Kaplan, R. S., & Norton, D. P. (1993). Putting the balanced scorecard to work. *Harvard Business Review*, September/October, 134-142.

Kasavana, M. L. (2002). eMarketing: Restaurant Websites that click. *Journal of Hospitality & Leisure Marketing*, 9 (3/4), 167-178.

Landis, J. R., & Koch, G. G. (1977). The measurement of observer agreement for categorical data. *Biometrics*, 33, 159-174.

Lanier, P., & Berman, J. (1993). Bed-and-breakfast inns come of age. *Cornell H.R.A. Quarterly*, 34 (2), 15-23.

Lituchy, T. R., & Rail, A. (2000). Bed and breakfasts, small inns, and the Internet: The impact of technology on the globalization of small businesses. *Journal of International Marketing*, 8 (2), 86-97.

Lodging Resources Workshops and Lanier Publishing. (2003). Retrieved June 30, 2003 from *http://www.lodgingresources.com/articles_article005.htm*.

Morrison, A. M., Pearce, P. L., Moscardo, G., Nadkarni, N., & O'Leary, J. T. (1996). Specialist accommodation: Definition, markets served, and roles in tourism development. *Journal of Travel Research*, 35 (1), 18-26.

Morrison, A. M., Taylor, J. S., Morrison, A. J., & Morrison, A. D. (1999). Marketing small hotels on the World Wide Web. *Information Technology & Tourism*, 2 (2), 97-113.

Morrow, E. P. (2001). *Internet marketing basics*. Advisor Today; Washington. 96 (6), 26.

NetMechanic. (2003). *Power tools for your website*. Retrieved May 24, 2003, from *http://www.netmechanic.com/toolbox/html-code.htm*.

Notarius, B., & Brewer, G. S. (2001). *Open your own bed and breakfast*. Canada: John Wiley & Sons, Inc.

Nunnaly, J. (1978). *Psychometric theory*. New York: McGraw-Hill.

Professional Association of Innkeepers International. (2003). *Definitions* Retrieved August 26, 2003, from *http://www.paii.org/tidbits/definitions.php*.

St. John, A. R., Kline, S. F., & Morrison, A. M. (2003). A study to determine effectiveness of Indiana bed and breakfast Websites. *Advances in Hospitality and Tourism Research, Volume 8: Proceedings of the Annual Graduate Education and Graduate Student Research Conference in Hospitality and Tourism*, 623-629.

Selz, D., & Schubert, P. (1998). *Web assessment: A model for the evaluation and the assessment of successful electronic commerce applications*. 31st HICS. Los Alamitos, CA.

Schleim, P., & Saint-Amour, P. (2001). The web: Hype or real? It's real! *Fifth Annual Tracking Innkeeper Tracking Study: 2001*. Retrieved June 30, 2003, from *http://www.digital-direct-marketing.com/surveys/reports/2001_part1.htm*.

Schwartz, S. (1999). *Using the Internet for health information: Legal issues*. Chicago, Illinois: American Medical Association.

Travel Industry Association of America. (2001, February). *Mature travelers comprise nearly one-third of all U.S. travel*. Retrieved February 25, 2003, from *http://www.tia.org/Press/012201mature.asp*.

Valhouli, C. (2002). The best B&Bs. Retrieved July 7, 2003, from *http://www.forbes.com/2002/06/13/0613feat.html*.

UCLA Academic Technology Services (2003). SPSS faq. *What does Cronbach's alpha mean?* Retrieved July 2, 2003, from *http://www.ats.ucla.edu/stat/spss/faq/alpha.html*.

Wuensch, K. L. (2000). *Inter-rater agreement*. Retrieved July 9, 2003, from *http://core.ecu.edu/psyc/wuenschk/docs30/InterRater.doc*.

Wuensch, K. L. (2002). *Nonparametric statistics*. Retrieved July 14, 2003, from *http://core.ecu.edu/psyc/wuenschk/SAS/nonparm.doc*.

Staying Afloat in the Tropics:
Applying a Structural Equation Model Approach
to Evaluating National Tourism Organization Websites
in the Caribbean

Alecia Douglas
Juline E. Mills

SUMMARY. This study examines the extent to which the top ten Caribbean destinations market their tourism product using their national tourism organization Websites. A comparison of the national tourism organization Websites of the Caribbean Tourism Organization member countries will be conducted to determine the differences in technical aspects, user friendliness, site attractiveness, and marketing effectiveness using the modified Balanced Scorecard (BSC) for Website evaluation. The modified BSC results were next used to develop and test a model of Caribbean NTO Website visitor retention. Third-order confirmatory factor analysis (CFA) was used to test the model. The model showed that the four aspects which comprise the modified BSC are important in the development of Caribbean NTO Websites. *[Article copies available for a fee from The Haworth Document Delivery Service: 1-800-HAWORTH. E-mail address: <docdelivery@haworthpress.com> Website: <http://www.HaworthPress.com> © 2004 by The Haworth Press, Inc. All rights reserved.]*

KEYWORDS. Caribbean, national tourism organizations, modified Balanced Scorecard, confirmatory factor analysis, Website visitor retention

INTRODUCTION

Described as an archipelago of sunny, tropical islands naturally decorated with exotic flora and fauna, and surrounded by blue seawater and gentle breezes, the Caribbean is a virtual tourist paradise (Jayawardena, 2002). This picture perfect haven of cascading water-falls, magnificent miles of white, black, and pink sand beaches accentuated with coconut groves and towering palm trees creates an intoxicating array of nature's finest. Travelers escape to enchanting islands with award winning hotels featuring "one-price-for-all" vacations, romantic rendezvous, and world class restaurants with magical island hospitality, all

---

Alecia Douglas is a Master's Candidate, Department of Hotel, Restaurant, and Institutional Management, University of Delaware. Juline E. Mills is Assistant Professor, Ecommerce in Hospitality and Tourism, Department of Hospitality and Tourism Management, Purdue University.

Address correspondence to Juline E. Mills (E-mail: millsj@cfs.purdue.edu).

[Haworth co-indexing entry note]: "Staying Afloat in the Tropics: Applying a Structural Equation Model Approach to Evaluating National Tourism Organization Websites in the Caribbean." Douglas, Alecia, and Juline E. Mills. Co-published simultaneously in *Journal of Travel & Tourism Marketing* (The Haworth Hospitality Press, an imprint of The Haworth Press, Inc.) Vol. 17, No. 2/3, 2004, pp. 269-293; and: *Handbook of Consumer Behavior, Tourism, and the Internet* (ed: Juline E. Mills, and Rob Law) The Haworth Hospitality Press, an imprint of The Haworth Press, Inc., 2004, pp. 269-293. Single or multiple copies of this article are available for a fee from The Haworth Document Delivery Service [1-800-HAWORTH, 9:00 a.m. - 5:00 p.m. (EST). E-mail address: docdelivery@haworthpress.com].

http://www.haworthpress.com/web/JTTM
© 2004 by The Haworth Press, Inc. All rights reserved.
Digital Object Identifier: 10.1300/J073v17n02_20

combined to enhance the visitor experience. Key visitor segments to the region include the cruise ship passengers, the all-inclusive or resort tourists, the "sun-lusters," the business travelers, the special interest tourists, and the eco-tourists (ARA Consulting Group, Systems Caribbean, Marshall & KPMG, 1996; Jayawardena, 2002). Yet the soul of the Caribbean is not merely the experience gained by the visitor, but also that of a brand that plays to the traveler's desires through the creation of high levels of message empathy that stimulates verbal, visual, and physiological responses as well as the ultimate desire to purchase (Caribbean Tourism Organization, 2002a; Leckenby, 1998).

Despite these well-defined products and visitor segments, the Caribbean over the past four years has experienced a decline in travelers to the region since 1999. The 1991 to 1998 statistics showed an annual growth rate of 5.5% that was consistently above the world average of 4.2%, thus placing the Caribbean sixth behind major league destinations such as the United States (U.S.), Italy, France, Spain, and the United Kingdom (U.K.) (Collins, 2003; Jayawardena, 2000). However, in 1999 the growth rate declined to 3.9%. This decline continued during 2001-2003 where the industry faced the perfect storm–a combination of stock market falls and a recession in the U.S., the rippling effects of the 9/11 World Trade Center bombing and terrorist attacks, the U.S.-Iraqi war, the Bali bombing, and the Severe Acute Respiratory Syndrome (SARS) epidemic in Asia and Canada (Baumgarten, 2003; Collins, 2003; Caribbean Tourism Organization, 2002a; Girvan, 2001). Statistics for the Winter 2002 season continued to be less than impressive as visitor arrivals were down 10.4% (Girvan, 2002). These statistics are certainly not comforting for a region highly dependent on the tourism trade for economic stability and employment. Approximately 25% of the Caribbean work force is employed in the tourism sector (The Namibian, 2003). In addition to the high dependence on travel for employment and wealth creation, the region finds itself at the center of a waging battle to attract visitors. Caribbean national tourism organizations (NTOs) are now more challenged than ever to improve on current marketing efforts.

This study therefore sought to determine the extent to which the Internet is being used to market tourism destinations from a Caribbean perspective. Using the island member states of the Caribbean Tourism Organization (CTO), this study evaluated the extent to which the top ten destinations market their tourism product using their NTO Websites. A comparison of the NTO Websites of CTO member countries was conducted to determine the differences in technical aspects, user friendliness, site attractiveness, and marketing effectiveness using the modified Balanced Scorecard (BSC) for Website evaluation based on Mills and Morrison (2000). The modified BSC results were next used to develop and test a model of Caribbean NTO Website visitor retention. Third-order confirmatory factor analysis (CFA) was used to test the model.

THE ROLE OF NTOs IN PROMOTING THE CARIBBEAN DESTINATION

Destination management organizations such as NTOs are best described as the official tourism bodies for their respective countries with a mandate to plan and execute strategic marketing programs for achieving stated organizational objectives (Buhalis, 2000; Formica & Littlefield, 2000). As Formica and Littlefield (2000) note, NTOs develop strategic partnerships with trade representatives, such as hotel and restaurant associations, to channel effective marketing activities geared towards promoting a strong destination brand. Other organizational goals may be mono-functional or multifunctional in nature and may expand beyond the areas of destination marketing, developing, planning, and visitor servicing into researching and lobbying as well as regulating practices and policies (Pearce, 1996). More often than not, NTOs appear in a variety of forms ranging from traditional government departments to legal bodies (Pearce, 1996). Funded by the industry through taxes or budgetary contributions from the government, NTOs are typically non-profit organizations that communicate their country's products and services through various media such as brochures, film, and television (Formica & Littlefield, 2000; United Nations Trade & Development Board, 2000). NTOs in addition to having local offices at the destination may also have locations in strategic main markets that the country sees as key revenue earners (Formica & Littlefield, 2000; Pearce, 1996).

Marketing initiatives such as the Jamaica Tourist Board's (JTB), Insider's Jamaica Programme is one example of how Caribbean NTOs are executing their responsibility to market their destinations. The JTB, a Caribbean NTO, developed the program in 1999 in response to smaller European Plan hotels that were affected by decreasing room occupancies and increasing competition from larger all-inclusive hotels. The program launched on InsidersJamaica.com, promotes a collection of 40 small hotels, inns, restaurants, and attractions on the island by offering vacation deals to travelers spending at least five nights at a small hotel (The Destination Group, 1999; The Jamaica Gleaner, 2000). By promoting the destination internationally, the NTO works best by pooling the marketing resources of the public and private sectors, thus providing benefits to local service providers such as lowered marketing costs, increased market reach, and enhanced access to niche markets (CANA, 2000; Faulkner, 1997; Gretzel, Yuan, & Fesenmaier, 2000).

In addition to marketing the products and services available, Caribbean NTOs also play a more critical role in improving the destination by developing human resources, activating tourism response centers, and ensuring sustainability of the tourism product (Caribbean Tourism Organization, 2003a). NTOs in the Caribbean invest in human resources by providing educational assistance in the form of scholarships and study grants to students and industry personnel to pursue higher education in the area of tourism and hospitality. In addition to these efforts, technical assistance and general training activities are designed to broaden and strengthen the skill sets of industry personnel from front-line to management positions. The activation of tourism response centers by Caribbean NTOs is also important for the destination when coping with emergency management issues such as national di-

sasters and disease control at the local and international level. In summation, these organizations oversee the "optimal use of natural, cultural, social, and financial resources for national development on an equitable and self-sustaining basis" (CTO, 2003a). By providing a unique visitor experience as well as enhancing the way of life for Caribbean nationals, NTOs further promote sustainable tourism through partnerships with their governments, the private sector, and local communities (CTO, 2003a). With e-commerce changing the tourism landscape, as well as the nature in which governments and businesses operate, Caribbean NTOs can use the technology to partner with these bodies to sustain their tourism product. Small hoteliers in the Caribbean have already made the move towards marketing and advertising on the Internet with government assistance (Jackson, 1999; Mitchell, 2000). Likewise, official tourism bodies such as the Barbados Tourism Authority (BTA) has embarked on an integrated, interactive Internet marketing program with partnering organizations such as travel agents (Barbados.org, 1997). The outlook for e-commerce could be promising for Caribbean destinations if benefits such as increased user access to the Internet, e-mail marketing possibilities, and worldwide 800 numbers are exploited (Bryan, 2001).

The charge for Caribbean NTOs to engage in aggressive Internet marketing programs is undeniable. NTOs in developing countries need to actively play the lead role in promoting the development of tourism online in the fulfillment of their obligation to disseminate quality information to visitors and suppliers alike (United Nations Trade and Development Board, 2000). With a strong focus on the customer contact experience, NTOs have developed a higher level of interest in Internet marketing because of its potential to attract more visitors by promoting destination offerings at a lower cost (World Tourism Business Council, 1999). As such, tourism marketers have come to recognize the Internet's importance in reaching today's e-consumers effectively, and as Tourism British Columbia (2000) emphasizes, NTOs must have an overall Internet strategy to compete. Further, the Canadian Tourism Commission argue that the current wave of NTO budget cuts will force NTOs more into Internet marketing strategies (Personal communication July 23, 2003, Canadian Tourism Commission letter to industry Executives). Caribbean destinations will therefore need to optimize the highly customized, interactive, and immersive marketing that can be facilitated by the Internet.

The need also exists for NTOs to capitalize on information technology by actively developing innovative concepts that translate into the relationship-building end of marketing and promotion (Gretzel et al., 2000). To date, the impact of information technology on tourism has been fundamental so much so that the need for data processing, marketing, distribution, coordination, and promotion within the industry is continuously increasing (Bryan, 2001). These technologies, as Bryan (2001) notes, can potentially improve intra-regional communication as well as information collection and analysis on the supply and demand sides of Caribbean tourism. The role of the Internet in Caribbean Tourism will become increasingly important as it facilitates relationship-building not only with visitors but also with suppliers to the industry.

CARIBBEAN TOURISM ON THE INTERNET

In a study conducted by Forrester Research (1999), Internet technologies surfaced as one of the key factors contributing to the growth of the tourism industry to the extent where Werthner and Klein (1999) estimated that between 33 to 50% of all consumer-based Internet transactions were tourism related. Additionally, travel offerings have been embraced as a good product fit for online marketing, as well as having the potential to leverage online relationships between consumers and providers (Kierzkowski, McQuade, Waitman, & Zeisser, 1996; Weber & Roehl, 1999). For U.S. travel consumers, the Internet continues to be the number one source for information used to plan travel over traditional forms of advertising and in 2002, online travel increased by 45% from $18.6 to $27.0 billion

(Marcussen, 2003; World Tourism Organization Business Council, 2001).

Internet marketing not only offers the potential to make information and booking facilities available to a larger number of tourists but also significantly reduces the associated costs with advertising and promoting the product (World Tourism Organization Business Council, 2001). Printed materials in the form of brochures and pamphlets become outdated quicker and are more costly to update than Websites (Ismail & Mills, 2002). Marketing expenses can also be reduced by eliminating the need to handle sales through telephone hotlines, as well as to capitalize on mass marketing and mass customization strategies (Morrison, Mills, Chuvessiriporn, & Ismail, 2002). Other benefits also include: availability where potential consumers can access the information 24 hours a day and timeliness in allowing travel inquiries to be responded to in a shorter timeframe (Mills & Morrison, 2002). As a result, Web marketing efforts will not only be as effective as those communicated through more traditional media but may also be more efficient in building brand alliances than radio, television, or print media (Gallagher, Foster, & Parsons, 2001; Korgaonkar & Wolin, 2002; Tierney, 2000). Consequently, tourism organizations are beginning to view Web marketing as critically important to the industry where a large percent of vacations are being planned online (World Tourism Organization, 2000). These activities are facilitated by allowing tourists to search for travel information, plan itineraries, book hotel rooms, tours, and flights, as well as to stimulate virtual experiences of the destination online (Hoffman & Novak, 1996; Kiani, 1998; Werthner & Klein, 2000).

Efforts have been made by the Caribbean Hotel Association Charitable Trust (CHACT) and the CTO to market all 34-member destinations as one product under the slogan "Life Needs the Caribbean" with the support of Expedia.com (Hospitality Net, 2002). Likewise, some service providers have sought to advertise heavily discounted vacation specials on the Internet in an effort to counteract competitive forces. Sandals Resorts, an all-inclusive resort hotel chain operating in Jamaica, St. Lucia, Bahamas, and Antigua, is currently promoting "Operation Relax" to active U.S. military on their Website (Sandals Resorts, 2003). Upon booking a vacation with Sandals, U.S. military personnel will receive a free three-night travel certificate valid for two. In similar attempts to compete in this dynamic travel market, SuperClubs the All-Inclusive Resort Chain, with hotels in Cuba, Bahamas, Curacao, and Jamaica and Sandals Resorts' biggest competitor, is currently promoting a 40% discount on reservations booked at all the resorts on their Website (SuperClubs, 2003). Offering free vacations and discounted holidays online may attract increased visitorship to the Website but unless the content is engaging and dynamic, visitor retention may not be guaranteed.

Web content for destination marketing sites is becoming increasingly important, especially as the image portrayed by the site and perceived by the user directly affects the overall impression of the destination (Beirne & Curry, 1999; Boolin, Burgess, & Cooper, 2002). In addition, the virtual experience for the travelers may impact their decisions on whether or not to visit the destination (Mac-Leod, 2001). While the use of technology in destination marketing has not displaced the desire for travel, tourist expectations are changing as the Internet reinforces the need for newer, better, and more precise information making real-time communication, reliable service, and Web experience important to online customer or e-satisfaction, and ultimately retention (Buhalis & Dombey, 2001). Results from a Caribbean tourism survey conducted in 1998 showed, that in choosing the preferred destinations in North America, the Caribbean, or Europe, respondents rated the Internet behind "word-of-mouth information" and "personal experience from previous visits" as the third most influential factor (Karma Centre for Knowledge and Research in Marketing, 1998). Likewise, when considering the type of vacation to purchase, whether all-inclusive, self-organized, or ocean cruises, respondents rated the Internet second behind word-of-mouth communication as most influential. These findings indicate that the Internet is a significant factor influencing the way visitors to the Caribbean choose to plan their vacation experience. The study concluded with the suggestion for Caribbean destination marketers to monitor the results of Internet marketing so as to fine-tune Website presentations as well as to identify new Web-based marketing applications.

In a similar survey on Caribbean destination Websites, the results revealed that "there was an uneven development and inability to manage the sites consistently or even to provide accurate and updated information" (CANA Business Interactive, 2000). A contributing factor to this dilemma may be that Caribbean governments and businesses are oftentimes apprehensive about using technology to meet the needs, expectations, and rapidly changing interests and desires of tourists. As Reddy, Langdale and Iyer (2002) asserted, effectively designed sites are becoming more important to enhancing Website visitor retention. If customers are not satisfied immediately with their current Website, they will simply view another competing site just a click away (Fortune, 2000). As Web surfers are increasingly wary about the time spent at a Website, e-commerce Web design is becoming more important. Stewart (2001) notes that:

... the typical tourist board office is becoming obsolete. Traditional approaches of meet and greet, though still valuable, is no longer adequate. The travel business is becoming more information based and 'Hi-tech' driven. The modern traveler is more educated, more aware of social, political and business issues and can therefore make more informed decisions. The days of a few flyers and brochures are over. New multi-media strategies involving the distribution of products through the Internet, frequent flyer databases and automated systems mean that the Caribbean will have to adjust their distribution systems to remain competitive.

One of the marketing strategies being employed by the Caribbean Tourism Organization (CTO) and individual member destinations is an increased focus on developing Websites that showcase the products and services being offered. The CTO has embarked on a variety of projects to revitalize their Web presence with a new regional collaborative marketing strategy. One such project is the "Global Gateway Station" hosted at Doitcaribbean.com. Using a new approach to Web design and Internet marketing, the new Website seeks to immerse visitors through communicating in six languages to general and niche markets in a fun, user-friendly environment, and to redirect visitors to any of the 34 destinations of their choice (CANA, 2000). In 2002, the U.K. version of the site received accolades from TravelMode magazine for being a good source of tourist information delivered in a thoroughly enjoyable environment, well thought out, and properly designed with an excellent use of color and imagery (CTO, 2002a).

Since destinations are amalgams of tourism products and services offering an integrated experience to consumers (Davidson & Maitland, 1997; Hall, 2000), their presence on the Web should likewise be an engaging experience for the users. Communicating the features of a destination on the Internet cannot be achieved solely by using traditional marketing efforts with very little interactivity or dynamic content. More specifically, Gretzel et al. (2000) asserted that destination Websites should attempt at all costs to attract travelers by stimulating their interest and participation with the hopes of retaining and ensuring their increased patronage. The Website should also learn about their travelers' preferences as well as to create feedback thus providing customized interactions. As a result of these capabilities, travel providers will be better equipped to anticipate the visitor's needs and target them individually in order to deliver customized products (Bloch & Segev, 1996). The success of NTOs in the Caribbean will, therefore, be based on the move away from passive marketing to a more interactive and integrated marketing effort, most often facilitated by using the Internet. With that view, Caribbean destinations should employ Internet marketing technologies that will build solid visitor relations, thus increasing the likelihood for visitor retention to the site.

WEBSITE VISITOR RETENTION (WVR) MODEL

The key to retaining customers is first being able to satisfy them. As such it can be ascertained that satisfaction is directly related to retention and that dissatisfaction could equate to loss of patronage (eLoyalty Corporation, 1999). This underlying factor is oftentimes underestimated by many businesses to the extent where it becomes more expensive to attract new customers than to retain existing customers. As Heath (1997) professed, a company can potentially increase its bottom line by 75 percent from a mere five percent increase in customer retention, thereby emphasizing the lifetime value of repeat customers to a business.

The concept does not only measure the value of a customer or visitor to the destination but also the potential contribution of the visitor over a period of time (Profitadvisors.com, 1998). It has been shown over time that past consumer behavior can predict future actions and, as such, a visitor who repeats their actions is likely to continue doing so, therefore increasing the future value to the business (Drilling-down.com, 2001). As a result, an increase in repeat visitors may potentially predict the strength of the destination's products and services in the future, whereas a decrease in visitorship may indicate lower arrivals to the destination. The concept of the lifetime value of a customer thus becomes important for the marketer and is possibly more demanding for destinations to achieve in an online environment.

It is estimated that four out of every five users of a Website never revisit a site (Hodgkins, 1999) making the challenge for marketers more difficult to satisfy and retain the average Web user. Kaminski (2003) contends that the most important aspects of the Website have to do with how well the design features, navigation, content, and visual appeal are all combined. Website retention or "stickiness" is, therefore, important as it is an indirect measure of the effectiveness, usability, and organization of the site (Nemzow, 1999). Defined as the amount of time a person spends at a Website, the term Website stickiness also refers to the ability of the company to retain users and drive them further into the site (Beddoe-Stephens, 1999). In an effort to strengthen the tourism product offered online and to drive visitors to the site and keep them there, it is necessary for Caribbean destination sites to identify the key Website features emphasized in the proposed model that they determine visitor retention.

The model for visitor retention at Caribbean Websites in Figure 1 was developed using the constructs of user friendliness, site attractiveness, and marketing effectiveness as the factors important for the creation of Website retention or stickiness. The model proposes that WVR is a third-order factor and is a function of three second-order factors (user friendliness, site attractiveness, and marketing effectiveness). These three factors are in turn a function of nine first-order factors (from Web mobility to trip planner in Figure 1). The constructs supporting user friendliness and site attractiveness enable the Website to become more customer-focused as well as highly interactive by attracting and engaging the user, while marketing effective-

ness serves as a function to educate users. Therefore, the second-order constructs are capable of generating interest and participation in the Website by providing intuitive navigation, interactive content, and user-generated content (Parsons, Zeisser & Waitman, 1998). A discussion of the second-order constructs in the model follows.

User Friendliness

User friendliness was broken down into two major components, that of Web mobility and ease of contact. These sub-groups influence the visitor's perception of a site by simulating the role of a concierge, thus providing navigational assistance and contact information. Perdue (2001) asserts that the user's perception of the Website may be driven by such factors as ease of navigation and site accessibility. Web mobility is determined by the availability of items such as a

FIGURE 1. Website Visitor Retention Model

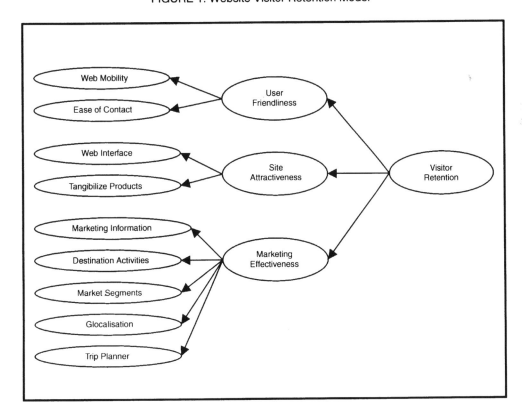

site map or index, a search engine facility, clear and effective navigation tools, and home buttons on all pages. Ease of contact provides several ways by which the users can communicate with the destination whether by phone, fax, e-mail or direct mail. As Websites have assumed a major marketing role in tourism by interfacing with the visitors, interaction both online and offline should be facilitated.

Site Attractiveness

This second-order construct is explained by the first-order constructs of Web interface and tangibilizes products, which facilitates the interactivity of the site. The interactivity of a Website is critical in enhancing the browser experience and increasingly being expected by users (Gretzel et al., 2000). Specific features contributing to the overall site attractiveness are the layout, general aesthetics, and appeal. In addition, the artistic use of background imagery, pictures, color, text, and use of space is vital if the Web page is to be visually attractive to the user. The site design should be simple with a touch of elegance. Reddy et al. (2002) argued that "fancy," glaring backgrounds, or too much graphics or animations may distract the attention of the viewers. As Hanna and Millar (1997) contended, "a site that features the latest in Web page appearance will attract users purely for the effect." The aim for Caribbean destination Websites is to emote the feeling of a fun, engaging, and interactive experience achieved through site attractiveness.

Marketing Effectiveness

Critical components of marketing effectiveness include marketing information, market segments, destination activities, trip planner, and "glocalisation." These factors are important to the model as they are at the forefront of communicating information often needed by users. In general, marketing effectiveness arises out of a need for NTOs to keep Websites up-to-date by not only posting current information but also changing page layouts to incorporate new features (Hanna & Millar, 1997). The first-order construct of marketing information is therefore driven by

items that inform users on hotels, restaurants, and events at the destination in addition to providing current and timely reports on local happenings. The construct of market segments is broken down into seven items, covering niche tourist groups such as business travelers, couples, honeymooners, children, tour groups, and meeting and convention groups. As such, information obtained from the Websites should be arranged according to the interest group, thus catering specifically to the needs and wants of the target market.

In addition to market segments, destination activities should also be arranged by interest areas such as culture and arts activities, recreation and excursions, and sporting activities. This construct enhances the ability of the Website to showcase special-interest features about the destination that give the site a competitive advantage over rival destinations. In an effort to sell the destination's offerings, the site must communicate to the visitor the excitement, adventure, and intrigue that awaits. For a more personalized experience, destination Websites should also offer a trip planner facility for users. The information in this section should be thorough and to the point so that visitors who wish to plan their own vacations can do so with limited assistance. This feature is especially well-suited for the more adventurous travelers who take pleasure in "do-it-yourself" pursuits. Key items in the trip planner should therefore include, but not be limited to, information on how to get around the destination, for example, public transportation, documents needed for international travel, local weather and bank postings, and things to do.

As some industries and countries have embraced the concept of globalization, another strategy that most developing countries are catching on to is "glocalisation." Defined as the combination of localization and globalization, glocalisation refers to the impact of global issues, trends, ideas, and events on the local environment and vice versa (Cheong, 2002; The Economic Times, 2002). Therefore, with the understanding that Web content is key to the overall perception of the destination in the minds of the visitor, information should be "glocalised," appropriate, and of high quality. Caribbean NTOs market their destinations internationally, hence the reason for them to communicate in the language of the visitor thus opening the international gateway to the local products and services. Glocalisation is not merely communicating in a different language, but also showcasing local attributes of the destination to the global market.

In the context of this study, Website visitor retention is not merely seen as exceeding expectations but more importantly ensuring a positive impact on their experience at the Website. The knowledgeable traveler is more independent, active and biased to their own desires; therefore, when planning a travel itinerary online, for example, personal satisfaction and experiences are deemed important (King, 2001). As users become more comfortable with the Internet, their experiences and expectations of Websites will continuously change, thus making it harder to achieve satisfaction and ultimately retention or Web stickiness. Hoffman and Novak (1996) state that the time spent at a Website could be significantly increased if the experience at the site is a positive one for the user.

Additionally, the ability for Caribbean Websites to evoke a desire for users to visit the destination could be a compelling case for these destinations to invest more in interactive Internet marketing. Research has already shown the influence of destination Websites on travel behavior. For example, the results of a survey by Tierney (2000) on the effectiveness of a tourism promotional Website revealed that 80.3% of the sample surveyed reported that the Website increased their likelihood of visiting the destination within the next two years. Emphasis should, therefore, be placed on the need for organizations to conduct Website evaluations that are instrumental in determining the effectiveness sites. Evaluations encourage organizations to continuously improve site functionality and effectiveness. The proposed WVR model is potentially one such source of evaluation.

METHODOLOGY

To examine the extent to which the top ten Caribbean destinations through their NTOs are investing in Web advertising and marketing technologies, this study was approached using a combined method of the modified Balanced Scorecard (BSC) method along with expert ratings. The data were analyzed using CFA. The methodology focused on the top ten Caribbean destinations as selected from the CTO's 2002 statistics followed by a concise description of the approach used to develop and collect the data based on the modified BSC and expert ratings.

Overview of the Top Ten Caribbean Island Destinations

The top ten Caribbean destinations for the study were determined from CTO statistics available on the total tourist visitor arrivals by main market (U.S., Canada, and Europe) in 2002 to the region (Caribbean Tourism Organization, 2003b). Table 1 shows a modified version of the results with a listing of the destinations in descending order from the highest total arrivals to the lowest. As such, the top ten islands in order of merit are the Dominican Republic, Cuba, Bahamas, Jamaica, Puerto Rico, Aruba, Barbados, U.S. Virgin Islands, Martinique, and St. Maarten. The NTO's Websites for the respective islands were obtained from the CTO's Global Gateway Station accessible at *www.doitcaribbean.com*. For the purposes of the study, Cancun, Mexico, often referred to as "the Mexican Caribbean," which reported a figure of 1.9 million in total visitor arrivals for 2002 was omitted, as although it is a member of the Caribbean, it was not listed among the islands on the CTO's Website. It should be noted that an attempt was made by the authors to include the destination by conducting a search for the official NTO Website using Google.com, but it was unsuccessful. A brief description of the primary products offered by each of the islands in the top ten is shown in Table 2.

Two-Step Approach to Survey Development and Execution

The Modified Balanced Score Card

The instrument used for this evaluation was developed based on Mills and Morrison's (2000) modified Balanced Scorecard (BSC) for Website

TABLE 1. Modified Tourist Arrivals by Main Market–2002. Source: Caribbean Tourism Organization (*www.onecaribbean.org*)

Modified Tourist Arrivals by Main Market–2002										
Destination	United States		Canada		Europe		Others		Total	
	Tourists	% ch	Tourists	% ch	Tourists	% ch	Tourists	% ch	Tourists	% ch
Dominican Republic	710,971	3.8	313,612	6.4	1,046,471	−9.7	722,527	−1.0	2,793,581	−2.6
Cuba	77,646	−1.5	348,468	−0.6	859,129	−4.3	400,919	−10.4	1,686,162	−5.0
Bahamas	n.a.	n.a.	n.a.	n.a.	n.a.	n.a.	n.a.	n.a.	1,428,209	−1.8
Jamaica	924,322	1.0	97,413	−12.4	179,089	−0.9	65,542	−5.7	1,266,366	−.08
Puerto Rico	917,793	4.7	9,279	−23.8	29,299	−5.7	109,091	2.2	1,065,462	3.8
Aruba	432,906	−2.3	17,601	−7.0	43,970	−1.6	148,150	−19.7	642,627	−7.1
Barbados	123,429	15.8	46,754	−10.7	219,023	−11.4	108,693	7.7	497,899	−1.8
U.S. Virgin Is.	393,470	−5.7	3,891	−27.7	4,850	−32.6	86,945	18.3	489,156	−2.3
Martinique	n.a.	n.a.	n.a.	n.a.	n.a.	n.a.	n.a.	n.a.	447,891	−2.7
St. Maarten	192,059	−0.4	23,460	−6.5	87,146	−10.6	77,636	−11.0	380,301	−5.6

*Non-Resident Air Arrivals. **Non-Resident Hotel Registrations only.
N.B.: The US Virgin Islands reported figures in this table are Hotel Registrations whereas they reported Stay Over totals are Air Arrivals.
N.B.: Figures are subject to revision by reporting countries.

TABLE 2. List of Top Ten Caribbean Destinations with Their Respective Descriptions

Caribbean Destination	Brief Country Biography	Key Product Features
Dominican Republic– "Experience Our Treasures" *www.dominicanrepublic.com*	• Largest all-inclusive inventory Popular holiday destination • Rain forests, lowlands, coastal swamps, desert and mountains	• Art and culture • Flora, fauna • Beaches
Cuba– "The Warmth You'd Remember" *www.cubatravel.cu*	• 90 miles south of Key West, FL • Largest Caribbean island • Vibrant culture, festive nights • 300 natural white sand beaches	• Beach, city • Eco-tourism • Events
Bahamas– "It Just Keeps Getting Better" *www.bahamas.com*	• 3 million visitors/year • 700 islands–30 occupied • Cruise destination	• Boating/sailing, diving • Ecotours • Family travel • Honeymoon, gaming
Jamaica– "Come. Feel Alright" *www.visitjamaica.com*	• Water sports, music scenes • White and black sand beaches • Over one million tourists/year	• Adventure, beaches • Family, golf • Spring break • Weddings/honeymoons
Puerto Rico– "The Shining Star" *www.gotopuertorico.com*	• Child-friendly destination • Art and entertainment • 272 miles of beaches	• Beaches and sports • Nature and adventure • Entertainment, nightlife
Aruba– "One Happy Island" *www.aruba.com*	• Occupies 70 square miles • White sand beaches • Modern hotels, festive nightlife	• Weddings • Kids r Us • Sightseeing
Barbados– "Just Beyond Your Imagination" *www.barbados.org*	• Turquoise beaches • Natural attractions: underground lakes and an array of caves • Flora and fauna	• Sightseeing • Sports and activities • Alternative health • Weddings
U.S. Virgin Islands– "America's Caribbean Paradise" *www.usvitourism.vi*	• Beaches, coves, coral reefs and untouched rainforests • 3 main islands–St. Thomas, St. Croix and St. John • 50 other islands and reefs	• Meetings • Weddings and honeymoons • Nature and wildlife • Dining
Martinique– "The French Caribbean Haven" *www.martinique.org*	• French culture • Harbor and marinas • Reefs for snorkeling, fishing villages, hot springs, rainforests and woods	• Cruises, lodging • Towns and villages • Culinary, sports
St. Maarten– "Twice the Vacation, Twice the Fun" *www.st-maarten.com*	• Vacation/shopping destination • Dual Dutch/French heritage • 500 pastel colored stores selling luxury goods at 25 to 50% below the normal price	• Weddings • Shopping • Art and culture • Sport

evaluations in tourism and hospitality businesses adapted from Kaplan and Norton's (1992) Balanced Scorecard approach. The modified BSC form designed for Caribbean NTOs Website evaluation was comprised of four main categories (see Table 3 for more details), the first of which was the technical features. This category examined the Website mechanics as it relates to link check, Hyper Text Markup Language (HTML) check, browser compatibility, load time, and spell check, and was determined by results obtained from NetMechanic.com. In addition to these, the category also addressed the link popularity of the site (accessible at *www.linkpopularity.com*), as well as determining the extent to which legal compliance is met.

The second category of the form was used to evaluate the user friendliness of the site and was broken down into sub-categories exploring Website mobility and ease of contact. Category three evaluated the Website based on scores obtained from the Web interface and tangibilizing of products subsections. The final category in this modified BSC encapsulated marketing effectiveness, which was evaluated based on the marketing information, market segments, destination activities, glocalisation, and trip planner. With a total of 56 questions ranging from Website design to destination marketing factors, the survey was distributed to and collected from a selected panel of evaluators via e-mail.

Expert Ratings

The decision to evaluate the Websites on expert ratings using the modified BSC was based on the importance of such ratings in identifying which factors would be the best predictors of quality of the site and, thereby, features that could potentially lead to Website

TABLE 3. Caribbean Website Balanced Scorecard (BSC) Categories

CATEGORIES	FACTORS EXAMINED	SCORE
Technical	*Net Mechanic* Link, Spell, and HTML check, Browser compatibility, Load time	25
	Link Popularity Altavista links, Google links, Hotbot links	15
	Legal Compliance Copyright disclaimers, Trademark display, Site usage, Privacy	20
User Friendliness	*Web Mobility (9 items)* Examples: Home button on all pages, Site map or index available, theme	45
	Ease of Contact Direct e-mail, Mailing address, Telephone number, Fax number	20
Site Attractiveness	*Web Interface (10 items)* Examples: Clear and readable text, Too long scrolling pages	50
	Tangibilizing of Product (4 items) Virtual tour, Testimonials, Photo Gallery, News Releases	20
Marketing Effectiveness	*Market Information (7 items)* Current and timely information, Separate links page, Map/directions Contact information gathered from visitors Hotels, Restaurants, Events	15 5 15
	Market Segments (7 items) Example: Business traveler, Children, Families, Couples	35
	Destination Activities (3 items) Sporting, Recreation, Culture and Arts	15
	Glocalisation (5 items) Hyperlinks to Partnering organizations Foreign language and special interest sites for International travelers Inquiries encouraged, FAQ, Guest-book	5 5 15
	Trip Planner (6 items) Examples: Getting around, Local weather information	30
	TOTAL SCORE	330

retention. As Amento, Terveen and Hill (2000) stated, the quality of a Website is a matter of human judgment of which site organization and layout as well as quantity and uniqueness of information are major factors influencing the expert's decision. These expert decisions are the expressions of learned opinion based on the intelligence and experience of the expert (Ortiz, Wheeler, Breeding, Hora, Meyer, & Keeney, 1991). Further, Booker and Meyer (2001) described experts as individuals qualified in specific subject areas, such as medicine, economics, and engineering, and are recognized in their discipline as being competent to address the problem.

On average, expert judgment may be used to either structure a technical problem, that is, to determine which data are appropriate for analysis, or to provide estimates or even determine failure or incidence rates (Booker & Meyer, 2001). To that end, experts are often required to evaluate items based on their knowledge and to determine the extent to which items reflect a construct's conceptual definition (Hardesty & Bearden, 2003). Typically, items evaluated by a panel of judges should be rated based on the judge's perception of whether or not the item is "clearly representative," "somewhat representative," or "not representative of the construct of interest" (Zaichkowsky, 1985). It should be noted that this is not the only procedure used in expert judging. For example, expert judges were used in previous research to: (1) rate the quality of a survey, and (2) to decide on a subset of items for use in additional analysis (Kohli & Zaltman, 1988; Malhotra, 1981). However, as Hardesty and Bearden (2003) stated, regardless of the method employed when using expert judgments, the decision of which items to take into further analysis is the responsibility of the authors.

A panel was recruited for this study because it entailed not only descriptive analysis but also quality ratings. It was felt that individuals with the knowledge of tourism marketing on the Internet would better understand the importance of the effectiveness of Website marketing and as such be in a position to rate them. The evaluation of the top ten Caribbean destinations was carried out by a team of seven panelists inclusive of six Master's students

and one undergraduate student with experience in Website development. These individuals are pursuing their respective degrees at the graduate and undergraduate level in Hospitality Information Management. In addition, their curriculum is centered on technology use in hospitality, hence they have benefited from courses in Web-based Marketing, Computer-Based Training, Data-Mining Analysis, Issues in Information Technology, and Management Systems in Hospitality. The panel was familiar with tourism marketing in the online environment to varying degrees as they either had experience with rating tourism Websites and/ or developing Websites both in and out of class either as part of their coursework, or in the latter's case for undergraduate assistantship job requirement. They were presented with the form indicating the four criteria stated earlier by which the evaluations were to be based. Panelists were asked to judge each Website based on the BSC categories of user friendliness, site attractiveness, and marketing effectiveness.

The task of analyzing these ten Websites was conducted over a two-week period where the experts had to peruse and evaluate each site based on their knowledge and experience. They were required to use a computer with minimum system requirements of at least 56k modem connection, Internet Explorer 5 or higher or Netscape 5 or higher, Macromedia Flash player (or a downloadable format obtained from the destination's Website), at least a 15" monitor with minimum screen resolution of 800×600, and computer speakers. The completed surveys were then entered into SPSSv11 for data analysis.

DATA ANALYSIS AND RESULTS

Scores obtained from NetMechanic.com and Linkpopularity.com for the technical aspects section were calculated for the respective Websites with the results shown in Table 4. Listed alphabetically, the countries were ranked from highest to lowest based on the scores earned for each subcategory of the technical ratings. For Web mechanics, Bahamas topped off the group by reporting the highest

TABLE 4. Modified Balanced Scorecard Results for Technical Aspect Ratings

TECHNICAL ASPECT RATINGS								
	Web Mechanics		Link Popularity		Legal Issues		Overall Total	
Caribbean Countries	Total	Rank	Total	Rank	Total	Rank	Total	Rank
Aruba	16	5	12	3	16	2	44	3
Bahamas	22	1	13	2	12	3	47	1
Barbados	17	4	14	1	11	4	42	4
Cuba	16	5	10	5	10	5	36	6
Dominican Republic	12	8	6	6	11	4	29	8
Jamaica	14	6	14	1	17	1	45	2
Martinique	20	2	6	6	16	2	42	4
Puerto Rico	20	2	11	4	11	4	42	4
St. Maarten	13	7	11	4	8	6	32	7
U.S. Virgin Islands	18	3	10	5	12	3	40	5
MAXIMUM SCORE	**25**		**15**		**20**		**60**	

score of 22 out of 25, while the Dominican Republic earned the lowest score of 12. Poor load time (in excess of 46 seconds), browser incompatibility (had more than 12 problems with the page display in browsers such as Netscape and Internet Explorer), and poor HTML check (had over 18 HTML design code flaws) were the contributing factors to the overall low score obtained by the Dominican Republic. The Bahamas posted maximum scores for link check, HTML check, and spell check, indicating that no dead links or design code problems were present, and that all words were spelt correctly on the Website.

Scores for link popularity ranged from six to fourteen with two countries–Barbados and Jamaica–earning high scores of 14 out of a maximum of 15, and another two earning low scores of 6 (Dominican Republic and Martinique). This category indicated the number of Websites that is linked to the site in question on major search engines such as Altavista, Google, and Hotbot. For legal issues, the maximum score obtainable was 20, with the results for the Websites ranging from a high of 17 for Jamaica to a low of 8 for St. Maarten. The Websites were required to be legally compliant based on how well their copyright disclaimer and trademark was prominently displayed, in addition to their site usage terms and privacy policy. As such, Jamaica was found to be more compliant in these areas than the other sites. Therefore, the top three Websites emerged as

Bahamas, Jamaica, and Aruba respectively from the overall scores for the technical aspects.

Results from the panel ratings on user friendliness, site attractiveness, and marketing effectiveness ranked Aruba as the best Website, followed by Jamaica and then the Bahamas. The results presented in Table 5 show the dominance of the top three Websites throughout the categories. Aruba had the highest mean score of 53.04 out of 65 for user friendliness, while St. Maarten and Martinique recorded the second and third highest scores of 48.28 and 45.20 respectively. Aruba's high scores can be attributed to the fact that for the items: navigate, home, site map, search, theme, and the entire category of ease of contact, the site earned scores of over 4.5 for each. Likewise, St. Maarten and Martinique recorded scores of at least 4.0 for the same categories as Aruba. From the tallies, Cuba's Website was the least user friendly with a mean score of 32.92 as the panelists felt that the category "ease of contact" was poorly represented on the site. Conversely, St. Maarten's earned the lowest score of 39.58 from a maximum of 70 for site attractiveness, while Aruba ranked first with 62.86 closely followed by Jamaica in second with 62.24. By using sharp, clear imagery, the two sites were visually and aesthetically appealing for the panelists, in addition to the use of virtual tours to tangibilize the product.

Once again, Aruba dominated the marketing effectiveness section by amassing the top

TABLE 5. Modified Balanced Scorecard Results for Quantitative Student Expert Ratings

RATINGS–QUANTITATIVE								
	User Friendliness		Site Attractiveness		Marketing Effectiveness		Overall Total	
Caribbean Countries	Mean	Rank	Mean	Rank	Mean	Rank	Total	Rank
Aruba	53.04	1	62.86	1	112.63	1	228.53	1
Bahamas	44.04	6	56.67	3	105.17	3	205.88	3
Barbados	37.42	8	42.10	9	93.63	5	173.15	7
Cuba	32.92	10	51.47	7	74.21	7	158.61	10
Dominican Republic	37.54	7	43.15	8	83.47	10	164.16	9
Jamaica	45.11	4	62.24	2	109.91	2	217.26	2
Martinique	45.20	3	54.67	5	86.45	6	186.32	5
Puerto Rico	44.40	5	56.27	4	93.60	4	194.27	4
St. Maarten	48.28	2	39.58	10	87.01	8	174.87	6
U.S. Virgin Islands	36.86	9	53.81	6	82.08	9	172.76	8
MAXIMUM SCORE	**65**		**70**		**135**		**270**	

mean score of 112.63 of 135 from the panelists, with Jamaica and the Bahamas settling for second and third respectively. Aruba was able to earn high scores for specific items in marketing effectiveness such as market information, market segments, destination activities, and trip planning. Interestingly, Jamaica had high scores in the same categories but had a higher score for market information than that of Aruba. To top off the category of marketing effectiveness, all the scores from the five sub-categories were tallied with the winner emerging as Aruba. Jamaica and the Bahamas were not strong enough to contest Aruba as the site outperformed its competitors with a total score of 228.53 from 270.

Having derived the means for the retention scores in Table 6 for each country, the panelists rated Jamaica as the top site with Aruba and Cuba following closely. Using a scale of 1 to 5, panelists were asked to rate their satisfaction and intent to return to the site after evaluating the user friendliness, site attractiveness, and marketing effectiveness. The Dominican Republic Website was the least satisfying having previously received low scores for Web mechanics, link popularity, user friendliness, site attractiveness, and marketing effectiveness. On the contrary, the destination site for Aruba consistently ranked in the top three for all areas, except for Web mechanics, where it had placed fifth and so it is quite logical for the site to be rated highest for satisfaction.

When the overall totals from Tables 4 and 5 were combined with the satisfaction mean scores from Table 6, Aruba (Aruba.com) emerged as the best overall Caribbean destination Website. Aruba.com was found to be highly interactive and delivered essential information about the destination in a simple, yet elegant and effective manner. The online experience at Aruba.com was engaging for the experts and from the results of the various segments of the survey, the Website, although not technically the best, had its merits for user friendliness, site attractiveness, marketing effectiveness, satisfaction, retention, and was highly recommendable.

WEBSITE VISITOR RETENTION (WVR) MODEL TESTING

In order to construct the best WVR model, the data collected was taken through a three-step process that included preliminary data analysis, principal component analysis for data reduction, and a confirmatory factor analysis to determine model fit respectively. First, second and third-order CFAs were then conducted to arrive at the final WVR model for Caribbean NTO Websites.

Preliminary Data Analysis for Model Testing

In order to carry out the analysis, the authors first addressed the question of whether or not the sample size was sufficient for multilevel modeling and the achievement of ade-

TABLE 6. Modified Balanced Scorecard Results for Qualitative Student Expert Ratings

INITIAL RETENTION RANKING BY COUNTRY								
Maximum Score–30								
Caribbean Countries	Expecta-tion	Experience	Satisfaction with Site	Recommend as Customer	Intention to Revisit as Customer	Recommend Professionally	Total	Rank
Aruba	3.86	3.86	4.71	4.00	4.29	3.71	24.42	2
Bahamas	3.29	3.14	4.00	3.14	3.86	3.71	21.14	7
Barbados	3.71	3.29	2.93	3.29	3.29	3.57	20.07	8
Cuba	4.43	4.14	3.50	4.29	3.57	4.14	24.07	3
Dominican Republic	3.29	3.29	2.71	3.29	3.00	3.57	19.14	10
Jamaica	3.86	4.00	4.43	4.14	4.43	3.71	24.57	1
Martinique	3.57	3.86	3.64	3.57	3.71	3.43	21.78	6
Puerto Rico	4.00	4.29	3.71	3.86	4.00	4.00	23.85	4
St. Maarten	3.29	3.29	2.79	3.43	3.14	3.43	19.36	9
U.S. Virgin Islands	4.14	3.71	3.71	4.00	3.71	3.71	23.00	5

quate model fit. The data set with seven experts rating in ten categories produced a sample size of 70. Based on Bentler and Chou's (1987) suggestion of a minimum of five cases per parameter when using maximum likelihood estimation under reasonable distributional conditions of continuous data in conjunction with Kaplan (2000) who states that sample size sensitivity is only relevant when the null hypothesis is false, and Marsh, Hau, Balla, and Grayson's (1998) recommendations of a minimum of 50 cases in order to achieve proper convergence and parameter accuracy the sample size was deemed appropriate to conduct the study. The data collected from the panelist survey was next checked for missing fields. For those variables with missing fields, the mean scores were entered as CFA analysis cannot be conducted with missing data (Bryne, 2001).

In checking the strength of the relationship between the independent variables, significant problems of multicollinearity were found, as is shown in Table 7. From the table, Item codes: "PAGES," "BACK_GR," "AESTHETI," "VISUAL," "SCROLLIN," and "APPEAL" were found to have Pearson's *r* greater than 0.70 and correlating with multiple other items. As such they were deleted from the dataset, thus reducing the data to 51 variables. Item numbers 1-8 in Table 7 also exceeded Pearson's *r* of 0.70. These items were grouped rather than deleted as they were measuring the same first-order constructs of Web mobility, ease of contact,

market information, and market segments in the proposed model. A further test of multicollinearity showed that the item codes MEET_GRP and BUS_TOUR were found to have Pearson's *r* of 0.715. Both variables were combined to create a new variable called "TOUR_GRP" as they represented the factor market segments thereby reducing the dataset to 40 variables and once rechecked, no evidence of multicollinearity was found. In examining for normality of the 40 variables in the data set, skewness and kurtosis tests were conducted to identify extreme departures from normality. The results of the normality test, which showed no departures from normality, are presented in Table 8.

Principal Component Analysis

The principal component analysis (PCA) procedure for the WVR was used to begin the reduction process of the final number of items that was to be used to represent each construct. PCA analysis was conducted based on the proposed first-order factors of Web mobility, ease of contact, Web interface, tangibilizing of products, marketing information, destination activities, market segments, glocalisation, and trip planner, as was previously shown in Figure 1. A total of nine PCAs were conducted with the results of the factor analysis for each construct shown in Table 9. Of the 40 items used in the first PCA, 11 items were dropped from Web mobility, marketing information,

TABLE 7. Multicollinearity Results

Item Codes	Pearson's Correlation	Omitted	Grouped	New Variables Created
1. NONFRAME to NON_GRAP	.947		Yes	FRAM_GPH
2. MAILING to FAX_NO	.865		Yes	CONTACT
3. HOTELS to RESTAURA	.743		Yes	
4. RESTAURA to EVENTS	.749		Yes	HOTRESEV
5. EVENTS to HOTELS	.746		Yes	
6. HNY_MOON to FAMILIES	.715		Yes	FAMMOON
7. TOUR_GROUP to BUS_TRVL	.715		Yes	BUS_TOUR
8. SPORTING to RECREATE	.885		Yes	ACTIVITY
9. CONTRAST to PAGES	.750	PAGES		
10. BACK_GR to PAGES	.711	Both Items		
11. SCROLLIN to PAGES	.770	Both Items		
12. APPEAL to PAGES	.792	Both Items		
13. CONTRAST to BACK_GR	.774	BACK_GR		
14. CONTRAST to VISUAL	.729	VISUAL		
15. BACK_GR to PICTURES	.733	BACK_GR		
16. BACK_GR to VISUAL	.828	Both Items		
17. PICTURES to AESTHETI	.783	AESTHETI		
18. PICTURES to VISUAL	.825	VISUAL		
19. AESTHETI to VISUAL	.790	Both Items		
20. APPEAL to CONTRAST	.752	APPEAL		
21. APPEAL to BACK_GR	.811	APPEAL		
22. APPEAL to PICTURES	.724	APPEAL		
23. APPEAL to AESTHETI	.795	Both Items		
24. APPEAL to VISUAL	.802	APPEAL		
25. APPEAL to SCROLLIN	.816	Both Items		
26. APPEAL to SPACE	.709	APPEAL		
27. SATISFY to SCROLLIN	.715	SCROLLIN		
28. SATISFY to APPEAL	.799	APPEAL		

glocalisation, and trip planner respectively as they reported values below the 0.50 threshold. As such, only 29 items remained in the data for further analysis. Factor loadings ranged from a low of 0.57 to a high of 0.91 while Eigenvalues returned ranged from 1.67 to 2.71. The majority of constructs had percentages of variance explained in the 60th percentile where the lowest variance was 52.58% and the highest, 83.75%. Kaiser-Meyer-Olkin (KMO) measure of sampling adequacy for the first run of the PCA reported figures from 0.500 to 0.807.

Using varimax rotation with Kaiser normalization to generate factor loadings, a second PCA procedure was then conducted for the initial first-order constructs based on their higher-order constructs. The authors chose to use PCA as it is capable of identifying if any items in a given factor loaded onto items of another factor. As such, items that may inhibit the confirmatory factor analysis procedure were removed from the dataset. Additionally, the method summarizes the least number of items from the majority of the initial variance (Jolliffe, 1986). The second-stage PCA for user friendliness and marketing effectiveness both confirmed the results of the first PCA. However, in the second stage PCA for site attractiveness, the item VIR_TOUR was removed as it was not significant. The reliability coefficients for all the factors derived from the second PCA were normal with results ranging from a low of 0.6833 to a high of 0.8686. The overall findings for the second-stage PCA procedure are shown in Table 10.

Confirmatory Factor Analysis (CFA)

To ensure that the data fit the proposed Website Visitor Retention model, CFA was

TABLE 8. Normality Results

Question	Item Code	Mean Statistic	Std. Deviation Statistic	Skewness Statistic	Kurtosis Statistic
1. Clear and effective navigation tools	NAVIGATE	4.2143	.94628	−.976	−.072
2. Home button available from all pages	HOME	4.0714	1.27770	−1.296	.598
3. Availability of a site map or index	SITE_MAP	2.5000	1.64184	.475	−1.471
4. Availability of a search engine	SEARCH	4.2940	1.25177	−1.819	2.059
5. Links to required plug-ins provided	PLUG_IN	3.1507	1.53600	−.271	−1.324
6. Direct email contact clearly available	EMAIL	3.8406	1.56616	−1.009	−.635
7. Telephone number clearly available	TELEPHON	4.0146	1.50836	−1.304	.073
8. Clear and readable text	TEXT	4.1571	.94233	−1.393	2.299
9. Sufficient contrast	CONTRAST	3.9571	1.04168	−1.100	1.053
10. Pictures to reinforce text	PICTURES	3.9571	1.08261	−.901	−.154
11. Effective use of Web page space	SPACE	3.7101	1.09149	−.629	−.122
12. Current and timely information	INFO	4.2286	1.11864	−1.365	.861
13. Maps and driving directions	MAPS	3.5686	1.46425	−.624	−.969
14. Contact information from visitors	VISITORS	2.5409	1.61132	.502	−1.322
15. Children	CHILDREN	2.3571	1.41458	.790	−.695
16. Couples	COUPLES	3.1143	1.46992	−.231	−1.331
17. Culture and arts activities provided	CULT_ART	3.9429	1.35010	−1.239	.371
18. Mission and purpose of organization	MISION	2.5901	1.52636	.239	−1.514
19. Stated theme carried throughout site	THEME	3.8677	1.16066	−1.040	.546
20. Virtual tour and/or map of city	VIR_TOUR	3.3634	1.42072	−.369	−1.103
21. Testimonials and/or awards posted	AWARDS	2.6500	1.36015	.294	−1.131
22. Photo gallery	PHOTOGAL	3.8823	1.35699	−.890	−.509
23. News releases	NEWS	4.0324	1.40359	−1.323	.331
24. Hyperlinks provided to partners	PARTNERS	4.2120	1.22196	−1.702	1.904
25. Foreign language, special interests	LANGUAGE	3.0934	1.64818	−.175	−1.606
26. Inquiries encouraged	INQUIRY	3.3133	1.31004	−.732	−.618
27. FAQ	FAQ	2.1126	1.41529	1.212	.131
28. Guest-book	GUEST_BK	2.5474	1.70827	.446	−1.565
29. Getting around	GETAROUN	3.8694	1.10221	−.669	−.339
30. Essential information	ESS_INFO	4.0857	1.07330	−1.261	1.205
31. Documents needed by	DOCUMENT	3.0571	1.62307	−.137	−1.615
32. Local weather information	WEATHER	4.2429	1.17258	−1.824	2.624
33. Local bank information	BANK	3.0714	1.58179	−.234	−1.545
34. Things to do	TODO	3.9714	1.15434	−1.281	1.072
35. Non-Frame/Non-Graph option	FRAM_GPH	1.6750	1.02778	1.837	2.157
36. Mailing address; fax number	CONTACT	3.2943	1.77825	−.346	−1.711
37. Honeymoon and families	FAMMOON	3.3214	1.35678	−.515	−.943
38. Sports/outdoor recreation	ACTIVITY	3.9210	1.25850	−1.102	.174
39. Hotel, restaurants and events	HOTRESEV	4.1152	1.12889	−1.208	.399
40. Meeting/tour groups, business travel	TOUR_GRP	3.1357	1.33764	−.226	−1.213

carried out for a thorough analysis of the underlying structure. As the nature of the data is continuous, the authors used maximum likelihood estimation procedure with covariance matrix. The procedure was used as it is considered to be theory-oriented, thereby emphasizing the transition from exploratory to confirmatory analysis. Model testing was conducted using Analysis of Moment Structures (AMOS 4.0). In assessing the model as a whole, the goodness-of-fit statistics were examined (Byrne, 2001). In addition, the comparative fit index (CFI) as proposed by Bentler (1990), which should be reported for small sample

TABLE 9. Initial Principal Component Analysis Solution

Construct	No. of Items	Range of Factor Loading	Items Dropped	Eigenvalue	% of Variance Explained	KMO
1. Web Mobility	8	.78-.82	5	1.93	64.34%	.678
2. Ease of Contact	3	.79-.88	0	2.13	71.17%	.683
3. Web Interface	4	.77-.88	0	2.71	67.87%	.771
4. Tangibilize Products	4	.62-.81	0	2.10	52.58%	.681
5. Marketing Information	4	.78-.85	1	2.07	69.17%	.688
6. Destination Activities	2	.91	0	1.67	83.75%	.500
7. Market Segments	4	.83-.87	0	2.87	71.87%	.807
8. Glocalisation	5	.57-.82	2	1.68	56.28%	.579
9. Trip Planner	6	.71-.83	3	1.83	61.05%	.639

TABLE 10. Rotated Principal Component Analysis Solution

User Friendliness			Site Attractiveness		
	Ease of Contact	Web Mobility		Web Interface	Tangibilize Products
Eigenvalues	*2.35*	*1.74*	*Eigenvalues*	*3.67*	*.1.18*
Alpha	*.7955*	*.7161*	*Alpha*	*.8406*	*.6833*
CONTACT	.887		CONTRAST	.886	
TELEPHON	.855		PICTURES	.806	
EMAIL	.774		SPACE	.773	
HOME		.832	TEXT	.681	
THEME		.798	PHOTOGAL		.878
NAVIGATE		.767	NEWS		.811
			AWARDS		.509
			VIR_TOUR*		
KMO = .677, Bartlett's test X^2 111.86; df = 15; p = 0.000			KMO = .794, Bartlett's test X^2 200.007; df = 28; p = 0.000		

Marketing Effectiveness			
	Market Segment	Destination Activities	Marketing Information	Glocalisation
Eigenvalues	*4.78*	*2.19*	*1.98*	*1.17*
Alpha	*.8686*	*.8010*	*.7409*	*.6702*
FAMMOON	.887			
COUPLES	.799			
CHILDREN	.795			
TOUR_GRP	.753			
WEATHER		.785		
CULT_ART		.718		
ESS_INFO		.672		
TODO		.657		
ACTIVITY		.628		
MAPS			.867	
HOTRESEV			.793	
LANGUAGE			.660	
INFO			.634	
GUEST_BK				.858
INQUIRY				.795
KMO = .779, Bartlett's test X^2 432.188; df = 105; p = 0.000			

*Values below 0.50 are suppressed.

sizes, was examined. For CFI values closer to 0.95 are considered representative of a well fitting model (Hu & Bentler, 1999).

Model Results

For all stages of the analysis from first-order to third-order, the standardized residual covariance did not display unusually large estimates (greater than 2.58). In the initial first-order model, negative covariances were noted between the latent constructs marketing information and ease of contact, ease of contact and Website interface, as well as between glocalisation and destination activities, and glocalisation and tangibilization of products. Based on the modification indices and the expected parameter change (EPC) statistic, a step-by-step removal process was used to achieve appropriate model fit. At the end of the first-order model testing, the constructs of glocalisation and marketing information were removed in addition to the items "PICTURES" and "TEXT." Model fit was achieved with $\chi^2 = 188.99$; df = 155; p = 0.033; CFI = 0.933; RMSEA = 0.056. All standardized estimates were substantively reasonable and statistically significant at the p = 0.001 level. The results of the CFA analysis for the first-order WVR model are displayed in Figure 2.

In the second-order CFA, based on the EPC statistic, improved model fit was achieved by the removal of five items "THEME," "TELE-PHONE," "FAM_MOON," "CHILDREN," and "WEATHER." The modification indices also noted that a correlation of the error terms between "EMAIL" and "MAIL/FAX" would also improve the final model statistic. This makes sense intuitively as inquiries by e-mail requesting information on a particular destination are often followed with the faxing or snail mailing of brochures and other paraphernalia not included at the destination's Website. The results of the CFA analysis for the second-order WVR model are shown in Figure 3.

In the third-order model, no items were removed to achieve model fit. The final model showed WVR was impacted by the second-order functions of user friendliness (0.76), site attractiveness (0.81), and marketing effectiveness (0.83). The results of the CFA analysis

for the third-order WVR model are shown in Figure 4.

DISCUSSION AND CONCLUSION

The first- to third-order CFA modeling-building process produced good model fitting results for the Caribbean NTO WVR model. The model presents a base for Caribbean NTOs and other regions to use for evaluating their Websites. Marketing effectiveness was most significant in the model with a regression weight of 0.83 indicating that with Caribbean NTOs are focusing on making their Websites more appealing by focusing on key market segments and bringing across their destination activities as evidenced by the information discussed in the literature review and shown in Table 2. Key marketing segments that remained in the model were couples and groups, which have traditionally been the focus of the sun, sea, and sand focus of advertisements depicting the Caribbean. Group business has also become popular particularly with convention business and spring break travelers. While the information available on the products and services of each destination are similar from destination to destination, marketing effectiveness becomes more important to the destinations as they look to differentiate from their competitors. Differentiation could thus be exploited through the first-order construct of destination activities which goes hand in hand to create marketing effectiveness.

Consistent with Website design literature, user friendliness and site attractiveness are seen as key to Caribbean NTO Websites. Owing to the fact that Caribbean destinations themselves exude a warm, welcoming feeling to visitors, the Websites have sought to reflect those same emotions to the online visitor in keeping with the customs of the islands. With the nature of the industry being highly people personal, it seems logical that user friendliness and site attractiveness has a strong relationship with visitor retention. In further dissection of the model, factor loadings for ease of contact were (0.32) and (0.47) respectively. These loadings were the lowest in the model and may indicate a need to restructure these items in the modified BSC instrument. Web

FIGURE 2. First-Order CFA Model for Caribbean NTO Website Visitor Retention

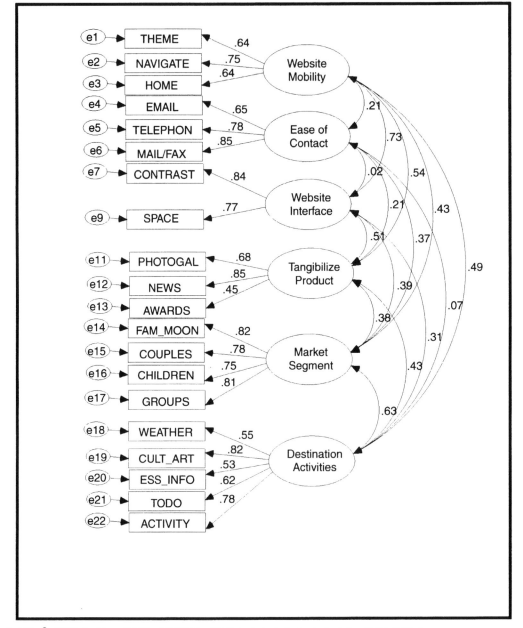

Model fit: χ^2 = 188.99; df = 155; p = .033; CFI = .933; RMSEA = .056. All standardized estimates significant at p = .0001 to .001 level.

mobility produced the highest factor loading in the model of .95 for "NAVIGATE" reflecting the emphasis these Websites placed on browsing through the site. The expert results therefore suggest the need for Websites to simulate "the help desk" scenario at the destination online. With the customer contact employee absent from Website interaction, it becomes increasingly important for the visitor to be able to travel through the site without

FIGURE 3. Second-Order CFA Model for Caribbean NTO Website Visitor Retention

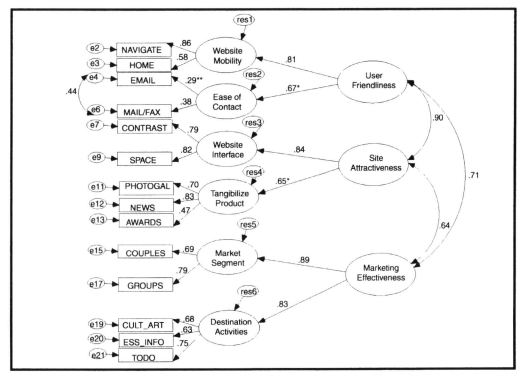

Model fit: χ^2 = 79.11; df = 73; p = .0292; CFI = .976; RMSEA = .035. All standardized estimates significant at p = .0001 level EXCEPT as noted (*); where *p = .007; **p = .11.

having any problems. One other explanation as to why ease of contact is less important could be because the experts recognize that it is better to design a Website where navigating is easily facilitated as well as to contribute to "hits" rather than to have a poorly designed site where visitors constantly use "contact us." The point here is not to argue the irrelevance of ease of contact but to introduce the theory that in an online environment, not every visitor will want to "talk to the machine" especially for an industry where interpersonal relations are essential. By all means, websites should provide contact information and more so in a variety of ways such as telephone, address, e-mail, and fax thus allowing the visitor to choose the medium he/she desires.

Interestingly, the results show that Website interface had a higher factor loading of .86 than tangibilized product with a loading of .66. This suggests that the appeal of the Web design considerably influences the perception of

its attractiveness. Additionally, it is important for Caribbean Websites to consider improvements to the methods currently used to physically represent the tourism product and service in the online environment. Factors such as the availability of current news on the island were deemed more important by the panelists whereas the option to view a photo gallery was the second most important.

Overall, the testing of a third-order CFA model with Caribbean NTOs provided evidence for the continued support and use of the modified BSC instrument for assessing various travel and hospitality-related Websites. The results of the survey and modeling process provide compelling evidence for Caribbean NTOs to adapt and continue to use an interactive Internet marketing strategy. However, the use of expert ratings in the evaluation of these Websites was not without any limitations and it is the opinion of the authors that these results may vary from one expert to another. Viewed

FIGURE 4. Third-Order CFA Model for Caribbean NTO Website Visitor Retention

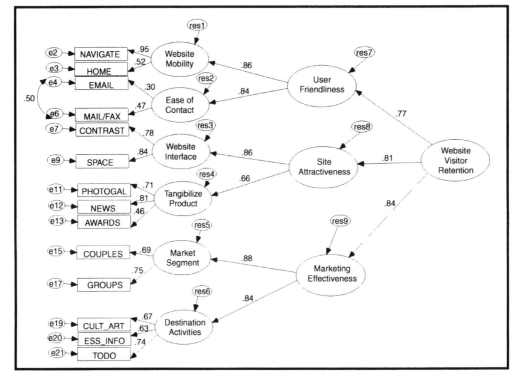

Model fit: χ^2 = 82.10; df = 75; p = .0269; CFI = .972; RMSEA = .037. All standardized estimates significant at p = .0001 to .02 level.

as a representation or a snapshot of the expert's state of knowledge at the time of the evaluation of the Website, the views can and should change as time moves on and the expert acquires new learning and experiences (Booker & Meyer, 2001; Keeney & Windterfedt, 1989). Thus, as Amento et al. (2000) argue, the degree of variability in the results from one expert to the next may significantly question the shared concept of Website quality exists. On the other hand, if the expert results show a high degree of accordance in their judgment, confidence in the quality of the Website is reinforced.

REFERENCES

Amento, B., Terveen, L., & Hill, W. (2000). Does "authority" mean quality? Predicting expert quality ratings of Web sites. In: Belkin, N. J., Ingwersen, P., Leong, M. (Eds.). *Proceedings of the 23rd Annual International ACM SIGIR Conference on Research and Development in Information Retrieval* (pp. 296-303). New York: ACM Press.

ARA Consulting Group Inc., Systems Caribbean Ltd., Marshall, I., KPMG Peat Marwick Barbados (1996, May 30). *A study to assess the economic impact of tourism on selected CDB borrowing member countries.* The Caribbean Development Bank, Barbados.

Barbados.org (1997). *Internet marketing of travel.* Retrieved July 17, 2003 from http://barbados.org/marketwatch.

Baumgarten, J. (2003). *Presentation: The third global travel and tourism summit.* Retrieved June 24, 2003 from http://www.wttc.org.

Beddoe-Stephens, P. (1999). Yahoo: gettin' sticky with it. *Wired News.* Retrieved July 7, 2003 from http://www.wired.com/news/culture/0,1284,18229,00.html.

Beirne, E. & Curry, P. (1999). The impact of the Internet on the information search process and tourism decision making. In: Buhalis, D. and Schertler, W. (Eds.). *Information and Communication Technologies in Tourism.* Wein, Austria: Springer-Verlag.

Bentler, P. M., & Chou, C. (1987). Practical issues in structural modeling. *Sociological Methods & Research,* 16, 78-117.

Bentler, P. (1990). Comparative fit indexes in structural models. *Psychological Bulletin*, 107, 238-246.

Bloch, M. & Segev, A. (1996, March). *Impact of electronic commerce on the travel industry, an analysis, methodology, and case study.* Retrieved June 29, 2003 from University of California, Berkeley, Walter Haas School of Business, The Fisher Center for Information Technology & Management Website: http://haas.berkeley.edu/~citm.

Booker, J. M. & Meyer, M. A. (2001). *Elicitation and analysis of expert judgment: A practical guide 2nd Edition.* ASA-SIAM Series on Statistics and Applied Probability. Philadelphia, PA: SIAM.

Boolin, B., Burgess, L. & Cooper, J. (2002). Evaluating the use of the Web for tourism marketing: A case study from New Zealand. *Tourism Management*, 23(5), 557-561.

Bryan, A. T., (2001). Caribbean tourism: Igniting the engines of sustainable growth. *The North-South Agenda*, 52, 1-30.

Buhalis, D. (1998). Information technologies in tourism: Implications for the tourism curriculum. In: Buhalis, D. and Jafari, J. (Eds.). *Information and Communications Technologies in Tourism* (pp. 289-297). Vienna, Austria: Springer-Verlag.

Buhalis, D. (2000). Marketing the competitive destination of the future. *Tourism Management*, 21(1), 97-116.

Buhalis, D., & Dombey, O. (2001). Changing distribution channels in the travel industry. *International Journal of Tourism Research*, 3(6), 507-511.

Byrne, B. (2001). *Structural equation modeling with AMOS: Basic concepts, applications, and programming.* New Jersey, NY: Lawrence Erlbaum Associates.

CANA Business Interactive (2000). *Internet thrust to market regional tourism.* Retrieved June 30, 2003 from http://www.cananews.com/cbi/businessupdate783.htm.

Caribbean Tourism Organization (2002a). *Life needs the Caribbean.* Retrieved June 10, 2003 from http://www.onecaribbean.org.

Caribbean Tourism Organization (2002b). *CTO Website promoting the Caribbean gets recognition from leading online tourism industry magazine.* Retrieved July 2, 2003 from http://www.onecaribbean.org.

Caribbean Tourism Organization (2003a). *Information centre.* Retrieved July 10, 2004 from http://www.onecaribbean.org.

Caribbean Tourism Organization (2003b). *Key tourism statistics January-March 2003.* Retrieved June 10, 2003 from http://www.onecaribbean.org.

Cheong, T. H. (2002). *Glocalisation (going global, staying local).* Retrieved July 3, 2003 from Ngee Ann Polytechnic Website: http://www.np.edu.sg/~dept-corpcomm/ar/.

Collins, J. (2003). State of Caribbean tourism mixed. *PymesDominicanas.com.* Retrieved June 25, 2003 from http://www.pymesdominicanas.com/english/articles/collins_state-of-caribbean.htm.

Davidson, R. & Maitland, R. (1997). *Tourism destinations.* London: Hodder & Stoughton.

eLoyalty Corporation (1999). *The customer relationship revolution–A methodology for creating golden customers.* Retrieved June 30, 2003 from http://www.eloyaltyco.com.

Faulkner, B. (1997). A model for the evaluation of national tourism destination marketing programs. *Journal of Travel Research*, 35(3), 23-32.

Formica, S. & Littlefield, J. (2000). National Tourism Organizations: A promotional plans framework. *Journal of Hospitality & Leisure Marketing*, 7(1), 103-119.

Forrester Research (1999). *Web site success transcends hits and page views, predicts Forrester Research.* Retrieved June 18, 2003 from http://www.forrester.com.

Fortune (2001). Design Matters. *Fortune Winter Technology Guide*, 142(12), 183-187.

Gallagher, K., Foster, K. D., & Parsons, J. (2001). The medium is not the message: Advertising effectiveness and content evaluation in print and on the Web. *Journal of Advertising Research*, 41(4), 57-70.

Girvan, N. (2001). *Rescuing Caribbean tourism.* Retrieved June 25, 2003 from http://www.acs-aec.org/column/index9.htm.

Girvan, N. (2002). *Can Caribbean tourism be reinvented?* Retrieved June 26, 2003 from http://www.acs-aec.org/column/index59.htm.

Gretzel, U., Yuan, Y., & Fesenmaier, D. R. (2000). Preparing for the new economy: Advertising strategies and change in destination marketing organizations. *Journal of Travel Research*, 39(2), 146-156.

Hall, C. M. (2000). *Tourism planning: Policies, processes, relationships.* UK: Prentice Hall.

Hanna, J. R. P. & Millar, R. J. (1997). Promoting tourism on the Internet. *Tourism Management*, 18(7), 469-470.

Hardesty, D. M. & Bearden, W. O. (2004). The use of expert judges in scale development: Implications for improving face validity of measures of unobservable constructs. *Journal of Business Research*, 57(2), 98-107.

Heath, R. (1997). Loyalty for sale: Everybody's doing frequency marketing–but only a few companies are doing it well. *Marketing Tools*, 4(7), 40.

Hodgkins, R. (1999). Increase the stickiness of your website. *Computer Weekly.* Retrieved July 7, 2003 from http://www.computerweekly.com/Article46033.htm.

Hoffman, D. L. & Novak, T. P. (1996). Marketing in hypermedia computer-mediated environments: Conceptual foundations. *Journal of Marketing*, 60, 50-68.

Hospitality Net (2002, September). *Caribbean hotel association charitable trust and Expedia, Inc. partner to boost area tourism with Gocaribbean.com.* Retrieved June 23, 2003 from http://www.hospitalitynet.org.

Hu, L. & Bentler, P. (1999). Cutoff criteria for fit indexes in covariance analysis: Conventional criteria versus new analysis. *Structural Equation Modeling: Multidisciplinary Journal*, 6, 1-55.

Ismail, J., Labropoulos, T., Mills, J. E., & Morrison, A. (2002). A snapshot in time: The marketing of culture in European Union NTO Websites. *Tourism, Culture & Communication*, 3(3), 165-179.

Ismail, J. & Mills, J. E. (2001). Contract disputes in travel and tourism: When the online deal goes bad. *Journal of Travel & Tourism Marketing*, 11(2/3), 63-82.

Jackson, P. F. (1999, June). *Caribbean hotels turn to the Internet.* Retrieved June 23, 2003 from http://www.jamaicagleaner.com.

Jayawardena, C. (2000). The future of tourism in the Caribbean. *The Jamaica Gleaner.* Retrieved June 25, 2003 from http://www.jamaica-gleaner.com/gleaner/20001019/news/news3.html.

Jayawardena, C. (2002). Mastering Caribbean tourism. *International Journal of Contemporary Hospitality Management*, 14(2), 88-93.

Jolliffe, I. T. (1986). *Principal Component Matrix.* New York: Springer-Verlag.

Kaminski, J. (2003). Stickiness: Attract & keep Website traffic. *BellaOnline.* Retrieved from http://www.bellaonline.com/articles/art1678.asp.

Kaplan, D. (2000). *Structural equation modeling: Foundations and extensions. Advanced quantitative techniques in the social science series.* Thousand Oaks, CA: SAGE Publications, Inc.

Kaplan, R. S. & Norton, D. P. (1992). The balanced scorecard–measures that drive performance. *Harvard Business Review*, January/February, 71-79.

Karma Centre for Knowledge and Research in Marketing (1998). *Caribbean tourism survey.* Retrieved June 30, 2003 from http://www.oas.org/TOURISM/tr_othe.htm.

Kiani, G. R. (1998). Marketing opportunities in the digital world. *Internet Research*, 8(2), 185-194.

Kierzkowski, A., McQuade, S., Waitman, R. & Zeisser, M. (1996). Marketing to the digital consumer. *McKinsey Quarterly*, 33, 4-21.

King, J. (2001). Destination marketing organizations–Connecting the experience rather than promoting the place. *Journal of Vacation Marketing*, 8(2), 105-108.

Kohli, A. K. & Zaltman, G. (1988). Measuring multiple buying influences. *Industrial Marketing Management*, 17(3), 197-204.

Korgaonkar, P. & Wolin, L. D. (2002). Web usage, advertising, and shopping: Relationship patterns. *Internet Research: Electronic Networking Applications and Policy*, 12(2), 191-204.

Leckenby, J. D. (1998). *Theories of persuasive communication and consumer decision making: Emotion in advertising.* Retrieved June 16, 2003 from http://www.ciadvertising.org/studies/student/98_fall/theory/weirtz/Emotion.htm.

MacLeod, S. (2001). *Gazing at the box: Tourism in the context of the Internet and globalization.* Retrieved June 25, 2003 from http://scottmacleod.com/anthropology/anth250v.htm.

Malhotra, N. K. (1981). A scale to measure self-concepts, person concepts, and product concepts. *Journal of Marketing Research*, 18(4), 456-464.

Marcussen, C. H. (2003). *Trends in U.S. online travel market.* Retrieved July 14, 2003 from http://www.crt.dk/uk/staff/chm/trends/USA_2003.pdf.

Marsh, H. W., Hau, K-T., Balla, J. R., & Grayson, D. (1998). Is more ever too much? The number of indicators per factor in confirmatory factor analysis. *Multivariate Behavioral Research*, 33, 181-220.

Mills, J. E. & Morrison, A. M. (2000). Updated Balanced Score Card Instrument. Available: http://www.htmresearch.atfreeweb.com/BSC.

Mills, J. E. & Morrison, A. M. (2002b). *Leaving the tried and true, embracing the new: A primer on the advantages of Web vs. traditional advertising.* Unpublished Manuscript, Purdue University, West Lafayette, Indiana.

Mitchell, K. (2000, December 6). *Transitioning to the global economy–Imperatives for the smaller economies.* CLAA Miami Conference. Unpublished manuscript.

Morrison, A. M., Mills, J. E., Chuvessiriporn, S. & Ismail, J. A. (2002). Where are we now? An initial analysis of Web-based marketing issues affecting travel and tourism. In Wober, K. W., Frew, A. J. & Hitz, M. (Eds.). *Information and Communications Technologies in Tourism 2002* (pp. 375-386). Springer Computer Science, Austria.

Nemzow, M. (1999). Ecommerce "stickiness" for customer retention. *Journal of Internet Banking and Commerce*, 4(1). Retrieved July 7, 2003 from http://www.array.dev.com/commerce/jibc/9908-03.htm.

Ortiz, N. R., Wheeler, T. A., Breeding, R. J., Hora, S., Meyer, M. A. & Keeney, R. L. (1991). Use of Expert Judgments in NUREG-1150. *Nuclear Engineering and Design*, 126, 313-331.

Parsons, A., Zeisser, M. & Waitman, R. (1998). Organizing today for the digital marketing of tomorrow. *Journal of Interactive Marketing*, 12(1), 31-46.

Pearce, D. G. (1996). Tourist organizations in Sweden. *Tourism Management*, 17(6), 413-424.

Perdue, R. R. (2001). Internet site evaluations: The influence of behavioral experience, existing images, and selected Website characteristics. *Journal of Travel & Tourism Marketing*, 11(2/3), 21-38.

Profitadvisors.com (1998). *Better business ideas #13: The lifetime value of a customer.* Retrieved July 17, 2003 from http://www.profitadvisors.com/customer.shtml.

Reddy, A. C., Langdale, H. & Iyer, R. (2002). Creating and maintaining effective E-commerce Websites. *Journal of Internet Marketing*, 2 (1). Retrieved June

19, 2003 from http://www.arraydev.com/commerce/jim/0203-05.htm.

Sandals Resorts (2003). *Operation Relax*. Retrieved June 29, 2003 from http://www.sandals.com/general/operation-relax.cfm.

Stewart, G. (2001, June). *The state of Caribbean tourism*. Chic conference 2001. Retrieved July 5, 2003 from http://www.caribbeanhotels.org/cha/conferences/Butch%20Stewart%20Speech.pdf.

SuperClubs (2003). *40% off all SuperClubs resorts in 2003!* Retrieved June 29, 2003 from http://www.superclubs.com/sc_specials_item.asp?newsUID=52.

The Economic Times (2002, June 16 & 23). *Glocalisation: Globalization plus localization*. Retrieved July 3, 2003 from http://www.swaminomics.org/et_articles/et20020623_glocalisation.htm.

The Destination Group (1999). *About Insider's Jamaica*. Retrieved June 30, 2003 from http://www.insidersjamaica.co.uk/index.html?left.htm&top.htm&about_us/index.htm.

The Jamaica Gleaner (2000, January 22). *Insiders' Jamaica deemed failure*. Retrieved June 26, 2003 from http://www.jamaica-gleaner.com/gleaner/20000122/news/n3.html.

The Namibian (2003, April 4). *Tourism in Caribbean threatened*. Retrieved June 25, 2003 from http://www.namibian.com.na/2003/march/world/03C404E6D9.html.

Tierney, P. (2000) Internet-based evaluation of tourism Web site effectiveness: Methodological issues and survey results. *Journal of Travel Research*, 39(2), 212-219.

Tourism British Columbia (2000). *Internet Marketing*. Tourism Business Essentials Series.

United Nations Trade & Development Board (2000). *Electronic commerce and tourism: New perspectives and challenges for developing countries*. Retrieved July 10, 2003 from http://r0.unctad.org/en/special/c3em9ag.htm.

Weber, K. & Roehl, W. (1999). Profiling people searching for and purchasing travel products on the World Wide Web. *Journal of Travel Research*, 37(3), 291-298.

Werthner, H. & Klein, S. (1999). *Information technology and tourism–A challenging relationship*. Wien, Austria: Springer-Verlag.

Werthner, H. & Klein, S. (2000). *Information technology and tourism–A challenging relationship*. Wien, New York: Springer Computer Science.

World Tourism Business Council (1999). *Marketing tourism destinations online–Strategies for the information age*. Retrieved July 10, 2003 from http://www.world-tourism.org.

World Tourism Organization (2000). *Tourism highlights 2000 (2nd Edition)*. Spain: World Tourism Organization Business Council.

World Tourism Organization Business Council (2001). *E-Business for tourism: Practical guideline for tourism destinations and businesses*. Retrieved July 1, 2003 from http://www.wto.org.

Zaichkowsky, J. L. (1994). The personal involvement inventory: Reduction, revision, and application to advertising. *Journal of Advertising*, 23(4), 59-70.

Zeff, R. L. & Aronson, B. (1999). *Advertising on the Internet, Second Edition*. John Wiley & Sons, Inc.

Developing a Content Analysis Evaluation Approach for the Examination of Limited-Service Lodging Properties

Sunny Ham

SUMMARY. This exploratory study investigates the Website effectiveness of limited-service chain lodging operations. Websites of the top 25 limited-service chain lodging operations in the U.S. were evaluated based on the criteria established for the study. The seven evaluation criteria included impression, content usefulness, accuracy, navigation, accessibility, online reservations, and timeliness of information. A detailed description was developed for each criterion. The results of this study offers a starting point for both Web researchers and practitioners in the limited-service segment of the lodging industry to determine specific areas of Website improvements. *[Article copies available for a fee from The Haworth Document Delivery Service: 1-800-HAWORTH. E-mail address: <docdelivery@ haworthpress.com> Website: <http://www.HaworthPress.com> © 2004 by The Haworth Press, Inc. All rights reserved.]*

KEYWORDS. Web effectiveness, limited-service chain lodging operations, evaluation criteria

INTRODUCTION

Substantial investments in the developing, maintaining, and advertising through Web-based mechanisms have made the evaluation of Website effectiveness essential (Tierney, 2000). Website evaluation studies for the travel and tourism sector encompass airline (Chu, 2001), travel (Law & Wong, 2003; Chu, 2001), state tourism offices (Tierney, 2000), regional tourism organizations (Benckendorff & Black, 2000; Doolin, Burgess, & Cooper, 2002), and lodging industry (Jeong & Lambert, 2001; Wan, 2002; Murphy, Forrest, Wotring, & Brymer, 1996). The evaluation of lodging-industry Websites covered international tourist hotels, global hotel industries through six continents, and tour wholesalers (Murphy et al., 1996; Wan, 2002; Wei, Ruys, van Hoof, & Combrink, 2001). However, these studies were focused mainly on luxury, upscale, or larger hotels. Little research has been devoted to the Websites of the limited-service lodging sector. Previous research (van Hoof & Combrink,

Sunny Ham is Assistant Professor, Hospitality and Tourism Management, University of Kentucky.

Address correspondence to Sunny Ham, Hospitality and Tourism, University of Kentucky, 121 Erikson Hall, Lexington, KY 40506 (E-mail: sham2@uky.edu).

The author is grateful to Wing Ka Yeung, a graduate student at the Hospitality and Dietetics Department, for her assistance to the project. The author also acknowledges two formal reviewers for their thorough and helpful suggestions.

[Haworth co-indexing entry note]: "Developing a Content Analysis Evaluation Approach for the Examination of Limited-Service Lodging Properties." Ham, Sunny. Co-published simultaneously in *Journal of Travel & Tourism Marketing* (The Haworth Hospitality Press, an imprint of The Haworth Press, Inc.) Vol. 17. No. 2/3, 2004, pp. 295-308; and: *Handbook of Consumer Behavior, Tourism, and the Internet* (ed: Juline E. Mills, and Rob Law) The Haworth Hospitality Press, an imprint of The Haworth Press, Inc., 2004, pp. 295-308. Single or multiple copies of this article are available for a fee from The Haworth Document Delivery Service [1-800-HAWORTH, 9:00 a.m. - 5:00 p.m. (EST). E-mail address: docdelivery@haworthpress.com].

1988) indicate that the limited-service lodging industry is less exposed to the Internet mainly due to financial reasons, and thus barely receive as much benefit as the full-service sector does. However, providing Internet access as well as developing effective Websites is inevitable for the limited-service sector to maintain or increase its target market as customers are becoming more technology-oriented.

Given the importance of the Internet to the lodging industry and the lack of attention paid to the limited-service lodging sector, this study proposed to examine the effectiveness of the Websites of the limited-service lodging operations in the United States. The research objectives were two-fold: (1) to establish evaluation criteria for Websites of the limited-service lodging sector, and (2) to identify opportunities for improvements for the Websites by evaluating the Websites of the sector based on the established criteria for the study. The results of the study may be beneficial to researchers investigating Website evaluation and to lodging practitioners who would like to know more about the current state of Websites in the limited-service lodging sector.

LIMITED-SERVICE CHAIN LODGING OPERATIONS

In opposite of "full-service" lodging properties, "limited-service" is defined as a hotel that provides a limited number of amenities and which does not provide food service (Hebert, 1997). Two distinct price categories are included within the broadly defined limited-service segment: budget/economy and moderate price. In addition to the traditional value-oriented economy property, this segment has the gamut of the lodging product types such as extended-stay, all suites, business class, and combinations of the three (Hebert, 1997).

A reopening of the bank finance market to small property developers in addition to strong capital flows from public and equity markets, growing customer recognition, as well as high returns forced the development of the limited-service lodging sector in the eighties. From 1993 through 1996, the limited-service sector posted a 73% increase in total room

openings in the lodging industry, with new room openings accounting for 89% of aggregate industry openings during the period (Hebert, 1997). After recovering from the recession of the early 1990s, the U.S. lodging market enjoyed over 65 percent occupancies throughout the late 1990s. However, in 1998, over one-quarter of the limited-service sector managed to have occupancy rates of less than 60%, while only 16.5% of full-service sector performed with less than 60% occupancy (Quek, 1999). By 2002, there were 33,334 limited-service lodging operations in the U.S., 2.6 times as many as the full-service sector. Both sectors had occupancy rates of around 60% with RevPAR (revenue per available room) of $38 and $62, respectively, for limited-service and full-service sectors (Smith Travel Research, 2003). Hospitality Research Group (2002) forecasted growth for both the full and limited-service sectors from 2003 through 2005. However, in comparison with RevPAR increases ranging from six to ten percent for the full-service sector the outlook for the limited-service market was not as optimistic with forecasted RevPAR increase of only 2.3 percent.

With regards to the use of the Internet, hotel managers are recognizing the value of Websites. Websites serve as strong marketing tools as well as attractive information sources for hotel products and services. In addition, the lodging Website is a communication medium between customers and the property by exchanging numerous inquiries and responses (Shaw, 1996). Lodging managers regard the Internet as the most effective when used as a marketing and advertising tool (Van Hoof & Combrink, 1998). However, managers in the limited-service sector perceived the marketing and advertising roles of the Internet less significantly than do managers in full-service and resort sectors. Limited-service lodging managers contend that that accessibility of the Internet was not as important to them as it was for managers in other property types. Passive attitudes of limited-service lodging managers may have originated from their lack of experience with the Internet (Van Hoof & Combrink, 1998).

WEBSITE AND TECHNOLOGY EVALUATION IN THE LODGING INDUSTRY

With a growing reliance on Internet marketing, a great deal of attention was given to studies regarding the effectiveness of the Web dealing specifically with lodging companies (Jeong & Lambert, 2001; Wan, 2002; Murphy et al., 1996; Wei et al., 2001). Previous Website evaluation studies for the lodging industry cover a variety of sectors, including international tourist hotels, tour wholesalers (Wan, 2002), global hotels (Wei et al., 2001), and chain and independent hotels (Murphy et al., 1996). Geographical locations of the studied hotels vary across six continents including the United States, Taiwan, and Wales. In regard to the methodologies involved, each research project developed criteria based on a review of literature and specific factors relevant to the segment under investigation to examine Website effectiveness of the respective sector. The researchers also attempted to objectively measure the Websites with rating scales. Different rating systems were employed from Likert type 5-point, 7-point, and 1 or 0 ordinal ratings.

Information quality of the lodging Website was found to be a key factor affecting customers' purchasing behavior. Jeong and Lambert (2002) evaluated simulated lodging Websites by 240 conference attendees. Information quality was measured in the areas of information content, information format, and physical environment, using a 7-point Likert-type scale. The study concluded that Web users looked for accurate, relevant, helpful, and important information to make their purchase decision. The study authors recommended that lodging companies incorporate qualified information to their Websites to reap a strategic advantage and excel in the current customer-focused e-market.

Wan (2002) performed Website evaluations of international tourist hotels and tour wholesalers in Taiwan. Three evaluation criteria were developed: user interface, variety of information, and online reservations. Websites of 30 tourist hotels and 39 tour wholesalers were examined following the three criteria using a 5-point rating scale. User interface was scored the highest, followed by online reservations, and variety of information. In respect of online reservations, 13% of Websites of tour wholesalers offered an online reservation service, but only five hotels and one tour wholesaler provided a credit card payment system.

Murphy and colleagues also released an article about online reservations of lodging operations. A study of hotel Websites in Florida (Murphy et al., 1996) found that less than 50% of the 36 hotel Websites (20 chain and 16 independent hotels) had reservation systems on the Internet. The discrepancy between the two countries (United States and Taiwan) indicated that the Website was not used in Taiwan's tourism/travel industry for marketing, but rather its main role was advertising. Regarding online reservations, Murphy and his colleagues (1996) pointed out that there was a huge gap between offering reservation features and providing a mechanism to complete the transaction. In their study of 20 chain and 16 independent hotels, only seven Websites offered a method to make payment, and only two sites offered secure (encrypted) online payment methods. This lack of security results in customers' concern over booking hotel reservations over the Internet. The online reservation issue was also the focus of other researchers as well. Wei et al. (2001) reported only a small proportion of reservations received from the Internet despite the fact that other features of Internet use were commonly used in the lodging industry. The study respondents did not feel secure about releasing financial and personal information, which might occur through these transactions. The investigators attributed a low reservation rate from the Web partly due to the lack of relevant information on the site.

Wei and colleagues (2001) looked into the uses of the Internet by surveying the members of Global Hoteliers, a 900-member organization of international hotel executives. Hotel size, star rating, hotel type and geographical location of hotels were found to have some significant effect on Internet use. Over 90% of the hotels provide Websites, which was not surprising given that a majority of the respondents worked at large hotels. This figure contrasted with the Taiwan study in which only 50% of the sampled hotels established the

Websites (Wan, 2002). Hotel size also had a significant effect on who designed the Websites. While many larger hotels had the Web built by media specialists, smaller hotels tended to delegate the task to the corporate office. E-mail use can be tracked by the hotel's star rating; four- and five-star hotels use e-mail significantly more often to communicate with line staff, other managers, and corporate officers. As to hotel type, larger numbers of conference hotels did have information about room availability, whereas a higher proportion of resort hotels included virtual tours of the property. The geographical location of the hotels had a significant effect on providing room availability information on the Website. Australian, Pacific, and European hotels offered more information about room availability than hotels in Central and South America and Africa.

A longitudinal study on the use of the Internet by hotels in Wales (Main, 2000) showed the technological trend in the hotel industry across sectors. The changes in the profile of technology from 1994 and 2000 showed that large hotel companies were at the forefront of the move to adopt IT; however, small- and medium-sized travel organizations kept abreast of the trend, and the use of technology, including the Internet, has been increasing in those sectors since 1994. One of the findings was that some demographic factors of the property (e.g., size) and managers (e.g., age, education, gender) played a crucial role in the use of technology, but there was no evidence that these factors made a significant impact in 2000. The study also showed that about 70% of the managers using technology had not attended a course in the past two years prior to the study period. Instead, they were self-taught or taught informally by friends or colleagues, and thus they might miss an opportunity to maximize the potential use of technology (hardware and software). The study suggested that training is a critical issue for hotel managers using technology in their operations.

Lorenz and Mills (2003) studied technology outsourcing as a technology adoption strategy by examining limited-service properties in the U.S. The findings are that 83% of the limited-service operations indicated outsourcing IT as an informal part of their tech-

nology strategy, indicating that formal technology strategies, which include Internet access, were not the standard for the studied limited-service operations. In most cases (64%), decisions for the selection and implementation of new technologies were made by the management company. In respect to outsourcing technology at the limited-service lodging sector, the general managers considered superior quality of services the most important factor followed by increased profits and reduced cost. Given that limited-service lodging properties lack the staff and knowledge to implement technologies at the property level, it was concluded that outsourcing technology was a good strategy at the limited-service lodging sector.

DEVELOPING WEBSITE EVALUATION FACTORS FOR LIMITED-SERVICE LODGING PROPERTIES

An extensive review of the literature yielded seven categories of Web evaluation criteria for limited-service lodging properties: impression, content usefulness, accuracy, navigation, accessibility, online reservations, and timeliness of information. Each category included different numbers of features or criterion. The study developed twenty-six features to measure the Website effectiveness of the limited-service lodging sector. A detailed description of each category is provided in Appendix A.

1. Impression–A Website is an ambassador of an organization on the Web, and the first impression of the site will be the first impression of the organization conducting their business on the Web. A key element to having an effective Website is to convey a good impression with a clear, professional image (Murphy et al., 1996). The Website should look professional with a simple domain name (Murphy et al., 1996; Waller, 2001), a nice contrast of texts and images and no compulsory pop-ups (MCIL, 2002).

2. Content usefulness–Kasavana (2002), Gilbert and Perry (2002), and Dutta and Biren (2001) mentioned that the main functions of lodging Websites are to increase awareness, enhance marketability, and advertise the property's service and products. As stated by Jeong and

Lambert (2001), customers' perceptions and uses of information are the major attributes to measure information quality; therefore, lodging Websites should provide useful, timely and reliable information to attract as many users and potential customers as possible. Information customers look for on lodging Websites includes virtual tours of the property, room information and availability, information on surrounding areas, and contact information.

3. Accuracy–Publications by Jeong and Lambert (2001) and other Internet references (Waller, 2001; Everhart, 1996) reported the importance of providing accurate information to customers. Accurate information should be free of spelling and grammatical errors. The Website should also contain a sentence guaranteeing accuracy of information.

4. Navigation–Kasavana (2002) insisted that a Website design should appeal to the largest possible number of users. While not all users or customers are experts with the computer or familiar with Websites, it is important for lodging Websites to be user-friendly. Easy-to-navigate Websites provide users a quick, efficient, and positive Web experience. The navigation category, in this study, is analogous to the term, "user interface," in Wan's study (2002), and "ease in navigation" of best practice Website features mentioned by Kasavana (2002).

5. Accessibility–Constructing a Website does not guarantee viewers (Kasavana, 2002). Attracting Web surfers is a fundamental part of having an effective Website. Search engines provide Websites with a great opportunity to attract new users to their sites. A good rating on a top search engine can significantly increase the flow of traffic to the site. The Internet resources (Everhart, 1996; MCIL, 2002) cited accessibility as one important evaluation category. In answering to the item, "accessibility through search engines," five commonly used search engines are utilized: Google, Yahoo, MSN, AOL, and Netscape. The list of the most popular search engines came from e-surveys on search engine ratings from Internet companies (SearchEngineWatch.com, 2003; OneStat.com, 2002).

6. Online reservations–The Internet is a new shopping media for consumers (Dutta &

Biren, 2001), while the online reservation functions of lodging Websites act as a marketing tool to provide a channel for transactions (Jeong & Lambert, 2001; Kasavana, 2002). Online purchasing technology provides a means for customers to conduct secure electronic transactions at lodging sites.

7. Timeliness of information–Information on lodging operations change continuously. Contents of lodging sites such as seasonal promotions and room features and availability should be updated as frequently as possible. Current information stimulates visitors' interests in the site. Timeliness of information was also included in Wan's (2002) study as an evaluation criterion for the travel and tourism industry.

METHODOLOGY

Sample

The research sample consisted of Websites of the top 25 limited-service chain lodging operations in the United States. The list for the sample was obtained from the *Hotel and Motel Management's 2002 Special Report* limited-service hotel chain survey (Hotel & Motel Management, 2003). The list of the top 25 limited-service chain lodging operations are presented in Table 1. Limited-service chains for the survey were comprised of the economy and mid-scale-without-food-and-beverage segments. The researcher identified the Website addresses of the research sample.

The selection of Website evaluation criteria is often subjective. Most current Web design checklists are based on individual author opinions or preferences (Zhang & von Dran, 2000). Following this assumption, a multifaceted approach with the integration of previously published articles on Website evaluation was designed to develop criteria for the study in an attempt to decrease author subjectivity. In keeping with Schwartz's assessment that the quality of a Website should be a comprehensive assessment rather than a single criterion (Schwartz, 1999), a total of 26 criterion points were developed to analyze the sampled Websites. A 5-point Likert scale or 1 or 0 rating scale, as demonstrated in the Website evaluation study by Wan (2002) was used. Nine crite-

TABLE 1. List of Top 25 Limited-Service Chain Lodging Companies

Ranking	Lodging Companies	Web Address
1	Days Inn Worldwide	http://www.daysinn.com
2	Super 8 Motels	http://www.super8.com
3	Hampton Inn/Inn & Suites	http://www.hamptoninn.com
4	Comfort Inn	http://www.comfortinn.com
5	Holiday Inn Express	http://www.sixcontinentshotels.com/hiexpress
6	Motel 6	http://www.motel6.com
7	Fairfield Inn	http://www.fairfieldinn.com
8	Travelodge Hotels	http://www.travelodge.com
9	Econolodge	http://www.econolodge.com
10	LaQuinta Inns	http://www.lq.com
11	Red Roof Inns	http://www.redroof.com
12	Extended Stay America Efficiency Studio	http://www.extendedstay.com
13	Ramada Ltd.	http://www.ramada.com
14	Comfort Suite	http://www.comfortsuite.com
15	Country Inns & Suites by Carlson	http://www.countryinns.com
16	Sleep Inn	http://www.sleepinn.com
17	Microtel Inns & Suites	http://www.microtelinn.com
18	Baymont Inns & Suites	http://www.baymontinns.com
19	InTown Suites	http://www.intownsuites.com
20	Suburban Lodge	http://www.suburbanlodge.com
21	Howard Johnson Express	http://www.hojo.com
22	Homestead Studio Suites Hotels	http://www.homesteadhotels.com
23	Drury Inns	http://www.drury-inn.com
24	Candlewood Suites	http://www.candlewoodsuites.com
25	Wingate Inn Hotels	http://www.wingateinns.com

ria took the form of a 5-point Likert rating scale while 17 were evaluated with yes/no questions. An effort was made to use a systematic rating system, either yes/no or 5-point Likert scale, to measure all the attributes identified for the study. However, based on the unique characteristics of each criteria such approach would not be logical. The evaluation criteria utilized for this study is shown in Table 2.

Data Collection

An investigation of Websites of limited-service chain lodging operations was conducted in March 2003. Multiple evaluators were involved in examining the chosen Websites in order to reduce bias in the evaluation process as suggested by Wan (2002). In addition to the author of this paper, four volunteers were recruited from the

Hospitality and Tourism Management program at the University of Kentucky to participate in the Website evaluation process in the fall of 2002. The volunteers had weekly meetings with the author to be briefed on the status of this research project.

First, the students researched and discussed articles on Web evaluation in the area of hospitality and travel/tourism industry through the semester. Through the series of practices, the volunteers were trained to objectively evaluate the Websites following the evaluation criteria for the current study. Practice sessions were conducted to ensure that the students were capable of assessing Websites as objectively as possible. Students practiced evaluating four different Website studies before conducting the present study. These se-

TABLE 2. Evaluation Criteria for Limited-Service Chain Lodging Operations

Criteria
Impression
Simple and appropriate URL/Domain Name
Clear professional image
Nice contrast of texts and images
Nice contrast between text and background
No compulsory pop-ups
Good multi-media interactions
Content Usefulness
Virtual tours of the property
Room information
Transportation and directions
Information on the surrounding areas
Frequently Asked Questions (FAQs)
Hyperlinks to other relevant Websites
Contact information
Accuracy
Free of spelling and grammatical errors
Guaranteed accurate information
Navigation
Ease of access information
Easy to read
Standardized format
Identifiable and logically grouped links
Same navigation bars are used
Internal search tool
Multi-language support
Accessibility
Accessibility through major search engines
Online Reservations
Means of transactions
Timeliness of information
The page has last updated date
The page has been updated recently

dard deviation were computed from the ratings of the developed criteria for each hotel Website. Finally, Friedman's test was conducted to rank the 25 hotel Websites in the limited-service lodging sector.

RESULTS

Tables 3 and 4 are the results of analyses from the Web evaluation for the 25 limited-service chain lodging operations. Table 3 includes the outcomes from the features evalu-

TABLE 3. Website Evaluation Results of Yes/No Rating Criteria for Limited-Service Chain Lodging Operations

Criteria	Yes (%)	No (%)
Impression		
Simple and appropriate URL/Domain Name	25 (100)	0 (0)
Clear professional image	25 (100)	0 (0)
Nice contrast between text and image	25 (100)	0 (0)
Nice contrast between text and background	25 (100)	0 (0)
No compulsory pop-ups	18 (72)	7 (28)
Good multi-media interactions	14 (56)	11 (44)
Accuracy		
Free of spelling and grammatical errors	25 (100)	0 (0)
Guaranteed accurate information	0 (0)	25 (100)
Navigation		
Ease of access information	25 (100)	0 (0)
Easy to read	25 (100)	0 (0)
Standardized format	25 (100)	0 (0)
Identifiable and logically grouped links	25 (100)	0 (0)
Same navigation bars are used	25 (100)	0 (0)
Internal search tool	20 (80)	5 (20)
Multi-language support	4 (16)	21 (84)
Timeliness of information		
Has last updated date	0 (0)	25 (100)
The page has been updated recently	17 (68)	8 (32)

mester-long meetings and training sessions aided the evaluators in becoming familiar with the rating system. The detailed description of the rating criteria is provided in Appendix A. Data obtained from the Website evaluation were analyzed using the Statistical Analysis System (SAS Institute, 2001). Mean and stan-

TABLE 4. Website Evaluation Results of 5-Point Rating Scale Criteria for Limited-Service Chain Lodging Operations

Criteria	Mean (SD)
Content Usefulness	
Virtual tours of the property	3.4 ± 1.3
Room information	3.2 ± 0.6
Transportation and directions	3.9 ± 0.5
Information on the surrounding areas	3.8 ± 0.6
Frequently Asked Questions (FAQs)	3.4 ± 1.3
Hyperlinks to other relevant Websites	3.6 ± 0.8
Contact information	4.8 ± 0.5
Accessibility	
Accessibility through major search engines	1.6 ± 1.1
Online Reservations	
Means of transactions	2.8 ± 0.6

ated with 1 or 0 ratings, impression, accuracy, navigation, and timeliness of information categories. The evaluation results for the other categories, evaluated with 5-point rating systems, content usefulness, accessibility, and online reservations, are shown in Table 4.

All 25 Websites satisfied the features of the impression category. They provided clear professional images with simple, appropriate, and easy-to-remember domain names. In addition, contrast between text, image, and background helped to maintain a good impression of the Website. Pop-ups distract customers upon entry to the Website. Eighteen sites (72%) revealed pop-ups when users accessed information at the site. As customers become more sophisticated, the more they enjoy interactions with multi-media. Sound effects, graphics, and videos were multi-media installed at the limited-service lodging operation Websites. Fourteen sites embedded at least one kind of multi-media effect. Only one site provided all three types of multi-media effects. Twenty-four sites (96%) provided a virtual tour, which contrasted with much lower percentages (21.2%) from the previous study for the global hotel industry (Wei et al., 2001). Eight sites (32%) scored excellent by demonstrating all four items of virtual tours. Seventeen Websites

(68%) contained at least two items of the features.

Wei et al. (2001) reported 22.4% of global hotels showing room availability information on their Websites in the 1998 study. This study, however, identified that it was no longer uncommon for hotels to publicize room availability information on their Websites. Transportation and direction scored the second highest (3.9) among the content usefulness category with all sites stating written directions to the hotel from nearby airports. Over 75% or (19) Websites included an enlargeable (can be zoomed) map and clear instructions from the airports and highway exits. Two sites added detailed directions from airports, highway exits, and other attractions. Information on the surrounding areas was the third highest scored (3.8) feature in the content usefulness segment. All Websites included a list of shops and attractions nearby. Seventeen sites (68%) included brief descriptions while two Websites had contact information or hyperlinks to the shop and attraction sites. The frequently asked questions (FAQs) feature was rated between fair and good (3.4). Four sites did not provide the feature through the Websites at all. On the other hand, over 50% (14) of the sites situated the feature under "about us," "help," or "first time here," which would make it harder for customers to find it. The limited-service chain lodging operations were good about supplying hyperlinks to relevant Websites. Twenty-four Websites provided hyperlinks to hotels in the chain, and twelve sites expanded the links to other chain hotels. The contact information feature was the highest among the content usefulness category with a score of 4.8. Most of the sites (22) had all of the contact information (fax, e-mail, telephone and address). Along with content usefulness, content accuracy is important to provide reliable information to customers. Even though no spelling or grammatical errors were found, no site included a statement guaranteeing the provision of accurate information.

All 25 sites were easy to read and provided access to information with standardized formats. Logically grouped links and the same navigation bars throughout the Websites also enhanced navigation. Twenty Websites featured an internal search, and multi-language items were the least-supported feature. Accessibility through search engines examined whether the Websites could be located in the first 60 results by using the five most popular search engines (Google, Yahoo, MSN, AOL, and Netscape). This feature received a very low rating, 1.6, indicating that the limited-service Websites could not be located in the first 60 results by any of the search engines or was only found by one search engine.

Online reservation is a critical feature for the customers to book hotel rooms conveniently while they look for hotel information. Four kinds of reservation methods were calculated through credit cards, fax, e-mail, and phone. This feature averaged 2.8, interpreted. This study found that all 25 Websites provided credit card transactions, while sixteen sites included more than one method of transaction whether by e-mail, fax, or phone, in addition to credit card transactions.

None of the lodging operation sites provided information on last updated date. Instead, they indicated the year they were updated. Stating the year 2003 for this feature was regarded as being updated recently. The majority of the sites (17) were updated in 2003. Six sites were updated in 2002, and the remaining six sites were done in 2001 or before.

Analysis of Rankings for the Websites

Each Website was ranked from one to twenty-five on each criterion of the seven categories. Table 5 shows the results. Rankings ranged from 10.69 through 15. Since the best Website is ranked 1, the smaller the number, the rank the higher. Extended Stay America did the best job with the best overall ranking, followed by Howard Johnson Express, Fairfield Inn, and Wingate Inn Hotels. Candlewood Suite and Super 8 Motel received the lowest overall ranking. Friedman's one-way nonparametric Analysis of Variance (ANOVA) was conducted to support the analysis. This test was employed to see if the numerous rounded ties in rankings had any effect. In particular the test is utilized to find out any possible groupings according to the rankings. The result was not statistically significant with the following statistics (p = .091, F = 1.415, and R^2 = .052).

TABLE 5. Friedman's Analysis of Website Rankings

Lodging Companies	Mean Rank of Websites
Extended Stay America Efficiency Studio	10.69
Howard Johnson Express	11.25
Fairfield Inn	11.82
Wingate Inn Hotels	11.82
Drury Inns	11.90
Red Roof Inns	12.69
Country Inns & Suites by Carlson	12.69
Microtel Inns & Suites	12.84
Comfort Inn	12.86
Econolodge	12.86
Comfort Suite	12.86
Sleep Inn	12.86
Motel 6	13.00
Ramada Ltd.	13.13
Suburban Lodge	13.17
Travelodge Hotels	13.26
Homestead Studio Suites Hotels	13.28
Baymont Inns & Suites	13.32
Hampton Inn/Inn & Suites	13.42
InTown Suites	13.55
Days Inn Worldwide	13.61
Holiday Inn Express	14.07
LaQuinta Inns	14.50
Super 8 Motels	14.59
Candlewood Suites	14.85

This indicates that all twenty-five hotels are grouped as one subset.

CONCLUSION

With the increasing interest in e-commerce in the lodging industry, this study intended to investigate the effectiveness of the Websites for limited-service chain lodging operations. The top 25 limited-service chain operations in the U.S. were evaluated based on the criteria established for this study. Seven categories of evaluation for limited-service chain lodging operations were developed: impression, content usefulness, accuracy, navigation, accessibility, online reservations, and timeliness of information. The Websites of the limited-service sector provided appropriate content that customers seek. Overall the Websites among the 25 lodging operations were rated better than fair (above 3 points) based on the 5-point Likert scale features. Over seventy percent of the Websites were identified with compulsory pop-ups which should be avoided as it distracts customers. Content usefulness features were rated more highly than in previous lodging related Website studies such as Wei et al. (2001). In addition to those features evaluated by previous Web evaluation studies for the lodging industry, this study added new features to the content usefulness category such as transportation and directions, information on the surrounding areas, frequently asked questions, and contact information. Accessibility of the Websites through five popular search engines resulted in the lowest rating of 1.6, indicating that limited-service lodging properties need to register their Websites with major search engines. Another recommended improvement is to specify the last revised date of the Website. The information on the Website should be current and accurate. Customers need assurance that the information is accurate and currently valid especially for room rate and room availability (Wei et al., 2001).

Regarding online reservations, though all the Websites provided the option for credit card transactions, less than half of the Websites (11) supported this option with a currency converter. Considering the globalization of the industry, installation of a currency converter is necessary to attract international travelers as well as language options other than English (MCIL, 2002). According to *HOTEL's 1998 Worldwide Technology Survey* (Gilbert & Perry, 2002), eighty-one percent of hoteliers were thought to be capable of accepting reservations over the Web in 1999. This report is consistent with our findings for the limited-service sector.

It must be noted that the small sample size was a limitation of the study. Hence, the results are not generalizable to all limited-service lodging operations. In order to better analyze information technology trends in the lodging industry, it is recommended, along with the criteria developed by this study, to repeat and expand this study longitudinally as uses of the Internet within the limited-service

lodging sector may vary within regions, and organizational structures. Another limitation lies in the validity of the study from a bias perspective. The study made every effort to reduce human bias from the two aspects: (1) a great number of previous Web evaluation studies were scrutinized to select appropriate criteria, and (2) multiple evaluators were chosen and trained to evaluate the Websites as accurately and consistently as possible. This study therefore serves as preliminary research to provide valuable insights for Web researchers and lodging practitioners to understand important Web evaluation issues in the limited-service lodging industry. The results of this study can be used as a basis for Web researchers in the limited-service lodging sector to improve and refine their Websites. Accordingly, the improved Websites could help enhance customers' perceived usefulness and positive attitudes toward limited-service lodging Websites.

REFERENCES

Benckendorff, P. J., & Black, N. L. (2000). Destination marketing on the Internet: A case study of Australian Regional Tourism Authorities. *Journal of Tourism Studies, 11*(1), 11.

Chu, R. (2001). What online Hong Kong travelers look for on airline/travel Websites? *International Journal of Hospitality Management, 20*, 95-100.

Doolin, B., Burgess, L., & Cooper, J. (2002). Evaluating the use of the Web for tourism marketing: A case study from New Zealand. *Tourism Management, 23*, 557-561.

Dutta, S., & Biren, B. (2001). Business Transformation on the Internet: Results from the 2000 study. *European Management Journal, 19*, 449-462.

Everhart, N. (1996). Web Page Evaluation Worksheet. St. John's University, Division of Library and Information Science. Available: *http://www.Duke.edu/~del/evaluate.html*

Gilbert, D., & Perry, J. P. (2002). Exploring Developments in Web Based Relationship Marketing Within the Hotel Industry. *Journal of Hospitality & Leisure Marketing, 9*(3/4), 141-159.

Hebert, D. (1997). Limited-service headed for a curve? *Hotel & Motel Management, 212*(1), 66-68.

Hospitality Research Group. (2002). Branded hotel occupancy to rise during 2003. Available: *http://www.pkfonline.com/hrgonline/whatsnew.news_view.cfm?pressReleaseID=51*

Hotel & Motel Management. (2003, February). Hotel & Motel Management's 2002 Limited-Service-Hotel-Chain Survey. Available: *http://www.hotelmotel.com/ hotelmotel/data/articlestandard/hotelmotel/052003/ 44538/article.pdf*

Jeong, M., & Lambert, C. U. (2001). Adaptation of an information quality framework to measure customers' behavioral intentions to use lodging Websites. *International Journal of Hospitality Management, 20*(2), 129-146.

Kasavana, M. L. (2002). eMarketing: Restaurant Websites That Click. *Journal of Hospitality & Leisure Marketing, 9*(3/4), 161-178.

Law, R., & Wong, J. (2003). Successful factors for a travel Website: Perceptions of online purchasers in Hong Kong. *Journal of Hospitality and Tourism Research, 27*(1), 118-124.

Lorenz, J., & Mills, J. E. (2003). Using information technology as a technology adoption strategy: An examination of limited service hotel properties in Newark, Delaware. *Proceedings of the Eighth Annual Graduate Education and Graduate Students Research Conference in Hospitality and Tourism*, Las Vegas, NV, January 5-7, 421-425.

Main, H. C. (2002). The use of the Internet by Hotels in Wales–A longitudinal study: 1994-2000. *International Journal of Hospitality Information Technology, 2*, 35-44.

Management Centre International Limited (MCIL). (2002). Website Effectiveness Review. Available: *http://www.mcil.co.uk/7-site-review-homepage.htm*

Murphy, J., Forrest, E. J., Wotring, E. C., & Brymer, R. A. (1996). Hotel Management and Marketing on the Internet; An Analysis of Sites and Features. *Cornell Hotel and Restaurant Administration Quarterly, 3*, 70-82.

OneStat.com. (2002). Google is the most popular search engine according to OneStat.com. Available: *http:// www.onestat.com/html/aboutus_pressbox3.html*

Quek, P. (1999, March). The Implications of Declining Occupancies. Available: *http://www.hotel-online.com/ Trends/PKF/Special/DecliningOccupancies_July99. html*

SAS Institute. (2001). *SAS/STAT User's Guide.* Cary, NC: SAS Institute Inc.

Schwartz, S. (1999). *Using the Internet for Health Information: Legal Issues.* Chicago, IL: The American Medical Association.

SearchEngineWatch.com. (2003). Nelson netratings search engine ratings. Available: *http://www.searchenginewatch. com/reports/article.php/2156451*

Shaw, R. (1996). Lodging online: Hotel Websites are becoming attractive marketing vehicles and profitable information generators. *Hotel & Motel Management, 211*(4), 52-54.

Smith Travel Research. (2003). *The Host Study 2002: Hotel Operating Statistics.* Hendersonville, TN: Smith Travel Research.

Tierney, P. (2000). Internet-based evaluation of tourism Website effectiveness: Methodological issues and survey results. *Journal of Travel Research, 39*, 212-219.

Van Hoof, V., & Combrink, T. E. (1998). US lodging managers and the Internet: Perceptions from the industry. *Cornell Hotel & Restaurant Administration Quarterly, 39*(2), 46-54.

Waller, R. (2001). Richard Waller Website Design and Creaton: Richard Waller Rating and Evaluation. Available: *http://www.waller.co.uk/evalhead.htm*

Wan, C. S. (2002). The Websites of international tourist hotels and tour wholesalers in Taiwan. *Tourism Management, 23*, 155-160.

Wei, S., Ruys, H. F., Hoof, H. B., & Combrink, T. E. (2001). Uses of the Internet in the global hotel industry. *Journal of Business Research, 54*, 235-241.

Zhang, P., & von Dran, G. M. (2000). Satisfiers and dissatisfiers: A two-factor model for Website design and evaluation. *Journal of American Society of Information Science, 51*, 253-1268.

APPENDIX A

Detailed Definition of the Rating System for Evaluating Websites

1. Impression

Q1: URL simple and appropriate
(1) Yes. Simple and meaningful URL, the domain name should be the name or abbreviation of the hotel.
(0) No. Meaningless URL, the domain name is not the name or abbreviation of the hotel.

Q2: Clear professional title
(1) Yes. Clear professional title in every page.
(0) No. Do not have clear professional title in every page.

Q3: Color of text and image nicely contrasted
(1) Yes. Text and image nicely contrasted.
(0) No. Text and image not nicely contrasted.

Q4: Background and text nicely contrasted
(1) Yes. Background and text nicely contrasted and text can be clearly seen.
(0) No. Background and text not nicely contrasted or text cannot be nicely seen.

Q5: Good interaction with multi-media by sound/graphics/videos
(1) Yes. Have at least one multi-media among sound effects, graphics, and videos.
(0) No. Do not have any kind of multi-media among the above three.

Q6: No compulsory pop-ups
(1) Yes. No compulsory pop-up upon entry to the Website.
(0) No. Have pop-up(s) upon entry to the Website.

2. Content Usefulness

Q1: Virtual tours of the property (enlarged picture, photo slide show, 360 degree panorama, multi-media virtual tour)
(1) Poor. Have none of the effects.
(2) Acceptable. Have 1 of the effects.
(3) Fair. Have 2 of the above effects.
(4) Good. Have 3 of the above effects.
(5) Excellent. Have all of the above effects.

Q2: Room information and availability (room availability, room rate, room service menu, pictures of the hotel room)
(1) Poor. Have none of the above items.
(2) Acceptable. Have 1 of the items.
(3) Fair. Have 2 of the items.
(4) Good. Have 3 of the items.
(5) Excellent. Have all of the items.

Q3: Transportation and directions
(1) Poor. Have no transportation and directions to the hotel information provided.
(2) Acceptable. Have written directions to the hotel from nearby airports or have a map(s) provided.
(3) Fair. Have a simple map(s) and written directions from airports only.
(4) Good. Have an enlargeable/can be zoom map(s) and clear instructions from airports and other highway exits.
(5) Excellent. Have an enlargeable map(s) and clear and detailed directions from airports, highway exits, and other attractions.

Q4: **Information on surrounding areas**

(1) Poor. No information on surrounding areas is provided.

(2) Acceptable. Only names of the shops/attractions nearby, without detailed descriptions nor directions to those places.

(3) Fair. A brief description on the shops/attractions nearby, but without directions.

(4) Good. A list of shops/attractions nearby with brief directions provided.

(5) Excellent. A list of shops/attractions nearby with brief directions and with the contact information or hyperlink to those sites.

Q5: **Frequent Asked Questions (FAQs) available**

(1) Poor. No FAQs are found.

(2) Acceptable. FAQs are found in the page, but the information is not useful or not comprehensive enough.

(3) Fair. FAQs are found only in reservation, and the information provided is only related to reservation.

(4) Good. FAQs are found under other icons, such as "about us," "help," "first time here," and comprehensive and useful information is provided.

(5) Excellent. FAQs are found in the main icon of the navigation bar, and comprehensive and useful information is provided.

Q6: **Hyperlinks to other Websites**

(1) Poor. No hyperlink to other Websites.

(2) Acceptable. Hyperlinks to other sponsored/advertised Websites, which is not useful to the readers.

(3) Fair. Hyperlinks to other hotel Websites within the hotel chain.

(4) Good. Hyperlinks to other hotel Websites within the hotel chain and other hotels.

(5) Excellent. Hyperlinks to other hotel Websites within the hotel chain and other hotels, and to other relevant Websites (e.g., attraction sites, tourism board homepage, etc.).

Q7: **Contact information (e-mail, fax, phone number, address)**

(1) Poor. No contact information is provided.

(2) Acceptable. Only 1 of the above items is provided.

(3) Fair. Two of the above items are provided.

(4) Good. Three of the above items are provided.

(5) Excellent. All of the above items are provided.

3. **Accuracy**

Q1: **Free of spelling and grammatical errors**

(1) Yes. No spelling and grammatical errors are found.

(0) No. Spelling and grammatical errors are found.

Q2: **Guaranteed accurate information**

(1) Yes. Statement of guaranteed accurate information is indicated in the Website.

(0) No. No statement of guaranteed accurate information is indicated in the Website.

4. **Navigation**

Q1: **Ease of access information**

(1) Yes. Contents are easy to find and sorted into appropriate categories.

(0) No. Contents are difficult to find and not sorted into appropriate categories.

Q2: **Easy to read**

(1) Yes. Contents are well presented with the appropriate use of texts or graphics.

(0) No. Contents are not well presented.

APPENDIX A (continued)

4.   Navigation

Q3:   Standardized format

(1)   Yes. Navigation is consistent throughout the Website.

(0)   No. Navigation is not consistent throughout the Website.

Q4:   Links easily identified and grouped

(1)   Yes. Links are easily identified and grouped properly.

(0)   No. Links are not easily identified and not grouped properly.

Q5:   Same navigation bars are used

(1)   Yes. One standard navigation bar is used throughout the Website.

(0)   No. No standard navigation bar is used throughout the Website.

Q6:   Internal search tool

(1)   Yes. Internal search function or site map is provided.

(0)   No. No internal search function nor site map is provided.

Q7:   Multi-language support

(1)   Yes. (An) Other language than English (is) are supported.

(2)   No. Only English is supported.

5.   Accessibility

Q1:   Accessibility through major search engines

(1)   Poor. The Website cannot be located in the first 60 results by using the 5 major search engines chosen for the study.

(2)   Acceptable. The Website can be located in the first 60 results of 1 search engine chosen for the study.

(3)   Fair. The Website can be located in the first 60 results of any 2 search engines chosen for the study.

(4)   Good. The Website can be located in the first 60 results of any 3 search engines chosen for the study.

(5)   Excellent. The Website can be located in the first 60 results of more than 3 search engines chosen for the study.

6.   Online Reservations

Q1:   Means of transactions

(1)   Poor. No online booking is provided.

(2)   Acceptable. Credit card booking is only provided.

(3)   Fair. Credit card booking plus one of other means of transactions (fax, e-mail, phone) provided.

(4)   Good. Credit card booking plus two other means of transactions provided.

(5)   Excellent. Credit card booking plus 3 other means of transactions provided.

7.   Timeliness of Information

Q1:   Last updated date provision

(1)   Yes. Last updated date (with month and year) is provided.

(0)   No. Last updated date (with month and year) is not provided.

Q2:   Has been updated recently

(1)   Yes. Updated in 2003.

(0)   No. Updated before 2003.

Index